women's words

women's words

The Columbia Book of Quotations by Women

Mary Biggs

• • • • •

COLUMBIA

UNIVERSITY

PRESS

NEW YORK

Columbia University Press

New York Chichester, West Sussex

Library of Congress Cataloging-in-Publication Data

Biggs, Mary.

   Women's words : the Columbia book of quotations by women /
Mary Biggs

       p. cm.

       Includes index.

       ISBN 0–231–07986–9

       1. Women—Quotations, maxims, etc. I. Title.

   PN6084.W6B47 1996

   305.4–dc20   95-47973

Printed in the United States of America

c 10 9 8 7 6 5 4 3 2 1

This book is dedicated to the memory of my mother,

Ruth Murray Gleason, 1906–1989

Contents

Introduction

This book began with my casual question to an assemblage of Westchester County librarians during coffee break at a professional meeting four years ago. "What sort of reference book should exist, but doesn't?" I asked. "A topically arranged collection of quotations by women," said the librarian sitting across from me. I recorded her suggestion, along with some others, and transmitted it to Columbia University Press, where I was then serving on a committee of librarians that offered advice from time to time.

That would have been the end of it, except that I was then promptly asked if I would be interested in compiling the book myself. A feminist librarian with a strong avocational interest in women's history and a lifelong fascination with quotation books (at fourteen, I saved up my babysitting income to buy Bartlett's *Familiar Quotations*), I could hardly dismiss the suggestion out of hand. Yet to undertake such a task alone was beyond imagining. I mentioned the project to friends, to librarians, to library school professors; all thought it worthy, thought they would like to read the resulting book, and showed some inclination to help out by submitting quotations. Those who taught promised to encourage their students to submit quotations. I envisioned my mailbox filling daily with verbal pearls for my delight and effortless transformation into manuscript.

Uh, no.

I had, of course, mistaken polite expressions of interest for commitment. I had overestimated the number of people in this world nerdy enough to buy Bartlett's at fourteen. And I had underestimated my bibliographic paranoia: every quotation submitted by someone else would have to be checked against its source. And what if I didn't like a quotation? I wanted the book to be readable, to be fun, to be . . . *mine*. And so it is.

From the beginning, I was determined to avoid checking other quotation books and to include only those quotations that I found intrinsically interesting. This resulted in the exclusion of many most-familiar quotations, such as Gertrude Stein saying that there's no there there (I am tired of hearing it quoted as Profound Wisdom, aren't you?), or Queen Victoria announcing that she was not amused; or Queen Elizabeth II's *annus horribilis,* etc. They didn't interest me—at least, not in themselves—and though they might interest my audience, they were available in numerous other books. John Bartlett's onerous responsibility was not mine.

Once a saying passed the test of captivating me, I had to consider that a colorful context might account partly for its charm. I decided to provide notes on context when desirable and when I could.

I structured the project as a compilation of women's observations on education, work, success, fame, and failure; on struggle, poverty, and prejudice; on money and business, government and politics, war and peace; on the arts and sciences; on nature, religion, and the search for meaning. And, less monumentally, on avocations: fashion, parties, reading, music, sports, travel, and the other things we do for fun.

This book is the selection of one woman, based on what that woman likes to read. Some famous quotations are here: Sojourner Truth's "A'n't I a Woman?," speech, for example; Susan B. Anthony's declaration that " . . . failure is impossible"; Queen Consort Elizabeth's announcement that she and the little Princesses Elizabeth and Margaret would remain in London while the bombs of World War II fell around them; and Lillian Hellman's celebrated refusal to "cut [her] conscience to fit this year's fashions." But they are not here *because* they are famous; fame simply happens to coincide with their eloquence.

The collection heavily emphasizes the United States and England in the last two centuries, both because those places and times are so rich in material, and because they are the places and times best known to me.

And what have I found? I certainly cannot claim to "prove" anything here about distinctions between male and female voice, but I will share my impressions. First of all, I do not believe that ways of using words vary detectably by gender. Give men and women identical ideas to be expressed; give me the resulting articulations, with authors kept anonymous; and I doubt that I'll be able to tell what gender wrote each with any more accuracy than guesswork would yield. Women write lengthily or laconically; they are flowery and elaborate or dry and to the point; they are sensitive, abrasive, lachrymose, witty, simplistic, ironic, scrupulously civil, and flamboyantly crude. Is Florynce Kennedy "feminine"? Is George Eliot "sentimental"? Does Adrienne Rich avert her eyes? Does Rhonda Cornum, sexually abused in wartime, talk like a "victim"? Do *any* of the African American or South African black women here, all subject to double, triple, or quadruple oppressions, talk like victims? Do the eighteenth- and nineteenth-century women sound more repressed than our contemporaries? Although some of the quoted sources claim that women speak in a special "language" or use words in a special way, I doubt it.

But the other components of utterance are topic and perspective, and here the differences between women's words and those of men are significant. In this book, women's references to warfare, government, and politics, for example, tend to be skeptical or even downright hostile. Women view the goal of worldly success from a distance, guardedly, sometimes even dismissively, and when they celebrate it, they celebrate in muted tones. By contrast, they repeatedly affirm service as an ideal (and painstakingly differentiate it from servility).

In addition, women writers highly value education and work—more highly, I think, than men do. For women, schooling and employment pave the road to independence; they liberate, and women do not take them for granted. The women quoted here do not, as a rule, bemoan the effort required to learn or to earn—nor do they dream of undeserved riches: the legacy from a rich (childless) bachelor-uncle, the hot tip, the lucky roll. They yearn to accomplish and to have their accomplishments rewarded: that's all. But those have always been such unusual occurrences for women that they may amount to our version of winning the lottery or hitting the jackpot.

The women here—admittedly, by definition a special group—are tough minded, articulate, strong, often angry, sometimes funny, and nearly always independent. They demand respect and are committed to equality of the sexes, of races, of classes, and of those with minority sexual orientations. They talk of literature, art, sports, music, nature, business, religion, the job—and of injustice, struggle, determination, hope, and the meaning of life. They are profoundly, sometimes even inexplicably, optimistic. They are their own people, whole and impressive.

I need this book, and I suspect that other people, men and women, boys and girls, need it too.

Acknowledgments

I owe thanks to James Raimes; to my project manager, Ivan Farkas; and especially to my sons, Nicholas and Nathan Mancuso. They are my best friends and biggest supporters, unfailingly interested in what I do and appreciative of the results. Thanks, guys.

women's words

Quotations

ABNORMALITY

1 Whenever I'm asked why Southern writers particularly have a penchant for writing about freaks, I say it is because we are still able to recognize one. To be able to recognize a freak, you have to have some conception of the whole man, and in the South the general conception of man is still, in the main, theological.

FLANNERY O'CONNOR (1925–1964), U.S. fiction writer and essayist. *Mystery and Manners,* part 2 (1969).

Written in 1957. O'Connor, a lifelong Georgian, invented many fictional characters often described as freakish or "grotesque." She was a committed Roman Catholic.

ABOLITIONISM

1 Dost thou ask what I mean by emancipation? . . . 1. It is "to reject with indignation, the wile and guilty phantasy, that man can hold *property* in man." 2. To pay the laborer his hire, for he is worthy of it. 3. No longer to deny him the right of marriage, but to "let every man have his own wife, and let every woman have her own husband," as saith the apostle. 4. To let parents have their own children, for they are the gift of the Lord to *them,* and no one else has any right to them. 5. No longer to withhold the advantages of education and the privilege of reading the bible. 6. To put the slave under the protection of equitable laws. Now, why should not *all* this be done immediately? Which of these things is to be done next year, and which the year after? and so on. *Our* immediate emancipation means, doing justice and loving mercy *to-day*—and this is what we call upon every slaveholder to do. I have seen too much of slavery to be a gradualist.

ANGELINA GRIMKÉ (1805–1879), U.S. abolitionist and feminist. *Letters to Catherine Beecher,* letter #2 (1837).

In a letter dated June 17, 1837.

2 We Abolition Women are turning the world upside down.

ANGELINA GRIMKÉ (1805–1879), U.S. abolitionist and feminist. As quoted in *The*

Grimke Sisters from South Carolina, ch. 1, by Gerda Lerner (1967).
Said on February 25, 1838.

3 Southern women are . . . all at heart abolitionists.

ELLA GERTRUDE CLANTON THOMAS, U.S. diarist. As quoted in *Divided Houses,* ch. 1, by Leeann Whites (1992).

In a journal entry dated January 2, 1858, referring to women of the "planter class," who chafed at their husbands' flagrant sex with slave women.

4 I had crossed de line of which I had so long been dreaming. I was free; but dere was no one to welcome me to de land of freedom. I was a stranger in a strange land, and my home after all was down in de old cabin quarter, wid de ole folks, and my brudders and sisters. But to dis solemn resolution I came; I was free, and dey should be free also; I would make a home for dem in de North, and de Lord helping me, I would bring dem all dere.

HARRIET TUBMAN (c. 1820–1913), African American abolitionist. As quoted in *Harriet, the Moses of Her People,* by Sarah Bradford (1969).

Bradford was the friend and first biographer of the great abolitionist and ex-slave who, after escaping to freedom, returned nineteen times to the South and ushered more than 300 other runaway slaves, including her parents and brothers, to freedom in the North. Here, Tubman was remembering what she thought when, as a fugitive slave, she finally reached free soil.

5 I was the conductor of the Underground Railroad for eight years, and I can say what most conductors can't say—I never ran my train off the track and I never lost a passenger.

HARRIET TUBMAN (c. 1820–1913), African American slave, liberator of slaves, and spy. As quoted in *Divided Houses,* ch. 7, by Lyde Cullen Sizer (1992).

Of her experience as slave-liberator via the secret network of way-stations known metaphorically as the Underground Railroad. Following her own escape from her Maryland slavemaster, Tubman returned to the South nineteen times to usher other slaves out of bondage; she freed 300–400 people.

6 . . . I am an abolitionist for the sake of my own race—Contact with the African degenerates our white race—I find the association with them injurious to my child—keenly as I watch to prevent it & his faithful nurse to help me . . . She is a good woman & so are many of them—Still the race is a degraded one . . .

ELIZABETH BLAIR LEE (1818–?), U.S. housewife. *Wartime Washington,* letter dated December 31, 1862 (1991).

Born in Kentucky, Lee later lived in Maryland and in Washington, D.C., with her husband and child. Her husband, Samuel Phillips Lee, was a Union naval commander in the Civil War, and she wrote this in a letter to him. The "faithful nurse," of course, was African American.

7 You are de cause of de brutality of these poor creeters. For you're de children of those who enslaved dem. . . . You are ready to help de heathen in foreign lands, but don't care for the heathen right about you. I want you to sign petitions to send to Washington. Dey say there dey will do what de people want. The majority rules. If dey want anything good dey git it. If dey want anything not right dey git it too. You send these petitions, and those men in Congress will have something to spout about.

SOJOURNER TRUTH (1797–1883), African American slave; later an itinerant preacher and advocate of various social reforms including abolition, woman suffrage, and temperance. As quoted in *The Narrative of Sojourner Truth*, part 2: "Book of Life," by Frances W. Titus (1875).
Said c. 1860 to a gathering in Rochester, New York.

8 Abolitionists were men of sharp angles. Organizing them was like binding crooked sticks in a bundle.

JANE GREY SWISSHELM (1815–1884), U.S. newspaperwoman, abolitionist, and human rights activist. *Half a Century*, ch. 18 (1880).
On writing for *The Spirit of Liberty*, an abolitionist publication, in the early 1840s. Later, in 1847, Swisshelm founded her own abolitionist paper, the *Pittsburg Saturday Visitor*.

9 ... women learned one important lesson—namely, that it is impossible for the best of men to understand women's feelings or the humiliation of their position. When they asked us to be silent on our question during the War, and labor for the emancipation of the slave, we did so, and gave five years to his emancipation and enfranchisement. ... I was convinced, at the time, that it was the true policy. I am now equally sure that it was a blunder.

ELIZABETH CADY STANTON (1815–1902), U.S. suffragist, author, and social reformer. *Eighty Years and More (1815–1897)*, ch. 16 (1898).
On suffragists' agreement to devote their energies to supporting the Union and the antislavery cause during the Civil War. Stanton and many other suffragists were angry and disillusioned when those with and for whom they had worked successfully failed to support the suffrage cause after military victory and emancipation of the slaves. They were also bitter that African American men were now enfranchised, while women of all races still were not.

ABORTION

1 ... an abortion is only horrible, but to deny life is satanic. Why then, I wonder, do priests and nuns remain unmarried? Why then are celibacy and self-control approved and exacted? What a priceless ideal for mothers to follow! To continue bearing children misshapen, deformed, hideous to the eyes, in the hope that Heaven may be filled! It's a monstrous doctrine, abhorrent of every civilized instinct in us.

MARGARET SANGER (1879–1966), U.S. birth control advocate. *My Fight for Birth Control*, ch. 17 (1931).
On the Roman Catholic Church's opposition to birth control and abortion.

2 If men could become pregnant, abortion would be a sacrament.

FLORYNCE KENNEDY (b. 1916), U.S. lawyer, author, activist, and humorist. As quoted in *The Decade of Women*, by Suzanne Levine and Harriet Lyons (1980).
Said in 1970.

3 The literal alternatives to [abortion] are suicide, motherhood, and, some would add, madness. Consequently, there is some confusion, discomfort, and cynicism greeting efforts to "find" or "emphasize" or "identify" alternatives to abortion.

CONNIE J. DOWNEY (b. 1934), U.S. feminist. As quoted in *The Decade of Women*, by Suzanne Levine and Harriet Lyons (1980).
From an internal working paper written by the director of the Women's Action Program, U. S. Department of Health, Education, and Welfare; the agency had been charged with identifying "alternatives" to abortion.

4 I began to realize that it was bigotry of the worst kind to say that it's bet-

ter to be dead than to be born re-
tarded or blind or without a limb.
It's a value judgment you're making
about someone's life, based on their
degree of perfection.

JULI LOESCH (b. c. 1953), U.S. sympa-
thizer with the anti-abortion movement. As
quoted in *The Great Divide,* book 2, section 1,
by Studs Terkel (1988).

The victim of a crippling case of rheumatoid ar-
thritis, Loesch was explaining why she opposed
abortion.

5 . . . abortion opponents love little
babies as long as they are in somebody else's uterus.

JOYCELYN ELDERS (b. 1933), U.S. pediatrician and medical educator; first woman, and
second African American, Surgeon General. As
quoted in the *New York Times,* p. A14 (December 31, 1993).

Elders said this c. 1990.

6 If the vice president thinks it's dis-
graceful for an unmarried woman
to bear a child, and if he believes
that a woman cannot adequately
raise a child without a father, then
he'd better make sure that abortion
remains safe and legal.

DIANE BRITISH (b. 1948), U.S. television
producer. As quoted in *Newsweek* magazine,
p. 17 (June 1, 1992).

Reacting to Vice-President Dan Quayle's criticism of her popular comedy show, *Murphy
Brown.* In that show, the middle-aged, unmarried, professionally-employed heroine had a
child. Quayle attacked the plot line, saying that
he was defending "family values;" he was also
a strong opponent of abortion rights.

7 The personal things should be left
out of platforms at conventions. . . .
You can argue yourself blue in the
face, and you're not going to

change each other's minds. It's a
waste of your time and my time.

BARBARA BUSH (b. 1925), First Lady of
the United States (1988–1992). As quoted in
Time magazine, p. 27 (August 24, 1992).

The wife of Republican President George Bush,
she was referring to abortion; her personal position on the issue was the reverse of her husband's, and the Republican Party's, anti-abortion stance.

8 We really need to get over this love
affair with the fetus and start worrying about children.

JOYCELYN ELDERS (b. 1933), U.S. pedia-
trician and educator; first woman (and second
African American) Surgeon General of the
United States. As quoted in the *New York Times
Magazine,* p. 19 (January 30, 1994).

Elders, who was U. S. Surgeon General at the
time, was discussing the anti-abortion movement and the effects of teenagers' unwanted
pregnancies on the teenagers themselves.

9 Morality becomes hypocrisy if it
means accepting mothers' suffering
or dying in connection with unwanted pregnancies and illegal abortions and unwanted children.

GRO HARLEM BRUNDTLAND (b. 1939),
Norwegian Prime Minister. As quoted in the
New York Times, pp. A1, A9 (September 6,
1994).

Speaking at the United Nations Conference on
Population and Development in Cairo, Egypt.
She was defying representatives of Roman Catholic and Islamic countries by calling for "a general legalization of abortion."

10 I suppose it would be nice to say
. . . that . . . I realized I was making
abortion-rights history. . . . But the
honest truth is that nothing like
that even occurred to me. I was simply at the end of my rope. At a dead
end. I just didn't know what else to
do.

NORMA MCCORVEY (b. 1947), U.S. speaker and Supreme Court case plaintiff. *I Am Roe*, ch. 10 (1994).

McCorvey was a reform school veteran, a lesbian, without money, and alone when, at twenty-one, she was impregnated with her third child during a brief heterosexual affair. Using the name "Jane Roe" to protect her privacy, she became the plaintiff in a historic court case, *Roe v. Wade*. It went to the U. S. Supreme Court and established women's right to abortion, which until then had been illegal in the United States. However, the decision was too late for McCorvey, who bore her child, surrendered it for adoption, and descended into a struggle with alcohol, drugs, and depression, from which she eventually emerged. The year after this book was published, McCorvey would express reservations about abortion and declare herself "pro-life."

ABUSE

1   . . . the virtue of female slaves is wholly at the mercy of irresponsible tyrants, and women are bought and sold in our slave markets, to gratify the brutal lust of those who bear the name of Christians.

SARAH M. GRIMKE (1792–1873), U.S. abolitionist and feminist. *Letters on the Equality of the Sexes and the Condition of Woman*, letter #8: dated 1837 (1838).

Grimke, the daughter of a wealthy South Carolina slaveowner, had witnessed slavery at first hand and was passionately opposed to it.

2   The woman may serve as a vehicle for the rapist expressing his rage against a world that gives him pain—because he is poor, or oppressed, or mad, or simply human. Then what of her? We have waded in the swamp of compassion for him long enough.

ROBIN MORGAN (b. 1941), U.S. author, feminist, and child actor. *The Word of a Woman*, part 1 (1992).

Written in 1974.

3   Rape fattens on the fantasies of the normal male
like a maggot in garbage.

MARGE PIERCY (b. 1936), U.S. poet, novelist, and political activist. "Rape Poem," lines 18–19 (1976).

4   I asked myself, "Is it going to prevent me from getting out of here? Is there a risk of death attached to it? Is it permanently disabling? Is it permanently disfiguring? Lastly, is it excruciating?" If it doesn't fit one of those five categories, then it isn't important.

RHONDA CORNUM, United States Army Major. As quoted in *Newsweek* magazine, "Perspectives" page (July 13, 1992).

On being sexually abused by Iraqi soldiers during the 1992 Persian Gulf War.

5   According to our social pyramid, all men who feel displaced racially, culturally, and/or because of economic hardships will turn on those whom they feel they can order and humiliate, usually women, children, and animals—just as they have been ordered and humiliated by those privileged few who are in power. However, this definition does not explain why there are privileged men who behave this way toward women.

ANA CASTILLO (b. 1953), Mexican–American poet, essayist, and feminist. *Massacre of the Dreamers*, ch. 3 (1994).

ACADEMIA

1   The popular colleges of the United States are turning out more edu-

cated people with less originality and fewer geniuses than any other country.

CAROLINE NICHOLS CHURCHILL (1833–?), U.S. author. *Active Footsteps,* ch. 24 (1909).

2 Ignorance of what real learning is, and a consequent suspicion of it; materialism, and a consequent intellectual laxity—both of these have done destructive work in the colleges.

KATHERINE FULLERTON GEROULD (1879–1944), U.S. author. *Modes and Morals,* ch. 4 (1920).

3 Here was a place where nothing was crystallized. There were no traditions, no customs, no college songs. . . . There were no rules and regulations. All would have to be thought of, planned, built up, created—what a magnificent opportunity!

MABEL SMITH DOUGLASS (1877–1933), U.S. educator. *The Early History of New Jersey College for Women* (1929). Recalling the early years of the New Jersey College for Women; Douglass became its first dean in 1918.

4 Professors could silence me then; they had figures, diagrams, maps, books. . . . I was learning that books and diagrams can be evil things if they deaden the mind of man and make him blind or cynical before subjection of any kind.

AGNES SMEDLEY (1890–1950), U.S. journalist and socialist. *Daughter of Earth,* part 7 (1943). In this autobiographical novel, the future journalist and political activist, who lived, worked, and organized in China, 1928–1941, was describing her experience with American university education.

5 The university is no longer a quiet place to teach and do scholarly work at a measured pace and contemplate the universe. It is big, complex, demanding, competitive, bureaucratic, and chronically short of money.

PHYLLIS DAIN (b. 1930), U.S. librarian, educator, and historian. *Aspirations and Mentoring in an Academic Environment,* by Mary Niles Maack and Joanne Passet, "Commentary" section (1994). From a speech given at the 1990 annual conference of the Association for Library and Information Science Education, in a program sponsored by the Gender Issues Special Interest Group. Dain was a faculty member at Columbia University.

6 I was so grateful to be independent of the academic establishment. I thought, how awful it would be to have my future hinge on such people and such decisions.

JANE JACOBS (b. 1916), U.S. urban analyst. As quoted in the *New York Times,* p. 18 (May 31, 1993). The author of several books, including the classic *Death and Life of Great American Cities,* Jacobs was describing an interaction with urban planners from Harvard University and the Massachusetts Institute of Technology. She never attended college.

7 If, as a feminist leader, I try to help out the career of a rising woman faculty leader—I'm sleeping with her.

THEO J. KALIKOW (b. 1941), U.S. educator. As quoted in the *Chronicle of Higher Education,* p. A16 (June 16, 1993). The interim president of Plymouth State College (New Hampshire) was remarking on the tendency toward unfounded speculation in academia about feminists', and women college presidents', sexual orientation and behavior.

8 Institutions of higher education in the United States are products of

Western society in which masculine values like an orientation toward achievement and objectivity are valued over cooperation, connectedness and subjectivity.

YOLANDA MOSES (b. 1946), U.S. educator. As quoted in the *New York Times*, p. 47 (September 12, 1993).

Moses was the recently-appointed President of City College in the City University of New York. The only CUNY trustee to vote against her appointment, Herman Badillo, cited this statement, made by Moses in an article published earlier, when explaining his opposition.

9 . . . in the minds of search committees there is the lingering question: Can she manage the football coach?

DONNA E. SHALALA (b. 1941), U.S. educator and government official. As quoted in the *New York Times*, p. C4 (October 20, 1994).

At this time, Shalala was the U. S. Secretary of Health and Human Services, as well as the former Chancellor of the University of Wisconsin. She was speaking of the reluctance of University President search committees to select women candidates.

10 The academy is not paradise. But learning is a place where paradise can be created.

BELL HOOKS (b. c. 1955), U.S. author and educator. *Teaching to Transgress*, ch. 14 (1994).

ACHIEVEMENT

1 I have such an intense pride of sex that the triumphs of women in art, literature, oratory, science, or song rouse my enthusiasm as nothing else can.

ELIZABETH CADY STANTON (1815–1902), U.S. suffragist, author, and social reformer. *Eighty Years and More (1815–1897)*, ch. 17 (1898).

2 Events that are predestined require but little management. They manage themselves. They slip into place while we sleep, and suddenly we are aware that the thing we fear to attempt, is already accomplished.

AMELIA E. BARR (1831–1919), U.S. author; born in Scotland. *All the Days of My Life*, ch. 10 (1913).

3 People Who Do things exceed my endurance;
God, for a man that solicits insurance!

DOROTHY PARKER (1893–1967), U.S. author and humorist. "Bohemia," lines 9–10 (c. late 1920s).

The poem is a put-down of tedious, self-absorbed "authors . . . artists . . . sculptors . . . singers . . . playwrights . . . poets . . . diarists . . . critics". Parker's first husband, Edwin Pond Parker II, sold insurance.

4 The higher one climbs the lonelier one is.

MARY BARNETT GILSON (1877– ?), U.S. factory personnel manager, economist, and educator. *What's Past is Prologue*, ch. 19 (1940).

5 The needs of a society determine its ethics, and in the Black American ghettos the hero is that man who is offered only the crumbs from his country's table but by ingenuity and courage is able to take for himself a Lucullan feast. Hence the janitor who lives in one room but sports a robin's-egg-blue Cadillac is not laughed at but admired, and the domestic who buys forty-dollar shoes is not criticized but is appreciated. We know that they have put to use their full mental and physical powers. Each single gain feeds into the gains of the body collective.

MAYA ANGELOU (b. 1928), African American poet, autobiographer, and performer. *I Know Why the Caged Bird Sings*, ch. 29 (1970).

6 I don't think the question needs to be genderized. It would feel great to anyone. But whether you're a girl or a boy or a Martian, you still have to go out and prove yourself again every day.

JULIE KRONE (b. 1963), U.S. jockey. As quoted in the *New York Times Magazine*, p. 20 (July 15, 1993).

On being asked, following her victory in the 1993 Belmont Stakes, how it felt to be the first woman jockey ever to win a prestigious Triple Crown horse race.

7 I'd take the bus downtown with my mother, and the big thing was to sit at the counter and get an orange drink and a tuna sandwich on toast. I thought I was living large! . . . When I was at the Ritz with the publisher a few months ago, I did think, *"Oh my God, I'm in the Ritz tearoom."* . . . The person who was so happy to sit at the Woolworths counter is now sitting at the Ritz, listening to the harp, and wondering what tea to order. . . . [ellipsis in source] *Am I awake?*

CONNIE PORTER (b. 1959), African American novelist and educator. As quoted in *Listen to Their Voices*, ch. 5, by Mickey Pearlman (1993).

8 (1) Do not cry. No matter what. (2) Use your appearance to create an image of strength. (3) Develop staying power. (4) Specialize. (5) Don't wear your sex like a badge on your sleeve. (6) Put in

more time than anyone else. (7) Be loyal. (8) Be a team player. (9) Never use your family as an excuse. (10) Learn how to be a manager. (11) Network.

DIANNE FEINSTEIN (b. 1933), U.S. politician. As quoted in *Dianne Feinstein*, chapters 1–9, 11–12, by Jerry Roberts (1994).

Feinstein was the former San Francisco Mayor and current United States Senator. Roberts labelled these "Dianne Feinstein's Rules for [women] Getting Ahead" and headed each of eleven chapters with one of them, in the order shown above.

ACTING

1 . . . unless the actor is able to discourse most eloquently without opening his lips, he lacks the prime essential of a finished artist.

JULIA MARLOWE (1870–1950), U.S. actor; born in England. As quoted in *Actors on Acting*, rev. ed., part 13, by Toby Cole and Helen Krich (1970).

Said in 1913.

2 As soon as I suspect a fine effect is being achieved by accident I lose interest. I am not interested . . . in unskilled labor. . . . The scientific actor is an *even* worker. Any one may achieve on some rare occasion an outburst of genuine feeling, a gesture of imperishable beauty, a ringing accent of truth; but your scientific actor knows how he did it. He can repeat it again and again and again. He can be depended on.

MINNIE MADDERN FISKE (1865–1932), U.S. actor. As quoted in *Mrs. Fiske: Her Views on Actors, Acting and the Problems of Production*, ch. 3, by Alexander Woollcott (1917).

Fiske had been a popular stage actor since the age of four (when she used her birth name, Minnie Maddern).

3 The essence of acting is the conveyance of truth through the medium of the actor's mind and person. The science of acting deals with the perfecting of that medium.

MINNIE MADDERN FISKE (1865–1932), U.S. actor. As quoted in *Mrs. Fiske: Her Views on Actors, Acting and the Problems of Production,* ch. 5, by Alexander Woollcott (1917).

Fiske had been a popular stage actor since the age of four (when she used her birth name, Minnie Maddern).

4 *The Temptress* has now been shown here—terrible. The story, Garbo, everything is extremely bad. It is no exaggeration to say that I was dreadful. I was tired, I couldn't sleep and everything went wrong. But the main reason is, I suppose, that I'm no actress.

GRETA GARBO (1905–1990), Swedish actor; relocated to the United States. As quoted in *The Divine Garbo,* ch. 4, by Frederick Sands and Sven Broman (1979).

Written in a letter to her Swedish friend, Lars Saxon, in 1926. *The Temptress* was Garbo's second American movie; during production, Garbo's sister had died and her director and mentor, fellow Swede Mauritz Stiller (1883–1928), had been fired by the studio executive. Though the film made her a star, this was her assessment of it. She would come to be judged by many critics the greatest actress in the history of the movies.

5 I have no acting technique. . . . I act instinctively. That's why I can't play any role that isn't based on something in my life.

ETHEL WATERS (1900–1977), U.S. actor and singer. As quoted in *Famous Actors and Actresses on the American Stage,* vol. 2, by William C. Young (1975).

First quoted by Henry Hewes in the *New York Times* on April 30, 1950 (section 1, p. 2).

6 Acting is a form of confession.

TALLULAH BANKHEAD (1903–1968), U.S. actress. *Tallulah,* ch. 16 (1952).

7 An actor rides in a bus or railroad train; he sees a movement and applies it to a new role. A woman in agony of spirit *might* turn her head just so; a man in deep humiliation probably would wring his hands in such a way. From straws like these, drawn from completely different sources, the fabric of a character may be built. The whole garment in which the actor hides himself is made of small externals of observation fitted to his conception of a role.

ELEANOR ROBSON BELMONT (1878–1979), U.S. stage actress and socialite. *The Fabric of Memory,* part 1 ch. 2 (1957).

Belmont was a stage actress in her youth, under her maiden name.

8 Personality is the most important thing to an actress's success.

MAE WEST (1892–1980), U.S. actor. *Goodness Had Nothing to Do With It,* ch. 1 (1959).

West was a flamboyant stage and screen actor known for her witty, audacious portrayals of sexually experienced women.

9 Every single night I'm nervous.

VIVIEN LEIGH (1913–1967), British actor; born in India. As quoted in *Famous Actors and Actresses on the American Stage,* vol. 2, by William C. Young (1975).

From an interview first published in *Actors Talk About Acting,* edited by Lewis Funke and John E. Booth (1961). The experienced screen and stage actress was referring to the stage fright that afflicted her before every performance; at the time, she was in her tenth month of performing in the play, *Duel of Angels.*

10 Today the young actors regard their environment with rage and disgust. They regard their Master not as disciples regard their Master, but as slaves regard their Master.

JUDITH MALINA (b. 1926), U.S. actor and stage producer. As quoted in *Actors on Acting,* rev. ed., part 13, by Toby Cole and Helen Krich (1970).

With her husband, Julian Beck, Malina founded and developed the Living Theatre, which attempted to break down the separation between performer and spectator, inviting intense interaction. Their theater grew increasingly improvisational, confrontational, chaotic, and daring.

11 I'm tired of playing worn-out depressing ladies in frayed bathrobes. I'm going to get a new hairdo and look terrific and go back to school and even if nobody notices, I'm going to be the most self-fulfilled lady on the block.

JOANNE WOODWARD (b. 1930), U.S. actor. As quoted in *Ms.* magazine, p. 54 (February 1975).

Woodward, an Academy Award-winning movie actor, was commenting on the uninteresting sameness of the roles available to her. She did indeed return to school; a number of years later, she and one of her daughters received their baccalaureates from Sarah Lawrence College on the same day.

12 Make them laugh, make them cry, and back to laughter. What do people go to the theatre for? An emotional exercise. . . . I am a servant of the people. I have never forgotten that.

MARY PICKFORD (1893–1979), U.S. actor. As quoted in *The International Dictionary of Films and Filmmakers, Volume III: Actors and Actresses,* by Elaine Mancini (1986).

13 I could live without acting. . . . Acting is a gift I've received. And I'm grateful for it and I enjoy it. But it's not the main point of my life. It never was.

JEANNE MOREAU (b. 1928), French actor. As quoted in the *New York Times,* p. B15 (January 3, 1994).

A major star of the French cinema, she said this during a 1993 interview.

14 Be a doctor! Be a lawyer! Be a leper missionary!

DIANE LADD (b. 1932), U.S. actor. As quoted in *People* magazine, p. 211 (March 4–17, 1994).

Advising her young daughter, Laura Dern—whose father, Bruce Dern, was also an actor—to enter any profession other than acting. Laura disregarded the advice.

ACTIVITY

1 If we don't act at all (express our imaginings either in work or a changing personality, so that we can learn and think again something better) we certainly rot.

BRENDA UELAND (1891–1985), U.S. author and writing teacher. *If You Want to Write,* 2nd. ed., ch. 5 (1938).

2 Without being forgiven, released from the consequences of what we have done, our capacity to act would . . . be confined to one single deed from which we could never recover; we would remain the victims of its consequences forever, not unlike the sorcerer's apprentice who lacked the magic formula to break the spell.

HANNAH ARENDT (1906–1975), U.S. philosopher. *The Human Condition,* ch. 33 (1958).

3 You are richer for doing things.

JESSICA TANDY (1909–1994), U.S. actress. As quoted in the *New York Times,* p. D11 (September 12, 1994).

Explaining why she continued to act, sometimes accepting inferior roles, into her eighties. Even near the end of her life, when she was very sick with cancer, she made several movies and television shows.

ACTORS

1 The actor can be compared to the soldier. The former dazzled by his triumphs, sighs continually for the struggles of stage-life; the latter filled with the glory he has acquired on the battlefield, cannot resign himself to peace.

ADELAIDE RISTORI (1822–1906), Italian actor. As quoted in *Famous Actors and Actresses on the American Stage,* vol. 2, by William C. Young (1975).
From *Memoirs and Artistic Studies,* which was first published in Italian in 1857, in English in 1888.

2 An actress must be a woman whose emotional perceptions are true, and to make them so, she must have a fine contempt for any art or thought that betrays them for something false.

NANCE O'NEIL (1874–1965), U.S. actor. As quoted in *Famous Actors and Actresses on the American Stage,* vol. 2, by William C. Young (1975).
From an article first published in *Theatre* magazine in 1920.

3 Once the curtain is raised, the actor ceases to belong to himself. He belongs to his character, to his author, to his public. He must do the impossible to identify himself with the first, not to betray the second, and not to disappoint the third.

SARAH BERNHARDT (1845–1923), French actor. *The Art of the Theatre,* ch. 3 (1924).

4 The actor should not play a part. Like the Aeolian harps that used to be hung in the trees to be played only by the breeze, the actor should be an instrument *played upon* by the character he depicts.

ALLA NAZIMOVA (1879–1945), U.S. actor; born in Russia. As quoted in *Actors on Acting,* rev. ed., part 13, by Toby Cole and Helen Krich (1970).
Said in 1937.

5 Please don't make me a joke.

MARILYN MONROE (1926–1962), U.S. actor. As quoted in *Ms.* magazine, p. 42 (August 1972).
Monroe, a beautiful movie star and "sex symbol," was often ridiculed; people tended to underrate both her acting ability and her intelligence. She concluded her last interview, with Patricia Newcomb in 1962, with this plea to Newcomb. Soon afterward, she was dead—probably of suicide.

6 I suspect there isn't an actor alive who was able to truthfully answer his family's questions after his first day's activity in his future profession.

SIMONE SIGNORET (1921–1985), French movie actor. *Nostalgia Isn't What It Used to Be,* ch. 3 (1976).
Referring to the dull and unpleasant, rather than glamorous, nature of a movie actor's first day of work.

7 . . . actresses are such very dull people off the stage. We are only delightful and brilliant when we are doing what we are told to do. Off stage we are awful chumps.

DAME EDITH EVANS (1888–1976), British actor. As quoted in *Dame Edith Evans,* ch. 12, by Bryan Forbes (1977).

8 I don't know why people think child actresses in particular are screwed up. I see kids everywhere who are totally bored. I've never been bored a day in my life.

JODIE FOSTER (b. 1962), U.S. actor. As quoted in *People* magazine, p. 316 (February 7–14, 1994).

Foster, once a child actor, had developed a highly successful adult career, twice winning the Academy Award for Best Actress.

ADVANCEMENT

1 So close is the bond between man and woman that you can not raise one without lifting the other. The world can not move ahead without woman's sharing in the movement, and to help give a right impetus to that movement is woman's highest privilege.

FRANCES ELLEN WATKINS HARPER (1825–1911), U.S. suffragist and rights advocate. As quoted in *Black Women in Nineteenth-Century American Life,* part 3, by Bert James Loewenberg and Ruth Bogin (1976).

From her 1893 speech at the Columbian Exposition in Chicago: "Woman's Political Future."

2 I have never yet spoken from a public platform about women in industry that someone has not said, "But things are far better than they used to be." I confess to impatience with persons who are satisfied with a dangerously slow tempo of progress for half of society in an age which requires a much faster tempo than in the days that "used to be." Let us use *what might be* instead of *what has been* as our yardstick!

MARY BARNETT GILSON (1877– ?), U.S. factory personnel manager, economist, and educator. *What's Past is Prologue,* ch. 26 (1940).

On the pace at which employment opportunities were opening for women.

3 Probably nothing in the experience of the rank and file of workers causes more bitterness and envy than the realization which comes sooner or later to many of them that they are "stuck" and can go no further.

MARY BARNETT GILSON (1877– ?), U.S. factory personnel manager, economist, and educator. *What's Past is Prologue,* ch. 7 (1940).

4 There was danger at times that women might not be judged by the highest standards, but more leniently because of their sex. "She is a remarkably good chemist—for a woman," you might hear a man say. It seemed to me essential, if the ablest young women scholars were to achieve the best work of which they were capable, that they should be held to the most rigorous standards. . . . To advance, a woman must do at least as good work as her male colleagues, usually better.

VIRGINIA CROCHERON GILDER-SLEEVE (1877–1965), U.S. educator. *Many a Good Crusade,* part 1 (1954).

5 Women have progressed far beyond the point of no return. They're in medical schools and law schools, and they're inching into the upper echelons of the corporate world. They've entered the political arena and are even beginning to make inroads into that ultimate male enclave, the U. S. Congress. They've had a taste of equality, even a taste of power. They've experienced the shift in the balance of power in a marriage that occurs when a wife is

earning as much money as her husband. They've experienced the autonomy that comes from being in control of their own reproductive lives. They will almost certainly have to fight for these things again and again, losing ground, gaining ground, running in place. But they will never go back.

BRETT HARVEY (b. 1936), U.S. author. *The Fifties,* Epilogue (1993).

6 Let's assume you guys know I got this job because of my competency and proven successes with this company and you're just as happy to have me here as I am to be here, and I won't ever think anything other than that.

DEBORAH S. KENT (b. 1953), African American assembly plant manager. As quoted in the *New York Times,* sect. 3 p. 7 (February 5, 1995).
The third of nine children raised by Leodas and Earline Stewart, a St. Louis laborer and housewife, Kent became the first woman ever to head a vehicle assembly plant for the Ford Motor Company. Shortly after her arrival, she met with the area managers and said this.

ADVENTURE

1 She might have been old once and now, miraculously, young again— but with the memory of that other life intact. She seemed to know the world down there in the dark hall and beyond for what it was. Yet knowing, she still longed to leave this safe, sunlit place at the top of the house for the challenge there.

PAULE MARSHALL (b. 1929), African American novelist. *Brown Girl, Brownstones,* ch. 1 (1959).

Ten-year-old Selina Boyce, the heroine of this novel set among West Indian immigrants living in Brooklyn, New York, during the Great Depression and World War II, contemplates life beyond her familiar apartment. Marshall, the daughter of immigrants from Barbados, grew up in Brooklyn and graduated from Brooklyn College.

2 I've stayed in the front yard all my life.
I want a peek at the back
Where it's rough and untended and hungry weed grows.
A girl gets sick of a rose.

GWENDOLYN BROOKS (b. 1917), African American author. "A song in the front yard," lines 1–4 (1968).

ADVERTISING

1 Advertising . . . legitimizes the idealized, stereotyped roles of woman as temptress, wife, mother, and sex object, and portrays women as less intelligent and more dependent than men. It makes women believe that their chief role is to please men and that their fulfillment will be as wives, mothers, and homemakers. It makes women feel unfeminine if they are not pretty enough and guilty if they do not spend most of their time in desperate attempts to imitate gourmet cooks and eighteenth-century scullery maids. It makes women believe that their own lives, talents, and interests ought to be secondary to the needs of their husbands and families and that they are almost totally defined by these relationships.

LUCY KOMISAR (b. 1942), U.S. author. *Woman in Sexist Society,* ch. 13 (1971).

2 Watching fifteen seconds of nasal passages unblocking sure beats watching thirty seconds.

BARBARA LIPPERT, U.S. advertising critic. As quoted in *Newsweek* magazine, p. 8 (June 16, 1986).

On the trend toward shorter television advertisements; Lippert was referring to excessively detailed antihistamine ads.

3 I'm a copywriter for an ad agency. It involves being a total asshole. I do it for the money, it's easy and horrible. I do nothing good for society.

ISABELLE KUPRIN (b. c. 1960), U.S. advertising copywriter. As quoted in *The Great Divide*, book 1, section 5, by Studs Terkel (1988).

ADVICE

1 . . . advice is one of those things it is far more blessed to give than to receive.

CAROLYN WELLS (1862–1942), U.S. author. *The Rest of My Life*, ch. 5 (1937).

2 I've been asked to give some words of advice for young women entering library/information science education. Does anyone ever take advice? The advice we give is usually what we would do or would have done if we had the chance, and the advice that's taken, if ever, is often what we wanted to hear in the first place.

PHYLLIS DAIN (b. 1930), U.S. librarian, educator, and historian. *Aspirations and Mentoring in an Academic Environment*, by Mary Niles Maack and Joanne Passet, "Commentary" section (1994).

From a speech given at the 1990 annual conference of the Association for Library and Informa-

tion Science Education, in a program sponsored by the Gender Issues Special Interest Group.

AESTHETICS

1 INTELLECTUALS DO NOT HAVE AESTHETIC EXPERIENCES.

MARGARET ANDERSON (1886–1973), U.S. editor and memoirist. *The Strange Necessity,* part 1 (1969).

Anderson referred to this as part of the "credo" for her renowned literary and arts journal, *The Little Review* (1914–1929).

AFRICAN AMERICAN RIGHTS

1 It's time for America to get right.

FANNIE LOU HAMER (1917–1977), African American civil rights activist. As quoted in *This Little Light of Mine*, ch. 8, by Hay Mills (1993).

Said on September 13, 1965, in a speech at a rally following a hearing before the United States House of Representatives' Subcommittee on Elections—at which she had also spoken.

AFRICAN AMERICAN WOMEN

1 The hearts of Afro-American women are too warm and too large for race hatred. Long suffering has so chastened them that they are developing a special sense of sympathy for all who suffer and fail of justice.

FANNIE BARRIER WILLIAMS (1855–1944), African American advocate of civil rights and women's rights. As quoted in *Black Women in Nineteenth-Century American Life,* ch. 3, by Bert James Loewenberg and Ruth Bogin (1976).

Born in Brockport, New York, to a distinguished free African American family, Williams had lived in the South before marrying a Chicago attorney. This is from "The Intellectual Progress of the Colored Women of the United States Since the Emancipation Proclamation," an 1893 speech she made in Chicago before the World's Congress of Representative Women.

2 . . . the Black woman in America can justly be described as a "slave of a slave."

FRANCES BEALE, African American feminist and civil rights activist. *The Black Woman,* ch. 14 (1970).

3 No other group in America has so had their identity socialized out of existence as have black women. . . . When black people are talked about the focus tends to be on black *men;* and when women are talked about the focus tends to be on *white* women.

BELL HOOKS (b. c. 1955), African American author, feminist, and civil rights advocate. *Ain't I a Woman?* Introduction (1981).

4 Let me just say, at once: I am not now nor have I ever been a white man. And, leaving aside the joys of unearned privilege, this leaves me feeling pretty good . . .

JUNE JORDAN (b. 1936), African American poet and social critic. *On Call,* ch. 10 (1985). Written in 1984.

5 I am a person. I have feelings. I have needs. I have wants. I'm sittin' here and nobody sees me. Everybody just looks over me and walks on past because I'm black, because I'm a woman, because I'm poor, because I have no education. But I'm still here.

CORA LEE JOHNSON (b. 1925), African American social activist. As quoted in *I Dream a World,* by Brian Lanker (1989).

A poor, uneducated African American woman from rural Soperton, Georgia, Johnson became

an unpaid activist who successfully pressed for changes in social service policy.

6 The myth of black women profiting at the expense of black men is the oldest rap around.

JOHNNETTA BETSCH COLE (b. 1936), African American educator. As quoted in *I Dream a World,* by Brian Lanker (1989).

At this time, Cole was the President of Spelman College, a historically African American women's institution.

7 The empowerment of black women constitutes . . . the empowerment of our entire community.

KIMBERLÉ CRENSHAW (b. 1959), African American author. *Race-ing Justice, En-gendering Power,* ch. 14 (1992).

8 . . . I am who I am *because* I'm a black female. . . . When I was health director in Arkansas . . . I could talk about teen-age pregnancy, about poverty, ignorance and enslavement and how the white power structure had imposed it—*only* because I was a black female. I mean, black people would have eaten up a white male who said what I did.

JOYCELYN ELDERS (b. 1933), U.S. pediatrician and educator; first woman (and second African American) Surgeon General of the United States. As quoted in the *New York Times Magazine,* p. 18 (January 30, 1994).

Elders, who was U. S. Surgeon General at the time, was explaining why she did not feel "oppressed" by her race or sex. Within a year, she was dismissed by President Bill Clinton for her outspokenness.

9 . . . black women have always found that in the social order of things we're the least likely to be believed—by anyone.

JOYCELYN ELDERS (b. 1933), U.S. pediatrician and educator; first woman (and second African American) Surgeon General of the United States. As quoted in the *New York Times Magazine*, p. 18 (January 30, 1994).

Reflecting on the treatment of Anita Hill, an African American attorney and law school professor who accused Judge Clarence Thomas, also African American and then a U. S. Supreme Court nominee, of sexual harassment when she had worked for him some years earlier. Hill was ridiculed by several Senators during Thomas's confirmation hearings. Ultimately, Thomas was appointed to the Court.

AFRICAN AMERICAN-JEWISH RELATIONSHIPS

1 ... the histories of Blacks and Jews in bondage and out of bondage, have been blood histories pursued through our kindred searchings for self-determination. Let this blood be a stain of honor that we share. Let us not now become enemies to ourselves and to each other.

JUNE JORDAN (b. 1936), African American poet and social critic. *On Call*, ch. 14 (1985).

At the time, relations between African Americans and Jews, who traditionally supported African American rights, had become tense.

AFRICAN AMERICANS

1 Take us generally as a people, we are neither lazy nor idle; and considering how little we have to excite or stimulate us, I am almost astonished that there are so many industrious and ambitious ones to be found; although I acknowledge, with extreme sorrow, that there are some who never were and never will be serviceable to society. And have you not a similar class among yourselves?

MARIA STEWART (1803–1879), African American abolitionist and schoolteacher. As quoted in *Black Women in Nineteenth-Century American Life*, part 3, by Bert James Loewenberg and Ruth Bogin (1976).

Stewart, a free African American, said this in a September 21, 1832 speech delivered at Franklin Hall in Boston.

2 What man or woman of common sense now doubts the intellectual capacity of colored people? Who does not know, that with all our efforts as a nation to crush and *annihilate the mind* of this portion of our race, we have never yet been able to do it.

ANGELINA GRIMKÉ (1805–1879), U.S. abolitionist and feminist. *Letters to Catherine Beecher*, letter #6 (1837).

In a letter dated July 20, 1837.

3 ... there is a place in the United States for the Negro. They are real American citizens, and at home. They have fought and bled and died, like men, to make this country what it is. And if they have got to suffer and die, and be lynched, and tortured, and burned at the stake, I say they are at home.

AMANDA BERRY SMITH (1837–1915), African American preacher and missionary. As quoted in *Black Women in Nineteenth-Century American Life*, part 3, by Bert James Loewenberg and Ruth Bogin (1976).

Reacting, in 1893, to the movement which was encouraging American blacks to emigrate to Liberia. Born a slave in Maryland, Smith had been liberated as a child when her father bought her freedom. She had later become an intinerant preacher and, for eight years, a missionary to Africa—mainly Liberia.

4 ... I was confronted with a virile idealism, an awareness of what man must have for manliness, dignity, and inner liberty which, by con-

trast, made me see how easy living had made my own group into childishly unthinking people. The Negro's struggles and despairs have been like fertilizer in the fields of his humanity, while we, like protected children with all our basic needs supplied, have given our attention to superficialities.

SARAH PATTON BOYLE, U.S. civil rights activist and author. *The Desegregated Heart,* part 1, ch. 19 (1962).

Boyle, a white Virginian who was an activist in the Civil Rights movement, was recalling the fall of 1951, when she first attended the Virginia Slave Conference of the NAACP.

5 I marvel at the many ways we, as black people, bend but do not break in order to survive. This astonishes me, and what excites me I write about. Everyone of us is a wonder. Everyone of us has a story.

KRISTIN HUNTER (b. 1931), African American author. *Black Women Writers at Work,* ch. 6, by Claudia Tate (1983).

6 I think it's unfair for people to try to make successful blacks feel guilty for not feeling guilty. . . . We're unique in that we're not supposed to enjoy the things we've worked so hard for.

PATRICIA GRAYSON, African American administrator. As quoted in *Time* magazine, p. 59 (March 13, 1989).

Grayson was Vice-President of National Medical Fellowships, which promoted the education of minority students in medicine.

AFTERLIFE

1 Are there not some pursuits that we practise because they are good in themselves, and some pleasures that

are final? And is not [reading] among them? I have sometimes dreamt, at least, that when the Day of Judgment dawns and the great conquerors and lawyers and statesmen come to receive their rewards . . . the Almighty will turn to Peter and say, not without a certain envy when He sees us coming with our books under our arms, "Look, these need no reward. We have nothing to give them here. They have loved reading."

VIRGINIA WOOLF (1882–1941), British novelist, essayist, and diarist. *The Second Common Reader,* ch. 22 (1932).

2 . . . the loss of belief in future states is politically, though certainly not spiritually, the most significant distinction between our present period and the centuries before. And this loss is definite. For no matter how religious our world may turn again, or how much authentic faith still exists in it, or how deeply our moral values may be rooted in our religious systems, the fear of hell is no longer among the motives which would prevent or stimulate the actions of a majority.

HANNAH ARENDT (1906–1975), U.S. philosopher and political theorist; born in Germany. *Between Past and Future,* ch. 3 (1961).

AGEISM

1 Prejudice against women . . . is many, many times intensified against older women. You are viewed not as an intellect but as a body. . . . Astonishingly, even women's liberation has paid extraordinarily little attention to the older woman and to the fact that her job is limited because she is [older]. They say that women shouldn't be sex objects, but you damned well better be a sex object if you want to get ahead in television.

Elinor Guggenheimer (b. 1912), U.S. television newswoman. As quoted in *Women in Television News,* ch. 3, by Judith S. Gelfman (1976).

Said on March 1, 1973. Guggenheimer has been co-host of the television news program, *Straight Talk.*

2 Think about the pressure to "pass" by lying about one's age . . . that familiar temptation to falsify a condition of one's birth or identity and pretend to be part of a more favored group. Fair-skinned blacks invented "passing" as a term, Jews escaping anti-Semitism perfected the art, and the sexual closet continues the punishment, but pretending to be a younger age is probably the most encouraged form of "passing," with the least organized support for "coming out" as one's true generational self.

Gloria Steinem (b. 1934), U.S. feminist, author, and editor. *Moving Beyond Words,* part 6 (1994).

AGING

1 I have enjoyed greatly the second blooming that comes when you finish the life of the emotions and of personal relations; and suddenly you find—at the age of fifty, say— that a whole new life has opened before you, filled with things you can think about, study, or read about. . . . It is as if a fresh sap of ideas and thoughts was rising in you.

Agatha Christie (1891–1976), British mystery novelist. *An Autobiography,* part 11 (1977).

Christie worked on this book sporadically from 1950 to 1965, though it was not published until after her death.

2 Logic and hope fade somewhat by thirty-six, when endings seem more like clear warnings than useful experience.

Jane O'Reilly, U.S. feminist and humorist. *The Girl I Left Behind,* ch. 2 (1980).

This is drawn from O'Reilly's famous essay first published in *Ms.* magazine: "Click! The Housewife's Moment of Truth."

3 The aging process is a part of most of our lives, and it remains one we try to ignore until it seems to pounce upon us. We evade all its signals. We stay blandly unprepared for some of its obnoxious effects, even though we have coped with the cracked voices and puzzling glands of our emerging natures, and have been guided no matter how clumsily through budding love-pains, morning sickness, and hot flashes. We do what our mentors teach us to do, but few of us acknowledge that the last years of our lives, if we can survive to live them out, are as physically predictable as infancy's or those of our full flowering. This seems impossible, but it is true.

M. F. K. Fisher (1908–1992), U.S. culinary writer and autobiographer. *Sister Age,* Afterword (1983).

4 [To an admirer who said, "You look gorgeous":] Oh, God, if you only knew how much work it takes.

JULIE WILSON (b. 1925), U.S. singer. As quoted in the *New York Times,* p. B3 (September 29, 1993).

This exchange took place at a gathering of women who had been Copacabana "showgirls" in the 1940s and fifties.

AGING: NEGATIVE ASPECTS

1 Oh, yes, I'd do it all again; the spirit is willing yet; I feel the same desire to do the work but the flesh is weak. It's too bad that our bodies wear out while our interests are just as strong as ever.

SUSAN B. ANTHONY (1820–1906), U.S. suffragist. As quoted in *Life and Work of Susan B. Anthony,* vol. 3 ch. 71, by Anna Howard Shaw, to Ida Husted Harper (1908).

In March 1906, on her death bed, in answer to the question of her sister suffragist, Rev. Anna Howard Shaw (1847–1919): " . . . as you look back on the past, if you had to live it over again, would you do the same?"

2 No amount of skill on the part of the actress can make up for the loss of youth.

ELLEN TERRY (1847–1928), British actor. *Ellen Terry's Memoirs,* 2nd. ed., ch. 13 (1932). Written in 1906 or 1907.

3 [My early stories] are the work of a living writer whom I know in a sense, but can never meet.

ELIZABETH BOWEN (1899–1973), British novelist, story writer, essayist, and memoirist; born in Ireland. *Seven Winters,* part 2, sect. 2, ch. 8 (1962).

From preface to the 1951 reprint of *Ann Lee's,* her second story collection.

4 The young . . . look into visages dull-eyed, long-toothed, wattle-necked, and chop-fallen, something they have never been and which they cannot imagine ever being. . . . If it occurs to a young person, looking at us, that this is the direction in which he himself travels, how can he forgive, let alone bear the sight of, us, who constantly bring him the bad news of our own faces, bitter signposts pointing to his own destination?

JESSAMYN WEST (1902–1984), U.S. novelist. *To See the Dream,* part 1 (1956).

5 . . . after being at the top, I don't think I could play senior tournaments, because you know how good you were. I don't know if I would enjoy that, being half of what I was.

CHRIS EVERT (b. 1954), U.S. tennis player. As quoted in *Sports Illustrated,* p. 61 (May 25, 1992).

Evert, who had recently retired from professional tennis, had been a top-ranked star for many years.

6 . . . we've allowed a youth-centered culture to leave us so estranged from our future selves that, when asked about the years beyond fifty, sixty, or seventy—all part of the average human life span providing we can escape hunger, violence, and other epidemics—many people can see only a blank screen, or one on which they project fear of disease and democracy.

GLORIA STEINEM (b. 1934), U.S. feminist, author, and editor. *Moving Beyond Words,* part 6 (1994).

AGING: POSITIVE ASPECTS

1   . . . the hey-day of a woman's life is on the shady side of fifty, when the vital forces heretofore expended in other ways are garnered in the brain, when their thoughts and sentiments flow out in broader channels, when philanthropy takes the place of family selfishness, and when from the depths of poverty and suffering the wail of humanity grows as pathetic to their ears as once was the cry of their own children.

ELIZABETH CADY STANTON (1815–1902), U.S. suffragist, social reformer, and author. *Eighty Years and More (1815–1897)*, ch. 27 (1898).

Written in June 1892.

2   The older I get, the greater power I seem to have to help the world; I am like a snowball—the further I am rolled the more I gain.

SUSAN B. ANTHONY (1820–1906), U.S. suffragist. As quoted in *The Life and Work of Susan B. Anthony*, ch. 46, by Ida Husted Harper (1898).

Said in 1896. Within four years, she would begin to suffer health problems and a reduced capacity for work.

3   To-morrow I will have finished four-score years. I have lived to rise from the most despised and hated woman in all the world of fifty years ago, until now it seems as if I am loved by you all. If this is true, then I am indeed satisfied.

SUSAN B. ANTHONY (1820–1906), U.S. suffragist. As quoted in *History of Woman Suffrage*, vol. 4 ch. 21, by Susan B. Anthony and Ida Husted Harper (1902).

Said on the closing day of the thirty-second annual convention of the National Woman Suffrage Association, held February 8–14, 1900, in Washington, D.C. Anthony had resigned the association's presidency after holding office in woman suffrage organizations continuously for forty-eight years. The next day, she turned eighty. Once widely resented and ridiculed for her advocacy of women's rights—especially suffrage—Anthony had become a respected personage, though suffrage still eluded American women.

4   Every time I think that I am getting old, and gradually going to the grave, something else happens.

LILLIAN CARTER (1898–1983), U.S. matriarch mother of American President Jimmy Carter. As quoted in *The Decade of Women*, by Suzanne Levine and Harriet Lyons (1980).

She was first quoted in *Ms.* magazine in 1976.

5   I've been in the twilight of my career longer than most people have had their career.

MARTINA NAVRATILOVA (b. 1956), U.S. tennis player; born and raised in Czechoslovakia. As quoted in the *New York Times*, p. B19 (September 30, 1993).

Once ranked the best woman tennis player in the world (and often judged the best in history), she had slipped to a number three ranking. She had been playing singles tennis competitively for twenty-one years and was easily old enough to be the mother of some of her opponents.

AGNOSTICISM

1   Agnosticism has nothing to impart. Its sermons are the exhortations of one who convinces you he stands on nothing and urges you to stand there too.

ANNA JULIA COOPER (1859–1964), U.S. educator and feminist. *A Voice from the South*, part 2 (1892).

ALCOHOL AND DRINKING

1 ... this I conceive to be no time to prate of moral influences. Our men's nerves require their accustomed narcotics and a glass of whiskey is a powerful friend in a sunstroke, and these poor fellows fall senseless on their heavy drills.

CLARA BARTON (1821–1912), U.S. Civil War nurse and founder of the American Red Cross. As quoted in *Angel of the Battlefield,* ch. 3, by Ishbel Ross (1956).

In an 1861 letter to her cousin Elvira. Once an opponent of tobacco, Barton now recognized the value of it and other intoxicating substances in wartime and supplied it to the Civil War soldiers herself. During World War II, after her death, the Red Cross would send 87 million packages of cigarettes abroad to service people.

2 The diagnosis of drunkenness was that it was a disease for which the patient was in no way responsible, that it was created by existing saloons, and non-existing bright hearths, smiling wives, pretty caps and aprons. The cure was the patent nostrum of pledge-signing, a lying-made-easy invention, which like calomel, seldom had any permanent effect on the disease for which it was given, and never failed to produce another and a worse. Here the care created an epidemic of forgery, falsehood and perjury.

JANE GREY SWISSHELM (1815–1884), U.S. newspaperwoman, abolitionist, and human rights activist. *Half a Century,* ch. 30 (1880).

3 I believe that the miseries consequent on the manufacture and sale of intoxicating liquors are so great as imperiously to command the at-

tention of all dedicated lives; and that while the abolition of American slavery was numerically first, the abolition of the liquor traffic is not morally second.

ELIZABETH STUART PHELPS (1844–1911), U.S. novelist and short story writer. *Chapters from a Life,* ch. 12 (1897).

Phelps worked for temperance. Prohibition would be enacted in 1920 when the 18th Amendment to the Constitution took effect, then abolished in 1933 by the 21st Amendment.

4 I can no more think of my own life without thinking of wine and wines and where they grew for me and why I drank them when I did and why I picked the grapes and where I opened the oldest procurable bottles, and all that, than I can remember living before I breathed.

M. F. K. FISHER (1908–1992), U.S. culinary writer and autobiographer. Preface (1984).

5 Unrecognized alcoholism is the ruling pathology among writers and intellectuals.

DIANA TRILLING (b. 1905), U.S. intellectual. *New York Times Book Review,* p. 15 (October 3, 1993).

AMBITION

1 I want to do everything in the world that can be done.

FANNY KEMBLE (1809–1893), British actress. *Journal of a Residence in America,* entry for September 11, 1832 (1835).

2 ... indefinite visions of ambition are weak against the ease of doing what is habitual or beguilingly agreeable.

George Eliot (1819–1880), British novelist. *Middlemarch,* ch. 60 (1871–1872).

3 I constantly felt (as I suppose many an ambitious girl has felt) a thumping from within unanswered by any beckoning from without.

Anna Julia Cooper (1859–1964), U.S. educator and feminist. *A Voice from the South,* part 1 (1892).

Of her frustration as a young student in a school offering inadequate intellectual stimulation. Cooper, the daughter of a former slave, would become a teacher and, at age 67, the fourth African American woman to earn a Ph.D. (at the University of Paris).

4 If God lets me live, I shall attain more than Mummy ever has done, I shall not remain insignificant, I shall work in the world and for mankind!

Anne Frank (1929–1945), Dutch Jewish diarist; born in Germany. *Diary of a Young Girl,* entry dated April 11, 1944 (1947).

Frank and her family were in hiding in Holland when she wrote this; her mother was a housewife. On August 4, their hiding place would be raided by the police, and they would be sent to German and Dutch concentration camps. All of them except Otto Frank, the father, would perish; Anne died in Bergen-Belsen, a German camp, just two months before the liberation of Holland.

5 One thing I am determined on is that by the time I die *my brain* shall weigh as much as a man's if study and learning can make it so.

M. Carey Thomas (1857–1935), U.S. educator. As quoted in *Carey Thomas of Bryn Mawr,* ch. 2, by Edith Finch (1947).

Written when she was denied access to doctoral studies in the United States because of her sex. Thomas earned a doctorate *summa cum laude* in Zurich, Switzerland, and went on to become president of Bryn Mawr College.

6 [Asked by an interviewer, "What do YOU want to be?"]: What people want me to be.

Joan Crawford (1908–1977), U.S. actor. As quoted in *American Dreams,* book 1, part 1, by Studs Terkel (1980).

Said to an interviewer in 1963. An internationally famous star and an Academy Award winner, Crawford was serving on the Board of Directors of Pepsi-Cola and was in the midst of a nationwide tour on Pepsi's behalf. She had made her film debut thirty-eight years earlier.

7 From age eleven to age sixteen I lived a spartan life without the usual adolescent uncertainty. I wanted to be the best swimmer in the world, and there was nothing else.

Diana Nyad (b. 1949), U.S. long–distance swimmer. *Other Shores,* ch. 2 (1978).

8 We cannot expect in the immediate future that all women who seek it will achieve full equality of opportunity. But if women are to start moving towards that goal, we must believe in ourselves or no one else will believe in us; we must match our aspirations with the competence, courage and determination to succeed.

Rosalyn Yalow (b. 1921), U.S. chemist; Nobel Laureate in medicine and physiology (1977). As quoted in *The Decade of Women,* by Suzanne Levine and Harriet Lyons (1980).

9 I'd like to come back as an independent woman who has more ambition than I have.

Jenny Bird (b. c. 1937), U.S. supermarket clerk. As quoted in *American Dreams,* book 1, part 2, by Studs Terkel (1980).

A 43–year-old divorcee with four grown children, Bird believed deeply in reincarnation.

10 I always knew I wanted to be somebody. I think that's where it begins. People decide, "I want to be somebody. I want to make a contribution. I want to leave my mark here." Then different factors contribute to how you will do that.

FAITH RINGGOLD (b. 1934), U.S. painter and sculptor. As quoted in *Lives and Works*, by Lynn F. Miller and Sally S. Swenson (1981).
Making the point that ambition may exist alone, may actually *precede* a woman's settling on an area of endeavor.

11 In time your relatives will come to accept the idea that a career is as important to you as your family. Of course, in time the polar ice cap will melt.

BARBARA DALE (b. 1940), U.S. cartoonist. *The Working Woman Book*, ch. 4 (1985).

12 I'm not an overly ambitious person; I don't feel like I have to excel.

CHRIS EVERT (b. 1954), U.S. tennis player. As quoted in *Sports Illustrated*, p. 61 (May 25, 1992).
Evert, now a wife and mother, had once enjoyed top ranking as a tennis champion.

13 I have the same goal I've had ever since I was a girl. I want to rule the world.

MADONNA (b. 1958), U.S. singer and actor. As quoted in *People* magazine (July 27, 1992).
An extremely flamboyant, independent, controversial, and financially successful public figure.

14 I can't be President since I am a naturalized citizen, but I figured everything else was fair game.

ARATI PRABHAKAR (b. c. 1959), U.S. technology analyst; born in India. As quoted in the *New York Times*, section 3, p. 8 (August 1, 1993).
At thirty-four, she was appointed head of the National Institute of Standards and Technology by President Clinton. She was the first woman to lead the 3,000-employee agency and among the few to be appointed from without rather than from within the agency. Earlier, she had been the first woman to earn a Ph.D. in applied physics from the California Institute of Technology (Caltech).

AMERICAN CHARACTER

1 . . . it were impossible for a people to be more completely identified with their government than are the Americans. In considering it, they seem to feel, "It is ours, we have created it, and we support it; it exists for our protection and service; it lives as the breath of our mouths; and, while it answers the ends for which we decreed it, so long shall it stand, and nought shall prevail against it."

FRANCES WRIGHT (1795–1852), U.S. social reformer and author; born and raised in Scotland. *Views of Society and Manners in America*, entry for November 1818 (1821).
Wright was on her first trip to America; she had been in the country for two months when she wrote this.

2 Those who sit in a glass house do wrong to throw stones about them; besides, the American glass house is rather thin, it will break easily, and the interior is anything but a gainly sight.

EMMA GOLDMAN (1869–1940), U.S. anarchist, labor organizer, and author. *Feminism*, ch. 5 (1910).
Referring to Americans' common belief that most United States prostitutes were immigrants and had in many cases been prostitutes earlier, in their native lands.

3 The American landscape has no foreground and the American mind no background.

EDITH WHARTON (1862–1937), U.S. author; relocated to France. As quoted in *Edith Wharton*, ch. 9, by R. W. B. Lewis (1985).

In a letter written to her friend Sara Norton in the early 1900s.

4 It is bitter to think of one's best years disappearing in this unpolished country.

GRETA GARBO (1905–1990), Swedish actor; relocated to the United States. As quoted in *The Divine Garbo*, ch. 4, by Frederick Sands and Sven Broman (1979).

Written in a letter to her friend, the Swede Lars Saxon, on February 2, 1926; less than a year earlier, Garbo had come to the United States to make movies.

5 In America we eat, collectively, with a glum urge for food to fill us. We are ignorant of flavour. We are as a nation taste-blind.

M. F. K. FISHER (1908–1992), U.S. author and food expert. *Serve it Forth*, ch. 13 (1937).

6 . . . America has enjoyed the doubtful blessing of a single-track mind. We are able to accommodate, at a time, only one national hero; and we demand that that hero shall be uniform and invincible. As a literate people we are preoccupied, neither with the race nor the individual, but with the type. Yesterday, we romanticized the "tough guy;" today, we are romanticizing the underprivileged, tough or tender; tomorrow, we shall begin to romanticize the pure primitive.

ELLEN GLASGOW (1873–1945), U.S. novelist. *The Woman Within*, ch. 21 (1954).

Written in 1937.

7 This is . . . a trait no other nation seems to possess in quite the same degree that we do—namely, a feeling of almost childish injury and resentment unless the world as a whole recognizes how innocent we are of anything but the most generous and harmless intentions.

ELEANOR ROOSEVELT (1884–1962), U.S. author, speaker, and First Lady. As quoted in *Eleanor: The Years Alone*, ch. 4, by Joseph P. Lash (1972).

From her "My Day" column, published in the *Ladies' Home Journal* on November 11, 1946.

8 I am convinced that our American society will become more and more vulgarized and that it will be fragmentized into contending economic, racial and religious pressure groups lacking in unity and common will, unless we can arrest the disintegration of the family and of community solidarity.

AGNES E. MEYER (1887–1970), U.S. journalist. *Out of These Roots*, ch. 1 (1953).

9 I don't measure America by its achievement, but by its potential.

SHIRLEY CHISHOLM (b. 1924), African American politician and feminist. *Unbought and Unbossed*, ch. 16 (1970).

10 America is not a melting pot. It is a sizzling cauldron.

BARBARA MIKULSKI (b. 1936), U.S. politician. As quoted in *The Decade of Women*, by Suzanne Levine and Harriet Lyons (1980).

Said in June 1970.

11 The American Dream, the idea of the happy ending, is an avoidance of responsibility and commitment.

JILL ROBINSON (b. 1936), U.S. novelist.
As quoted in *American Dreams*, book 1 part 1,
by Studs Terkel (1980).
The daughter of movie producer Dore Schary,
Robinson had grown up in Hollywood and was
referring obliquely to the movie industry's preference for happy endings.

12 The American Dream is really
money.

JILL ROBINSON (b. 1936), U.S. novelist.
As quoted in *American Dreams*, part 1, by
Studs Terkel (1980).
The daughter of movie producer Dore
Schary, Robinson had grown up rich in Holly-
wood.

ANARCHISM

1 Anarchism is the great liberator
of man from the phantoms that
have held him captive; it is the
arbiter and pacifier of the two
forces for individual and social
harmony.

EMMA GOLDMAN (1869–1940), U.S.
anarchist and author; born in Russia. *Anarchism and Other Essays,* 3rd rev. ed., ch. 1
(1917).

2 I became increasingly anarchistic. I
began to find people of my own
class vicious, people in clean collars
uninteresting. I even accepted
smells, personal as well as official.
Everyone who came to the studio
smelled either of machine oil or her-
ring.

MARGARET ANDERSON (1886–1973),
U.S. literary editor and autobiographer. *My
Thirty Years' War,* ch. 2 (1930).
Of her (passing) infatuation, in her early twenties, with Emma Goldman (1869–1940) and anarchism. Anderson had met Goldman after writing and publishing an article which was sympathetic to anarchism.

ANGER

1 There are characters which are continually creating collisions and
nodes for themselves in dramas
which nobody is prepared to act
with them. Their susceptibilities will
clash against objects that remain in-
nocently quiet.

GEORGE ELIOT (1819–1880), British novelist. *Middlemarch,* ch. 19 (1871–1872).

2 It was a time of madness, the sort
of mad-hysteria that always pres-
ages war. There seems to be nothing
left but war—when any population
in any sort of a nation gets violently
angry, civilization falls down and religion forsakes its hold on the consciences of human kind in such
times of public madness.

REBECCA LATIMER FELTON (1835–
1930), U.S. author. *Country Life in Georgia in
the Days of My Youth,* ch. 1 (1919).
Recalling the period preceding the Civil War.

3 I never felt that getting angry would
do you any good other than hurt
your own digestion—keep you
from eating, which I liked to do.

SEPTIMA CLARK (1898–1987), African
American civil rights activist. *Ready from
Within,* part 1, ch. 2 (1986).
Clark, a native of Kentucky, was recalling the
rather curious fact that she did not become
angry in the days when "Jim Crow" laws still obtained in the South and she had to yield her bus
seat to a white person.

4 Even the most subjected person has
moments of rage and resentment so
intense that they respond, they act
against. There is an inner uprising
that leads to rebellion, however
short-lived. It may be only momen-

tary but it takes place. That space within oneself where resistance is possible remains.

BELL HOOKS (b. c. 1955), African American feminist author and educator. *Yearning*, ch. 2 (1990).

5 Anger becomes limiting, restricting. You can't see through it. While anger is there, look at that, too. But after a while, you have to look at something else.

THYLIAS MOSS, African American poet. As quoted in the *Wall Street Journal* (May 12, 1994).

ANGLO-IRISH RELATIONS

1 I went to a very militantly Republican grammar school and, under its influence, began to revolt against the Establishment, on the simple rule of thumb, highly satisfying to a ten-year-old, that Irish equals good, English equals bad.

BERNADETTE DEVLIN (b. 1947), Irish politician. *The Price of My Soul*, ch. 4 (1969).

ANIMALS

1 I am secretly afraid of animals. . . . I think it is because of the *us*ness in their eyes, with the underlying *not-us*ness which belies it, and is so tragic a reminder of the lost age when we human beings branched off and left them: left them to eternal inarticulateness and slavery. Why? their eyes seem to ask us.

EDITH WHARTON (1862–1937), U.S. author; later relocated to France. As quoted in *Edith Wharton*, by R.W.B. Lewis (1975). From a journal entry dated 1924.

2 In their sympathies, children feel nearer animals than adults. They frolic with animals, caress them, share with them feelings neither has words for. Have they ever stroked any adult with the love they bestow on a cat? Hugged any grownup with the ecstasy they feel when clasping a puppy?

JESSAMYN WEST (1907–1984), U.S. novelist and autobiographer. *The Life I Really Lived*, part 1 (1979).

3 I don't want her to have a cat because she'll end up talking baby talk to the cat. That's the way it is, and how can a P.I. do that?

SUE GRAFTON (b. 1940), U.S. mystery novelist. As quoted in the *New York Times*, p. C10 (August 4, 1994).

On why Kinsey Millhone, the private-investigator heroine of her popular series of mystery novels, will never have a cat.

ANTI-FEMINISM

1 Perhaps the fact that I am not a Radical or a believer in the all powerful ballot for women to right her wrongs and that I do not scorn womanly duties, but claim it as a privilege to clean up and sort of supervise the room and sew things, etc., is winning me stronger allies than anything else.

ELLEN HENRIETTA SWALLOW RICHARDS (1842–1911), U.S. chemist and educator. As quoted in *The Life of Ellen H. Richards*, ch. 5, by Caroline L. Hunt (1912).

Written on February 11, 1871, in the month following her entry into the Massachusetts Institute of Technology as its first woman student.

2 I don't want to smoke cigars or go to stag parties, wear jockey shorts or pick up the check.

SHELLEY WINTERS (b. 1922), U.S. actor. As quoted in *Movers and Shakers,* ch. 4, by June Sochem (1973).
Said in 1950.

APARTHEID

1 Women are the people who are going to relieve us from all this oppression and depression. The rent boycott that is happening in Soweto now is alive because of the women. It is the women who are on the street committees educating the people to stand up and protect each other.

NONTSIKELELO ALBERTINA SISULU (b. 1919), South African black anti–apartheid activist. As quoted in *Lives of Courage,* ch. 10, by Diana E. H. Russell (1989).
Said in 1987. Soweto was a group of townships southwest (hence the acronym) of Johannesburg reserved for blacks.

2 I don't have any doubts that there will be a place for progressive white people in this country in the future. I think the paranoia common among white people is very unfounded. I have always organized my life so that I could focus on political work. That's all I want to do, and that's all that makes me happy.

HETTIE V., South African white anti-apartheid activist and feminist. As quoted in *Lives of Courage,* ch. 21, by Diana E. H. Russell (1989).
Said in a 1987 interview.

3 The women made a plan to dig their own graves and they said, "We will stand beside our graves because we are not moving from here. You can shoot and we will lie in our land forever."

SHEENA DUNCAN (b. 1932), South African white anti–apartheid activist. As quoted in *Lives of Courage,* ch. 24, by Diana E. H. Russell (1989).
Said in a 1987 interview. The white daughter of the founder of Black Sash, an anti-apartheid women's organization, Duncan succeeded her mother as Black Sash president. Here she described the members' determination to resist.

ARCHITECTURE

1 To approach a city . . . as if it were [an] . . . architectural problem . . . is to make the mistake of attempting to substitute art for life. . . . The results . . . are neither life nor art. They are taxidermy.

JANE JACOBS (b. 1916), U.S. author and urban design critic. *The Death and Life of Great American Cities,* ch. 19 (1961).

2 It was always the work that was the gyroscope in my life. I don't know who could have lived with me. As an architect you're absolutely devoured. A woman's cast in a lot of roles and a man isn't. I couldn't be an architect and be a wife and mother.

ELEANORE KENDALL PETTERSEN (b. 1916), U.S. architect. As quoted in *Past and Promise,* part 4, by June Shatken (1990).
In an interview with the author on February 4, 1987. Pettersen was the first woman architect in New Jersey to open her own office—which she did in 1952 in Saddle River. She was also the first woman president of the New Jersey State Board of Architects (1975–76) and the New Jersey Society of Architects (1984–85).

ART

1 It is painful to be told that anything is very fine and not be able to feel that it is fine—something like being blind, while people talk of the sky.

GEORGE ELIOT (1819–1880), British novelist. Dorothea Brooke Casaubon, the heroine of *Middlemarch,* ch. 21 (1871–1872).
About art criticism.

2 . . . a master-piece . . . may be unwelcome but it is never dull.

GERTRUDE STEIN (1874–1946), U.S. author and patron of the arts; relocated to France. *What Are Masterpieces and Why Are There So Few of Them* (1936).

3 . . . art transcends its limitations only by staying within them.

FLANNERY O'CONNOR (1925–1964), U.S. fiction writer and essayist. *Mystery and Manners,* part 5 (1969).
Written in 1964.

4 We use important words too frequently and they lose value; for instance, *charm* and *great.* An actor or musician often is proclaimed *great* when we really mean he is *outstanding.*

ELEANOR ROBSON BELMONT (1878–1979), U.S. stage actress and socialite. *The Fabric of Memory,* part 7, ch. 5 (1957).

An actress in her youth, under her maiden name, she later married August Belmont and became a social luminary and founder of the Metropolitan Opera Guild in New York City.

5 . . . if art speaks clearly about something relevant to people's lives it can change the way they perceive reality.

JUDY CHICAGO (b. 1939), U.S. artist. As quoted in *The Political Palate,* ch. 3, by Betsey Beaven, et al. (1980).

6 . . . when I was in my studio I didn't give a damn what sex I was. . . . I thought art is art.

ALICE NEEL (1900–1984), U.S. painter. As quoted in *Lives and Works,* by Lynn F. Miller and Sally S. Swenson (1981).
Neel was a supporter of the Women's Liberation Movement.

7 One line typed twenty years ago can be blazed on a wall in
  spraypaint
to glorify art as detachment
or torture of those we
did not love but also
did not want to kill.

ADRIENNE RICH (b. 1929), U.S. poet and essayist. "North American Time," part 2, lines 8–13 (1983).

8 Art is not living. It is the use of living.

AUDRE LORDE (1934–1992), U.S. author. *Black Women Writers at Work,* ch. 8, by Claudia Tate (1985).

ARTISTS

1 There is a wilderness of commonplace and much that is ugly and poor. . . . there seems no inspiration, no evolvement of the beautiful, no intricate poetic conception, no freshness. It is all "technique, technique." There is little independence of vision; all "treatment" with no apprehension of the thing to treat. . . . They are adventurous, these artists. They draw admirably; they do not color so well, and they have few ideals. . . . that ideal which was once the real world of the artist seems to have fled, and that present world, "all around us lying," does not seem to have revealed itself to the artist with its truest and most tender grace.

M. E. W. SHERWOOD (1826–1903), U.S. socialite, traveller, and author. *An Epistle to Posterity,* ch. 13 (1897).
Of contemporary art in the 1880s and 1890s.

2   The artist must be an egotist because, like the spider, he draws all his building material from his own breast. But just the same the artist alone among men knows what true humility means. His reach forever exceeds his grasp. He can never be satisfied with his work. He knows when he has done well, but he knows he has never attained his dream. He knows he never can.

RHETA CHILDE DORR (1866–1948), U.S. journalist. *A Woman of Fifty,* 2nd. ed., ch. 3 (1924).

3   . . . artists were intended to be an ornament to society. As a society in themselves they are unthinkable.

ELIZABETH BOWEN (1899–1973), British novelist, story writer, essayist, and memoirist; born in Ireland. As quoted in *Elizabeth Bowen,* ch. 8, by Victoria Glendinning (1979).
In a letter to the author Charles Ritchie, her lover, written during the 1940s.

4   It is . . . despair at the mutability of all created things that links the Artist and the Ascetic—a desire to purify and preserve—to set oneself apart—somehow—from the river flowing onward to the grave.

MICHELE MURRAY (1933–1974), U.S. author. As quoted in *The Writer on Her Work,* by Janet Sternburg (1980).
From a journal entry dated January 8, 1961.

5   No other creative field is as closed to those who are not white and male as is the visual arts. After I decided to be an artist, the first thing that I had to believe was that I, a black woman, could penetrate the art scene, and that, further, I could do so without sacrificing one iota of my blackness or my femaleness or my humanity.

FAITH RINGGOLD (b. 1934), African American painter and sculptor. As quoted in *Ms.* magazine, p. 55 (January 1973).
Ringgold was a very prolific and admired visual artist.

6   I was given the gifts of the artist, and the trouble that goes with them: So I have that blessing, and there was never a time that I questioned it or doubted it. . . . For forty years, I wanted to jump out of windows.

LOUISE NEVELSON (1900–1988), U.S. sculptor. As quoted in *The Decade of Women,* by Suzanne Levine and Harriet Lyons (1980). Said in 1975.

7   The twentieth-century artist who uses symbols is alienated because the system of symbols is a private one. After you have dealt with the symbols you are still private, you are still lonely, because you are not sure anyone will understand it except yourself. The ransom of privacy is that you are alone.

LOUISE BOURGEOIS (b. 1911), U.S. sculptor. As quoted in *Lives and Works,* by Lynn F. Miller and Sally S. Swenson (1981).

8   . . . when I'm [working in my studio], at that moment, it's all worth it, it's worth the struggle, it's worth the fact that I have no money, it's

worth the fact that my life is ridiculous in most people's terms.

SUSAN SCHWALB (b. 1944), U.S. artist. As quoted in *Lives and Works,* by Lynn F. Miller and Sally S. Swenson (1981).

9 The black artist is dangerous. Black art controls the "Negro's" reality, negates negative influences, and creates positive images.

SONIA SANCHEZ (b. 1934), African American poet. *Black Women Writers at Work,* ch. 10, by Claudia Tate (1985).

10 I never had the sense of myself as an accomplished artist, and I always had to work three times as hard as anyone else to make my pieces as good as they could be. I am never completely satisfied. There always seems to be something just beyond my reach.

TOSHIKO TAKAEZU (b. 1922), U.S. artist. As quoted in *Past and Promise,* part 4, by Gertrude W. Dubrovsky (1990).

Said in an interview with the author on May 18, 1986. Takaezu, Hawaiian-born of Japanese parents, was a ceramicist, weaver, and sculptor.

11 The painter . . . does not fit the paints to the world. He most certainly does not fit the world to himself. He fits himself to the paint. The self is the servant who bears the paintbox and its inherited contents.

ANNIE DILLARD (b. 1945), U.S. author. *The Writing Life,* ch. 5 (1989).

Using painting as an exemplar of all creative endeavors.

ARTS, THE

1 . . . that softening influence of the fine arts which makes other people's hardships picturesque . . .

GEORGE ELIOT (1819–1880), British novelist. *Middlemarch,* ch. 39 (1871–1872).

2 What would life be without art? Science prolongs life. To consist of what—eating, drinking, and sleeping? What is the good of living longer if it is only a matter of satisfying the requirements that sustain life? All this is nothing without the charm of art.

SARAH BERNHARDT (1845–1923), French actor. *The Art of the Theatre,* ch. 3 (1924).

3 . . . the creator of the new composition in the arts is an outlaw until he is a classic.

GERTRUDE STEIN (1874–1946), U.S. author and patron of the arts; relocated to France. *Composition as Explanation* (1926).

4 Every man is in a state of conflict, owing to his attempt to reconcile himself and his relationship with life to his conception of harmony. This conflict makes his soul a battlefield, where the forces that wish this reconciliation fight those that do not and reject the alternative solutions they offer. Works of art are attempts to fight out this conflict in the imaginative world.

REBECCA WEST (1892–1983), British author. *The Strange Necessity,* ch. 6 (1928).

5 Self-expression is not enough; experiment is not enough; the recording of special moments or cases is not enough. All of the arts have broken faith or lost connection with

their origin and function. They have ceased to be concerned with the legitimate and permanent material of art.

JANE HEAP (*c.* 1880–1964), U.S. artist and editor. As quoted in *My Thirty Years' War,* ch. 6, by Margaret Anderson (1930).
From her farewell editorial, published in the last issue of *The Little Review,* a prominent, eccentric, influential literary and arts magazine founded by Anderson in 1914 and coedited by Heap from 1916 until its demise in 1929.

6 A writer should write with his eyes and a painter paint with his ears.

GERTRUDE STEIN (1874–1946), U.S. author and patron of the arts; relocated to France. As quoted in *What Are Masterpieces,* afterword, by Robert Haas (1970).
Said in a January 1946 interview with Haas.

7 A work of art is one through which the consciousness of the artist is able to give its emotions to anyone who is prepared to receive them. There is no such thing as bad art.

MURIEL RUKEYSER (1913–1980), U.S. poet. *The Life of Poetry,* ch. 4 (1949).

8 Art to me was a state, it didn't need to be an accomplishment. By any of the standards of production, achievement, performance, I was not an artist. But I always thought of myself as one.

MARGARET ANDERSON (1886–1973), U.S. editor and memoirist. *The Fiery Fountains,* part 1 (1951).
Anderson did some writing and played the piano, but her main contribution to the arts, except for her three idiosyncratic volumes of memoirs, was to found and edit an influential magazine which promoted the arts: *The Little Review* (1914–1929).

9 If art has a purpose, it is to interpret life, reproduce it in fresh visions.

CATHERINE DRINKER BOWEN (1897–1973), U.S. biographer. *Adventures of a Biographer,* ch. 10 (1959).
Though Bowen was referring to the "art" of writers, she was also a musician, and musicians had been her first biographical subjects.

10 I am dead against art's being self-expression. I see an inherent failure in any story which fails to detach itself from the author—detach itself in the sense that a well-blown soap-bubble detaches itself from the bowl of the blower's pipe and spherically takes off into the air as a new, whole, pure, iridescent world. Whereas the ill-blown bubble, as children know, timidly adheres to the bowl's lip, then either bursts or sinks flatly back again.

ELIZABETH BOWEN (1899–1973), British novelist, story writer, essayist, and memoirist; born in Ireland. *Seven Winters,* part 2, sect. 2, ch. 5 (1962).

11 TO EXPRESS THE EMOTIONS OF LIFE IS TO LIVE. TO EXPRESS THE LIFE OF EMOTIONS IS TO MAKE ART.

JANE HEAP (*c.* 1880–1964), U.S. artist and editor. As quoted in *The Strange Necessity,* Foreword 1, by Margaret Anderson (1969).
Heap was coeditor, with Anderson, of *The Little Review* (1914–1929), an idiosyncratic, extremely interesting, and important literary and arts journal; she formulated these statements as its "credo."

12 Art is "should be."

MARGARET ANDERSON (1886–1973), U.S. editor and memoirist. *The Strange Necessity,* part 1 (1969).

13 ... does it seem to you that it is possible to speak of Art? It would be the same as explaining love!

ELEONORA DUSE (1858–1924), Italian actor. As quoted in *Actors on Acting*, rev. ed., part 11, by Toby Cole and Helen Krich (1970).

14 Art is beauty, and every exposition of art, whether it be music, painting, or the drama, should be subservient to that one great end. As long as nature is a means to the attainment of beauty, so-called realism is necessary and permissable [sic], but it must be realism enhanced by idealism and uplifted by the spirit of an inner life or purpose.

JULIA MARLOWE (1866–1950), U.S. actor; born in England. As quoted in *Famous Actors and Actresses on the American Stage*, vol. 2, by William C. Young (1975).

15 A successful artist of any kind has to work so hard that she is justified in refusing to lay down her sceptre until she is placed on the bier.

DAME EDITH EVANS (1888–1976), British actor. As quoted in *Dame Edith Evans*, ch. 13, by Bryan Forbes (1977).

16 Our role is to support anything positive in black life and destroy anything negative that touches it. You have no other reason for being. I don't understand art for art's sake. Art is the guts of the people.

ELMA LEWIS (b. 1921), African American artist. As quoted in *The Decade of Women*, by Suzanne Levine and Harriet Lyons (1980).

On the mission of the Elma Lewis School in Roxbury, Massachusetts. This quotation was first published in a 1977 issue of *Ms.* magazine.

17 Minority art, vernacular art, is marginal art. Only on the margins does growth occur.

JOANNA RUSS (b. 1937), U.S. science fiction writer and feminist. *How to Suppress Women's Writing*, Epilogue (1983).

18 ... the function of art is to do more than tell it like it is—it's to imagine what is *possible*.

BELL HOOKS (b. c. 1955), African American author, feminist, and human rights advocate. *Outlaw Culture*, ch. 19 (1994).

19 The disaster ... is not the money, although the money will be missed. The disaster is the disrespect—this belief that the arts are dispensable, that they're not critical to a culture's existence.

TWYLA THARP (b. 1941), U.S. dancer and choreographer. As quoted in *Newsweek* magazine, p. 64 (January 23, 1995).

On proposals to abolish the National Endowment for the Arts, which gave grants to a wide range of American fine and performing arts activities.

ASSASSINATION

1 Be of good cheer, for you will never want, for the bullet was meant for me, though it hit you.

ELIZABETH I (1533–1603), Queen of England (1558–1603). As quoted in *The Sayings of Queen Elizabeth*, ch. 13, by Frederick Chamberlin (1923).

"To one of her boatmen who was shot when within six feet of her on her barge in the Thames. She took off her scarf and gave it to him to bind over his wound, which was bleeding profusely."

2 Today, San Francisco has experienced a double tragedy of incredible proportions. As acting mayor, I order an immediate state of mourning in our city. The city and county of San Francisco must and will pull itself together at this time. We will carry on as best as we possibly can. . . . I think we all have to share the same sense of shame and the same sense of outrage.

DIANNE FEINSTEIN (b. 1933), U.S. politician. As quoted in *Dianne Feinstein*, ch. 10, by Jerry Roberts (1994).

Feinstein, then President of the San Francisco Board of Supervisors, made the first of these two statements at a 12:30 p.m. press conference on November 27, 1978; less than two hours earlier, Supervisor Dan White had murdered Supervisor Harvey Milk and Mayor George Moscone in their offices at City Hall. Feinstein, who had also been in her office, had heard shots in Milk's office and had discovered his body; she had actually spoken briefly to White in the moments between the two murders, without realizing that Moscone had been shot. She made the second statement at a Board meeting on November 27, 1978, at its regularly scheduled time of 2:00 p.m.; determined to start the meeting on time so as to reassure the city that its government was still in order, she said this, called for silent prayer, and then recessed the Board. She was lauded for her calming, organized behavior in time of crisis. With the Mayor's death, she had succeeded to the Acting Mayoralty; she was elected Mayor in 1979 and 1983, was narrowly defeated for the Governorship of California in 1990, and was elected to the United States Senate in 1992 and 1994.

ASSERTIVENESS

1 I do not weep at the world—I am too busy sharpening my oyster knife.

ZORA NEALE HURSTON (1891–1960), African American author. *How It Feels to be Colored Me* (1928).

2 I've been described as a tough and noisy woman, a prize fighter, a man-hater, you name it. They call me Battling Bella, Mother Courage, and a Jewish mother with more complaints than Portnoy. There are those who say I'm impatient, impetuous, uppity, rude, profane, brash, and overbearing. Whether I'm any of those things, or all of them, you can decide for yourself. But whatever I am —and this ought to be made very clear—I am a very serious woman.

BELLA ABZUG (b. 1920), U.S. Jewish politician. *Bella!* Introduction (1972).

When she said this, Abzug was a member of the United States House of Representatives.

3 . . . you have to keep fighting them off and realize that nobody would be interested in attacking you personally unless you were trying to do some things that are bothering them.

JOYCELYN ELDERS (b. 1933), U.S. pediatrician and educator; first woman (and second African American) Surgeon General of the United States. As quoted in the *New York Times Magazine,* p. 19 (January 30, 1994).

Elders, who was U. S. Surgeon General at the time, was commenting on the "personal attacks" she and President Bill Clinton were experiencing. She had been criticized for her 28-year-old son's arrest for selling cocaine. The President had been repeatedly attacked for alleged adultery and, more recently, for possible ethical violations related to his and the First Lady's investments; also, his brother had suffered from cocaine addiction.

ATHEISM

1 I do not mind if I lose my soul for all eternity. If the kind of God exists Who would damn me for not working out a deal with Him, then that is unfortunate. I should not care to spend eternity in the company of such a person.

MARY McCARTHY (1912–1989), U.S. author. *Memories of a Catholic Girlhood,* ch. 1 (1957).

ATOMIC BOMB

1 For more than twenty-five years my mind had been deeply troubled by the fact that these mechanical and scientific achievements of man had outrun his intellectual and spiritual power.... Throughout the Second World War this terrible problem hung in the back of my mind. As I write these words the problem and the danger are as threatening as ever. We hope our nation will survive, but in its effort to survive will it transform itself intellectually and spiritually into the image of the thing against which we fought?

VIRGINIA CROCHERON GILDERSLEEVE (1877–1965), U.S. educator. *Many a Good Crusade,* part 4 (1954).

Gildersleeve was the Dean of Barnard College in New York City and an activist in international affairs, working for peace and cooperation among nations.

2 In the atom's fizz and pop we heard possibility
uncorked. Taffeta wraps whispered on davenports.
A new planet bloomed above us; in its light
the stumps of cut pine gleamed like dinner plates.
The world was beginning all over again, fresh and hot;
we could have anything we wanted.

LYNN EMANUEL (b. 1949), U.S. poet. "The Planet Krypton" [poem], lines 23–28 (1992).

On watching atomic bomb testing in Nevada.

AUDIENCES

1 ... most of all [the actor] will love the boys and girls, the men and women, who sit in the cheapest seats, in the very last row of the top gallery. They have given more than they can afford to come. In the most self-effacing spirit of fellowship they are listening to catch every word, watching to miss no slightest gesture or expression. To save his life the actor cannot help feeling these nearest and dearest. He cannot help wishing to do his best for *them.* He cannot help loving them best of all.

MINNIE MADDERN FISKE (1865–1932), U.S. actor. As quoted in *Mrs. Fiske: Her Views on Actors, Acting and the Problems of Production,* ch. 3, by Alexander Woollcott (1917).

Fiske had been a popular stage actor since the age of four (when she used her birth name, Minnie Maddern).

2 Above all, ignore the audience....

MINNIE MADDERN FISKE (1865–1932), U.S. actor. As quoted in *Actors on Acting,* rev. ed., part 13, by Toby Cole and Helen Krich (1970).

Said in 1917, to Alexander Woollcott. Fiske, who had been a popular stage actor since she was four, offered this advice to actors.

3 ... in the happy laughter of a theatre audience one can get the most immediate and numerically impressive guarantee that there is nothing in one's mind which is not familiar to the mass of persons living at the time.

Rebecca West (1892–1983), British author. *The Strange Necessity*, ch. 12 (1928).

4 An actor must communicate his author's given message—comedy, tragedy, serio-comedy; then comes his unique moment, as he is confronted by the looked-for, yet at times unexpected, reaction of the audience. This split second is his; he is in command of his medium; the effect vanishes into thin air; but that moment has a power all its own and, like power in any form, is stimulating and alluring.

Eleanor Robson Belmont (1878–1979), U.S. stage actress and socialite. *The Fabric of Memory*, part 1, ch. 2 (1957).

Belmont was a stage actress in her youth, under her maiden name.

5 When I am on a stage, I am the focus of thousands of eyes and it gives me strength. I feel that something, some energy, is flowing from the audience into me. I actually feel stronger because of these waves. Now when the play's done, the eyes taken away, I feel just as if a circuit's been broken. The power is switched off. I feel all gone and empty inside of me—like a balloon that's been pricked and the air's let out.

Lynn Fontanne (1887–1983), U.S. actor; born in England. As quoted in *Actors on Acting*, rev. ed., part 13, by Toby Cole and Helen Krich (1970).

Said c. 1960.

AUTOBIOGRAPHY

1 It is too late—the world is too dark for any thought ahead. *Others* are writing my biography, and let it rest as they elect to make it. I have lived my life, well and ill, always less well than I wanted it to be but it is, *as* it is, and as it has been; *so small* a thing, to have had so much about it!

Clara Barton (1821–1912), U.S. nurse and founder of the Red Cross. As quoted in *Angel of the Battlefield*, ch. 20, by Ishbel Ross (1956).

On being asked in 1904, upon her resignation as President of the American Red Cross, to write her autobiography.

2 A proper autobiography is a deathbed confession. A true man finds so much work to do that he has no time to contemplate his yesterdays; for to-day and to-morrow are here, with their impatient tasks. The world is so busy, too, that it cannot afford to study any man's unfinished work; for the end may prove it a failure, and the world needs masterpieces.

Mary Antin (1881–1949), U.S. socialite and author; born in Russia. *The Promised Land*, Introduction (1912).

This, Antin's own autobiography, was written before her thirtieth birthday.

3 I have always hated biography, and more especially, autobiography. If biography, the writer invariably finds it necessary to plaster the subject with praises, flattery and adulation and to invest him with all the Christian graces. If autobiography, the same plan is followed, but the writer apologizes for it.

Carolyn Wells (1862–1942), U.S. author. *The Rest of My Life*, ch. 1 (1937).

Written in her own autobiography.

4 Autobiographies are . . . only useful as the lives you read about and analyze may suggest to you something that you may find useful in your own journey through life.

ELEANOR ROOSEVELT (1884–1962), First Lady of the United States, author, speaker, and diplomat. *This Is My Story,* ch. 23 (1937).

5 . . . any fiction . . . is bound to be transposed autobiography.

ELIZABETH BOWEN (1899–1973), British novelist, story writer, essayist, and memoirist; born in Ireland. *Seven Winters,* part 2, sect. 2, ch. 5 (1962).

From the preface to her 1959 *Selected Stories.*

6 They're all the same—it's always rags-to-riches or I-slept-with-so-and-so. Damned if I'm going to say that.

DEBORAH KERR (b. 1921), British actor; born in Scotland. As quoted in *Newsweek* magazine, p. 19 (November 19, 1986).

On movie-star autobiographies, and why she did not want to write one.

7 . . . all fiction may be autobiography, but all autobiography is of course fiction.

SHIRLEY ABBOTT (b. 1934), U.S. memoirist. As quoted in *Listen to Their Voices,* ch. 12, by Mickey Pearlman (1993).

AUTOMATION

1 The more we reduce ourselves to machines in the lower things, the more force we shall set free to use in the higher.

ANNA C. BRACKETT (1836–1911), U.S. author. *The Technique of Rest,* ch. 2 (1892).

Adopting a metaphor of the Industrial Revolution.

2 It is a society of laborers which is about to be liberated from the ferrets of labor, and this society does no longer know of those other higher and more meaningful activities for the sake of which this freedom would deserve to be won.

HANNAH ARENDT (1906–1975), U.S. philosopher. *The Human Condition,* prologue (1958).

On the prospect of human liberation from labor through automation.

3 . . . the promise of automation seemed to exert a magnetic force, a seduction that promised to fulfill a dream of perfect control and heal egos wounded by their needs for certainty. The dream contains the image of "people serving a smart machine," but in the shadow of the dream, human beings have lost the experience of critical judgment that would allow them to no longer simply respond but to know better than, to question, to say no.

SHOSHANA ZUBOFF (b. 1951), U.S. social scientist. *In the Age of the Smart Machine,* Conclusion (1988).

AUTOMOBILES AND DRIVING

1 What if we fail to stop the erosion of cities by automobiles? . . . In that case America will hardly need to ponder a mystery that has troubled men for millennia: What is the purpose of life? For us, the answer will be clear, established and for all practical purposes indisputable: The purpose of life is to produce and consume automobiles.

JANE JACOBS (b. 1916), U.S. urban analyst. *The Death and Life of Great American Cities,* ch. 18 (1961).

Jacobs lived in the lively, diverse Greenwich Village section of Manhattan (New York City).

2 Good driving has nothing to do with sex. It's all above the collar.

ALICE HUYLER RAMSEY (1887–1983), U.S. driver. As quoted in *Ms.* magazine, p. 17 (February 1975).

In 1909, she had become the tenth person, and first woman, to drive from Hell's Gate in New York City to the Golden Gate in San Francisco: 3,800 miles.

AWARDS AND PRIZES

1 I was just glad to get the Grammy. I didn't know what the thing was. It's the honor what I loved.

ELIZABETH COTTEN (1892–1987), African American musical performer. As quoted in *I Dream a World,* by Brian Lanker (1989).

On winning a Grammy award for her album, *Elizabeth Cotten Live!,* which was voted the "Best ethnic or traditional folk recording" of 1984. A "singer, storyteller, composer, guitarist, and banjo player," she began performing professionally at age sixty-seven, after decades spent working as a housekeeper, and continued until her death twenty-eight years later.

2 I doubt that I would have taken so many leaps in my own writing or been as clear about my feminist and political commitments if I had not been anointed as early as I was. Some major form of recognition seems to have to mark a woman's career for her to be able to go out on a limb without having her credentials questioned.

RUTH BEHAR (b. 1956), U.S. anthropologist. *Chronicle of Higher Education,* p. A44 (November 4, 1992).

On the professional effect of winning the extremely prestigious MacArthur Fellowship.

AWARENESS

1 The writer, unlike his non-writing adult friend, has no predisposed outlook; he seldom observes deliberately. He sees what he did not intend to see; he remembers what does not seem wholly possible. Inattentive learner in the schoolroom of life, he keeps some faculty free to veer and wander. His is the roving eye.

ELIZABETH BOWEN (1899–1973), British novelist, story writer, essayist, and memoirist; born in Ireland. *Seven Winters,* part 2, sect. 1, ch. 1 (1962).

Written in 1959.

2 Awareness requires a rupture with the world we take for granted; then old categories of experience are called into question and revised.

SHOSHANA ZUBOFF (b. 1951), U.S. social scientist. *In the Age of the Smart Machine,* Introduction (1988).

3 One must always be aware, to notice—even though the cost of noticing is to become responsible.

THYLIAS MOSS, African American poet. As quoted in the *Wall Street Journal* (May 12, 1994).

BANKS

1 The world is a puzzling place today. All these banks sending us credit cards, with our names on them. Well, we didn't order any credit cards! We don't spend what we don't have. So we just cut them in half and throw them out, just as soon as we open them in the mail. Imagine a bank sending credit cards

to two ladies over a hundred years old! What are those folks thinking?

SARAH LOUISE DELANY (b. 1889), U.S. educator. *Having Our Say,* ch. 3 (1992).

Delany was speaking for herself and her sister Annie Elizabeth, who, at 101, was two years her junior.

BASEBALL

1 If women were umpiring none of this [rowdyism] would happen. Do you suppose any ball player in the country would step up to a good-looking girl and say to her, "You color-blind, pickle-brained, cross-eyed idiot, if you don't stop throwing the soup into me I'll distribute your features all over your countenance!" Of course he wouldn't.

AMANDA CLEMENT (1888–1971), U.S. baseball umpire. As quoted in *Women in Baseball,* ch. 4, by Gai Ingham Berlage (1994).

Said in 1907. Clement, the "first official woman umpire in men's baseball," worked for semi-professional teams "from about 1905 through 1911."

2 I think a lot of people believe I'm going to fall flat on my face, and they're still waiting for it to happen. I hope they wait forever, and I hope they keep coming to watch me.

CHRISTINE WREN, U.S. baseball umpire. As quoted in *WomenSports* magazine, p. 15 (October 1975).

Wren was the second woman umpire in professional baseball; the career of the first, Bernice Gera, had begun and ended in 1972 with one game.

3 Anyone with any real blood in his or her . . . veins cannot help being a fan. . . . Being a true American and being a fan are synonymous.

LULU GLASER (1874–1958), U.S. comic opera performer. As quoted in *Women in Baseball,* ch. 1, by Gai Ingham Berlage (1994).

BEAUTY

1 Plain women he regarded as he did the other severe facts of life, to be faced with philosophy and investigated by science.

GEORGE ELIOT (1819–1880), British novelist. *Middlemarch,* ch. 11 (1871–1872).

Of Lydgate, a young doctor in the novel.

2 . . . I had been fed, in my youth, a lot of old wives' tales about the way men would instantly forsake a beautiful woman to flock around a brilliant one. It is but fair to say that, after getting out in the world, I had never seen this happen. . . .

DOROTHY PARKER (1893–1967), U.S. author and humorist. *Constant Reader,* ch. 22 (1970).

From a column dated November 17, 1928.

3 . . . beauty, like ecstasy, has always been hostile to the commonplace. And the commonplace, under its popular label of the normal, has been the supreme authority for *Homo sapiens* since the days when he was probably arboreal.

ELLEN GLASGOW (1873–1945), U.S. novelist. *The Woman Within,* ch. 21 (1954).

Written in 1937.

4 . . . I wasn't at all prepared for the avalanche of criticism that overwhelmed me. You would have thought I had murdered someone, and perhaps I had, but only to give her successor a chance to live. It

was a very sad business indeed to be made to feel that my success depended solely, or at least in large part, on a head of hair.

MARY PICKFORD (1893–1979), U.S. actor. *Sunshine and Shadow,* ch. 20 (1955).
On deciding, in her early thirties, to cut the long curls which had grown uninterruptedly since her birth. She hoped that by doing so, she would affirm her adulthood and determination to begin playing women, rather than children and adolescents, in films. But the public adored her as "little Mary" and never accepted her as a bobbed-hair adult. She later mused, "I sometimes wonder whether I had the right to cut off my hair. Were the choice given to me again, I am positive I would not do it."

5 Beautiful women seldom want to act. They are afraid of emotion and they do not try to extract anything from a character that they are portraying, because in expressing emotion they may encourage crow's feet and laughing wrinkles. They avoid anything that will disturb their placidity of countenance, for placidity of countenance insures a smooth skin.

LAURETTE TAYLOR (1887–1946), U.S. actor. As quoted in *Actors on Acting,* rev. ed., part 13, by Toby Cole and Helen Krich (1970).
Taylor, a fine stage actor, was not a beauty.

6 Every day, in every way, the billion-dollar beauty business tells women they are monsters in disguise. . . . women are told they are the fair sex, but at the same time that their "beauty" needs lifting, shaping, dyeing, painting, curling, padding. Women are really being told that "the beauty" is a beast.

UNA STANNARD (b. 1927), U.S. author. *Woman in Sexist Society,* ch. 7 (1971).

7 They say it's worse to be ugly. I think it must only be different. If you're pretty, you are subject to one set of assaults; if you're plain you are subject to another.

ALIX KATES SHULMAN (b. 1932), U.S. author. *Memoirs of an Ex-Prom Queen,* ch. 2 (1972).

8 . . . when you do get a job everybody says, "Well, they wanted a black woman," which necessarily puts you on a level where you have to prove yourself above being a woman and being black. . . . Now, I would say, in certain situations, it helped me simply because I was mildly attractive, not because I was black or a woman. That gets you more mileage than anything else. . . . God help you if you're not an attractive woman.

THERESA BROWN (b. 1957), African American television newswoman. As quoted in *Women in Television News,* ch. 5, by Judith S. Gelfman (1976).
Said on April 3, 1973.

9 Although they tell you you are most beautiful when you're pregnant, all the models who epitomize beauty have skinny waistlines. So they're shitting you right from the start.

FLORYNCE KENNEDY (b. 1916), U.S. lawyer, activist, speaker, and author. *Color Me Flo,* ch. 3 (1976).
From the June 21, 1975, keynote speech delivered in San Francisco at the Second National Hookers' Convention. Kennedy had never been either a prostitute or a mother.

10 So successful has been the camera's role in beautifying the world that photographs, rather than the world,

have become the standard of the beautiful.

Susan Sontag (b. 1933), U.S. author. *On Photography*, ch. 4 (1977).

11 I longed to arrest all beauty that came before me, and at length the longing has been satisfied.

Julia Margaret Cameron (1815–1879), U.S. photographer. As quoted in *On Photography*, Appendix, by Susan Sontag (1977).

12 It is very fashionable for good-looking ladies to say how hard it is to be beautiful, but that's not true. There are times when it depresses and bothers me to see just how easy things are made for a beautiful woman.

Catherine Deneuve (b. 1943), French actress. As quoted in *People* magazine, p. 315 (March 4–17, 1994).

Deneuve was an exceptionally beautiful movie star.

BEAUTY CONTESTS

1 No one knows anybody's name because nobody has a name. You're just your state. I got to where somebody would say "Virginia," and I'd answer. I was just "Virginia." I wasn't me any more.

Wendy Dascomb Long (b. c. 1950), U.S. beauty queen. As quoted in *Ms.* magazine, p. 36 (September 1972).

Miss U.S.A. for 1969–1970, Long was describing the pageant, in which she competed successfully after having won the title of Miss Virginia.

2 Miss U.S.A. is in the same graveyard that [Amanda Jones] the twelve-year-old is. Where the six-

teen-year-old is. All the past selves. There comes a time when you have to bury those selves because you've grown into another one.

Amanda Jones, U.S. beauty contest winner, Miss U.S.A., 1973. As quoted under the pseudonym "Emma Wright" in *American Dreams*, Prologue, by Studs Terkel (1980).

3 You have to be nice and congenial and enthusiastic. What makes that so difficult is you have to be nice, congenial, and enthusiastic three hundred and sixty-five days in a row! . . . You can't have a day off.

Shirley Cothran-Barnet (b. c. 1955), U.S. beauty contest winner, Miss America, 1975 (as Shirley Cothran). As quoted in *Miss America,* ch. 17, by Ann-Marie Bivans (1991).

Recalling her year "in office."

4 Who's gonna take me seriously with this on my head?

Leanza Corbett (b. c. 1973), U.S. beauty queen. As quoted in the *New York Times*, sect. 9, p. 12 (September 12, 1993).

The 1993 Miss America was referring to the rhinestone crown traditionally worn by Miss Americas. Corbett, a serious and thoughtful person, had spoken publicly in support of AIDS research and had argued successfully that Miss America contestants should henceforth fix their own hair and makeup rather than bringing along professional assistants. She made a practice of *holding* rather than *wearing* her crown; she did wear a small crown-shaped pin and a red ribbon signifying support for AIDS victims.

BEST-SELLERS

1 In trying to understand the appeal of best-sellers, it is well to remember that whistles can be made sounding certain notes which are clearly audible to dogs and other of

the lower animals, though man is incapable of hearing them.

REBECCA WEST (1892–1983), British author. *The Strange Necessity,* ch. 11 (1928).

BICYCLING

1 [Bicycling] has done more to emancipate woman than any one thing in the world. I rejoice every time I see a woman ride by on a wheel. It gives her a feeling of self-reliance and independence the moment she takes her seat; and away she goes, the picture of untrammelled womanhood.

SUSAN B. ANTHONY (1820–1906), U.S. suffragist. As quoted in *The Life and Work of Susan B. Anthony,* ch. 46, by Ida Husted Harper (1898).

Said in 1896.

2 This, my first [bicycle] had an intrinsic beauty. And it opened for me an era of all but flying, which roads emptily crossing the airy, gold-gorsy Common enhanced. Nothing since has equalled that birdlike freedom.

ELIZABETH BOWEN (1899–1973), British novelist, essayist, and memoirist; born in Ireland. *Pictures and Conversations,* ch. 1 (1975).

On her first bicycle, which she acquired at age 13.

BIOGRAPHY

1 ... my last work is no sooner on the stands than letters come, suggesting a subject. The grandmothers of strangers are crying from the grave, it seems, for literary recognition; it is bewildering, the number

of salty grandfathers, aunts and uncles that languish unappreciated.

CATHERINE DRINKER BOWEN (1897–1973), U.S. biographer. *Adventures of a Biographer,* ch. 10 (1959).

Bowen wrote popular biographies of Tchaikovsky, Oliver Wendell Holmes, John Adams, and Francis Bacon, among others.

2 i am terrified of biographies,
. . .
"born in australia in the emerald
studded
pouch of a sable coated kangaroo
my right eye is a perfect star
sapphire."
i am in favor of myths.

LYNNE SAVITT, U.S. poet. "On Being Asked for Biographical Information," lines 1, 19–22 (1979).

BIRTH CONTROL

1 I don't believe there is one woman within the confines of this state who does not believe in birth control. I never met one. That is, I never met one who thought that she should be kept in ignorance of contraceptive methods. Many I have met who valued the knowledge they possessed, but thought there were certain other classes who would be better kept in ignorance. The old would protect the young. The rich would keep the poor in ignorance. The good would keep their knowledge from the bad, the strong from the weak.

CRYSTAL EASTMAN (1881–1928), U.S. author and political activist. *On Women and Revolution,* part 1 (1978).

From an article originally published in *Birth Control Review* (January 1918). To dispense information about birth control was then illegal.

2 . . . only a controlled fertility in human beings can maintain any progress. No system of society depending for its continuation on intelligent humans can stand long
unless it encourages the control of
the birth rate and includes contraceptive knowledge as a right. Without it no system, no matter what its
ideals, can withstand the overpow-
ering force of uncontrolled, unre-
stricted fecundity.

MARGARET SANGER (1879–1966), U.S.
birth control advocate. *My Fight for Birth Control*, ch. 4 (1931).

Of insights gained during her 1913 trip to Glasgow, Scotland. At the time, distribution of birth
control information was illegal in the United
States.

3 . . . given a choice between hearing
my daughter say "I'm pregnant" or
"I used a condom," most mothers
would get up in the middle of the
night and buy them herself.

JOYCELYN ELDERS (b. 1933), U.S. pediatrician and medical educator; first woman (and
second African American) Surgeon General. As
quoted in the *New York Times*, p. 6 (July 24,
1993).

Testifying before the U.S. Senate's Labor and
Human Resources Committee following her
designation by President Clinton as his candidate for Surgeon General. Elders was explaining
her support for sex education in the schools.

4 If I could be the "condom queen"
and get every young person who engaged in sex to use a condom in the
United States, I would wear a
crown on my head with a condom
on it! I would!

JOYCELYN ELDERS (b. 1933), U.S. pedia-
trician and educator; first woman (and second
African American) Surgeon General of the
United States. As quoted in the *New York Times
Magazine*, p. 19 (January 30, 1994).

Elders, who was U. S. Surgeon General at the
time, was a passionate advocate of the controversial practice of providing contraceptives to
teenagers. This was her reaction to being con-
temptuously nicknamed the "condom queen"
by the Traditional Values Coalition, a conservative lobbying organization.

5 . . . the black girls didn't get these
pills because their black ministers
were up on the pulpit saying that
birth control pills were black genocide. What I'm saying is that black
men have exploited black women.
. . . They didn't want them to have
any choice about their reproductive
health. And if you can't control
your reproduction, you can't control your life.

JOYCELYN ELDERS (b. 1933), U.S. pedia-
trician and educator; first woman (and second
African American) Surgeon General of the
United States. As quoted in the *New York Times
Magazine*, p. 18 (January 30, 1994).

Elders, who was U. S. Surgeon General at the
time, was citing one reason white girls were taking birth control pills at a higher rate (and having out-of-wedlock babies at a lower rate) than
African American girls.

BIRTH CONTROL MOVEMENT

1 . . . the ocean could not be swept
back with a broom. The truth was
out. It illuminated the world. Motherhood no longer cringed before the
relentless laws of fecundity.

MARGARET SANGER (1879–1966), U.S.
birth control advocate. *My Fight for Birth Control*, ch. 21 (1931).

On her success, in 1922, in obtaining New
York State incorporation for the American Birth
Control League. Sanger was President of the
League.

2 I resolved that women should have
knowledge of contraception. They

have every right to know about their own bodies. I would strike out—I would scream from the housetops. I would tell the world what was going on in the lives of these poor women. *I would* be heard. No matter what it should cost. *I would be heard.*

MARGARET SANGER (1879–1966), U.S. birth control advocate. *My Fight for Birth Control,* ch. 3 (1931).

Of the resolve she made in 1912 while serving as a nurse to the poor on New York City's lower east side.

BLASPHEMY

1 Now a doll found naked in a ditch eyes rusted open, is blasphemy.

DEBORAH DIGGES (b. 1950), U.S. author. "The Man in the Circle," last two lines (1986).

BLINDNESS

1 In general the newly sighted see the world as a dazzle of color-patches. They are pleased by the sensation of color, and learn quickly to name the colors, but the rest of seeing is tormentingly difficult. . . . It oppresses them to realize, if they ever do at all, the tremendous size of the world, which they had previously conceived of as something touchingly manageable. It oppresses them to realize that they have been visible to people all along, perhaps unattractively so, without their knowledge or consent. A disheartening number of them refuse to use their new vision, continuing to go over objects with their tongues, and lapsing into apathy and despair.

ANNIE DILLARD (b. 1945), U.S. essayist and autobiographer. *Pilgrim at Tinker Creek,* ch. 2 (1974).

BODY

1 Though the sex to which I belong is considered weak . . . you will nevertheless find me a rock that bends to no wind.

ELIZABETH I (1533–1603), British monarch, Queen of England (1558–1603). As quoted in *The Sayings of Queen Elizabeth,* ch. 11, by Frederick Chamberlin (1923).
To the French Ambassador.

2 The truth, the absolute truth, is that the chief beauty for the theatre consists in fine bodily proportions.

SARAH BERNHARDT (1845–1923), French actor. *The Art of the Theatre,* ch. 3 (1924).
Written in 1923.

3 The dream of the typical American girl-next-door still doesn't include a good pair of quadriceps. . . . But there's been a big change in attitudes. Muscles are becoming O.K. for women; it's even O.K. to sweat.

MAREN SEIDLER (b. 1953), U.S. shot put champion. As quoted in *WomenSports* magazine, p. 58 (February 1977).
Seidler was 6'2" tall and powerfully built.

BOOKS

1 . . . I have depended on books not only for pleasure and for the wisdom they bring to all who read, but also for that knowledge which comes to others through their eyes and their ears. . . . books have

meant so much more in my education than in that of others . . .

HELEN KELLER (1880–1968), U.S. author. *The Story of My Life,* ch. 21 (1905). Keller was rendered deaf and blind at the age of nineteen months. But in 1904, she had graduated *cum laude* from Radcliffe College.

2   I would not, if I could, give up the memory of the joy I have had in books for any advantage that could be offered in other pursuits or occupations. Books have been to me what gold is to the miser, what new fields are to the explorer.

MARGARET E. SANGSTER (1838–1912), U.S. author. *An Autobiography from My Youth Up,* ch. 6 (1909).

3   . . . if we have a dollar to spend on some wild excess, we shall spend it on a book, not on asparagus out of season.

KATHERINE FULLERTON GEROULD (1879–1944), U.S. author. *Modes and Morals,* ch. 1 (1920).

4   I can imagine living without food. I cannot imagine living without books.

ALICE FOOTE MACDOUGALL (1867–1945), U.S. businesswoman. *The Autobiography of a Business Woman,* ch. 2 (1928). Recalling her childhood self-education in her grandfather's library, where she read works by Lewis Carroll, Edward Lear, Louisa May Alcott, Shakespeare, Smollett, Shelley, Spenser, Browning, Emerson, and George Eliot, among other writers.

5   It is the interest one takes in books that makes a library. And if a library have interest it is; if not, it isn't.

CAROLYN WELLS (1862–1942), U.S. author. *The Rest of My Life,* ch. 16 (1937). Wells primarily wrote popular novels.

6   . . . if this world were anything near what it should be there would be no more need of a Book Week than there would be of a Society for the Prevention of Cruelty to Children.

DOROTHY PARKER (1893–1967), U.S. author and humorist. *Constant Reader,* column dated February 11, 1928 (1970).

7   It had been startling and disappointing to me to find out that story books had been written by *people,* that books were not natural wonders, coming up of themselves like grass. Yet regardless of where they came from, I cannot remember a time when I was not in love with them—with the books themselves, cover and binding and the paper they were printed on, with their smell and their weight and with their possession in my arms, captured and carried off to myself. Still illiterate, I was ready for them, committed to all the reading I could give them.

EUDORA WELTY (b. 1909), U.S. fiction writer. *One Writer's Beginnings,* ch. 1 (1984).

8   Life-transforming ideas have always come to me through books.

BELL HOOKS (b. c. 1955), African American author, feminist, and human rights advocate. *Outlaw Culture,* ch. 8 (1994).

BOSNIAN WAR

1   I keep asking why? What for? Who's to blame? I ask but there's no answer. All I know is that we are living in misery.

ZLATA FILIPOVIC (b. c. 1981), Yugoslavian diarist. As quoted in *Newsweek* magazine, p. 26 (February 28, 1994).

A 13–year-old Sarajevan and the author of *Zlata's Diary: A Child's Life in Sarajevo,* Filipovic wrote this on June 18, 1992, about the civil war that was tearing her country apart.

2 International relations is security, it's trade relations, it's power games. It's not good-and-bad. But what I saw in Yugoslavia was pure evil. Not ethnic hatred—that's only like a label. I really had a feeling there that I am observing unleashed human evil . . .

NATASHA DUDINSKA (b. c. 1967), Czechoslovakian Jew; attending college in America. As quoted in the *New York Times,* sect. 4 p. 7 (June 13, 1993).

A former anti-Communist student activist in Czechoslovakia, she was pondering the 1992–1993 "ethnic cleansing" movement in the fractured country once called Yugoslavia. One day earlier, Dudinska had been awarded a Master's degree in International Relations from Columbia University (New York City).

3 We want Sarajevo to stay alive. We will shoot at them each year with one child. Whatever they do, they can't stop us.

GORDONA KITIC (b. 1962), Bosnian expectant mother. As quoted in *Newsweek* magazine, p. 60 (January 3, 1994).

A Bosnian living in the midst of civil war, Kitic was eight months pregnant.

BOXING

1 Getting hit really isn't that bad. The worst part is getting beat.

BOBBIE LYNN BOWEN (b. c. 1960), U.S. boxer. As quoted in *WomenSports* magazine, p. 15 (January 1976).

Bowen was Miss Junior Golden Gloves.

2 Boxing has become America's tragic theater.

JOYCE CAROL OATES (b. 1938), U.S. author. *On Boxing* (1987).

3 I've been complimented for my scorekeeping, and sometimes it's hard to tell whether it's a backhanded compliment or not. Are the men surprised when a woman does a good job as a judge?

SHEILA HARMON-MARTIN, U.S. political scientist and boxing judge. As quoted in the *Chronicle of Higher Education,* pp. A13–A14 (June 2, 1993).

Harmon-Martin was "one of about a dozen women who are sanctioned internationally to judge professional bouts."

BULLFIGHTING

1 I was so sick and faint, so overcome at the brutality of this fiendish sport, that I hardly heard the shouts of "Bravo! bravo!" and the fanfaronade of trumpets. . . . I do not know which astonished me the most, the strikingly curious, brilliant *coup d'oeil,* the dexterity of the men, the intrepidity of the animals, the miserable unfair play, or the pleasure of the spectators.

M. E. W. SHERWOOD (1826–1903), U.S. socialite, traveller, and author. *An Epistle to Posterity,* ch. 18 (1897).

On seeing her first bullfight—at the Plaza de los Toros in Madrid in 1889.

BUSINESS

1 I do not claim that all women, or a large portion of them, should enter into independent business relations with the world, but I do claim that all women should cultivate and respect in themselves an ability to make money.

ELLEN DEMAREST (1824–1898), U.S. businesswoman. As quoted in *Feminine Ingenuity,* ch., by Anne L. MacDonald (1992).

Said in 1872. Active in many business enterprises, Demarest also was co-owner of a ship named *Madame Demarest,* which had an all-woman crew.

2 The plodding thrift and scrupulous integrity and long-winded patient industry of our business men of the last century are out of fashion in these "giddy-paced" times, and England is forgetting that those who make haste to be rich can hardly avoid much temptation and some sin.

FANNY KEMBLE (1809–1893), British actor. *Further Records, 1848–1883,* vol. 2; Entry dated December 22, 1853 (1891).

3 ... the ... thing I am proudest of in my whole business life is that I do not take, that I never took in all my life, and never, never! will take, one single penny more than 6% on any loan or any contract.

HETTY GREEN (1834–1916), U.S. investor and businesswoman. As quoted in *The Witch of Wall Street,* ch. 31, by Boyden Sparkes and Samuel Taylor Moore (1935).

In a letter, written c. 1907, to the financial editor of a New York newspaper. Green had parlayed a large inherited fortune into a much larger one.

4 ... women especially seem to have very little idea of the importance of business time.

CAROLINE NICHOLS CHURCHILL (1833–?), U.S. author. *Active Footsteps,* ch. 8 (1909).

5 This is a woman's industry. No man will vote our stock, transact

our business, pronounce on women's wages, supervise our factories. Give men whatever work is suitable, but keep the governing power. ... Here is a mission, let it be fulfilled.

AMANDA THEODOSIA JONES (1835–1914), U.S. inventor, businesswoman, and psychic. *A Psychic's Autobiography,* ch. 31 (1910).

In an address to the employees of the Women's Canning and Preserving Company, a successful business which she had founded in Chicago after inventing a canning process.

6 ... if the production of any commodity necessitates the sacrifice of human life, society should do without that commodity, but it can not do without that life.

EMMA GOLDMAN (1869–1940), U.S. anarchist and author; born in Russia. *Anarchism and Other Essays,* 3rd rev. ed., ch. 3 (1917).

7 God protect us from the efficient, go-getter businesswoman whose feminine instincts have been completely sterilized. Wherever women are functioning, whether in the home or in a job, they must remember that their chief function as women is a capacity for warm, understanding and charitable human relationships.

AGNES E. MEYER (1887–1970), U.S. journalist. *Out of These Roots,* ch. 16 (1953).

8 The world is not merely *the* world. It is our world. It is not merely an industrial world. It is, above all things, a human world.

AGNES E. MEYER (1887–1970), U.S. journalist. *Out of These Roots,* ch. 13 (1953).

Meyer was concerned about the negative impact of technological progress on human happiness.

9 ... men and women are not yet free. . . . The slavery of greed endures. Little child workers, the hope of the future, are sacrificed to industry. Young men are sent out by the billion to die for profits. . . . We must destroy industrial slavery and build industrial democracy. . . . The people everywhere must come into possession of the earth [second, third, and fourth ellipses in source].

SARA BARD FIELD (1882–1974), U.S. feminist. As quoted in *On Women and Revolution*, part 1, by Crystal Eastman (1978). From an article published in *The Liberator* in April 1921. From Field's speech at a ceremony in which the Woman's Party presented the U. S. Congress with a statue of the pre-eminent suffragists Susan B. Anthony (1820–1906), Lucretia Mott (1793–1880), and Elizabeth Cady Stanton (1815–1902). Field was asserting that American feminists' work was not completed with passage of the Nineteenth Amendment to the Constitution, which had taken effect the year before and enfranchised women.

10 The more important the title, the more self-important the person, the greater the amount of time spent on the Eastern shuttle, the more suspicious the man and the less vitality in the organization.

JANE O'REILLY, U.S. feminist and humorist. *The Girl I Left Behind*, ch. 5 (1980). This was the last of O'Reilly's twelve "rules of Upward Failure." Among the others were "If you are outside the Establishment try to work at something no one really understands" (number 8) and "There is no such thing as bad publicity" (number 6).

11 This morning I threw up at a board meeting. I was sure the cat was out of the bag, but no one seemed to think anything about it; apparently it's quite common for people to throw up at board meetings.

JANE WAGNER (b. 1935), U.S. playwright. *The Search for Signs of Intelligent Life in the Universe* (1986). In this section of the book based on a one-person play, a pregnant woman is explaining that she is keeping her pregnancy secret for fear it may negatively affect her employment.

12 I would go to all these dinners with people who told me how much money they made. It didn't excite me at all.

LAURA SCHER, U.S. businesswoman. As quoted in the *New York Times*, section 3, p. 8 (November 7, 1993). A Harvard Business School graduate, she was remembering being recruited by companies. She eventually accepted a comparatively small salary to run a Working Assets Funding Service, a company that systematizes charitable donations through payments of credit card, telephone, and other bills.

13 We didn't want any men in our group. They drink their loans, they don't work their stores. Why should we have to pay for their irresponsibilities?

BRACHIATE GUIOTH DE ESPINOSA, Colombian storekeeper. As quoted in the *New York Times*, p. A6 (July 15, 1994). Abandoned five years earlier by her husband, Guioth de Espinosa ran a store in Colombia and belonged to a cooperative association of women storekeepers. In recent years, the number of Colombian women in the workforce had increased greatly.

CANNIBALISM

1 We have done scant justice to the reasonableness of cannibalism. There are in fact so many and such excellent motives possible to it that mankind has never been able to fit all of them into one universal scheme, and has accordingly contrived various diverse and contradictory systems the better to display its virtues.

Ruth Benedict (1887–1948), U.S. anthropologist. *An Anthropologist at Work,* part 1 (1959).
From "The Uses of Cannibalism," a paper written c. 1925.

CAPITALISM

1 Work of all kinds is got from poor women, at prices that will not keep soul and body together, and then the articles thus made are sold for prices that give monstrous prices to the capitalist, who thus grows rich on the hard labor of our sex.

Catherine E. Beecher (1800–1878), U.S. educator and author. As quoted in *Catherine Beecher,* ch. 12, by Kathryn Kish Sklar (1973).
Written in 1844.

2 ... the greatest bulwark of capitalism is militarism.

Emma Goldman (1869–1940), U.S. anarchist and author; born in Russia. *Anarchism and Other Essays,* 3rd rev. ed., ch. 5 (1917).

3 ... in a capitalist society a man is expected to be an aggressive, uncompromising, factual, lusty, intelligent provider of goods, and the woman, a retiring, gracious, emotional, intuitive, attractive consumer of goods.

Toni Cade (b. 1939), African American author and political activist. *The Black Woman,* ch. 15 (1970).
Excerpted from "The Scattered Sopranoes," an autobiographical essay delivered as a lecture to the Livingston College Black Woman's Seminar in December 1969. Cade would become well known for her fiction, written under the name Toni Cade Bambara.

CATHEDRALS

1 ... the first cathedral you see remains with you forever as *the* cathedral of the world.

M. E. W. Sherwood (1826–1903), U.S. socialite, traveller, and author. *An Epistle to Posterity,* ch. 8 (1897).

CAUTION

1 A fool too late bewares when all the peril is past.

Elizabeth I (1533–1603), Queen of England (1558–1603). As quoted in *The Sayings of Queen Elizabeth,* ch. 11, by Frederick Chamberlin (1923).
To Sir Henry Sidney, governor of Ireland.

2 Moderation has never yet engineered an explosion. ...

Ellen Glasgow (1873–1945), U.S. novelist. *The Woman Within,* ch. 21 (1954).
Written in 1937.

CENSORSHIP

1 If there is anything I really fear it is the mind of a young girl.

Jane Heap (c. 1880–1964), U.S. artist and editor. As quoted in *The Strange Necessity,* part 1, by Margaret Anderson (1969).
Said in 1920, when Heap and her co-editor, Margaret Anderson, were on trial for publishing sections of the Irish novelist James Joyce's controversial masterpiece, *Ulysses,* in their literary journal, *The Little Review.* Two years later, the American expatriate Sylvia Beach, who had become a Parisian bookseller, published the complete *Ulysses* in book form. Here, Heap was reacting privately to the prosecutor's assertion in court that reading *Ulysses* would endanger "the minds of young girls." Ultimately, Anderson and Heap were convicted and fined $100.

2 God forbid that any book should be banned. The practice is as indefensible as infanticide.

REBECCA WEST (1892–1983), British author. *The Strange Necessity,* ch. 11 (1928).

3 . . . gathering news in Russia was like mining coal with a hatpin.

MARY HEATON VORSE (1874–1966), U.S. journalist and labor activist. *A Footnote to Folly,* ch. 24 (1935).

On Russia in 1921, following the Revolution. Vorse was there as a Hearst newspaper correspondent.

4 I think they are the slobber-heartedest lily-mindedest piously conniving crowd in the modern world.

FLANNERY O'CONNOR (1925–1964), U.S. novelist, story writer, and essayist. As quoted in *The Habit of Being* (1979).

From a letter, dated September 1, 1963, to her anonymous correspondent "A." She was speaking of an interview conducted with her by a writer for an Atlanta magazine; before publication, their discussion of the "race question" was amended by an editor to the "social" crisis, "so that none of it makes much sense."

CHALLENGER SPACE SHUTTLE

1 Just opening up the door, having this ordinary person fly, says a lot for the future. You can always equate astronauts with explorers who were subsidized. Now you are getting someone going just to observe. And then you'll have the settlers.

CHRISTA MCAULIFFE (1948–1986), U.S. schoolteacher. As quoted in *Newsweek* magazine, p. 29 (February 10, 1986).

McAuliffe had been chosen from among thousands of teacher-applicants to accompany the crew of the Challenger on a space mission. The spaceship took off on January 28, 1986, and exploded in midair. McAuliffe would have been the first non-astronaut to travel in space.

2 The report reflects incredibly terrible judgments, shockingly sparse concern for human life, instances of officials lacking the courage to exercise the responsibilities of their high office and some very bewildering thought processes.

JANE JARRELL SMITH, U.S. widow of American astronaut Michael J. Smith. As quoted in *Newsweek* magazine, p. 13 (June 30, 1986).

On the Rogers Commission report which described the circumstances surrounding the explosion of the Challenger, the American space shuttle on which her husband and the other six crew members were killed. As it turned out, the explosion was caused by faulty "O-ring" seals.

CHANGE

1 There are no such oysters, terrapin, or canvas-back ducks as there were in those days; the race is extinct. It is strange how things degenerate. . . . I passed, the other day, the deserted house of Mrs. Gerry, which I used to think so lordly. It stands alone now amid the surrounding sky-scrapers, and reminds me of Don Quixote going out to fight the windmills. It should always remain to mark the difference between the past and the present.

M. E. W. SHERWOOD (1826–1903), U.S. socialite, traveller, and author. *An Epistle to Posterity,* ch. 11 (1897).

Sherwood, a New Yorker, was remembering the city's genteel social life and cuisine in the 1870s, when she lived at 6 West 11th Street, worshipped at nearby Ascension Church, took her children to pick their "first dandelions" in Washington Square, and attended a magnificent ball at "Mrs. Gerry's," or Mr. Peter Goelet's house, at the corner of 19th Street and Broadway.

2 All changes are more or less tinged with melancholy, for what we are

leaving behind is part of ourselves.

AMELIA E. BARR (1831–1919), U.S. au-
thor; born in Scotland. *All the Days of My Life,*
ch. 16 (1913).

3   . . . all big changes in human history
have been arrived at slowly and
through many compromises.

ELEANOR ROOSEVELT (1884–1962), U.S.
First Lady, author, and speaker. As quoted in *Eleanor and Franklin,* ch. 27, by Joseph P. Lash
(1971).

Stated in 1925.

4   Change is the only constant. Hanging on is the only sin.

DENISE MCCLUGGAGE (b. 1927), U.S.
race car driver. As quoted in *WomenSports*
magazine, p. 18 (June 1977).

5   Poetry is not only dream and vision; it is the skeleton architecture
of our lives. It lays the foundations
for a future of change, a bridge
across our fears of what has never
been before.

AUDRE LORDE (1934–1992), African
American poet, autobiographer, and lesbian
feminist. *Sister Outsider,* ch. 3 (1984).

From "Poetry is Not a Luxury," an essay first
published in *Chrysalis,* number 3 (1977).

6   Nobody can resist a ripe idea. The
idea today is change.

TANSU CILLER (b. 1946), Turkish politician. As quoted in the *New York Times,* p. 4
(July 3, 1993).

Upon being elected the first woman Prime Minister in the history of Turkey. Thirty years earlier,
she had married and not only refused to take
her husband's name but persuaded him to take
hers.

7   . . . wariness about change is a kind
of prairie wisdom.

KATHLEEN NORRIS (b. 1947), U.S. poet
and farmer. *Dakota,* ch. 9 (1993).

CHARACTER

1   Innocence is lovely in the child, because in harmony with its nature;
but our path in life is not backward
but onward, and virtue can never
be the offspring of mere innocence.
If we are to progress in the knowledge of good, we must also progress
in the knowledge of evil. Every experience of evil brings its own temptation and according to the degree
in which the evil is recognized and
the temptations resisted, will be the
value of the character into which
the individual will develop.

MRS. H. O. WARD (1824–1899), U.S. author. *Sensible Etiquette of the Best Society Customs, Manners, Morals, and Home Culture,
Compiled from the Best Authorities,* ch. 12
(1878).

CHARITY

1   I don't feel sure about doing good
in any way now; everything seems
like going on a mission to a people
whose language I don't know.

GEORGE ELIOT (1819–1880), British novelist. *Middlemarch,* ch. 3 (1871).

Said by the novel's devout and dedicated heroine, Dorothea Brooke (later Casaubon).

2   Let . . . individuals make the most
of what God has given them, have
their neighbors do the same, and
then do all they can to serve each
other. There is no use in one man,
or one nation, to try to do or be everything. It is a good thing to be de-

pendent on each other for something, it makes us civil and peaceable.

SOJOURNER TRUTH (c. 1797–1883), African American suffragist and abolitionist. As quoted in *History of Woman Suffrage,* appendix—ch. 19, by Elizabeth Cady Stanton (1882).

The former slave, itinerant preacher, and beloved activist in the woman suffrage movement said this during an 1867 visit with Elizabeth Cady Stanton and her family. This is from a letter that Stanton wrote to the *World,* which, she said, "seemed to please Sojourner more than any other journal." Truth was illiterate but enjoyed having newspapers read aloud to her.

3   Arrive in the afternoon, the late
    light slanting
    In diluted gold bars across the boulevard brag
    Of proud, seamed faces with mercy
    and murder hinting
    here, there, interrupting, all deep
    and debonair,
    The pink paint on the innocence of
    fear;
    Walk in a gingerly manner up the
    hall.

GWENDOLYN BROOKS (b. 1917), African American poet and fiction writer. "The Lovers of the Poor," lines 1–6 (1960).

On the condescending charity of wealthy Chicago suburban matrons toward inner-city poor African Americans.

4   Charity is a cop-out so traditionally female in its apparent self-effacement that there seems resonant comfort in it. We're no longer supposed to serve the imaginations of men who have dominated us. We are to give up ourselves instead to those whose suffering is greater than our own. Looking down is just as distorting as looking up and as

dangerous in perpetuating hierarchies.

JANE RULE (b. 1931), Canadian fiction writer and essayist; born in the U.S. *A Hot-Eyed Moderate,* part 1 (1985).

CHARM

1   You must have this charm to reach the pinnacle. It is made of everything and of nothing, the striving will, the look, the walk, the proportions of the body, the sound of the voice, the ease of the gestures. It is not at all necessary to be handsome or to be pretty; all that is needful is charm.

SARAH BERNHARDT (1845–1923), French actor. *The Art of the Theatre,* ch. 2 (1924). Written in 1923.

2   The rarest of all things in American life is charm. We spend billions every year manufacturing fake charm that goes under the heading of "public relations." Without it, America would be grim indeed.

ANITA LOOS (1888–1981), U.S. screenwriter, author, and humorist. *Kiss Hollywood Good-by,* ch. 11 (1974).

CHILDHOOD

1   Childhood is not from birth to a
    certain age and at a certain age
    The child is grown, and puts away
    childish things.
    Childhood is the kingdom where
    nobody dies.

EDNA ST. VINCENT MILLAY (1892–1950), U.S. poet. "Childhood Is the Kingdom Where Nobody Dies," lines 1–3 (1934).

2 At the age of twelve I was finding the world too small: it appeared to me like a dull, trim back garden, in which only trivial games could be played.

ELIZABETH BOWEN (1899–1973), British novelist, story writer, essayist, and memoirist; born in Ireland. *Seven Winters,* part 2, sect. 4, ch. 1 (1962).

From a 1947 British Broadcasting Company (BBC) radio program in which Bowen discussed *She,* a novel by H. Rider Haggard.

3 We hear a great deal of lamentation these days about writers having all taken themselves to the colleges and universities where they live decorously instead of going out and getting firsthand information about life. The fact is that anybody who has survived his childhood has enough information about life to last him the rest of his days.

FLANNERY O'CONNOR (1925–1964), U.S. fiction writer and essayist. *Mystery and Manners,* part 3 (1969).

Written c. 1960. O'Connor suffered from lupus and was an invalid for much of her adult life, living with her mother on the family farm in Georgia. So, although she was not a college faculty member, she did not lead a notably adventuresome life.

4 . . . a country encapsulates our childhood and those lanes, byres, fields, flowers, insects, suns, moons and stars are forever reoccurring.

EDNA O'BRIEN (b. c. 1932), Irish author; relocated to England. *Mother Ireland,* ch. 7 (1976).

5 The hardest part about being a kid is knowing you have got your whole life ahead of you.

JANE WAGNER (b. 1935), U.S. author. *Edith Ann* (1994).

CHILDREN

1 We are told that every American boy has the chance of being president. I tell you that these little boys in the iron cages would sell their chance any day for good square meals and a chance to play.

MOTHER JONES (1830–1930), U.S. labor organizer. *The Autobiography of Mother Jones,* ch. 10 (1925).

Addressing a crowd at a wild animal show at Coney Island, New York, in 1903. She was accompanied by striking child textile workers from Kensington, Pennsylvania, whom she had locked in empty iron animal cages to make a symbolic point.

2 What if all the forces of society were bent upon developing [poor] children? What if society's business were making people instead of profits? How much of their creative beauty of spirit would remain unquenched through the years? How much of this responsiveness would follow them through life?

MARY HEATON VORSE (1874–1966), U.S. journalist and labor activist. *A Footnote to Folly,* ch. 23 (1935).

On the responsiveness of poor children in New York City to a New Year's Eve party given for them by the Amalgamated Clothing Workers in 1921 during a strike.

3 . . . all children have creative power.

BRENDA UELAND (1891–1985), U.S. author and writing teacher. *If You Want to Write,* 2nd. ed., ch. 1 (1938).

4 . . . children do not take war seriously as war. War is soldiers and soldiers have not to be war but they have to be soldiers. Which is a nice thing.

GERTRUDE STEIN (1874–1946), U.S. author; relocated to France. *Wars I Have Seen* (1945).
Written in 1943.

5   O the night of the weeping children!
O the night of the children branded for death!
Sleep may not enter here.
Terrible nursemaids
Have usurped the place of mothers . . .

NELLY SACHS (1891–1970), German Jewish poet and translator; relocated to Sweden. "O the night of the weeping children!" Lines 1–5, translated by Michael Hamburger, et al. (1967; first edition in German: 1946).
Sachs was cowinner of the 1966 Nobel Prize for Literature.

6   Just as everybody has the vote including women, I think children should, because as a child is conscious of itself then it has to me an existence and has a stake in what happens.

GERTRUDE STEIN (1874–1946), U.S. author and patron of the arts; relocated to France. As quoted in *What Are Masterpieces,* afterword, by Robert Haas (1970).
Said in a January 1946 interview with Haas.

7   The idea of feminine authority is so deeply embedded in the human subconscious that even after all these centuries of father-right the young child instinctively regards the mother as the supreme authority. He looks upon the father as equal with himself, equally subject to the woman's rule. Children have to be taught to love, honor, and respect the father.

ELIZABETH GOULD DAVIS (b. 1910), U.S. feminist and author. *The First Sex,* ch. 7 (1971).

8   Children cannot eat rhetoric and they cannot be sheltered by commissions. I don't want to see another commission that studies the needs of kids. We need to help them.

MARIAN WRIGHT EDELMAN (b. 1939), African American lawyer. As quoted in *I Dream a World,* by Brian Lanker (1989).
A graduate of Yale University Law School, and the first African American woman admitted to the bar in Mississippi, Edelman founded the Children's Defense Fund in 1973.

9   So much missing, no sense of self, no core, no trust. Only a deep hollow we need to fill.

SISTER MICHELE, Indian nun. As quoted in the *New York Times Magazine,* p. 35 (January 16, 1994).
On child prostitutes in Thailand, whom she counselled.

CHILDREN'S LITERATURE

I   There are too many coy books full of talking animals, whimsical children, and condescending adults. (Some of the most famous animals in the world have talked, but they talked real talk and they weren't called silly names like Doody and Mooloo. They were called names like The Cheshire Cat and they asked sensible questions like "Did you say pig, or fig?")

KATHARINE S. WHITE (1892–1977), U.S. editor. As quoted in *Onward and Upward,* ch. 5, by Linda H. Davis (1986).
Said in 1935. White reviewed children's books for the *New Yorker,* and her husband, E. B. White, wrote several important children's books (*Stuart Little, Charlotte's Web,* etc.).

CHIVALRY

1 . . . I scarcely am able to govern my muscles, when I see a man start with eager, and serious solicitude, to lift a handkerchief, or shut a door, when the *lady* could have done it herself, had she only moved a pace or two.

MARY WOLLSTONECRAFT (1759–1797), British feminist. *A Vindication of the Rights of Woman,* ch. 4 (1792).

2 We are told that men protect us; that they are generous, even chivalric in their protection. Gentlemen, if your protectors were women, and they took all your property and your children, and paid you half as much for your work, though as well or better done than your own, would you think much of the chivalry which permitted you to sit in street-cars and picked up your pocket-handkerchief?

MARY B. CLAY, U.S. suffragist. As quoted in *History of Woman Suffrage,* vol. 4, ch. 3, by Susan B. Anthony and Ida Husted Harper (1902).

In a hearing on woman suffrage held by the Judiciary Committee of the United States House of Representatives on March 8, 1884; Clay was from Kentucky.

3 The clause which lived twenty-four hours in the Alabama Constitution, granting to taxpaying women owning $500 worth of property the suffrage on questions of bonded indebtedness, was killed by a disease peculiar to the genus homo known as chivalry. In the case in point, the diagnosis revealed that the fairest, purest and brightest jewels that ever shone under the brilliant rays of God's shining sun would be immeasurably lowered by voting upon questions relating to the taxation of their own property. Yet, under the vagaries of this disease, this same convention conferred on husbands the right to vote on their wives' property. This is the same character of chivalry which gives the wages of the brightest, fairest jewels to the husband, which makes impossible equal pay for equal work and which classes the jewels with the idiots, insane and criminals in that and other States.

ANNA GORDON (1853–1931), U.S. temperance activist and suffragist. As quoted in *History of Woman Suffrage,* vol. 5, ch. 2, by Ida Husted Harper (1922).

Speaking in February 1902 before the thirty-fourth annual convention of the National Woman Suffrage Association. "Idiots, insane [people] and criminals" were the only male citizens denied suffrage.

CHOICE

1 The point of cities is multiplicity of choice.

JANE JACOBS (b. 1916), U.S. urban analyst. *The Death and Life of Great American Cities,* ch. 18 (1961).

Jacobs lived in the lively, diverse Greenwich Village neighborhood of Manhattan (New York City).

CHRISTIANITY

1 If there were two princes in Christendom who had good will and courage, it would be very easy to reconcile the religious difficulties; there is only one Jesus Christ and one faith, and all the rest is a dispute over trifles.

ELIZABETH I (1533–1603), Queen of England (1558–1603). As quoted in *The Sayings of Queen Elizabeth,* ch. 10, by Frederick Chamberlin (1923).

Referring to the ongoing arguments between Protestants (of which Elizabeth was one) and Roman Catholics in England and other parts of Europe. She said this to the French Ambassador, whose country was Catholic.

2 If Jesus, or his likeness, should now visit the earth, what church of the many which now go by his name would he enter? Or, if tempted by curiosity, he should incline to look into all, which do you think would not shut the door in his face? . . . It seems to me . . . that as one who loved peace, taught industry, equality, union, and love, one towards another, Jesus were he alive at this day, would recommend you to come out of your churches of faith, and to gather into schools of knowledge.

FRANCES WRIGHT (1795–1852), Scottish author and speaker; relocated to America. *Course of Popular Lectures,* lecture 6 (1829).

3 Only let the North exert as much moral influence over the South, as the South has exerted demoralizing influence over the North, and slavery would die amid the flame of Christian remonstrance, and faithful rebuke, and holy indignation.

ANGELINA GRIMKÉ (1805–1879), U.S. abolitionist and feminist. *Letters to Catherine Beecher,* letter #4 (1837).
In a letter dated July 1837.

4 Dat little man in black dar, he say women can't have as much rights as men, 'cause Christ wan't a woman! Whar did your Christ come from?

Whar did your Christ come from? From God and a woman! Man had nothin' to do wid Him.

SOJOURNER TRUTH (1797–1883), African American human rights activist and preacher. As represented by Frances D. Gage and printed in *The History of Woman Suffrage,* vol. 1 ch. 6 (1881).

Remarks made on the second day of the Woman's Rights Convention held in Akron, Ohio, May 28–29, 1851; Truth was responding to a point made by a man in attendance. Gage, the President of the Convention, wrote up Truth's remarks from memory. Born a slave in Ulster County, New York, and named Isabella Baumfree, Truth had been freed by New York State law in 1827. In 1843, she had a religious vision which led her to change her name and become an itinerant preacher. She also became a prominent and beloved figure in the woman suffrage and anti-slavery movements.

5 I understand that only the rich can be members of Dr. C—'s church. The Lord Christ, also, is therefore ineligible. I will remain outside with Him.

AMELIA E. BARR (1831–1919), U.S. author; born in Scotland. *All the Days of My Life,* ch. 20 (1913).

Said in the early 1870s to a New York City church officer, on being refused permission to join his church. At the time, Barr was a financially strained widow and struggling writer with three dependent daughters.

6 Rationally considered, nothing can be more absurd than the baptism of infants under any circumstances. No statement, no matter by whom it may be said to have been uttered, can make that true which is radically false. If an innocent child, unconscious of good or evil, irresponsible to God and man, incapable of thought or action, is not already, in accordance with Christian theology, a member of Christ, then no vicarious promise or priestly ablution can make him one. For if this were so, a similar ceremony under devil worship could make him a member of Satan.

TENNESSEE CLAFLIN (1846–1923), U.S. journalist, lecturer, and social reform advocate; relocated to England. *Talks and Essays,* vol. 4 ch. 11 (1897).

7 . . . it was religion that saved me. Our ugly church and parochial school provided me with my only aesthetic outlet, in the words of the Mass and the litanies and the old Latin hymns, in the Easter lilies around the altar, rosaries, ornamented prayer books, votive lamps, holy cards stamped in gold and decorated with flower wreaths and a saint's picture.

MARY MCCARTHY (1912–1989), U.S. author. *Memories of a Catholic Girlhood,* ch. 1 (1957).
Raised in a strictly Catholic, unsympathetic, Irish-American home, McCarthy would later become an unbeliever.

8 . . . while the South is hardly Christ-centered, it is most certainly Christ-haunted.

FLANNERY O'CONNOR (1925–1964), U.S. fiction writer and essayist. *Mystery and Manners,* part 2 (1969).
Written in 1957.

9 . . . in Northern Ireland, if you don't have basic Christianity, rather than merely religion, all you get out of the experience of living is bitterness.

BERNADETTE DEVLIN (b. 1947), Northern Irish political activist and Member of Parliament. *The Price of My Soul,* ch. 2 (1969).

CHRISTMAS

1 . . . Christmas is a season of such infinite *labour,* as well as expense in the shopping and present-making line, that almost every woman I know is good for nothing in purse and person for a month afterwards, done up physically, and broken down financially.

FANNY KEMBLE (1809–1893), British actor. *Further Records, 1848–1883,* Vol. 1; Entry dated December 31, 1874 (1891).

2 For this your mother sweated in the cold,
For this you bled upon the bitter tree:
A yard of tinsel ribbon bought and sold;
A paper wreath; a day at home for me.

EDNA ST. VINCENT MILLAY (1892–1950), U.S. poet. "To Jesus on His Birthday," lines 1–4 (1928).

3 I hear that in many places something has happened to Christmas; that it is changing from a time of merriment and carefree gaiety to a holiday which is filled with tedium; that many people dread the day and the obligation to give Christmas presents is a nightmare to weary, bored souls; that the children of enlightened parents no longer believe in Santa Claus; that all in all, the effort to be happy and have pleasure makes many honest hearts grow dark with despair instead of beaming with good will and cheerfulness.

JULIA PETERKIN (1880–1961), U.S. author. *A Plantation Christmas* (1934).

4   There is no end to the work of salvage
In the drowning high seas of
Christmas
when loneliness, in the name of
Christ
(That longing!), attacks the world.

MAY SARTON (1912–1995), U.S. poet, novelist, and memoirist. "Christmas Letter to a Psychiatrist," part 2 lines 6–9 (1970).

5   As if being eighty-five or ninety
and terrified and talked down to
loudly
and pushed around in wheelchairs
by the staff
all day weren't bad enough,
for tonight's entertainment the local
Brownies
have come to sing Christmas
carols. . . .

MARY JO SALTER (b. 1954), U.S. poet. "Brownie Troop #722 Visits the Nursing Home," lines 1–6 (1994).

CHURCH

1   When I married Humphrey I made up my mind to like sermons, and I set out by liking the end very much. That soon spread to the middle and the beginning, because I couldn't have the end without them.

GEORGE ELIOT (1819–1880), British novelist. *Middlemarch,* ch. 34 (1871–1872).

Said by the novel's character named Mrs. Cadwallader, wife of the Rector of Tipton and Freshitt.

2   In the county there are thirty-seven churches
and no butcher shop. This could be taken

as a matter of all form and no content.

MAXINE KUMIN (b. 1925), U.S. Jewish poet. "Living Alone with Jesus," lines 10–12 (1975).
Written while living in Danville, Kentucky.

CIRCUS

1   I have lived in both worlds. And I think I prefer, to the indifferent, haphazard, money-mad hurry of the Outside World, that of my world; that sympathy and understanding grown shadowy since I have been away from it so long, still is more real to me than the world I am in now. Not only the spangles and the gay trappings made it colorful; there was an inner color that warmed the soul. And that I miss.

JOSEPHINE DEMOTT ROBINSON (1865–1948), U.S. circus performer. *The Circus Lady,* ch. 1 (1926).

CITIES AND CITY LIFE

1   The distractions, the exhaustions, the savage noises, the demands of town life, are, for me, mortal enemies to thought, to sleep, and to study; its extremes of squalor and of splendor do not stimulate, but sadden me; certain phases of its society I profoundly value, but would sacrifice them to the heaven of country quiet, if I had to choose between.

ELIZABETH STUART PHELPS (1844–1911), U.S. novelist and short story writer. *Chapters from a Life,* ch. 12 (1897).
Phelps lived in Gloucester, Massachusetts, in the country and near the sea.

2 Everything that was ever to happen to me in the future had its germ or impulse in the conditions of my life on Dover Street. My friendships, my advantages and disadvantages, my gifts, my habits, my ambitions—these were the materials out of which I built my after life, in the open workshop of America. My days in the slums were pregnant with possibilities; it only needed the ripeness of events to make them fruit forth in realities. Steadily as I worked to win America, America advanced to lie at my feet. I was an heir, on Dover Street, awaiting maturity. I was a princess waiting to be led to the throne.

MARY ANTIN (1881–1949), U.S. socialite and author; born in Russia. *The Promised Land*, ch. 19 (1912).

A Russian Jew, Antin emigrated to the United States at age fifteen with her family and settled on Dover Street in Boston's slums. She attended prestigious Barnard College and made her way up in Boston society.

3 . . . in the cities there are thousands of rolling stones like me. We are all alike; we have no ties, we know nobody, we own nothing. When one of us dies, they scarcely know where to bury him. . . . We have no house, no place, no people of our own. We live in the streets, in the parks, in the theatres. We sit in restaurants and concert halls and look about at the hundreds of our own kind and shudder.

WILLA CATHER (1873–1947), U.S. novelist. *O Pioneers!* Part 2 (1913).

In this novel; Carl Linstrum, an engraver, has returned from the city to the Nebraska farmland where he grew up.

4 he had crowded the city so full that men could not grasp beauty, beauty was over them, through them, about them, no crevice unpacked with honey, rare, measureless.

H.D. (1886–1961), U.S. poet and fiction writer. "Cities," lines 30–35 (1916).
"He" is "the maker of cities."

5 It could be so beautiful here if the Americans themselves had not made it so ugly with their big buildings, their millions of cars, and noise . . .

GRETA GARBO (1905–1990), Swedish actor; relocated to the United States. As quoted in *The Divine Garbo*, ch. 4, by Frederick Sands and Sven Broman (1979).

Written in a letter to her friend, the Swede Lars Saxon, in autumn 1925, soon after arriving in California to make movies. She would eventually choose to make New York City her home.

6 Cities [are] problems in organized complexity, like the life sciences.

JANE JACOBS (b. 1916), U.S. urban analyst. *The Death and Life of Great American Cities*, ch. 19 (1961).

Jacobs lived in the lively, diverse Greenwich Village section of Manhattan (New York City).

7 There they are.
Thirty at the corner.
Black raw, ready.
Sores in the city
that do not want to heal.

GWENDOLYN BROOKS (b. 1917), African American author. "The Blackstone Rangers," part 1 (1968).

8 What is a slum? . . . it is something that mostly exists in the imaginations of middle-class do-gooders and bureaucrats: people who do not have to live in them in the first place and do not have to live in what they put up afterwards once they have pulled them all down. One person's slum is another person's community.

May Hobbs (b. 1938), British author. *Born to Struggle,* "Prelude," (1973).

Hobbs was born and raised on Hoxton Street in the London borough of Hackney, in the city's East End—a neighborhood that was destroyed by a government slum clearance project.

9 The meaning of the Street in all ways and at all times is the need for sharing life with others and the search for community.

Virginia Hamilton (b. 1936), African American writer of children's books. *Illusion and Reality.*

Referring to the streets in urban black neighborhoods.

CIVIL DISOBEDIENCE

I We are told to maintain constitutions because they are constitutions, and what is laid down in those constitutions? . . . Certain great fundamental ideas of right are common to the world, and . . . all laws of man's making which trample on these ideas, are null and void— wrong to obey, right to disobey. The Constitution of the United States recognizes human slavery; and makes the souls of men articles of purchase and of sale.

Anna Elizabeth Dickinson (1842– 1932), U.S. suffragist. As quoted in *History of Woman Suffrage,* vol. 2, ch. 16, by Elizabeth Cady Stanton, Susan B. Anthony, and Matilda Joslyn Gage (1882).

In a speech at Kennett Square in Philadelphia, c. 1860. Dickinson was an eloquent, bold, teen-aged activist whom the press often compared to Joan of Arc.

2 Trust me that as I ignore all law to help the slave, so will I ignore it all to protect an enslaved woman.

Susan B. Anthony (1820–1906), U.S. suffragist. As quoted in *The Life and Work of Susan B. Anthony,* vol. 1, ch. 12, by Ida Husted Harper (1898).

In an 1860 letter to William Lloyd Garrison and Wendell Phillips, defending her decision to assist a woman who had run away, with her child, from an abusive husband. Garrison and Phillips were abolitionists who favored assisting runaway slaves.

CIVIL RIGHTS MOVEMENT

I There are many persons ready to do what is right because in their hearts they know it is right. But they hesitate, waiting for the other fellow to make the first move—and he, in turn, waits for you. The minute a person whose word means a great deal dares to take the open-hearted and courageous way, many others follow. Not everyone can be turned aside from meanness and hatred, but the great majority of Americans is heading in that direction. I have a great belief in the future of my people and my country.

Marian Anderson (1897–1993), African American singer. *My Lord, What a Morning,* ch. 28 (1956).

Born in south Philadelphia, Anderson had developed into one of the most talented and famous singers in the world. But she had suffered greatly from racial discrimination along the way and had been prevented from achieving the major operatic career that many believed should have been hers by right of ability. When she wrote this, the civil rights movement was just getting underway.

2 . . . two great areas of deafness existed in the South: White Southerners had no ears to hear that which threatened their Dream. And colored Southerners had none to hear that which could reduce their anger.

SARAH PATTON BOYLE, U.S. civil rights activist and author. *The Desegregated Heart*, part 1, ch. 16 (1962).

Boyle, a white Virginian, was remembering what the American South was like at the commencement of the 1950s civil rights movement.

3 . . . there is one thing you have got to learn about our movement. Three people are better than no people.

FANNIE LOU HAMER (1917–1977), African American civil rights activist. As quoted in *This Little Light of Mine*, ch. 8, by Arthur Kinoy, in a February 19, 1990 interview with Hay Mills (1993).

Said in 1964, of a Mississippi civil rights meeting that drew only three attendees.

4 . . . I always said if I lived to get grown and had a chance, I was going to try to get something for my mother and I was going to do something for the black man of the South if it would cost my life; I was determined to see that things were changed.

FANNIE LOU HAMER (1917–1977), African American civil rights activist. As quoted in *Freedomways*, p. 232 (Second quarter, 1965).

On growing up poor in Mississippi, the youngest of twenty children. Hamer's mother wore ragged clothes and went blind following an accident, because she could not get proper medical care.

5 What had begun as a movement to free all black people from racist oppression became a movement with its primary goal the establishment of black male patriarchy.

BELL HOOKS (b. c. 1955), African American author, feminist, and civil rights advocate. *Ain't I a Woman?* Introduction (1981).

6 They were fighting tradition and change. It just wasn't my time.

AUTHERINE LUCY (b. 1929), African American civil rights pioneer. As quoted in *I Dream a World*, by Brian Lanker (1989).

In February 1956, Lucy became the first African American student to integrate the University of Alabama. Riots broke out, and she was expelled after three days. Thirty-two years later, the university wrote her a letter notifying her that the expulsion had been revoked and she could re-enroll.

7 This will be a black baby born in Mississippi, and thus where ever he is born he will be in prison . . . If I go to jail now it may help hasten that day when my child and all children will be free.

DIANE NASH (b. 1938), African American civil rights activist. As quoted in *American Women in the 1960s*, ch. 2, by Blanche Linden-Ward and Carol Hurd Green (1993).

To the judge when being sentenced to two years in prison for "civil disobedience." The wife of Southern Christian Leadership Conference (SCLC) activist James Bevel, she was pregnant at the time but refused to use her condition as a reason to appeal or post bond.

CIVIL WAR

I My country is bleeding, my people are perishing around me. But I feel as a South Carolinian, I am bound to tell the North, go on! go on! Never falter, never abandon the principles which you have adopted.

ANGELINA GRIMKÉ (1805–1879), U.S. abolitionist and feminist. As quoted in *The Grimke Sisters from South Carolina*, ch. 19, by Gerda Lerner (1967).

Speaking on May 14, 1863, at a national convention of women called to consider how Northern women might best aid the Union war effort. Raised in South Carolina, Grimke had moved North in 1829 to escape constant contact with slavery, which she abhorred.

2 The nation is in a death-struggle. It must either become one vast slave-ocracy of petty tyrants, or wholly the land of the free.

Angelina Grimké (1805–1879), U.S. abolitionist and feminist. As quoted in *The Grimke Sisters from South Carolina*, ch. 19, by Gerda Lerner (1967).

From a paper read on May 14, 1863, at the final session of a convention of Northern women which was held to discuss how women might aid the Union effort.

3 There is great fear expressed on all sides lest this war shall be made a war for the negro. I am willing that it shall be. It is a war to found an empire on the negro in slavery, and shame on us if we do not make it a war to establish the negro in freedom—against whom the whole nation, North and South, East and West, in one mighty conspiracy, has combined from the beginning.

Susan B. Anthony (1820–1906), U.S. suffragist. As quoted in *History of Woman Suffrage*, vol. 2 ch. 16, by Elizabeth Cady Stanton, Matilda Joslyn Gage, and herself (1882).

Speaking on May 14, 1863, at a national convention of the Woman's National Loyal League.

4 It is a life-and-death conflict between all those grand, universal, man-respecting principles which we call by the comprehensive term democracy, and all those partial, person-respecting, class-favoring elements which we group together under that silver-slippered word

aristocracy. If this war does not mean that, it means nothing.

Antoinette Brown Blackwell (1825–1921), U.S. minister, suffragist, abolitionist, and temperance advocate. As quoted in *History of Woman Suffrage*, vol. 2 ch. 16, by Elizabeth Cady Stanton, Susan B. Anthony, and Matilda Joslyn Gage (1882).

Speaking on May 14, 1863, at a national convention of the Woman's National Loyal League.

5 *Resolved,* There can never be a true peace in this Republic until the civil and political rights of all citizens of African descent and all women are practically established. *Resolved,* that the women of the Revolution were not wanting in heroism and self-sacrifice, and we, their daughters, are ready, in this War, to pledge our time, our means, our talents, and our lives, if need be, to secure the final and complete consecration of America to freedom.

Woman's Loyal League (founded May 1861), As quoted in *Eighty Years and More (1815–1897)*, ch. 15, by Elizabeth Cady Stanton (1898).

Resolutions adopted at a meeting of women called by Stanton (1815–1902) and Susan B. Anthony (1820–1906) in May 1861, soon after the outbreak of the Civil War. At this meeting, the Woman's Loyal League was formed.

6 It was the most ungrateful and unjust act ever perpetrated by a republic upon a class of citizens who had worked and sacrificed and suffered as did the women of this nation in the struggle of the Civil War only to be rewarded at its close by such unspeakable degradation as to be reduced to the plane of subjects to enfranchised slaves.

Anna Howard Shaw (1847–1919), U.S. minister, suffragist, and speaker; born in

England. As quoted in *History of Woman Suffrage*, vol. 5 ch. 6, by Ida Husted Harper (1922).

Speaking in February 1906 before the thirty-eighth annual convention of the National Woman Suffrage Association. At the time Shaw said this, typical attitudes toward African American men were very different than they are today. This statement would not have sounded as illiberal in 1906 as it does now. Most suffragists had been staunch foes of slavery and had supported the Union during the Civil War; many were still bitter that, despite this record, they remained disfranchised even after African American men were granted suffrage by the 15th Amendment to the Constitution (1870).

7 What armies and how much of war I have seen, what thousands of marching troops, what fields of slain, what prisons, what hospitals, what ruins, what cities in ashes, what hunger and nakedness, what orphanages, what widowhood, what wrongs and what vengeance.

CLARA BARTON (1821–1912), U.S. Civil War nurse and founder of the American Red Cross. As quoted in *Angel of the Battlefield*, ch. 20, by Ishbel Ross (1956).

Said c. 1909.

8 It was a marvel, an enigma in abolition latitudes, that the slaves did not rise en-masse, at the beginning of hostilities.

REBECCA LATIMER FELTON (1835–1930), U.S. author. *Country Life in Georgia in the Days of My Youth*, ch. 2 (1919).

By "the hostilities," Felton meant the Civil War. She was a slaveowner who came to disbelieve in slavery. This remark is from Felton's 1919 synopsis of a 1900 address she gave in Augusta, Georgia, to the Daughters of the Confederacy.

CIVILIZATION

1 . . . the history of the race, from infancy through its stages of barbarism, heathenism, civilization, and

Christianity, is a process of *suffering*, as the lower principles of humanity are gradually subjected to the higher.

CATHERINE E. BEECHER (1800–1878), U.S. educator and author. *Common Sense Applied to Religion, or the Bible and the People*, ch. 4 (1857).

2 Civilization is merely an advance in taste: accepting, all the time, nicer things, and rejecting nasty ones.

KATHERINE FULLERTON GEROULD (1879–1944), U.S. author. *Modes and Morals*, ch. 7 (1920).

3 The civilizing process has increased the distance between behavior and the impulse life of the animal body.

SHOSHANA ZUBOFF (b. 1951), U.S. social scientist. *In the Age of the Smart Machine*, ch. 2 (1988).

CLASS DIFFERENCES

1 To most middle-class feminists, as to most middle-class non-feminists, working-class women remain mysterious creatures to be "reached out to" in some abstract way. No connection. No solidarity.

IRENA KLEPFISZ (b. 1941), U.S. Jewish lesbian author; born in Poland. *Dreams of an Insomniac*, part 1 (1990).

Klepfisz was a feminist from a working-class background.

CLASS SYSTEM

1 . . . his rank penetrated them as though it had been an odour.

GEORGE ELIOT (1819–1880), British novelist. *Middlemarch*, ch. 58 (1871–1872).

Of a baronet's son being introduced to guests at the home of a physician of modest circumstances. This fictional scene took place in a small English village in the early 1830s.

2 It is impossible for one class to appreciate the wrongs of another.

ELIZABETH CADY STANTON (1815–1902), U.S. suffragist, social reformer, and author. *History of Woman Suffrage,* vol. 2, ch. 19 (1882).

By "wrongs of," she meant "wrongs suffered by."

3 During the long ages of class rule, which are just beginning to cease, only one form of sovereignty has been assigned to all men—that, namely, over all women. Upon these feeble and inferior companions all men were permitted to avenge the indignities they suffered from so many men to whom they were forced to submit.

MARY PUTNAM JACOBI (1842–1906), U.S. suffragist. *"Common Sense" Applied to Woman Suffrage,* ch. 4 (1894).

4 Social distinctions concern themselves ultimately with whom you may and may not marry.

KATHERINE FULLERTON GEROULD (1879–1944), U.S. author. *Modes and Morals,* ch. 7 (1920).

5 I am so tired of talking to others translating my life for the deaf, the blind,
the "I really want to know what your life is like without giving up any of my privileges
to live it" white women
the "I want to live my white life with Third World women's style and keep my skin
class privileges" dykes

LORRAINE BETHEL, African American lesbian feminist poet. "What Chou Mean *We,* White Girl?" Lines 49–54 (1979).

"Dykes" was a slang term for lesbians; although considered an insult when used by non-lesbians, it was often used by lesbians themselves—sometimes humorously, sometimes insultingly, sometimes defiantly, and sometimes as simply an alternative term.

6 Quite frankly, if you bed people of belowstairs class, they go to the papers.

JANE CLARK, British millionaire politician's wife. As quoted in *Newsweek* magazine, p. 15 (June 13, 1994).

On a judge's wife having told a tabloid that Clark's husband, Alan Clark, had seduced her and her two daughters.

7 One of the strengths I derive from my class background is that I am accustomed to contempt.

DOROTHY ALLISON (b. 1949), U.S. author and lesbian feminist. *Skin,* ch. 2 (1994).

Allison grew up in a very poor, dysfunctional South Carolina family.

8 Class is rarely talked about in the United States; nowhere is there a more intense silence about the reality of class differences than in educational settings.

BELL HOOKS (b. c. 1955), African American author and educator. *Teaching to Transgress,* ch. 12 (1994).

hooks had been raised in very modest circumstances in Hopkinsville, Kentucky.

CLERGY

1 . . . the hired preachers of all sects, creeds, and religions, never do, and never can, teach any thing but what is in conformity with the opinions of those who pay them.

FRANCES WRIGHT (1795–1852), Scottish author and speaker; relocated to America. *Course of Popular Lectures,* lecture 3 (1829).

2   . . . I do deeply deplore, of the sake of the cause, the prevalent notion, that the clergy must be had, either by persuasion or by bribery. They will not need persuasion or bribery, if their hearts are with us; if they are not, we are better without them. It is idle to suppose that the kingdom of heaven cannot come on earth, without their cooperation.

SARAH M. GRIMKÉ (1792–1873), U.S. abolitionist and feminist. *Letters on the Equality of the Sexes and the Condition of Woman,* letter #15: dated October 20, 1837 (1838).

The "cause" was two-fold: abolition of slavery and establishment of women's rights, especially suffrage. Some abolitionists and feminists thought it essential to win the support of clergymen.

3   Only men of moral and mental force, of a patriotic regard for the relationship of the two races, can be of real service as ministers in the South. Less theology and more of human brotherhood, less declamation and more common sense and love for truth, must be the qualifications of the new ministry that shall yet save the race from the evils of false teaching.

FANNIE BARRIER WILLIAMS (1855–1944), African American women's rights and rights activist. As quoted in *Black Women in Nineteenth-Century American Life,* part 3, by Bert James Loewenberg and Ruth Bogin (1976).

Born free in Brockport, New York, Williams had taught in the South before her marriage. She said this in 1893.

4   A successful woman preacher was once asked "what special obstacles have you met as a woman in the ministry?" "Not one," she answered, "except the lack of a minister's wife."

ANNA GARLIN SPENCER (1851–1931), U.S. educator, author, feminist, and Unitarian minister. *Woman's Share in Social Culture,* ch. 3 (1913).

5   Let priests and bishops denounce— let the hierarchy roar! They cannot push the chick back into the shell.

MARGARET SANGER (1879–1966), U.S. birth control advocate. *My Fight for Birth Control,* ch. 17 (1931).

On the futility of the Roman Catholic Church's opposition to birth control and abortion.

6   Are we talking about a church founded by the Son of God made man? Or are we talking about simply a social gathering that we can rebuild as we wish?

DONNA STEICHEN, U.S. opponent of women in the ministry. As quoted in *Time* magazine, p. 54 (November 23, 1992).

7   They can stop me from being ordained, but they can't stop me from being a priest.

NANCY SMALL (b. 1963), U.S. Roman Catholic feminist, pacifist, and counselor. As quoted in the *New York Times,* p. 29 (January 30, 1994).

Small held a Master of Divinity degree; was a leader in the protest against women's exclusion from the Roman Catholic priesthood; was the New York coordinator of Pax Christi, a Roman Catholic pacifist organization; and was a principal in the Women's Liturgy Group, in which women were worshipping together and celebrating a liturgy reserved to men. She also was active in community organizing and prayer counseling.

CLERICAL WORK

I   . . . the wife of an executive would be a better wife had she been a secretary first. As a secretary, you learn to adjust to the boss's moods. Many marriages would be happier if the wife would do that.

ANNE BOGAN, U.S. executive secretary. As quoted in *Working,* book 1, by Studs Terkel (1973).

2 I just can't conceive of a mentality that says, "I don't file."

ANONYMOUS, U.S. secretary. As quoted in *Ms.* magazine, p. 46, by Lily Tomlin (January 1974).

CLINTON, HILLARY RODHAM

I Hilary Clinton's great sin was that she left the nicely wallpapered domestic sphere with a slam of the door, took up public life on her own, leaving big feminist footprints all over the place, and without so much as an apology.

PATRICIA J. WILLIAMS (b. 1942), U.S. author. As quoted in the *Chronicle of Higher Education,* p. A7 (April 7, 1993).

Hillary Rodham Clinton (b. 1947), who was First Lady of the United States at the time, had previously been a successful attorney in Arkansas. She was being criticized for, among other things, her visibility in her husband's (President Bill Clinton's) administration and her lucrative investments.

2 A man who graduated high in his class at Yale Law School and made partnership in a top law firm would be celebrated. A man who invested wisely would be admired, but a woman who accomplishes this is treated with suspicion.

BARBRA STREISAND (b. 1942), U.S. entertainer and moviemaker. As quoted in the *New York Times,* p. 22 (April 16, 1994).

Speaking at April 14, 1994 Humanitarian Award Dinner given by the Elie Wiesel Founda-

tion. Attorney and First Lady Hillary Rodham Clinton, the award recipient, had long been regarded with reservations by some because of her professional success. Recently, her extremely profitable commodities investments had come under scrutiny.

CLOTHING

I "I spent one hundred hours," said an educated and cultivated lady recently, ". . . in embroidering my winter suit. . . ." One hundred hours! One could almost learn a language, or make the acquaintance of a science, or apprentice one's self to a business, or nurse a consumptive to the end of her sufferings, or save a soul, in one hundred well-selected hours. One—hundred— hours!

ELIZABETH STUART PHELPS, U.S. author. *What to Wear?* Ch. 2 (1873).

Referring to the elaborate outfits and decoration then considered fashionable, and to women's misplaced priorities.

COEDUCATION

I I regard the effort to introduce women into colleges for young men as very undesirable, and for many reasons. That the two sexes should be united, both as teachers and pupils, in the same institution seems very desirable, but rarely in early life by a method that removes them from parental watch and care, and the protecting influences of a home.

CATHERINE E. BEECHER (1800–1878), U.S. educator and author. *Woman Suffrage and Woman's Profession* (1871).

COLLEGE STUDENTS

1 What I often forget about students, especially undergraduates, is that surface appearances are misleading. Most of them are at base as conventional as Presbyterian deacons.

MURIEL BEADLE (b. 1915), U.S. author and community organizer. *Where Has All the Ivy Gone?* Ch. 25 (1972).

Beadle was the wife of George Beadle, who served as President of the University of Chicago, 1960–1968, during part of the time that the university was besieged by a series of student anti-Vietnam War protests and social reform demands.

COMMERCIALISM

1 The cultivation of one set of faculties tends to the disuse of others. The loss of one faculty sharpens others; the blind are sensitive in touch. Has not the extreme cultivation of the commercial faculty permitted others as essential to national life, to be blighted by disease?

J. ELLEN FOSTER (1840–1910), U.S. attorney, temperance activist, and suffragist. *What America Owes to Women,* ch. 33 (1893).

Reflecting on America's national prosperity.

2 . . . too many young painters of the day work for the crowd, and not for art. But, then, should not the painters of the day work for the education of the crowd?

M. E. W. SHERWOOD (1826–1903), U.S. socialite, traveller, and author. *An Epistle to Posterity,* ch. 13 (1897).

3 I'm so sick of Nancy Drew I could vomit.

MILDRED AUGUSTUS WIRT BENSON (b. c. 1906), U.S. author. As quoted in the *New York Times,* sect. 4, p. 7 (May 9, 1993).

On the heroine of the extremely popular mystery series for teenage girls that she initiated in 1930, using the pseudonym "Carolyn Keene," with publication of *The Secret of the Old Clock.*

COMMITMENT

1 To stand up on the stage is to say to many people: "Look at me." How can you do that without speaking the only truth you know? There is no such thing as an uncommitted actor.

JUDITH MALINA (b. 1926), U.S. actor and stage producer. As quoted in *Actors on Acting,* rev. ed., part 13, by Toby Cole and Helen Krich (1970).

2 The main thing is to care. Care very hard, even if it is only a game you are playing.

BILLIE JEAN KING (b. 1943), U.S. tennis player. *Billie Jean,* ch. 16 (1982).

3 I don't want to express alienation. It isn't what I feel. I'm interested in various kinds of passionate engagement. All my work says be serious, be passionate, wake up.

SUSAN SONTAG (b. 1933), U.S. author. As quoted in the *New York Times Magazine,* "Susan Sontag Finds Romance," by Leslie Garis (August 2, 1992).

A noted intellectual and essayist, Sontag was commenting on just having written a romantic novel (*The Volcano Lover*).

COMMON SENSE

1 Horses and children, I often think, have a lot of the good sense there is in the world.

JOSEPHINE DEMOTT ROBINSON (1865–1948), U.S. circus performer. *The Circus Lady,* ch. 16 (1926).

During her circus career, she performed on horseback.

COMMUNICATION

1   The inability to listen and to depict in the countenance what others have said has spoiled many a good actress.

JULIA MARLOWE (1870–1950), U.S. actor; born in England. As quoted in *Actors on Acting*, rev. ed., part 13, by Toby Cole and Helen Krich (1970).

A distinguished stage actor in both modern and Shakespearean plays, Marlowe was commenting on the tendency of actors to concentrate only on their own characters and lines. She said this in 1913.

2   Instead of seeing society as a collection of clearly defined "interest groups," society must be reconceptualized as a complex network of groups of interacting individuals whose membership and communication patterns are seldom confined to one such group alone.

DIANA CRANE (b. 1933), U.S. sociologist. *Invisible Colleges*, ch. 8 (1972).

The closing statement of her groundbreaking study of the "diffusion of knowledge in scientific communities."

3   the true nature of poetry. The drive to connect. The dream of a common language.

ADRIENNE RICH (b. 1929), U.S. poet, essayist, and lesbian feminist. "Origins and History of Consciousness," part 1, lines 11–12 (1972–1974).

4   Poetry is a search for ways of communication; it must be conducted with openness, flexibility, and a constant readiness to listen.

FLEUR ADCOCK (b. 1934), New Zealand poet. As quoted in *Contemporary Poets*, 3rd ed., by James Vinson (1980).

5   For the writer, there is nothing quite like having someone say that he or she understands, that you have reached them and affected them with what you have written. It is the feeling early humans must have experienced when the firelight first overcame the darkness of the cave. It is the communal cooking pot, the Street, all over again. It is our need to know we are not alone.

VIRGINIA HAMILTON (b. 1936), African American writer of children's books. *Illusion and Reality.*

COMMUNITY

1   There is a communion of more than our bodies when bread is broken and wine drunk.

M. F. K. FISHER (1908–1992), U.S. culinary writer and autobiographer. *The Gastronomical Me*, Foreword (1943).

2   The people needed to be rehoused, but I feel disgusted and depressed when I see how they have done it. It did not suit the planners to think how they might deal with the community, or the individuals that made up the community. All they could think was, "Sweep it away!" The bureaucrats put their heads together, and if anyone had told them, "A community is people," they would not have known what they were on about.

MAY HOBBS (b. 1938), British author. *Born to Struggle*, "Prelude," (1973).

Of the way the government had implemented "slum clearance" in her childhood neighborhood in London's East End.

3   Women's art, though created in solitude, wells up out of community. There is, clearly, both enormous hunger for the work thus being diffused, and an explosion of creative energy, bursting through the coercive choicelessness of the system on whose boundaries we are working.

ADRIENNE RICH (b. 1929), U.S. lesbian feminist poet and essayist. Book review of *Housework*, by Joan Larkin (1977).

COMPASSION

I   It is a natural virtue incident to our sex to be pitiful of those that are afflicted.

ELIZABETH I (1533–1603), British monarch, Queen of England (1558–1603). As quoted in *The Sayings of Queen Elizabeth*, ch. 11, by Frederick Chamberlin (1923).

"To Doctor Dale, to say to the Queen-Mother of France, Catherine de' Medici, in behalf of a woman in exile for her religion." Elizabeth was a Protestant; France was a Roman Catholic country.

COMPETITION

I   Competition *is.* In every business, no matter how small or how large, someone is just around the corner forever trying to steal your ideas and build his success out of your imagination, struggling after that which you have toiled endless years to secure, striving to outdo you in each and every way. If such a competitor would work as hard to origi-

nate as he does to copy, he would much more quickly gain success.

ALICE FOOTE MACDOUGALL (1867–1945), U.S. businesswoman. *The Autobiography of a Business Woman,* ch. 5 (1928).

MacDougall was a highly successful, self-made merchant and restaurateur in New York City.

2   . . . women become far more cruel than men when they hurl themselves into ruthless competition with the opposite sex.

AGNES E. MEYER (1887–1970), U.S. journalist. *Out of These Roots,* ch. 16 (1953).

3   I don't go that fast in practice, because I need the excitement of the race, the adrenalin. The others might train more and be in better shape, but when I'm racing, I put winning before everything else. I don't stop until the world gets gray and fuzzy around the edges.

CANDI CLARK (b. c. 1950), U.S. kayaker. As quoted in *WomenSports* magazine, p. 43 (October 1975).

Clark was top-ranked in her sport.

4   Competition can be a very intense experience and a very rewarding one, or it can be enormously destructive. External pressure, whether it's exerted by a coach, a school, a ski club, or a country, is what can make it a negative thing. When they use you to satisfy their need to succeed, when they impose their value system on you, then competition isn't personally rewarding anymore. . . . You're either a winner or a loser. . . . There's no way in my mind that you can divide humanity into those two categories.

ANDREA MEAD LAWRENCE (b. 1932),
U.S. skier. As quoted in *WomenSports* magazine, p. 26 (January 1977).
Lawrence was the first alpine skier to win two gold medals at a single Olympics (1952).

One of the rare young photographers who continues to develop her pictures chemically in a darkroom rather than shooting and processing them through computerized means.

COMPETITIVENESS

1 When women finally get liberated, they'll do the same that men do— dog eat dog— that's what our culture is. . . . Not cooperation but assassination. Women will cooperate until they attain certain goals. Then one will begin to destroy the other.

ALICE NEEL (1900–1984), U.S. painter. As quoted in *Lives and Works,* by Lynn F. Miller and Sally S. Swenson (1981).
Neel was a supporter of the Women's Liberation Movement.

2 You listen to artists fighting with each other, competing to the death like gladiators, in order to see who is going to get into a show, who is going to make it, who isn't: who is going to get a full-page ad and who is going to get a half-page. Then I think, "Wouldn't it be wonderful to go off somewhere and just do your work?"

HOWARDENA PINDELL (b. 1943), U.S. artist. As quoted in *Lives and Works,* by Lynn F. Miller and Sally S. Swenson (1981).

COMPUTERS

1 The romance and mystery is [sic] gone. Computer-processed images have no delicacy, no craftsmanship, no substance, and no soul. No love.

KIM NIBBLETT (b. c. 1969), U.S. photographer. As quoted in *Silicon Snake Oil,* ch. 6, by Clifford Stoll (1995).

CONGRESS (U. S.)

1 Congress seems drugged and inert most of the time. . . . Its idea of meeting a problem is to hold hearings or, in extreme cases, to appoint a commission.

SHIRLEY CHISHOLM (b. 1924), African American politician. *Unbought and Unbossed,* ch. 10 (1970).
Chisholm was a Congresswoman from a poor district of Brooklyn.

CONSERVATISM

1 Among the best traitors Ireland has ever had, Mother Church ranks at the very top, a massive obstacle in the path to equality and freedom. She has been a force for conservatism, not on the basis of preserving Catholic doctrine or preventing the corruption of her children, but simply to ward off threats to her own security and influence.

BERNADETTE DEVLIN (b. 1947), Irish Catholic politician. *The Price of My Soul,* ch. 5 (1969).

2 My characters never die screaming in rage. They attempt to pull themselves back together and go on. And that's basically a conservative view of life.

JANE SMILEY (b. 1949), U.S. novelist. As quoted in *Listen to Their Voices,* ch. 8, by Mickey Pearlman (1993).

CONSISTENCY

1 Consistency is the horror of the world.

BRENDA UELAND (1891–1985), U.S. author and writing teacher. *If You Want to Write*, 2nd. ed., ch. 17 (1938).

CONSTITUTION (U.S.)

1 . . . all the slaveholding laws violate the fundamental principles of the Constitution of the United States. In the preamble of that instrument, the great objects for which it was framed are declared to be "to establish justice, to promote the *general* welfare, and to secure the blessings of *liberty* to us and to our posterity." The slave laws are flagrant violations of these fundamental principles. Slavery subverts justice, promotes the welfare of the *few* to the manifest injury of the many, and robs thousands of the *posterity* of their forefathers of the blessings of liberty.

ANGELINA GRIMKÉ (1805–1879), U.S. abolitionist and feminist. *Letters to Catherine Beecher*, letter #2 (1837).
In a letter dated June 17, 1837.

2 Can you conceive what it is to native-born American women citizens, accustomed to the advantages of our schools, our churches and the mingling of our social life, to ask over and over again for so simple a thing as that "we, the people," should mean women as well as men; that our Constitution should mean exactly what it says?

MARY F. EASTMAN, U.S. suffragist. As quoted in *History of Woman Suffrage*, vol. 4 ch. 5, by Susan B. Anthony and Ida Husted Harper (1902).
Speaking before the eighteenth annual convention of the National Woman Suffrage Association, held February 17–19, 1886, in Washington, D.C. Eastman was from Massachusetts.

3 We have been here over forty years, a longer period than the children of Israel wandered through the wilderness, coming to this Capitol pleading for this recognition of the principle that the Government derives its just powers from the consent of the governed. Mr. Chairman, we ask that you report our resolution favorably if you can but unfavorably if you must; that you report one way or the other, so that the Senate may have the chance to consider it.

ANNA HOWARD SHAW (1847–1919), U.S. minister, suffragist, and speaker; born in England. As quoted in *History of Woman Suffrage*, vol. 5 ch. 10, by Ida Husted Harper (1922).
Speaking on April 19, 1910, before a hearing of the United States Senate Judiciary Committee; it was chaired by Senator Alexander S. Clay of Georgia. Shaw, who was then President of the National Woman Suffrage Association, presented petitions and said: ". . . we petitioners pray this honorable body to submit to the Legislatures of the several States for ratification an amendment to the Federal Constitution which will enable American women to vote."

4 . . . the separation of church and state means separation—absolute and eternal—or it means nothing.

AGNES E. MEYER (1887–1970), U.S. journalist. *Out of These Roots*, ch. 14 (1953).

5 One of the things I considered a delightful experience in school was the Constitution and the Bill of Rights.

I didn't realize the gap was so big from the Founding Fathers until now. And I didn't realize they weren't talking about me.

MAXINE WATERS (b. 1938), African American politician. As quoted in *I Dream a World,* by Brian Lanker (1989).

CONVERSATION

1 If the minds of women were enlightened and improved, the domestic circle would be more frequently refreshed by intelligent conversation, a means of edification now deplorably neglected, for want of that cultivation which these intellectual advantages would confer.

SARAH M. GRIMKÉ (1792–1873), U.S. abolitionist and feminist. *Letters on the Equality of the Sexes and the Condition of Woman,* letter #15: dated October 20, 1837 (1838).

2 Woman has been systematically educated to spend her conversational ability upon the most frivolous topics. This has the effect to belittle her range of thought so that she can comprehend only superficialities.

CAROLINE NICHOLS CHURCHILL (1833–?), U.S. author. *Active Footsteps,* ch. 24 (1909).

3 . . . the random talk of people who have no chance of immortality and thus can speak their minds out has a setting, often, of lights, streets, houses, human beings, beautiful or grotesque, which will weave itself into the moment for ever.

VIRGINIA WOOLF (1882–1941), British novelist, essayist, and diarist. *The Common Reader,* ch. 21 (1925).

4 I had been curiously depressed all day. In the night I wakened. First precise thought: I know why I'm depressed—nothing inspired is going on. Second: I demand that life be inspired every moment. Third: the only way to guarantee this is to have inspired conversation every moment. Fourth: most people never get so far as conversation; they haven't the stamina, and there is no time. Fifth: if I had a magazine I could spend my time filling it up with the best conversation the world has to offer. Sixth: marvelous idea—salvation. Seventh: decision to do it. Deep sleep.

MARGARET ANDERSON (1886–1973), U.S. literary editor and autobiographer. *My Thirty Years' War,* ch. 2 (1930). On why, in her twenties and with no capital, she decided to begin publishing *The Little Review* (1914–1929), which became a charming, prominent, and influential—though never financially successful—magazine.

5 . . . nothing could bother me more than the way a thing goes dead once it has been said.

GERTRUDE STEIN (1874–1946), U.S. author and patron of the arts; relocated to France. *What Are Masterpieces and Why Are There So Few of Them* (1936).

6 The conversational overachiever is someone whose grasp exceeds his reach. This is possible but not attractive.

FRAN LEBOWITZ (b. 1950), U.S. humorist. *Metropolitan Life,* part 1 (1978).

7 Great people talk about ideas, average people talk about things, and

small people talk about wine.

FRAN LEBOWITZ (b. 1950), U.S. humorist. *Social Studies,* ch. 1 (1981).

8 Polite conversation is rarely either.

FRAN LEBOWITZ (b. 1950), U.S. humorist. *Social Studies,* ch. 1 (1981).

9 It was odd how one found oneself making trivial conversation on important occasions. Perhaps it was because one could not say what was really in one's mind.

BARBARA PYM (1913–1980), British novelist. *An Unsuitable Attachment,* ch. 22 (1982).

10 When cafe life thrives, talk is a shared limberness of the mind that improves appetite for conversation: an adequate sentence maker is then made good, a good one excellent, an excellent one extraordinary.

VIVIAN GORNICK (b. 1935), U.S. author. *New York Times Book Review,* p. 24 (July 31, 1994).

CONVICTIONS

I It is always disagreeable to take stands. It is always easier to compromise, always easier to let things go. To many women, and I am one of them, it is extraordinarily difficult to care about anything enough to cause disagreement or unpleasant feelings, but I have come to the conclusion that this must be done for a time until we can prove our strength and demand respect for our wishes. We cannot even be of real service in the coming campaign and speak as a united body of women unless we have the respect of the men and show that when we express a wish, we are willing to stand by it.

ELEANOR ROOSEVELT (1884–1962), First Lady of the United States, author, speaker, and diplomat. As quoted in *Eleanor and Franklin,* ch. 28, by Joseph P. Lash (1971).

From a speech given at the women's dinner, New York Democratic State Convention of 1924; this was before Roosevelt's husband, Franklin Delano Roosevelt, had yet been elected President.

2 . . . it has always been the depth of my belief, my faith, or my love that was the mainspring of my behavior. When once I believed in doing a thing, nothing could prevent my doing it.

MARGARET SANGER (1879–1966), U.S. birth control advocate. *My Fight for Birth Control,* ch. 1 (1931).

3 Life has taught me one supreme lesson. This is that we must—if we are really to *live* at all, if we are to enjoy the life more abundant promised by the Sages of Wisdom—we must put our convictions into action. My remuneration has been that I have been privileged to act out my faith.

MARGARET SANGER (1879–1966), U.S. birth control rights activist. *My Fight for Birth Control,* ch. 27 (1931).

4 We are too ready (women especially) not to stand by what we have said or done.

BRENDA UELAND (1891–1985), U.S. author and writing teacher. *If You Want to Write,* 2nd. ed., ch. 18 (1938).

5   A man's real and deep feelings are surely those which he acts upon when challenged, not those which, mellow-eyed and soft-voiced, he spouts in easy times.

SARAH PATTON BOYLE, U.S. civil rights activist and author. *The Desegregated Heart,* part 2, ch. 13 (1962).

6   . . . there is a difference between being convinced and being stubborn. I'm not certain what the difference is, but I do know that if you butt your head against a stone wall long enough, at some point you realize the wall is stone and that your head is flesh and blood.

MAYA ANGELOU (b. 1928), U.S. author and performer. As quoted in *Reel Women,* part 4, by Ally Acker (1991).

Said in 1979, on giving up her attempt to be named director of the television version of the first volume of her autobiography, *I Know Why the Caged Bird Sings.*

7   If I feel strongly, I say it. I know I can do more good by being vocal than by staying quiet. I'd have a whole lot more money if I lied, but I wouldn't enjoy spending it.

MARTINA NAVRATILOVA (b. 1956), U.S. tennis player; born in Czechoslovakia. As quoted in *Sports Illustrated,* p. 61 (December 2, 1991).

On losing lucrative endorsement contracts because of her openness about, among other things, being a lesbian.

8   You show people what you're willing to fight for when you fight your friends.

HILLARY RODHAM CLINTON (b. 1947), First Lady of the United States and attorney. As quoted in *The Agenda,* ch. 14, by Bob Woodward (1994).

Commenting on the value and occasional necessity of defying one's political supporters.

COOKING

1   Architecture might be more sportive and varied if every man built his own house, but it would not be the art and science that we have made it; and while every woman prepares food for her own family, cooking can never rise beyond the level of the amateur's work.

CHARLOTTE PERKINS GILMAN (1860–1935), U.S. author and feminist. *Women and Economics,* ch. 11 (1898).

Perkins favored the centralization and professionalization of much housework, both to improve its quality and (more importantly) to free women for other pursuits.

2   . . . cooking is just like religion. Rules don't no more make a cook than sermons make a saint.

ANONYMOUS, U.S. cook. As quoted in *I Dream a World,* by Leah Chase, who was quoted in turn by Brian Lanker (1989).

Chase, a Creole chef in New Orleans, was quoting a saying that had been passed down and was supposedly uttered c. 1901.

3   I tell people all the time, you have to be in love with that pot. You have to put all your love in that pot. If you're in a hurry, just eat your sandwich and go. Don't even start cooking, because you can't do anything well in a hurry. I love food. I love serving people. I love satisfying people.

LEAH CHASE (b. 1923), U.S. chef. As quoted in *I Dream a World,* by Brian Lanker (1989).

Chase was a "master chef in the Creole tradition" in New Orleans.

COOPERATION

1 We fatuously hoped that we might pluck from the human tragedy itself a consciousness of a common destiny which should bring its own healing, that we might extract from life's very misfortunes a power of cooperation which should be effective against them.

JANE ADDAMS (1860–1935), U.S. social worker and social reformer. *Twenty Years at Hull-House,* ch. 7 (1910).

Addams, the white middle-class cofounder twenty-one years earlier of the first American "Settlement House"—Hull-House—in a Chicago tenement district, was recalling her and her colleagues' idealistic, naive early expectations.

2 I long to create something that can't be used to keep us passive:
I want to write
a script about plumbing, how every pipe
is joined
to every other.

ADRIENNE RICH (b. 1929), U.S. poet and feminist. "Essential Resources," lines 17–22 (1973).

3 It is all right for the lion and the lamb to lie down together if they are both asleep, but if one of them begins to get active it is dangerous.

CRYSTAL EASTMAN (1881–1928), U.S. social/political activist and author. *On Women and Revolution,* part 1 (1978).

CORRESPONDENCE

1 He who receives a great many letters demanding answer, sees himself as if engaged in a hopeless struggle of one man against the rest of the world.

ANNA C. BRACKETT (1836–1911), U.S. author. *The Technique of Rest,* ch. 4 (1892).

2 The telephone conversation is, by its very nature, reactive, not reflective. Immediacy is its prime virtue. The immediacy delivers quick company, instant stimulation; the stimulation is cathartic; catharsis pushes back anxiety; into open space flows the kind of thought generated by electric return. The letter, written in absorbed solitude, is an act of faith; it assumes the presence of humanity; world and self are generated from within; loneliness is courted, not feared. To write a letter is to be alone with my thoughts in the conjured presence of another person. I keep myself imaginative company. I occupy the empty room. I alone infuse the silence.

VIVIAN GORNICK (b. 1935), U.S. sociologist and author. *New York Times Book Review,* p. 24 (July 31, 1994).

3 Thirty-five years ago, when I was a college student, people wrote letters. The businessman who read, the lawyer who traveled; the dressmaker in evening school, my unhappy mother, our expectant neighbor: all conducted an often large and varied correspondence. It was the accustomed way of ordinarily educated people to occupy the world beyond their own small and immediate lives.

VIVIAN GORNICK (b. 1935), U.S. author. *New York Times Book Review,* p. 3 (July 31, 1994).

COUNTRY LIFE

1 She had never known before how much the country meant to her. The chirping of the insects in the long grass had been like the sweetest music. She had felt as if her heart were hiding down there, somewhere, with the quail and the plover and all the little wild things that crooned or buzzed in the sun. Under the long shaggy ridges, she felt the future stirring.

WILLA CATHER (1873–1947), U.S. novelist. *O Pioneers!* Part 1 (1913).

In this novel; Alexandra Bergson, the young daughter of Swedish immigrant farmers in Nebraska and inheritor of her recently-deceased father's dreams and expectations, will manage the family's land to a remarkable prosperity.

COURAGE

1 I have the heart of a man, not a woman, and I am not afraid of anything.

ELIZABETH I (1533–1603), British monarch, Queen of England (1558–1603). As quoted in *The Sayings of Queen Elizabeth,* ch. 3, by Frederick Chamberlin (1923).

Said to the Swedish Ambassador early in her reign.

2 Children, I talks to God and God talks to me. I goes out and talks to God in de fields and de woods. Dis morning I was walking out, and I got over de fence. I saw de wheat a holding up its head, looking very big. I goes up and takes holt ob it. You b'lieve it, dere was *no* wheat dare? I says, God, what *is* de matter wid *dis* wheat? and he says to me, "Sojourner, dere is a little weasel in it." Now I hears talkin' about de Constitution and de rights of man. I comes up and I takes hold of dis Constitution. it looks *mighty big,* and I feels for *my* rights, but der aint any dare. Den, I says, God, what *ails* dis Constitution? He says to me, "Sojourner, dere is a little *weasel* in it."

I carry no weapon; the Lord will reserve [i.e., preserve] me without weapons, I feel safe even in the midst of my enemies; for the truth is powerful and will prevail.

SOJOURNER TRUTH (c. 1777–1883), African American slave; later an itinerant preacher and advocate of various social reforms including abolition, woman suffrage, and temperance. As quoted in *The Narrative of Sojourner Truth,* part 2: "Book of Life," by Frances W. Titus (1875).

Thousands of acres of wheat had been destroyed by weevils recently. From an account written by "J.A.D.," who lived "near Mt. Pleasant, Iowa," and first published in 1863 in the *National Anti-Slavery Standard.* Truth said this at "a religious meeting where some speaker had alluded to the government of the United States, and had uttered sentiments in favor of its Constitution." Said in 1862 to friends who advised her to carry a "sword or pistol" into a hostile meeting which she was scheduled to address in Angola, Indiana. Townspeople had threatened to burn down the building if she attempted to speak. They did not, and she spoke without being harmed.

3 People glorify all sorts of bravery except the bravery they might show on behalf of their nearest neighbours.

GEORGE ELIOT (1819–1880), British novelist. *Middlemarch,* ch. 72 (1871–1872).

4 . . . the big courageous acts of life are those one never hears of and only suspects from having been through like experience. It takes real courage to do battle in the un-

spectacular task. We always listen for the applause of our co-workers. He is courageous who plods on, un-lettered and unknown. . . . In the last analysis it is this courage, devel-oping between man and his limita-tions, that brings success.

ALICE FOOTE MACDOUGALL (1867–1945), U.S. businesswoman. *The Autobiography of a Business Woman,* ch. 7 (1928).

5 That way of life against which my generation rebelled had given us grim courage, fortitude, self-disci-pline, a sense of individual responsi-bility, and a capacity for relentless hard work.

ROSE WILDER LANE (1886–1968), U.S. author. As quoted in *The Ghost in the Little House,* ch. 2, by William V. Holtz (1993). Written in 1935.

6 . . . I discovered that I could take a risk and survive. I could march in Philadelphia. I could go out in the street and be gay even in a dress or a skirt without getting shot. Each victory gave me courage for the next one.

MARTHA SHELLEY, U.S. author and social activist. As quoted in *Making History,* part 3, by Eric Marcus (1992).
On the lessons learned and courage gained as a radical gay rights activist in the Gay Liberation Front of the 1960s.

CREATIVE WRITING CLASSES

1 But suppose, asks the student of the professor, we follow all your struc-tural rules for writing, what about that "something else" that brings the book alive? What is the formula

for that? The formula for that is not included in the curriculum.

FANNIE HURST (1889–1968), U.S. novel-ist. *Anatomy of Me,* book 4 (1957).

CREATIVITY

1 Creative genius is a divinely be-stowed gift which is the coronation of the few.

MARGARET E. SANGSTER (1838–1912), U.S. author. *An Autobiography from My Youth Up,* ch. 20 (1909).

2 It is hard to describe the thrill of creative joy which the artist feels when the conviction seizes her that at last she has caught the very soul of the character she wishes to por-tray, in the music and action which reveal it.

MARIA JERITZA (1887–1982), Austrian op-era singer. *Sunlight and Song,* ch. 21 (1924).

3 It is very natural that every one who makes anything inside themselves that is makes it entirely out of what is in them does naturally have to have two civilizations. They have to have the civilization that makes them and the civilization that has nothing to do with them.

GERTRUDE STEIN (1874–1946), U.S. au-thor and patron of the arts; relocated to France. *An American and France* (1936).
Born, raised, and educated in America, Stein settled in Paris, where she built her reputation as an innovative writer and patron of young art-ists and avant-garde art.

4 . . . *no* writing is a waste of time,— no creative work where the feelings, the imagination, the intelligence must work.

BRENDA UELAND (1891–1985), U.S. author and writing teacher. *If You Want to Write,* 2nd. ed., ch. 2 (1938).

5 Exchange is creation.

MURIEL RUKEYSER (1913–1980), U.S. poet. *The Life of Poetry,* ch. 11 (1949).

6 Tension is . . . a prerequisite for creative living.

AGNES E. MEYER (1887–1970), U.S. journalist. *Out of These Roots,* ch. 17 (1953).

7 . . . like a woman made frigid, I had to learn response, to trust this possibility for fruition that had not been before.

TILLIE OLSEN (b. 1912), U.S. essayist and story writer. *Silences,* part 1 (1978). Written in 1962, on trying to compose fiction after many years of being "silenced" by the demands of raising four children, keeping house, and holding a full-time job.

8 . . . woman is frequently praised as the more "creative" sex. She does not need to make poems, it is argued; she has no drive to make poems, because she is privileged to make babies. A pregnancy is as fulfilling as, say, Yeats' *Sailing to Byzantium.* . . . To call a child a poem may be a pretty metaphor, but it is a slur on the labor of art.

CYNTHIA OZICK (b. 1928), U.S. author. *Woman in Sexist Society,* ch. 19 (1971). Written in 1969. William Butler Yeats (1865–1939) was a great Irish poet; "Sailing to Byzantium" was one of his best-loved poems.

9 The one happiness is to shut one's door upon a little room, with a table before one, and to create; to create life in that isolation from life.

ELEONORA DUSE (1858–1924), Italian actor. As quoted in *Actors on Acting,* rev. ed., part 11, by Toby Cole and Helen Krich (1970).

10 If I had not come to America, where I felt free to formulate tentatively insights at which I had empathically arrived, I would have accomplished very little. I would never have begun to publish, to teach, to undertake research. Because if one does not find an assenting echo to one's ideas, if one is passed over, as I was in Vienna, then one cannot create. To create, after all, is to believe that what one says will count.

MARGARET S. MAHLER (1897–1985), U.S. psychoanalyst and author; born in Austria. *The Memoirs of Margaret S. Mahler,* compiled and edited by Paul E. Stepansky, ch. 6 (1988). Said sometime in the 1970s. Mahler, a Jew, left Vienna after the annexation of Austria by Nazi Germany in 1938. She became an important figure in her field, specializing in childhood psychosis.

11 . . . a bit of conversational sex makes a pleasant climate for creative effort . . .

ANITA LOOS (1888–1981), U.S. screenwriter, author, and humorist. *Kiss Hollywood Good-by,* ch. 5 (1974). Remembering the pleasure of co-writing the screenplay for *Red-Headed Woman,* a 1932 film, with Albert Lewin.

12 It is the lesbian in us who is creative, for the dutiful daughter of the fathers in us is only a hack.

ADRIENNE RICH (b. 1929), U.S. poet, essayist, and lesbian feminist. "It Is the Lesbian In Us Who Is Creative," (1976).

13 I have great belief in the fact that whenever there is chaos, it creates wonderful thinking. I consider chaos a gift.

SEPTIMA CLARK (1898–1987), African American civil rights activist. As quoted in *I Dream a World,* by Brian Lanker (1989). Clark, a native of South Carolina, said this in 1986.

14 A work in progress quickly becomes feral. It reverts to a wild state overnight. It is barely domesticated, a mustang on which you one day fastened a halter, but which now you cannot catch. It is a lion you cage in your study. As the work grows, it gets harder to control; it is a lion growing in strength. You must visit it every day and reassert your mastery over it. If you skip a day, you are, quite rightly, afraid to open the door to its room.

ANNIE DILLARD (b. 1945), U.S. author. *The Writing Life,* ch. 3 (1989).

CRIME

1 When a man comes to me and tries to convince me that he is not a thief, then I take care of my coppers.

ERNESTINE L. ROSE (1810–1892), U.S. suffragist. As quoted in *History of Woman Suffrage,* vol. 2, ch. 22, by Elizabeth Cady Stanton, Susan B. Anthony, and Matilda Joslyn Gage (1882).
Speaking at a May 12, 1869, anniversary celebration of the Equal Rights Association.

2 With five to ten hundred pureminded young women threading the streets of the village every evening unattended, vice must slink away, like frost before the rising sun . . .

ANNA JULIA COOPER (1859–1964), U.S. educator and feminist. *A Voice from the South,* part 1 (1892).
On why the crime rate was low in Oberlin, Ohio, where coeducational Oberlin College was located.

3 It might easily be made a physical impossibility for criminals, hereditary paupers, imbeciles, profligates, and others suffering from gross bodily or mental defects, to propagate their failings and their vices. In no long time our prisons, workhouses, and asylums would be empty. . . . Prostitution would become a forgotten calling. Pauperism would cease. Disease would be almost unknown. By the same methods which breeders adopt, our race could be raised to the highest pitch of perfection and of excellence. The people who shall first have the moral courage to do this, will take the lead among the nations of the world.

TENNESSEE CLAFLIN (1846–1923), U.S. journalist, lecturer, and social reform advocate; relocated to England. *Talks and Essays,* vol. 1, ch. 4 (1897).
Advocating selective forced sterilization and scientific "breeding" of human beings.

4 . . . while one-half of the people of the United States are robbed of their inherent right of personal representation in this freest country on the face of the globe, it is idle for us to expect that the men who thus rob women will not rob each other as individuals, corporations and Government.

SUSAN B. ANTHONY (1820–1906), U.S. suffragist. As quoted in *Life and Work of Susan*

B. Anthony, vol. 3, ch. 57, by Ida Husted Harper (1908).
Written to a women's organization in 1900.

5 Crime is naught but misdirected energy. So long as every institution of today, economic, political, social, and moral, conspires to misdirect human energy into wrong channels; so long as most people are out of place doing the things they hate to do, living a life they loathe to live, crime will be inevitable.

EMMA GOLDMAN (1869–1940), U.S. anarchist and author; born in Russia. *Anarchism and Other Essays*, 3rd rev. ed., ch. 1 (1917).

6 Stories of law violations are weighed on a different set of scales in the Black mind than in the white. Petty crimes embarrass the community and many people wistfully wonder why Negroes don't rob more banks, embezzle more funds and employ graft in the unions. . . . This . . . appeals particularly to one who is unable to compete legally with his fellow citizens.

MAYA ANGELOU (b. 1928), African American poet, autobiographer, and performer. *I Know Why the Caged Bird Sings*, ch. 29 (1970).

7 I thought that a Jewish state would be free of the evils afflicting other societies: theft, murder, prostitution. . . . But now we have them all. And that's a thing that cuts to the heart . . .

GOLDA MEIR (1898–1978), Israeli Prime Minister; born in Russia. As quoted in *Ms.* magazine, p. 75 (April 1973).

8 He took control of me for forty-five minutes. This time I'll have control over him for the rest of his life. If he gets out fifteen years from now, I'll know. I'll check on him every three months through police computers. If he makes one mistake he's going down again. I'll make sure. I'm his worst enemy now.

ELIZABETH WILSON, U.S. crime victim. As quoted in *People* magazine, p. 88 (May 31, 1993).

Wilson was raped for forty-five minutes at knifepoint by a night-time intruder in her apartment. Joel Valdez confessed to the crime, but initially, a grand jury refused to indict him because he had donned a condom after Wilson, fearful of AIDS, begged him to do so; the grand jury saw this request as implying consent. After pressure from Wilson and women's groups, a second grand jury was empaneled and indicted Valdez. He was found guilty and was sentenced to forty years in prison.

CRITICISM

1 If you keep your feathers well oiled the water of criticism will run off as from a duck's back.

ELLEN HENRIETTA SWALLOW RICHARDS, (1842–1911) U.S. chemist and educator. As quoted in *The Life of Ellen H. Richards*, ch. 9, by Caroline L. Hunt (1912).
Written in the 1870s to a woman student whom she was educating through correspondence courses. Richards had been the first woman to graduate from the Massachusetts Institute of Technology (MIT).

2 Mortals are easily tempted to pinch the life out of their neighbour's buzzing glory, and think that such killing is no murder.

GEORGE ELIOT (1819–1880), British novelist. *Middlemarch*, ch. 21 (1871–1872).

3 . . . criticism . . . makes very little dent upon me, unless I think there is some real justification and something should be done.

ELEANOR ROOSEVELT (1884–1962), U.S. First Lady, author, and speaker. As quoted in *Eleanor and Franklin*, ch. 39, by Joseph P. Lash (1971).

In a letter to feminist Carrie Chapman Catt dated April 18, 1936. As First Lady (1933–1945), Roosevelt was constantly criticized (as well as admired) for her highly visible, substantive, independent political activities and writings.

4 i am always amazed at their certainty
about the past how it could have been
different could have been turned around
with what ease they transport themselves
to another time
place taking the comfort
confidence of an after dinner drink

IRENA KLEPFISZ (b. 1941), U.S. Jewish poet and essayist; born in Poland. "Perspectives on the Second World War," lines 43–48 (1975).

On those who make retrospective judgments on the Holocaust. Klepfisz's father, a fighter for Jewish rights, died in the Warsaw Uprising. She and her mother fled Poland and eventually settled in New York City.

CRITICISM OF WOMEN

1 I have often thought how strange it is that men can at once and the same moment cheerfully consign our sex to lives either of narrowest toil or senseless luxury and vanity, and then sneer at the smallness of our aims, the pettiness of our thoughts, the puerility of our conversation!

FRANCES POWER COBBE (1822–1904), U.S. author and feminist. *The Duties of Women*, lecture 6 (1882).

2 . . . so long as woman labors to second man's endeavors and exalt his sex above her own, her virtues pass unquestioned; but when she dares to demand rights and privileges for herself, her motives, manners, dress, personal appearance, and character are subjects for ridicule and detraction.

ELIZABETH CADY STANTON (1815–1902), U.S. suffragist, author, and social reformer. *Eighty Years and More (1815–1897)*, ch. 15 (1898).

3 The master class seldom lose a chance to insult a woman who has the ability for something besides service to his lordship.

CAROLINE NICHOLS CHURCHILL (1833–?), U.S. author. *Active Footsteps*, ch. 7 (1909).

4 . . . until opportunity is as free from sex discrimination as the right to vote finally came to be, no man has any right to criticize women for failure to measure up to men.

MARY BARNETT GILSON (1877–?), U.S. factory personnel manager, economist, and educator. *What's Past is Prologue*, ch. 9 (1940).

5 A man has to be Joe McCarthy to be called ruthless. All a woman has to do is put you on hold.

MARLO THOMAS (b. 1943), U.S. actor. As quoted in *The Decade of Women*, by Suzanne Levine and Harriet Lyons (1980).

Senator Joseph McCarthy (1909–1957) of Wisconsin was a relentless anti-Communist who held televised Senate hearings on the subject of Communism, an ideology that, he believed, had penetrated the highest reaches of American government. He proved to be wrong.

6 This is one of the most serious intrusions into personal life that I can think of, and it's as bad as anything I've ever experienced.

ELLEN WOOD HALL (b. 1945), U.S. educator. As quoted in the *Chronicle of Higher Education*, p. A16 (June 16, 1993).

"Forced to resign" a month earlier as president of all-woman Converse College (Spartanburg, S. C.), Hall was describing the personal toll taken by ridicule of her appearance and rumors that she was a lesbian, although she was married. An accompanying photograph showed her to be an average-looking woman with no obvious appearance problem.

CULTURAL DIVERSITY

1 Success and failure in our own national economy will hang upon the degree to which we are able to work with races and nations whose social order and whose behavior and attitudes are strange to us.

RUTH BENEDICT (1887–1948), U.S. anthropologist. *An Anthropologist at Work*, part 5 (1959).

2 It is important to note that multiculturalism does not share the postmodernist stance. Its passions are political; its assumptions empirical; its conception of identities visceral. For it, there is no doubting that history is something that happened and that those happenings have left their mark within our collective consciousness. History for multiculturalists is not a succession of dissolving texts, but a tense tangle of past actions that have reshaped the landscape, distributed the nation's wealth, established boundaries, engendered prejudices, and unleashed energies.

JOYCE APPLEBY (b. 1929), U.S. historian. "Recovering America's Historic Diversity," *Journal of American History*, p. 430 (September 1992).

3 What we have to do . . . is to find a way to celebrate our diversity and debate our differences without fracturing our communities.

HILLARY RODHAM CLINTON (b. 1947), U.S. attorney; First Lady of the United States. P. A17 (May 18, 1993).

From the First Lady's commencement speech a day earlier at the University of Pennsylvania, which had recently experienced racial conflicts.

CULTURE

1 . . . in the fierce competition of modern society the only class left in the country possessing leisure is that of women supported in easy circumstances by husband or father, and it is to this class we must look for the maintenance of cultivated and refined tastes, for that value and pursuit of knowledge and of art for their own sakes which can alone save society from degenerating into a huge machine for making money, and gratifying the love of sensual luxury.

MRS. H. O. WARD (1824–1899), U.S. author. *Sensible Etiquette of the Best Society Customs, Manners, Morals, and Home Culture, Compiled from the Best Authorities*, ch. 10 (1878).

2 Before the birth of the New Woman the country was not an intellectual desert, as she is apt to suppose. There were teachers of the highest grade, and libraries, and countless circles in our towns and villages of scholarly, leisurely folk, who loved books, and music, and Nature, and lived much apart with them. The mad craze for money, which clutches at our souls to-day as *la grippe* does at our bodies, was hardly known then.

REBECCA HARDING DAVIS (1831–1910), U.S. author. *Bits of Gossip*, ch. 4 (1904).

3 . . . every one is as their land is, as the climate is, as the mountains and the rivers or their oceans are as the wind and rain and snow and ice and heat and moisture is, they just are and that makes them have their way to eat their way to drink their way to act their way to think and their way to be subtle, and even if the lines of demarcation are only made with a ruler after all what is inside those right angles is different from those on the outside of those right angles, any American knows that.

GERTRUDE STEIN (1874–1946), U.S. author; relocated to France. *Wars I Have Seen* (1945).
Written in occupied France in 1944, during World War II. Stein was finding that she missed the United States, where she had been born, raised, and educated, and where she still maintained citizenship, though she had long ago resettled permanently in France.

4 Those who speak of our culture as dead or dying have a quarrel with life, and I think they cannot understand its terms, but must endlessly repeat the projection of their own desires.

MURIEL RUKEYSER (1913–1980), U.S. poet. *The Life of Poetry*, ch. 3 (1949).

5 Culture relates to objects and is a phenomenon of the world; entertainment relates to people and is a phenomenon of life.

HANNAH ARENDT (1906–1975), U.S. philosopher and political theorist; born in Germany. *Between Past and Future*, ch. 6 (1961).

6 . . . good and evil appear to be joined in every culture at the spine.

FLANNERY O'CONNOR (1925–1964), U.S. fiction writer and essayist. *Mystery and Manners*, part 5 (1969).
Written in 1963.

7 There are many of us who cannot but feel dismal about the future of various cultures. Often it is hard not to agree that we are becoming culinary nitwits, dependent upon fast foods and mass kitchens and megavitamins for our basically rotten nourishment.

M. F. K. FISHER (1908–1992), U.S. culinary writer and autobiographer. Preface (1984). The book's author is Lou Seibert Pappas.

8 Who decides what is margin and what is text? Who decides where the borders of the homeland run? Absences and silences are potent. It is the eloquent margins which frame the official history of the land. As for geography, there are divisions and boundary lines that fissure any state more deeply than the moat it digs around the nationhood. In every country there are gaping holes. People fall through them and disappear. Yet on every side there are also doors to a wider place, a covert geography under sleep where all the waters meet.

JANETTE TURNER HOSPITAL (b. 1951), Australian novelist (born in Australia; raised in New Zealand; dividing residency between Australia and Canada). As quoted in *Listen to Their Voices*, ch. 3, by Mickey Pearlman (1993).

(1566–1625; King of Scotland, 1567–1625; King of England, 1603–1625). In 1586, he had broken with his mother, who was Elizabeth's rival for the throne and had schemed against her, to ally himself with Elizabeth. Mary was executed in 1587.

DANCE

1 The Gods have meant
That I should dance
And by the Gods
I will!

RUTH ST. DENIS (1877–1968), U.S. dancer, choreographer, and dance teacher. "Calling," lines 1–4 (1932).

These lines are engraved on her tombstone.

2 People come to see beauty, and I dance to give it to them.

JUDITH JAMISON (b. 1944), U.S. dancer. As quoted in *WomenSports* magazine, p. 14 (September 1975).

3 Dance is bigger than the physical body. . . . When you extend your arm, it doesn't stop at the end of your fingers, because you're dancing bigger than that; you're dancing spirit.

JUDITH JAMISON (b. 1943), U.S. dancer. *Dancing Spirit,* ch. 21 (1993).

DEATH AND DYING

1 The name of a successor is like the tolling of my own death-bell!

ELIZABETH I (1533–1603), British monarch, Queen of England (1558–1603). As quoted in *The Sayings of Queen Elizabeth,* ch. 24, by Frederick Chamberlin (1923).

Said near the end of her life. Elizabeth, who never married and died without an heir, refused, despite much urging, to name a successor until she was on her deathbed. He was Mary, Queen of Scots' son, James VI, King of Scotland, who became King James I of England

2 I'd like to live another hundred years yet—and I don't know but I will, too. My teeth are good, and if I can get enough to eat, I don't know why I should die. There's no use in dying—you ain't good for anything after you are dead.

SILVIA DUBOIS (1788?–1889), African American slave and hog breeder. As quoted in *Silvia Dubois, a Biografy of the Slav Who Whipt Her Mistres and Gand Her Fredom,* interview dated January 27, 1883, by C. W. Larison (1883).

3 Down, down, down into the
darkness of the grave
Gently they go, the beautiful, the
tender, the kind;
Quietly they go, the intelligent, the
witty, the brave.
I know, But I do not approve. And
I am not resigned.

EDNA ST. VINCENT MILLAY (1892–1950), U.S. poet. "Dirge Without Music," lines 13–16 (1928).

4 There is in every one of us an unending see-saw between the will to live and the will to die.

REBECCA WEST (1892–1983), British author. *The Strange Necessity,* ch. 10 (1928).

5 All is changed. All looks strange to me and gives me a feeling which I would rather get away from, although I know it to be the carrying out of natural laws. And I am not complaining. I am doing the same as many old people have done, I suppose, who have led an active life and suddenly find themselves living without a purpose. Oh, my heart is so full. I could write a big book on the subject of going out of this world gracefully.

MARIA D. BROWN (1827–1927), U.S. homemaker. As quoted in *Grandmother Brown's Hundred Years,* ch. 9, by Harriet Connor Brown (1929).

In a letter written c. 1906, soon after the death of her husband. Within a few months, however, she regained her spirits and began to travel widely by train and lead a vigorous life. Even in her last year, she continued to read, write letters, knit, and enjoy long automobile rides.

6 When sleep enters the body like smoke
and man journeys into the abyss
like an extinguished star that is
  lighted elsewhere,
then all quarrel ceases,
overworked nag that has tossed the
  nightmare grip
of its rider.

NELLY SACHS (1891–1970), German Jewish poet and translator; relocated to Sweden. "When sleep enters the body like smoke," lines 1–6, translated by Michael Hamburger, et al. (1967; first edition in German: 1949).

Sachs was cowinner of the 1966 Nobel Prize for Literature.

7 I think we should look forward to death more than we do. Of course everybody hates to go to bed or miss anything, but dying is really the only chance we'll get to rest.

FLORYNCE KENNEDY (b. 1916), U.S. lawyer, activist, speaker, and author. *Color Me Flo,* ch. 2 (1976).

8 I bet the worst part about dying is the part where your whole life passes before you.

JANE WAGNER (b. 1935), U.S. playwright. *The Search for Signs of Intelligent Life in the Universe* (1986).

9 The cemetery isn't really a place to make a statement.

MARY ELIZABETH BAKER, U.S. cemetery committee head. As quoted in *Newsweek* magazine, p. 15 (June 13, 1988).

Head of a Concord, Massachusetts, cemetery committee, she was referring to a tombstone located near those of the great authors Ralph Waldo Emerson (1803–1882) and Henry David Thoreau (1817–1862); it read, "Who the hell is Sheila Shea?"

10 On the day that will always belong
  to you,
lunar clockwork had faltered
and I was certain. Walking
the streets of Manhattan I thought:
Remember this day. I felt already
like an urn, filling with wine.

RITA DOVE (b. 1952), U.S. poet and fiction writer. "Your Death," lines 1–6 (1989).

11 When it's over I don't want to
  wonder
if I have made of my life something
  particular, and real.
I don't want to find myself sighing
  and frightened,
or full of argument.
I don't want to end up simply
  having visited this world.

MARY OLIVER (b. 1935), U.S. poet. "When Death Comes," lines 24–28 (c. 1991).

12 This could be the day.
I could slip anchor and wander
to the end of the jetty
uncoil into the waters
a vessel of light moonglade
ride the freshets to sundown

AUDRE LORDE (1934–1992), U.S. author. "Today is Not the Day," stanza 7, lines 1–6 (April 22, 1992).

When she wrote this poem, which she dated precisely, Lorde was dying of breast cancer.

DEATH PENALTY

1 Many of us do not believe in capital punishment, because thus society takes from a man what society cannot give.

KATHERINE FULLERTON GEROULD (1879–1944), U.S. author. *Modes and Morals,* ch. 7 (1920).

2 Once you are involved in politics, the most difficult thing is to go for hang [be sentenced to death]. . . . We can't cry over what has happened to us because other people suffer lots more than we suffer. . . . until you are killed, you can't say that you have really suffered.

ELA RAMGOBIN (b. 1941), South African Indian anti–apartheid activist. As quoted in *Lives of Courage,* ch. 9, by Diana E. H. Russell (1989).

Said in 1987.

3 . . . people are more than the worst thing they have ever done in their lives.

HELEN PREJEAN (b. 1940), U.S. nun and activist against the death penalty. As quoted in the *New York Times Magazine,* p. 31 (May 9, 1993).

Explaining her opposition to the death penalty and her commitment to ministering to the spiritual needs of death row inmates.

4 . . . if I were to be murdered I would not want my murderer executed. I would not want my death avenged. *Especially by government—*

which can't be trusted to control its own bureaucrats or collect taxes equitably or fill a pothole, much less decide which of its citizens to kill.

HELEN PREJEAN (b. 1940), U.S. nun and activist against the death penalty. *Dead Man Walking,* ch. 1 (1993).

5 As a Christian, as an individual, as a doctor, I am absolutely opposed to the death penalty.

JOYCELYN ELDERS (b. 1933), U.S. pediatrician and educator; first woman (and second African American) Surgeon General of the United States. As quoted in the *New York Times Magazine,* p. 16 (January 30, 1994).

Recalling the murder of her brother and explaining why she would not have advocated the death penalty for his murderer.

DECADENCE

1 The attraction of horror is a mental, or even an intellectual, excitement, but the fascination of the repulsive, so noticeable in contemporary writing, can spring openly from some rotted substance within our civilization . . .

ELLEN GLASGOW (1873–1945), U.S. novelist. *The Woman Within,* ch. 21 (1954).

Written in 1937.

DEDICATION

1 If it is the mark of the artist to love art before everything, to renounce everything for its sake, to think all the sweet human things of life well lost if only he may attain something, do some good, great work— then I was never an artist.

ELLEN TERRY (1847–1928), British actor. *Ellen Terry's Memoirs*, 2nd. ed., ch. 4 (1932). Written in 1906 or 1907.

2 He did his job to the end as he would want you to do.

ELEANOR ROOSEVELT (1884–1962), U.S. First Lady, author, and speaker. As quoted in *Eleanor and Franklin*, ch. 56, by Joseph P. Lash (1971).

In a cable to her sons on April 12, 1945, the day of the death of her husband, President Franklin Delano Roosevelt (1882–1945).

DEFEAT

1 It is the small doubts of timid souls that accomplish their ruin. It is the narrow vision, the fear and trembling hesitation, that constitute defeat.

ALICE FOOTE MACDOUGALL, (1867–1945) U.S. businesswoman. *The Autobiography of a Business Woman*, ch. 7 (1928).

2 My race groaned. It was our people falling. It was another lynching, yet another Black man hanging on a tree. One more woman ambushed and raped. A Black boy whipped and maimed. It was hounds on the trail of a man running through slimy swamps.

MAYA ANGELOU (b. 1928), African American poet, autobiographer, and performer. *I Know Why the Caged Bird Sings*, ch. 19 (1970). Remembering a world heavyweight championship fight of African American boxer Joe Louis (1914–1981), the defending champion, against Primo Carnera (1906–1967), a white Italian challenger and former heavyweight champion. Angelou's grandmother ran a store in the small, strictly segregated, brutally racist town of Stamps, Arkansas. Her family and neighbors crowded the store to listen to the fight on radio. At this point, Carnera had Louis on the ropes and was pummelling him. But Louis would fight back and prevail. Louis, who had won the championship in 1937 by defeating James J. Braddock, held it until his first retirement in 1949; he had defended the title successfully twenty-five times, scoring twenty-one knockouts. He returned to fighting in 1950 and retired permanently the following year, ironically after being knocked out by a white Italian-American: Rocky Marciano (1924–1969). It was only his third defeat in seventy-one professional fights.

DEMOCRACY

1 If our vaunted *"rule of the people"* does not breed nobler men and women than monarchies have done—it must and will inevitably give place to something better.

ANNA JULIA COOPER (1859–1964), U.S. educator and feminist. *A Voice from the South*, part 2 (1892).

2 Don't talk to the people until you've listened to the people.

ANN KLEIN (1923–1986), U.S. politician. As quoted in *Past and Promise*, part 4, by Noel Robinson (1990). Klein, a New Jersey Democrat, held various political posts and advocated such causes as abortion rights, improved Medicaid, the rights of institutionalized people, and opposition to child abuse.

DEMOCRACY: NEGATIVE ASPECTS

1 Jefferson's posthumous works were very generally circulated whilst I was in America. They are a mighty mass of mischief. He wrote with more perspicuity than he thought, and his hot-headed democracy has done a fearful injury to his country. Hollow and unsound as his doctrines are, they are but too palatable to a people, each individual of

whom would rather derive his importance from believing that none
are above him, than from the consciousness that in his station he
makes part of a noble whole.

FRANCES TROLLOPE (1780–1863), British
author. *Domestic Manners of the Americans*,
ch. 29 (1832).

Trollope had recently travelled extensively in
the United States. Here, she referred to the writings of former President Thomas Jefferson
(1743–1826), author of the Declaration of Independence, who had died the year before she
commenced her trip.

DEMOCRACY: PROBLEMS

I . . . individual freedom and individual equality cannot co-exist. I dare
say no one since Thomas Jefferson
. . . has really believed it.

KATHERINE FULLERTON GEROULD
(1879–1944), U.S. author. *Modes and Morals*,
ch. 4 (1920).

DEMOCRACY: THE CONCEPT

I I . . . observed the great beauty of
American government to be, *that
the simple machines of representation, carried through all its parts,
gives facility for a being moulded at
will to fit with the knowledge of the
age;* that thus, *although it should be
imperfect in any or all of its parts, it
bears within it a perfect principle the
principle of improvement.*

FRANCES WRIGHT (1795–1852),
Scottish author and speaker; relocated to
America. *Course of Popular Lectures*, lecture 2
(1829).

From a lecture given on July 4, 1829. Wright
had recently become an American citizen. She
gave this "Fourth of July address" in the Philadelphia Theatre.

2 Women and negroes, being seven-
twelfths of the people, are a majority; and according to our republican
theory, are the rightful rulers of the
nation.

ELIZABETH CADY STANTON (1815–
1902), U.S. suffragist, social reformer, and author. As quoted in *History of Woman Suffrage*,
vol. 2, ch. 20, by Susan B. Anthony, Matilda Joslyn Gage, and herself (1882).

Speaking to the New York Constitutional Convention on January 23, 1867.

3 If the women of the United States,
with their free schools and all their
enlarged liberties, are not superior
to women brought up under mo-
narchical forms of government,
then there is no good in liberty.

ANNA HOWARD SHAW (1847–1919),
U.S. suffragist and minister; born in England. As
quoted in *Life and Work of Susan B. Anthony*,
vol. 3, ch. 55, by Ida Husted Harper (1908).
Said in 1899.

4 The essence of democracy is its assurance that every human being
should so respect himself and
should be so respected in his own
personality that he should have opportunity equal to that of every
other human being to "show what
he was meant to become."

ANNA GARLIN SPENCER (1851–1931),
U.S. suffragist, feminist, and author. *Woman's
Share in Social Culture*, ch. 7 (1913).

Stated in the context of an argument for wom-
en's suffrage and other rights, and independence.

5 Perhaps our national ambition to
standardize ourselves has behind it
the notion that democracy means
standardization. But standardization is the surest way to destroy the
initiative, to benumb the creative

impulse above all else essential to the vitality and growth of democratic ideals.

IDA M. TARBELL (1857–1944), U.S. author. *All in the Day's Work,* ch. 19 (1939).
On the American pressure for cultural assimilation of different nationalities.

6   You can't talk about a kind of democracy unless those who are affected by decisions make those decisions whether the institutions in question be the welfare department, the university, the factory, the farm, the neighborhood, the country.

CASEY HAYDEN (b. c. 1940), U.S. social and political activist. As quoted in *American Women in the 1960s,* ch. 6, by Blanche Linden-Ward and Carol Hurd Green (1993).
Hayden said this in the 1960s. She was an activist in the Student Non-Violent Coordinating Committee (SNCC) and the Economic Research and Action Project (ERAP) sponsored by the Students for a Democratic Society (SDS). ERAP organized the inner-city poor to better their conditions through political activism.

DEMOCRACY: THE PRACTICE

1   . . . every sapient prophecy with regard to America has been disproved. We were forewarned that she was too free, and her liberty has proved her security; too peaceable, and she has been found sufficient for her defence; too large, and her size has ensured her union. The bonds of union, indeed, are more numerous and intimate than can be easily conceived by foreigners. A people who have bled together for liberty, who equally appreciate and equally enjoy that liberty which their own blood or that of their fathers has purchased, who feel, too,

that the liberty which they love has found her last asylum on their shores—such a people are bound together by ties of amity and citizenship far beyond what is usual in national communities.

FRANCES WRIGHT (1795–1852), Scottish author and speaker; relocated to America. *Views of Society and Manners in America,* February 1820 entry (1821).
Speaking of the United States forty-four years after the Revolution.

2   It is singular to look round upon a country where the dreams of sages, smiled at as utopian, seem distinctly realized, a people voluntarily submitting to laws of their own imposing, with arms in their hands respecting the voice of a government which their breath created and which their breath could in a moment destroy!

FRANCES WRIGHT (1795–1852), Scottish author and speaker; relocated to America. *Views of Society and Manners in America,* January 1820 entry (1821).
The Scotswoman had been travelling in the United States since September 1818.

3   The American nation, in its march onward and upward, can not publicly choke the intellectual and political activity of half its citizens by narrow statutes. The will of the entire people is the true basis of republican government, and a free expression of that will by the public vote of all citizens, without distinctions of race, color, occupation, or sex, is the only means by which that will can be ascertained.

VICTORIA CLAFLIN WOODHULL (1838–1927), U.S. suffragist, social reformer, author, and publisher; relocated to England in

1877. As quoted in *History of Woman Suffrage,* vol. 2, ch. 23, by Elizabeth Cady Stanton, Susan B. Anthony, and Matilda Joslyn Gage (1882). From an address delivered before the Judiciary Committee of the U.S. House of Representatives on January 11, 1871. The previous year, Woodhull and her sister, Tennessee Claflin, had founded *Woodhull and Claflin's Weekly,* a journal which advocated, among other reforms, woman suffrage, socialism, and free love. In 1872, the first English translation of the *Communist Manifesto* would appear in its pages, and Woodhull would become the first woman candidate for the Presidency of the United States, nominated by the People's party with the famous former slave Frederick Douglass as her running mate. Douglass, too, supported woman suffrage.

4 ... the most important effect of the suffrage is psychological. The permanent consciousness of power for effective action, the knowledge that their own thoughts have an equal chance with those of any other person ... this is what has always rendered the men of a free state so energetic, so acutely intelligent, so powerful.

MARY PUTNAM JACOBI (1842–1906), U.S. suffragist. *"Common Sense" Applied to Woman Suffrage,* ch. 9 (1894).

5 It is not revolutionary on our part to ask a share in our Government. We are demanding it because it is in accord with American ideals and absolutely essential to the establishment of true democracy. A democratic form of government is right or it is not right—it is either right that the people should be self-governed or that they should not. If it is not right, then we ought to know it; the whole people ought to know it. If it is right, then the whole people ought to have equal opportunities in self-government. ... Some

one asked Wendell Phillips if Christianity were not a failure and he replied, "It has not yet been tried." So we can say in regard to democracy.

ANNA HOWARD SHAW (1847–1919), U.S. minister, suffragist, and speaker; born in England. As quoted in *History of Woman Suffrage,* vol. 5, ch. 10, by Ida Husted Harper (1922).

Speaking on April 19, 1910, before a hearing of the United States Senate Judiciary Committee; it was chaired by Senator Alexander S. Clay of Georgia. Wendell Phillips (1811–1884) was an abolitionist and an advocate of various other social reforms, including woman suffrage.

6 We need not fear any isms if our democracy is achieving the ends for which it was established ...

ELEANOR ROOSEVELT (1884–1962), U.S. First Lady, author, and speaker. As quoted in *Eleanor and Franklin,* ch. 48, by Joseph P. Lash (1971).

In her September 26, 1938, "My Day" column. She was concerned about "the constant battle between those who would have us fear the communists and those who would have us fear the fascists."

7 To find ways of practicing democracy, not ways of orating about it, is our great problem.

MARY BARNETT GILSON (1877– ?), U.S. factory personnel manager, economist, and educator. *What's Past is Prologue,* ch. 27 (1940).

8 ... some people are democrats by choice, and some by necessity.

LILLIAN HELLMAN (1905–1984), U.S. playwright and memoirist. *Another Part of the Forest,* Act 2 (1946).

Said by the character named Marcus Hubbard, a member of a distinguished Alabama family in the year 1880.

9 ... democracy is not only service, action, brotherhood—it is spirit—

spirit free, indefinable, all-pervasive, that holds us to its revelations even when we seek to escape them.

AGNES E. MEYER (1887–1970), U.S. journalist. *Out of These Roots*, ch. 17 (1953).

10 With the people, for the people, by the people. I crack up when I hear it; I say, with the handful, for the handful, by the handful, 'cause that's what really happens.

FANNIE LOU HAMER (1917–1977), African American civil rights activist. As quoted in *This Little Light of Mine*, ch. 8, by Hay Mills (1993).

When Hamer, a Mississippian, said this, African Americans in Mississippi were still effectively denied the vote.

DEPENDENCE

1 It is vain to expect virtue from women till they are, in some degree, independent of men . . . Whilst they are absolutely dependent on their husbands they will be cunning, mean, and selfish, and the men who can be gratified by the fawning fondness of spaniel-like affection, have not much delicacy, for love is not to be bought, in any sense of the words, its silken wings are instantly shrivelled up when any thing beside a return in kind is sought.

MARY WOLLSTONECRAFT (1759–1797), British feminist. *A Vindication of the Rights of Woman*, ch. 9 (1792).

2 . . . the prevalent custom of educating young women only for marriage, and not for the duties and responsibilities consequent on marriage—only for appendages and dead weights to husbands—of

bringing them up without an occupation, profession, or employment, and thus leaving them dependent on anyone but themselves—is an enormous evil, and an unpardonable sin.

HARRIOT K. HUNT (1805–1875), U.S. physician and feminist. *Glances and Glimpses*, ch. 4 (1856).

3 There is not the woman born who desires to eat the bread of dependence, no matter whether it be from the hand of father, husband, or brother; for any one who does so eat her bread places herself in the power of the person from whom she takes it.

SUSAN B. ANTHONY (1820–1906), U.S. suffragist. As quoted in *History of Woman Suffrage*, vol. 2, ch. 22, by Elizabeth Cady Stanton, Matilda Joslyn Gage, and herself (1882).

Speaking at a May 12, 1869, anniversary celebration of the Equal Rights Association, held in New York.

4 . . . the planters began by stealing the liberty of their slaves, by stealing their labour, by stealing, in fact, all they had; and the natural result was that the slaves stole back all they could. So in the case of women. Reduced to the condition of dependency and with no other avenue for acquirement of success than the one which lies through their mastery or influence over the opposite sex, their natural powers to charm and seduce are, of course, reinforced by astuteness and trickery.

TENNESSEE CLAFLIN (1846–1923), U.S. journalist, lecturer, and social reform advocate; relocated to England. *Talks and Essays*, vol. 2, ch. 4 (1897).

5 [Woman's] life-long economic parasitism has utterly blurred her conception of the meaning of equality.

EMMA GOLDMAN (1869–1940), U.S. anarchist and author; born in Russia. *Anarchism and Other Essays*, 3rd rev. ed., ch. 9 (1917).

6 If women have young children, they are one man away from welfare.

GLORIA STEINEM (b. 1934), U.S. feminist, author, and editor. *Moving Beyond Words*, part 5 (1994).

Referring to mothers without the education or skills required for economic self-sufficiency.

DEPRESSION (1930s)

1 The chief lesson of the Depression should never be forgotten. Even our liberty-loving American people will sacrifice their freedom and their democratic principles if their security and their very lives are threatened by another breakdown of our free enterprise system. We can no more afford another general depression than we can afford another total war, if democracy is to survive.

AGNES E. MEYER (1887–1970), U.S. journalist. *Out of These Roots*, ch. 7 (1953).

2 Unless you are political or intellectual, events like the Depression are seen as personal events. We thought of the Depression as something that made the pipes freeze; we thought it hit us because Daddy didn't move his taxi stand and because he broke his hip. It was only later I found out it was a national phenomenon.

FLORYNCE KENNEDY (b. 1916), African American lawyer, activist, speaker, and author. *Color Me Flo*, ch. 2 (1976).

Kennedy was a daughter of a black family of modest means in Kansas City, Missouri.

DESIRE

1 If you want to touch the other shore badly enough, barring an impossible situation, you will. If your desire is diluted for any reason, you'll never make it.

DIANA NYAD (b. 1949), U.S. long–distance swimmer. *Other Shores*, ch. 7 (1978).

DESPAIR

1 . . . despair is often only the painful eagerness of unfed hope.

GEORGE ELIOT (1819–1880), British novelist. *Middlemarch*, ch. 47 (1871–1872).

2 We joined long wagon trains moving south; we met hundreds of wagons going north; the roads east and west were crawling lines of families traveling under canvas, looking for work, for another foothold somewhere on the land. . . . The country was ruined, the whole world was ruined; nothing like this had ever happened before. There was no hope, but everyone felt the courage of despair.

ROSE WILDER LANE (1886–1968), U.S. author. As quoted in *The Ghost in the Little House*, ch. 1, by William V. Holtz (1993).

Written in 1935, recalling her family's migration from drought-stricken South Dakota to the Missouri Ozarks in 1894; the 650-mile trip had taken them six weeks. Incidentally, Lane was the daughter of Laura Ingalls Wilder, author of the famous "Little House" books for children.

3 One of the things that is most striking about the young generation is that they never talk about their own futures, there are no futures for this generation, not any of them and so naturally they never think of them. It is very striking, they do not live in the present they just live, as well as they can, and they do not plan. It is extraordinary that whole populations have no projects for a future, none at all.

GERTRUDE STEIN (1874–1946), U.S. author; relocated to France. *Wars I Have Seen* (1945).
Written in occupied France in 1944, during World War II.

4   At its best our age is an age of searchers and discoverers, and at its worst, an age that has domesticated despair and learned to live with it happily.

FLANNERY O'CONNOR (1925–1964), U.S. fiction writer and essayist. *Mystery and Manners*, part 5 (1969).
From "Novelist and Believer," a paper given in March 1963 at a symposium at Sweet Briar College, Virginia.

DESTRUCTION

I   . . . a family I know . . . bought an acre in the country on which to build a house. For many years, while they lacked the money to build, they visited the site regularly and picnicked on a knoll, the site's most attractive feature. They liked so much to visualize themselves as always there, that when they finally built they put the house on the knoll. But then the knoll was gone. Somehow they had not realized they would destroy it and lose it by supplanting it with themselves.

JANE JACOBS (b. 1916), U.S. urban analyst. *The Death and Life of Great American Cities*, ch. 13 (1961).

DEVOTION

I   Ye may have a greater prince, but ye shall never have a more loving prince.

ELIZABETH I (1533–1603), Queen of England (1558–1603). As quoted in *The Sayings of Queen Elizabeth*, ch. 2, by Frederick Chamberlin (1923).
In 1588, following the defeat of the Spanish Armada, in a speech to a crowd of her subjects.

DIFFERENCES AMONG PEOPLE

I   . . . it is nearly impossible to understand those who are beyond our sight, who are not explained to us by ties of birth or the contact of the flesh.

REBECCA WEST (1892–1983), British author. *The Strange Necessity*, ch. 10 (1928).

2   Institutionalized rejection of *difference* is an absolute necessity in a profit economy which needs outsiders as surplus people. As members of such an economy, we have *all* been programmed to respond to the human differences between us with fear and loathing and to handle that difference in one of three ways: ignore it, and if that is not possible, copy it if we think it is dominant, or destroy it if we think it is subordinate. But we have no patterns for relating across our human differences as equals. As a result, those differences have been

misnamed and misused in the service of separation and confusion.

AUDRE LORDE (1934–1992), African American poet, autobiographer, and lesbian feminist. *Sister Outsider,* ch. 12 (1984). From a paper delivered at the Copeland Colloquium, Amherst College, in April 1980. The paper was entitled "Age, Race, Class, and Sex: Women Redefining Difference."

3 We are rarely able to interact only with folks like ourselves, who think as we do. No matter how much some of us deny this reality and long for the safety and familiarity of sameness, inclusive ways of knowing and living offer us the only true way to emancipate ourselves from the divisions that limit our minds and imaginations.

BELL HOOKS (b. 1955), African American author, educator, feminist, and human rights advocate. *Chronicle of Higher Education,* p. A44 (July 13, 1994).

4 Class, race, sexuality, gender—and all other categories by which we categorize and dismiss each other— need to be excavated from the inside.

DOROTHY ALLISON (b. 1949), U.S. author and lesbian feminist. *Skin,* ch. 2 (1994). Allison had grown up in a very poor and dysfunctional South Carolina family.

DISAPPOINTMENT

1 At sixty I look back on a life of deep disappointments, of withered hopes, of unlooked for suffering, of severe discipline.

SARAH M. GRIMKÉ (1792–1873), U.S. abolitionist and feminist. As quoted in *The Grimke Sisters from South Carolina,* ch. 18, by Gerda Lerner (1969).

In an 1853 letter to her friend, the noted physician Harriot Hunt. With her sister Angelina, Sarah had long been a prominent speaker and writer advocating women's rights and abolition of slavery; the major goals of neither cause had yet been achieved. Sarah had also taught in a school run by Angelina's husband and had helped out in their household. She herself never married.

2 The last speaker alluded to this movement as being that of a few disappointed women. From the first years to which my memory stretches, I have been a disappointed woman. . . . I was disappointed when I came to seek a profession worthy an immortal being— every employment was closed to me, except those of the teacher, the seamstress, and the housekeeper. In education, in marriage, in religion, in everything, disappointment is the lot of woman. It shall be the business of my life to deepen this disappointment in every woman's heart until she bows down to it no longer.

LUCY STONE (1818–1893), U.S. suffragist. As quoted in *Feminism: The Essential Historical Writings,* part 3, by Miriam Schnier (1972). Extemporaneous remarks following a speaker's comments at the 1855 National Woman's Rights Convention in Cincinnati, Ohio.

3 . . . there are perhaps only one or two things in the world which are not far more charming in desire than they are in possession.

ANNA C. BRACKETT (1836–1911), U.S. author. *The Technique of Rest,* ch. 3 (1892).

4 Persons who insist to themselves that under one set of conditions

only can they lead interesting and satisfying lives lay themselves open to bitter disappointments and frustrations.

HORTENSE ODLUM (1892– ?), U.S. businesswoman. *A Woman's Place*, ch. 16 (1939).

5 A vegetable garden in the beginning looks so promising and then after all little by little it grows nothing but vegetables, nothing, nothing but vegetables.

GERTRUDE STEIN (1874–1946), U.S. author; relocated to France. *Wars I Have Seen* (1945).
Written in 1943.

DISCIPLINE

1 ... the surest test of discipline is its absence.

CLARA BARTON (1821–1912), U.S. nurse; founder of the American Red Cross. *The Story of My Childhood* (1907).
Recalling her early days as a New Jersey schoolteacher.

DISHONESTY

1 I pray to God that I shall not live one hour after I have thought of using deception.

ELIZABETH I (1533–1603), British monarch, Queen of England (1558–1603). As quoted in *The Sayings of Queen Elizabeth*, ch. 22, by Frederick Chamberlin (1923).
To Fenelon, the French Ambassador.

2 It is a poor cause which has to be lied for regularly.

KATHERINE FULLERTON GEROULD (1879–1944), U.S. author. *Modes and Morals,* ch. 8 (1920).

DISTANCE

1 ... near a war it is always not very near.

GERTRUDE STEIN (1874–1946), U.S. author; relocated to France. *Wars I Have Seen* (1945).
Written in 1943.

DIVERSITY

1 ... city areas with flourishing diversity sprout strange and unpredictable uses and peculiar scenes. But this is not a drawback of diversity. This is the point ... of it.

JANE JACOBS (b. 1916), U.S. urban analyst. *The Death and Life of Great American Cities,* ch. 10 (1961).
Jacobs lived in the lively, diverse Greenwich Village neighborhood in Manhattan (New York City).

2 Our strategy is how we cope—how we measure and weigh what is to be said and when, what is to be done and how, and to whom and to whom and to whom, daily deciding/risking who it is we can call an ally, call a friend (whatever that person's skin, sex or sexuality). We are women without a line. We are women who contradict each other.

CHERRÍE MORAGA (b. 1952), Hispanic American lesbian feminist author. *This Bridge Called My Back,* Preface (1983).

3 *How do we work together?* For if we want liberation for women, then we're committed to building a society in which these distances—of class and economics—dissolve, and all our authentic differences—cultures, personalities, sexualities, talents, and aspirations—emerge and are equally nourished.

IRENA KLEPFISZ (b. 1941), U.S. Jewish lesbian author; born in Poland. *Dreams of an Insomniac,* part 1 (1990).

DIVORCE

1 . . . the courts cannot garnish a father's salary, nor freeze his account, nor seize his property on behalf of his children, in our society. Apparently this is because a kid is not a car or a couch or a boat.

JUNE JORDAN (b. 1936), U.S. poet, essayist, and social critic. *On Call,* ch. 3 (1985).

Written in 1981, on the refusal of American law courts to enforce child support orders and agreements, although they did enforce installment-payment contracts. Jordan's own husband had left her and their eight-year-old child for another woman.

DOMESTIC SCIENCE MOVEMENT

1 The care of a house, the conduct of a home, the management of children, the instruction and government of servants, are as deserving of scientific treatment and scientific professors and lectureships as are the care of farms, the management of manure and crops, and the raising and care of stock.

CATHERINE E. BEECHER (1800–1878), U.S. educator and author. *Woman Suffrage and Woman's Profession* (1871).

Beecher was a leader in the domestic science, or home economics, movement, which aspired to systematize and "scientize" housework and home management.

DOMESTIC WORK

1 . . . the time will come when no servant will be hired without a diploma from some training school, and a girl will as much expect to fit herself for house-maid or cook, as for dressmaker or any trade.

LYDIA HOYT FARMER (1842–1903), U.S. author. *What America Owes to Women,* ch. 10 (1893).

Farmer's editorial showed the influence of the domestic science movement, which attempted to scientize and professionalize housework.

2 I had a long day's work, starting at eight in the morning and ending after nine at night, but in those days [we] . . . did not think of our day in terms of hours. We liked our work, we were proud to do it well, and I am afraid that we were very, very happy.

LOUIE MAYER (b. c. 1914), British housekeeper. As quoted in *Ms.* magazine, p. 71 (November 1972).

Recalling her work in the 1930s as housekeeper for the important novelist Virginia Woolf (1882–1941) and her husband Leonard Woolf.

3 The cleaning lady deals with the patient on a human level. She's scrubbing the floor in the room and the patient says, "My son didn't come to visit me today." The cleaning lady smiles and says, "I know how you feel. I know how I'd feel if my son didn't come to visit me if I was sick." The cleaning lady doesn't see the patient as a renal failure or an ileostomy. She just sees a poor lady who's sick.

KITTY SCANLAN, U.S. occupational therapist. As quoted in *Working,* book 8, by Studs Terkel (1973).

Scanlan worked at a major rehabilitation hospital.

4 Mighty few young black women are doin' domestic work. And I'm glad. That's why I want my kids to go to school. This one lady told me, "All you people are gettin' like that." I said, "I'm glad." There's no more gettin' on their knees.

MAGGIE HOLMES, African American domestic worker. As quoted in *Working,* book 3, by Studs Terkel (1973).

Raised poor, uneducated, Holmes had been a domestic all her life.

5 . . . we never worked for white people in their homes. No, sir, not even once! That is one of the accomplishments in my life of which I am the most proud, yes, sir!

ANNIE ELIZABETH DELANY (1891–1995), African American dentist. *Having Our Say,* ch. 12 (1992).

Speaking of herself and her sister, who lived with her and was two years her senior. They were two of ten children born to an ex-slave and his wife.

DOUBLE STANDARD

I I prize the purity of *his* character as highly as I do that of hers. As a moral being, *whatever it is morally wrong for her to do, it is morally wrong for him to do.* The fallacious doctrine of male and female virtues has well nigh ruined all that is morally great and lovely in his character: he has been quite as deep a sufferer by it as woman, though mostly in different respects and by other processes.

ANGELINA GRIMKÉ (1805–1879), U.S. abolitionist and feminist. *Letters to Catherine Beecher,* letter #12 (1837).

In a letter dated October 2, 1837.

2 [If a woman athlete who had contracted the AIDS virus admitted that she] had been with one hundred or two hundred men, they'd call her a slut, and the corporations would drop her like a lead balloon.

MARTINA NAVRATILOVA (b. 1956), U.S. tennis player; born and raised in Czechoslovakia. As quoted in *Sports Illustrated,* p. 58 (December 2, 1991).

On the outpouring of sympathy for, and near-idolization of, basketball star Magic Johnson after he revealed that he had contracted the AIDS virus after years of extreme heterosexual promiscuity. Retiring from basketball as a result, he won sports commentary assignments and retained his endorsement contracts. Navratilova was surprised at the outraged public reaction to her comment, which was published first in the *New York Post.* She mused: "I could have said that President Bush is a cross-dresser, and I wouldn't have gotten this much response" (p. 61 of above issue). A few years earlier, Navratilova had been criticized and dropped by sponsors after admitting that she was a lesbian.

DREAMS

I Our fathers had their dreams; we have ours; the generation that follows will have its own. Without dreams and phantoms man cannot exist.

OLIVE SCHREINER (1855–1920), British novelist. *The Story of an African Farm,* ch. 13 (1883).

First published under the pseudonym "Ralph Iron."

2 What else are we gonna live by if not dreams? We need to believe in something. What would really drive us crazy is to believe this reality we run into every day is all there is. If I don't believe there's that happy ending out there—that will-you-marry-me in the sky—I can't keep working today.

JILL ROBINSON (b. 1936), U.S. novelist. As quoted in *American Dreams*, part 1, by Studs Terkel (1980).

The daughter of movie producer Dore Schary, Robinson had grown up rich in Hollywood; her notions of the world were shaped by the movies in which she was immersed.

3 I had been sitting in my mother's house in a small town in Rhode Island watching the Miss America Pageant, as we always did. After the telecast, I went into the kitchen with my bathrobe tied around by neck singing, "Therrrre She Is, Miss A-mer-i-caaa!" And that *very next year* I was there on that stage, with God knows how many people watching, and millions of seventeen-year-old women sitting in their living rooms watching the Miss America Pageant. Well, I was so emotionally touched by the whole moment that I was hysterical crying! That I was *there*, and that there were millions of people watching me, dreaming about doing it someday.

MICHELE PASSARELLI (b. c. 1954), U.S. beauty contest winner, Miss Rhode Island, 1972. As quoted in *Miss America*, ch. 14, by Ann-Marie Bivans (1991).

Passarelli, who failed to be selected as a top-ten finalist in the 1972 Miss America Pageant, was explaining why the pageant was, nonetheless, memorable for her.

4 My dreams have become puny with the reality my life has become.

IMELDA MARCOS (b. 1931), Former Philippine First Lady. As quoted in *Newsweek* magazine, p. 29 (April 20, 1992).

Once the big-spending wife of Philippine president Ferdinand Marcos, she had been driven into exile with him when he was deposed.

DRESS REFORM

1 Women are in bondage; their clothes are a great hindrance to their engaging in any business which will make them pecuniarily independent, and since the soul of womanhood never can be queenly and noble so long as it must beg bread for its body, is it not better, even at the expense of a vast deal of annoyance, that they whose lives deserve respect and are greater than their garments should give an example by which woman may more easily work out her own emancipation?

LUCY STONE (1818–1893), U.S. suffragist. As quoted in *The Life and Work of Susan B. Anthony*, vol. 1, ch. 7, by Ida Husted Harper (1898).

In an 1854 letter to her friend and sister suffragist Susan B. Anthony, who had written that the abuse she was receiving for wearing a short-skirt-and-bloomer ensemble in the interest of comfort and dress reform, had become intolerable. Stone, too, and eventually all of the few feminists who had worn bloomers, abandoned them before long.

2 I feel no more like a man now than I did in long skirts, unless it be that enjoying more freedom and cutting off the fetters is to be like a man. I suppose in that respect we are more mannish, for we know that in dress, as in all things else, we have been and are slaves, while man in dress and all things else is free.

AMELIA BLOOMER (1818–1894), U.S. suffragist and dress reformer. As quoted in *The Life and Work of Susan B. Anthony*, vol. 1, ch. 7, by Ida Husted Harper (1898).

From an 1854 letter. She was referring to the short skirt and Turkish-style trousers—dubbed "bloomers" in her honor—whose wearing she pioneered. The accepted women's dress of the period was complicated and inhibiting, restricting women's activity. Very few women were bold enough to adopt bloomers, and almost none who did so wore them as long as Bloomer did: eight years. Finally, the women's rights activists of the time abandoned dress reform as too radical a goal.

3 I believe in women; and in their right to their own best possibilities in every department of life. I believe that the methods of dress practiced among women are a marked hindrance to the realization of these possibilities, and should be scorned or persuaded out of society.

ELIZABETH STUART PHELPS (1844–1911), U.S. novelist and short story writer. *Chapters from a Life*, ch. 12 (1897).

Phelps was referring to the long, wide, uncomfortable, and movement-inhibiting skirts and the waist-cinching corsets then in fashion.

DUTY

1 Obligation may be stretched till it is no better than a brand of slavery stamped on us when we were too young to know its meaning.

GEORGE ELIOT (1819–1880), British novelist. *Middlemarch*, ch. 39 (1871–1872).

2 Our sense of duty must often wait for some work which shall take the place of dilettanteism [sic] and make us feel that the quality of our action is not a matter of indifference.

GEORGE ELIOT (1819–1880), British novelist. *Middlemarch*, ch. 46 (1871–1872).

3 When I had youth I had no money; now I have the money I have no time; and when I get the time, if I ever do, I shall have no health to enjoy life. I suppose it's the discipline I need; but it's rather hard to love the things I do, and see them go by because duty chains me to my galley. If I ever come into port with all sails set, that will be my reward perhaps.

LOUISA MAY ALCOTT (1832–1888), U.S. author. As quoted in *Louisa May*, ch. 17, by Martha Saxton (1977).

Written in 1873. Alcott, who had remained single and worked hard to support her family—especially her parents—was wistful about what her sacrifices had cost her. She died of natural but unclear causes two days after the death of her father, writer/philosopher Bronson Alcott.

EASE

1 . . . to many of us ease is far more soul-destroying than trouble.

ALICE FOOTE MACDOUGALL, (1867–1945) U.S. businesswoman. *The Autobiography of a Business Woman*, ch. 2 (1928).

EATING

1 Life wants padding.

GEORGE ELIOT (1819–1880), British novelist. *Middlemarch*, ch. 13 (1871–1872).

Said by the character in the novel named Mr. Vincy to his brother-in-law Mr. Bulstrode, a cautious eater.

2 . . . gastronomical perfection can be reached in these combinations: one person dining alone, usually upon a couch or a hill side; two people, of no matter what sex or age, dining in a good restaurant; six people, of no matter what sex or age, dining in a good home.

M. F. K. FISHER (1908–1992), U.S. author and food expert. *An Alphabet for Gourmets,* "From A to Z" chapter (1949).

3   It is puzzling to me that otherwise sensitive people develop a real docility about the obvious necessity of eating, at least once a day, in order to stay alive. Often they lose their primal enjoyment of flavors and odors and textures to the point of complete unawareness. And if ever they question this progressive numbing-off, they shrug helplessly in the face of mediocrity everywhere. Bit by bit, hour by hour, they say, we are being forced to accept the not-so-good as the best, since there is little that is even good to compare it with.

M. F. K. FISHER (1908–1992), U.S. culinary writer and autobiographer. Preface (1982). The book's author is Richard Sax.

EDUCATION

1   . . . all education must be unsound which does not propose for itself some object; and the highest of all objects must be that of living a life in accordance with God's Will.

CATHERINE E. BEECHER (1800–1878), U.S. educator and author. *Principles of Education, Drawn from Nature and Revelation, and Applied to Female Education* i the Upper Classes, ch. 32 (1866).

2   Obedience . . . is the primary object of all sound education.

ELIZABETH MISSING SEWELL (1815–1906), British author. *Principles of Education, Drawn from Nature and Revelation, and Applied to Female Education in the Upper Classes,* ch. 6 (1866).

3   The whole world of thought lay unexplored before me,—a world of which I had already caught large and tempting glimpses, and I did not like to feel the horizon shutting me in, even to so pleasant a corner as this.

LUCY LARCOM (1824–1893), U.S. poet and teacher. *A New England Girlhood,* ch. 9 (1889).

On her yearning for the education denied her when her family's poverty forced her into mill work at age 11 and later into assisting with her older sister's domestic work. Eventually, Larcom became a teacher and a noted poet.

4   A republican government should be based on free and equal education among the people. While we have class and sectarian schools the parties supporting them will not give their fullest aid toward building up the public school system. If all of the rich and all of the church people should send their children to the public schools they would feel bound to concentrate their money and energies on improving these schools until they met the highest ideals. To be a success a republic must have a homogeneous people, and to do this it must have homogeneous schools. . . . I grow more and more opposed to [sectarian schools].

SUSAN B. ANTHONY (1820–1906), U.S. suffragist. As quoted in *Life and Work of Susan B. Anthony,* vol. 3, ch. 57, by Ida Husted Harper (1908).

Written in 1900 to a friend, Dr. Sarah R. Dolley, of Rochester, New York, who had praised Roman Catholic schools.

5   I am always glad to think that my education was, for the most part, in-

formal, and had not the slightest reference to a future business career. It left me free and untrammeled to approach my business problems without the limiting influence of specific training.

ALICE FOOTE MACDOUGALL, (1867–1945) U.S. businesswoman. *The Autobiography of a Business Woman,* ch. 2 (1928).

She had been, to a considerable extent, self-educated through reading the books in her grandfather's extensive library.

6 . . . often in the heat of noonday, leaning on a hoe, looking across valleys at the mountains, so blue, so close, my only conscious thought was, "*How* can I ever get away from here? How can I get to where they have books, where I can be educated?" I worked hard, always waiting for something to happen to change things. There came a time when I knew I must make them happen; that no one would do anything about it for me. And I did.

BELINDA JELLIFFE (1892–1979), U.S. nurse and autobiographer. *For Dear Life,* ch. 1 (1936).

Jelliffe was one of ten children born to hardworking North Carolina tobacco farmers. Eventually, she escaped farming and became a nurse.

7 Let woman out of the home, let man into it, should be the aim of education. The home needs man, and the world outside needs woman.

PEARL S. BUCK (1892–1973), U.S. author; born in China. *Of Men and Women,* ch. 8 (1941).

8 Education is not so important as people think.

ELIZABETH BOWEN (1899–1973), Irish author; born in Ireland. *Bowen's Court,* ch. 5 (1942).

9 Next to our free political institutions, our free public-school system ranks as the greatest achievement of democratic life in America . . .

AGNES E. MEYER (1887–1970), U.S. journalist. *Out of These Roots,* ch. 14 (1953).

10 The ability to think straight, some knowledge of the past, some vision of the future, some skill to do useful service, some urge to fit that service into the well-being of the community,—these are the most vital things education must try to produce.

VIRGINIA CROCHERON GILDERSLEEVE, (1877–1965) U.S. educator. *Many a Good Crusade,* part 6 (1954).

Gildersleeve was Professor of English and then Dean at Barnard, a women's college in New York City.

11 We must continually remind students in the classroom that expression of different opinions and dissenting ideas affirms the intellectual process. We should forcefully explain that our role is not to teach them to think as we do but rather to teach them, by example, the importance of taking a stance that is rooted in rigorous engagement with the full range of ideas about a topic.

BELL HOOKS (b. 1955), African American author, educator, feminist, and human rights advocate. *Chronicle of Higher Education,* p. A44 (July 13, 1994).

hooks was thinking of the students she encountered as a professor of English at City College of the City University of New York.

12 The classroom, with all its limitations, remains a location of possibility. In that field of possibility we have the opportunity to labor for freedom, to demand of ourselves and our comrades, an openness of mind and heart that allows us to face reality even as we collectively imagine ways to move beyond boundaries, to transgress. This is education as the practice of freedom.

BELL HOOKS (b. c. 1955), African American author and educator. *Teaching to Transgress*, ch. 14 (1994).

EDUCATION OF AFRICAN AMERICANS

1 I envy neither the heart nor the head of any legislator who has been born to an inheritance of privileges, who has behind him ages of education, dominion, civilization, and Christianity, if he stands opposed to the passage of a national education bill, whose purpose is to secure education to the children of those who were born under the shadow of institutions which made it a crime to read.

FRANCES ELLEN WATKINS HARPER, (1825–1911) African American suffragist and rights advocate. As quoted in *Black Women in Nineteenth-Century American Life*, part 3, by Bert James Loewenberg and Ruth Bogin (1976). Harper said this in 1893. Born free, she was advocating education for African American children. It had been a crime to teach slaves to read.

2 Whatever may be our just grievances in the southern states, it is fitting that we acknowledge that, considering their poverty and past relationship to the Negro race, they have done remarkably well for the cause of education among us. That the whole South should commit itself to the principle that the colored people have a right to be educated is an immense acquisition to the cause of popular education.

FANNIE BARRIER WILLIAMS (1855–1944), African American advocate of civil rights and women's rights. As quoted in *Black Women in Nineteenth-Century American Life*, ch. 3, by Bert James Loewenberg and Ruth Bogin (1976). Born in Brockport, New York, to a distinguished free African American family, Williams had taught school in the South before marrying a Chicago attorney. This is from "Religious Duty to the Negro," an 1893 speech she made in Chicago before the World's Parliament of Religions.

3 . . . we have the satisfaction of knowing that because all of us believed, we inspired, motivated, and liberated some of the most beautiful people on earth—young, gifted, and black.

MARY ALLISON BURCH (b. 1906), African American advocate for children. As quoted in *Past and Promise*, part 4, by Georgetta Merritt Campbell and Daryl Boylan (1990). From an interview conducted on November 22, 1986 by Campbell and Boylan. Burch settled in Newark, New Jersey, and in 1949 established a group called "The Leaguers," which assisted young people through scholarships, tutoring, and other efforts.

4 We have what I would call educational genocide. I'm concerned about learning totally, but I'm immersed in the disastrous record of how many black kids are going into science. They are very few and far between. I've said that when I see more black students in the laboratories than I see on the football field, I'll be happy.

JEWEL PLUMMER COBB (b. 1924), African American biologist and educator. As quoted in *I Dream a World*, by Brian Lanker (1989).

Cobb was the President of California State University at Fullerton.

5 I think what everybody calls a miracle is just common sense. . . . You can look at the attitudes when people come in. That's why they call it a miracle. These are black kids and they're not supposed to know the things they know and achieve the way they are achieving.

MARVA NETTLES COLLINS (b. 1936), African American educator. As quoted in *I Dream a World,* by Brian Lanker (1989).

Collins became nationally renowned for founding the Westside Preparatory School in Chicago (1975), which was remarkably successful ("miraculously" successful, some said) in educating poor, inner-city children.

6 Once I had a professor say to me, "You know you have as much education as a lot of white people." I answered, "Doctor, I have *more* education than most white people."

JOYCELYN ELDERS (b. 1933), U.S. pediatrician and educator; first woman (and second African American) Surgeon General of the United States. As quoted in the *New York Times Magazine*, p. 18 (January 30, 1994).

Elders, who was the U. S. Surgeon General at the time, was recalling her days as a student at the University of Arkansas Medical School in the 1950s.

EDUCATION OF CHILDREN

1 Unusual precocity in children, is usually the result of an unhealthy state of the brain; and, in such cases, medical men would now direct, that the wonderful child should be deprived of all books and

study, and turned to play or work in the fresh air.

CATHERINE E. BEECHER (1800–1878), U.S. educator and author. *Treatise on Domestic Economy for the Use of Young Ladies at Home and at School*, ch. 18 (1843).

Beecher had girls in mind, especially. A pioneer in female education, she was very concerned about excessive mental stimulation, which, she claimed, could lead to "idiocy or an early grave."

2 . . . the school should be an appendage of the family state, and modeled on its primary principle, which is, *to train the ignorant and weak by self-sacrificing labor and love; and to bestow the most on the weakest, the most undeveloped, and the most sinful.*

CATHERINE E. BEECHER (1800–1878), U.S. educator and author. *Woman Suffrage and Woman's Profession* (1871).

3 It is cruelty to children to keep five-year-olds sitting still, gazing into vacancy even for one hour at a time. We have little idea of the torture we thus inflict.

ELLEN HENRIETTA SWALLOW RICHARDS, (1842–1911) U.S. chemist and educator. As quoted in *The Life of Ellen H. Richards*, ch. 10, by Caroline L. Hunt (1912).

Written in 1881, criticizing traditional methods of primary education.

4 The poorest children in a community now find the beneficent kindergarten open to them from the age of two-and-a-half to six years. Too young heretofore to be eligible to any public school, they have acquired in their babyhood the vicious tendencies of their own depraved neighborhoods; and to their environment at that tender age had been due the loss of decency and self-respect that no after example of education has been able to restore to them.

VIRGINIA THRALL SMITH (1836–1903), U.S. educator and social reformer. As quoted in *The Fair Women,* ch. 13, by Jeanne Madeline Weimann (1981).

From a speech, "The Kindergarten," given at the Congress of Women at the World's Columbian Exposition, Chicago, 1893. Smith established the first free kindergarten in Connecticut and pressed successfully for passage of a state law requiring public kindergartens.

5 We put [young children] into kindergarten where their reasoning powers are ruined; or, if we can afford it, we buy Montessori outfits that were invented for semi-imbeciles in Italian slums; or we send them to outdoor schools and give them prizes for sleeping.

KATHERINE FULLERTON GEROULD (1879–1944), U.S. author. *Modes and Morals,* ch. 4 (1920).

6 ... in America ... children are instructed in the virtues of the system they live under, as though history had achieved a happy ending in American civics.

MARY McCARTHY (1912–1989), U.S. author. *Memories of a Catholic Girlhood,* ch. 1 (1957).

7 Schools are generally feminine places, institutions where conformity is valued, taught largely by conformist women.

JUDITH M. BARDWICK (b. 1933), U.S. sociologist. *Woman in Sexist Society,* ch. 9 (1971).

8 What I wanted was to create *thoughtful citizens*—people who be-

lieved they could live interesting lives and be productive and socially useful. So I tried to create a community of children and adults where the adults shared and respected the children's lives.

DEBORAH MEIER (b. 1931), U.S. educator. As quoted in *New York* magazine, p. 78 (December 21–28, 1992).

An urban educator, she co-founded the innovative Central Park East High School in the Harlem neighborhood of New York City.

EDUCATION OF FEMALES

1 If you complain of neglect of education in sons, what shall I say with regard to daughters, who every day experience the want of it? With regard to the education of my own children, I find myself soon out of my depth, destitute and deficient in every part of education. I most sincerely wish ... that our new Constitution may be distinguished for encouraging learning and virtue. If we mean to have heroes, statesmen, and philosophers, we should have learned women.

ABIGAIL ADAMS (1744–1818), U.S. matriarch; wife and mother of United States President. *Familiar Letters of John Adams and His Wife Abigail Adams, During the Revolution,* letter dated August 14, 1776 (1875).

In a letter to her husband John Adams, who was away at war. She was reacting to his letter of August 3, in which he lamented his "countrymen's" lack of "art and address" and "knowledge of the world."

2 ... in the education of women, the cultivation of the understanding is always subordinate to the acquirement of some corporeal accomplishment ...

MARY WOLLSTONECRAFT (1759–1797), British feminist. *A Vindication of the Rights of Woman,* ch. 2 (1792).

3   . . . the whole tenour of female education . . . tends to render the best disposed romantic and inconstant; and the remainder vain and mean.

MARY WOLLSTONECRAFT (1759–1797), British feminist. *A Vindication of the Rights of Woman,* ch. 4 (1792).

4   It is not my design to render my sex any less Feminine, but to develop as fully as may be the powers of womanhood, and furnish women with the means of usefulness, happiness and honor, now withheld from them.

SOPHIA SMITH (1796–1870), U.S. philanthropist. As quoted in *Feminine Ingenuity,* ch. 6, by Anne L. MacDonald (1992).

From the Last Will and Testament of the founder of Smith College for women.

5   Among families, so rich as to be above labour, the daughters are hurried through the routine of boarding school instruction, and at an early period introduced into the gay world; and, thenceforth, their only object is amusement.—Mark the different treatment, which the sons of these families receive. While their sisters are gliding through the mazes of the midnight dance, they employ the lamp, to treasure up for future use the riches of ancient wisdom; or to gather strength and expansion of the mind, in exploring the wonderful paths of philosophy.

EMMA HART WILLARD (1787–1870), U.S. educator and feminist. As quoted in *The Female Experience,* ch. 40, by Gerda Lerner (1977).

From "An Address to the Public; Particularly to the Members of the Legislature of New York, Proposing a Plan for Improving Female Education." The second edition of this address, which Lerner was quoting, was published in 1819. Two years later, Willard moved her all-female Waterford School to Troy, New York, where it became the Troy Female Seminary and set new, comparatively high, standards for female education.

6   Oh, had I received the education I desired, had I been bred to the profession of the law, I might have been a useful member of society, and instead of myself and my property being taken care of, I might have been a protector of the helpless, a pleader for the poor and unfortunate.

SARAH M. GRIMKÉ (1792–1873), U.S. abolitionist and feminist. As quoted in *The Grimke Sisters from South Carolina,* ch. 5, by Gerda Lerner (1969).

Said in 1827. The daughter of a wealthy South Carolina family, Grimke received an education that was good for the time, but insubstantial as compared with boys'.

7   In opening your doors to woman, it is mind that will enter the lecture room, it is intelligence that will ask for food; *sex* will never be felt where science leads for the atmosphere of thought will be around every lecture.

HARRIOT K. HUNT (1805–1875), U.S. physician and feminist. *Glances and Glimpses,* ch. 18 (1856).

In a letter dated November 12, 1850, to the "Gentlemen of the Medical Faculty of Harvard College," asking that they admit women to their lectures.

8   Let the girl be thoroughly developed in body and soul, not modeled, like a piece of clay, after some artificial specimen of humanity,

with a body like some plate in Godey's book of fashion, and a mind after the type of Father Gregory's pattern daughters, loaded down with the traditions, proprieties, and sentimentalities of generations of silly mothers and grandmothers, but left free to be, to grow, to feel, to think, to act. Development is one thing, that system of cramping, restraining, torturing, perverting, and mystifying, called education, is quite another.

ELIZABETH CADY STANTON (1815–1902), U.S. feminist, social reformer, and author. As quoted in *The Female Experience,* ch. 75, by Gerda Lerner (1977).

In a speech delivered on May 25, 1851, at the Woman's Rights Convention held in Akron, Ohio.

9 I see by the papers that you have once more stirred that pool of intellectual stagnation, the educational convention.

ELIZABETH CADY STANTON (1815–1902), U.S. suffragist, social reformer, and author. As quoted in *The Life and Work of Susan B. Anthony,* vol. 1, ch. 10, by Ida Husted Harper (1898).

In an 1857 letter to Susan B. Anthony, her close friend and sister activist, who had created a sensation at the State Teachers' Convention in Binghamton, NY, by advocating equal treatment of African Americans, girls, and women in education—as both students and teachers.

10 Any strain upon a girl's intellect is to be dreaded, and any attempt to bring women into competition with men can scarcely escape failure.

ELIZABETH MISSING SEWELL (1815–1906), British author. *Principles of Education, Drawn from Nature and Revelation, and Applied to Female Education in the Upper Classes,* ch. 32 (1866).

11 The only trouble here is they won't let us study enough. They are so afraid we shall break down and you know the reputation of the College is at stake, for the question is, can girls get a college degree without ruining their health?

ELLEN HENRIETTA SWALLOW RICHARDS, (1842–1911) U.S. chemist and educator. As quoted in *The Life of Ellen H. Richards,* ch. 3, by Caroline L. Hunt (1912).

Written in an October 4, 1868, letter to her parents when she was a student at Vassar College. At the time, some people believed that women's health was delicate, and their health would be damaged if they were subjected to rigorous study.

12 The well-educated young woman of 1950 will blend art and sciences in a way we do not dream of; the science will steady the art and the art will give charm to the science. This young woman will marry—yes, indeed, but she will take her pick of men, who will by that time have begun to realize what sort of men it behooves them to be.

ELLEN HENRIETTA SWALLOW RICHARDS, (1842–1911) U.S. chemist and educator. As quoted in *The Life of Ellen H. Richards,* ch. 11, by Caroline L. Hunt (1912).

Written sometime during the 1870s in a paper entitled "The College Woman in 1950." Richards was responding implicitly to the often-expressed fear that education would reduce women's attractiveness to men and competitiveness for marriage offers.

13 I have inspected the accommodations and find them entirely satisfactory, and as for those young men, who are of appropriate ages to be my grandsons, they will not trouble me in the least.

CATHERINE E. BEECHER (1800–1878), U.S. educator and author. As quoted in *Catherine Beecher,* ch. 18, by Kathryn Kish Sklar (1973).

While in her seventies, Beecher decided to take a course at Cornell University, then an all-male institution. President Andrew D. White explained to her that there were no dormitories for women; this was Beecher's response. She stayed in the men's dorm and "enjoyed the course."

14 When institutions are endowed to train women for all departments connected with the family state, domestic labor, now so shunned and disgraced, will become honorable, will gain liberal compensation, and will enable every woman to secure an independence in employments suited to her sex. And when this is attained, there will be few or none who wish to enter the professions of men or take charge of civil government.

Catherine E. Beecher (1800–1878), U.S. educator and author. *Woman Suffrage and Woman's Profession* (1871).

Though passionately committed to education for girls and women, Beecher opposed woman suffrage.

15 ... there is a lightness about the feminine mind—a touch and go— music, the fine arts, that kind of thing—they should study those up to a certain point, women should; but in a light way, you know.

George Eliot (1819–1880), British novelist. *Middlemarch*, ch. 7 (1871–1872).

Said by the character named Mr. Brooke, uncle of Dorothea Brooke, whose desire for knowledge and a serious classical education is so great that it misleads her into a disastrous marriage.

16 What happiness did poor Mother's studies bring her? It is the melancholy tendency of such studies to separate people from their friends and neighbors and fellow crea-

tures in whom alone lies one's happiness.

Mary Potter Playne (c. 1850– ?), British housewife; sister of Beatrice Webb. As quoted in *Beatrice Webb*, ch. 1, by Carole Seymour-Jones (1992).

In a letter to Beatrice Potter Webb, dated October 16, 1883. Playne was referring to Lawrencina Potter, the intellectually accomplished but emotionally distant and unhappy mother of nine daughters. Beatrice Webb would, working with her husband Sidney Webb, become a distinguished theoretician of socialism.

17 The education of females has been exclusively directed to fit them for displaying to advantage the charms of youth and beauty. ... though well to decorate the blossom, it is far better to prepare for the harvest.

Emma Hart Willard (1787–1870), U.S. educator. As quoted in *The Technique of Rest*, ch. 1, by Anna C. Brackett (1892).

In a speech to the New York State legislature.

18 Consider the value to the race of one-half of its members being enabled to throw aside the intolerable bondage of ignorance that has always weighed them down!

Bertha Honore Potter Palmer, (1849–1918) U.S. socialite. "Address to the Dedicatory Ceremonies [of the Woman's Building, World's Columbian Exposition, Chicago, 1893]," (October 21, 1893).

On the desirability of girls and women acquiring formal education, from which they had, until fairly recently, been barred.

19 ... wasting the energies of the race by neglecting to develop the intelligence of the members to whom its most precious resources must be entrusted, already seems a childish absurdity.

Anna Eugenia Morgan (1845–1909), U.S. college professor. *What America Owes to Women*, ch. 25 (1893).

A professor at Wellesley, a women's college, Morgan was speaking of the constraints on education for women.

20 The young women, what can they not learn, what can they not achieve, with Columbia University annex thrown open to them? In this great outlook for women's broader intellectual development I see the great sunburst of the future.

M. E. W. SHERWOOD (1826–1903), U.S. socialite, traveller, and author. *An Epistle to Posterity,* ch. 19 (1897).

On the expanding, though still far from equal, educational opportunities for New York City women.

21 They let the girls in.

SUSAN B. ANTHONY (1820–1906), U.S. suffragist. As quoted in *Life and Work of Susan B. Anthony,* vol. 3, ch. 58, by Ida Husted Harper (1908).

With this line written in her diary on September 10, 1900, Anthony noted the success of a long and costly campaign to get women admitted to the University of Rochester on the same basis as men. Despite her advanced age, she had played a major role in the effort. She apparently made the diary entry immediately after returning home from a meeting with the University of Rochester's Board of Trustees.

22 I can't say that the college-bred woman is the most contented woman. The broader her mind the more she understands the unequal conditions between men and women, the more she chafes under a government that tolerates it.

SUSAN B. ANTHONY (1820–1906), U.S. suffragist. As quoted in *Life and Work of Susan B. Anthony,* vol. 3, ch. 67, by Ida Husted Harper (1908).

In a 1905 interview with Edwin Tracey of the New York *Press.*

23 If any proof were needed of the progress of the cause for which I have worked, it is here tonight. The presence on the stage of these college women, and in the audience of all those college girls who will some day be the nation's greatest strength, will tell their own story to the world.

SUSAN B. ANTHONY (1820–1906), U.S. suffragist. As quoted in *History of Woman Suffrage,* vol. 5, ch. 6, by Ida Husted Harper (1922).

Speaking in February 1906 before the thirty-eighth annual convention of the National Woman Suffrage Association—and the last one that she would attend. Anthony, who was very ill and weak, lacked the strength to give a full-length speech. Though primarily a suffragist, she also actively supported college education for women; a few years earlier, she had been instrumental in changing admission policy at the University of Rochester so that women were admitted.

24 I hope there will be no effort to put up a shaft or any monument of that sort in memory of me or of the other women who have given themselves to our work. The best kind of a memorial would be a school where girls could be taught everything useful that would help them to earn an honorable livelihood; where they could learn to do anything they were capable of, just as boys can. I would like to have lived to see such a school as that in every great city of the United States.

SUSAN B. ANTHONY (1820–1906), U.S. suffragist. As quoted in *Life and Work of Susan B. Anthony,* vol. 3, ch. 71, by Anna Howard Shaw, to Ida Husted Harper (1908).

In March 1906, on her death bed, speaking to her sister suffragist, Rev. Anna Howard Shaw (1847–1919).

25 There used to be housekeepers with more energy than sense—the everlasting scrubber; the over-neat woman. Since the better education of woman has come to stay, this type of woman has disappeared almost, if not entirely.

CAROLINE NICHOLS CHURCHILL (1833–?), U.S. author. *Active Footsteps*, ch. 18 (1909).

26 . . . fain would I turn back the clock and devote to French or some other language the hours I spent upon algebra, geometry, and trigonometry, of which not one principle remains with me. Stay! There is one theorem painfully drummed into my head which seems to have inhabited some corner of my brain since that early time: "The square on the hypotenuse of a right-angled triangle is equal to the sum of the squares on the other two sides!" There it sticks, but what of it, ye gods, what of it?

JESSIE B. RITTENHOUSE (1869– ?), U.S. author. *My House of Life*, ch. 14 (1934). On studying mathematics at the Genesee Wesleyan Seminary in her late teens.

27 A man is educated and turned out to work. But a woman is educated—and turned out to grass.

PEARL S. BUCK (1892–1973), U.S. author; born in China. *Of Men and Women*, ch. 4 (1941).

28 Finishing schools in the fifties were a good place to store girls for a few years before marrying them off, a satisfactory rest stop between college weekends spent husband hunting. It was a haven for those of us adept at styling each other's hair, playing canasta, and chain smoking Pall Mall extra-long cigarettes.

BARBARA HOWAR (b. 1934), U.S. socialite and author. *Laughing all the Way*, ch. 2 (1973). The daughter of an affluent North Carolina family, Howar had been sent to Holton-Arms, a private girls' school in Washington, DC., in 1952.

29 These young women have had four years of very special space. . . . This has been special space. This has been safe space. But when they graduate, they will begin to deal on a daily basis, all day long, month after month, year after year, with the realities that still haunt our nation.

JOHNNETTA BETSCH COLE (b. 1936), African American educator. P. 1 (Spring 1993). Cole was the President of Spelman College, a historically African American, all-women's college in Atlanta; she was referring to her students' college years in an institution that was, by its nature, virtually free of racism and sexism.

30 . . . my education was to become a Miss. [You mean a Mrs.? To get married?] No, no. A *Miss*. Like Miss Venezuela, Miss World . . .

CLAUDIA SCHIFFER (b. c. 1970), German fashion model. As quoted in the *New York Times Magazine*, p. 43 (January 15, 1995).

EDUCATION OF GIRLS

1 From infancy, almost, the average girl is told that marriage is her ultimate goal; therefore her training and education must be directed toward that end. Like the mute beast fattened for slaughter, she is prepared for that.

EMMA GOLDMAN (1869–1940), U.S. anarchist, labor organizer, and author. *Feminism*, ch. 5 (1910).

2 . . . as for helping me in the outside world, the Convent taught me only that if you spit on a pencil eraser, it will erase ink.

DOROTHY PARKER (1893–1967), U.S. author and humorist. As quoted in *The Late Mrs. Dorothy Parker*, ch. 2, by Leslie Frewin (1986). At age six, Parker—though the daughter of a Jewish father—began attending the Blessed Sacrament Convent school in New York City. She was a rebellious student, and when she was thirteen, the nuns asked her parents to withdraw her.

EDUCATION OF MALES

1 Females serve as ever-present reminders to developing males of what they must not become.

ETHEL STRAINCHAMPS, U.S. author. *Woman in Sexist Society*, ch. 16 (1971).

EFFORT

1 . . . pleasure lies in pursuit, not in the attainment. It is because of this, that society is never satisfied, and, however, wearied, is always on the race-track, straining every nerve to reach the goal.

ANNA C. BRACKETT (1836–1911), U.S. author. *The Technique of Rest*, ch. 3 (1892).

EGOTISM

1 We are all of us born in moral stupidity, taking the world as an udder to feed our supreme selves . . .

GEORGE ELIOT (1819–1880), British novelist. *Middlemarch*, ch. 21 (1871–1872).

2 Conceit is an insuperable obstacle to all progress.

ELLEN TERRY (1847–1928), British actor. *Ellen Terry's Memoirs*, 2nd. ed., ch. 5 (1932). Written in 1906 or 1907.

3 The affair between Margot Asquith and Margot Asquith will live as one of the prettiest love stories in all literature.

DOROTHY PARKER (1893–1967), U.S. author and humorist. As quoted in *The Late Mrs. Dorothy Parker*, ch. 28, by Leslie Frewin (1986). In a review, probably written in the early 1920s, of the autobiography of Margot Asquith (1864–1945).

4 The world of the egotist is, inevitably, a narrow world, and the boundaries of self are limited to the close horizon of personality. . . . But, within this horizon, there is room for many attributes that are excellent. . . .

ELLEN GLASGOW (1873–1945), U.S. novelist. *The Woman Within*, ch. 19 (1954). Written in 1944.

5 I'm so glad I never *feel* important, it does complicate life!

ELEANOR ROOSEVELT (1884–1962), U.S. author, speaker, and First Lady. As quoted in *Eleanor: The Years Alone*, ch. 2, by Joseph P. Lash (1972). Said in 1946, the year after the death of her husband, President Franklin Delano Roosevelt (1882–1945).

6 Egocentrics are attracted to the inept. It gives them one more excuse for patting themselves on the back.

HELEN HAYES (1900–1993), U.S. actor. *On Reflection*, ch. 10 (1968).

7 Pleasure in irony . . . is an ego trip.

JESSAMYN WEST (1907–1984), U.S. novelist and autobiographer. *The Life I Really Lived*, part 6 (1979).

ELITISM

| | . . . the living, vital truth of social and economic well-being will become a reality only through the zeal, courage, the non-compromising determination of intelligent minorities, and not through the mass.

EMMA GOLDMAN (1869–1940), U.S. anarchist and author; born in Russia. *Anarchism and Other Essays,* 3rd rev. ed., ch. 2 (1917).

EMOTION

| | . . . women are supposed to be unfit to vote because they are hysterical and emotional and of course men would not like to have emotion enter into a political campaign. They want to cut out all emotion and so they would like to cut us out. I had heard so much about our emotionalism that I went to the last Democratic national convention, held at Baltimore, to observe the calm repose of the male politicians. I saw some men take a picture of one gentleman whom they wanted elected and it was so big they had to walk sidewise as they carried it forward; they were followed by hundreds of other men screaming and yelling, shouting and singing the "Houn' Dawg". . . . I saw men jump up on the seats and throw their hats in the air and shout: "What's the matter with Champ Clark?" Then, when those hats came down, other men would kick them back into the air, shouting at the top of their voices: "He's all right!!" . . . No hysteria about it—just patriotic loyalty,

splendid manly devotion to principle. And so they went on and on until 5 o'clock in the morning—the whole night long. I saw men jump up on their seats and jump down again and run around in a ring. I saw two men run towards another man to hug him both at once and they split his coat up the middle of his back and sent him spinning around like a wheel. All this with the perfect poise of the legal male mind in politics! I have been to many women's conventions in my day but I never saw a woman leap up on a chair and take off her bonnet and toss it up in the air and shout: "What's the matter with" somebody. I never saw a woman knock another woman's bonnet off her head as she screamed, "She's all right!". . . . But we are willing to admit that we are emotional. I have actually seen women stand up and wave their handkerchiefs. I have even seen them take hold of hands and sing, "Blest be the tie that binds." Nobody doubts that women are excitable.

ANNA HOWARD SHAW (1847–1919), U.S. minister, suffragist, and speaker; born in England. As quoted in *History of Woman Suffrage,* vol. 5, ch. 13, by Ida Husted Harper (1922).

Speaking before the forty-fifth annual convention of the National Woman Suffrage Association, which was held in Washington, D.C., November 29–December 5, 1913. Champ Clark (1850–1921), whose full name was James Beauchamp Clark, was a United States Representative from Kentucky; he was Speaker of the House from 1911 to 1919. At the Democratic Convention of 1912, Clark was the leading candidate for the Presidential nomination until the influential William Jennings Bryan (1860–1925), a three-time unsuccessful Presidential nominee, switched his support to Woodrow Wilson (1856–1924), who went on to win the election. In the days before television, political conventions were often considerably less restrained than they are today.

2 I positively like the sense, when I dine out, and stoop to rescue a falling handkerchief, that I am not going to rub my shoulder against a heart. What are hearts doing on sleeves?

KATHERINE FULLERTON GEROULD (1879–1944), U.S. author. *Modes and Morals,* ch. 7 (1920).

3 He who is incapable of feeling strong passions, of being shaken by anger, of living in every sense of the word, will never be a good actor . . .

SARAH BERNHARDT (1845–1923), French actor. *The Art of the Theatre,* ch. 3 (1924). Written in 1923.

4 Poetry is, above all, an approach to the truth of feeling. . . . A fine poem will seize your imagination intellectually—that is, when you reach it, you will reach it intellectually too— but the way is through emotion, through what we call feeling.

MURIEL RUKEYSER (1913–1980), U.S. poet. *The Life of Poetry,* ch. 1 (1949).

5 Acting is the physical representation of a mental picture and the projection of an emotional concept.

LAURETTE TAYLOR (1887–1946), U.S. actor. As quoted in *Actors on Acting,* rev. ed., part 13, by Toby Cole and Helen Krich (1970).

EMPLOYMENT

1 To have the external pressure of a job removed is very astonishing.

Your own will is now your only motor and it has no horse-power. Sometimes I think that perhaps the most competent business men, and lawyers and doctors, who must be at the office at nine o'clock every morning, do not realize this and take more credit for initiative and industry than they deserve. And it is why all the bright women of the world, who if more were expected of them, might do important work, but who instead have a chronic feeling of ineffectiveness and sloth.

BRENDA UELAND (1891–1985), U.S. magazine writer. *Me,* ch. 6 (1939). On leaving her job as a staff writer at *Liberty* magazine to become a free-lance writer.

2 The word *career* is a divisive word. It's a word that divides the normal life from business or professional life.

GRACE PALEY (b. 1922), U.S. story writer, poet, and peace activist. As quoted in *Listen to Their Voices,* ch. 1, by Mickey Pearlman (1993).

EMPLOYMENT OF WOMEN

1 The ability to secure an independent livelihood and honorable employ suited to her education and capacities is the only true foundation of the social elevation of woman, even in the very highest classes of society. While she continues to be educated only to be somebody's wife, and is left without any aim in life till that somebody either in love, or in pity, or in selfish regard at last grants her the opportunity, she can never be truly independent.

CATHERINE E. BEECHER (1800–1878), U.S. educator and author. As quoted in *Catherine Beecher*, ch. 15, by Kathryn Kish Sklar (1973).
Written in 1851. Though never a classic feminist—e.g., she opposed woman suffrage—Beecher devoted her life to female education and vocational training. She herself always worked and never married.

2   Had I made capital on my prettiness, I should have closed the doors of public employment to women for many a year, by the very means which now makes them weak, underpaid competitors in the great workshop of the world.

JANE GREY SWISSHELM (1815–1884), U.S. newspaperwoman, abolitionist, and human rights activist. *Half a Century*, ch. 21 (1880).
On her founding of the abolitionist newspaper, the *Pittsburg Saturday Visiter*.

3   The human race is not so rich in talent, genius, and useful curative energy, that it can afford to allow any considerable proportion of these valuable attributes to be wasted or unproductive, even though they may be possessed by women.

BERTHA HONORÉ POTTER PALMER, (1849–1918) U.S. socialite. "Address to the Dedicatory Ceremonies [of the Woman's Building, World's Columbian Exposition, Chicago, 1893]," (October 21, 1893).

4   Every woman who vacates a place in the teachers' ranks and enters an unusual line of work, does two excellent things: she makes room for someone waiting for a place and helps to open a new vocation for herself and other women.

FRANCES E. WILLARD (1839–1898), U.S. temperance leader and social reformer. *What America Owes to Women*, ch. 29 (1893).

5   . . . there are important considerations in the world beyond plain sewing and teaching dull little boys the alphabet. Any woman who has brains and willing hands finds twenty remunerative occupations open to her where formerly she would have found merely the inevitable two—plain sewing, or the dull little boys. All she had to do is to make her choice and then buckle on her armor of perseverance, while the world applauds.

CLARA (MARQUISE) LANZA (1859–1939), U.S. author. *What America Owes to Women*, ch. 44 (1893).

6   I may be old-fashioned. I don't like this modern movement. . . . And yet, there are certain sorts of work a woman may well do; teaching, being governess, or any taking care of children.

JULIA DENT GRANT (1826–1902), First Lady of the United States (1869–1877). As quoted in *The Fair Women*, ch. 8, by Jeanne Madeline Weimann (1981).
In conversation with sculptor Enid Yandell, who was creating statuary for the landmark Woman's Building at the 1893 World's Columbian Exposition in Chicago. Grant was then the widow of former United States President Ulysses S. Grant (1822–1885).

7   Write, if you *must*; not otherwise. Do not write, if you can earn a fair living at teaching or dressmaking, at electricity or hod-carrying. Make shoes, weed cabbages, survey land, keep house, make ice-cream, sell cake, climb a telephone pole. Nay, be a lightning-rod peddler or a book agent, before you set your heart upon it that you shall write for a living. . . . Living? It is more

likely to be dying by your pen; despairing by your pen; burying hope and heart and youth and courage in your ink-stand.

ELIZABETH STUART PHELPS (1844–1911), U.S. novelist and short story writer. *Chapters from a Life*, ch. 4 (1897).

8 Fifty years ago it was taken for granted that marriage was the goal of every young woman's inmost thought, and the aim for her of her father and mother. While it is everlastingly true that home is woman's kingdom, and that she who is happily married reaches a divine reality of blessedness surpassing that of her mateless sister, still single women are not objects of pity. There are numberless avenues for their occupation, and a girl with ordinary gifts has but to choose that employment for which she is best fitted.

MARGARET E. SANGSTER (1838–1912), U.S. author. *An Autobiography from My Youth Up*, ch. 23 (1909).

9 What is the problem of women's freedom? It seems to me to be this: how to arrange the world so that women can be human beings, with a chance to exercise their infinitely varied gifts in infinitely varied ways, instead of being destined by the accident of their sex to one field of activity—housework and child-raising. And second, if and when they choose housework and child-raising to have that occupation recognized by the world as work, requiring a definite economic reward and not merely entitling the performer to be dependent on some man.

CRYSTAL EASTMAN (1881–1928), U.S. social/political activist and author. *On Women and Revolution*, part 1 (1978). From an article first published in *The Liberator* in December 1920.

Published at the end of the year when, after a 72-year struggle, American women were finally enfranchised.

10 I haven't strength of mind not to need a career.

RUTH BENEDICT (1887–1948), U.S. anthropologist. As quoted in *An Anthropologist at Work*, part 1, by Margaret Mead (1959).

From a prefatory essay to this collection of Benedict's writings: "Search: 1920–1930." According to Mead, Benedict used to say this, "with a rueful smile," during her early years of studying and practicing anthropology—i.e., c. in her early thirties.

11 Long as there's lunch counters, you can always find work.

MOTHER AND AUNTS OF DOROTHY ALLISON, U.S. waitresses. As quoted in *Skin*, ch. 2, by Dorothy Allison (1994).

In the 1960s and seventies, Allison was told this by her female relatives—Southern women with little education or opportunity.

12 While waiting to get married, several forms of employment were acceptable. Teaching kindergarten was for those girls who stayed in school four years. The rest were secretaries, typists, file clerks, or receptionists in insurance firms or banks, preferably those owned or run by the family, but respectable enough if the boss was an upstanding Christian member of the community.

BARBARA HOWAR (b. 1934), U.S. socialite and author. *Laughing all the Way*, ch. 2 (1973).

The daughter of affluent North Carolinians, Howar was describing expectations of well-to-do young women in the 1950s.

13 Black women . . . work because
their husbands can't make enough
money at their jobs to keep everything going. . . . They don't go to
work to find fulfillment, or adventure, or glamour and romance, like
so many white women think they
are doing. Black women work out
of necessity.

WILMA RUDOLPH (1940–1994), African
American runner. *Wilma*, ch. 14 (1977).
Rudolph, a track champion, was raised in a
modest Tennessee home as the twentieth of
twenty-two children. To help support them,
her mother cleaned houses and cooked in a
diner.

14 Unless we include a job as part of
every citizen's right to autonomy
and personal fulfillment, women
will continue to be vulnerable to
someone else's idea of what "need"
is.

GLORIA STEINEM (b. 1934), U.S. author,
editor, and feminist. As quoted in *The Decade
of Women*, by Suzanne Levine and Harriet Lyons (1980).

15 I used to join the murmurings
about "Where are the qualified
women?" As we murmured, we
would all gaze about the room, up
toward the chandelier, into the corner behind the potted palm, under
the napkin, hoping perhaps that
qualified women would pop out
like leprechauns.

JANE O'REILLY, U.S. feminist and humorist. *The Girl I Left Behind*, ch. 5 (1980).
On the often-heard employers' excuse for not
hiring women: i.e., that none with the needed
qualifications could be found.

16 Balancing a job and a family is not
the hardest thing to achieve. It's second. (Right after world peace.)

BARBARA DALE (b. 1940), U.S. cartoonist. *The Working Woman Book*, ch. 1
(1985).

17 If you put a woman in a man's position, she will be more efficient, but
no more kind . . .

FAY WELDON (b. 1931), U.S. author. As
quoted in *Listen to Their Voices*, ch. 6, by
Mickey Pearlman (1993).

ENJOYMENT

1 . . . all enjoyment is dependent
upon the frailty of human life and
human desires . . . if we were to
have all we want and to live forever,
all enjoyment would be gone.

ELLEN HENRIETTA SWALLOW RICH-
ARDS, (1842–1911) U.S. chemist and educator. As quoted in *The Life of Ellen H. Richards*,
ch. 9, by Caroline L. Hunt (1912).
Written in the 1870s.

2 Life for me has been exactly what I
thought it would be—a cake, which
I have eaten and had too.

MARGARET ANDERSON (1886–1973),
U.S. editor and memoirist. *The Fiery Fountains*,
part 1 (1951).
The founder and editor of an influential arts
journal, *The Little Review* (1914–1929), Anderson—a beautiful and stylish woman—had
known many important writers and artists, had
lived in France for nearly twenty years, had experienced at least three great loves, had played
and enjoyed fine music, and had largely managed to eke out a living without doing work
that she disliked—or, much of the time, any
work at all.

ENVIRONMENTALISM

1 . . . the fundamental principles of
ecology govern our lives wherever
we live, and . . . we must wake up to
this fact or be lost.

KARIN SHELDON (b. c. 1945), U.S. lawyer specializing in environmental protection. As quoted in *Ms.* magazine, p. 28 (September 1973).

2 I think an erotics of place may be one of the reasons why environmentalists are seen as subversive. There is a backlash now: . . . [ellipsis in source] take all the regulations away; weaken existing legislation; the endangered species act is too severe, too restrictive; let there be carte blanche for real-estate developers. Because if we really have to confront wildness, solitude, and serenity, both the fierceness and compassionate nature of the land, then we ultimately have to confront it in ourselves, and it's easier to be numb, to be distracted, to be disengaged.

TERRY TEMPEST WILLIAMS, U.S. author and environmentalist. As quoted in *Listen to Their Voices,* ch. 10, by Mickey Pearlman (1993).
Speculating on the reason for anti-environmentalism. Williams was a naturalist-in-residence at the Utah Museum of Natural History.

ENVY

1 There is a sort of jealousy which needs very little fire; it is hardly a passion, but a blight bred in the cloudy, damp despondency of uneasy egoism.

GEORGE ELIOT (1819–1880), British novelist. *Middlemarch,* ch. 21 (1871–1872).

2 It is queer to contemplate how many people there are in any community who labor under the hallucination that if one is engaged in any occupation different from their own, that they are just having a good time, with no possible hardships to encounter.

CAROLINE NICHOLS CHURCHILL (1833–?), U.S. author. *Active Footsteps,* ch. 8 (1909).

3 I kept in mind that the minute it got too rough, the minute the fourteen-hour days became too long, the minute people started to be naggy and frustrating, I knew that I could walk away and there were over seventy-nine thousand women who would trade shoes with me in a second.

KAYE LANI RAE RAFKO (b. c. 1968), U.S. beauty contest winner, Miss America, 1988. As quoted in *Miss America,* ch. 17, by Ann-Marie Bivans (1991).

EQUAL RIGHTS AMENDMENT

1 Section 1. Equality of rights under the law shall not be denied or abridged by the United States or by any state on account of sex. Section 2. The Congress shall have the power to enforce, by appropriate legislation, the provisions of this article. Section 3. This amendment shall take effect two years after the date of ratification.

EQUAL RIGHTS AMENDMENT, Text. *Full* (1970).
This proposed amendment to the United States Constitution, which was passed by both houses of Congress in 1972, needed ratification by 38 states to become a Constitutional amendment. Only 35 did so; in 1982, time ran out, and it was declared to be defeated. Opponents had made many spurious but emotionally effective claims: e.g., that it would legalize homosexual marriages, outlaw the paying of alimony and child support, extend the military draft and active combat duty to women, and outlaw sex-segregated rest rooms. A constitutional amend-

ment to establish equal rights for women in the United States had first been introduced in 1923.

2 I'll do anything to pass the ERA [Equal Rights Amendment], even if it means wearing babydoll night-gowns and padded bras, if that will make people less afraid.

JOAN HACKETT (1934–1983), U.S. actor. As quoted in *Ms.* magazine, p. 53 (June 1978). Speaking of the proposed Equal Rights Amendment to the U. S. Constitution; ultimately, it would be defeated.

EQUALITY

I To throw obstacles in the way of a complete education is like putting out the eyes; to deny the rights of property is like cutting off the hands. To refuse political equality is like robbing the ostracized of all self-respect, of credit in the market place, of recompense in the world of work, of a voice in choosing those who make and administer the law, a choice in the jury before whom they are tried, and in the judge who decides their punishment.

ELIZABETH CADY STANTON (1815–1902), U.S. suffragist, social reformer, and author. *The Solitude of Self* (February 20, 1894). From a famous speech delivered before a Senate committee which was considering arguments in favor of woman suffrage. Printed in the *Congressional Record* and reprinted in the *Women's Tribune,* the speech was remarkable for its refusal to engage the usual practical and democratic pro-suffrage arguments.

EQUALITY OF THE RACES

I A great many will find fault in the resolution that the negro shall be

free and equal, because our equal not every human being can be; but free every human being has a right to be. He can only be equal in his rights.

MRS. CHALKSTONE, U.S. suffragist. As quoted in *History of Woman Suffrage,* vol. 2, ch. 16, by Elizabeth Cady Stanton, Susan B. Anthony, and Matilda Joslyn Gage (1882). Speaking on May 14, 1863, at a national convention of the Woman's National Loyal League. Chalkstone had travelled from California to attend.

EQUALITY OF THE SEXES

I When human beings are regarded as *moral* beings, *sex,* instead of being enthroned upon the summit, administering upon rights and responsibilities, sinks into insignificance and nothingness. My doctrine then is, that whatever it is morally right for man to do, it is morally right for woman to do. Our duties originate, not from difference of sex, but from the diversity of our relations in life, the various gifts and talents committed to our care, and the different eras in which we live.

ANGELINA GRIMKÉ, (1805–1879) U.S. abolitionist and feminist. *Letters to Catherine Beecher,* letter #12 (1837). In a letter dated October 2, 1837.

2 I want my sex to claim nothing from their brethren but what their brethren may justly claim from them . . .

SARAH M. GRIMKÉ (1792–1873), U.S. abolitionist and feminist. *Letters on the Equality of the Sexes and the Condition of Woman,* letter #15: dated October 20, 1837 (1838). Opposing unreciprocated acts of chivalry and deference toward women.

3 Demands for equality for women are threats to men's self-esteem and sense of sexual turf.

ALICE S. ROSSI (b. 1922), U.S. sociologist. *Dissent*, p. 539 (November-December 1970).

EQUALITY OF THE SEXES: IN PRACTICE

I Woman's happiness and development are of more importance than all man's institutions. If constitutions and statute laws stand in the way of woman's emancipation, they must be amended to meet her wants and needs, of which she is a better judge than man possibly can be. If church canons and scriptures do not admit of women's equal recognition in all the sacred offices, then they must be revised in harmony with that idea. If the present family life is necessarily based on man's headship, then we must build a new domestic altar, at which the mother shall have equal dignity, honor and power; and we do not propose to wait another century to secure all this; the time has come.

ELIZABETH CADY STANTON (1815–1902), U.S. suffragist, social reformer, and author. As quoted in *History of Woman Suffrage*, vol. 4, ch. 11, by Susan B. Anthony and Ida Husted Harper (1902).

In an address entitled "The Degradation of Disfranchisement," delivered before the first triennial convention of the National Council of Women, a prosuffrage organization that had been founded in 1888; the convention was held in February 1891.

2 I thought that the chief thing to be done in order to equal boys was to

be learned and courageous. So I decided to study Greek and learn to manage a horse.

ELIZABETH CADY STANTON (1815–1902), U.S. suffragist, author, and social reformer. *Eighty Years and More (1815–1897)*, ch. 2 (1898).

Of the death of her brother, the only boy of the family's six children, in 1826, when she was eleven. Aware that her bereaved father had longed for another son, she vowed to him "to be all my brother was."

3 You can't protect women without handicapping them in competition with men. If you demand equality you must accept equality. Women can't have it both ways.

MARY BELL-RICHARDS, As quoted in *On Women and Revolution*, part 1, by Crystal Eastman (1978). From an article first published in *Equal Rights* on October 3, 1925.

4 Now men and women are separate and unequal. We should be hand in hand; in fact, we should have our arms around each other.

CLORIS LEACHMAN (b. 1930), U.S. actress. As quoted in *Ms.* magazine, p. 55 (June 1978).

Speaking of her support for the proposed Equal Rights Amendment to the U. S. Constitution; ultimately, it would be defeated.

EQUALITY OF THE SEXES: IN PRINCIPLE

I Had Adam tenderly reproved his wife, and endeavored to lead her to repentance instead of sharing in her guilt, I should be much more ready to accord to man that superiority which he claims; but as the facts stand disclosed by the sacred historian, it appears to me that to say the least, there was as much weakness exhibited by Adam as by Eve. They both fell from innocence, and consequently from happiness, *but not from equality.*

SARAH M. GRIMKÉ (1792–1873), U.S. abolitionist and feminist. *Letters on the Equality of the Sexes and the Condition of Woman,* letter #1: dated July 11, 1837 (1838).

2   . . . in America, alone . . . women are raised to an equality with the other sex; and . . . both in theory and practice, their interests are regarded as of equal value. They are made subordinate in station, only where a regard to their best interests demands it, while, as if in compensation for this, by custom and courtesy, they are always treated as superiors. Universally, in this Country, through every class of society, precedence is given to woman, in all the comforts, conveniences, and courtesies of life.

CATHERINE E. BEECHER (1800–1878), U.S. educator and author. *Treatise on Domestic Economy for the Use of Young Ladies at Home and at School,* ch. 3 (1843).

Beecher, a pioneer in education for women, would emerge as an antisuffragist in later years when the woman suffrage movement developed and gained force.

3   . . . strike the words "white male" from all your constitutions, and then, with fair sailing, let us sink or swim, live or die, survive or perish together.

ELIZABETH CADY STANTON (1815–1902), U.S. suffragist, social reformer, and author. As quoted in *Feminism: The Essential Historical Writings,* part 3, by Miriam Schnier (1972).

The conclusion of her 1860 address to the New York State legislature.

4   A woman who occupies the same realm of thought with man, who

can explore with him the depths of science, comprehend the steps of progress through the long past and prophesy those of the momentous future, must ever be surprised and aggravated with his assumptions of leadership and superiority, a superiority she never concedes, an authority she utterly repudiates.

ELIZABETH CADY STANTON (1815–1902), U.S. suffragist, social reformer, and author. *History of Woman Suffrage,* vol. 2, ch. 19 (1882).

5   We seem to be pariahs alike in the visible and the invisible world, with no foothold anywhere, though by every principle of government and religion we should have an equal place on this planet.

ELIZABETH CADY STANTON (1815–1902), U.S. suffragist, social reformer, and author. As quoted in *History of Woman Suffrage,* vol. 4, ch. 19, by Susan B. Anthony and Ida Husted Harper (1902).

In a letter read by Susan B. Anthony (1820–1906) before the thirty-first annual convention of the National Woman Suffrage Association, which was held April 27–May 3, 1899, in Grand Rapids, Michigan.

6   To grant woman an equality with man in the affairs of life is contrary to every tradition, every precedent, every inheritance, every instinct and every teaching. The acceptance of this idea is possible only to those of especially progressive tendencies and a strong sense of justice, and it is yet too soon to expect these from the majority.

SUSAN B. ANTHONY (1820–1906), U.S. suffragist and author. *History of Woman Suffrage,* vol. 4, introduction (1902).

7   In the adjustment of the new order of things, we women demand an

equal voice; we shall accept nothing less.

CARRIE CHAPMAN CATT (1859–1947), U.S. suffragist, journalist, and educator. As quoted in *Feminism: The Essential Historical Writings*, part 5, by Miriam Schnier (1972). The closing line of Catt's notable speech delivered in Stockholm, Sweden, in 1911. She served two terms as President of the National Woman Suffrage Association (1900–1904 and 1915–1920) and founded the International Woman Suffrage Alliance.

8   Can a woman become a genius of the first class? Nobody can know unless women in general shall have equal opportunity with men in education, in vocational choice, and in social welcome of their best intellectual work for a number of generations.

ANNA GARLIN SPENCER (1851–1931), U.S. educator, author, feminist, and Unitarian minister. *Woman's Share in Social Culture*, ch. 3 (1913).

9   Men and women should own the world as a mutual possession.

PEARL S. BUCK (1892–1973), U.S. author; born in China. *Of Men and Women*, ch. 8 (1941).

10 It is a hidden fear that somehow, if they are only given a chance, women will suddenly do as they have been done by.

EVA FIGES (b. 1932), British author; born in Germany. As quoted in *The Decade of Women*, by Suzanne Levine and Harriet Lyons (1980).

11 When we reach the point where the women athletes are getting their pick of dates just as easily as the men athletes, then we've really and truly arrived. Parity at last!

BILLIE JEAN KING (b. 1943), U.S. tennis player. *Billie Jean*, ch. 12 (1982).

Referring humorously to the female "groupies" who pursued popular male athletes.

EVIL

1   . . . by desiring what is perfectly good, even when we don't quite know what it is and cannot do what we would, we are part of the divine power against evil—widening the skirts of light and making the struggle with darkness narrower.

GEORGE ELIOT (1819–1880), British novelist. *Middlemarch*, ch. 39 (1871–1872).

2   When this immediate evil power has been defeated, we shall not yet have won the long battle with the elemental barbarities. Another Hitler, it may be an invisible adversary, will attempt, again, and yet again, to destroy our frail civilization. Is it true, I wonder, that the only way to escape a war is to be in it? When one is a part of an actuality does the imagination find a release?

ELLEN GLASGOW (1873–1945), U.S. novelist. *The Woman Within*, ch. 22 (1954). Written in 1944, near the end of World War II.

3   Evil is simply
    a grammatical error:
    a failure to leap
    the precipice
    between "he"
    and "I."

LINDA PASTAN (b. 1932), U.S. poet. "Instructions to the Reader," lines 28–33 (1982).

EVOLUTION

1   Evolution was all over my chldhood, walks abroad with an

evolutionist and the world was full of evolution, biological and botanical evolution.

GERTRUDE STEIN (1874–1946), U.S. author; relocated to France. *Wars I Have Seen* (1945).
Written in 1943.

EXCELLENCE

I ... we never do any thing well, unless we love it for its own sake.

MARY WOLLSTONECRAFT (1759–1797), British feminist. *A Vindication of the Rights of Woman*, ch. 5 (1792).

2 The requirements of the theatre are very great—a strong constitution, energy and unflagging purpose, charm of feature, these alone do not necessarily mean anything, and they must not be relied upon as assurances of an easy conquest of the public heart. It is not only a question of fitness for the work, but of long years of most diligent effort to master the technique of the theatre, and to develop whatever of the art instinct we may possess upon the simplest, broadest, and most human lines.

JULIA MARLOWE (1866–1950), U.S. actor; born in England. As quoted in *Famous Actors and Actresses on the American Stage*, vol. 2, by William C. Young (1975).
From an article first published in *Metropolitan* (September 1909).

3 If a person goes to his job with a firm determination to give of himself the best of which he is capable, that job—no matter what it is— takes on dignity and importance.

HORTENSE ODLUM (1892– ?), U.S. businesswoman. *A Woman's Place*, ch. 6 (1939).

4 One of the greatest satisfactions one can ever have, comes from the knowledge that he can do some one thing superlatively well.

HORTENSE ODLUM (1892– ?), U.S. businesswoman. *A Woman's Place*, ch. 17 (1939).

5 The best that an individual can do is to concentrate on what he or she can do, in the course of a burning effort to do it better.

ELIZABETH BOWEN (1899–1973), British novelist, story writer, essayist, and memoirist; born in Ireland. *Seven Winters*, part 2, sect. 2, ch. 5 (1962).
Written in 1959.

6 When you are beginning, you will find you give better performances in the evening if you stay quiet during the day—no lunches, and certainly no cocktail parties. Remember you are overpaid, so take your money at the end of the week with as clear a conscience as you can.

LYNN FONTANNE (1887–1983), U.S. actor; born in England. As quoted in *Actors on Acting*, rev. ed., part 13, by Toby Cole and Helen Krich (1970).
Offering advice to aspiring actors, c. 1960.

7 I don't want to make money, I just want to be wonderful.

MARILYN MONROE (1926–1962), U.S. actor. As quoted in *Ms.* magazine, p. 41 (August 1972).
Monroe, a popular movie star, made a great deal of money but was dissatisfied with her level of skill and privately studied acting after she was already famous.

8 ... excellence is the best deterrent to racism or sexism.

OPRAH WINFREY (b. 1954), African American television personality and actress. As quoted in *I Dream a World*, by Brian Lanker (1989).

Born in Mississippi, she became the first African American woman to host a nationally syndicated weekday television talk show and the first to found her own television and film production company. She was also among the few to be nominated for an Academy Award (for Best Supporting Actress in *The Color Purple* [1985]).

9 I don't want to be graded on a curve.

MARY CARILLO (b. 1957), U.S. tennis player. As quoted in *Sports Illustrated*, p. 89 (June 17, 1991).

On being called "the best woman tennis expert or anything else with the word woman in it."

10 You work hard to be good and then to be great, but when you're great, you don't just want to be good.

PAT BRADLEY (b. 1951), U.S. golfer. As quoted in the *New York Times*, sect. 8, p. 1, by Nancy Lopez (July 11, 1993).

Lopez (b. 1957), a Hall of Fame golfer, was quoting Bradley in an attempt to explain her declining patience and enthusiasm for her sport. Lopez's three children, ranging in age from twenty months to nine years, were accompanying her on the Ladies' Professional Golf Association Tour.

11 The question is not . . . if art is enough to fulfill my life, but if I am true to the path I have set for myself, if I am the best I can be in the things I do. Am I living up to the reasons I became a singer in the first place?

KATHLEEN BATTLE (b. 1948), U.S. opera singer. As quoted in *New York* magazine, p. 44–45 (July 12, 1993).

At the time, Battle was one of the world's greatest opera singers. She was known for her perfectionism.

12 It looks like I've been here. Yes, it looks like I've been here.

ELAINE STRONG (b. 1934), U.S. maid. As quoted in the *New York Times*, sect. 14, p. 12 (May 8, 1994).

Surveying a New York City apartment she had just cleaned and expressing pride in her work. She usually cleaned two apartments per eight-hour day at $7.25 per hour.

13 I remember a very important lesson that my father gave me when I was twelve or thirteen. He said, "You know, today I welded a perfect seam and I signed my name to it." And I said, "But, Daddy, no one's going to see it!" And he said, "Yeah, but I know it's there." So when I was working in kitchens, I did good work.

TONI MORRISON (b. 1931), African American author. As quoted in the *New York Times Magazine*, p. 73 (September 11, 1994).

Morrison, winner of the 1993 Nobel Prize for Literature, was recalling her days as a domestic worker.

EXILE

1 The politics of the exile are fever, revenge, daydream, theater of the aging convalescent. You wait in the wings and rehearse. You wait and wait.

MARGE PIERCY (b. 1936), U.S. poet, novelist, and political activist. "The Organizer's Bogeyman," lines 20–24 (1969).

Written during the Vietnam War, on expulsion from an activist organization governed by radical political ideology. Piercy was prominent among the opponents of American involvement in that war.

EXPATRIATISM

1 Even people whose lives have been made various by learning, sometimes find it hard to keep a fast hold on their habitual views of life, on their faith in the Invisible—nay, on the sense that their past joys and sorrows are a real experience, when they are suddenly transported to a new land, where by beings around them know nothing of their history, and share none of their ideas— where their mother earth shows another lap, and human life has other forms than those on which their souls have been nourished. Minds that have been unhinged from their old faith and love, have perhaps sought this Lethean influence of exile, in which the past becomes dreamy because its symbols have all vanished, and the present too is dreamy because it is linked with no memories.

GEORGE ELIOT (1819–1880), British novelist. *Silas Marner,* ch. 2 (1861).

2   Three characteristics mark all confirmed expatriates: (1) slowness on the up-take, (2) the tendency to personalize the impersonal—interpreting in terms of politeness or of policy what should be kept clearly in terms of ideas, (3) the tendency to orientalize one's attitude toward women.

MARGARET ANDERSON (1886–1973), U.S. literary editor and autobiographer. *My Thirty Years' War,* ch. 6 (1930).

Anderson lived as an expatriate in Paris during the late 1920s and early 1930s.

3   There is something in this native land business and you cannot get away from it, in peace time you do not seem to notice it much particularly when you live in foreign parts

but when there is a war and you are all alone and completely cut off from knowing about your country well then there it is, your native land is your native land, it certainly is.

GERTRUDE STEIN (1874–1946), U.S. author; relocated to France. *Wars I Have Seen* (1945).

Written in occupied France in 1944, during World War II. Stein felt cut off from reliable information about events in the United States, where she had been born, raised, and educated, and where she still maintained citizenship, though she had long ago resettled permanently in France.

4   . . . expatriated Americans, even Henry James himself, have always seemed to me somewhat anchorless, rudderless, drifting before the wind.

VIRGINIA CROCHERON GILDERSLEEVE, (1877–1965) U.S. educator. *Many a Good Crusade,* part 3 (1954).

Gildersleeve, Dean of Barnard College, was active for decades in international political work and lived in England much of the time with her "intimate friend," the Englishwoman Caroline Spurgeon. Henry James (1843–1916), an important American novelist, left the United States to settle first in Paris and then, in 1876, in England, where he remained for the rest of his life.

5   I had got away. That was my victory. The real quarrel with Ireland began to burgeon in me then; I thought of how it had warped me, and those around me, and their parents before them, all stooped by a variety of fears—fear of church, fear of gombeenism, fear of phantoms, fear of ridicule, fear of hunger, fear of annihilation, and fear of their own deeply ingrained agression [sic] that can only strike a blow at each other, not having the innate authority to strike at those who are

higher. Pity arose too, pity for a land so often denuded, pity for a people reluctant to admit that there is anything wrong. That is why we leave. Because we beg to differ. Because we dread the psychological choke. But leaving is only conditional. The person you are is anathema to the person you would like to be.

EDNA O'BRIEN (b. c. 1932), Irish author; relocated to England. *Mother Ireland,* ch. 7 (1976).

6 All my life I have lived and behaved very much like [the] sandpiper— just running down the edges of different countries and continents, "looking for something" . . . having spent most of my life timorously seeking for subsistence along the coastlines of the world.

ELIZABETH BISHOP (1911–1979), U.S. poet; relocated to Brazil. As quoted in *Contemporary Poets,* 3rd ed., by James Vinson (1980).

A native of Worcester, Massachusetts, Bishop spent much of her life living reclusively in Brazil.

7 I am a citizen of the world.

SYLVIA BEACH (1887–1962), U.S. bookseller and publisher; relocated to France. As quoted in *Sylvia Beach and the Lost Generation,* ch. 20, by Noel Fitch (1983).

An American who settled in Paris at age 30, Beach was best known for her bookstore and lending library, Shakespeare and Company, which became a gathering place for the Parisian literati and arts community, and for being the first book publisher of the great Irish novelist James Joyce.

8 I became the butterfly. I got out of the cocoon, and I *flew.*

LYNN REDGRAVE (b. 1943), British actor; relocated to America. As quoted in the *New York Times Magazine,* p. 80 (June 6, 1993).

The daughter and sister of famous and oppressive English actors, Redgrave was describing her resettlement from England to California, which was followed by a successful diet, marriage, and acting career.

EXPECTATIONS

1 I can't imagine going on when there are no more expectations.

DAME EDITH EVANS (1888–1976), British actor. As quoted in *Dame Edith Evans,* ch. 5, by Bryan Forbes (1977).

Evans had had a brilliantly successful stage career.

2 I've always got such high expectations for myself. I'm aware of them, but I can't relax them.

MARY DECKER SLANEY (b. 1958), U.S. runner. As quoted in *Sports Illustrated,* p. 52 (July 29, 1991).

At thirty-three, Slaney had been running competitively for eighteen years; at age fifteen, she had already been ranked fourth in the world. She had suffered setbacks recently and was professionally threatened by emerging African track stars.

EXPERIENCE

1 . . . should one sit down to paint the scenes among which he has grown, he will find that the facts creep in upon him. Those brilliant phases and shapes which the imagination sees in far-off lands are not for him to portray. Sadly he must squeeze the colour from his brush, and dip it into the grey pigments around him. He must paint what lies before him.

OLIVE SCHREINER (1855–1920), South African author. *The Story of an African Farm,* Preface (1883).

On why her semi-autobiographical novel, which was about South African farm life, dealt with relatively homely situations rather than "wild adventure," as one critic had suggested it should. Schreiner wrote under the pseudonym "Ralph Iron."

2 Go into the streets, into the slums, into the fashionable quarters. Go into the day courts and the night courts. Become acquainted with sorrow, with many kinds of sorrow. Learn of the wonderful heroism of the poor, of the incredible generosity of the very poor—a generosity of which the rich and the well-to-do have, for the most part, not the faintest conception. Go into the modest homes, into the out-of-the-way corners, into the open country. Go where you can find something fresh to bring back to the stage.

MINNIE MADDERN FISKE (1865–1932), U.S. actress. As quoted in *Mrs. Fiske: Her Views on Actors, Acting and the Problems of Production,* ch. 3, by Alexander Woollcott (1917). This was Fiske's advice to actors. She had been a popular stage actor since the age of four (when she used her birth name, Minnie Maddern).

3 . . . every day is any day.

GERTRUDE STEIN (1874–1946), U.S. author; relocated to France. *Wars I Have Seen* (1945). Written in 1943.

4 Doesn't all experience crumble in the end to mere literary material?

ELLEN GLASGOW (1873–1945), U.S. novelist. *The Woman Within,* ch. 18 (1954). Written in 1944, of her expectation that a sudden attraction to a man would not endure.

5 . . . it is not only our fate but our business to lose innocence, and once we have lost that it is futile to attempt a picnic in Eden.

ELIZABETH BOWEN (1899–1973), British novelist, story writer, essayist, and memoirist; born in Ireland. As quoted in *Elizabeth Bowen,* ch. 2, by Victoria Glendinning (1979). Written in 1946.

6 Whatever can happen to anyone can happen to me.

MURIEL RUKEYSER (1913–1980), U.S. poet. "Waterlily Fire," part 5, line 26 (1962).

7 . . . the basic experience of everyone is the experience of human limitation.

FLANNERY O'CONNOR (1925–1964), U.S. fiction writer and essayist. *Mystery and Manners,* part 4 (1969). Written in 1963.

8 The old-fashioned idea that the simple piling up of experiences, one on top of another, can make you an artist, is, of course, so much rubbish. If acting were just a matter of experience, then any busy harlot could make Garbo's *Camille* pale.

HELEN HAYES (1900–1993), U.S. actor. *On Reflection,* ch. 6 (1968). *Camille* was the American version of Alexandre Dumas, *fils'* 1852 French play, *La Dame aux Camelias.* A sentimental tale of the tragic love of a beautiful courtesan, it was made into a popular movie in 1937 starring Greta Garbo.

9 Tremble: your whole life is a rehearsal for the moment you are in now.

JUDITH MALINA (b. 1926), U.S. actor and stage producer. As quoted in *Actors on Acting,* rev. ed., part 13, by Toby Cole and Helen Krich (1970).

10 The only thing experience teaches you is what you can't do. When you start, you think you can do anything. And then you start to get a little tired.

ELAINE MAY (b. 1932), U.S. comedienne and movie–maker. As quoted in *Reel Women*, part 2, by Ally Acker (1991). Said in 1975.

Larcom became a mill worker at age 11 to Alleviate her family's poverty after her father died.

11 I've never been convinced that experience is linear, circular, or even random. It just is. I try to put it in some kind of order to extract meaning from it, to bring meaning to it.

TONI CADE BAMBARA (b. 1939), U.S. fiction writer. *Black Women Writers at Work*, ch. 2, by Claudia Tate (1983).

12 . . . ordinary experience has to be made extraordinary in order to become accessible to reflection.

SHOSHANA ZUBOFF (b. 1951), U.S. social scientist. *In the Age of the Smart Machine*, Introduction (1988).

13 If you want an expert on war, you get a retired general. I'm not exactly a general, but I am retired.

SYDNEY BIDDLE BARROWS (b. 1952), Ex-"madam." As quoted in *Newsweek* magazine, p. 33 (November 21, 1994).

Barrows, once the proprietress of a "high-class" prostitution service, was known as the "Mayflower Madam" because of her wealthy, distinguished, "old" family background. She was commenting on being hired as a cable-TV commentator on the trial of Heidi Fleiss, who had allegedly supplied high-priced prostitutes to Hollywood personalities.

FACTORY WORK

1 I defied the machinery to make me its slave. Its incessant discords could not drown the music of my thoughts if I would let them fly high enough.

LUCY LARCOM (1824–1893), U.S. poet and teacher. *A New England Girlhood*, ch. 8 (1889).

2 If factory-labor is not a means of education to the operative of to-day, it is because the employer does not do his duty. It is because he treats his work-people like machines, and forgets that they are struggling, hoping, despairing human beings.

HARRIET H. ROBINSON (1825–1911), U.S. author and former mill worker. *Loom and Spindle, or Life Among the Early Mill Girls*, ch. 9 (1898).

3 . . . you can have a couple of seconds to rest in. I mean *seconds*. You have about two seconds to wait while the blanker is on the felt drawing the moisture out. You can stand and relax those two seconds—three seconds at most. You wish you didn't have to work in a factory. When it's all you know what to do, that's what you do.

GRACE CLEMENTS, U.S. factory worker. As quoted in *Working*, book 5, by Studs Terkel (1973).

A felter in the luggage division of ARMCO Corp., Clements had become a company organizer for the United Auto Workers and, after the union came in, chair of the grievance committee.

4 . . . working at the factory . . . gave my time value. It gave my body value. It gave *me* value.

LINDA FERRARA (b. c. 1945), U.S. factory worker. As Quoted In *Ms.* Magazine, p. 87 (November 1979).

On the way in which getting a job—at a food processing plant—changed her life.

FAILURE

1   All who strive to live for something beyond mere selfish aims find their capacities for doing good very inadequate to their aspirations. They do so much less than they *want* to do, and so much less than they, at the outset, *expected* to do, that their lives, viewed retrospectively, inevitably look like failure.

LYDIA MARIA CHILD (1802–1880), U.S. author, abolitionist, and suffragist. *Selected Letters, 1817–1880*, ch. 9 (1982).

Written in 1868 to John Fraser, who was married to a niece of David Child, her husband. Lydia Maria Child had just turned sixty-six.

2   Failure after long perseverance is much grander than never to have a striving good enough to be called a failure.

GEORGE ELIOT (1819–1880), British novelist. *Middlemarch*, ch. 22 (1871–1872).

3   In all failures, the beginning is certainly the half of the whole.

GEORGE ELIOT (1819–1880), British novelist. *Middlemarch*, ch. 31 (1871–1872).

4   I have never worked for fame or praise, and shall not feel their loss as I otherwise would. I have never for a moment lost sight of the humble life I was born to, its small environments, and the consequently little right I had to expect much of myself, and shall have the less to censure, or upbraid myself with for the failures I must see myself make.

CLARA BARTON (1821–1912), U.S. Civil War nurse and founder of the American Red Cross. As quoted in *Angel of the Battlefield*, ch. 19, by Ishbel Ross (1956).

Barton wrote this in 1903, at a time when her Presidency of the American Red Cross was being challenged. She had been born one of five children to a North Oxford, Massachusetts family in modest circumstances.

5   There have been others also just as true and devoted to the cause—I wish I could name every one—but with such women consecrating their lives, failure is impossible!

SUSAN B. ANTHONY (1820–1906), U.S. suffragist. As quoted in *Life and Work of Susan B. Anthony*, vol. 3, ch. 70, by Ida Husted Harper (1908).

At a celebration of her eighty-sixth birthday held in Washington, D.C., on February 15, 1906. Anthony had outlived virtually all of the other founders of the woman suffrage movement. She was in ill health and had struggled to attend the event; these would be the last words she would ever speak to a public gathering. "Failure is impossible," is one of her most famous utterances; she seems to have pronounced it on other occasions as well and certainly believed it. At it turned out, she was correct, though women would not be granted the vote for another fourteen years, a century after her birth.

6   Never mind if you fall far short of the thing you want to do,—encourage your effort. If no one else will say it to you, say it to yourself. "Not so bad." It will make the next effort easier and better.

JOSEPHINE DEMOTT ROBINSON (1865–1948), U.S. circus performer. *The Circus Lady*, ch. 11 (1926).

On beginning to train once again as a circus performer after being retired for fifteen years.

7   I simply don't believe in failure. In itself, it doesn't exist. We create it. We make ourselves fail.

ALICE FOOTE MACDOUGALL, (1867–1945) U.S. businesswoman. *The Autobiography of a Business Woman*, ch. 4 (1928).

MacDougall was a successful coffee house proprietor and coffee, tea, and cocoa merchant.

8 With ruin staring you in the face, there is nothing worse to live through than a siege of waiting and hoping. If you manage to live through it, nothing can ever jar your nerves after that.

SUE SANDERS, U.S. oil producer. *Our Common Herd,* ch. 20 (1940).

Of panic in the oil production business in the early 1920s.

9 . . . there are persons who seem to have overcome obstacles and by character and perseverance to have risen to the top. But we have no record of the numbers of able persons who fall by the wayside, persons who, with enough encouragement and opportunity, might make great contributions.

MARY BARNETT GILSON (1877– ?), U.S. factory personnel manager, economist, and educator. *What's Past is Prologue,* ch. 12 (1940).

10 It felt dark. It felt like midnight.

MARTINA NAVRATILOVA (b. 1956), U.S. tennis player; born and raised in Czechoslovakia. As quoted in *Sports Illustrated,* p. 27 (July 15, 1991).

After failing, for the first time in fourteen years, to advance at least as far as the semifinal round at Wimbledon, the world's most prestigious tennis tournament and one that she had already won a record nine times. Strained by her former lover's recent suit for half the assets she had accumulated during their relationship, and distracted by an overnight rain delay, Navratilova had just lost to teenager Jennifer Capriati in the quarterfinals.

11 I spend so many times for skating, and I gave up so many hobbies for this . . . the Olympics are four years in time. And I am old.

YE QIAOBO (b. 1965), Chinese ice skater. As quoted in *Time* magazine, p. 50 (February 24, 1992).

The first Chinese athlete ever to win a Winter Olympics medal, Qiaobo had just won two silvers and, in tears, expressed her disappointment and frustration at not winning a gold. At the next Olympics, she would be thirty-one, perhaps too old to compete.

FAITH

1 There is one thing higher than Royalty: and that is religion, which causes us to leave the world, and seek God.

ELIZABETH I (1533–1603), British monarch, Queen of England (1558–1603). As quoted in *The Sayings of Queen Elizabeth,* ch. 9, by Frederick Chamberlin (1923).

Said to one of her attendants; reported by Fenelon, the French ambassador.

2 In all the wide gamut of human experience, nothing plays so important a part as faith. . . . Faith that is as broad as the heavens and as wide as the earth. Faith that comprehends in its vast sympathies everything human as well as divine, and carries one with the swift sure wings of the angels directly to his goal.

ALICE FOOTE MACDOUGALL, (1867–1945) U.S. businesswoman. *The Autobiography of a Business Woman,* ch. 7 (1928).

3 I didn't have any looks, I didn't have any talent, and it was easy for me to say to the Lord, "I don't *have* anything." If you only knew where I came from . . . this *leetle*-bitty town with no more than twelve hundred people in it. *So* . . . anything I am today, *He* is the one who has done it [ellipses in source].

KATHRYN KUHLMAN (1907–1976), U.S. faith healer. As quoted in *Ms.* magazine, p. 13 (January 1975).

4 There is a place where we are always alone with our own mortality, where we must simply have something greater than ourselves to hold onto—God or history or politics or literature or a belief in the healing power of love, or even righteous anger. . . . A reason to believe, a way to take the world by the throat and insist that there is more to this life than we have ever imagined.

DOROTHY ALLISON (b. 1949), U.S. author and lesbian feminist. *Skin*, ch. 18 (1994).

Allison had suffered a poverty-stricken, violence-ridden, Southern childhood.

FAME

1 When I received this [coronation] ring I solemnly bound myself in marriage to the realm; and it will be quite sufficient for the memorial of my name and for my glory, if, when I die, an inscription be engraved on a marble tomb, saying, "Here lieth Elizabeth, which reigned a virgin, and died a virgin."

ELIZABETH I (1533–1603), British monarch, Queen of England (1558–1603). As quoted in *The Sayings of Queen Elizabeth*, ch. 7, by Frederick Chamberlin (1923).

Said "to the Speaker, Knights, and Burgesses of the Lower House who [in 1559, the second year of her reign] laid an address before her in the great gallery of Whitehall Palace urging her to marry." For years thereafter, Elizabeth would vacillate about her marital intentions, sometimes declaring that to marry would be "necessary." However, despite many aggressive overtures from European nobility and imperative urging from within England, she never did, thus ruling alone and leaving behind no heir.

2 Fame is a bee.
It has a song—
It has a sting—
Ah, too, it has a wing.

EMILY DICKINSON (1831–1886), U.S. poet. "Fame is a bee": poem no. 1763 in her *Collected Poems*, entire poem (date not known).

3 . . . I, his wife, rested and was warmed in the sunlight of his loyal love, and glorious fame, and now, even though his beautiful life has gone out, it is as when some far off planet disappears from the heavens, the light of his great fame still falls upon and warms me.

JULIA DENT GRANT (1825–1902), First Lady of the United States (1869–1877), wife of Ulysses S. Grant. *What America Owes to Women*, ch. 7 (1893).

On surviving her husband, who was a General and the 18th President of the United States.

4 Alas, we are the victims of advertisement. Those who taste the joys and sorrows of fame when they have passed forty, know how to look after themselves. They know what is concealed beneath the flowers, and what the gossip, the calumnies, and the praise are worth. But as for those who win fame when they are twenty, they know nothing, and are caught up in the whirlpool.

SARAH BERNHARDT (1845–1923), French actor. *The Art of the Theatre*, ch. 3 (1924).

By her early twenties, Bernhardt was attracting notice for her performances at the Odeon theater; by age 30, she was a star with the Comedie Francaise.

5 You know when there's a star, like in show business, the star has her name in lights on the marquee! Right? And the star gets the money because the people come to see the star, right? Well, I'm the star, and all of you are in the chorus.

BABE DIDRIKSON ZAHARIAS (1911–1956), U.S. athlete. As quoted in *WomenSports* magazine, p. 55 (December 1977).
Said in the 1940s to her sister golfers at a meeting she had called of the Ladies' Professional Golf Association.

HELEN HAYES (1900–1993), U.S. actor. *On Reflection,* ch. 6 (1968).
Hayes, a professional actress from age five until into her seventies, was by this time routinely referred to as the "First Lady of the Theater."

9 Stardom can be a gilded slavery.

HELEN HAYES (1900–1993), U.S. actor. *On Reflection,* ch. 14 (1968).
Often dubbed "The First Lady of the Theater," Hayes began acting at age five and had become well known by early adulthood. Although she was primarily a stage actor, she won the 1931 Best Actress "Oscar" for her first movie, *The Sin of Madelon Claudet.*

6 I was going to get myself recognized at any price. . . . If I could not win fame by goodness, I was ready to do it by badness. . . .

MARY MCCARTHY (1912–1989), U.S. author. *Memories of a Catholic Girlhood,* ch. 5 (1957).
On determining to distinguish herself when in the eighth grade of a convent school.

7 People feel fame gives them some kind of privilege to walk up to you and say anything to you, of any kind of nature—and it won't hurt your feelings—like it's happening to your clothing.

MARILYN MONROE (1926–1962), U.S. actor. As quoted in *Ms.* magazine, p. 40 (August 1972).
Monroe was an extremely famous movie star and "sex symbol." She seemed to be very vulnerable emotionally; her early death was ruled a suicide.

8 The flattering, if arbitrary, label, First Lady of the Theatre, takes its toll. The demands are great, not only in energy but eventually in dramatic focus. It is difficult, if not impossible, for a star to occupy an inch of space without bursting seams, cramping everyone else's style and unbalancing a play. No matter how self-effacing a famous player may be, he makes an entrance as a casual neighbor and the audience interest shifts to the house next door.

10 I was the toast of two continents: Greenland and Australia.

DOROTHY PARKER (1893–1967), U.S. author and humorist. As quoted in *You Might as Well Live,* part 1, ch. 6, by John Keats (1970).
Parker was recalling her 1920s reputation as a rather silly "smartcracker."

11 The more I had won that year, the less it meant . . . and the more tired and sad I became. And the more I won, the more people wanted a part of me. I will tell you King's First Law of Recognition: You never get it when you want it, and then when it comes, you get too much.

BILLIE JEAN KING (b. 1943), U.S. tennis player. *Billie Jean,* ch. 3 (1982).
Of 1972, when she won three of the four Grand Slam tennis tournaments (not having entered the fourth, the Australian Open).

12 Sometimes it takes years to really grasp what has happened to your life. What do you do after you are world-famous and nineteen or twenty and you have sat with prime ministers, kings and queens, the Pope? What do you do after that? Do you go back home and take a job? What do you do to keep your sanity? You come back to the real world.

WILMA RUDOLPH (1940–1994), U.S. runner. As quoted in *I Dream a World*, by Brian Lanker (1989).

In Rome in 1960, Rudolph had become the first American woman to win three gold medals in track and field at a single Olympics.

13 Mickey Mouse . . . [is] always there—he's part of my life. That really is something not everyone can call their claim to fame.

ANNETTE FUNICELLO (b. 1942), U.S. entertainer. As quoted in the *New York Times*, sect. 9, p. 9 (November 21, 1993).

Funicello was a child performer on the popular *Mickey Mouse Club* television show in the 1950s, wearing a cap with mock "mouse ears."

FAMILY

1 Every member of the family of the future will be a producer of some kind and in some degree. The only one who will have the right of exemption will be the mother . . .

RUTH C. D. HAVENS, U.S. suffragist. As quoted in *History of Woman Suffrage*, vol. 4, ch. 13, by Susan B. Anthony and Ida Husted Harper (1902).

Speaking in 1893 at the twenty-fifth annual convention of the National Woman Suffrage Association. Havens was from Washington, D.C.; her address was entitled "The Girl of the Future."

2 Families are great murderers of the creative impulse, particularly husbands.

BRENDA UELAND (1891–1985), U.S. author and writing teacher. *If You Want to Write*, 2nd. ed., ch. 1 (1938).

3 . . . what's been building since the 1980's is a new kind of social Dar-

winism that blames poverty and crime and the crisis of our youth on a breakdown of the family. That's what will last after this flurry on family values.

STEPHANIE COONTZ (b. 1944), U.S. social historian. *Chronicle of Higher Education*, p. A13 (November 4, 1992).

Reacting to recent appeals to "family values" by both the Democratic and the Republican parties' leadership. Coontz specialized in research on the subject of the American family.

FANATICISM

1 If a weakly mortal is to do anything in the world besides eat the bread thereof, there must be a determined subordination of the whole nature to the one aim—no trifling with time, which is passing, with strength which is only too limited.

BEATRICE WEBB (1858–1943), British author and socialist. As quoted in *Beatrice Webb*, ch. 8. by Carole Seymour-Jones (1992).

Written in her diary on July 24, 1882. The future socialist theorist was expressing guilty regrets over a week "spent unworthily" in a flirtation.

2 It is . . . marvellous . . . to have a period of apparent fanaticism. No obstacle can discourage you. The single vision of your quest obscures defeat and lifts you over mountainous difficulties.

MARGARET SANGER (1879–1966), U.S. birth control rights activist. *My Fight for Birth Control*, ch. 5 (1931).

On her refusal, in 1914–1915, to abandon her search for a printer for her pamphlet entitled "Family Limitation," which provided birth control information that was illegal to disseminate. Eventually, she found an independent printer who did it anonymously after regular business hours.

FANTASY

1 Fantasy is toxic: the private cruelty and the world war both have their start in the heated brain.

ELIZABETH BOWEN (1899–1973), Irish author; born in Ireland. *Bowen's Court,* afterword (1942).

2 ... one of my motivating forces has been to recreate the world I know into a world I wish I could be in. Hence my optimism and happy endings. But I've never dreamed I could actually reshape the real world.

KRISTIN HUNTER (b. 1931), African American author. *Black Women Writers at Work,* ch. 6, by Claudia Tate (1983).

FARMING

1 ... farming conservatism, which consisted in holding that whatever is, is bad, and any change is likely to be worse.

GEORGE ELIOT (1819–1880), British novelist. *Middlemarch,* ch. 39 (1871–1872).

2 My weary limbs are scarcely stretched for repose, before red dawn peeps into my chamber window, and the birds in the whispering leaves over the roof, apprise me by their sweetest notes that another day of toil awaits me. I arise, the harness is hastily adjusted and once more I step upon the treadmill.

"E. B.", U.S. farmer. As quoted in *Feminine Ingenuity,* by Anne L. MacDonald (1992). From a letter written c. 1878 to a journal, *The Household.*

3 On the farm I had learned how to meet realities without suffering either mentally or physically. My initiative had never been blunted. I had freedom to succeed—freedom to fail. Life on the farm produces a kind of toughness.

BERTHA VAN HOOSEN (1863–1952), U.S. physician. *Petticoat Surgeon,* ch. 8 (1947). On why her farm background prepared her well for medical school and practice.

4 The prairies were dust. Day after day, summer after summer, the scorching winds blew the dust and the sun was brassy in a yellow sky. Crop after crop failed. Again and again the barren land must be mortgaged for taxes and food and next year's seed. The agony of hope ended when there was not harvest and no more credit, no money to pay interest and taxes; the banker took the land. Then the bank failed.

ROSE WILDER LANE (1886–1968), U.S. author. *On the Way Home,* ch. 1 (1962). Lane, the only child of Laura Ingalls Wilder, who wrote the famous "Little House" books for children, was recalling her and her parents' years in South Dakota. In 1897, drought forced them to travel by covered wagon to the Ozarks in search of a new life.

5 Girls, get an education and escape slavery.

RENA RIETVELD VERDUIN, U.S. farm woman. As quoted in *The Female Experience,* ch. 45, by Gerda Lerner (1977). Said in a 1907 debate organized by the Lansing Country Culture Club. She was reacting to the typical hard life of a farm woman.

6 Self-centeredness and selfishness has [sic] become the farmer's way of life ... instead of neighborliness, conservation, and families.

LOU ANNE KLING, U.S. government worker. As quoted in *The Great Divide*, book 1, section 3, by Studs Terkel (1988).

Kling was state coordinator for the farm advocate program of the Minnesota Department of Agriculture.

7 They were masculine toys. They were tall wishes. They were the ribs of the modern world.

RITA DOVE (b. 1952), U.S. poet and fiction writer. "Silos," last paragraph of the prose poem (1989).

FASHION

1 ... too much attention is paid to dress by those who have neither the excuse of ample means nor of social claims. ... The injury done by this state of things to the morals and the manners of our lower classes is incalculable.

MRS. H. O. WARD (1824–1899), U.S. author. *Sensible Etiquette of the Best Society Customs, Manners, Morals, and Home Culture, Compiled from the Best Authorities*, ch. 8 (1878).

2 The principle of fashion is ... the principle of the kaleidoscope. A new year can only bring us a new combination of the same elements; and about once in so often we go back and begin again.

KATHERINE FULLERTON GEROULD (1879–1944), U.S. author. *Modes and Morals*, ch. 2 (1920).

3 A completely indifferent attitude toward clothes in women seems to me to be an admission of inferiority, of perverseness, or of a lack of realization of her place in the world

as a woman. Or—what is even more hopeless and pathetic—it's an admission that she has given up, that she is beaten, and refuses longer to stand up to the world.

HORTENSE ODLUM (1892– ?), U.S. businesswoman. *A Woman's Place*, ch. 11 (1939).

Odlum was president of Bonwit Teller, a New York City women's store.

4 Dressing up is a bore. At a certain age, you decorate yourself to attract the opposite sex, and at a certain age, I did that. But I'm past that age.

KATHARINE HEPBURN (b. 1909), U.S. actor. As quoted in *Famous Actors and Actresses on the American Stage*, vol. 2, by William C. Young (1975).

First quoted in *Time* magazine (November 7, 1969), when she was sixty years old. She was said to own "20 pairs of beige slacks, white shirts and black sweaters" so that: "When she gets up in the morning, she knows what she's going to wear."

5 Fashion is an imposition, a rein on freedom.

GOLDA MEIR (1898–1978), Israeli Prime Minister; born in Russia. As quoted in *Ms.* magazine, p. 104 (April 1973).

FATE

1 ... no human being is master of his fate, and ... we are all motivated far more than we care to admit by characteristics inherited from our ancestors which individual experiences of childhood can modify, repress, or enhance, but cannot erase.

AGNES E. MEYER (1887–1970), U.S. journalist. *Out of These Roots*, ch. 7 (1953).

2 Fate is unalterable only in the sense that given a cause, a certain result must follow, but no cause is inevitable in itself, and man can shape his world if he does not resign himself to ignorance.

PEARL S. BUCK (1892–1973), U.S. author. *My Several Worlds* (1954).

3 . . . fate is not an eagle, it creeps like a rat.

ELIZABETH BOWEN (1899–1973), British novelist, story writer, essayist, and memoirist; born in Ireland. As quoted in *Elizabeth Bowen,* ch. 13, by Victoria Glendinning (1979).

FATHER-DAUGHTER RELATIONSHIPS

1 When I tried to talk to my father about the kind of work I might do after college, he said, "You know, Charlotte, I've been giving a lot of thought to that, and it seems to me that the world really needs good, competent secretaries. Your English degree will help you." He said this with perfect seriousness. I was an A student at Bryn Mawr . . .

CHARLOTTE PALMER (b. c. 1925), U.S. homemaker. As quoted in *The Fifties,* ch. 3, by Brett Harvey (1993).

Palmer was an interviewee in Harvey's oral history of the 1950s.

2 Father told me if I could get my fingers
to ballet the typewriter keys
to Nureyev the steno pad
everything would be perfect.

LYNNE SAVITT, U.S. poet. "Self Worth and the Typist," lines 1–4 (1979).

Rudolf Nureyev (1938–1993) was a great Russian ballet dancer who defected to the United States in 1961.

3 I stand where Papa stood. I wear Papa's robes.

DEBORAH PARTRIDGE WOLFE (b. 1916), U.S. minister and educator. As quoted in *Past and Promise,* part 4, by Ellen J. Wayman (1990).

Said in an interview with the author on January 10, 1986. She was referring to herself becoming a Baptist minister like her father when she was 54. She also spent thirty-five years as a faculty member at Queens College (New York).

4 Dad and I had breakfast this morning. We had a look at each other's speeches. He would have used mine, but he's not a lesbian. I would have used his, but I'm not a Republican.

DIANE MOSBACHER, U.S. psychiatrist. As quoted in *Newsweek* magazine, p. 15 (July 18, 1991).

The daughter of United States Secretary of Commerce Robert Mosbacher, she said this in a commencement address at Pitzer College.

5 My father's ashes are not yet interred. . . . strangely, I find the fact that he isn't properly laid to rest helps me when I'm doing this play.

LYNN REDGRAVE (b. 1943), British actor; relocated to America. As quoted in the *New York Times Magazine,* p. 88 (June 6, 1993).

On how personal experience informs acting. Redgrave was the daughter of the great Shakespearean actor Sir Michael Redgrave (1908–1985) and the sister of actors Vanessa (b. 1937) and Corin (b. 1939) Redgrave. The play in question was *Shakespeare for My Father.*

FATHER-SON RELATIONSHIPS

1 I'll come up the steps to the house and the gardener will be clipping away at the hedges and he'll say, "Good evening, Mr. Younger." And I'll say, "Hello, Jefferson, how are you this evening?" And I'll go inside and Ruth will come downstairs and meet me at the door and we'll kiss each other and she'll take my arm and we'll go up to your room to see you sitting on the floor with the catalogues of all the great schools in America around you. . . . All the great schools in the world! And—and I'll say, all right son—it's your seventeenth birthday, what is it you've decided? . . . Just tell me, what it is you want to be—and you'll *be* it. . . . Whatever you want to be—Yessir! You just name it, so . . . and I hand you the world!

LORRAINE HANSBERRY (1930–1965), African American playwright. *A Raisin in the Sun*, act 2, scene 2 (1959).

Walter Lee Younger, the ne'er-do-well protagonist of this play about a family in a poor African American Chicago neighborhood, describes to his young son what life would be like if he ever attained the wealth he dreams of. Ruth is Walter Lee's wife.

FEAR

1 A clear and innocent conscience fears nothing.

ELIZABETH I (1533–1603), British monarch, Queen of England (1558–1603). As quoted in *The Sayings of Queen Elizabeth*, ch. 11, by Frederick Chamberlin (1923).

To the Spanish Ambassador.

2 . . . religion can only change when the emotions which fill it are changed; and the religion of personal fear remains nearly at the level of the savage.

GEORGE ELIOT (1819–1880), British novelist. *Middlemarch*, ch. 61 (1871–1872).

3 One of the greatest faults of the women of the present time is a silly fear of things, and one object of the education of girls should be to give them knowledge of what things are really dangerous.

ELLEN HENRIETTA SWALLOW RICHARDS, (1842–1911) U.S. chemist and educator. As quoted in *The Life of Ellen H. Richards*, ch. 17, by Caroline L. Hunt (1912).

Said sometime in the early 1900s.

4 I have actually gotten to like fear . . .

PEARL WHITE (1889–1938), U.S. actor. *Just Me* (1919).

White starred in *The Perils of Pauline*, a movie adventure series that featured dangerous stunt work.

5 . . . an institution cannot be run progressively on a basis of fear.

MARY B. HARRIS (1874–1957), U.S. prison administrator. *I Knew Them in Prison*, ch. 4 (1936).

6 . . . to be scared is such a release from all the logy weight of procrastination, of dallying and pokiness! You burn into work. It is as though gravity were removed and you walked lightly to the moon like an angel.

BRENDA UELAND (1891–1985), U.S. magazine writer. *Me*, ch. 6 (1939).

On overcoming lethargy and a tendency to procrastinate when, having decided to divorce her husband, she was suddenly faced with the need to support herself and her baby daughter.

7 *Love your enemies.* I saw this admonition now as simple, sensible advice. I knew I could face an angry, murderous mob without even the beginning of fear if I could love them. Like a flame, love consumes fear, and thus make true defeat impossible.

SARAH PATTON BOYLE, U.S. civil rights activist and author. *The Desegregated Heart,* part 2, ch. 2 (1962).

Boyle, a white Virginian who, beginning in the early 1950s, publicly advocated integration, recalled her empowering compassion and "love" even for those whites who bitterly opposed her.

8 Life, from beginning to end, is fear. Yes, it is pain, yes, it is desire, but more than anything it is fear; a certain amount rational, an enormous amount irrational. All political cruelties stem from that overwhelming fear. To push back the threatening forces, to offer primitive sacrifices, to give up some in the hope that others will be saved . . . that is the power struggle. That is the outsidedness of the poor, the feeble, the infantile. That is the outsidedness of Jews. That is the outsidedness of blacks. That is the outsidedness of women.

VIVIAN GORNICK (b. 1935), U.S. sociologist. *Woman in Sexist Society,* ch. 4 (1971).

9 I wanted to learn to fly, not because it was the smart thing to do in the 1920s, but because I was afraid of anything that flew. . . . I reasoned that if I learned to fly, I might conquer my fear of it. The remedy worked.

JOY BRIGHT HANCOCK (1898–1986), U.S. naval officer. *Lady in the Navy,* ch. 3 (1972).

In 1925, Hancock's husband of fifteen months had died in a plane crash. Here she was explaining why she became a student pilot in the late 1920s. Later, she would become an officer in the WAVES, the U. S. Navy's women's division.

10 I write for those women who do not speak, for those who do not have a voice because they were so terrified, because we are taught to respect fear more than ourselves. We've been taught that silence would save us, but it won't.

AUDRE LORDE (1934–1992), African American lesbian author and feminist. *Black Women Writers at Work,* ch. 8, by Claudia Tate (1985).

Lorde was an African American lesbian feminist poet and autobiographer.

11 . . . heaven may be only the mind's fear of the wonders it imagines.

DEBORAH DIGGES (b. 1950), U.S. author. "Ancestral Lights," lines 35–36 (1986).

12 What I fear is being in the presence of evil and doing nothing. I fear that more than death.

OTILIA DE KOSTER, Panamanian civil rights monitor. As quoted in *Newsweek* magazine, p. 15 (December 19, 1988).

On being asked "if she feared for her life or her family."

FEARFULNESS

1 I am afraid if there is anything to be afraid of. A precipice cannot hurt you. Lions and tigers can. The streets of New York I consider more dangerous than the Matterhorn to a thoroughly competent and careful climber.

ANNIE SMITH PECK (1850–1935), U.S. mountain climber. As quoted in *WomenSports* magazine, p. 15 (December 1977).

Said c. 1925 by the pioneering climber who, at seventy-five, was still scaling mountains. She conquered her last peak at age 82: the 5,363–foot Mt. Madison in New Hampshire.

2   I have not ceased being fearful, but I have ceased to let fear control me. I have accepted fear as a part of life, specifically the fear of change, the fear of the unknown, and I have gone ahead despite the pounding in the heart that says: turn back, turn back, you'll die if you venture too far.

ERICA JONG, U.S. author. In an essay in *The Writer on Her Work,* ch. 13 (1980).

FEMALE SUPREMACY

1   I consider women a great deal superior to men. Men are physically strong, but women are morally better. . . . It is woman who keeps the world in balance.

MRS. CHALKSTONE, U.S. suffragist. As quoted in *History of Woman Suffrage,* vol. 2, ch. 16, by Elizabeth Cady Stanton, Susan B. Anthony, and Matilda Joslyn Gage (1882).

Speaking on May 14, 1863, at a national convention of the Woman's National Loyal League. Chalkstone had travelled from California to attend.

2   Could it not be that just at the moment masculinity has brought us to the brink of nuclear destruction or ecological suicide, women are beginning to rise in response to the Mother's call to save her planet and create instead the next stage of evolution? Can our revolution mean anything else than the reversion of social and economic control to Her representatives among Womankind,

and the resumption of Her worship on the face of the Earth? *Do we dare demand less?*

JANE ALPERT (b. 1947), U.S. anti–Vietnam war activist and terrorist. *Ms.* magazine, p. 94 (August 1973).

These are the closing lines of Alpert's famous "letter" to her "Sisters in the Weather Underground" articulating a "new feminist theory" and assuming women's biological superiority and "mother right." She, and those to whom she was ostensibly writing (though the letter was sent directly to *Ms.*) were fugitives from justice at the time, having committed violent crimes in the service of political goals.

FEMININITY

1   . . . a woman who is not feminine is a monster in creation.

ELIZABETH MISSING SEWELL (1815–1906), British author. *Principles of Education, Drawn from Nature and Revelation, and Applied to Female Education in the Upper Classes,* ch. 32 (1866).

2   When a woman starts out in the world on a mission, secular or religious, she should leave her feminine charms at home.

JANE GREY SWISSHELM (1815–1884), U.S. newspaperwoman, abolitionist, and human rights activist. *Half a Century,* ch. 21 (1880).

3   Men insist that they don't mind women succeeding so long as they retain their "femininity". Yet the qualities that men consider "feminine"—timidity, submissiveness, obedience, silliness, and self-debasement—are the very qualities best guaranteed to assure the defeat of even the most gifted aspirant.

ELIZABETH GOULD DAVIS (b. 1910), U.S. feminist and author. *The First Sex,* ch. 22 (1971).

4 When I put the shot, it's feminine, because I'm female. Athletic motion doesn't have a gender.

MAREN SEIDLER (b. 1953), U.S. shot put champion. As quoted in *WomenSports* magazine, p. 58 (February 1977).
Seidler was 6'2" tall.

5 By act of Congress, male officers are gentlemen, but by act of God, we are ladies. We don't have to be little mini-men and try to be masculine and use obscene language to come across. I can take you and flip you on the floor and put your arms behind your back and you'll never move again, without your ever knowing that I can do it.

SHERIAN GRACE CADORIA (b. 1940), African American military officer. As quoted in *I Dream a World,* by Brian Lanker (1989).
A Brigadier General, she was then the highest-ranking African American woman in the United States armed forces and one of only four woman Army generals.

FEMINISM

1 . . . such are the secret outcomes of revolution! that two women can meet
. . .
as two eyes in one brow receiving at one moment the rainbow of the world.

ADRIENNE RICH (b. 1929), U.S. poet and feminist. "To Judith, Taking Leave," lines 81–83 and 86–88 (1962).
More than a decade later, Rich would "come out" as a lesbian.

2 I have met many feminists who were not Lesbians—but I have never met a Lesbian who was not a feminist.

MARTHA SHELLEY (b. c. 1942), U.S. lesbian author and political activist. *Notes of a Radical Lesbian (essay)* (1969).

3 Bitches are aggressive, assertive, domineering, overbearing, strong-minded, spiteful, hostile, direct, blunt, candid, obnoxious, thick-skinned, hard-headed, vicious, dogmatic, competent, competitive, pushy, loud-mouthed, independent, stubborn, demanding, manipulative, egoistic, driven, achieving, over-whelming, threatening, scary, ambitious, tough, brassy, masculine, boisterous and turbulent. A Bitch takes shit from no one. You may not like her, but you cannot ignore her.

JOREEN, U.S. feminist and author. As quoted in *The Decade of Women,* by Suzanne Levine and Harriet Lyons (1980).

FEMINISM: EARLY 20TH CENTURY

1 I . . . have never been able to find out precisely what feminism is. I only know that people call me a feminist when I express sentiments that differentiate me from a doormat, or a prostitute.

REBECCA WEST (1892–1983), British author. As quoted in *Time* magazine, p. 51 (March 9, 1992).
Written in 1913.

2 . . . feminism is the attempt of women to grow up, to accept the responsibilities of life, to outgrow those characteristics of childhood—selfishness and unworldliness—that we require our boys to outgrow, but that we permit and by our social system encourage our girls to retain.

Henrietta Rodman (1878–?), U.S. feminist. As quoted in the *New York Times*, section 5, p. 9 (January 24, 1915).

Rodman, a rather flamboyant activist, organized the Feminist Alliance in April 1914.

3 If the feminist program goes to pieces on the arrival of the first baby, it's false and useless.

Crystal Eastman (1881–1928), U.S. social/political activist and author. *On Women and Revolution*, part 1 (1978).

Written in 1920, the same year that the Nineteenth Amendment to the Constitution took effect, enfranchising women after a 72-year struggle for suffrage.

4 Feminism, like Boston, is a state of mind. It is the state of mind of women who realize that their whole position in the social order is antiquated, as a woman cooking over an open fire with heavy iron pots would know that her entire housekeeping was out of date.

Rheta Childe Dorr (1866–1948), U.S. journalist. *A Woman of Fifty,* 2nd. ed., ch. 16 (1924).

5 Feminists have emphasized for a long time the importance of each woman's individual entity and the necessity of economic independence. Perhaps it was necessary. But now I think we need some emphasis on the instinctive side of life, sex and motherhood. . . . Life isn't all earning your living. Unfortunately we fall in love and Feminism must take that into consideration.

Dora Black Russell (1894–1986), Quoted in *On Women and Revolution*, part 1, by Crystal Eastman (1978). From an article first published in *Equal Rights* on June 5, 1926.

Black was married to the British philosopher Bertrand Russell.

6 I was always a feminist, for I liked intellectual revolt as much as I disliked physical violence. On the whole, I think women have lost something precious, but have gained, immeasurably, by the passing of the old order.

Ellen Glasgow (1873–1945), U.S. novelist. *The Woman Within,* ch. 14 (1954).

FEMINISM: LATE 20TH CENTURY

1 . . . I want men
to take us seriously.
I am tired wanting them to think
about right and wrong.
I want them to fear.

Susan Griffin (b. 1943), U.S. author and feminist. "I Like to Think of Harriet Tubman," lines 74–78 (c. 1970).

This poem is a protest against inadequate government measures to provide food for poor children. Tubman (*c.* 1820–1913) was an escaped slave who, armed with a loaded revolver, ushered hundreds of other runaway slaves to freedom via the network of secret safe houses known as the Underground Railroad.

2 To the "feminist" of both sexes, femininity is synonymous with the eternal female principle, connoting strength, integrity, wisdom, justice, dependability, and a psychic power foreign and therefore dangerous to the plodding masculists of both sexes.

Elizabeth Gould Davis (b. 1910), U.S. feminist and author. *The First Sex,* ch. 22 (1971).

"Masculist" is a coined word meant to correlate grammatically with "feminist."

3 I am a writer and a feminist, and the two seem to be constantly in conflict. . . . ever since I became loosely involved with it, it has seemed to me one of the recurring ironies of this movement that there is no way to tell the truth about it without, in some small way, seeming to hurt it.

NORA EPHRON (b. 1941), U.S. author and humorist. *Crazy Salad,* ch. 13 (1973).

4 We are trying to live as if we were an experiment conducted by the future

MARGE PIERCY (b. 1936), U.S. poet, novelist, and political activist. "Rough Times," lines 1–3 (1976).
On women's trying to construct lives that break with traditional sex roles.

5 . . . feminism is a political term and it must be recognized as such: it is political in women's terms. What are these terms? Essentially it means making connections: between personal power and economic power, between domestic oppression and labor exploitation, between plants and chemicals, feelings and theories; it means making connections between our inside worlds and the outside world.

ANICA VESEL MANDER, U.S. author and feminist. As quoted in *The Political Palate,* ch. 5, by Betsey Beaven et al. (1980).

6 Today masses of black women in the U.S. refuse to acknowledge that they have much to gain by feminist struggle. They fear feminism. They have stood in place so long that they are afraid to move. They fear change. They fear losing what little they have.

BELL HOOKS (b. c. 1955), African American author, feminist, and civil rights advocate. *Ain't I a Woman?* Ch. 5 (1981).

7 I think that any woman who sets goals for herself and takes her own life seriously and moves to achieve the goals that she wants as a person in her own right is a feminist.

FRANCES KUEHN (b. 1943), U.S. artist. As quoted in *Lives and Works,* by Lynn F. Miller and Sally S. Swenson (1981).

8 A central tenet of modern feminist thought has been the assertion that "all women are oppressed." This assertion implies that women share a common lot, that factors like class, race, religion, sexual preference, etc. do not create a diversity of experience that determines the extent to which sexism will be an oppressive force in the lives of individual women.

BELL HOOKS (b. 1955), African American author and educator. *Feminist Theory,* ch. 1 (1984).
hooks had grown up poor in Hopkinsville, Kentucky.

9 [Feminists are] Women in limousines who give each other awards.

LISA SLIWA (b. 1953), U.S. national director of the Guardian Angels, a militant urban security organization. As quoted in *Newsweek* magazine, p. 13 (July 7, 1986).

10 If you say, "I'm for equal pay," that's a reform. But if you say. "I'm a feminist," that's . . . a transformation of society.

GLORIA STEINEM (b. 1934), U.S. feminist, author, and editor. As quoted in *Time*, p. 56 (March 9, 1992).

membering her upbringing. Feinstein was sometimes criticized as inadequately committed to feminist causes.

11 Nonwhite and working-class women, if they are ever to identify with the organized women's movement, must see their own diverse experiences reflected in the practice and policy statements of these predominantly white middle-class groups.

KIMBERLÉ CRENSHAW (b. 1959), African American author. *Race-ing Justice, En-gendering Power*, ch. 14 (1992).

12 If you excommunicate one of us there will be 10 more to step up and take her place. Excommunicate those 10 and there will be 100 to take their places.

LYNN KNAVEL WHITESIDES, U.S. Mormon feminist. As quoted in the *New York Times*, p. 7 (October 2, 1993).

The President of the feminist Mormon Women's Forum, Whitesides had been "disfellowshipped" by the church for advocating an expanded role for women in it and greater freedom of expression for the faculty at Brigham Young University, which is owned by the Mormons. Whitesides said this on a Salt Lake City television program.

13 There was no need for a feminist philosophy. My mother never stopped to think that she couldn't do something. . . . You didn't have to change the rules. Just be a strong and skilled individual, work hard, do your homework, and you can do it.

KATHERINE BERMAN MARIANO (b. 1957), U.S. housewife. As quoted in *Dianne Feinstein*, ch. 15, by Jerry Roberts (1994).

Mariano, the only child of Dianne Feinstein (b. 1933), former San Francisco Mayor and current United States Senator from California, was re-

14 . . . feminists solidarity rooted in a commitment to progressive politics must include a space for rigorous critique, for dissent, or we are doomed to reproduce in progressive communities the very forms of domination we seek to oppose.

BELL HOOKS (b. c. 1955), African American author, feminist, and human rights advocate. *Outlaw Culture*, ch. 19 (1994).

hooks was criticizing the feminists who closed ranks behind Anita Hill (b. 1956), a conservative African American law professor who in 1991 accused Clarence Thomas (b. 1948), an African American conservative Supreme Court nominee, of past sexual harassment. Heralding Hill as a heroine, these feminists often failed to consider that her general political stance was antithetical to theirs.

FEMINISM: THE CONCEPT

1 One may divide women in the woman's movement into two groups: the Feminists and the reformers who are not in the least Feminists; who do not care tuppence about equality for itself. . . . Now, almost every women's organization recognizes that reformers are far more common than Feminists, that the passion to decide to look after your fellow-men, and especially women, to do good to them in your way is far more common than the desire to put into everyone's hand the power to look after themselves.

LADY MARGARET RHONDDA (1883–1958), British feminist. As quoted in *Everyone Was Brave*, ch. 8, by William L. O'Neill (1969).

From a speech made by the English militant before a National Woman's Party luncheon in Paris. The speech was printed in the June 19, 1926, issue of the Party's journal, *Equal Rights*.

FICTION

1 Possibly the Creator did not make the world chiefly for the purpose of providing studies for gifted novelists; but if he had done so, we can scarcely imagine that He could have offered anything much better in the way of material . . .

ELIZABETH STUART PHELPS (1844–1911), U.S. novelist and short story writer. *Chapters from a Life*, ch. 12 (1897).

2 "The proper stuff of fiction" does not exist; everything is the proper stuff of fiction, every feeling, every thought; every quality of brain and spirit is drawn upon; no perception comes amiss.

VIRGINIA WOOLF (1882–1941), British novelist, essayist, and diarist. *The Common Reader*, ch. 13 (1925).

3 No one can write a best-seller by taking thought. The slightest touch of insincerity blurs its appeal. The writer who keeps his tongue in his cheek, who knows that he is writing for fools and that, therefore, he had better write like a fool, makes a respectable living out of serials and novelettes; but he will never make the vast, the blaring, half a million success. That comes of blended sincerity and vitality.

REBECCA WEST (1892–1983), British author. *The Strange Necessity*, ch. 11 (1928).

4 Writing fiction is . . . an endless and always defeated effort to capture some quality of life without killing it.

ROSE WILDER LANE (1886–1965), U.S. author. *Old Hometown*, ch. 1 (1935).

In addition to writing books of her own, Lane helped her mother, Laura Ingalls Wilder (1867–1957), develop her famous series of autobiographical "Little House" books for children.

5 Fiction reveals truths that reality obscures.

JESSAMYN WEST (1902–1984), U.S. novelist. *To See the Dream*, part 1 (1956).

6 What is a novel? I say: an invented story. At the same time a story which, though invented has the power to ring true. True to what? True to life as the reader knows life to be or, it may be, feels life to be. And I mean the adult, the grown-up reader. Such a reader has outgrown fairy tales, and we do not want the fantastic and the impossible. So I say to you that a novel must stand up to the adult tests of reality.

ELIZABETH BOWEN (1899–1973), British novelist, story writer, essayist, and memoirist; born in Ireland. *Seven Winters*, part 2, sect. 4, ch. 2 (1962).

From "Truth and Fiction," a 1956 talk which Bowen gave on a British Broadcasting Company (BBC) Home Service radio program.

7 The beginning of human knowledge is through the senses, and the fiction writer begins where human perception begins. He appeals through the senses, and you cannot appeal to the senses with abstractions.

FLANNERY O'CONNOR (1925–1964), U.S. fiction writer and essayist. *Mystery and Manners*, part 3 (1969).

Written c. 1960.

8 . . . the main concern of the fiction writer is with mystery as it is incarnated in human life.

FLANNERY O'CONNOR (1925–1964), U.S. fiction writer and essayist. *Mystery and Manners*, part 5 (1969). Written in 1964.

9 I expect that any day now, I will have said all I have to say; I'll have used up all my characters, and then I'll be free to get on with my real life.

ANNE TYLER (b. 1941), U.S. novelist. As quoted in *The Writer on Her Work*, ch. 2, by Janet Sternburg (1980).

10 Morality for the novelist is expressed not so much in the choice of subject matter as in the plot of the narrative, which is perhaps why in our morally bewildered time novelists have often been timid about plot.

JANE RULE (b. 1931), Canadian fiction writer and essayist; born in the U. S.. *Outlander*, part 2, essay 1 (1981).

Many of Rule's story and novel plots centered around lesbian relationships.

11 Greater than scene . . . is situation. Greater than situation is implication. Greater than all of these is a single, entire human being, who will never be confined in any frame.

EUDORA WELTY (b. 1909), U.S. fiction writer. *One Writer's Beginnings*, ch. 3 (1984).

12 It was like taking a beloved person to the airport and returning to an empty house. I miss the people. I miss the world.

SUSAN SONTAG (b. 1933), U.S. author. As quoted in the *New York Times Magazine*, "Su-

san Sontag Finds Romance," by Leslie Garis (August 2, 1992).

On leaving the last section of her latest novel, *The Volcano Lover*, at her publisher's office.

13 . . . fiction never exceeds the reach of the writer's courage.

DOROTHY ALLISON (b. 1949), U.S. author and lesbian feminist. *Skin*, ch. 22 (1994).

Allison wrote novels and short stories, as well as poetry and essays.

FICTIONAL CHARACTERS

1 It was strange to think that all the great women of fiction were, until Jane Austen's day, not only seen by the other sex, but seen only in relation to the other sex. And how small a part of woman's life is that . . .

VIRGINIA WOOLF (1882–1941), British author. *A Room of One's Own*, ch. 5 (1929). Jane Austen (1775–1817), an Englishwoman, was the first important woman novelist.

2 I became, and remain, my characters' close and intent watcher: their director, never. Their creator I cannot feel that I was, or am.

ELIZABETH BOWEN (1899–1973), British novelist, essayist, and memoirist; born in Ireland. *Pictures and Conversations*, ch. 1 (1975).

FIRST LADIES OF THE UNITED STATES

1 Always be on time. Never try to make any personal engagements. Do as little talking as humanly possible. Never be disturbed by anything. Always do what you're told to do as quickly as possible. Remember to lean back in a parade, so that people can see your husband. Don't get too fat to ride three on a seat. Get out of the way as quickly as you're not needed.

ELEANOR ROOSEVELT (1884–1962), U.S. First Lady, author, and speaker. As quoted in *Eleanor and Franklin*, ch. 50, by Joseph P. Lash (1971).

Written c. 1940, on what the wife of a "public man" must do. Roosevelt was the wife of President Franklin Delano Roosevelt (1882–1945; President, 1933–1945).

FLATTERY

1 Eulogy is nice, but one does not learn anything from it.

ELLEN TERRY (1847–1928), British actor. *Ellen Terry's Memoirs*, 2nd. ed., ch. 5 (1932).

Written in 1906 or 1907. Terry, a beloved stage star, was much eulogized.

FLIGHT

1 Flight is intolerable contradiction.

MURIEL RUKEYSER (1913–1980), U.S. poet. "Theory of Flight," line 8 (1935).

FLIGHT ATTENDANTS

1 If a girl's a stewardess, she might as well forget it after twenty-six. They no longer have compulsory retirement, but the girls get into a rut at that age. A lot of them start showing the rough life they've lived.

BERYL SIMPSON, U.S. employment counselor; former airline reservationist. As quoted in *Working*, book 2, by Studs Terkel (1973).

2 I don't think of myself as a sex symbol or a servant. I think of myself as somebody who knows how to open

the door of a 747 in the dark, upside down, and under water.

U.S. flight attendant (name not given). As quoted in *The Decade of Women*, by Suzanne Levine and Harriet Lyons (1980).

3 If you are trying to run a whorehouse in the sky, then get a license.

MARTHA GRIFFITHS (b. 1912), U.S. politician. As quoted in *American Women in the 1960s*, ch. 14, by Blanche Linden-Ward and Carol Hurd Green (1991).

4 Here I am. . . . You get the parts of me you like and also the parts that make you uncomfortable. You have to understand that other people's comfort is no longer my job. I am no longer a flight attendant.

PATRICIA IRELAND (b. 1935), U.S. feminist. As quoted in the *New York Times Magazine*, p. 38 (March 1, 1992).

Ireland, who was President of the National Organization for Women, was reacting to some people's uneasiness at the disclosure that she had both a husband and a woman "companion."

FOOD

1 There are very few men and women, I suspect, who cooked and marketed their way through the past war without losing forever some of the nonchalant extravagance of the Twenties. They will feel, until their final days on earth, a kind of culinary caution: butter, no matter how unlimited, is a precious substance not lightly to be wasted; meats, too, and eggs, and all the far-brought spices of the world, take on a new significance, having once been so rare. And that is good, for there can be no more shameful

carelessness than with the food we eat for life itself. When we exist without thought or thanksgiving we are not men, but beasts.

M. F. K. FISHER (1908–1992), U.S. culinary writer and autobiographer. *How to Cook a Wolf,* rev. ed., Introduction to the Revised Edition (1951).

The first edition of this book had been published in 1942, when World War II was still in progress. It seems likely that even before that war, the "nonchalant extravagance of the Twenties" was checked by the Great Depression of the 1930s.

2 Salad is roughage and a French idea.

U.S. grandmother. As quoted in "Once a Tramp, Always . . . ," by M. F. K. Fisher (1969).

Fisher was quoting her own grandmother.

3 Wine and cheese are ageless companions, like aspirin and aches, or June and moon, or good people and noble ventures . . .

M. F. K. FISHER (1908–1992), U.S. culinary writer and autobiographer. Introduction (1981).

In English, the title of this book (which was written and published in the United States) is "Wine and Cheese." The book's authors are Marylou Scavarda and Kate Sater.

FOOLISHNESS

I There is small disproportion betwixt a fool who useth not wit because he hath it not and him that useth it not when it should avail him.

ELIZABETH I (1533–1603), Queen of England (1558–1603). As quoted in *The Sayings of Queen Elizabeth,* ch. 11, by Frederick Chamberlin (1923).

Said c. 1587 to Baron Buckhurst (born Thomas Sackville, first Earl of Dorset), on a diplomatic mission to the Netherlands, where he displeased her.

2 . . . the yearly expenses of the existing religious system . . . exceed in these United States twenty millions of dollars. Twenty millions! For teaching what? Things unseen and causes unknown! . . . Twenty millions would more than suffice to make us wise; and alas! do they not more than suffice to make us foolish?

FRANCES WRIGHT (1795–1852), Scottish author and speaker; relocated to America. *Course of Popular Lectures,* lecture 3 (1829).

3 Only a fool would refuse to enter a fool's paradise—when that's the only paradise he'll ever have a chance to enter.

JESSAMYN WEST (1902–1984), U.S. novelist. *To See the Dream,* part 1 (1956).

FOOTBALL

I I don't know if everybody is ready to hear a woman tell them so-and-so is going to run off left tackle. But you know what? They're going to hear it.

LESLEY VISSER, U.S. sports reporter and announcer. As quoted in *Sports Illustrated,* p. 85 (June 17, 1991).

FRANK, ANNE

I . . . I was hoping she would still come back and that I would be able to give it to her. I wanted to see her smile at me.

MIEP GIES (b. c. 1908), Dutch former secretary; born in Austria. As quoted in the *New York Times,* p. 27 (March 11, 1995).

At the beginning of World War II, Gies, a Christian, was a secretary in the food chemicals business of Otto Frank, a Jew. To escape the Nazis, Frank, his family, and four other Jews moved into a secret apartment above the business. Gies was one of five people aware of their hideout and took food to them daily; after the Jews were discovered and taken away on August 4, 1944, for delivery to concentration camps, Gies defied Nazi orders to stay out of the no-longer-secret apartment. There she found strewn across the floor the handwritten diary pages of Frank's younger daughter, Anne (1929–1945); at great personal risk, she retrieved and kept them. Here she was explaining why she waited until she was certain that Anne was dead before she gave the diary to Otto Frank, the only member of the family who survived the camps. He arranged for its publication in 1947, and it became an extraordinarily poignant and important document of Nazi oppression.

FREEDOM

1   I looked at my hands, to see if I was de same person now I was free. Dere was such a glory ober eberything, de sun came like gold trou de trees, and ober de fields, and I felt like I was in heaven.

HARRIET TUBMAN (c. 1820–1913), African American abolitionist. As quoted in *Harriet, the Moses of Her People,* by Sarah Bradford (1869).
Bradford was the friend and first biographer of the great abolitionist and ex-slave who, after escaping to freedom, returned nineteen times to the South and ushered more than 300 other runaway slaves to freedom in the North. Here, Tubman was remembering how she felt when, as a fugitive slave, she finally reached free soil.

2   . . . the mistakes that we male and female mortals make when we have our own way might fairly raise some wonder that we are so fond of it.

GEORGE ELIOT (1819–1880), British novelist. *Middlemarch,* ch. 9 (1871–1872).

3   All real freedom springs from necessity, for it can be gained only

through the exercise of the individual will, and that will can be roused to energetic action only by the force of necessity acting upon it from the outside to spur it to effort.

ANNA C. BRACKETT (1836–1911), U.S. author. *The Technique of Rest,* ch. 3 (1892).

4   The poor, stupid, free American citizen! Free to starve, free to tramp the highways of this great country, he enjoys universal suffrage, and by that right, he has forged chains around his limbs. The reward that he receives is stringent labor laws prohibiting the right of boycott, of picketing, of everything, except the right to be robbed of the fruits of his labor.

EMMA GOLDMAN (1869–1940), U.S. anarchist and author; born in Russia. *Anarchism and Other Essays,* 3rd rev. ed., ch. 9 (1917).

5   You realize the futility of worry. You learn to hate the small and the little. Life is a pie which you cut in large slices, not grudgingly, not sparingly. You know your limitations and proceed to eliminate them; your abilities, and proceed to develop them. You are free.

ALICE FOOTE MACDOUGALL, (1867–1945) U.S. businesswoman. Ch. 7 (1928).
On the liberating effect of struggling to establish a business and succeeding.

6   The question is whether personal freedom is worth the terrible effort, the never-lifted burden and risks of self-reliance.

ROSE WILDER LANE (1886–1968), U.S. author. As quoted in *The Ghost in the Little House,* prologue, by William V. Holtz (1993). Said in 1936.

7 ... liberty is the one thing no man can have unless he grants it to others.

RUTH BENEDICT (1887–1948), U.S. anthropologist. *An Anthropologist at Work,* part 4 (1959).
From "Primitive Freedom," a paper written in 1942.

8 ... the one thing that everybody wants is to be free, to talk to eat to drink to walk to think, to please, to wish, and to do it now.

GERTRUDE STEIN (1874–1946), U.S. author; relocated to France. *Wars I Have Seen* (1945).
Written in 1943.

9 A society in which everyone works is not necessarily a free society and may indeed be a slave society; on the other hand, a society in which there is widespread economic insecurity can turn freedom into a barren and vapid right for the millions of people.

ELEANOR ROOSEVELT (1884–1962), U.S. author, speaker, and First Lady. As quoted in *Eleanor: The Years Alone,* ch. 3, by Joseph P. Lash (1972).
Said in 1948, responding to the representative from the Soviet Union who criticized the existence of unemployment in the United States.

10 Surely the day will come when color means nothing more than skin tone, when religion is seen uniquely as a way to speak one's soul; when birth places have the weight of a throw of the dice and all men are born free, when understanding breeds love and brotherhood.

JOSEPHINE BAKER (1906–1975), French dancer and singer; born in United States. *Josephine,* ch. 16 (1977).

Written in 1963. Baker, a black performer, married a white Frenchman and assembled a multiracial, multireligion family of adopted children.

11 It is only when we speak what is right that we stand a chance at night of being blown to bits in our homes. Can we call this a free country, when I am afraid to go to sleep in my own home in Mississippi? ... I might not live two hours after I get back home, but I want to be a part of setting the Negro free in Mississippi.

FANNIE LOU HAMER (1917–1977), African American civil rights activist. As quoted in *This Little Light of Mine,* ch. 8, by Hay Mills (1993).
Said on September 13, 1965, in a hearing before the United States House of Representatives' Subcommittee on Elections.

12 ... how have I used rivers, how have I used wars
to escape writing of the worst thing of all—
not the crimes of other, not even our own death,
but the failure to want our freedom passionately enough
so that blighted elms, sick rivers, massacres would seem
mere emblems of that desecration of ourselves?

ADRIENNE RICH (b. 1929), U.S. poet and lesbian feminist. *Twenty-One Love Poems,* poem #7, lines 8–13 (1974–76).

13 ... the space left to freedom is very small. ... ends are inherent in human nature and the same for all.

HANNAH ARENDT (1906–1975), U.S. philosopher and political theorist; born in Germany. *The Life of the Mind,* vol. 2: *Willing,* ch. 7 (1978).

14 Like a lot of Black women, I have always had to invent the power my freedom requires . . .

JUNE JORDAN (b. 1936), African American poet and social critic. *On Call,* ch. 9 (1985). Written in 1984.

15 Bit by bit . . . she had claimed herself. Freeing yourself was one thing; claiming ownership of that freed self was another.

TONI MORRISON (b. 1931), African American novelist and essayist. *Beloved,* part 1 (1987).

Of the heroine, Sethe, twenty-eight days after she had escaped from slavery.

16 The "real movement" of history, it turns out, is fueled not by matter but by spirit, by the will to freedom.

GERTRUDE HIMMELFARB (b. 1922), U.S. historian. *On Looking Into the Abyss,* ch. 3 (1994).

Written in 1990.

FREEDOM OF EXPRESSION

1 Some of us who sit upon this platform have many a time been clamored down, and told that we had no right to speak, and that we were out of our place in public meetings; far be it from us, when women assemble, and a man has a thought in his soul, burning for utterance, to retaliate upon him.

SUSAN B. ANTHONY (1820–1906), U.S. suffragist. As quoted in *History of Woman Suffrage,* vol. 2, ch. 16, by Elizabeth Cady Stanton, Matilda Joslyn Gage, and herself (1882).

Speaking on May 14, 1863, at a national convention of the Woman's National Loyal League; a man who was attempting to speak had been shouted down by women claiming he had no right to speak or vote.

2 In our period, they say there is free speech.
They say there is no penalty for poets,
There is no penalty for writing poems.
They say this. This is the penalty.

MURIEL RUKEYSER (1913–1980), U.S. poet. "In Our Time," (1968).

3 For me, writing something down was the only road out.

ANNE TYLER (b. 1941), U.S. novelist. As quoted in *The Writer on Her Work,* ch. 2, by Janet Sternburg (1980).

4 As liberty of thought is absolute, so is liberty of speech, which is "inseparable" from the liberty of thought. Liberty of speech, moreover, is essential not only for its own sake but for the sake of truth, which requires absolute liberty for the utterance of unpopular and even demonstrably false opinions.

GERTRUDE HIMMELFARB (b. 1922), U.S. historian. *On Looking Into the Abyss,* ch. 4 (1994).

From "Liberty: 'One Very Simple Principle'," a paper written for a 1992 colloquium organized by the Institut fur die Vissenschaften vom Menschen.

5 The political core of any movement for freedom in the society has to have the political imperative to protect free speech.

BELL HOOKS (b. 1955), African American author, feminist, and human rights advocate. *Outlaw Culture,* ch. 5 (1994).

Reflecting on the tendency of some feminists and African American rights activists to advocate selective suppression—e.g., some feminists' advocacy of censoring pornography.

FREEDOM OF RELIGION

I   . . . a Christian has neither more nor less rights in our association than an atheist. When our platform becomes too narrow for people of all creeds and of no creeds, I myself cannot stand upon it.

SUSAN B. ANTHONY (1820–1906), U.S. suffragist. As quoted in *History of Woman Suffrage,* vol. 4, ch. 16, by Susan B. Anthony and Ida Husted Harper (1902).

Said at the twenty-eighth annual convention of the National Woman Suffrage Association, held January 23–28, 1896, in Washington, D.C.

FREEDOM OF THOUGHT

I   Persecution for opinion is the master vice of society.

FRANCES WRIGHT (1795–1852), Scottish author and speaker; relocated to America. *Course of Popular Lectures,* lecture 6 (1829).

FREEDOM, POLITICAL

I   I have given the best of myself and the best work of my life to help obtain political freedom for women, knowing that upon this rests the hope not only of the freedom of men but of the onward civilization of the world.

MARY S. ANTHONY (1827–1907), U.S. suffragist. As quoted in *History of Woman Suffrage,* vol. 5, ch. 7, by Ida Husted Harper (1922).

From a statement dictated a few days before her death in February 1907 and sent to the thirty-ninth annual convention of the National Woman Suffrage Association, which was convened later that month. It was read aloud by the association's president, the Rev. Anna Howard Shaw. Sister of the much better-known suffragist, Susan B. Anthony (1820–1906), Mary S. Anthony had become involved in women's rights activity even earlier. She had attended the famous Seneca Falls, N.Y., convention in 1848,

which was the first American convention dedicated to women's rights, and for many years had presided over the Political Equality Club of Rochester, N.Y.

FRIENDSHIP

I   In thought and sympathy we were one, and in the division of labor we exactly complemented each other. In writing we did better work than either could do alone. While she is slow and analytical in composition, I am rapid and synthetic. I am the better writer, she the better critic. She supplied the facts and statistics, I the philosophy and rhetoric, and, together, we have made arguments that have stood unshaken through the storms of long years. . . . So closely interwoven have been our lives, our purposes and experiences that, separated, we have a feeling of incompleteness—united, such strength of self-assertion that no ordinary obstacles, difficulties, or dangers ever appear to us insurmountable.

ELIZABETH CADY STANTON (1815–1902), U.S. suffragist, author, and social reformer. *Eighty Years and More (1815–1897),* chapters 10 and 11 (1898).

Of her long and fruitful association with sister suffragist Susan B. Anthony (1820–1906), whom she met in 1850.

2   So closely interwoven have been our lives, our purposes, and experiences that, separated, we have a feeling of incompleteness—united, such strength of self-association that no ordinary obstacles, difficulties, or dangers ever appear to us insurmountable.

ELIZABETH CADY STANTON (1815–1902), U.S. author, suffragist, and social reformer. *Elizabeth Cady Stanton as Revealed in her Letters, Diary and Reminiscences,* vol. 1, ch. 10 (1922).
Of her long friendship and professional association with Susan B. Anthony (1820–1906).

FRONTIER

I   Two deep human desires were at war . . . the longing for stability, for form, for permanence, which in its essence is the desire for death, and the opposing hunger for movement, change, instability and risk, which are life. Men came from the east and built these American towns because they wished to go no farther, and the towns they built were shaped by the urge to go onward.

ROSE WILDER LANE (1886–1965), U.S. author. *Old Hometown,* ch. 1 (1935).
Lane had grown up in a small Nebraska town.

2   . . . one thing that distinguishes a frontier is the precarious nature of the human hold on it.

KATHLEEN NORRIS (b. 1947), U.S. poet and farmer. *Dakota,* ch. 22 (1993).
Norris lived and farmed in rural Lemmon, South Dakota.

FUTILITY

I   It is the fixed that horrifies us, the fixed that assails us with the tremendous force of mindlessness. The fixed is a Mason jar, and we can't beat it open. . . . The fixed is a world without fire—dead flint, dead tinder, and nowhere a spark. It is motion without direction, force without power, the aimless proces-

sion of caterpillars round the rim of a vase, and I hate it because at any moment I myself might step to that charmed and glistening thread.

ANNIE DILLARD (b. 1945), U.S. essayist and autobiographer. *Pilgrim at Tinker Creek,* ch. 4 (1974).

FUTURE, THE

I   Living each day as a preparation for the next is an exciting way to live. Looking forward to something is much more fun than looking back at something—and much more constructive. If we can prepare ourselves so that we never have to think, "Oh, if I had only known, if I had only been ready," our lives can really be the great adventure we so passionately want them to be.

HORTENSE ODLUM (1892– ?), U.S. businesswoman. *A Woman's Place,* ch. 16 (1939).

2   By the year 2020, the year of perfect vision, the old will outnumber the young.

MAGGIE KUHN (b. 1905), U.S. senior rights activist. As quoted in *The Great Divide,* book 2, section 6, by Studs Terkel (1988).
Kuhn was the grand convener of the Gray Panthers, a militant organization that advocated the rights of the elderly.

3   The future depends entirely on what each of us does every day . . . a movement is only people moving.

GLORIA STEINEM (b. 1934), U.S. feminist, author, and editor. As quoted in *Time,* p. 57 (March 9, 1992).

4   . . . disconnecting from change does not recapture the past. It loses the future.

KATHLEEN NORRIS (b. 1947), U.S. poet and farmer. *Dakota*, ch. 9 (1993).

5 I have to live for the day, and not worry about or try to know what tomorrow brings. . . . if I've learned one thing from all that's happened to me, it's that if you would know what tomorrow brings, you may not want to live it.

MONICA SELES (b. 1973), Yugoslavian tennis player; relocated to America. As quoted in *Tennis* magazine, p. 44 (March 1994).
The former top-ranked woman singles tennis player in the world, she was reflecting on the experience of being stabbed a year earlier by Gunther Parche, a deranged fan of rival player Steffi Graf.

GAY LIBERATION MOVEMENT

1 The terrifying message of gay liberation is that men are capable of loving their brothers. It should be sweet news to every woman in the world, for, if the capacity of men to love whom they have been taught to treat as competitors and enemies can transcend their education, the world can begin to heal.

JANE RULE (b. 1931), Canadian lesbian, feminist, fiction writer, and essayist; born in America. *A Hot-Eyed Moderate*, part 2 (1985).

GENERATIONS

1 There is singularly nothing that makes a difference a difference in beginning and in the middle and in ending except that each generation has something different at which they are all looking. By this I mean so simply that anybody knows it that composition is the difference which makes each and all of them then different from other generations and this is what makes everything different otherwise they are all alike and everybody knows it because everybody says it.

GERTRUDE STEIN (1874–1946), U.S. author and patron of the arts; relocated to France. *Composition as Explanation* (1926).

2 . . . the task of youth is not only its own salvation but the salvation of those against whom it rebels, but in that case there must be something vital to rebel against and if the elderly stiffly refuse to put up a vigorous front of their own, it leaves the entire situation in a mist.

JANE ADDAMS (1860–1935), U.S. social reformer. *The Second Twenty Years at Hull-House, September 1909–September 1929*, Introduction (1930).

3 In time of war you know much more what children feel than in time of peace, not that children feel more but you have to know more about what they feel. In time of peace what children feel concerns the lives of children as children but in time of war there is a mingling there is not children's lives and grown up lives there is just lives and so quite naturally you have to know what children feel.

GERTRUDE STEIN (1874–1946), U.S. author; relocated to France. *Wars I Have Seen* (1945).
Written in 1943.

4 There are two barriers that often prevent communication between the young and their elders. The first is middle-aged forgetfulness of the

fact that they themselves are no longer young. The second is youthful ignorance of the fact that the middle aged are still alive.

JESSAMYN WEST (1902–1984), U.S. novelist. *To See the Dream,* part 1 (1956).

5 MAMA: Son—how come you talk so much 'bout money?
WALTER: Because it is life, Mama!
MAMA: Oh—So now it's life. Money is life. Once upon a time freedom used to be life—now it's money. I guess the world really do change . . .
WALTER: No—it was always money, Mama. We just didn't know about it.
MAMA: No . . . something has changed. You something new, boy. In my time we was worried about not being lynched and getting to the North if we could and how to stay alive and still have a pinch of dignity too. . . . Now here come you and Beneatha—talking 'bout things we ain't never even thought about hardly, me and your daddy. You ain't satisfied or proud of nothing we done. I mean that you had a home; that we kept you out of trouble till you was grown; that you don't have to ride to work on the back of nobody's streetcar—You my children—but how different we done become.

LORRAINE HANSBERRY (1930–1965), African American playwright. *A Raisin in the Sun,* act 1, scene 2 (1959).
The play concerns three generations of Youngers, a black family living together in a Chicago ghetto: Mama Younger, a widow; her grown children Walter Lee and Beneatha; and Walter's wife and son. Walter yearns to make big money, while Beneatha, a college student, has become interested in African culture and what would later be called "black pride."

6 Children and old people and the parents in between should be able to live together, in order to learn how to die with grace, together. And I fear that this is purely utopian fantasy . . .

M. F. K. FISHER (1908–1992), U.S. culinary writer and autobiographer. *Sister Age,* Afterword (1983).

7 The danger lies in forgetting what we had. The flow between generations becomes a trickle, grandchildren tape-recording grandparents' memories on special occasions perhaps—no casual storytelling jogged by daily life, there being no shared daily life what with migrations, exiles, diasporas, rendings, the search for work. Or there is a shared daily life riddled with holes of silence.

ADRIENNE RICH (b. 1929), U.S. poet, essayist, and lesbian feminist. *What Is Found There,* ch. 11 (1993).

GENIUS

1 . . . men of highest genius have been too frequently of extremely shaky morals.

TENNESSEE CLAFLIN (1846–1923), U.S. journalist, lecturer, and social reform advocate; relocated to England. *Talks and Essays,* vol. 3, ch. 9 (1897).

2 Only a great actor finds the difficulties of the actor's art infinite.

ELLEN TERRY (1847–1928), British actor. *Ellen Terry's Memoirs,* 2nd. ed., ch. 5 (1932). Written in 1906 or 1907.

3 It is fair to assume that when women in the past have achieved even a second or third place in the ranks of genius they have shown far more native ability than men have needed to reach the same eminence. Not excused from the more general duties that constitute the cement of society, most women of talent have had but one hand free with which to work out their ideal conceptions.

Anna Garlin Spencer (1851–1931), U.S. feminist, educator, author, and Unitarian minister. *Woman's Share in Social Culture,* ch. 3 (1913).
Referring to the "duties" of housework, childbearing, and child and husband care.

4 ... actors of the first water are not more plentiful than playwrights of genius.

Sarah Bernhardt (1845–1923), French actor. *The Art of the Theatre,* ch. 3 (1924). Written in 1923.

5 It seems as if an age of genius must be succeeded by an age of endeavour; riot and extravagance by cleanliness and hard work.

Virginia Woolf (1882–1941), British novelist, essayist, and diarist. *The Common Reader,* ch. 21 (1925).

6 There is no logical reason why the camel of great art should pass through the needle of mob intelligence.

Rebecca West (1892–1983), British author. *The Strange Necessity,* ch. 9 (1928).

7 ... the great artists ... do not want security, egoistic or materialistic.

Brenda Ueland (1891–1985), U.S. author and writing teacher. *If You Want to Write,* 2nd. ed., ch. 4 (1938).

GENTILITY

1 ... no gentleman lies, on any occasion, with unmixed pleasure. He feels, rather, as if he had put on rags.

Katherine Fullerton Gerould (1879–1944), U.S. author. *Modes and Morals,* ch. 8 (1920).

GERMANY

1 I know what Germans are. They are a funny people. They are always choosing someone to lead them in a direction which they do not want to go.

Gertrude Stein (1874–1946), U.S. author; relocated to France. *Wars I Have Seen* (1945). Written in 1943.

GOALS

1 We set up a certain aim, and put ourselves of our own will into the power of a certain current. Once having done that, we find ourselves committed to usages and customs which we had not before fully known, but from which we cannot depart without giving up the end which we have chosen. But we have no right, therefore, to claim that we are under the yoke of necessity. We might as well say that the man whom we see struggling vainly in the current of Niagara could not have helped jumping in.

ANNA C. BRACKETT (1836–1911), U.S. author. *The Technique of Rest,* ch. 3 (1892).

2 . . . a fixed aim furnishes us with a fixed measure, by which we can decide whether such or such an action proposed is worth trying for or not, and as aims must vary with the individual, the decisions of any two people as to the desirableness of an action may not be the same.

ANNA C. BRACKETT (1836–1911), U.S. author. *The Technique of Rest,* ch. 3 (1892).

3 Aim for the chopping block. If you aim for the wood, you will have nothing. Aim past the wood, aim through the wood; aim for the chopping block.

ANNIE DILLARD (b. 1945), U.S. author. *The Writing Life,* ch. 3 (1989).

GODDESSES

1 Goddesses never die. They slip in and out of the world's cities, in and out of our dreams, century after century, answering to different names, dressed differently, perhaps even disguised, perhaps idle and unemployed, their official altars abandoned, their temples feared or simply forgotten.

PHYLLIS CHESLER (b. 1941), U.S. author and feminist. As quoted in *The Political Palate,* ch. 2, by Betsey Beaven, et al.(1980).

GOSSIP

1 The higher, the more exalted the society, the greater is its culture and refinement, and the less does gossip

prevail. People in such circles find too much of interest in the world of art and literature and science to discuss, without gloating over the shortcomings of their neighbors.

MRS. H. O. WARD (1824–1899), U.S. author. *Sensible Etiquette of the Best Society Customs, Manners, Morals, and Home Culture, Compiled from the Best Authorities,* ch. 4 (1878).

2 This habit of free speaking at ladies' lunches has impaired society; it has doubtless led to many of the tragedies of divorce and marital unhappiness. Could society be deaf and dumb and Congress abolished for a season, what a happy and peaceful life one could lead!

M. E. W. SHERWOOD (1826–1903), U.S. socialite, traveller, and author. *An Epistle to Posterity,* ch. 11 (1897).

3 I sometimes wonder whether, in the still, sleepless hours of the night, the consciences of . . . professional gossips do not stalk them. I myself believe in a final reckoning, when we shall be held accountable for our misdeeds. Do they? If so, they have cause to worry over many scoops that brought them a day's dubious laurels and perhaps destroyed someone's peace forever.

MARY PICKFORD (1893–1979), U.S. actor. *Sunshine and Shadow,* ch. 22 (1955). Of her much-publicized break with her beloved second husband, Douglas Fairbanks (1883–1939).

4 Women born at the turn of the century have been conditioned not to speak openly of their wedding nights. Of other nights in bed with

other men they speak not at all. Today a woman having bedded with a great general feels free to tell us that in bed the general could not present arms. Women of my generation would have spared the great general the revelation of this failure.

JESSAMYN WEST (1907–1984), U.S. novelist and autobiographer. *The Life I Really Lived,* part 7 (1979).

5 Good gossip is just what's going on. Bad gossip is stuff that is salacious, mean and bitchy—the kind most people really enjoy.

LIZ SMITH (b. 1923), U.S. gossip columnist. As quoted in the *Newsweek* magazine, p. 17 (January 13, 1992).

6 The river of sludge will go on and on. It isn't about me.

JACQUELINE KENNEDY ONASSIS (1929–1994), U.S. editor and former First Lady of the United States. As quoted in *Newsweek* magazine, p. 33 (August 30, 1994).

In 1992, on being asked how she dealt with the constant stream of tabloid stories that were written about her. She was the widow of assassinated United States President John F. Kennedy (1917–1963).

GOVERNMENT

1 Where might is mixed with wit, there is too good an accord in a government.

ELIZABETH I (1533–1603), Queen of England (1558–1603). As quoted in *The Sayings of Queen Elizabeth,* ch. 13, by Frederick Chamberlin (1923).

To Sir Henry Sidney, governor of Ireland.

2 The reins of government have been so long slackened, that I fear the people will not quietly submit to those restraints which are necessary

for the peace and security of the community.

ABIGAIL ADAMS (1744–1818), U.S. matriarch; wife and mother of United States President. *Familiar Letters of John Adams and His Wife Abigail Adams, During the Revolution,* letter dated November 27, 1775 (1875).

In a letter to her husband John Adams, who was away fighting in the American colonies' revolution against Britain.

3 . . . the happiness of a people is the only rational object of government, and the only object for which a people, free to choose, can have a government at all.

FRANCES WRIGHT (1795–1852), Scottish author and speaker; relocated to America. *Course of Popular Lectures,* address 1 (1829).

From a lecture given on July 4, 1828.

4 Even more important than the discovery of Columbus, which we are gathered together to celebrate, is the fact that the general government has just discovered women.

BERTHA HONORE POTTER PALMER, (1849–1918) U.S. socialite. As quoted in *The Fair Women,* ch. 10, by Jeanne Madeline Weimann (1981).

Palmer, President of the Board of Lady Managers for the World's Columbian Exposition in Chicago, was speaking on October 21, 1892, at the fair's dedication ceremony. Columbus had sailed to America 400 years earlier—landing on October 12, however, not October 21.

5 . . . the keynote of government is injustice.

EMMA GOLDMAN (1869–1940), U.S. anarchist and author; born in Russia. *Anarchism and Other Essays,* 3rd rev. ed., ch. 1 (1917).

Arguing that all government is to be deplored because it violates the supremacy of the individual.

6 Educational . . . legislation nowadays is largely in the hands of illiterate people, and the illiterate will take good care that their illiteracy is not made a reproach on them.

KATHERINE FULLERTON GEROULD (1879–1944), U.S. author. *Modes and Morals,* ch. 4 (1920).

7 . . . governing is occupying but not interesting, governments are occupying but not interesting . . .

GERTRUDE STEIN (1874–1946), U.S. author and patron of the arts; relocated to France. *What Are Masterpieces and Why Are There So Few of Them* (1936).

8 The thing that is most interesting about government servants is that they believe what they are supposed to believe, they really do believe what they are supposed to believe.

GERTRUDE STEIN (1874–1946), U.S. author; relocated to France. *Wars I Have Seen* (1945).

Written in 1943.

GRATITUDE

1 When one is altering the face of the universe one cannot remember small helpful acts.

ALICE FOOTE MACDOUGALL, (1867–1945) U.S. businesswoman. *The Autobiography of a Business Woman,* ch. 3 (1928).

On her failure to acknowledge a small, but important, order placed with her in the early years of her wholesale coffee business, when she was struggling to establish herself against great odds.

2 . . . gratitude is not a healthy emotion in the long run . . .

AGNES E. MEYER (1887–1970), U.S. journalist. *Out of These Roots,* ch. 10 (1953).

Reflecting on Britain's gratitude for American assistance during World War II.

3 . . . it is a dangerous thing to ask why someone else has been given more. It is humbling—and indeed healthy—to ask why you have been given so much.

CONDOLEEZZA RICE (b. 1954), African American university administrator. As quoted in the *Chronicle of Higher Education,* p. B3 (June 15, 1994).

Rice, provost of elite Stanford University, was the granddaughter of impoverished people who had managed to send their children to college. She said this in a commencement speech at the University of Alabama.

GRIEF

1 We orphans we lament to the world:
World, why have you taken our soft mothers from us
And the fathers who say: My child, you are like me!
We orphans are like no one in this world any more!
O world
We accuse you!

NELLY SACHS (1891–1970), German Jewish poet and translator; relocated to Sweden. "Chorus of the Orphans," lines 25–30, translated by Michael Hamburger, et al. (1967; first edition in German: 1946).

Sachs was cowinner of the 1966 Nobel Prize for Literature.

2 . . . most bereaved souls crave nourishment more tangible than prayers: they want a steak. What is more, they need a steak. Preferably they need it rare, grilled, heavily salted, for that way it is most easily digested, and most quickly turned into the glandular whip their tired adrenals cry for.

M. F. K. Fisher (1908–1992), U.S. author and food expert. *An Alphabet for Gourmets,* "S is for Sad" chapter (1949).

GUILT

1 Guilt plays a large part in my life.

Christine Zajac, U.S. fifth-grade teacher. As quoted in *Among Schoolchildren,* "September" section, part 3, by Tracy Kidder (1989).

Reflecting on an error she made in handling a recalcitrant pupil.

HANDICAPS

1 The goal for all blind skiers is more freedom. You don't have to see where you're going, as long as you go. In skiing, you ski with your legs and not with your eyes. In life, you experience things with your mind and your body. And if you're lacking one of the five senses, you adapt.

Lorita Bertraun, Blind American skier. As quoted in *WomenSports* magazine, p. 29 (January 1976).

HAPPINESS

1 That milkmaid's lot is better than mine, and her life merrier.

Elizabeth I (1533–1603), Queen of England (1558–1603). As quoted in *The Sayings of Queen Elizabeth,* ch. 1, by Frederick Chamberlin (1923).

Said to one of her attendants in 1554, when she was still Princess Elizabeth, during her imprisonment for treason; she had heard a milkmaid singing at her work.

2 A good education is another name for happiness.

Ann Plato (1820– ?), U.S. teacher and author. As quoted in *Black Women in Nineteenth-Century American Life,* part 2, by Bert James Loewenberg and Ruth Bogin (1976).

Plato, a free African American who was a schoolmistress in Hartford, Connecticut, said this in 1841.

3 One cannot divine nor forecast the conditions that will make happiness; one only stumbles upon them by chance, in a lucky hour, at the world's end somewhere, and hold fast to the days, as to fortune or fame.

Willa Cather (1876–1947), U.S. novelist. *Willa Cather in Europe,* ch. 13 (1956).

Written on September 10, 1902.

4 The root of the discontent in American women is that they are too well educated. . . . There will be no real content among American women unless they are made and kept more ignorant or unless they are given equal opportunity with men to use what they have been taught. And American men will not be really happy until their women are.

Pearl S. Buck (1892–1973), U.S. novelist and essayist. *Harper's Magazine,* pp. 229, 232 (August 1938).

5 You must work and do good, not be lazy and gamble, if you wish to earn happiness. Laziness may *appear* attractive, but work *gives* satisfaction. . . . I can't understand people who don't like work . . .

Anne Frank (1929–1945), Dutch Jewish diarist; born in Germany. *Diary of a Young Girl,* entry dated July 6, 1944 (1947).

Frank and her family were in hiding in Holland when she wrote this. On August 4, their hiding place would be raided by the police, and they would be sent to German and Dutch concentration camps. All of them except Otto Frank, the father, would perish; Anne died in Bergen-Belsen, a German camp, just two months before the liberation of Holland.

6 And if sun comes
How shall we greet him?
Shall we not dread him,
Shall we not fear him
After so lengthy a
Session with shade?

GWENDOLYN BROOKS (b. 1917), African American poet and fiction writer. "The Womanhood," part 9: "truth," lines 1–6 (1949).

7 . . . you have to have been desperately unhappy before you can play comedy, so that nothing can frighten you any more. And you can't do tragedy before you know absolute happiness, because having known that, you are safe.

DAME EDITH EVANS (1888–1976), British actor. As quoted in Dame Edith Evans, ch. 12, by Bryan Forbes (1977).

A brilliantly successful actress, Evans identified both her "desperate unhappiness" and her "absolute happiness" with her husband, George "Guy" Booth, with whom she had fallen in love in 1904; he died in 1935.

8 The ultimate end of human acts is *eudaimonia,* happiness in the sense of "living well," which all men desire; all acts are but different means chosen to arrive at it.

HANNAH ARENDT (1906–1975), U.S. philosopher and political theorist; born in Germany. The Life of the Mind, vol. 2: Willing, ch. 7 (1978).

9 I never meet anyone nowadays who admits to having had a happy childhood. Everyone appears to think happiness betokens a lack of sensitivity.

JESSAMYN WEST (1907–1984), U.S. novelist and autobiographer. The Life I Really Lived, part 1 (1979).

10 the hatchlings wake in the swaying branches,
in the silver baskets,
and love the world.
Is it necessary to say any more?
Have you heard them singing in the wind, above the final fields?
Have you ever been so happy in your life?

MARY OLIVER (b. 1935), U.S. poet. "Goldfinches," lines 31–36 (c. 1991).

11 . . . no one with a happy childhood ever amounts to much in this world. They are so well adjusted, they never are driven to achieve anything.

SUE GRAFTON (b. 1940), U.S. murder mystery novelist. As quoted in the New York Times, p. C10 (August 4, 1994).

Grafton, author of a popular series of detective novels, was the daughter of two alcoholics and described their parenting as "benign neglect."

HARDSHIP

1 . . . care and labor are as much correlated to human existence as shadow is to light . . .

HARRIET BEECHER STOWE (1811–1896), U.S. author. Household Papers and Stories, part 2, ch. 4 (1864).

2 . . . we can bear with great philosophy the sufferings of others, especially if we do not actually see them.

ALBION FELLOWS BACON (1865–1933), U.S. social worker and housing reform advocate. Beauty for Ashes, ch. 6 (1914).

3   . . . the hard work and poverty of my childhood . . . turned out to be my greatest asset in later years. Nothing could ever seem too hard after that.

SUE SANDERS, U.S. oil producer. *Our Common Herd,* ch. 30 (1940).

Through the death of her father when she was five and marriage to a luckless farmer when she was fourteen, Sanders had experienced great financial and emotional stress. Separating from her husband at age eighteen, with their two babies in tow, she went on to become a successful businesswoman.

4   The human condition is such that pain and effort are not just symbols which can be removed without changing life itself; they are rather the modes in which life itself, together with the necessity to which it is bound, makes itself felt. For mortals, the "easy life of the gods" would be a lifeless life.

HANNAH ARENDT (1906–1975), U.S. philosopher. *The Human Condition,* ch. 16 (1958).

5   . . . suffering does not ennoble. It destroys. To resist destruction, self-hatred, or lifelong hopelessness, we have to throw off the conditioning of being despised, the fear of becoming the *they* that is talked about so dismissively, to refuse lying myths and easy moralities, to see ourselves as human, flawed, and extraordinary. All of us—extraordinary.

DOROTHY ALLISON (b. 1949), U.S. author and lesbian feminist. *Skin,* ch. 2 (1994).

Allison had grown up in a very poor and dysfunctional South Carolina family.

HEALTH

1   Medication alone is not to be relied on. In one half the cases medicine is not needed, or is worse than useless. Obedience to spiritual and physical laws—hygeine [sic] of the body, and hygeine of the spirit—is the surest warrant for health and happiness.

HARRIOT K. HUNT (1805–1875), U.S. physician. *Glances and Glimpses,* ch. 11 (1856).

2   A woman's health is her capital.

HARRIET BEECHER STOWE (1811–1896), U.S. author. *Household Papers and Stories,* part 2, ch. 5 (1864).

3   . . . health is the obstacle, which . . . must stand in the way of a girl's acquiring the intellectual strength, which . . . is so invaluable to a boy.

ELIZABETH MISSING SEWELL (1815–1906), British author. *Principles of Education, Drawn from Nature and Revelation, and Applied to Female Education in the Upper Classes,* ch. 32 (1866).

4   This program has helped me to keep physically healthy and to eat the right foods . . . and that's really what the swimsuit competition is about.

KAYE LANI RAE RAFKO (b. 1968), U.S. beauty contest winner, Miss America, 1988. As quoted in *Miss America,* ch. 7, by Ann-Marie Bivans (1991).

On the controversial "swimsuit competition," in which contestants paraded in swimsuits and high heels. Later, in an attempt to respond to criticism that requiring young women to display themselves in this manner was sexist, pageant officials deleted the high heels.

5   It is unconscionable that we ration health care by the ability to pay. . . . your heart breaks. Health care should be a given.

KATHRYN ANASTOS (b. 1950), U.S. physician. As quoted in *New York* magazine, p. 90 (December 21–28, 1992).

Anastos was at this time serving as medical director of an ambulatory-care unit of HIV primary-care services at Bronx-Lebanon Hospital in New York City. A feminist and social reformer, she was an advocate of health care for women and the poor.

HEAVEN

1 . . . it is easier for a camel to pass through the needle's eye than for anything really *chic* to enter the Kingdom of Heaven.

KATHERINE FULLERTON GEROULD (1879–1944), U.S. author. *Modes and Morals,* ch. 1 (1920).

2 Once our idea of heaven meant
all the dead relatives waiting
on the kept lawn of the many mansions
as if, suddenly sinless, they had nothing
to do. . . .

DEBORAH DIGGES (b. 1950), U.S. author. "Custody," lines 5–9 (1986).

HEROISM

1 We all felt that the men about us were making history, and that we were looking at heroes, if we could only find them out.

M. E. W. SHERWOOD (1826–1903), U.S. socialite, traveller, and author. *An Epistle to Posterity,* ch. 5 (1897).

Remembering Washington, D.C., in 1862–1863, when it was a Civil War camp. Sherwood's "favorite" of the men was General McClellan.

2 A nice war is a war where everybody who is heroic is a hero, and

everybody more or less is a hero in a nice war. Now this war is not at all a nice war.

GERTRUDE STEIN (1874–1946), U.S. author; relocated to France. *Wars I Have Seen* (1945).

Written in 1943 about World War II, which was then in progress.

3 I had to kick their law into their teeth in order to save them.
However I have heard that sometimes you have to deal
Devilishly with drowning men in order to swim them to shore.
Or they will haul themselves and you to the trash and the fish beneath.

GWENDOLYN BROOKS (b. 1917), African American poet and fiction writer. "Negro Hero," lines 1–4 (1945).

Of an African American man who saved the lives of whites.

4 . . . if there are no waving flags and marching songs at the barricades as Walter marches out with his little battalion, it is not because the battle lacks nobility. On the contrary, he has picked up in his way, still imperfect and wobbly in his small view of human destiny. . . . He becomes, in spite of those who are too intrigued with despair and hatred of man to see it, King Oedipus refusing to tear out his eyes, but attacking the oracle instead. He is that last Jewish patriot manning his rifle at Warsaw. . . . He is Anne Frank, still believing in people; he is the nine small heroes of Little Rock; he is Michelangelo creating David and Beethoven bursting forth with the Ninth Symphony. He is all these

things because he has finally reached out in his tiny moment and caught that sweet essence which is human dignity, and it shines like the old star-touched dream that is in his eyes.

LORRAINE HANSBERRY (1930–1965), African American playwright. An Author's Reflections: Walter Lee Younger, Willy Loman and He Who Must Live (1959).

Walter Lee Younger, the deeply flawed African American leading character of Hansberry's play A Raisin in the Sun (1959), finally stands up to intimidation and moves his family from a Chicago ghetto into a white neighborhood.

5 This might be the end of the world. If Joe lost we were back in slavery and beyond help. It would all be true, the accusations that we were lower types of human beings. Only a little higher than apes. True that we were stupid and ugly and lazy and dirty and, unlucky and worst of all, that God Himself hated us and ordained us to be hewers of wood and drawers of water, forever and ever, world without end.

MAYA ANGELOU (b. 1928), African American poet, autobiographer, and performer. I Know Why the Caged Bird Sings, ch. 19 (1970).

Remembering the significance to African American Southerners of a world heavyweight championship bout fought by African American boxer Joe Louis (1914–1981), the defending champion, against Primo Carnera (1906–1967), a white Italian challenger and former heavyweight champion. Angelou's grandmother ran a store in the small, strictly segregated, brutally racist town of Stamps, Arkansas. Her family and neighbors crowded the store to listen to the fight on radio. As it turned out, Louis won this and every one of his other twenty-four title defenses until his first retirement in 1949.

6 It is the fate of heroines to be laughed at.

JANE O'REILLY, U.S. feminist and humorist. The Girl I Left Behind, ch. 7 (1980).

7 I'm not an American hero. I'm a person that loves children.

CLARA MCBRIDE HALE (1905–1992), African American child care worker. As quoted in I Dream a World, by Brian Lanker (1989).

Hale was a poor mother of two who was widowed when her children were only five and six years old. She went on to raise forty foster children to successful adulthoods and to found Hale House (b. 1973) in the Harlem section of New York City. Hale House was a shelter for the babies of drug-addicted mothers. In 1985, President Ronald Reagan had cited her as "an American hero."

8 What's a hero? I didn't even think about it.

ULI DERICKSON (b. c. 1944), Flight attendant. As quoted in People magazine, p. 111 (March 7–14, 1994).

Working on TWA flight 847 from Athens to Rome, which was hijacked for seventeen days by Lebanese terrorists in 1985, she persuaded the hijackers to spare the lives of all but one person on board and maintained calm throughout the ordeal. Rejecting the "hero" label, she insisted that she was only doing her job.

HETEROSEXISM

1 Women who assume authority are unnatural. Unnatural women are lesbians. Therefore all the leaders of the women's movement were presumed to be lesbians.

JANE O'REILLY, U.S. feminist and humorist. The Girl I Left Behind, ch. 8 (1980).

O'Reilly, a heterosexual, was active in the women's rights movement. Here, she was describing common assumptions of antifeminists in the late 1960s and the 1970s.

2 The lie of compulsory female heterosexuality today afflicts not just feminist scholarship, but every profession, every reference work, every curriculum, every organizing attempt, every relationship or conversation over which it hovers. It cre-

ates, specifically, a profound false-ness, hypocrisy, and hysteria in the heterosexual dialogue, for every heterosexual relationship is lived in the queasy strobe light of that lie. However we choose to identify ourselves, however we find ourselves labeled, it flickers across and distorts our lives.

ADRIENNE RICH (b. 1929), U.S. poet, essayist, and lesbian feminist. *Blood, Bread and Poetry*, ch. 3 (1986).

Written in 1980, not long after Rich had begun publicly to acknowledge her lesbianism. She had once been married and was the mother of three sons.

3 Coming out, all the way out, is offered more and more as the political solution to our oppression. The argument goes that, if people could see just how many of us there are, some in very important places, the negative stereotype would vanish overnight. . . . It is far more realistic to suppose that, if the tenth of the population that is gay became visible tomorrow, the panic of the majority of people would inspire repressive legislation of a sort that would shock even the pessimists among us.

JANE RULE (b. 1931), Canadian fiction writer and essayist; born in the U. S. *Outlander,* part 2, essay 10 (1981).

Rule was a lesbian. Her assumption that a "tenth" of the population was gay or lesbian was widespread at the time, based largely on the famous Kinsey studies of sexuality. More recently, that percentage has been questioned as perhaps too high, especially if exclusive or almost exclusive homosexuality, rather than simply some homosexual activity, is the issue.

4 Female athletes are stereotyped by the general population—and usually as homosexuals.

BILLIE JEAN KING (b. 1943), U.S. tennis player. *Billie Jean,* ch. 15 (1982).

Married and a tennis champion in the 1960s and 70s, King was revealed as a bisexual in 1981 when her former lover, Marilyn Barnett, sued her for "palimony."

HISTORY

1 The history of the past is but one long struggle upward to equality.

ELIZABETH CADY STANTON (1815–1902), U.S. suffragist, social reformer, and author. As quoted in *History of Woman Suffrage,* vol. 2, ch. 16, by Susan B. Anthony, Matilda Joslyn Gage, and herself (1882).

From a March 1863 circular calling for a National Convention of the Woman's National Loyal League. It was held two months later in New York City.

2 You should read history—look at ostracism, persecution, martyrdom, and that kind of thing. They always happen to the best men, you know.

GEORGE ELIOT (1819–1880), British novelist. *Middlemarch,* ch. 38 (1871–1872).

Said by the novel's character named Mr. Brooke, a likable but comic figure described as "nearly sixty, of acquiescent temper, miscellaneous opinions, and uncertain vote."

3 When the temperamental and unconventional people are not mere plagiarists of dead eccentrics, they lack, in almost every case, the historic sense.

KATHERINE FULLERTON GEROULD (1879–1944), U.S. author. *Modes and Morals,* ch. 7 (1920).

4 It is the soothing thing about history that it does repeat itself.

GERTRUDE STEIN (1874–1946), U.S. author; relocated to France. *Wars I Have Seen* (1945).

Written in 1943.

5 History
Coming too close
Is monstrous, like a doll
That is alive and bigger than the
child
Who tries to hold it.
BABETTE DEUTSCH (1895–1982), U.S.
poet. "History," lines 15–19 (1944).

6 History counts its skeletons in
round numbers.
A thousand and one remains a
thousand,
as though the one had never
existed:
an imaginary embryo, an empty
cradle,
. . .
emptiness running down steps toward the garden,
nobody's place in line.
WISLAWA SZYMBORSKA (b. 1923), Polish poet. "Hunger Camp at Jaslo," lines 6–9,
12–13, translated by Grazyna Drabik and Austin Flint.
I know that Symborska's first book of poetry
was published in 1948, but I don't know
whether this poem was in it. In any event, that
book was attacked by her government and had
to be withdrawn. Neither do I know the date of
the translation.

7 . . . every event has had its cause,
and nothing, not the least wind that
blows, is accident or causeless. To
understand what happens now one
must find the cause, which may be
very long ago in its beginning, but
is surely there, and therefore a
knowledge of history as detailed as
possible is essential if we are to
comprehend the past and be prepared for the future.
PEARL S. BUCK (1892–1973), U.S. author.
My Several Worlds (1954).

8 Bias, point of view, fury—are they
. . . so dangerous and must they be
ironed out of history, the hills flattened and the contours leveled? The
professors talk . . . about passion
and point of view in history as a
Calvinist talks about sin in the bedroom.
CATHERINE DRINKER BOWEN (1897–
1973), U.S. biographer. Adventures of a Biographer, ch. 6 (1959).
Bowen wrote widely read biographies of Tchaikovsky, Oliver Wendell Holmes, John Adams,
and Francis Bacon, among others, but did not
have formal academic training in history or biography. Here she was referring to many modern historians' insistence upon scrupulously
"objective" presentations.

9 As photographs give people an
imaginary possession of a past that
is unreal, they also help people to
take possession of space in which
they are insecure.
SUSAN SONTAG (b. 1933), U.S. author. On
Photography, ch. 1 (1977).

10 False history gets made all day, any
day,
the truth of the new is never on the
news
False history gets written every day
. . .
the lesbian archaeologist watches
herself
sifting her own life out from the
shards she's piecing,
asking the clay all questions but her
own.
ADRIENNE RICH (b. 1929), U.S. poet, essayist, and lesbian feminist. "Turning the
Wheel," section 2, lines 1–3 and 5–7 (1981).

11 I've never cared that much for ce-
menting my place in history. Sports

is so transitory, so ephemeral. It just seems like so much nonsense comparing me to Helen Wills Moody or Suzanne Lenglen or anybody else from some other time. One lesson you learn from sports is that life goes on without you.

BILLIE JEAN KING (b. 1943), U.S. tennis player. *Billie Jean*, ch. 2 (1982).

Moody (b. 1905) was a champion tennis player in the 1920s and 30s, Lenglen (1899–1938) in the 1920s.

12 We have seen over and over that white male historians in general have tended to dismiss any history they didn't themselves write, on the grounds that it is unserious, unscholarly, a fad, too "political," "merely" oral and thus unreliable.

ADRIENNE RICH (b. 1929), U.S. poet, essayist, and feminist. *Blood, Bread and Poetry*, ch. 8 (1986).

From the Clark Lecture which she delivered at Scripps College in Claremont, California, on February 15, 1983.

HOLLYWOOD, CA

I The bite of existence did not cut into one in Hollywood. . . .

MAE WEST (1892–1980), U.S. actor. *Goodness Had Nothing to Do With It*, ch. 13 (1959).

2 This is where I have wasted the best years of my life.

GRETA GARBO (1905–1990), Swedish actor; relocated to the United States. As quoted in *The Divine Garbo*, ch. 6, by Frederick Sands and Sven Broman (1979).

Originally quoted by Cecil Beaton (1904–1980), an English designer and photographer who claimed to have had a romance with Garbo. She said this to him in the late 1940s, a few years after her retirement, when he accompanied her on a trip to Hollywood.

HOLOCAUST

I Who has inflicted this upon us? Who has made us Jews different from all other people? Who has allowed us to suffer so terribly up till now? It is God that has made us as we are, but it will be God, too, who will raise us up again. If we bear all this suffering and if there are still Jews left, when it is over, then Jews, instead of being doomed, will be held up as an example.

ANNE FRANK (1929–1945), Dutch Jewish diarist; born in Germany. *Diary of a Young Girl*, entry dated April 11, 1944 (1947).

Frank and her family were in hiding in Holland when she wrote this. On August 4, their hiding place would be raided by the police, and they would be sent to German and Dutch concentration camps. All of them except Otto Frank, the father, would perish; Anne died in Bergen-Belsen, a German camp, just two months before the liberation of Holland.

2 Not for me the glad tidings of forthcoming salvation; everything is lost and I so want to live.

ESTER WAJCBLUM (1924–1945), German Jewish victim of the Auschwitz concentration camp. As quoted in *Newsweek* magazine, p. 54 (January 16, 1995).

In a letter to her sister Anna, written in late 1944 when she was being kept in a prison block and tortured. Wajcblum was executed on January 6, 1945, along with three other women—Roza Robota, Ala Gertner, and Regina Safirsztain—for aiding in a plot to blow up the Auschwitz gas chambers and attack the guards. This was the last public execution at Auschwitz; two weeks later, the Germans abandoned the camp.

3 O the chimneys
On the ingeniously devised habitations of death
When Israel's body drifted as smoke
Through the air —

Nelly Sachs (1891–1970), German Jewish poet and translator; relocated to Sweden. "O the chimneys," lines 1–4, translated by Michael Hamburger, et al. (1967; first edition in German: 1946).

Sachs was cowinner of the 1966 Nobel Prize for Literature.

4   The symmetrical piles of white
     bodies,
  the round white breast-shapes of
     the heaps,
  the smell of the smoke, the dogs the
     wires the
  rope the hunger. It had happened
     to others.
  There was a word for us. I was: a
     Jew.

Sharon Olds (b. 1942), U.S. Jewish poet. "That Year," lines 24–28 (1980).

On seeing, in social studies class, photographs from Auschwitz, a Nazi concentration camp located in Poland, where more than one million Jews were killed during World War II.

5   These words are dedicated to those
     who survived
  because life is a wilderness and they
     were savage
  because life is an awakening and
     they were alert
  because life is a flowering and they
     blossomed
  because life is a struggle and they
     struggled
  because life is a gift and they were
     free to accept it

Irena Klepfisz (b. 1941), U.S. Jewish poet and essayist; born in Poland. "Bashert: These Words are Dedicated to Those Who Survived," lines 26–31 (1981).

Klepfisz and her mother escaped the Warsaw Uprising, in which her father died, and emigrated first to Sweden, then to the United States. These lines are dedicated to the survivors of the Holocaust.

6   i can't go back
  where i came from was
  burned off the map
  i'm a jew
  anywhere is someone else's land

Melanie Kaye–Kantrowitz, U.S. Jewish poet. As quoted in "Inhospitable Soil," Epigram, by Irena Klepfisz (1982).

7   . . . the Holocaust has been like a
  fad, a rock group losing its original
  sound, a fashionable form of dress
  that outlives its popularity . . . it has
  been commercialized, metaphored
  out of reality, glamorized, been severed from the historical fact.

Irena Klepfisz (b. 1941), U.S. Jewish author; born in Poland. Dreams of an Insomniac, part 2 (1990).

Klepfisz, a Jew born in Poland in 1941, escaped the 1943 Warsaw Uprising; her father had been killed on the second day of the Uprising. They emigrated to Sweden, then, in 1949, to New York City.

8   What was lost in the European cataclysm was not only the Jewish
  past—the whole life of a civilization—but also a major share of the
  Jewish future. . . . [ellipsis in source]
  It was not only the intellect of a
  people in its prime that was excised,
  but the treasure of a people in its
  potential.

Cynthia Ozick (b. 1928), U.S. Jewish novelist and story writer. As quoted in Dreams of an Insomniac, part 4, by Irena Klepfisz (1990).

9   It makes worries like what you wear
  today seem stupid.

Rebecca Neel (b. c. 1981), U.S. schoolgirl. As quoted in the New York Times Magazine, p. 44 (February 12, 1995).

The eighth-grader said this after visiting the Holocaust Museum in Washington, DC.

10 I am not a hero. I just did what any decent person would have done.

MIEP GIES (b. c. 1908), Dutch former secretary; born in Austria. As quoted in the *New York Times*, p. 27 (March 11, 1995).

At the beginning of World War II, Gies, a Christian, was a secretary in the food chemicals business of Otto Frank, a Jew. To escape the Nazis, Frank, his family, and four other Jews moved into a secret apartment above the business. Gies was one of five people aware of their hideout and took food to them daily; after the Jews were discovered and taken away to concentration camps on August 4, 1944, Gies defied Nazi orders to stay out of the no-longer-secret apartment. There she found strewn across the floor the handwritten diary pages of Frank's younger daughter, Anne (1929–1945); at great personal risk, she retrieved and kept them. After learning that Anne had died in Bergen-Belsen, Gies gave her diary to Otto Frank, the only member of the family who survived the camps. He arranged for its publication in 1947, and it became an extraordinarily poignant and important document of Nazi oppression.

HOME

1 The home is a woman's natural background. . . . From the beginning I tried to have the policy of the store reflect as nearly as it was possible in the commercial world, those standards of comfort and grace which are apparent in a lovely home.

HORTENSE ODLUM (1892– ?), U.S. businesswoman. *A Woman's Place*, ch. 7 (1939).

A longtime homemaker, Odlum had assumed the presidency of Bonwit Teller, a women's store in New York City, at the request of her husband, who had a financial interest in it. Though she had never held a job before, she saved the failing store and guided it to prosperity.

2 A long war like this makes you realise the society you really prefer, the home, goats chickens and dogs and casual acquaintances. I find myself not caring at all for gardens flowers or vegetables cats cows and rabbits, one gets tired of trees vines and hills, but houses, goats chickens dogs and casual acquaintances never pall.

GERTRUDE STEIN (1874–1946), U.S. author; relocated to France. *Wars I Have Seen* (1945).

Written in France in 1944, during World War II.

3 A stranger always has his homeland in his arms like an orphan for which he may be seeking nothing but a grave.

NELLY SACHS (1891–1970), German Jewish poet and translator; relocated to Sweden. "Someone Comes," closing lines, translated by Michael Hamburger, et al. (1967; first edition in German: 1958).

Sachs was cowinner of the 1966 Nobel Prize for Literature. A German Jew who escaped to Sweden in 1940, she was always keenly conscious of being a survivor of the Holocaust and an exile from her native land.

HOMOSEXUALITY

1 I've been thinking about the comments that are always made about the shower rooms and the lack of privacy. . . . How easy it would be just to hang a shower curtain . . .

MARGARETHE CAMMERMEYER (b. 1942), U.S. nurse and former military officer. As quoted in *Time* magazine, p. 63 (July 6, 1992).

On a common argument against allowing gays to serve in the military. Cammermeyer herself admitted her homosexuality during a routine background check and was dismissed after a career in which she had earned a Bronze Star for Vietnam War duty and was once the Veterans Administration Nurse of the Year.

2 We are your daughters, your sisters, your sons, your nurses, your mechanics, your athletes, your police,

your politicians, your fathers, your
doctors, your soldiers, your mothers. We live with you, care for you,
help you, protect you, teach you,
love you, and need you. All we ask is
that you let us. We are no different.
We want to serve, like you. Need
love, like you. Feel pain, like you.
And we deserve justice, like you.

MARGARETHE CAMMERMEYER (b.
1942), U.S. nurse and U. S. Army officer. *Serving in Silence*, ch. 12 (1994).

In 1992, Colonel Cammermeyer was dis-
charged from the U.S. Army three years after
stating, during routine questioning for a top-se-
curity clearance, that she was a lesbian. At the
time of her discharge, Cammermeyer was Chief
Nurse of the Washington State National Guard.
A twenty-six-year veteran, she had been the
1985 Veterans Administration Nurse of the Year
and had won the Bronze Star for her duty in the
Vietnam War. These words are from the conclusion of her autobiography.

HONESTY

1   When I wrote of the women in
their dances and wildness, it was a
mask,
on their mountain, gold-hunting,
singing, in orgy,
it was a mask; when I wrote of the
god,
fragmented, exiled from himself, his
life, the love gone down with song,
it was myself, split open, unable to
speak, in exile from myself.
. . .
No more masks! No more
mythologies!

MURIEL RUKEYSER (1913–1980), U.S.
poet. "The Poem as Mask," lines 1–5 and 10
(1968).

2   I'm not fancy. I'm what I appear to
be.

JANET WOOD RENO (b. 1938), U.S. attorney. As quoted in *People* magazine, p. 62 (December 27, 1993–January 3, 1994).

The first woman U.S. Attorney General was explaining her strong appeal to celebrities and the
public.

HOPE

1   The inevitable has always found me
ready and hopeful . . .

AMELIA E. BARR (1831–1919), U.S. author; born in Scotland. *All the Days of My Life*,
ch. 4 (1913).

2   Begin with loss and see
how the world contradicts you,
how the horizon implies that
beyond it
the water is not empty
but full of ships
all docking at another island.

LYNN EMANUEL (b. 1949), U.S. poet.
"Robinson Crusoe Talks to Friday," lines 1–6
(1979).

HORSE RACING

1   Oh yeah, the fun I had while I was
doing it was great. Not everybody
ends up this way.

SIDNEY UNDERWOOD (b. 1963), U.S.
jockey. As quoted in the *Trenton Times* (July 30,
1990).

On whether she would become a jockey if she
had it to do over again. Underwood had been
hospitalized a month earlier after a racing accident that left her paralyzed from the sternum
down; her doctors were predicting that she
would never walk again.

2   His nature just speaks to me. I
didn't want him too far back to
get dirt in his face, to get discouraged.

JULIE KRONE (b. 1963), U.S. jockey. As quoted in the *New York Times,* sect. 8, p. 7 (June 6, 1993).

Describing her "mystical relationship" with Colonial Affair, the horse that she rode to the first-ever victory by a woman jockey in a prestigious Triple Crown race: the Belmont Stakes on June 5, 1993.

ANNIE ELIZABETH DELANY (1891–1995), U.S. dentist. *Having Our Say,* ch. 4 (1992).

Delany was speaking for herself and her sister Sarah Louise, who, at 103, was two years her senior.

HOTELS

I **I have been spending my first night in an American "summer hotel," and I despair of the Republic! Such dreariness, such whining callow women, such utter absence of the amenities, such crass food, crass manners, crass landscape! . . . What a horror it is for a whole nation to be developing without a sense of beauty, and eating bananas for breakfast.**

EDITH WHARTON (1862–1937), U.S. author; relocated to France. As quoted in *Edith Wharton,* ch. 9, by R. W. B. Lewis (1975).

Written in August 1904 to her friend Sara Norton after Wharton's car broke down in Petersham, Massachusetts, and she was forced to stay at a "fashionable" new hotel called the Nichewang. Wharton came from a privileged background, had elegant taste, and lived lavishly. Beginning in the early 1900s, she spent most of her time in Paris.

HOSPITALS

I **I had gone into the hospital with the stupid notion that its primary object was the care and comfort of the sick and wounded. It was long after that I learned that a vast majority of all benevolent institutions are gotten up to gratify the aesthetic tastes of the public; exhibit the wealth and generosity of the founders, and furnish places for officers. The beneficiaries of the institutions are simply an apology for their existence, and having furnished that apology, the less said about them the better.**

JANE GREY SWISSHELM (1815–1884), U.S. newspaperwoman, abolitionist, and human rights activist. *Half a Century,* ch. 60 (1880).

Recalling her work in Campbell Hospital, Washington, DC, during the Civil War.

2 **. . . we avoid hospitals because . . . they'll kill you there. They overtreat you. And when they see how old you are, and that you still have a mind, they treat you like a curiosity: like "Exhibit A" and "Exhibit B." Like, "Hey. nurse, come on over here and looky-here at this old woman, she's in such good shape. . . ." . Most of the time they don't even treat you like a person, just an object.**

HOUSEWIVES

I **I put away my brushes; resolutely crucified my divine gift, and while it hung writhing on the cross, spent my best years and powers cooking cabbage. "A servant of servants shall she be," must have been spoken of women, not Negroes.**

JANE GREY SWISSHELM, (1815–1884) U.S. newspaperwoman, abolitionist, and human rights activist. *Half a Century,* ch. 8 (1880).

On giving up her artistic work to keep house for her husband. Later, she would become a journalist and the founder of an abolitionist newspaper, the *Pittsburgh Saturday Visiter.*

2 ... up to this date, I have never been shut up in a separate room, or hedged off with any observances. My study, all the study I have attained to, is the little 2nd drawing room where all the (feminine) life of the house goes on; and I don't think I have ever had two hours undisturbed (except at night, when everybody is in bed) during my whole literary life.

MARGARET OLIPHANT (1828–1897), Scottish author. As quoted in *Woman in Sexist Society*, ch. 20, by Elaine Showalter (1971). Widowed at thirty-one, she was forced to support not only her own three children but her brother and his family. She took up writing and was extremely prolific, producing biographies, histories, guidebooks, and many popular novels. She wrote this in 1888.

3 The bread-winner must toil as in the fruitless effort of a troubled dream while the expenditure of an uneducated wife discounts the income in the lack of understanding to discern the broad possibilities of an intelligent economy.

ANNA EUGENIA MORGAN (1845–1909), U.S. college professor. *What America Owes to Women*, ch. 25 (1893).
A Wellesley College professor, Morgan was concerned about uneducated housewives' ability to manage a household budget wisely.

4 The fact that women in the home have shut themselves away from the thought and life of the world has done much to retard progress. We fill the world with the children of 20th century A.D. fathers and 20th century B.C. mothers.

CHARLOTTE PERKINS GILMAN (1860–1935), U.S. feminist, social reformer, and author. As quoted in *History of Woman Suffrage*, vol. 5, ch. 5, by Ida Husted Harper (1922).

From an address entitled "Woman's World," delivered in the summer of 1905 to the thirty-seventh annual convention of the National Woman Suffrage Association.

5 When I hear that there are 5,000,000 working women in this country, I always take occasion to say that there are 18,000,000 but only 5,000,000 receive their wages.

ANNA HOWARD SHAW (1847–1919), U.S. minister, suffragist, and speaker; born in England. As quoted in *History of Woman Suffrage*, vol. 5, ch. 8, by Ida Husted Harper (1922).
Speaking in October 1908 before the fortieth annual convention of the National Woman Suffrage Association.

6 No record ... can ... name the women of talent who were so submerged by child-bearing and its duties, and by "general housework," that they had to leave their poems and stories all unwritten.

ANNA GARLIN SPENCER (1851–1931), U.S. feminist, educator, author, and Unitarian minister. *Woman's Share in Social Culture*, ch. 3 (1913).

7 ... the lives of most women are ... vaguely unsatisfactory. They are always doing secondary and menial things (that do not require all their gifts and ability) for *others* and never anything for *themselves*.

BRENDA UELAND (1891–1985), U.S. author and writing teacher. *If You Want to Write*, 2nd. ed., ch. 10 (1938).

8 The woman who does her job for society inside the four walls of her home must not be considered by her husband or anyone else an economic "dependent," reaching out her hands in mendicant fashion for financial help.

MARY BARNETT GILSON (1877– ?), U.S. factory personnel manager, economist, and educator. *What's Past is Prologue,* ch. 26 (1940).

Gilson never married or raised a child.

9 I have spent so long erecting partitions around the part of me that writes—learning how to close the door on it when ordinary life intervenes, how to close the door on ordinary life when it's time to start writing again—that I'm not sure I could fit the two parts of me back together now.

ANNE TYLER (b. 1941), U.S. novelist. As uoted in *The Writer on Her Work,* ch. 2, by Janet Sternburg (1980).

Tyler balanced her career as a prolific, celebrated novelist with duties as wife and mother.

HOUSEWORK

1 . . . much less time should be given to school, and much more to domestic employments, especially in the wealthier classes. A little girl may begin, at five or six years of age, to assist her mother: and, if properly trained, by the time she is ten, she can render essential aid. From this time, until she is fourteen or fifteen, it should be the principal object of her education to secure a strong and healthy constitution, and a thorough practical knowledge of all kinds of domestic employments. During this period, though some attention ought to be paid to intellectual culture, it ought to be made altogether secondary in importance.

CATHERINE E. BEECHER (1800–1878), U.S. educator and author. *Treatise on Domestic Economy for the Use of Young Ladies at Home and at School,* ch. 4 (1843).

2 We work harder than ever, and I cannot see the advantages in cooperative living.

LYDIA ARNOLD, U.S. commune supervisor (of the North American Phalanx, Red Bank, New Jersey, 1843– 1855). As quoted in *Past and Promise,* part 2: article on Rebecca Buffum Spring, by Marie Marmo Mullaney (1990).

Written in a mid-1800s letter to her sister-in-law, Rebecca Buffum Spring (1811–1911). Arnold supervised the North American Phalanx's domestic work.

3 It would be as wise to set up an accomplished lawyer to saw wood as a business as to condemn an educated and sensible woman to spend all her time boiling potatoes and patching old garments. Yet this is the lot of many a one who incessantly stitches and boils and bakes, compelled to thrust back out of sight the aspirations which fill her soul.

SARAH M. GRIMKÉ (1792–1873), U.S. abolitionist and feminist. As quoted in *The Female Experience,* ch. 87, by Gerda Lerner (1977). Written in 1852.

4 You do not expect a distinguished lawyer to clean his own clothes, a doctor to groom his horse, a teacher to take care of the schoolhouse furnace, a preacher to half-sole his shoes. . . . Yet a woman who enters upon any line of achievement is invariably hampered, for at least the early years, with the inbred desire to add to the labor of her profession all the so-called feminine duties, which, fulfilled to-day, are yet to be done to-morrow, which bring her neither comfort, gain nor reputation, and which by their perpetual demand diminish her powers for a higher quality of work.

RUTH C. D. HAVENS, U.S. suffragist. As quoted in *History of Woman Suffrage,* vol. 4, ch. 13, by Susan B. Anthony and Ida Husted Harper (1902).

Speaking in 1893 at the twenty-fifth annual convention of the National Woman Suffrage Association. Havens was from Washington, D.C.; her address was entitled "The Girl of the Future."

5 You cannot make women contented with cooking and cleaning and *you need not try.*

ELLEN HENRIETTA SWALLOW RICH-ARDS, (1842–1911) U.S. chemist and educator. As quoted in *The Life of Ellen H. Richards,* ch. 15, by Caroline L. Hunt (1912).

Said c. the 1890s to a conference of educators.

6 Woman was originally the inventor, the manufacturer, the provider. She has allowed one office after another gradually to slip from her hand, until she retains, with loose grasp, only the so-called housekeeping. . . . Having thus given up one by one the occupations which required knowledge of materials and processes, and skill in using them . . . she rightly feels that what's left is mere deadening drudgery.

ELLEN HENRIETTA SWALLOW RICH-ARDS, (1842–1911) U.S. chemist and educator. *The Outlook* magazine, p. 1079 (April 24, 1897).

Richards, the first woman student ever admitted to the Massachusetts Institute of Technology, was "one of the chief organizers and theoreticians of the domestic-science movement," which sought to professionalize housekeeping by establishing a scientific knowledge base for it and formulating standards.

7 The labor of women in the house, certainly, enables men to produce more wealth than they otherwise could; and in this way women are economic factors in society. But so are horses.

CHARLOTTE PERKINS GILMAN (1860–1935), U.S. author and feminist. *Women and Economics,* ch. 1 (1898).

8 Men will not give up their privilege of helplessness without a struggle. The average man has a carefully cultivated ignorance about household matters—from what to do with the crumbs to the grocer's telephone number—a sort of cheerful inefficiency which protects him better than the reputation for having a violent temper.

CRYSTAL EASTMAN (1881–1928), U.S. social/political activist and author. *On Women and Revolution,* part 1 (1978). From an article first published in *The Liberator* in December 1920.

Published at the end of the year when, after a 72-year struggle, American women were finally enfranchised.

9 I am an inveterate homemaker, it is at once my pleasure, my recreation, and my handicap. Were I a man, my books would have been written in leisure, protected by a wife and a secretary and various household officials. As it is, being a woman, my work has had to be done between bouts of homemaking.

PEARL S. BUCK (1892–1973), U.S. author. *My Several Worlds* (1954).

10 Behind every working woman is an enormous pile of unwashed laundry.

BARBARA DALE (b. 1940), U.S. cartoonist. *The Working Woman Book,* ch. 2 (1985).

HUDSON RIVER

1 Nothing could be more beautiful than our passage down the Hudson [River]. . . . The change, the contrast, the ceaseless variety of beauty, as you skim from side to side, the liquid smoothness of the broad mirror which reflects the scene, and most of all, the clear bright air through which you look at it; all this can only be seen and believed by crossing the Atlantic. . . . The magnificent boldness of the Jersey shore on the one side, and the luxurious softness of the shady lawns on the other, with the vast silvery stream that flows between them, altogether form a picture which may well excuse a traveller for saying, once and again, that the Hudson river can be surpassed in beauty by none on the outside of Paradise.

FRANCES TROLLOPE (1780–1863), British author. *Domestic Manners of the Americans*, ch. 34 (1832).

On her trip down the Hudson River from Albany to New York City.

HUMAN INTERESTS

1 Human beings are interested in two things. They are interested in the reality and interested in telling about it.

GERTRUDE STEIN (1874–1946), U.S. author and patron of the arts; relocated to France. As quoted in *What Are Masterpieces*, afterword, by Robert Haas (1970).

Said in a January 1946 interview with Haas.

HUMAN NATURE

1 . . . it is not the color of the skin that makes the man or the woman, but the principle formed in the soul. Brilliant wit will shine, come from whence it will; and genius and talent will not hide the brightness of its lustre.

MARIA STEWART (1803–1879), African American abolitionist and schoolteacher. As quoted in *Black Women in Nineteenth-Century American Life*, part 3, by Bert James Loewenberg and Ruth Bogin (1976).

Stewart, a free African American, said this in her September 21, 1833 "Farewell Address to Her Friends" in Boston. She moved on to New York, where she became a schoolteacher.

2 Simplicity is an acquired taste. Mankind, left free, instinctively complicates life.

KATHERINE FULLERTON GEROULD (1879–1944), U.S. author. *Modes and Morals*, ch. 3 (1920).

3 Don't think of yourself as an intestinal tract and tangle of nerves in the skull, that will not work unless you drink coffee. Think of yourself as incandescent power, illuminated perhaps and forever talked to by God and his messengers. . . . Think if Tiffany's made a mosquito, how wonderful we would think it was!

BRENDA UELAND (1891–1985), U.S. author and writing teacher. *If You Want to Write*, 2nd. ed., ch. 18 (1938).

Referring to the firm founded in New York City by Charles Lewis Tiffany (1812–1902), a jeweler and silversmith.

HUMAN NEEDS

1 All the average human being asks is something he can call a home; a family that is fed and warm; and now and then a little happiness; once in a long while an extravagance.

MOTHER JONES (1830–1930), U.S. labor

organizer. *The Autobiography of Mother Jones,* ch. 27 (1925).

2 If there were no poetry on any day in the world, poetry would be invented that day. For there would be an intolerable hunger.

MURIEL RUKEYSER (1913–1980), U.S. poet. *The Life of Poetry,* ch. 10 (1949).

3 What we grieve for is not the loss of a grand vision, but rather the loss of common things, events and gestures. . . . ordinariness is the most precious thing we struggle for, what the Jews of the Warsaw Ghetto fought for. Not noble causes or abstract theories. But the right to go on living with a sense of purpose and a sense of self-worth—an ordinary life.

IRENA KLEPFISZ (b. 1941), U.S. Jewish poet, essayist, and educator; born in Poland. *Dreams of an Insomniac,* part 3 (1990).

From an April 19, 1988, address delivered at a memorial ceremony marking the forty-fifth anniversary of the Warsaw Ghetto Uprising. Klepfisz and her mother survived the uprising, in which her 30–year-old father, a Jewish rights activist, was killed. The rest of her family died during World War II, most of them in the Treblinka death camp.

4 I do not think [poetry] is more, or less, necessary than food, shelter, health, education, decent working conditions. It is as necessary.

ADRIENNE RICH (b. 1929), U.S. poet and essayist. *What Is Found There,* preface (1993). Written in February 1993.

HUMAN RIGHTS

1 Human beings have *rights,* because they are *moral* beings: the rights of *all* men grow out of their moral nature; and as all men have the same moral nature, they have essentially the same rights. These rights may be wrested from the slave, but they cannot be alienated: his title to himself is as perfect *now,* as is that of Lyman Beecher: it is stamped on his moral being, and *is,* like it, imperishable.

ANGELINA GRIMKÉ (1805–1879), U.S. abolitionist and feminist. *Letters to Catherine Beecher,* letter #12 (1837).

In a letter dated October 2, 1837. Lyman Beecher (1775–1863) was Catherine Beecher's father, an esteemed clergyman and author.

2 I recognize no rights but human rights—I know nothing of Men's rights and women's rights . . .

ANGELINA GRIMKÉ (1805–1879), U.S. abolitionist, suffragist, feminist, and author. *Letters to Catherine E. Beecher,* letter #12 (1838).

From a letter dated October 2, 1837. Beecher, a prominent educator of women, was an anti-suffragist.

3 . . . I know nothing of *man's* rights, or *woman's* rights; *human* rights are all that I recognise.

SARAH M. GRIMKÉ (1792–1873), U.S. abolitionist and feminist. *Letters on the Equality of the Sexes and the Condition of Woman,* letter #15: dated October 20, 1837 (1838).

4 ... non-use of rights does not destroy them.

MATILDA JOSLYN GAGE (1826–1898), U.S. suffragist. As quoted in *The History of Woman Suffrage,* vol. 3, ch. 27, by Elizabeth Cady Stanton, Susan B. Anthony, and herself (1886).

Speaking before the U. S. House of Representatives on March 31, 1876, as President of the National Woman Suffrage Association.

5 I have known nothing the last thirty years save the struggle for human rights on this continent. If it had been a class of men who were disfranchised and denied their legal rights, I believe I should have devoted my life precisely as I have done in behalf of my own sex.

SUSAN B. ANTHONY (1820–1906), U.S. suffragist. As quoted in *The Life and Work of Susan B. Anthony,* vol. 2, ch. 31, by Ida Husted Harper (1898).

From a speech given on February 19, 1883, at a reception held in her honor in Philadelphia; it was organized by the Citizens' Suffrage Association.

6 The most fitting monuments this nation can build are schoolhouses and homes for those who do the work of the world. It is no answer to say that they are accustomed to rags and hunger. In this world of plenty every human being has a right to food, clothes, decent shelter, and the rudiments of education.

ELIZABETH CADY STANTON (1815–1902), U.S. suffragist, author, and social reformer. *Eighty Years and More (1815–1897),* ch. 24 (1898).

7 Where, after all, do universal human rights begin? In small places, close to home—so close and so small that they cannot be seen on any map of the world. Yes they *are* the world of the individual persons: The neighborhood he lives in; the school or college he attends; the factory, farm or office where he works. Such are the places where every man, woman and child seeks equal justice, equal opportunity, equal dignity without discrimination. Unless these rights have meaning there, they have little meaning anywhere. Without concerted citizen action to uphod them close to home, we shall look in vain for progress in the larger world.

ELEANOR ROOSEVELT (1884–1962), U.S. author, diplomat, and First Lady. "Statements at Presentation of *In Your Hands: A Guide for Community Action for the Tenth Anniversary of the Universal Declaration of Human Rights,* typescript (March 27, 1958).

From a speech delivered before the United Nations.

HUMANISM

1 I support all people on earth who have bodies like and unlike my body,
skins and moles and old scars, secret and public hair, crooked toes. I support those who have done nothing large.

NAOMI SHIHAB NYE (b. 1952), U.S. poet. "Those Whom We Do Not Know," part 2, lines 1–6 (1994).

HUMANITIES

1 ... though mathematics may teach a man how to build a bridge, it is what the Scotch Universities call *the humanities*, that teach him to be civil and sweet-tempered.

AMELIA E. BARR (1831–1919), U.S. author; born in Scotland. *All the Days of My Life,* ch. 22 (1913).

On being treated rudely by a mathematics teacher.

2 The adequate study of culture, our own and those on the opposite side of the globe, can press on to fulfillment only as we learn today from the humanities as well as from the scientists.

RUTH BENEDICT (1887–1948), U.S. anthropologist. *An Anthropologist at Work,* part 5 (1959).

From the conclusion of "Anthropology and the Humanities," the address that she gave in December 1947 as Retiring President of the American Anthropological Association.

HUMILITY

1 What are they applauding for?

SUSAN B. ANTHONY (1820–1906), U.S. suffragist. As quoted in *History of Woman Suffrage,* vol. 5 ch. 2, by Ida Husted Harper (1922).

From a *Washington Times* report of the thirty-fourth annual convention of the National Woman Suffrage Association, held in Washington, D.C., in February 1902. Anthony, who had been a suffrage leader for fifty years and would celebrate her eighty-second birthday during the convention, looked around the room and said

this when greeted by "a thunder of applause" from the delegates.

HUMOR AND SATIRE

1 [The satirist] must fully possess, at least in the world of the imagination, the quality the lack of which he is deriding in others.

REBECCA WEST (1892–1983), British author. *The Strange Necessity,* ch. 7 (1928).

2 Wit has truth in it ... wisecracking is simply calisthenics with words.

DOROTHY PARKER (1893–1967), U.S. author and humorist. As quoted in *The Late Mrs. Dorothy Parker,* ch. 9, by Leslie Frewin (1986).

Parker was reputed to be the wittiest woman of her time.

HUNGER

1 I was not at all apprehensive about ... disease ... [it] had no terrors for me. The thing I most feared in the world was hunger. That was something of which I had personal knowledge.

MADELEINE [BLAIR], U.S. prostitute and "madam." *Madeleine,* ch. 4 (1919).

Explaining her carelessness about exposing herself to venereal disease when she was a young and desperate prostitute.

2 Poverty is the result of bad adjustment between the soul and its desires. ... In the days of great poverty, I did not mind the sensation of hunger. ... But ... to be deprived of tooth paste, to brush the

teeth without it, was a dreadful thing, a daily discomfort.

ALICE FOOTE MACDOUGALL, (1867–1945) U.S. businesswoman. *The Autobiography of a Business Woman,* ch. 7 (1928).
Recalling the period of deep poverty that followed her affluent childhood and preceded her eventual business success.

3   Hunger makes a human being lapse into a state of lethargy, especially city hunger. Is there any place else in the world where a human being is supposed to go hungry amidst plenty without an outcry, without protest, where only the boldest steal or kill for bread, and the timid crawl the streets, hunger like the beak of a terrible bird at night?

MERIDEL LE SUEUR (b. 1900), U.S. author. *Women on the Breadlines,* lines 1 and 26–30 (1932).
These are the first and last lines of the poem. Written in America during the Great Depression.

4   The world is out of shape . . . when there are hungry men.

LILLIAN HELLMAN (1905–1984), U.S. playwright and memoirist. *Watch on the Rhine,* Act 3 (1941).
Spoken by the character named Kurt Muller.

5   People ask me: "Why do you write about food, and eating, and drinking? Why don't you write about the struggle for power and security, and about love, the way the others do?" . . . The easiest answer is to say that, like most other humans, I am hungry.

M. F. K. FISHER (1908–1992), U.S. culinary writer and autobiographer. *The Gastronomical Me,* Foreword (1943).

6   It seems to me that our three basic needs, for food and security and love, are so mixed and mingled and entwined that we cannot straightly think of one without the others. So it happens that when I write of hunger, I am really writing about love and the hunger for it, and warmth and the love of it and the hunger for it . . . and then the warmth and richness and fine reality of hunger satisfied . . . and it is all one.

M. F. K. FISHER (b. 1908), U.S. author and food expert. *Dubious Honors,* part 2 (1988).
Written in 1943.

7   The decision to feed the world
is the real decision. No revolution
has chosen it. For that choice
    requires
that women shall be free.

ADRIENNE RICH (b. 1929), U.S. poet and feminist. "Hunger," section 4, lines 1–4 (1974–75).

8   Language is filled
with words for deprivation
images so familiar
it is hard to crack language open
into that other country
the country of being.

SUSAN GRIFFIN (b. 1943), U.S. author and feminist. "Hunger," lines 42–47 (1986).
This poem's epigraph reads: "after photographs of refugees from famine in the Sahel, taken by Sebastian Selgado, exhibited in Paris, May, 1986." The Sahel is a semiarid region of Africa between the Sahara (north) and the savannas (south). It has seen repeated droughts and fam-

ines, most recently in the mid 1980s and early
1990s.

9 Hunger makes you restless. You
dream about food—not just any
food, but perfect food, the best
food, magical meals, famous and
awe-inspiring, the one piece of
meat, the exact taste of buttery
corn, tomatoes so ripe they split
and sweeten the air, beans so crisp
they snap between the teeth, gravy
like mother's milk singing to your
bloodstream.

Dorothy Allison (b. 1953), U.S. novelist and poet. *Bastard Out of Carolina,* ch. 6
(1992).

From the autobiographical novel based on
memories of her poverty-stricken youth in
South Carolina.

10 One can endure everything except
hunger. If I were a man, maybe I fill
my stomach. But as a woman, I became a prostitute.

"**Manju**" (b. c. 1973), Nepalese prostitute;
relocated to India. As quoted in *Time* magazine, p. 51 (June 21, 1993).

She had been forced into prostitution at age thirteen.

HUNTING

1 The only ones who are really grateful for the war are the wild ducks,
such a lot of them in the marshes of
the Rhone and so peaceful . . . because all the shot-guns have been
taken away completely taken away
and nobody can shoot with them
nobody at all and the wild ducks

are very content. They act as of they
had never been shot at, never, it is
so easy to form old habits again, so
very easy.

Gertrude Stein (1874–1946), U.S. author; relocated to France. *Wars I Have Seen*
(1945).

Written in 1943.

HYPOCRISY

1 Because hypocrisy stinks in the nostrils one is likely to rate it as a more
powerful agent for destruction than
it is.

Rebecca West (1892–1983), British author. *The Strange Necessity,* ch. 7 (1928).

2 We can love an honest rogue, but
what is more offensive than a false
saint?

Jessamyn West (1902–1984), U.S. novelist. *To See the Dream,* part 1 (1956).

ICE SKATING

1 It almost alarms me how free I feel
on the ice. I don't think about the
hospital or the groceries or the
kids—I'm just in touch with myself.
It's exciting when your whole body
is moving in synchronous motion.

Tenley Albright (b. 1935), U.S. ice
skater and physician. As quoted in *Women-Sports* magazine, p. 16 (January 1975).

In 1956, Albright had become the first United
States woman to win an Olympic gold medal
for singles figure skating. Later, she studied medicine.

2 If I'm on skates, I feel at home no
matter what I'm doing. If they

wanted me to sing and dance I think I could do it just because I was on skates. When I'm not on skates, though, I feel very strange.

DOROTHY HAMILL (b. 1956), U.S. ice skater. As quoted in *WomenSports* magazine, p. 48 (June 1977).

In the preceding year, Hamill had won the Olympic gold medal for women's figure skating.

IDEALISM

I   It is well worth the efforts of a lifetime to have attained knowledge which justifies an attack on the root of all evil—viz. the deadly atheism which asserts that because forms of evil have always existed in society, therefore they must always exist; and that the attainment of a high ideal is a hopeless chimera.

ELIZABETH BLACKWELL (1821–1910), U.S. physician. *Pioneer Work for Women*, ch. 7 (1895).

Blackwell had been the first American woman physician.

2   A noble company gathered to develop a society that would create harmony, love, and usefulness. Now I sit on the grave of great hopes. . . . I look back to see a light that went out from it—small, but bright and pure and true.

REBECCA BUFFUM SPRING (1811–1911), U.S. abolitionist and educator. As quoted in *Past and Promise*, part 2, by Marie Marmo Mullaney (1990).

In a letter to J. L. Kearney dated October 25, 1897. She was remembering Eagleswood, a progressive, coeducational boarding school in Perth Amboy, New Jersey, founded and operated by her and her husband, Marcus Spring, from 1853 to 1868. It eventually became an

overwhelming responsibility for them, and they closed it. Also, despite her Quaker upbringing and convictions, they had found it necessary to provide military training for boys.

3   If we love-and-serve an ideal we reach backward in time to its inception and forward to its consummation. To grow is sometimes to hurt; but who would return to smallness?

SARAH PATTON BOYLE, U.S. civil rights activist and author. *The Desegregated Heart*, part 3, ch. 3 (1962).

IDEALIZATION OF WOMEN

I   A pedestal is as much a prison as any other small space.

ANONYMOUS WOMAN (c. mid–1800s), African American feminist. As quoted in *Moving Beyond Words*, part 4, by Gloria Steinem (1994).

Said sometime in the latter half of the nineteenth century. Steinem first heard this while organizing in the American south in the early 1970s. It was attributed to an anonymous African American woman of the suffragist/abolitionist era, who supposedly said it to white Southern women, with reference to their social situation.

2   We are tired of the pretense that we have special privileges and the reality that we have none; of the fiction that we are queens, and the fact that we are subjects; of the symbolism which exalts our sex but is only a meaningless mockery.

LILLIE DEVEREUX BLAKE (1835–1913), U.S. suffragist. As quoted in *History of Woman Suffrage*, vol. 4, ch. 2, by Susan B. Anthony and Ida Husted Harper (1902).

In a speech entitled "The Unknown Quantity in Politics," delivered at an 1884 convention of the National Woman Suffrage Association; Blake was a delegate from New York.

IDEALS

1 . . . my whole existence is governed by abstract ideas. . . . the ideal must be preserved regardless of fact.

MARY CORINNA PUTNAM (1842–1906), U.S. physician, pharmacist, and feminist. As quoted in *The Female Experience*, ch. 3, by Gerda Lerner (1977).

Written to a friend in 1858, referring to her family's expectation that she give higher priority to learning to play the piano and to caring for her younger siblings than to her own education and work. She would become the first woman ever admitted to the Ecole de Medecin in Paris, receiving an M.D. degree in 1871. She had been awarded an M.D. by the less prestigious Woman's Medical College of Pennsylvania in 1864. After her marriage, Putnam was known as Mary Putnam Jacobi.

2 To live for a principle, for the triumph of some reform by which all mankind are to be lifted up—to be wedded to an idea—may be, after all, the holiest and happiest of marriages.

ELIZABETH CADY STANTON (1815–1902), U.S. suffragist, social reformer, speaker, author, and editor. As quoted in *The Life and Work of Susan B. Anthony*, ch. 50, by Ida Husted Harper (1898–1908).

Said in the late 1800s, reflecting on her longtime friend and colleague, Susan B. Anthony, who had never married. Stanton, on the other hand, was married and the mother of seven children.

3 . . . ideals, standards, aspirations,—those are chameleon words, and take color from their speakers,—often false tints. A scholarly man of my acquaintance once told me that he traveled a thousand miles into the desert to get away from the word *uplift*, and it was the first word he heard after he reached his destination.

CAROLYN WELLS (1862–1942), U.S. author. *The Rest of My Life*, ch. 4 (1937).

4 He was one whose glory was an inner glory, one who placed culture above prosperity, fairness above profit, generosity above possessions, hospitality above comfort, courtesy above triumph, courage above safety, kindness above personal welfare, honor above success.

SARAH PATTON BOYLE, U.S. civil rights activist and author. *The Desegregated Heart*, part 1, ch. 1 (1962).

A native of Virginia, she was describing the Virginian's ideal self-image.

IDEAS

1 . . . women are more quiet. They don't feel called to mount a barrel and harangue by the hour every time they imagine they have produced an idea.

ANNA JULIA COOPER (1859–1964), U.S. educator and feminist. *A Voice from the South*, part 1 (1892).

Distinguishing between men and women of "mental attainment."

2 . . . I knew I wanted to be permanently self-supporting and I vaguely thought I might work somewhere in the realm of ideas. I felt that I had within me an undeveloped fount of ideas. I did not know exactly what my ideas were, but whatever they were I wanted to convert people to them.

RHETA CHILDE DORR (1866–1948), U.S. journalist. *A Woman of Fifty,* 2nd. ed., ch. 2 (1924).

On growing up and envisioning her future in the late 1800s. She eventually became an important journalist, suffragist, and social reform advocate.

3 . . . when the Spaniards persecuted
heretics they may have been crude,
but they were not being unreasonable or unpractical. They were at
least wiser than the people of to-day
who pretend that it does not matter
what a man believes, as who should
say that the flavour and digestibility
of a pudding will have nothing to
do with its ingredients.

REBECCA WEST (1892–1983), British author. *The Strange Necessity,* ch. 10 (1928).
Of the Spanish Inquisition, which existed
1480–1808.

4 These people who are always briskly
doing something and as busy as
waltzing mice, they have little,
sharp, staccato ideas. . . . But they
have no slow, big ideas. And the
fewer consoling, noble, shining,
free, jovial, magnanimous ideas that
come, the more nervously and desperately they rush and run from office to office and up and downstairs, thinking by action at last to
make life have some warmth and
meaning.

BRENDA UELAND (1891–1985), U.S. au-
thor and writing teacher. *If You Want to Write,*
2nd. ed., ch. 4 (1938).

5 I have always fought for ideas—until I learned that it isn't ideas but
grief, struggle, and flashes of vision
which enlighten.

MARGARET ANDERSON (1886–1973),
U.S. editor and memoirist. *The Strange Necessity,* part 1 (1969).

6 A new idea is rarely born like Venus
attended by graces

More commonly it's modeled of
baling wire and acne.
More commonly it wheezes and
tips over.

MARGE PIERCY (b. 1936), U.S. poet, novelist, and political activist. "Rough Times," lines
20–22 (1976).

7 . . . it is through poetry that we give
name to those ideas which are—until the poem—nameless and form-
less, about to be birthed, but already felt. That distillation of experience from which true poetry
springs births thought as dreams
birth concept, as feeling births idea,
as knowledge births (precedes) understanding.

AUDRE LORDE (1934–1992), African
American poet, autobiographer, and lesbian
feminist. *Sister Outsider,* ch. 3 (1984).
From "Poetry is Not a Luxury," an essay first
published in *Chrysalis,* number 3 (1977).

IDENTITY

1 What we buy, and pay for, is part of
ourselves.

AMELIA E. BARR (1831–1919), U.S. au-
thor; born in Scotland. *All the Days of My Life,*
ch. 13 (1913).

2 I am I because my little dog knows
me but, creatively speaking the little
dog knowing that you are you and
your recognising that he knows,
that is what destroys creation. That
is what makes school.

GERTRUDE STEIN (1874–1946), U.S. au-
thor and patron of the arts; relocated to France.
*What Are Masterpieces and Why Are There So
Few of Them* (1936).

3 Our foreparents were mostly brought from West Africa. . . . We were brought to America and our foreparents were sold; white people bought them; white people changed their names . . . my maiden name is supposed to be Townsend, but really, what is my maiden name? What is my name?

FANNIE LOU HAMER (1917–1977), African American civil rights activist. As quoted in *This Little Light of Mine,* ch. 7, by Hay Mills (1993).

The Mississippi civil rights leader, granddaughter of a slave, was reflecting in the 1960s on black Americans' situation after visiting an African country (Guinea) for the first time.

4 In some extremely important ways, people are what you expect them to be, or at least they behave as you expect them to behave.

NAOMI WEISSTEIN, U.S. psychologist, feminist, and author. *Psychology Constructs the Female* (1969).

5 When those who have the power to name and to socially construct reality choose not to see you or hear . you . . . when someone with the authority of a teacher, say, describes the world and you are not in it, there is a moment of psychic disequilibrium, as if you looked in the mirror and saw nothing. It takes some strength of soul—and not just individual strength, but collective understanding—to resist this void, this non-being, into which you are thrust, and to stand up, demanding to be seen and heard.

ADRIENNE RICH (b. 1929), U.S. poet, essayist, and lesbian feminist. *Blood, Bread and Poetry,* ch. 13 (1986).

From an essay written in 1984.

6 I'm neither Czech nor Slovak . . . I'm still trying to figure out who I am. I think I'm Jewish. But first I want to be human.

NATASHA DUDINSKA (b. c. 1967), Czechoslovakian Jew; attending college in America. As quoted in the *New York Times,* sect. 4, p. 7 (June 13, 1993).

A Czechoslovakian citizen and New York City resident, Dudinska was reflecting on the downfall of the Communist regime in her native country. She disapproved of the subsequent division of the country into the Czech and Slovak republics.

IDLENESS

I How many women . . . waste life away the prey of discontent, who might have practised as physicians, regulated a farm, managed a shop, and stood erect, supported by their own industry, instead of hanging their heads surcharged with the dew of sensibility, that consumes the beauty to which it at first gave lustre . . .

MARY WOLLSTONECRAFT (1759–1797), British feminist. *A Vindication of the Rights of Woman,* ch. 9 (1792).

2 . . . she was a woman. She had been taught from her earliest childhood to make use of this talent which God had endowed her, would be an outrage against society; so she lived for a few years, going through the routine of breakfasts and dinners, journeys and parties, that society demanded of her, and at last sank into her grave, after having been of little use to the world or herself.

MATILDA JOSLYN GAGE (1826–1898), U.S. suffragist. As quoted in *Feminine Ingenuity,* ch. 2, by Anne L. MacDonald (1992).

Of a friend who wished to become an engineer and, had she been male, would have done so.

3 Work is the best of narcotics, providing the patient be strong enough to take it. . . . I . . . dread idleness as if it were Hell.

BEATRICE WEBB (1858–1943), British author and socialist. As quoted in *Beatrice Webb,* ch. 10, by Carole Seymour-Jones (1992).
Written in her diary on March 8, 1885, upon throwing herself into charitable work after a romance ended.

4 We might all place ourselves in one of two ranks—the women who do something, and the women who do nothing; the first being of course the only creditable place to occupy.

LUCY LARCOM (1824–1893), U.S. poet and teacher. *A New England Girlhood,* ch. 9 (1889).
Larcom began earning her living as a mill worker in Lowell, Massachusetts, at age 11.

5 The day has gone by into the dim vista of the past when idleness was considered a virtue in woman.

CAROLINE A. HULING (1857–1941), U.S. businesswoman. As quoted in *What America Owes to Women,* ch. 42, by Lydia Hoyt Farmer (1893).
Huling was Vice-President of the Woman's Baking Company of Chicago, a substantial business founded, owned, and run entirely by women.

6 . . . to *work,* to work hard, to see work steadily, and see it whole, was the way to be reputable. I think I always respected a good blacksmith more than a lady of leisure.

ELIZABETH STUART PHELPS (1844–1911), U.S. novelist and short story writer. *Chapters from a Life,* ch. 3 (1897).

7 . . . we have come to think of all idleness as hoggish, not as creative and radiant.

BRENDA UELAND (1891–1985), U.S. author and writing teacher. *If You Want to Write,* 2nd. ed., ch. 6 (1938).

8 . . . idleness is an evil. I don't think man can maintain his balance or sanity in idleness. Human beings must work to create some coherence. You do it only through work and through love. And you can only count on work.

BARBARA TERWILLIGER (b. c. 1940), U.S. unemployed woman. As quoted in *Working,* book 7, by Studs Terkel (1973).
A single woman with an independent income, she was not working. In her younger years, she had held various jobs.

9 I can't remember what I was doing before running. I guess shopping, sewing, watching TV—gaining nothing.

MIKI GORMAN (b. 1935), U.S. marathon runner; born in China. As quoted in *WomenSports* magazine, p. 28 (November 1977).
Gorman, a marathon champion, had begun running at age 33.

10 . . . pessimism is a product of inactivity.

STELLA NOWICKI (*c.* 1905–?), U.S. labor organizer. As quoted in *American Dreams,* book 1, part 2, by Studs Terkel (1980).
A labor organizer and member of the Young Communist League in the 1930s, Nowicki was one of three labor movement veterans featured in the 1976 documentary film, *Union Maids.*

11 If you rest, you rust.

HELEN HAYES (1900–1993), U.S. actor. *My Life in Three Acts,* ch. 19 (1990).
An actor from age five until into her seventies, and thereafter a speaker and an activist on be-

half of the elderly, Hayes used to tell this to the audiences at her speeches.

GEORGE ELIOT (1819–1880), British novelist. *Middlemarch*, ch. 35 (1871–1872).

IDOLATRY

1 . . . we need to interrogate "reverence," for idolization can be another way one is objectified and not really taken seriously.

BELL HOOKS (b. c. 1955), African American feminist author and educator. *Yearning*, ch. 10 (1990).

IGNORANCE

1 . . . there are no chains so galling as the chains of ignorance—no fetters so binding as those that bind the soul, and exclude it from the vast field of useful and scientific knowledge. O, had I received the advantages of early education, my ideas would, ere now, have expanded far and wide; but, alas! I possess nothing but moral capability—no teachings but the teachings of the Holy Spirit.

MARIA STEWART (1803–1879), African American abolitionist and schoolteacher. As quoted in *Black Women in Nineteenth-Century American Life*, part 3, by Bert James Loewenberg and Ruth Bogin (1976).

Stewart, a free African American, said this in a September 21, 1832 speech delivered at Franklin Hall in Boston. She asserted that, bad as Southern slavery was, the condition of uneducated free Northern African Americans was "but little better."

2 We are all humiliated by the sudden discovery of a fact which has existed very comfortably and perhaps been staring at us in private while we have been making up our world entirely without it.

ILLEGITIMACY

1 No legislation can suppress nature; all life rushes to reproduction; our procreative faculties are matured early, while passion is strong, and judgment and self-restraint weak. We cannot alter this, but we can alter what is conventional. We can refuse to brand an act of nature as a crime, and to impute to vice what is due to ignorance.

TENNESSEE CLAFLIN (1846–1923), U.S. journalist, lecturer, and social reform advocate; relocated to England. *Talks and Essays*, vol. 3, ch. 8 (1897).

Arguing against British laws that limited the rights of illegitimate offspring.

ILLNESS

1 To you illness is negligible. You have learned that you can dominate yourself. You know that your body lags, but your soul proceeds upon its triumphant way.

ALICE FOOTE MACDOUGALL, (1867–1945) U.S. businesswoman. *The Autobiography of a Business Woman*, ch. 7 (1928).

On the lessons learned through struggling to become a success in business.

2 You play through it. That's what you do. You just play through it.

HEATHER FARR (1965–1993), U.S. golfer. As quoted in the *New York Times*, p. B12 (November 22, 1993).

In 1992, the star golfer, who had been battling cancer for three years, explained her method of dealing with her health problem. She died of it a year later.

ILLUSION

1 . . . effective magic is transcendent nature . . .

GEORGE ELIOT (1819–1880), British novelist. *Middlemarch,* ch. 39 (1871–1872).

2 Bewitched is half of everything.

NELLY SACHS (1891–1970), German Jewish poet and translator; relocated to Sweden. "Bewitched is half of everything," line 1, translated by Michael Hamburger, et al. (1967; first edition in German: 1957).

Sachs was cowinner of the 1966 Nobel Prize for Literature.

IMAGINATION

1 We are all of us imaginative in some form or other, for images are the brood of desire . . .

GEORGE ELIOT (1819–1880), British novelist. *Middlemarch,* ch. 34 (1871–1872).

2 The literary artist will . . . portray what he knows, and little else. Imagination is built upon knowledge, and his dreams will rest upon his facts. He is worth to the world just about what he has learned from it, and no more.

ELIZABETH STUART PHELPS (1844–1911), U.S. novelist and short story writer. *Chapters from a Life,* ch. 11 (1897).

3 Imagination, industry, and intelligence—"the three I's"—are all indispensable to the actress, but of these three the greatest is, without any doubt, imagination.

ELLEN TERRY (1847–1928), British actor. *Ellen Terry's Memoirs,* 2nd. ed., ch. 2 (1932). Written in 1906 or 1907.

4 Personality is more important than beauty, but imagination is more important than both of them.

LAURETTE TAYLOR (1887–1946), U.S. actor. As quoted in *Actors on Acting,* rev. ed., part 13, by Toby Cole and Helen Krich (1970). About the qualities most needed by actors.

5 . . . an actor is exactly as big as his imagination.

MINNIE MADDERN FISKE (1865–1932), U.S. actor. As quoted in *Mrs. Fiske: Her Views on Actors, Acting and the Problems of Production,* ch. 3, by Alexander Woollcott (1917).

6 . . . the imagination needs moodling,—long, inefficient, happy idling, dawdling and puttering.

BRENDA UELAND (1891–1985), U.S. author and writing teacher. *If You Want to Write,* 2nd. ed., ch. 4 (1938).

7 Imagination of my kind is most caught, most fired, most worked upon by the unfamiliar: I have thriven . . . on the changes and chances, the dislocations and . . . contrasts which have made up so much of my life.

ELIZABETH BOWEN (1899–1973), British novelist, essayist, and memoirist; born in Ireland. *Pictures and Conversations,* ch. 1 (1975).

8 Write about winter in the summer. Describe Norway as Ibsen did, from a desk in Italy; describe Dublin as James Joyce did, from a desk in Paris. Willa Cather wrote her prairie novels in New York City; Mark Twain wrote *Huckleberry Finn* in Hartford, Connecticut. Recently, scholars learned that Walt Whitman rarely left his room.

ANNIE DILLARD (b. 1945), U.S. author. *The Writing Life*, ch. 5 (1989).

IMMIGRATION AND IMMIGRANTS

1 . . . the aspiring immigrant . . . is not content to progress alone. Solitary success is imperfect success in his eyes. He must take his family with him as he rises.

MARY ANTIN (1881–1949), U.S. socialite and author; born in Russia. *The Promised Land*, ch. 19 (1912).
A Jew born in Russia, Antin emigrated to America with her family when she was 15 and settled in a Boston slum.

2 . . . the more we recruit from immigrants who bring no personal traditions with them, the more America is going to ignore the things of the spirit. No one whose consuming desire is either for food or for motor-cars is going to care about culture, or even know what it is.

KATHERINE FULLERTON GEROULD (1879–1944), U.S. author. *Modes and Morals*, ch. 4 (1920).

3 Our national experience in Americanizing millions of Europeans whose chief wish was to become Americans has been a heady wine which has made us believe, as perhaps no nation before us has ever believed, that, given the slimmest chance, all peoples will pattern themselves upon our model.

RUTH BENEDICT (1887–1948), U.S. anthropologist. *An Anthropologist at Work*, part 5 (1959).

4 I have a huge need for financial security; the emigrant in me has a fear of ending up homeless and in the gutter.

RUTH BEHAR (b. 1956), U.S. anthropologist. *Chronicle of Higher Education*, p. A44 (November 4, 1992).
Winner of the extremely prestigious (and remunerative) MacArthur Fellowship, Behar was the granddaughter of a Russian Jew who emigrated to Cuba in 1924 and much later, after the Cuban Revolution, to the United States.

IMMORTALITY

1 Nothing is more consuming, or more illogical, than the desire for remembrance.

ELLEN GLASGOW (1873–1945), U.S. novelist. *The Woman Within*, ch. 21 (1954). Written in 1937.

2 . . . the reason I keep doing it is for the tremendous rush I get at the end of any great swim. . . . there is . . . nothing greater than touching the shore after crossing some great body of water knowing that I've done it with my own two arms and legs. . . . I'm overwhelmed by the strength of my body and the power of my mind. For one moment, just one second, I feel immortal.

DIANA NYAD (b. 1949), U.S. long-distance swimmer. As quoted in *WomenSports* magazine, p. 38 (March 1976).
On why she continued marathon swimming despite its gruelling nature and her dislike of the requisite tough training.

INDEPENDENCE

1 No genuine equality, no real freedom, no true manhood or woman-

hood can exist on any foundation save that of pecuniary independence. As a right over a man's subsistence is a power over his moral being, so a right over a woman's subsistence enslaves her will, degrades her pride and vitiates her whole moral nature.

SUSAN B. ANTHONY (1820–1907), U.S. suffragist. As quoted in *The Life of Susan B. Anthony,* vol. 1, ch. 11, by Ida Husted Harper (1897).
In an 1859 letter to an organization called the Friends of Human Progress.

2   Men will say that in supporting their wives, in furnishing them with houses and food and clothes, they are giving the women as much money as they could ever hope to earn by any other profession. I grant it; but between the independent wage-earner and the one who is given his keep for his services is the difference between the free-born and the chattel.

ELIZABETH M. GILMER (1861–1951), U.S. author. As quoted in *History of Woman Suffrage,* vol. 5, ch. 3, by Ida Husted Harper (1922).
From an address entitled "The Woman with the Broom," delivered in March 1903 at the thirty-fifth annual convention of the National Woman Studies Association.

3   Indeed, I thought, slipping the silver into my purse . . . what a change of temper a fixed income will bring about. No force in the world can take from me my five hundred pounds. Food, house and clothing are mine for ever. Therefore not merely do effort and labour cease,

but also hatred and bitterness. I need not hate any man; he cannot hurt me. I need not flatter any man; he has nothing to give me.

VIRGINIA WOOLF (1882–1941), British author. *A Room of One's Own,* ch. 2 (1929).
On inheriting 500 pounds per year from her aunt, Mary Beton.

4   With only one life to live we can't afford to live it only for itself. Somehow we must each for himself, find the way in which we can make our individual lives fit into the pattern of all the lives which surround it. We must establish our own relationships to the whole. And each must do it in his own way, using his own talents, relying on his own integrity and strength, climbing his own road to his own summit.

HORTENSE ODLUM (1892– ?), U.S. businesswoman. *A Woman's Place,* ch. 17 (1939).

5   Autonomy means women defining themselves and the values by which they will live, and beginning to think of institutional arrangements which will order their environment in line with their needs. . . . Autonomy means moving out from a world in which one is born to marginality, to a past without meaning, and a future determined by others—into a world in which one acts and chooses, aware of a meaningful past and free to shape one's future.

GERDA LERNER (b. 1920), U.S. historian and feminist. *The Female Experience,* Introduction (1977).

6   I have a sense of going my own way, and I don't really think much about whether it's going against the grain. I don't really want to spend a lot of time worrying about how I am perceived by other people.

KATHLEEN COLLINS (1931–1988), African American filmmaker. As quoted in *Reel Women*, part 4, by Ally Acker (1991). Said in 1986, in response to criticisms of her films' content: e.g., a negative depiction of an African American marriage.

INDEPENDENCE OF WOMEN

1 [Girls] study under the paralyzing idea that their acquirements cannot be brought into practical use. They may subserve the purposes of promoting individual domestic pleasure and social enjoyment in conversation, but what are they in comparison with the grand stimulation of independence and self-reliance, of the capability of contributing to the comfort and happiness of those whom they love as their own souls?

SARAH M. GRIMKE (1792–1873), U.S. abolitionist and feminist. As quoted in *The Female Experience*, ch. 87, by Gerda Lerner (1977). Written in 1852.

2 I have defeated them all. . . . I was left with some money to battle with the world when quite young, and at the present time have much to feel proud of. . . . The Lord gave me talent, and I know I have done good with it. . . . For my brains have made me quite independent and without the help of any man.

HARRIET A. BROWN, U.S. inventor and educator. As quoted in *Feminine Ingenuity*, ch. 8, by Anne L. MacDonald (1992). Said in 1871. Brown headed the Boston Dress-cutting College, said to be "the only dress-cutting and making college in the United States."

3 When women can support themselves, have entry to all the trades and professions, with a house of their own over their heads and a bank account, they will own their bodies and be dictators in the social realm.

ELIZABETH CADY STANTON (1815–1902), U.S. author, suffragist, and social reformer. *Elizabeth Cady Stanton as Revealed in her Letters, Diary and Reminiscences*, vol. 2, diary entry dated December 27, 1890 (1922).

4 The isolation of every human soul and the necessity of self-dependence must give each individual the right to choose his own surroundings. The strongest reason for giving woman all the opportunities for higher education, for the full development of her faculties, her forces of mind and body; for giving her the most enlarged freedom of thought and action; a complete emancipation from all forms of bondage, of custom, dependence, superstition; from all the crippling influences of fear—is the solitude and personal responsibility of her own individual life.

ELIZABETH CADY STANTON (1815–1902), U.S. suffragist, author, and social reformer. *The Solitude of Self* (1894). First presented on February 20, 1894 as a speech to a Senate subcommittee. It has endured as one of the most eloquent and original arguments ever made for women's rights.

5 Your small hands, precisely equal to
my own—
only the thumb is larger, longer—in
these hands
I could trust the world, or in many
hands like these,
handling power-tools or steering-
wheel
or touching a human face . . .

ADRIENNE RICH (b. 1929), U.S. poet and
lesbian feminist. *Twenty-One Love Poems,*
poem #6, lines 1–5 (1974–76).
On the notion of a world managed by women.

6 I've really never accepted the idea
that a woman can't do whatever the
hell it is she wants.

SYLVIA CHASE (b. 1938), U.S. television
newswoman. As quoted in *Women in Television News,* ch. 2, by Judith S. Gelfman (1976).
Chase was an early television newswoman.

7 [My daughter] says she wants to
marry a rich man, so she can have a
Porsche. My rejoinder always is: Go
out and get rich yourself, so you
can buy your own.

CAROL ROYCE (b. 1942), U.S. radio station administrator. As quoted in *The Great
Divide,* book 1, section 2, by Studs Terkel
(1988).
Royce, a divorcee who administered a classi-
cal-music station, was speaking of her daughter,
a pizza parlor employee and vocational-school
student.

8 Madonna has total control over her
life, and not many women have
that.

MONICA SELES (b. 1973), Yugoslavian ten-
nis player; relocated to America. As quoted in
Sports Illustrated, p. 63 (May 27, 1991).
On why she admired the controversial, rich,
and flamboyantly independent rock star,
Madonna.

9 I'm tough, I'm ambitious, and I
know exactly what I want. If that
makes me a bitch, OK.

MADONNA (b. 1958), U.S. singer and actor.
As quoted in *People* magazine (July 27, 1992).
Madonna was an extremely flamboyant, original, controversial, and financially successful
public figure.

INDIVIDUALISM

I The strongest reason why we ask
for woman a voice in the government under which she lives; in the
religion she is asked to believe;
equality in social life, where she is
the chief factor; a place in the trades
and professions, where she may
earn her bread, is because of her
birthright to self-sovereignty; because, as an individual, she must
rely on herself.

ELIZABETH CADY STANTON (1815–
1902), U.S. suffragist, social reformer, and author. As quoted in *History of Woman Suffrage,*
vol. 4, ch. 12, by Susan B. Anthony and Ida
Husted Harper (1902).
From the 1892 address which was perhaps the
great suffragist's most famous: "The Solitude of
the Self."

2 Before any woman is a wife, a sister
or a mother she is a human being.
We ask nothing as women but everything as human beings.

IDA C. HULTIN, U.S. minister and suffragist. As quoted in *History of Woman Suffrage,*
vol. 4, ch. 17, by Susan B. Anthony and Ida
Husted Harper (1902).
Speaking before the twenty-ninth annual convention of the National Woman Suffrage Association, held January 26–29, 1897, in Des
Moines, Iowa. Hultin's address was entitled
"The Point of View"; she was from Illinois.

3 [Anarchism] is the philosophy of the sovereignty of the individual. It is the theory of social harmony. It is the great, surging, living truth that is reconstructing the world, and that will usher in the Dawn.

EMMA GOLDMAN (1869–1940), U.S. anarchist and author; born in Russia. *Anarchism and Other Essays*, 3rd rev. ed., ch. 1 (1917).

2 The artist's personality must be left in his dressing-room; his soul must be denuded of its own sensations and clothed with the base or noble qualities he is called upon to exhibit. . . . [he] must leave behind him the cares and vexations of life, throw aside his personality for several hours, and move in the dream of another life, forgetting everything.

SARAH BERNHARDT (1845–1923), French actor. *The Art of the Theatre*, ch. 3 (1924). Written in 1923.

INDIVIDUALITY

1 The point I wish plainly to bring before you on this occasion is the individuality of each human soul—our Protestant idea, the right of individual conscience and judgment—our republican idea, individual citizenship. In discussing the rights of woman, we are to consider, first, what belongs to her as an individual, in a world of her own, the arbiter of her own destiny, an imaginary Robinson Crusoe with her woman Friday on a solitary island. Her rights under such circumstances are to use all her faculties for her own safety and happiness.

ELIZABETH CADY STANTON (1815–1902), U.S. suffragist, social reformer, and author. *The Solitude of Self* (February 20, 1894). These are the opening lines of a famous speech delivered before a Senate committee which was considering arguments in favor of woman suffrage. Printed in the *Congressional Record* and reprinted in the *Women's Tribune*, the speech was remarkable for its refusal to engage the usual practical and democratic pro-suffrage arguments. Also speaking on this occasion were three of Stanton's best-known sister suffragists: Susan B. Anthony (1820–1906), Lucy Stone (1818–1893), and Isabella Beecher Hooker (1822–1907).

INFLUENCE

1 It is in vain that we would circumscribe the power of one half of our race, and that half by far the most important and influential. If they exert it not for good, they will for evil; if they advance not knowledge, they will perpetuate ignorance. Let women stand where they may in the scale of improvement, their position decides that of the race.

FRANCES WRIGHT (1795–1852), Scottish author and speaker; relocated to America. *Course of Popular Lectures*, lecture 2 (1829).

2 All places where women are excluded tend downward to barbarism; but the moment she is introduced, there come in with her courtesy, cleanliness, sobriety, and order.

HARRIET BEECHER STOWE (1811–1896), U.S. author. *Household Papers and Stories*, part 2, ch. 2 (1864).

3 I believe that the influence of woman will save the country before every other power.

LUCY STONE (1818–1893), U.S. suffragist. As quoted in *History of Woman Suffrage*, vol. 2, ch. 22, by Elizabeth Cady Stanton, Susan B. Anthony, and Matilda Joslyn Gage (1882).
Arguing for woman suffrage at a May 12, 1869, anniversary celebration of the Equal Rights Association.

4 You will not find science annihilating personality from the government of the Universe and making of God as ungovernable, unintelligible, blind, often destructive physical force; you will not find jurisprudence formulating as an axiom the absurdity that man and wife are one, and that one the man—that the married woman may not hold or bequeath her own property save as subject to her husband's direction; you will not find political economists declaring that the only possible adjustment between laborers and capitalists is that of selfishness and rapacity—that each must get all he can and keep all that he gets, while the world cries *laissez faire* and the lawyers explain, "it is the beautiful working of the law of supply and demand;" in fine, you will not find the law of love shut out from the affairs of men after the feminine half of the world's truth is completed.

ANNA JULIA COOPER (1859–1964), U.S. educator and feminist. *A Voice from the South*, part 1 (1892).

5 It is not the intelligent woman v. the ignorant woman; nor the white

woman v. the black, the brown, and the red,—it is not even the cause of woman v. man. Nay, 'tis woman's strongest vindication for speaking that *the world needs to hear her voice.*

ANNA JULIA COOPER (1859–1964), African American educator and feminist. *A Voice from the South*, part 1 (1892).

6 . . . it is as true in morals as in physics that all force is imperishable; therefore the consequences of a human action never cease.

TENNESSEE CLAFLIN (1846–1923), U.S. journalist, lecturer, and social reform advocate; relocated to England. *Talks and Essays*, vol. 1, ch. 7 (1897).

7 Who can measure the advantages that would result if the magnificent abilities of these women could be devoted to the needs of government, society and home, instead of being consumed in the struggle to obtain their birthright of individual freedom? Until this be gained we can never know, we can not even prophesy the capacity and power of women for the uplifting of humanity.

SUSAN B. ANTHONY (1820–1906), U.S. suffragist. As quoted in *Life and Work of Susan B. Anthony*, vol. 3, ch. 53, by Ida Husted Harper (1908).
From an address entitled "Position of Women in the Political Life of the United States," delivered on June 27, 1899, to the International Council of Women in London. She was referring to the large amounts of time, over more than five decades, that she and dozens of other women had devoted to the struggle for suffrage.

8 They tell us that women can bring better things to pass by indirect influence. Try to persuade any man that he will have more weight, more influence, if he gives up his vote, allies himself with no party and relies on influence to achieve his ends! By all means let us use to the utmost whatever influence we have, but in all justice do not ask us to be content with this.

Mrs. William C. Gannett, U.S. suffragist. As quoted in *History of Woman Suffrage,* vol. 5, ch. 8, by Ida Husted Harper (1922).
Speaking in October 1908 before the fortieth annual convention of the National Woman Suffrage Association, with reference to the common antisuffrage argument that women did not need the vote because they exerted even stronger influence upon events through their private family roles. The speaker was identified only as the "wife of the Unitarian minister, William C. Gannett of Rochester, N.Y." and as a "loving friend" of the late suffragist leader Susan B. Anthony (1820–1906).

9 Woman's success in lifting men out of their way of life nearly resembling that of the beasts—who merely hunted and fished for food, who found shelter where they could in jungles, in trees, and caves—was a civilizing triumph.

Mary Beard (1876–1958), U.S. historian. *Woman as Force in History,* ch. 12 (1946).

10 . . . so long as the serpent continues to crawl on the ground, the primary influence of woman will be indirect . . .

Ellen Glasgow (1873–1945), U.S. novelist. *The Woman Within,* ch. 16 (1954).
Despite this conviction, Glasgow had campaigned actively for woman suffrage—which was granted in 1920.

INFORMATION

1 Do not seek for information of which you cannot make use.

Anna C. Brackett (1836–1911), U.S. author. *The Technique of Rest,* ch. 2 (1892).

INJUSTICE

1 Much suspected of me,
Nothing proved can be,
Quoth Elizabeth, prisoner.

Elizabeth I (1533–1603), Queen of England (1558–1603). As quoted in *The Sayings of Queen Elizabeth,* ch. 1, by Frederick Chamberlin (1923).
Written with a diamond on a glass window in 1554, when she was still Princess Elizabeth, during her unjust imprisonment for treason.

2 There are answers which, in turning away wrath, only send it to the other end of the room, and to have a discussion coolly waived when you feel that justice is all on your own side is even more exasperating in marriage than in philosophy.

George Eliot (1819–1880), British novelist. *Middlemarch,* ch. 29 (1871–1872).

3 Goodbye, boys; I'm under arrest. I may have to go to jail. I may not see you for a long time. Keep up the fight! Don't surrender! Pay no attention to the injunction machine at Parkersburg. The Federal judge is a scab anyhow. While you starve he plays golf. While you serve humanity, he serves injunctions for the money powers.

Mother Jones (1830–1930), U.S. labor organizer. *The Autobiography of Mother Jones,* ch. 7 (1925).

Addressing a June 1902 meeting of miners in Clarksburg, West Virginia, after just having been placed under arrest by a United States Marshal. An injunction had been obtained to prevent her from speaking.

4 All my life long I have been sensible of the injustice constantly done to women. Since I have had to fight the world single-handed, there has not been one day I have not smarted under the wrongs I have had to bear, because I was not only a woman, but a woman doing a man's work, without any man, husband, son, brother or friend, to stand at my side, and to see some semblance of justice done me. Icannot forget, for injustice is a sixth sense, and rouses all the others.

AMELIA E. BARR (1831–1919), U.S. author; born in Scotland. *All the Days of My Life*, ch. 26 (1913).
Widowed in her late thirties and left with three daughters to support entirely by herself, Barr had managed to become a popular writer of fiction, poetry, and nonfiction. Though not an active suffragist, she supported woman suffrage and other social reforms.

5 The good die young—but not always. The wicked prevail—but not consistently. I am confused by life, and I feel safe within the confines of the theatre.

HELEN HAYES (1900–1993), U.S. actor. *On Reflection*, ch. 14 (1968).

6 Justice is not blind—she very often "peeks" to determine the race, economic status, sex, and religion of persons prior to determination of guilt.

CONNIE SLAUGHTER (b. c. 1946), African American civil rights attorney and activist. As quoted in *Ms.* magazine, p. 47 (January 1973).
Slaughter was the first African American woman elected president of Tougaloo College student body and the first to graduate from the University of Mississippi.

7 For all the injustices in our past and our present, we have to believe that in the free exchange of ideas, justice will prevail over injustice, tolerance over intolerance and progress over reaction.

HILLARY RODHAM CLINTON (b. 1947), U.S. attorney; First Lady of the United States. P. A17 (May 18, 1993).
From the First Lady's commencement speech a day earlier at the University of Pennsylvania, which had recently experienced racial conflicts.

INNOCENCE

1 . . . pure and intelligent women can be deceived and misled by the baser sort, their very innocence and experience making them credulous and the helpless tools of the guilty and bold.

CATHERINE E. BEECHER (1800–1878), U.S. educator and author. *Woman's Profession as Mother and Educator, with Views in Opposition to Woman Suffrage, "An Address to the Christian Women of America,"* (1872).
She was framing an argument against woman suffrage, claiming that "pure" women would be easily led to unfortunate voting choices.

2 The innocent are so few that two of them seldom meet—when they do meet, their victims lie strewn around.

ELIZABETH BOWEN (1899–1973), British novelist, story writer, essayist, and memoirist; born in Ireland. As quoted in *Elizabeth Bowen*, ch. 7, by Victoria Glendinning (1979).

3 Innocence always calls mutely for protection, when we would be much wiser to guard ourselves against it . . . innocence is like a dumb leper who has lost his bell, wandering the world meaning no harm.

ELIZABETH BOWEN (1899–1973), British novelist, story writer, essayist, and memoirist; born in Ireland. As quoted in *Elizabeth Bowen*, ch. 5, by Victoria Glendinning (1979).

INNOVATION

1 There is all the difference in the world between departure from recognised rules by one who has learned to obey them, and neglect of them through want of training or want of skill or want of understanding. Before you can be eccentric you must know where the circle is.

ELLEN TERRY (1847–1928), British actor. *Ellen Terry's Memoirs*, 2nd. ed., ch. 5 (1932). Written in 1906 or 1907, discussing the necessity of thorough training in dramatic technique.

2 No one is ahead of his time, it is only that the particular variety of creating his time is the one that his contemporaries who also are creating their own time refuse to accept.

GERTRUDE STEIN (1874–1946), U.S. author and patron of the arts; relocated to France. *Composition as Explanation* (1926).

INSECURITY

1 Ours has been called a culture of narcissism. The label is apt but can be misleading. It reads colloquially as selfishness and self-absorption. But these images do not capture the anxiety behind our search for mirrors. We are insecure in our understanding of ourselves, and this insecurity breeds a new preoccupation with the question of who we are. We search for ways to see ourselves. The computer is a new mirror, the first psychological machine. Beyond its nature as an analytical engine lies its second nature as an evocative object.

SHERRY TURKLE (b. 1948), U.S. sociologist and psychologist. *The Second Self*, ch. 9 (1984). Turkle was on the faculty of the Massachusetts Institute of Technology's program in Science, Technology and Society.

INSTITUTIONS

1 One of the baffling things about life is that the purposes of institutions may be ideal, while their administration, dependent upon the faults and weaknesses of human beings, may be bad.

MARY BARNETT GILSON (1877– ?), U.S. factory personnel manager, economist, and educator. *What's Past is Prologue*, ch. 27 (1940). Speaking specifically of trade unions.

2 . . . no woman is really an insider in the institutions fathered by masculine consciousness.

ADRIENNE RICH (b. 1929), U.S. poet, essayist, and feminist. *Blood, Bread and Poetry*, ch. 1 (1986). From a 1979 commencement address delivered at Smith College, Northampton, Massachusetts.

INTEGRITY

1 If our web be framed with rotten handles, when our loom is well nigh done, our work is new to begin. God send the weaver true prentices again, and let them be denizens.

ELIZABETH I (1533–1603), Queen of England (1558–1603). As quoted in *The Sayings of Queen Elizabeth,* ch. 11, by Frederick Chamberlin (1923).

To Sir Henry Sidney, governor of Ireland.

2 It is better to be true to what you believe, though that be wrong, than to be false to what you believe, even if that belief is correct.

ANNA HOWARD SHAW (1847–1919), U.S. minister and suffragist. As quoted in *History of Woman Suffrage,* vol. 4, ch. 15, by Susan B. Anthony and Ida Husted Harper (1902).

In a sermon preached to the National Woman Suffrage Association during its twenty-seventh annual convention, held January 31–February 5, 1895, in Atlanta, Georgia.

3 I would rather be known as an advocate of equal suffrage than to speak every night on the best-paying platforms in the United States and ignore it.

ANNA HOWARD SHAW (1847–1919), U.S. suffragist, minister, and speaker; born in England. As quoted in *History of Woman Suffrage,* vol. 5, ch. 1, by Ida Husted Harper (1922).

In an address delivered in 1901 to the thirty-third annual convention of the National Woman Suffrage Association. She was recalling the advice she had received from a man who told her that if she "would only give up for a time" the causes of woman suffrage and prohibition, she could "earn enough money on the regular lecture platform in a few years to live on for the rest of your life." Shaw, who was a minister, was also one of the suffrage movement's most powerful speakers.

4 Faultless honesty is a *sine qua non* of business life. Not alone the honesty according to the moral code and the Bible. When I speak of honesty I refer to the small, hidden, evasive meannesses of our natures. I speak of the honesty of ourselves to ourselves.

ALICE FOOTE MACDOUGALL, (1867–1945) U.S. businesswoman. *The Autobiography of a Business Woman,* ch. 7 (1928).

MacDougall was a successful coffee house proprietor and coffee, tea, and cocoa merchant.

5 So long as you write what you wish to write, that is all that matters; and whether it matters for ages or only for hours, nobody can say. But to sacrifice a hair of the head of your vision, a shade of its colour, in deference to some Headmaster with a silver pot in his hand or to some professor with a measuring-rod up his sleeve, is the most abject treachery, and the sacrifice or wealth and chastity, which used to be said to be the greatest of human disasters, a mere flea-bite in comparison.

VIRGINIA WOOLF (1882–1941), British author. *A Room of One's Own,* ch. 6 (1929).

6 I cannot and will not cut my conscience to fit this year's fashions . . .

LILLIAN HELLMAN (1905–1984), U.S. playwright and memoirist. *Scoundrel Time* (1976).

From a letter dated May 19, 1952, to John S. Wood, Chair of the House Committee on Un-American Activities, refusing to appear before that Committee and testify about other people suspected of being Communist sympathizers.

7 Without being bound to the fulfillment of promises, we would never be able to keep our identities;

we would be condemned to wander helplessly and without direction in the darkness of each man's lonely heart, caught in its contradictions and equivocalities—a darkness which only the light shed over the public realm through the presence of others, who confirm the identity between the one who promises and the one who fulfills, can dispel.

HANNAH ARENDT (1906–1975), U.S. philosopher. *The Human Condition,* ch. 33 (1958).

8   I'm stronger knowing that while Donna Rice could be sold, she could not be bought.

DONNA RICE (b. c. 1962), U.S. model and actress. As quoted in *People* magazine, p. 266 (March 7–14, 1994).

The ex-lover of Gary Hart, a married U.S. Senator and former candidate for the Democratic Presidential nomination, she was commenting on her refusal to profit from the scandal that followed disclosure of their affair.

INTELLECTUAL FREEDOM

1   Men's minds must be free, and that means the minds of all, not the minds of a select few.

MARY BARNETT GILSON (1877– ?), U.S. factory personnel manager, economist, and educator. *What's Past is Prologue,* ch. 27 (1940).

2   As a writer, I must be free to say what is in all the diversity I can command. I regret the distorting prejudices that surround me, whether they affect homosexuals or men or the physically handicapped and I can't alone defeat them. They will not defeat me, either as a lesbian or a writer.

JANE RULE (b. 1931), Canadian lesbian, feminist, fiction writer, and essayist; born in the U.S. *A Hot-Eyed Moderate,* part 1 (1985).

INTELLECTUAL STIMULATION

1   There are women in middle life, whose days are crowded with practical duties, physical strain, and moral responsibility . . . they fail to see that some use of the mind, in solid reading or in study, would refresh them by its contrast with carking cares, and would prepare interest and pleasure for their later years. Such women often sink into depression, as their cares fall away from them, and many even become insane. They are mentally starved to death.

ELLEN HENRIETTA SWALLOW RICHARDS, (1842–1911) U.S. chemist and educator. As quoted in *The Life of Ellen H. Richards,* ch. 9, by Caroline L. Hunt (1912).

Written in the 1860s.

INTELLECTUALS

1   Only those who know the supremacy of the intellectual life—the life which has a seed of ennobling thought and purpose within it—can understand the grief of one who falls from that serene activity into the absorbing soul-wasting struggle with worldly annoyances.

GEORGE ELIOT (1819–1880), British novelist. *Middlemarch,* ch. 73 (1871–1872).

2   At the outstart of discussions of women's intellectual attainments, it

is well to remember how few are the men of the first rank.

ANNA GARLIN SPENCER (1851–1931), U.S. educator, author, feminist, and Unitarian minister. *Woman's Share in Social Culture*, ch. 3 (1913).

3   In the combined names of Social Intercourse, Meeting Interesting People, and Getting Out of a Rut, I have taken, in my time, some terrible beatings. I have listened to poets rendering their own odes. I have had the plots of yet unwritten plays given me in tiniest detail, I have assisted in charades, I have been politely mystified by card tricks, I have even been sent out of the room and been forced, on my return, to ask the assembled company such questions as I hoped might reveal to me what Famous Character in Fiction they represented. I have spent entire evenings knee-deep in derry-down-derries, listening to quaint old English ballads done without accompaniment; I have been backed into cold corners by pianos while composers showed me how that thing they wrote three years before Gershwin did "The Man I Love" went; I knew a young man who has an inlaid ukelele. You see these gray hairs? Well, making whoopee with the intelligentsia was the way I earned them.

DOROTHY PARKER (1893–1967), U.S. author and humorist. *Constant Reader*, column dated April 7, 1928 (1970).

4   . . . I didn't consider intellectuals intelligent, I never liked them or their thoughts about life. I defined them as people who care nothing for argument, who are interested only in information; or as people who have a preference for learning things rather than experiencing them. They have opinions but no point of view. . . . Their talk is the gloomiest type of human discourse I know. . . . This is a red flag to my nature. Intellectuals, to me have no natures . . .

MARGARET ANDERSON (1886–1973), U.S. editor and memoirist. *The Fiery Fountains*, part 1 (1951).

Anderson founded and edited a charming, iconoclastic, highly visible and influential arts magazine, *The Little Review* (1914–1929). She knew many intellectuals but preferred artists and writers; she loved stimulating conversation.

5   Nothing . . . is so ungrateful as a rising generation; yet, if there is any faintest glimmer of light ahead of us in the present, it was kindled by the intellectual fires that burned long before us.

ELLEN GLASGOW (1873–1945), U.S. novelist. *The Woman Within*, ch. 12 (1954).

6   Some men tend to cling to old intellectual excitements, just as some belles, when they are old ladies, still cling to the fashions and coiffures of their exciting youth.

JANE JACOBS (b. 1916), U.S. urban analyst. *The Death and Life of Great American Cities*, ch. 18 (1961).

7   Intellectuals are too sentimental for me.

MARGARET ANDERSON (1886–1973), U.S. editor and memoirist. *The Strange Necessity*, part 1 (1969).

8 . . . friendship . . . is essential to intellectuals. You can date the evolving life of a mind, like the age of a tree, by the rings of friendship formed by the expanding central trunk.

MARY McCARTHY (1912–1989), U.S. author. *How I Grew,* ch. 1 (1987).

INTELLIGENCE

1 I'll wager that it was impossible after we got mixed together to tell an anti from a suffragist by her clothes. There might have been a difference, though, in the expression of the faces and the shape of the heads.

SUSAN B. ANTHONY (1820–1906), U.S. suffragist. As quoted in *Life and Work of Susan B. Anthony,* vol. 3, ch. 55, by Ida Husted Harper (1908).

Reflecting on an annual convention of the National Suffrage Association, held in Washington, D. C., in February 1900; for the first time, antisuffragists had made an appearance.

2 One thing is certain: the riddle of mind, long a topic for philosophers, has taken on new urgency. Under pressure from the computer, the question of mind in relation to machine is becoming a central cultural preoccupation. It is becoming for us what sex was to the Victorians— threat and obsession, taboo and fascination.

SHERRY TURKLE (b. 1948), U.S. sociologist and psychologist. *The Second Self,* ch. 9 (1984).

Turkle was on the faculty of the Massachusetts Institute of Technology's program in Science, Technology and Society.

3 He seems like an average type of man. He's not, like smart. I'm not trying to rag on him or anything. But he has the same mentality I have—and I'm in the eighth grade.

VANESSA MARTINEZ (b. c. 1978), U.S. eighth-grade student. As quoted in *Newsweek* magazine, p. 17 (June 1, 1992).

Commenting on Vice-President Dan Quayle (b. 1947; Vice-President, 1989–1992) after he visited the Bret Harte Middle School in south-central Los Angeles, California. Quayle was often criticized as an unimpressive public speaker and as having mediocre intellectual ability.

INTENSITY

1 . . . intensity commands form.

MAY SARTON (1912–1995), U.S. author. As quoted in *Women Writers Talking,* ch. 1, by Janet Todd (1983).

Referring to formal poetry, as distinguished from free verse.

INTERNATIONAL RELATIONS

1 There is a close tie of affection between sovereigns and their subjects; and as chaste wives should have no eyes but for their husbands, so faithful liegemen should keep their regards at home and not look after foreign crowns. For my part I like not for my sheep to wear a stranger's mark nor to dance after a foreigner's whistle.

ELIZABETH I (1533–1603), Queen of England (1558–1603). As quoted in *The Sayings of Queen Elizabeth,* ch. 13, by Frederick Chamberlin (1923).

"To an official, who had asked her opinion of the right of Sir Thomas Arundel to precedence in England because of a foreign honour which he had received."

2 While you are divided from us by geographical lines, which are imaginary, and by a language which is not the same, you have not come to an alien people or land. In the realm of the heart, in the domain of the mind, there are no geographical lines dividing the nations.

ANNA HOWARD SHAW (1847–1919), U.S. minister, suffragist, and speaker; born in England. As quoted in *History of Woman Suffrage*, vol. 5, ch. 2, by Ida Husted Harper (1922).
In an address delivered in February 1902 to international delegates attending the thirty-fourth annual convention of the National Woman Suffrage Association.

3 International relationships are . . . preordained to be clumsy gestures based on imperfect knowledge.

REBECCA WEST (1892–1983), British author. *The Strange Necessity*, ch. 10 (1928).

4 The most profound effect of World War I on me . . . was that it committed me to international affairs as the principal work of my life. . . . I have sometimes regretted that my avocation or chief hobby happened to be such a gloomy one. . . . When I look at the world today . . . I sometimes wonder whether [my efforts] were not nearly all in vain. Perhaps it would have been better if I had adopted as my chief hobby the cultivation of chrysanthemums or the breeding of West Highland White Terriers or even, as did one of my friends, the collection of Japanese swordguards.

VIRGINIA CROCHERON GILDER-SLEEVE, (1877–1965) U.S. educator. *Many a Good Crusade*, part 1 (1954).

INTERPRETATION

1 Your pier-glass or extensive surface of polished steel . . . will be minutely and multitudinously scratched in all directions; but place now against it a lighted candle as a centre of illumination, and lo! the scratches will seem to arrange themselves in a fine series of concentric circles round that little sun. It is demonstrable that the scratches are going everywhere impartially, and it is only your candle which produces the flattering illusion of a concentric arrangement, its light falling with an exclusive optical selection. These things are a parable. The scratches are events, and the candle is the egoism of any person now absent.

GEORGE ELIOT (1819–1880), British novelist. *Middlemarch*, ch. 27 (1871–1872).

INVENTION

1 It is only following out nature. As a child, I never cared for things that girls usually do; dolls never possessed any charms for me. I couldn't see the sense of cuddling bits of porcelain with senseless faces; the only things I wanted were a jack-knife, a gimlet, and pieces of wood. My friends were horrified. . . . I sighed sometimes, because I was not like other girls, but wisely concluded that I couldn't help it, and sought further consolation from my tools. . . . I was famous for my kites; and my sleds were the envy and admiration of all the boys in town. I'm not surprised at what I've done. I'm only sorry I couldn't have had as good a chance as a boy, and have been put to my trade regularly.

MARGARET KNIGHT (1838–1914), U.S. inventor. As quoted in *Feminine Ingenuity,* ch. 3, by Anne L. MacDonald (1992). Written in 1872.

2   I believe my ardour for invention springs from his loins. I can't say that the brassiere will ever take as great a place in history as the steamboat, but I did invent it.

CARESSE CROSBY (1892–1970), U.S. literary editor and inventor. As quoted in *Feminine Ingenuity,* ch. 12, by Anne L. MacDonald (1992). Said in the early 1900s. The inventor of the backless brassiere (under her earlier name, Mary Phelps Peabody) was citing her descendence from Robert Fulton (1765–1815), inventor of the steamboat, as a possible explanation for her ingenuity.

3   Central heating, French rubber goods, and cookbooks are three amazing proofs of man's ingenuity in transforming necessity into art, and of these, cookbooks are perhaps most lastingly delightful.

M. F. K. FISHER (1908–1992), U.S. author and food expert. *Serve it Forth,* ch. 4 (1937).

4   If necessity is the mother of invention, then resourcefulness is the father.

BEULAH LOUISE HENRY, U.S. inventor. As quoted in *Feminine Ingenuity,* ch. 13, by Anne L. MacDonald (1992). Said in 1962; Henry had invented a type of umbrella.

IRELAND AND THE IRISH

1   . . . though one can be callous in Ireland one cannot be wholly opaque or material. An unearthly disturbance works in the spirit; reason can never reconcile one to life; nothing allays the wants one cannot explain.

ELIZABETH BOWEN (1899–1973), Irish author; born in Ireland. *Bowen's Court,* ch. 8 (1942).

2   One American said that the most interesting thing about Holy Ireland was that its people hate each other in the name of Jesus Christ. And they do!

BERNADETTE DEVLIN (b. 1947), Irish politician. *The Price of My Soul,* ch. 4 (1969).

3   Irish? In truth I would not want to be anything else. It is a state of mind as well as an actual country. It is being at odds with other nationalities, having quite different philosophy about pleasure, about punishment, about life, and about death. At least it does not leave one pusillanimous.

EDNA O'BRIEN (b. c. 1932), Irish author; relocated to England. *Mother Ireland,* ch. 7 (1976).

4   Ireland is a great country to die or be married in.

ELIZABETH BOWEN (1899–1973), British novelist, story writer, essayist, and memoirist; born in Ireland. As quoted in *Elizabeth Bowen,* ch. 1, by Victoria Glendinning (1979). The Anglo-Irish novelist, born in Dublin, was married in Northamptonshire, England, and died in Hythe, England. She was buried in Ireland near her father.

5 Grandmother, born in County Tyrone, believed as a good Irishwoman that there were only three kinds of tea fit to drink, none of them storebought. The first quality was kept, sensibly enough, in China. The second picking was sent directly to Ireland. The third and lowest grade went, of course, to the benighted British. And all the tea used in our house came once a year, in one or two beautiful soldered tin boxes, from Dublin. Then only would we know it to be second to what the Dowager Empress of China was drinking, while the other Old Lady in Buckingham Palace sipped our dregs, as served her right. . . . My grandmother died before tea bags. I am grateful. My mother never admitted their existence.

M. F. K. FISHER (1908–1992), U.S. culinary writer and autobiographer. *The Tea Lover's Treasury,* Introduction (1982).
The book's author is James Norwood Platt.

The great stage actor had an omnipresent aura of sadness and was reticent and retiring.

3 Shut out from the world with its blare and glare, life in an institution moves softly. The ears become attuned to gentle notes and a subdued tone.

MARY B. HARRIS (1874–1957), U.S. prison administrator. *I Knew Them in Prison,* ch. 33 (1936).

4 Terrified of being alone, yet afraid of intimacy, we experience widespread feelings of emptiness, of disconnection, of the unreality of self. And here the computer, a companion without emotional demands, offers a compromise. You can be a loner, but never alone. You can interact, but need never feel vulnerable to another person.

SHERRY TURKLE (b. 1948), U.S. sociologist and psychologist. *The Second Self,* ch. 9 (1984).
Turkle was on the faculty of the Massachusetts Institute of Technology's program in Science, Technology and Society.

ISOLATION

1 Of all the bewildering things about a new country, the absence of human landmarks is one of the most depressing and disheartening.

WILLA CATHER (1873–1947), U.S. novelist. *O Pioneers!* Part 1, ch. 2 (1913).

2 If I had my will I would live in a ship on the sea, and never come nearer to humanity than that!

ELEONORA DUSE (1858–1924), Italian actor. As quoted in *Actors on Acting,* rev. ed., part 11, by Toby Cole and Helen Krich (1970).

JOURNALISM

1 A woman had started a political paper! A woman! Could he believe his eyes? A woman! Instantly he sprang to his feet and clutched his pantaloons, shouted to the assistant editor, when he, too, read and grasped frantically at his cassimeres, called to the reporters and pressmen and typos and devils, who all rushed in, heard the news, and seized their nether garments and joined the general chorus, "My breeches! oh, my

breeches!" Here was a woman resolved to steal their pantaloons,
their trousers, and when these were
gone they might cry, "Ye have taken
away my gods, and what have I
more?"

JANE GREY SWISSHELM (1815–1884),
U.S. newspaperwoman, abolitionist, and human rights activist. *Half a Century*, ch. 22
(1880).

On male editors' reaction to her founding, in
1847, an abolitionist newspaper called the *Pittsburg Saturday Visiter*.

2 It was somewhere in the '70's that
the fiend gossip came into New
York society to stay. The first newspaper outburst that I remember was
after the Beecher trial, which was a
terrible beginning. Then the papers
began with attacks upon women.
There were stories of kleptomani-
acs, and of a young and fashionable
man who had stolen his cousin's
ring at a dinner-party, etc., etc.
None of this sort of story was allowed at the dinner of Mrs. Astor,
Mrs. Belmont, or Mrs. Fish. I can
imagine the fine face of the latter
freezing into marble had any one
opened such a door of Bluebeard's
closet in her stately presence.

M. E. W. SHERWOOD (1826–1903), U.S.
socialite, traveller, and author. *An Epistle to Posterity*, ch. 11 (1897).

The three ladies mentioned were eminent society hostesses in New York City in the 1870s. In
1875, Rev. Henry Ward Beecher (1813–1887),
who was a distinguished public speaker and
Congregational minister, was sued by journalist
Theodore Tilton (1835–1907) for committing
adultery with his wife; the Tiltons had been
Beecher's parishioners. The jury was unable
to reach a verdict. (Beecher was the brother
of Catherine Beecher and Harriet Beecher
Stowe, both of whom are quoted in this
book.)

3 To write weekly, to write daily, to
write shortly, to write for busy people catching trains in the morning
or for tired people coming home in
the evening, is a heartbreaking task
for men who know good writing
from bad. They do it, but instinctively draw out of harm's way anything precious that might be damaged by contact with the public, or
anything sharp that might irritate
its skin.

VIRGINIA WOOLF (1882–1941), British
novelist, essayist, and diarist. *The Common
Reader*, ch. 19 (1925).

4 . . . you learned to compress almost
everything in the first sentence, and
the only phrase you needed was
"plans were made to organize." It
took me a day to learn this, and
that is all you have to learn in newspaper writing.

BRENDA UELAND (1891–1985), U.S. magazine writer. *Me*, ch. 3 (1939).

On becoming a journalist in 1913, when she
obtained her first job: covering women's club
activities for the *Minneapolis Tribune*.

5 Our family talked a lot at table, and
only two subjects were taboo: politics and personal troubles. The first
was sternly avoided because Father
ran a nonpartisan daily in a small
town, with some success, and did
not wish to express his own opinions in public, even when in private.

M. F. K. FISHER (1908–1992), U.S. culinary writer and autobiographer. Introduction
(1968).

6 Avoid this crowd like the plague.
And if they quote you, make damn
sure they heard you.

BARBARA BUSH (b. 1925), First Lady of the United States (1988–1992). As quoted in *Newsweek* magazine, p. 25 (November 30, 1992).

Her husband, President George Bush, having been defeated for re-election by Governor Bill Clinton, Bush was giving the incoming first lady, Hillary Rodham Clinton, a tour of the White House. They were surrounded by representatives of the news media, and Bush gave Clinton this advice.

JOY

1 . . . how I understand that love of living, of being in this wonderful, astounding world even if one can look at it only through the prison bars of illness and suffering! *Plus je vois,* the more I am thrilled by the spectacle.

EDITH WHARTON (1862–1937), U.S. author; relocated to France. As quoted in *Edith Wharton,* ch. 9, by R. W. B. Lewis (1985).

In a letter written to her friend Sara Norton in spring 1906, commenting on a mutual friend who was seriously ill yet still spirited.

2 Cruelty is a mystery, and the waste of pain. But if we describe a word to compass these things, a world that is a long, brute game, then we bump against another mystery: the inrush of power and delight, the canary that sings on the skull.

ANNIE DILLARD (b. 1945), U.S. essayist and autobiographer. *Pilgrim at Tinker Creek,* ch. 1 (1974).

3 Our goal should be to achieve joy.

ANA CASTILLO (b. 1953), Mexican–American poet, essayist, and feminist. *Massacre of the Dreamers,* ch. 7 (1994).

JUDAISM AND JEWISH PEOPLE

1 . . . I am an outsider, a lesbian, a *shikse.* The Jewish community is not my community. But as a Jew—as a Jew in a Christian, anti-Semitic society—the Jewish community is, and will always remain, my community. Enemy and ally.

IRENA KLEPFISZ (b. 1941), U.S. Jewish lesbian author; born in Poland. *Dreams of an Insomniac,* part 2 (1990).

JUSTICE

1 I hope there are some who will brave ridicule for the sake of common justice to half the people in the world.

BARBARA LEIGH SMITH BODICHON, (1827–1891) British feminist. As quoted in *Barbara Bodichon,* Introduction, by Candida Lacey (1987).

Written in 1849, shen she was twenty-two. Bodichon was a radical activist who formulated the unsuccessful Married Women's Property Bill in England in 1857.

2 It used to be said in antislavery days that a people who would tacitly consent to the enslavement of 4,000,000 human beings were incapable of being just to each other, and I believe this same rule holds with regard to the injustice practiced by men towards women. So long as all men conspire to rob women of the citizen's right to perfect equality in all the privileges and immunities of our so-called "free" government, we can not expect these same men to be capable of perfect justice to each other.

SUSAN B. ANTHONY (1820–1906), U.S. suffragist. As quoted in *The Life and Work of Su-*

san B. Anthony, ch. 46, by Ida Husted Harper (1898).
Said in 1895.

3 We are taught for a comfort in this life that in the future there will certainly be more equity in distributing justice; that fully one-half of the judges shall be of either sex, so that all law and custom shall not be made in the interests of part of the race and executed for one party's whims, to the detriment of the other party's rights. In the future life no such condition shall prevail.

CAROLINE NICHOLS CHURCHILL (1833–?), U.S. author. *Active Footsteps*, ch. 16 (1909).

4 We ask not pardon for ourselves but justice for all American women.

ALISON LOW TURNBULL HOPKINS, (1880–1951) U.S. suffragist. As quoted in *Past and Promise*, part 3, by Janet Gibbs-Albanesius (1990).
Arrested for pro-suffrage picketing on July 14, 1917 (Bastille Day) at the White House, Hopkins was sentenced to sixty days in prison but pardoned by President Woodrow Wilson at the behest of her husband. Hopkins, however, claimed that Wilson had acted only to save himself political embarrassment and stood alone at the White House gates with a sign bearing this statement. Women were granted the right to vote in 1919, with passage of the Nineteenth Amendment to the Constitution.

5 Unless we maintain correctional institutions of such character that they create respect for law and government instead of breeding resentment and a desire for revenge, we are meeting lawlessness with stupidity and making a travesty of justice.

MARY B. HARRIS (1874–1957), U.S. prison administrator. *I Knew Them in Prison*, ch. 34 (1936).
When she wrote this, Harris was Superintendent of the Federal Industrial Institution for Women.

6 It would be . . . better to be judged by one's superiors than by one's peers. . . . In a trial before his superiors, *any* criminal would stand a chance of justice.

MARGARET ANDERSON (1886–1973), U.S. editor and memoirist. *The Strange Necessity*, part 1 (1969).

7 . . . censorship often boils down to some male judges getting to read a lot of dirty books—with one hand.

ROBIN MORGAN (b. 1941), U.S. author, feminist, and child actor. *The Word of a Woman*, part 1 (1992).
Written in 1974.

8 I was reborn when that jury said, "Guilty!"

MYRLIE EVERS (b. 1933), African American activist. As quoted in the *New York Times Magazine*, p. 70 (November 27, 1994).
The widow of Medgar Evers, a civil rights activist assassinated in 1963 in Mississippi, she was referring to the conviction of her husband's murderer, Byron De La Beckwith, on February 5, 1994. In 1964, two all-white juries had deadlocked on the question of Beckwith's guilt, resulting in mistrials and the eventual dismissal of the charge against him. Evers had managed to reopen the case and exert enough pressure to bring it to trial again.

KILLING

1 . . . there has never been a period in history when there have been necessary killings which has not been instantly followed by a period when there have been unnecessary killings.

REBECCA WEST (1892–1983), British author. *The Strange Necessity,* ch. 10 (1928).

2 I'd rather you shot at tin cans in the back yard, but I know you'll go after birds. Shoot all the bluejays you want, if you can hit 'em, but remember it's a sin to kill a mockingbird. . . . Mockingbirds don't do one thing but make music for us to enjoy. They don't eat up people's gardens, don't nest in corncribs, they don't do one thing but sing their hearts out for us. That's why it's a sin to kill a mockingbird.

HARPER LEE (b. 1926), U.S. novelist. *To Kill a Mockingbird,* ch. 10 (1960).
Atticus Finch, the Southern Alabama father and hero of this novel, instructs his teenage son when he gets his first air-rifle. The section following the ellipsis is an explanation of these instructions by Miss Maudie Atkinson, a neighbor.

3 . . . if we believe that murder is wrong and not admissible in our society, then it has to be wrong for everyone, not just individuals but governments as well.

HELEN PRÉJEAN (b. 1940), U.S. nun and activist against the death penalty. *Dead Man Walking,* ch. 6 (1993).

KINDNESS

1 Fear not, we are of the nature of the lion, and cannot descend to the destruction of mice and such small beasts.

ELIZABETH I (1533–1603), British monarch, Queen of England (1558–1603). As quoted in *The Sayings of Queen Elizabeth,* ch. 22, by Frederick Chamberlin (1923).
Said soon after she became queen to a member of the household staff of Queen Mary I, who had been Elizabeth's half-sister and predecessor. The household staff member had treated Elizabeth cruelly during Mary's reign and now sought her mercy.

2 . . . very little achievement is required in order to pity another man's shortcomings.

GEORGE ELIOT (1819–1880), British novelist. *Middlemarch,* ch. 21 (1871–1872).

3 The presence of a noble nature, generous in its wishes, ardent in its charity, changes the lights for us: we begin to see things again in their larger, quieter masses, and to believe that we too can be seen and judged in the wholeness of our character.

GEORGE ELIOT (1819–1880), British novelist. *Middlemarch,* ch. 76 (1871–1872).

4 Really to succeed, we must give; of our souls to the soulless, of our love to the lonely, of our intelligence to the dull. Business is quite as much a process of giving as it is of getting.

ALICE FOOTE MACDOUGALL, (1867–1945) U.S. businesswoman. Ch. 6 (1928).

KNOWLEDGE

1 The power of generalizing ideas, of drawing comprehensive conclusions from individual observations, is the only acquirement, for an immortal being, that really deserves the name of knowledge.

MARY WOLLSTONECRAFT (1759–1797), British feminist. *A Vindication of the Rights of Woman,* ch. 4 (1792).

2 Knowledge signifies *things known.* Where there are no *things known,* there is no *knowledge.* Where there are no *things to be known,* there *can be no knowledge.* We have observed that every science, that is, every branch of knowledge, is compounded of certain facts, of which our sensations furnish the evidence. Where no such evidence is supplied, we are without *data;* we are without first premises; and when, without these, we attempt to build up *a science,* we do as those who raise edifices without foundations. And what do such builders construct? *Castles in the air.*

FRANCES WRIGHT (1795–1852), Scottish author and speaker; relocated to America. *Course of Popular Lectures,* lecture 4 (1829). Wright was criticizing religion.

3 The world moves, but we seem to move with it. When I studied physiology before . . . there were two hundred and eight bones in the body. Now there are two hundred and thirty-eight.

ELLEN HENRIETTA SWALLOW RICHARDS, (1842–1911) U.S. chemist and educator. As quoted in *The Life of Ellen H. Richards,* ch. 4, by Caroline L. Hunt (1912). Written on February 13, 1870, when she was a student at Vassar College.

4 There is hardly any contact more depressing to a young ardent creature than that of a mind in which years full of knowledge seem to have issued in a blank absence of interest or sympathy.

GEORGE ELIOT (1819–1880), British novelist. *Middlemarch,* ch. 20 (1871–1872).

5 . . . men know best about everything, except what women know better.

GEORGE ELIOT (1819–1880), British novelist. *Middlemarch,* ch. 72 (1871–1872).

6 . . . to know what one knows is frightening to live what one lives is soothing and though everybody likes to be frightened what they really have to have is soothing . . .

GERTRUDE STEIN (1874–1946), U.S. author and patron of the arts; relocated to France. *What Are Masterpieces and Why Are There So Few of Them* (1936).

7 How ignorant we are! How ignorant everyone is! We can cut across only a small area of the appallingly expanding fields of knowledge. No human being can know more than a tiny fraction of the whole. It must have been satisfactory in ancient times when one's own land seemed to be the universe; when research studies, pamphlets, books did not issue in endless flow; when laboratories and scientists were not so rapidly pushing back frontiers of knowledge that the process of unlearning the old left you gasping for breath.

MARY BARNETT GILSON (1877– ?), U.S. factory personnel manager, economist, and educator. *What's Past is Prologue,* ch. 25 (1940).

On the overwhelming amount of material she found to learn when, after years in industry, she studied for a doctorate in economics at Columbia University and prepared to teach for the first time—at the University of Chicago.

8 I have always suspected that too much knowledge is a dangerous thing. It is a boon to people who

don't have deep feelings; their pleasure comes from what they know
about things, and their pride from
showing off what they know. But
this only emphasizes the difference
between the artist and the scholar.

MARGARET ANDERSON (1886–1973),
U.S. editor and memoirist. *The Strange Necessity,* part 1 (1969).
Countering the aphorism that "a little knowledge is a dangerous thing."

9   To help, to continually help and
share, that is the sum of all knowledge; that is the meaning of art.

ELEONORA DUSE (1858–1924), Italian
actor. As quoted in *Actors on Acting,* rev. ed.,
part 11, by Toby Cole and Helen Krich (1970).

10 Computerization brings about an
essential change in the way the
worker can know the world and,
with it, a crisis of confidence in the
possibility of certain knowledge.

SHOSHANA ZUBOFF (b. 1951), U.S. social
scientist. *In the Age of the Smart Machine,* ch. 2
(1988).

11 I don't believe that you have to be a
cow to know what milk is.

ANN LANDERS (b. 1918), U.S. advice columnist. As quoted in *Time* (August 21, 1989).
Explaining why, despite her untroubled Midwestern upbringing, she felt qualified to advise
people with serious problems.

12 Contention is inseparable from creating knowledge. It is not contention we should try to avoid, but
discourses that attempt to suppress
contention.

JOYCE APPLEBY (b. 1929), U.S. historian.
"Recovering America's Historic Diversity," *Journal of American History,* p. 431 (September
1992).

LABOR

1   . . . continual hard labor deadens
the energies of the soul, and be-
numbs the faculties of the mind;
the ideas become confined, the
mind barren, and, like the scorching sands of Arabia, produces nothing; or, like the uncultivated soil,
brings forth thorns and thistles.
Again, continual hard labor irritates
our tempers and sours our disposi-
tions; the whole system become
worn out with toil and fatigue; nature herself becomes almost exhausted, and we care but little
whether we live or die.

MARIA STEWART (1803–1879), African
American abolitionist and schoolteacher. As
quoted in *Black Women in Nineteenth-Century
American Life,* part 3, by Bert James Loewenb-
erg and Ruth Bogin (1976).
Stewart, a free African American, said this in a
September 21, 1832 speech delivered at Frank-
lin Hall in Boston. She was arguing for educa-
tion to improve the lot of Northern African
Americans—especially girls.

2   I hear . . . foreigners, who would
boycott an employer if he hired a
colored workman, complain of
wrong and oppression, of low wages
and long hours, clamoring for
eight-hour systems . . . ah, come
with me, I feel like saying, I can
show you workingmen's wrong and
workingmen's toil which, could it
speak, would send up a wail that
might be heard from the Potomac
to the Rio Grande; and *should it
unite and act,* would shake this
country from Carolina to California.

ANNA JULIA COOPER (1859–1964), African American educator and feminist. *A Voice
from the South,* part 2 (1892).

Cooper was born in North Carolina to a slave and her white master.

MARY HEATON VORSE (1874–1966), U.S. journalist and labor activist. *A Footnote to Folly*, ch. 23 (1935).

3 It's not the suffering of birth, death, love that the young reject, but the suffering of endless labor without dream, eating the spare bread in bitterness, being a slave without the security of a slave.

MERIDEL LE SUEUR (b. 1900), U.S. author. *Women on the Breadlines* (1932). Written in America during the Great Depression.

3 . . . I lost myself in my work and never felt that marriage would give me the security I wanted. I thought that through the trade union movement we working women could get better conditions and security of mind.

MARY ANDERSON (1872–1964), U.S. trade union activist. As quoted in *Women at Work* magazine, ch. 7 (1951).

4 Labor came to humanity with the fall from grace and was at best a penitential sacrifice enabling purity through humiliation. Labor was toil, distress, trouble, fatigue—an exertion both painful and compulsory. Labor was our animal condition, struggling to survive in dirt and darkness.

SHOSHANA ZUBOFF (b. 1951), U.S. social scientist. *In the Age of the Smart Machine*, ch. 1 (1988).

4 I married a miner myself. I had ten children. I've got seven now; thirty-one grandchildren and eight great-grandchildren. And I'm happy to say not a one's ever crossed a picket line.

FLORENCE REESE (c. 1900–?), U.S. labor movement activist. As quoted in *American Dreams*, book 1, part 3, by Studs Terkel (1980). Reese wrote the labor movement's powerful rallying song, "Which Side Are You On?"

LABOR UNIONS

1 The newly-formed clothing unions are ready to welcome her; but woman shrinks back from organization, Heaven knows why! It is perhaps because in organization one find the truest freedom, and woman has been a slave too long to know what freedom means.

KATHARINE PEARSON WOODS (1853–1923), U.S. author, teacher, and social service worker. *What America Owes to Women*, ch. 43 (1893).

LABOR MOVEMENT

1 . . . I learned in the early part of my career that labor must bear the cross for others' sins, must be the vicarious sufferer for the wrongs that others do.

MOTHER JONES (1830–1930), U.S. labor organizer. *The Autobiography of Mother Jones*, ch. 1 (1925).

2 . . . no one knows anything about a strike until he has seen it break down into its component parts of human beings.

2 The rank and file have let their servants become their masters and dic-

tators. . . . Provision should be made in all union constitutions for the recall of leaders. Big salaries should not be paid. Career hunters should be driven out, as well as leaders who use labor for political ends. These types are menaces to the advancement of labor.

MOTHER JONES (1830–1930), U.S. labor organizer. *The Autobiography of Mother Jones,* ch. 27 (1925).

3 What happens in a strike happens not to one person alone. . . . It is a crisis with meaning and potency for all and prophetic of a future. The elements in crisis are the same, there is a fermentation that is identical. The elements are these: a body of men, women and children, hungry; an organization of feudal employers out to break the back of unionization; and the government Labor Board sent to "negotiate" between this hunger and this greed.

MERIDEL LE SUEUR (b. 1900), U.S. author. *What Happens in a Strike* (1934). Written in America during the Great Depression.

LABOR-MANAGEMENT RELATIONS

1 . . . there are no limits to which powers of privilege will not go to keep the workers in slavery.

MOTHER JONES (1830–1930), U.S. labor organizer. *The Autobiography of Mother Jones,* ch. 3 (1925).

2 The industrial world would be a more peaceful place if workers were called in as collaborators in the pro-

cess of establishing standards and defining shop practices, matters which surely affect their interests and well-being fully as much as they affect those of employers and consumers.

MARY BARNETT GILSON (1877– ?), U.S. factory personnel manager, economist, and educator. *What's Past is Prologue,* ch. 5 (1940).

3 If the technology cannot shoulder the entire burden of strategic change, it nevertheless can set into motion a series of dynamics that present an important challenge to imperative control and the industrial division of labor. The more blurred the distinction between what workers know and what managers know, the more fragile and pointless any traditional relationships of domination and subordination between them will become.

SHOSHANA ZUBOFF (b. 1951), U.S. social scientist. *In the Age of the Smart Machine,* ch. 2 (1988).

LANGUAGE

1 Children who hear acquire language without any particular effort; the words that fall from others' lips they catch on the wing, as it were, delightedly, while the little deaf child must trap them by a slow and often painful process. But whatever the process, the result is wonderful. Gradually from naming an object we advance step by step until we have traversed the vast distance between our first stammered syllable and the sweep of thought in a line of Shakespeare.

HELEN KELLER (1880–1968), U.S. author. *The Story of My Life*, ch. 1 (1905).

Keller was rendered deaf and blind at the age of nineteen months.

2 We have decided that manners shall consist entirely of morals. It is just possible that, in the days when morals consisted largely of manners, fewer people were contaminated. You cannot shock a person practically whom you are totally unwilling to shock verbally; and if you are perfectly willing to shock an individual verbally, the next thing you will be doing is to shock him practically. Above all, when we become incapable of the shock verbal, there will be nothing left for the unconventional people but the shock practical.

KATHERINE FULLERTON GEROULD (1879–1944), U.S. author. *Modes and Morals*, ch. 7 (1920).

3 . . . often when I write I am trying to make words do the work of line and colour. I have the painter's sensitivity to light. Much (and perhaps the best) of my writing is verbal painting.

ELIZABETH BOWEN (1899–1973), British novelist, story writer, essayist, and memoirist; born in Ireland. As quoted in *Elizabeth Bowen*, ch. 3, by Victoria Glendinning (1979). Written c. 1949.

4 . . . whatever men do or know or experience can make sense only to the extent that it can be spoken about. There may be truths beyond speech, and they may be of great relevance to man in the singular, that is, to man in so far as he is not a political being, whatever else he may be. Men in the plural, that is, men in so far as they live and move and act in this world, can experience meaningfulness only because they can talk with and make sense to each other and to themselves.

HANNAH ARENDT (1906–1975), U.S. philosopher. *The Human Condition*, Prologue (1958).

5 Our ideal . . . must be a language as clear as glass—the person looking out of the window knows there *is* glass there, but he is not concerned with it; what concerns him is what comes through from the other side.

ELIZABETH BOWEN (1899–1973), British novelist, story writer, essayist, and memoirist; born in Ireland. *Seven Winters*, part 2, sect. 1, ch. 6 (1962).

6 . . . word-sniffing . . . is an addiction, like glue—or snow—sniffing in a somewhat less destructive way, physically if not economically. . . . As an addict . . . I am almost guiltily interested in converts to my own illness, and in a pinch I can recommend nearly any reasonable solace, whether or not it qualifies as a true descendant of Noah Webster.

M. F. K. FISHER (1908–1992), U.S. culinary writer and autobiographer. *Cook's and Diner's Dictionary*, Introduction (1968).

By "snow-sniffing," Fisher presumably meant inhaling cocaine.

7 When I was quite young I fondly imagined that all foreign languages were codes for English. I thought that "hat," say, was the real and actual name of the thing, but that people in other countries, who obstinately persisted in speaking the code of their forefathers, might use the word "ibu," say, to designate not merely the concept hat, but the English *word* "hat." I knew only one foreign word, "oui," and since it had three letters as did the word for which it was a code, it seemed, touchingly enough, to confirm my theory.

ANNIE DILLARD (b. 1945), U.S. essayist and autobiographer. *Pilgrim at Tinker Creek,* ch. 7 (1974).

8 Language is as real, as tangible, in our lives as streets, pipelines, telephone switchboards, microwaves, radioactivity, cloning laboratories, nuclear power stations.

ADRIENNE RICH (b. 1929), U.S. poet, essayist, and feminist. *The Work of a Common Woman,* by Judy Grahn, introductory essay (1978).

9 According to the dictionary: "In modern apprehension man as thus used" [in the sense of "person"] "primarily denotes the male sex, though by implication referring also to women." I am not sure that "by implication" fully expresses the degree to which I wish to feel included in the human race.

JANE O'REILLY, U.S. feminist and humorist. *The Girl I Left Behind,* ch. 6 (1980). On why she opposed the then-common use of the word "man" to designate *all* people.

10 Now that our sexual experience is increasingly available to us as a subject for contemplation, we have to extend our language to express our new consciousness until we have as many words for sexuality as the Eskimo has for snow, that pervasive, beautiful, and mortal climate in which we all live.

JANE RULE (b. 1931), Canadian fiction writer and essayist; born in the U. S.. *Outlander,* part 2, essay 1 (1981). Rule was a lesbian who wrote extensively about sexuality and sexual relationships (both heterosexual and homosexual) in her fiction and essays.

11 . . . I . . . believe that words *can* help us move or keep us paralyzed, and that our choices of language and verbal tone have something—a great deal—to do with how we live our lives and whom we end up speaking with and hearing; and that we can deflect words, by trivialization, of course, but also by ritualized respect, or we can let them enter our souls and mix with the juices of our minds.

ADRIENNE RICH (b. 1929), U.S. poet, essayist, and feminist. *Blood, Bread and Poetry,* ch. 5 (1986). From "Toward a More Feminist Criticism," an address delivered by Rich at the opening of the "Feminist Studies in Literature" symposium, University of Minnesota, 1981.

12 If we lived in a democratic state our language would have to hurtle, fly, curse, and sing, in all the common American names, all the undeniable and representative and participating voices of everybody here.

JUNE JORDAN (b. 1936), African American poet and social critic. *On Call,* ch. 4 (1985). Written in 1982, on schools' and other social institutions' insistence upon "standard English."

13 Dictionaries are always fun, but not always reassuring.

M. F. K. FISHER (1908–1992), U.S. author and food expert. *Dubious Honors*, part 2 (1988).
From a 1984 book review of *Square Meals*, by Jane and Michael Stern.

14 Yiddish acted as the cement that bound the Jewish community together on a socialist foundation. What language we spoke was critical. It reflected our identity, our loyalty, our distinctness not only from the gentile environment, but from other Jews as well. The use of Yiddish was an expression not only of love of a language, but of pride in ourselves as a people; it was an acknowledgement of a historical and cultural *yerushe*, heritage, a link to generations of Jews who came before and to the political activists of Eastern Europe. Above all it was the symbol of resistance to assimilation, an insistence on remaining who we were.

IRENA KLEPFISZ (b. 1941), U.S. Jewish author; born in Poland. *Dreams of an Insomniac*, part 4 (1990).
Klepfisz, a Jew born in Poland in 1941, escaped the 1943 Warsaw Uprising after her father was killed in its second day. After some years in Sweden, she and her mother emigrated to New York City–the only members of either side of the family to survive the Holocaust. She became an expert in, and teacher of, Yiddish.

15 Like desire, language disrupts, refuses to be contained within boundaries.

BELL HOOKS (b. c. 1955), U.S. author and educator. *Teaching to Transgress*, ch. 11 (1994).

LAW

1 . . . so far from thinking that a slaveholder is bound by the *immoral* and *unconstitutional* laws of the Southern States, *we* hold that he is solemnly bound as a man, as an American, to *break* them, and that *immediately* and openly . . .

ANGELINA GRIMKÉ (1805–1879), U.S. abolitionist and feminist. *Letters to Catherine Beecher*, letter #2 (1837).
In a letter dated June 17, 1837.

2 Of all my prosecutors . . . not one is my peer, but each and all are my political sovereigns; and had your honor submitted my case to the jury, as was clearly your duty, then I should have had just cause of protest, for not one of those men was my peer; but, native or foreign born, white or black, rich or poor, educated or ignorant, sober or drunk, each and every man of them was my political superior; hence, in no sense, my peer.

SUSAN B. ANTHONY (1820–1906), U.S. suffragist. As quoted in *Feminism: The Essential Historical Writings*, part 3, by Miriam Schnier (1972).
Said by the famous woman suffrage leader in federal court on June 18, 1873, upon its being judged that she "did knowingly, wrongfully and unlawfully vote for a Representative in the Congress of the United States"; the case was *United States vs. Susan B. Anthony*. Anthony was alluding to the American legal requirement that a person accused of a crime be tried by a jury of "peers." American women would not gain the right to vote for another forty-seven years.

3 [When asked: "If women voted, would they not have to sit on juries?":] Many women would be glad of a chance to sit on anything. There are women who stand up and wash six days in the week at 75 cents a day who would like to take a vacation and sit on a jury at $1.50.

ANNA HOWARD SHAW (1847–1919), U.S. minister, suffragist, and speaker; born in England. As quoted in *History of Woman Suffrage,* vol. 5, ch. 3, by Ida Husted Harper (1922).
Speaking in March 1903 at the thirty-fifth annual convention of the National Woman Suffrage Association.

4 The most absurd apology for authority and law is that they serve to diminish crime. Aside from the fact that the State is itself the greatest criminal, breaking every written and natural law, stealing in the form of taxes, killing in the form of war and capital punishment, it has come to an absolute standstill in coping with crime. It has failed utterly to destroy or even minimize the horrible scourge of its own creation.

EMMA GOLDMAN (1869–1940), U.S. anarchist and author; born in Russia. *Anarchism and Other Essays,* 3rd rev. ed., ch. 1 (1917).

5 . . . I have not found that the people who cling to the letter are always the people who cling to the spirit of the law.

KATHERINE FULLERTON GEROULD (1879–1944), U.S. author. *Modes and Morals,* ch. 8 (1920).

6 There are so bewilderingly many laws in the Outside World. We of the circus know only one law—simple and unfailing. *The Show must go on.*

JOSEPHINE DEMOTT ROBINSON (1865–1948), U.S. circus performer. *The Circus Lady,* ch. 1 (1926).

7 . . . laws haven't the slightest interest for me—except in the world of

science, in which they are always changing; or in the world of art, in which they are unchanging; or in the world of Being in which they are, for the most part, unknown.

MARGARET ANDERSON (1886–1973), U.S. editor and memoirist. *The Fiery Fountains,* part 1 (1951).

8 I enjoyed the courtroom as just another stage—but not so amusing as Broadway.

MAE WEST (1892–1980), U.S. actor. *Goodness Had Nothing to Do With It,* ch. 7 (1959).
The sexy stage and film performer was commenting on her 1926 New York City trial for writing and starring in an allegedly objectionable play, *SEX.* She was found guilty, sentenced to ten days in jail, and fined $500.

9 I defied nothing at all. I ignored the law because I didn't know it existed. It didn't occur to me that anyone would want to curb my inspiration.

MARGARET ANDERSON (1886–1973), U.S. editor and memoirist. *The Strange Necessity,* part 1 (1969).
For several months in the teens of the century, Anderson and a small entourage connected with *The Little Review* (1914–1929), an important but unremunerative arts magazine that she had founded, set up five tents on a public beach along Lake Michigan north of Chicago. They could not afford rent and had dedicated themselves to spending what little money they had on publishing the magazine. Upon its being pointed out to her later that she had "defied the law" by living on the beach, she said this.

10 . . . tobacco kills 52,000 people a year from lung cancer, and there's no telling how many lives have been ruined through drinking. But to my knowledge, no one has ever died of a blow job.

FLORYNCE KENNEDY (b. 1916), U.S. lawyer, activist, speaker, and author. *Color Me Flo,* ch. 1 (1976).

On the illogicality of prostitution being illegal while tobacco and alcohol are legal.

11 I believe the citizens of Marion County and the United States want to have judges who have feelings and who are human beings.

Paula Lopossa, U.S. judge. As quoted in the *New York Times*, p. B9 (May 21, 1993).

Lopossa, Superior Court Judge of Marion County, Indiana, was reflecting on whether she had behaved inappropriately when she broke down in tears in the courtroom after Portia Douglas, the victim of a rape and attempted murder, said that she did not seek revenge against her attacker, Rodney Cook. Cook's attorney unsuccessfully charged Lopossa with bias. Douglas, who was herself an attorney, observed: "I've seen male judges yell and scream and pound the table at defendants, and that's acceptable. What's the difference between anger toward the defendant or compassion toward a victim? Judge Lopossa did nothing different from what I've seen male judges do; she just did it in a different way."

LAWYERS

1 I had always been so much taken with the way all English people I knew always were going to see their lawyer. Even if they have no income and do not earn anything they always have a lawyer.

Gertrude Stein (1874–1946), U.S. author; relocated to France. *Wars I Have Seen* (1945).

Written in 1943.

2 The question arises . . . whether all lawyers are the same. This is like asking whether everything that gets into a sewer is garbage.

Florynce Kennedy (b. 1916), U.S. lawyer, activist, speaker, and author. *Color Me Flo*, ch. 3 (1976).

3 We have a responsibility to "make a difference" in the legal system and the administration of justice. My hope is that when historians assess the impact of this early wave of successful women entering all corners of the legal profession, they will not find us wanting.

Gladys Kessler, U.S. appellate court judge. As quoted in *Fordham Magazine*, p. 11 (Spring/Summer 1994).

From an article that originally appeared in *District Lawyer* magazine in 1983.

4 I'll never forget my father's response when I told him I wanted to be a lawyer. He said, "If you do this, no man will ever want you."

Cassandra Dunn (b. c. 1931), U.S. lawyer. As quoted in *The Fifties*, ch. 8, by Brett Harvey (1993).

Dunn was an interviewee in Harvey's oral history of the 1950s.

5 The good lawyer is the great salesman.

Janet Wood Reno (b. 1938), U.S. Attorney General. As quoted in the *New York Times Magazine*, p. 43 (May 15, 1994).

LAZINESS

1 Human nature is above all things— lazy.

Harriet Beecher Stowe (1811– 1896), U.S. author. *Household Papers and Stories*, ch. 6 (1864).

LEADERSHIP

1 . . . what a family is without a steward, a ship without a pilot, a flock without a shepherd, a body without a head, the same, I think, is a king-

dom without the health and safety of a good monarch.

ELIZABETH I (1533–1603), Queen of England (1558–1603). As quoted in *The Sayings of Queen Elizabeth,* ch. 1, by Frederick Chamberlin (1923).

Written c. 1550 to her half-brother, the "boy king" Edward VI (1537–1553).

2 I should say tact was worth much more than wealth as a road to leadership. . . . I mean that subtle apprehension which teaches a person how to do and say the right thing at the right time. It coexists with very ordinary qualities, and yet many great geniuses are without it. Of all human qualities I consider it the most convenient—not always the highest; yet I would rather have it than many more shining qualities.

M. E. W. SHERWOOD (1826–1903), U.S. socialite, traveller, and author. *An Epistle to Posterity,* ch. 19 (1897).

3 To the highest leadership among women it is given to hold steadily in one hand the sacred vessels that hold the ancient sanctities of life, and in the other a flaming torch to light the way for oncoming generations.

ANNA GARLIN SPENCER (1851–1931), U.S. educator, author, feminist, and Unitarian minister. *Woman's Share in Social Culture,* Introduction (1913).

4 I believe that no man who holds a leader's position should ever accept favors from either side. He is then committed to show favors. A leader must stand alone.

MOTHER JONES (1830–1930), U.S. labor organizer. *The Autobiography of Mother Jones,* ch. 11 (1925).

5 . . . the self respect of individuals ought to make them demand of their leaders conformity with an agreed-upon code of ethics and moral conduct.

MARY BARNETT GILSON (1877– ?), U.S. factory personnel manager, economist, and educator. *What's Past is Prologue,* ch. 27 (1940).

6 We have got to stop the nervous Nellies and the Toms from going to the Man's place. I don't believe in killing, but a good whipping behind the bushes wouldn't hurt them. . . . These bourgeoisie Negroes aren't helping. It's the ghetto Negroes who are leading the way.

FANNIE LOU HAMER (1917–1977), African American civil rights activist. As quoted in *This Little Light of Mine,* ch. 8, by Thelma Barnes—to whom Hamer said this in a November 17, 1989 interview—to Hay Mills (1993).

Said in a 1965 speech delivered to support twelve African American farm workers in the Delta, who were attempting to organize the Mississippi Freedom Labor Union. By "Nellies" and "Toms," she meant accommodationist African Americans; the "Man" referred generically to white men with power. The union did not succeed.

7 I don't think America's the center of the world anymore. I think African women will lead the way [in] . . . women's liberation . . . The African woman, she's got a country, she's got the flag, she's got her own army, got the navy. She doesn't have a racism problem. She's not afraid that if she speaks up, her man will say goodbye to her.

FAITH RINGGOLD (b. 1934), African American painter and sculptor. As quoted in *Lives and Works,* by Lynn F. Miller and Sally S. Swenson (1981).

8 It is very hard to be a female leader. While it is assumed that any man, no matter how tough, has a soft side . . . any female leader is assumed to be one-dimensional.

BILLIE JEAN KING (b. 1943), U.S. tennis player. *Billie Jean*, ch. 11 (1982).

In addition to playing championship tennis, King had assumed leadership in the campaign for better treatment of women tennis players, had been a co-founder of the Women's Tennis Association, and had begun the magazine *WomenSports*.

9 Being prime minister is a lonely job. . . . you cannot lead from the crowd.

MARGARET THATCHER (b. 1925), British politician; Prime Minister (1979–1990). *The Downing Street Years*, ch. 1 (1993).

LEARNING

1 I have eyes to see now what I have never seen before.

ANONYMOUS, U.S. correspondence student. As quoted in *The Life of Ellen H. Richards*, ch. 9, by Caroline L. Hunt, quoting Ellen Swallow Richards (1912).

Written in the late 1870s by a correspondence student of Richards', who was a chemist and educator. The student was learning through the Society to Encourage Studies at Home, which had been founded in 1873.

2 What we learn for the sake of knowing, we hold; what we learn for the sake of accomplishing some ulterior end, we forget as soon as that end has been gained. This, too, is automatic action in the constitution of the mind itself, and it is fortunate and merciful that it is so, for otherwise our minds would be soon only rubbish-rooms.

ANNA C. BRACKETT (1836–1911), U.S. author. *The Technique of Rest*, ch. 2 (1892).

3 If you should put a knife into a French girl's learning it would explode and blow away like an *omelette soufflee* . . .

M. E. W. SHERWOOD (1826–1903), U.S. socialite, traveller, and author. *An Epistle to Posterity*, ch. 16 (1897).

Of a beautiful young Parisian, "born for the splendid side of the tapestry."

4 All claims of education notwithstanding, the pupil will accept only that which his mind craves.

EMMA GOLDMAN (1869–1940), U.S. anarchist and author; born in Russia. *Anarchism and Other Essays*, 3rd rev. ed., ch. 1 (1917).

5 . . . nobody nobody wants to learn either by their own or anybody else's experience, nobody does, no they say they do but no nobody does, nobody does. Yes nobody does.

GERTRUDE STEIN (1874–1946), U.S. author; relocated to France. *Wars I Have Seen* (1945).

Written in France in January 1944, during World War II.

6 My grandmother stood among her
    kettles and ladles.
Smiling, in faulty grammar,
She praised my fortune and urged
    my lofty career.
So to please her I studied—but I
    will remember always
How she poured confusion out,
    how she cooled and labeled
All the wild sauces of the brimming
    year.

MARY OLIVER (b. 1935), U.S. poet. "Answers," lines 11–16 (1972).

LESBIANISM

1 So what if people say terrible things? Whatever they call me, I say, "Yes, and my name is Mary." I refuse to be afraid. And I do this out of an obligation not to the community but to myself. Nobody should have a say in who I am.

MARY HANSEN (b. c. 1975), U.S. gay/lesbian rights activist. As quoted in the New York Times, sect. 9, p. 7 (June 13, 1993). Hansen, a lesbian, was a recent graduate of New York City's Harvey Milk High School for gay and lesbian students.

2 When I get all these accolades for being true to myself, I say, "Who else can I be? I can't be Chris Evert."

MARTINA NAVRATILOVA (b. 1956), U.S. tennis player; born and raised in Czechoslovakia. As quoted in the New York Times, sect. 9, p. 4 (August 1, 1993). Referring to gays' and lesbians' praise of her openness about her lesbianism. Evert, a former tennis star and Navratilova's good friend and frequent opponent on court, was notably heterosexual. The veteran of several affairs with well-known men and of one failed marriage to a professional tennis player, she was by this time retired, remarried to a former Olympic skier, and the mother of a baby.

3 Why is it so difficult to see the lesbian—even when she is there, quite plainly, in front of us? In part because she has been "ghosted"—or made to seem invisible—by culture itself. . . . Once the lesbian has been defined as ghostly—the better to drain her of any sensual or moral

authority—she can then be exorcised.

TERRY CASTLE, U.S. lesbian author. The Apparitional Lesbian, ch. 1 (1993).

LIBERALISM

1 . . . liberal intellectuals . . . tend to have a classical theory of politics, in which the state has a monopoly of power; hoping that those in positions of authority may prove to be enlightened men, wielding power justly, they are natural, if cautious, allies of the "establishment."

SUSAN SONTAG (b. 1933), U.S. author. What's Happening in America (1966). Written in response to a summer 1966 questionnaire sent to her and other prominent American intellectuals by Partisan Review. All of their answers were published in the magazine's Winter 1967 issue, but Sontag also published hers separately as an essay. Sontag was herself a liberal.

2 A genuine Left doesn't consider anyone's suffering irrelevant or titilating; nor does it function as a microcosm of capitalist economy, with men competing for power and status at the top, and women doing all the work at the bottom. . . . Goodbye to all that.

ROBIN MORGAN (b. 1941), U.S. author, feminist, and child actor. Goodbye to All That (January 1970). Reacting to male chauvinism in the "New Left" movement against the Vietnam War, capitalism, and social injustice. Morgan had been a New Left activist.

LIBERATION

1 Woman—with a capital letter—should by now have ceased to be a specialty. There should be no more

need of "movements" on her behalf, and agitations for her advancement and development . . . than for the abolition of negro slavery in the United States.

MARION HARLAND (1830–1922), U.S. author. *What America Owes to Women*, ch. 10 (1893).

At this time, women could not vote in national elections and lacked many critical legal protections, though they had begun to be admitted to some colleges and universities. The Thirteenth Amendment to the Constitution (1865) had outlawed slavery, and the Fifteenth Amendment (1870) had granted suffrage to African American men.

2   The steps toward the emancipation of women are first intellectual, then industrial, lastly legal and political. Great strides in the first two of these stages already have been made of millions of women who do not yet perceive that it is surely carrying them towards the last.

ELLEN BATTELLE DIETRICK, U.S. suffragist. As quoted in *History of Woman Suffrage*, vol. 4, ch. 13, by Susan B. Anthony and Ida Husted Harper (1902).

Speaking in 1893 at the twenty-fifth annual convention of the National Woman Suffrage Association. Dietrick was from Massachusetts; her address was entitled "The Best Methods of Interesting Women in Suffrage."

3   . . . the absolute freedom of woman will be the dawn of the day of man's regeneration. In raising her he will elevate himself.

TENNESSEE CLAFLIN (1846–1923), U.S. journalist, lecturer, and social reform advocate; relocated to England. *Talks and Essays*, vol. 1, ch. 4 (1897).

4   The greatest block today in the way of woman's emancipation is the church, the canon law, the Bible and the priesthood.

ELIZABETH CADY STANTON (1815–1902), U.S. suffragist, social reformer, and author. As quoted in *History of Woman Suffrage*, vol. 5, ch. 1, by Ida Husted Harper (1922).

From a paper sent to the thirty-third annual convention of the National Woman Suffrage Association and read aloud on May 30, 1901, by her longtime colleague and closest friend, Susan B. Anthony (1820–1906). At this point, Anthony and Stanton, both in their eighties, were "Honorary Presidents" of the Association. Anthony had opposed Stanton's submitting this paper, urging her instead to send one of her usual rousing arguments on behalf of suffrage. Stanton refused, saying that such statements were passe; creator of a controversial *Woman's Bible* (1895–1898), she had become very interested in the roles played by theology and the church in suppressing women's rights.

5   The right to vote, or equal civil rights, may be good demands, but true emancipation begins neither at the polls nor in courts. It begins in woman's soul.

EMMA GOLDMAN (1869–1940), U.S. anarchist and author; born in Russia. *Anarchism and Other Essays*, 3rd rev. ed., ch. 10 (1917).

6   Anarchism . . . stands for the liberation of the human mind from the dominion of religion; the liberation of the human body from the dominion of property; liberation from the shackles and restraint of government. Anarchism stands for a social order based on the free grouping of individuals for the purpose of producing real social wealth; an order that will guarantee to every human being free access to the earth and full enjoyment of the necessities of life, according to individual desires, tastes, and inclinations.

EMMA GOLDMAN (1869–1940), U.S. anarchist and author; born in Russia. *Anarchism and Other Essays*, 3rd rev. ed., ch. 1 (1917).

7 Will women find themselves in the same position they have always been? Or do we see liberation as solving the conditions of women in our society? . . . If we continue to shy away from this problem we will not be able to solve it after independence. But if we can say that our first priority is the emancipation of women, we will become free as members of an oppressed community.

RUTH MOMPATI (b. 1925), South African black political activist. As quoted in *Lives of Courage*, ch. 7, by Diana E. H. Russell (1989). Said in 1987. Mompati was a prominent activist in the anti-apartheid African National Congress.

LIBERTINISM

1 . . . it is one thing to sow your wild oats in talk, and quite another to live by your own kaleidoscopic paradoxes.

KATHERINE FULLERTON GEROULD (1879–1944), U.S. author. *Modes and Morals*, ch. 7 (1920).

LIBRARIES

1 To take pride in a library kills it. Then, its motive power shifts over to the critical if admiring visitor, and apologies are necessary and acceptable and the fat is in the fire.

CAROLYN WELLS (1862–1942), U.S. author. *The Rest of My Life*, ch. 16 (1937).

2 In early days, I tried not to give librarians any trouble, which was where I made my primary mistake. Librarians like to be given trouble; they exist for it, they are geared to

it. For the location of a mislaid volume, an uncatalogued item, your good librarian has a ferret's nose. Give her a scent and she jumps the leash, her eye bright with battle.

CATHERINE DRINKER BOWEN (1897–1973), U.S. biographer. *Adventures of a Biographer*, ch. 9 (1959).
Bowen wrote popular biographies of Tchaikovsky, Oliver Wendell Holmes, John Adams, and Francis Bacon, among others. Lacking traditional academic training in history or biography, she was heavily dependent on the assistance of librarians.

3 I feel free as a bird. I'm in a unique position because I'm the boss. I buy what I like. I initiate things. I can experiment with all kinds of things I think the kids might be interested in. Nobody interferes. For me, it's no chore to go to work. Most people never get to do this at any time in their lives.

SARAH HOUGHTON, U.S. librarian. As quoted in *Working*, book 9, by Studs Terkel (1973).
Houghton ran a one-woman library in a private school.

LIFE

1 . . . it is the greatest of all mistakes to begin life with the expectation that it is going to be easy, or with the wish to have it so.

LUCY LARCOM (1824–1893), U.S. poet and teacher. *A New England Girlhood*, ch. 11 (1889).
Larcom was forced to become a mill worker at age 11 after her father died, leaving a destitute widow and eight young children.

2 Life must be something more than dilettante speculation.

ANNA JULIA COOPER (1859–1964), U.S.

educator and feminist. *A Voice from the South,* part 2 (1892).

3 The trouble with life isn't that there is no answer, it's that there are so many answers.

RUTH BENEDICT (1887–1948), U.S. anthropologist. *An Anthropologist at Work,* part 2 (1959).

Written in her journal on January 7, 1913.

4 I'm tired and nervous and I'm in America. Here you don't know that you live.

GRETA GARBO (1905–1990), Swedish actress; relocated to the United States. As quoted in *The Divine Garbo,* ch. 4, by Frederick Sands and Sven Broman (1979).

Written in a letter to her friend, the Swede Lars Saxon, on August 20, 1927; two years earlier, Garbo had come to the United States to make movies.

5 ... the precipitate of sorrow is happiness, the precipitate of struggle is success. Life means opportunity, and the thing men call death is the last wonderful, beautiful adventure.

ALICE FOOTE MacDOUGALL, (1867–1945) U.S. businesswoman. *The Autobiography of a Business Woman,* ch. 7 (1928).

On having overcome poverty, loneliness, and inexperience to succeed in business.

6 Life is not precious, a thing to be cherished. The soul and the mind are the instruments God gives us for our use and half of us don't begin to use them. We put Life and Health on two little pedestals and spend most of our time performing acts of devotion before them. Instead of using them as a carpenter his tools, as a helmsman the rudder,

to hammer or steer our way to victory, we turn ourselves into Vestal Virgins with nothing on the face of the earth to do but to feed the feeble flames of our comfort. Life is no craven thing, lurking coward-like in a corner. It is big, broad, splendid in opportunity. It is to be used, not cherished. It is to be spent, not saved.

ALICE FOOTE MacDOUGALL, (1867–1945) U.S. businesswoman. *The Autobiography of a Business Woman,* ch. 7 (1928).

MacDougall was highly successful, self-made, New York City merchant and restaurateur.

7 ... the great thing to learn about life is, first, not to do what you don't want to do, and, second, to do what you do want to do.

MARGARET ANDERSON (1886–1973), U.S. literary editor and autobiographer. *My Thirty Years' War,* ch. 1 (1930).

Anderson eschewed "the higher joys of country clubs and bridge," which her parents had expected her to pursue after college, for publishing what would become an influential literary and arts magazine, *The Little Review* (1914–1929). She also renounced marriage and motherhood for a fairly flamboyant lesbian life.

8 As I look at the human story I see two stories. They run parallel and never meet. One is of people who live, as they can or must, the events that arrive; the other is of people who live, as they intend, the events they create.

MARGARET ANDERSON (1886–1973), U.S. editor and memoirist. *The Fiery Fountains,* part 1 (1951).

Anderson, a spirited and original personality, placed herself in the second category.

9 I have always rebelled against the unadorned, the unbefitting, the un-

awakened, the unresisting, the undesirable, the unplanned, the un-
shapely, the uncommitted, the unat-
tempted—all leading to the
unintended. I believe in the unsub-
missive, the unfaltering, the unas-
sailable, the irresistible, the unbe-
lievable—in other words, in an art
of life.

MARGARET ANDERSON (1886–1973),
U.S. editor and memoirist. *The Strange Necessity,* part 1 (1969).

A devotee, editor, publisher, and promoter of
the arts—especially the avant-garde—Anderson
often survived on very little income and never
held a "regular" job. She was beautiful, stylish,
and flamboyant. Openly lesbian, she lived at
various times in Chicago, New York, and Paris,
becoming familiar with the visual and literary
artists of each locale. She consciously shaped
her life to her interests rather than treading conventional paths.

10   . . . our lives are like soap operas.
We can go for months and not tune
in to them, then six months later
we look in and the same stuff is going on.

JANE WAGNER (b. 1935), U.S. playwright.
*The Search for Signs of Intelligent Life in the
Universe* (1986).

11   I can entertain the proposition that
life is a metaphor for boxing—for
one of those bouts that go on and
on, round following round, jabs,
missed punches, clinches, nothing
determined, again the bell and
again and you and your opponent
so evenly matched it's impossible
not to see that your opponent *is*
you. . . . Life *is* like boxing in many
unsettling respects. But boxing is
only like boxing.

JOYCE CAROL OATES (b. 1938), U.S. author. *On Boxing* (1987).

12   Life is so messy that the temptation
to straighten it up is very strong.
And the results always illusory.

ANNA QUINDLEN (b. 1953), U.S. author.
New York Times, section 4, p. 17 (November
14, 1993).
Concluding a newspaper column on simplistic
explanations of a complexly motivated legal
case.

13   . . . here he is, fully alive, and it is
hard to picture him fully dead.
Death is thirty-three hours away
and here we are talking about the
brain size of birds and bloodhounds
and hunting in the woods. You can
only attend to death for so long before the life force sucks you right in
again.

HELEN PREJÉAN (b. 1940), U.S. nun and
activist against the death penalty. *Dead Man
Walking,* ch. 4 (1993).
Serving as "spiritual advisor" to Death Row inmate Pat Sonnier, Prejean discussed his Louisiana childhood with him fewer than two days
before he was scheduled to be executed.

14   We see daily that our lives are terrible and little, without continuity,
buyable and salable at any moment,
mere blips on a screen, that this is
the way we live now. Memory marketed as nostalgia; terror reduced to
mere suspense, to melodrama.

ADRIENNE RICH (b. 1929), U.S. poet
and essayist. *What is Found There,* ch. 3
(1993).

LIFE PATTERNS

1   Surely one of the peculiar habits of
circumstances is the way they follow, in their eternal recurrence, a
single course. If an event happens
once in a life, it may be depended

upon to repeat later its general design.

ELLEN GLASGOW (1873–1945), U.S. novelist. *The Woman Within,* ch. 11 (1954).
Written in 1944.

2   The worst constructed play is a
Bach fugue when compared to
life.

HELEN HAYES (1900–1993), U.S. actor.
On Reflection, ch. 14 (1968).

3   Our life is a faint tracing on the surface of mystery, like the idle, curved
tunnels of leaf miners on the face of
a leaf. We must somehow take a
wider view, look at the whole landscape, really see it, and describe
what's going on here. Then we can
at least wail the right question into
the swaddling band of darkness, or,
if it comes to that, choir the proper
praise.

ANNIE DILLARD (b. 1945), U.S. essayist
and autobiographer. *Pilgrim at Tinker Creek,* ch.
1 (1974).

LITERARY CRITICISM

1   A literary woman's best critic is her
husband . . .

ELIZABETH STUART PHELPS (1844–
1911), U.S. novelist and short story writer.
Chapters from a Life, ch. 11 (1897).
Phelps's husband, Herbert D. Ward, was, like
her, a popular author.

2   Many scholars forget . . . that our
enjoyment of the great works of literature depends more upon the
depth of our sympathy than upon
our understanding. . . . very few of
their laborious explanations stick in

the memory. The mind drops them
as a branch drops its overripe
fruit.

HELEN KELLER (1880–1968), U.S.
author. *The Story of My Life,* ch. 20 (1905).
Keller was rendered deaf and blind at the age of
nineteen months. But in 1904, she had graduated *cum laude* from Radcliffe College.

3   If behind the erratic gunfire of the
press the author felt that there was
another kind of criticism, the opinion of people reading for the love of
reading, slowly and unprofession-
ally, and judging with great sympathy and yet with great severity,
might this not improve the quality
of his work? And if by our means
books were to become stronger,
richer, and more varied, that would
be an end worth reaching.

VIRGINIA WOOLF (1882–1941), British
novelist, essayist, and diarist. *The Second Common Reader,* ch. 22 (1932).

4   With a few exceptions, the critics of
children's books are remarkably le-
nient souls. . . . Most of us assume
there is something good in every
child; the critics go from this to assume there is something good in every book written for a child. It is
not a sound theory.

KATHARINE S. WHITE (1892–1977),
U.S. editor. As quoted in *Onward and Upward,*
ch. 5, by Linda H. Davis (1986).
Said in 1939. White reviewed children's books
for the *New Yorker,* and her husband, E. B.
White, wrote several important children's books
(*Stuart Little, Charlotte's Web,* etc.).

5   I waited and worked, and watched
the inferior exalted for nearly thirty
years; and when recognition came
at last, it was too late to alter

events, or to make a difference in living.

Ellen Glasgow (1873–1945), U.S. novelist. *The Woman Within,* ch. 13 (1954).
Written in 1944. The important American Southern "regional" novelist was remembering her long wait for critical recognition.

6 I feel that the task of criticizing my poetry is best left to others (i.e. critics) and would much rather have it take place after I am dead. If at all.

Margaret Atwood (b. 1939), Canadian poet and novelist. As quoted in *Contemporary Poets,* 3rd ed., by James Vinson (1980).

7 The techniques are all means of dealing with one simple idea: *She wrote it.* (That is, the "wrong" person—in this case, female—has created the "right" value—i.e., art.) Denial of Agency: *She didn't write it.* Pollution of Agency: *She shouldn't have written it.* Double Standard of Content: *Yes, but look what she wrote about.* False Categorizing: *She is not really she* [an artist] *and it is not really it* [serious, of the right genre, aesthetically sound, important, etc.] *so how could "she" have written "it"?*
Or simply: Neither "she" nor "it" exists (simple exclusion).

Joanna Russ (b. 1937), U.S. science fiction writer and feminist. *How to Suppress Women's Writing,* ch. 6 (1983).
Satirizing mainstream sexist reactions to high-quality writing by women.

LITERATURE

1 . . . not only do . . . women suffer . . . indignities in daily life, but the literature of the world proclaims their inferiority and divinely decreed subjection in all history, sacred and profane, in science, philosophy, poetry, and song.

Elizabeth Cady Stanton (1815–1902), U.S. suffragist, social reformer, and author. *History of Woman Suffrage,* vol. 2, ch. 19 (1882).

2 . . . literature is my Utopia. Here I am not disfranchised. No barrier of the senses shuts me out from the sweet, gracious discourse of my book-friends. They talk to me without embarrassment or awkwardness.

Helen Keller (1880–1968), U.S. author. *The Story of My Life,* ch. 21 (1905).
Keller was rendered deaf and blind at the age of nineteen months. But in 1904, she had graduated *cum laude* from Radcliffe College.

3 I don't care very much for literary shrines and haunts . . . I knew a woman in London who boasted that she had lodgings from the windows of which she could throw a stone into Carlyle's yard. And when I said, "Why throw a stone into Carlyle's yard?" she looked at me as if I were an imbecile and changed the subject.

Carolyn Wells (1862–1942), U.S. author. *The Rest of My Life,* ch. 8 (1937).
Thomas Carlyle (1795–1881) was an English historian and essayist.

4 . . . stare into the lake of sunset as it runs
boiling, over the west past all control
rolling and swamps the heartbeat and repeats

sea beyond sea after unbearable
suns;
think: poems fixed this landscape:
Blake, Donne, Keats.

MURIEL RUKEYSER (1913–1980), U.S. poet. "Homage to Literature," lines 10–14 (1938).

William Blake (1757–1827), John Donne (1572–1631), and John Keats (1795–1821) were important English poets.

5   I have watched . . . many literary fashions shoot up and blossom, and then fade and drop. . . . Yet with the many that I have seen come and go, I have never yet encountered a mode of thinking that regarded itself as simply a changing fashion, and not as an infallible approach to the right culture.

ELLEN GLASGOW (1873–1945), U.S. novelist. *The Woman Within,* ch. 12 (1954).

Written in 1944.

6   To me, literature is a calling, even a kind of salvation. It connects me with an enterprise that is over 2,000 years old. What do we have from the past? Art and thought. That's what lasts. That's what continues to feed people and given them an idea of something better. A better state of one's feelings or simply the idea of a silence in one's self that allows one to think or to feel. Which to me is the same.

SUSAN SONTAG (b. 1933), U.S. author. As quoted in the *New York Times Magazine,* "Susan Sontag Finds Romance," by Leslie Garis (August 2, 1992).

LOGIC

I   There is no morality by instinct. . . . There is no social salvation—in the

end—without taking thought; without mastery of logic and application of logic to human experience.

KATHERINE FULLERTON GEROULD (1879–1944), U.S. author. *Modes and Morals,* ch. 1 (1920).

2   The nineteenth century was completely lacking in logic, it had cosmic terms and hopes, and aspirations, and discoveries, and ideals but it had no logic.

GERTRUDE STEIN (1874–1946), U.S. author; relocated to France. *Wars I Have Seen* (1945).

Written in 1943.

LONELINESS

I   . . . what loneliness is more lonely than distrust?

GEORGE ELIOT (1819–1880), British novelist. *Middlemarch,* ch. 44 (1871–1872).

2   I don't think I've ever felt so lost as I did then.

JANET WOOD RENO (b. 1938), U.S. Attorney General. As quoted in the *New York Times Magazine,* p. 42 (May 15, 1994).

The first woman to hold the post of America's top attorney, Reno was remembering her first day of law school.

LOSS

I   A queen driven from her throne, naked, in winter snows, like Elizabeth of Hungary, suffers more than she who wanders from a snow-beleaguered hut every day; the woman who has had the most suffers the most.

M. E. W. SHERWOOD (1826–1903), U.S. socialite, traveller, and author. *An Epistle to Posterity,* ch. 16 (1897).

Sherwood, an avid traveller and prolific writer on travel and "manners," had always been wealthy and a member of New York City's fashionable "society." The Hungarian Queen (1837–1898) would be assassinated in Geneva, Switzerland, the following year.

2 There is something to be said for losing one's possessions, after nothing can be done about it. I had loved my Nanking home and the little treasures it had contained, the lovely garden I had made, my life with friends and students. Well, that was over. I had nothing at all now except the old clothes I stood in. I should have felt sad, and I was quite shocked to realize that I did not feel sad at all. On the contrary, I had a lively sense of adventure merely at being alive and free, even of possessions. No one expected anything of me. I had no obligations, no duties, no tasks. I was nothing but a refugee, someone totally different from the busy young woman I had been.

PEARL S. BUCK (1892–1973), U.S. author. *My Several Worlds* (1954).

On losing everything in 1927, during the Chinese Revolution. The daughter of American missionaries to China, Buck had spent her childhood and most of her adulthood in that country. However, with the revolution, she and her family, who were white, were forced to flee.

3 I was a sophomore in college when everything went down the drain. I never thought it would happen. It was like the end of the world. We had those great plush years. I remember the house. The kid's [sic] say, "Is that *your* house?" The schools we went to, Palm Springs, inviting your friends down for the weekends, swimming pools, fancy

dresses. It was all tied up with my father. Finally I had to face my father being a real person.

LOIS KEELEY, U.S. As quoted in *Working,* book 7, by Studs Terkel (1973).

Keeley's father, a former business executive, lost his job at age sixty-four following a merger.

4 It was like stepping into a negative rather than a photograph. I was overcome by the sudden realization of the scale of the loss.

IRENA KLEPFISZ (b. 1941), U.S. Jewish author; born in Poland. *Dreams of an Insomniac,* part 4 (1990).

On visiting Poland with her mother in 1983, on the occasion of the fortieth anniversary of the Warsaw Uprising, in which her father, a Jewish rights activist, was killed. The rest of the two women's family also died in Poland during the Holocaust.

LOVE

1 I do not want a husband who honours me as a queen, if he does not love me as a woman.

ELIZABETH I (1533–1603), British monarch, Queen of England (1558–1603). As quoted in *The Sayings of Queen Elizabeth,* ch. 7, by Frederick Chamberlin (1923).

Said to Fenelon, the French Ambassador, who urged her to marry into the French royalty. Elizabeth remained single and died leaving no heir.

2 True love ennobles and dignifies the material labors of life; and homely services rendered for love's sake have in them a poetry that is immortal.

HARRIET BEECHER STOWE (1811– 1896), U.S. author. *Household Papers and Stories,* part 2, ch. 4 (1864).

3 When we lose love, we lose also our identification with the universe and with eternal values—an identification which alone makes it possible for us to lay our lives on the altar for what we believe.

SARAH PATTON BOYLE, U.S. civil rights activist and author. *The Desegregated Heart,* part 3, ch. 2 (1962).

Boyle, a white Virginian, had publicly advocated integration despite great opposition, social isolation, and threats of violence.

4 People love pretty much the same things best. A writer looking for subject inquires not after what he loves best, but after what he alone loves at all.

ANNIE DILLARD (b. 1945), U.S. author. *The Writing Life,* ch. 5 (1989).

5 The moment we choose to love we begin to move against domination, against oppression. The moment we choose to love we begin to move towards freedom, to act in ways that liberate ourselves and others. That action is the testimony of love as the practice of freedom.

BELL HOOKS (b. c. 1955), African American author, feminist, and human rights advocate. *Outlaw Culture,* ch. 19 (1994).

LUCK

1 ... we went on to Douglas, Arizona, and ... got in ahead of time. I asked the pilot the reason, and he told me we had a tail wind, which meant fast going. Right then it struck me that a tail wind was a mighty handy thing to have, in a lot of ways besides flying. I could look back over my life and think of quite a few times when a tail wind would have been right useful.

SUE SANDERS, U.S. oil producer. *Our Common Herd,* ch. 28 (1940).
Describing an insight gained in 1936, after taking her first flight. Sanders was a successful self-made businesswoman.

LYNCHING

1 ... lynching was ... a woman's issue: it had as much to do with ideas of gender as it had with race.

PAULA GIDDINGS (b. 1948), African American author. *Race-ing Justice, En-gendering Power,* ch. 15 (1992).

MALE DOMINANCE

1 Men have made out, that only they can run the world. It's in about as bad a state as it well can be, but they are proud of their work.

ANN ODDY, U.S. housekeeper. As quoted in *All the Days of My Life,* ch. 2 (1913).
Said to novelist Amelia E. Barr in the mid-1830s, when Barr was a child. Oddy cared for the household and the children.

2 All history attests that man has subjected woman to his will, used her as a means to promote his selfish gratification, to minister to his sensual pleasures, to be instrumental in promoting his comfort; but never has he desired to elevate her to that rank she was created to fill. He has done all he could to debase and enslave her mind; and now he looks triumphantly on the ruin he has wrought, and say, the being he has thus deeply injured is his inferior.

SARAH M. GRIMKÉ (1792–1873), U.S. abolitionist and feminist. *Letters on the Equality of the Sexes and the Condition of Woman,* letter #2: dated July 17, 1837 (1838).

3 The history of mankind is the history of repeated injuries and usurpations on the part of man toward woman, having in direct object the establishment of an absolute tyranny over her.

SENECA FALLS CONVENTION, As quoted in *Feminism: The Essential Historical Writings,* part 3, by Miriam Schnier (1972).
From the "Seneca Falls Declaration," formulated at the first women's rights convention, held in Seneca Falls, N.Y. in 1848. Here, for the first time, American women demanded suffrage and other rights thus far denied them. Among those who organized the convention were Lucretia Mott (1793–1880) and Elizabeth Cady Stanton (1815–1902), who would become two of the century's most famous suffragists and social reformers.

4 There is a great stir about colored men getting their rights, but not a word about colored women, and if colored men get their rights, and not colored women theirs, you see the colored men will be masters over the women, and it will be just as bad as it was before. So I'm for keeping the thing going while things are stirring; because if we wait till it is still, it will take a great while to get it going again.

SOJOURNER TRUTH (1797–1883), African American human rights activist and preacher. As quoted in *Feminism: The Essential Historical Writings,* part 3, by Miriam Schnier (1972).
Speaking at an 1867 meeting of the American Equal Rights Association held in New York City. Black men would be granted the right to vote by the Fifteenth Amendment to the U. S. Constitution in 1870; the Nineteenth Amendment, granting the same right to women, would not take effect until fifty years later. Born a slave in Ulster County, New York, and named Isabella Baumfree, Truth had been freed by New York State law in 1827. In 1843, she had a religious vision which led her to change her name and become an itinerant preacher. She also became a prominent and beloved figure in the woman suffrage and anti-slavery movements.

5 It is one thing to say, "Some men shall rule," quite another to declare, "All men shall rule," and that in virtue of the most primitive, the most rudimentary attribute they possess, that namely of sex.

MARY PUTNAM JACOBI (1842–1906), U.S. suffragist. *"Common Sense" Applied to Woman Suffrage,* ch. 4 (1894).

6 No man is good enough to govern any woman without her consent.

SUSAN B. ANTHONY (1820–1906), U.S. suffragist. As quoted in *The Life and Work of Susan B. Anthony,* ch. 45, by Ida Husted Harper (1898).
At an Independence Day celebration in San Francisco on July 4, 1895. Anthony was paraphrasing Abraham Lincoln's antislavery statement, "No man is good enough to govern another man without his consent."

7 The world is made by man—for man alone. I, who have lived as a man among men, realize it. I, who have talked with men as a man, know it. And whatever man may say about "the hand that rocks the cradle rules the world," they know that nothing rules men but their desires and there is no ruler in this world but sex.

CORA ANDERSON, U.S. male impersonator. As quoted in *Gay American History,* part 3, by Jonathan Katz (1976).
Said in 1914; for the previous thirteen years, Anderson had successfully impersonated a man, permitting her to earn a better living than she could as a woman.

8 [Women's] apparent endorsement of male supremacy is . . . a pathetic striving for self-respect, self-justification, and self-pardon. After fifteen hundred years of subjection to men, Western woman finds it almost unbearable to face the fact that she has been hoodwinked and enslaved by her *inferiors*—that the master is lesser than the slave.

ELIZABETH GOULD DAVIS (b. 1910), U.S. feminist and author. *The First Sex*, ch. 21 (1971).

9   Women are a colonized people.

ROBIN MORGAN (b. 1941), U.S. author, feminist, and child actor. *The Word of a Woman*, part 1 (1992).
Written in 1974.

10   The discourse of black resistance has always equated freedom with manhood, the economic and material domination of black men with castration, emasculation. Accepting these sexual metaphors forged a bond between oppressed black men and their white male oppressors. They shared the patriarchal belief that revolutionary struggle was really about the erect phallus, the ability of men to establish political dominance that could correspond to sexual dominance.

BELL HOOKS (b. c. 1955), African American author and educator. *Yearning*, ch. 7 (1990).

MALE-FEMALE RELATIONSHIPS

1   . . . instead of being a help meet to man, in the highest, noblest sense of the term, as a companion, a co-worker, an equal; she has been a mere appendage of his being, an instrument of his convenience and pleasure, the pretty toy with which he wiled [sic] away his leisure moments, or the pet animal whom he

humored into playfulness and submission.

ANGELINA GRIMKÉ (1805–1879), U.S. abolitionist and feminist. *Letters to Catherine Beecher*, letter #12 (1837).
In a letter dated October 2, 1837.

2   . . . he held it one of the prettiest attitudes of the feminine mind to adore a man's pre-eminence without too precise a knowledge of what it consisted in.

GEORGE ELIOT (1819–1880), British novelist. *Middlemarch*, ch. 27 (1871–1872).

3   . . . the majority of colored men do not yet think it worth while that women aspire to higher education. . . . The three R's, a little music and a good deal of dancing, a first rate dress-maker and a bottle of magnolia balm, are quite enough generally to render charming any woman possessed of tact and the capacity for worshipping masculinity.

ANNA JULIA COOPER (1859–1964), African American educator and feminist. *A Voice from the South*, part 1 (1892).
Though she specified "colored men" because she herself was half black, Cooper would probably have agreed that this judgment applied to men of other races as well.

4   . . . men, accustomed to think of men as possessing sex attributes and other things besides, are accustomed to think of women as having sex, and nothing else.

MARY PUTNAM JACOBI (1842–1906), U.S. suffragist. *"Common Sense" Applied to Woman Suffrage*, ch. 5 (1894).
On men's opposition to women's rights, especially suffrage.

5   . . . as women become free, economic, social factors, so becomes possible the full social combination of individuals in collective industry. With such freedom, such independence, such wider union, becomes possible also a union between man and woman such as the world has long dreamed of in vain.

CHARLOTTE PERKINS GILMAN (1860–1935), U.S. author, editor, feminist, and social reformer. *Women and Economics*, ch. 7 (1898).

Married for the first time in 1884 to a man whom she considered a good husband, Gilman nonetheless became desperately unhappy very soon. The birth of her beloved daughter in 1885 only deepened her depression and sense of confinement. Ultimately, she and her husband were divorced, he was remarried to her best friend, and Gilman allowed them to raise her daughter, for which she was harshly criticized. At age forty, Gilman herself was happily remarried to a man seven years her junior; they had no children.

6 A gentleman opposed to their enfranchisement once said to me, "Women have never produced anything of any value to the world." I told him the chief product of the women had been the men, and left it to him to decide whether the product was of any value.

ANNA HOWARD SHAW (1847–1919), U.S. minister and suffragist. As quoted in *History of Woman Suffrage*, vol. 4, ch. 19, by Susan B. Anthony and Ida Husted Harper (1902).

Speaking before the thirty-first annual convention of the National Woman Suffrage Association on April 29, 1899; her address was entitled "Working Partners."

7 ... the day will come when man will recognize woman as his peer, not only at the fireside but in the councils of the nation. Then, and not until then, will there be the perfect comradeship, the ideal union, between the sexes that shall result

in the highest development of the race.

SUSAN B. ANTHONY (1820–1906), U.S. suffragist. As quoted in *Life and Work of Susan B. Anthony*, vol. 3, ch. 53, by Ida Husted Harper (1908).

From an address entitled "Position of Women in the Political Life of the United States," delivered on June 27, 1899, to the International Council of Women in London.

8 [Bachelors'] approach to gastronomy is basically sexual, since few of them under seventy-nine will bother to produce a good meal unless it is for a pretty woman.

M. F. K. FISHER (1908–1992), U.S. author and food expert. *An Alphabet for Gourmets*, "B is for Bachelors" chapter (1949).

9 I got quite bored, serving in the bar. Since I was there, the customers wouldn't talk about women, and with half their subject matter denied them, it was: horses, silence; horses, silence.

BERNADETTE DEVLIN (b. 1947), Irish politician. *The Price of My Soul*, ch. 6 (1969).

The fiery Northern Irish political activist was remembering a summer spent working in her uncle's pub, where the "forbidden subject" of conversation was "politics."

10 ... men need women more than women need men; and so, aware of this fact, man has sought to keep woman dependent upon him economically as the only method open to him of making himself necessary to her.

ELIZABETH GOULD DAVIS (b. 1910), U.S. feminist and author. *The First Sex*, ch. 22 (1971).

11 Every time a man and a woman are at the water cooler, Anita Hill's right there between them.

ANDREA SANKAR, As quoted in *The Real Anita Hill*, introduction, by David Brock (1993). Said in 1991 about the inhibiting effect in the workplace of attorney Anita Hill's (b. 1956) claim that she had been sexually harassed by Clarence Thomas (b. 1948) long before he became a United States Supreme Court Justice.

12 Never be intimidated when you deal with men. Curse, don't cry.

ANONYMOUS, U.S. professional woman. As quoted in *Aspirations and Mentoring in an Academic Environment*, ch. 4, by Mary Niles Maack and Joanne Passet (1994).

Said by a woman who served as a "mentor" to a woman library school dean when the latter had been getting started in her career.

MANNERS

1 . . . there is nothing so sad as lack of fine manners in a gentleman, except the lack of them in a lady.

MRS. H. O. WARD (1824–1899), U.S. author. *Sensible Etiquette of the Best Society Customs, Manners, Morals, and Home Culture, Compiled from the Best Authorities*, ch. 3 (1878).

2 No matter what your fight, don't be ladylike! God Almighty made women and the Rockefeller gang of thieves made the ladies.

MOTHER JONES (1830–1930), U.S. labor organizer. *The Autobiography of Mother Jones*, ch. 22 (1925).

From her address to a 1915 dinner assemblage of 500 women, most of them suffragists. Jones herself was never active on behalf of woman suffrage. The Rockefellers were a wealthy family of industrialists.

3 Conventional manners are a kind of literacy test for the alien who comes among us.

KATHERINE FULLERTON GEROULD (1879–1944), U.S. author. *Modes and Morals*, ch. 7 (1920).

4 Courtesy is breeding. Breeding is an excellent thing. Always remember that.

LILLIAN HELLMAN (1905–1984), U.S. playwright and memoirist. *The Children's Hour*, act 1 (1934).

Spoken by the character named Mrs. Lily Mortar.

5 . . . all my life I've been terrible at remembering people's names. I once introduced a friend of mine as Martini. Her name was actually Olive.

TALLULAH BANKHEAD (1903–1968), U.S. actress. As quoted in *Tallulah*, photograph section at back, by Brendan Gill (1972).

The Southern-born actress was explaining "why she calls everybody 'dahling.' " Parenthetically, Bankhead was known to be a heavy drinker.

MARRIAGE

1 I felt more determined than ever to become a physician, and thus place a strong barrier between me and all ordinary marriage. I must have something to engross my thoughts, some object in life which will fill this vacuum and prevent this sad wearing away of the heart.

ELIZABETH BLACKWELL (1821–1910), U.S. physician. *Pioneer Work for Women*, ch. 2 (1895).

From a journal entry made in 1845, when she was first considering the study of medicine. Eventually, she became the first American woman physician.

2 . . . we are not dreamers or fanatics; and we know that the ballot when we get it, will achieve for woman no more than it has achieved for man. . . . The ballot is not even half the loaf; it is only a crust—a crumb. The ballot touches only those interests, either of women or men, which take their root in political questions. But woman's chief discontent is not with her political, but with her social, and particularly her marital bondage. The solemn and profound question of marriage . . . [ellipsis in source] is of more vital consequence to woman's welfare, reaches down to a deeper depth in woman's heart, and more thoroughly constitutes the core of the woman's movement, than any such superficial and fragmentary question as woman's suffrage.

LAURA BULLARD, U.S. feminist and author. As quoted in *Everyone Was Brave*, ch. 1, by William L. O'Neill (1971).

From an article entitled "What Flag Shall We Fly?," which was first published in the October 27, 1870, issue of *Revolution*, a weekly journal edited by the most prominent suffragists of their time, Susan B. Anthony (1820–1906) and Elizabeth Cady Stanton (1815–1902).

3 Twenty-five or thirty years ago it was natural for a girl to look forward to marriage as embodying all that was of consequence in life. Not to have done so would have stamped the bold Philistine with the fatal brand of eccentricity; and had she perchance gone yet farther and dared to fling conventionality to the winds by earning her bread in a sphere of employment hitherto confined to the sterner sex, her genteel acquaintances would have passed by on the other side, not so much

from a snobbish sense of superiority as from a deep-rooted conviction that the unfortunate woman in question had deliberately plunged into the very vortex of sin and humiliation.

CLARA (MARQUISE) LANZA (1859–1939), U.S. author. *What America Owes to Women*, ch. 44 (1893).

4 I never felt I could give up my life of freedom to become a man's housekeeper. When I was young, if a girl married poverty, she became a drudge; if she married wealth, she became a doll. Had I married at twenty-one, I would have been either a drudge or a doll for fifty-five years. Think of it!

SUSAN B. ANTHONY (1820–1906), U.S. suffragist, speaker, and editor. As quoted in *The Life and Work of Susan B. Anthony*, ch. 46, by Ida Husted Harper (1898–1908).
Said in 1896; Anthony never married.

5 I do not consider divorce an evil by any means. It is just as much a refuge for women married to brutal men as Canada was to the slaves of brutal masters.

SUSAN B. ANTHONY (1820–1906), U.S. suffragist. As quoted in *The Life and Work of Susan B. Anthony*, vol. 3, ch. 67, by Ida Husted Harper (1898).
Said in March 1905, at a Washington, D.C., meeting of the National Council of Women. She was objecting to a proposal that the Council "cooperate with Church and State to lessen the evil of divorce." Anthony had never married.

6 To the moralist prostitution does not consist so much in the fact that the woman sells her body, but rather that she sells it out of wedlock.

EMMA GOLDMAN (1869–1940), U.S. anarchist and author; born in Russia. *Anarchism and Other Essays*, 3rd rev. ed., ch. 8 (1917).

7 You need not be proud of me. . . . I'm only being *active* till you can be again—it isn't such a great desire on my part to serve the world and I'll fall back into habits of sloth quite easily!

ELEANOR ROOSEVELT (1884–1962), U.S. First Lady, author, and speaker. As quoted in *Eleanor and Franklin*, ch. 28, by Joseph P. Lash (1971).

In a letter to her husband, the future president Franklin Delano Roosevelt, dated February 5, 1924. She had become active politically while he recovered from polio and was forced to abandon political work. This letter was an attempt to reassure and console him. In fact, Roosevelt maintained and broadened her independent political activity (speaking, writing, etc.) throughout her life.

8 A friend of mine spoke of books that are dedicated like this: "To my wife, by whose helpful criticism . . ." and so on. He said the dedication should really read: "To my wife. If it had not been for her continual criticism and persistent nagging doubt as to my ability, this book would have appeared in *Harper's* instead of *The Hardware Age.*"

BRENDA UELAND (1891–1985), U.S. author and writing teacher. *If You Want to Write*, 2nd. ed., ch. 1 (1938).

9 I know a lot of wonderful men married to pills, and I know a lot of pills married to wonderful women. So one shouldn't judge that way.

BARBARA BUSH (b. 1925), First Lady of the United States (1988–1992). As quoted in *Time* magazine, p. 27 (August 24, 1992).

Opposing Republican attacks on Democratic Presidential candidate Bill Clinton which focused on his wife, Hillary Rodham Clinton. Bush was married to Republican President George Bush, whom Clinton defeated in the November election.

10 I had reconciled myself to a life without marriage or children for the sake of my career. And then my brothers got married. I realized I didn't even have a home, that in the future I couldn't do politics when I had to ask permission from their wives as to whether I could use the dining room or the telephone. I couldn't rent a home because a woman living on her own can be suspected of all kinds of scandalous associations. So keeping in mind that many people in Pakistan looked to me, I decided to make a personal sacrifice in what I thought would be, more or less, a loveless marriage, a marriage of convenience.

BENAZIR BHUTTO (b. 1953), Pakistani Prime Minister. As quoted in the *New York Times Magazine*, p. 39 (May 15, 1994).

Explaining why she acceded to a conventional arranged marriage in 1987 to a near-stranger, Asif Ali Zadari; as it turned out, the marriage was loving and happy.

MARRIAGE: AVOIDANCE

1 . . . spinsterhood [is considered to be] an abnormality of small proportions and small consequence, something like an extra finger or two on the body, presumably of temporary duration, and never of any social significance.

MARY PUTNAM JACOBI (1842–1906), U.S. suffragist. *"Common Sense" Applied to Woman Suffrage*, ch. 2 (1894).

MARRIAGE: DESIRABILITY

1 We [actors] are indeed a strange lot! There are times we doubt that we have any emotions we can honestly call our own. I have approached every dynamic scene change in my life the same way. When I married Charlie MacArthur, I sat down and wondered how I could play the best wife that ever was. . . . My love for him was the truest thing in my life; but it was still important that I love him with proper effect, that I *act* loving him with great style, that I achieve the ultimate in wifedom.

HELEN HAYES (1900–1993), U.S. actor. *On Reflection,* ch. 1 (1968).

Hayes began acting at age five, making her New York stage debut in 1909. She married the wayward, witty, charismatic playwright Charles MacArthur (1895–1956) in 1928; the marriage survived until his death.

2 . . . a supportive husband is an absolute requirement for professional women. . . . He is something she looks for, and when she finds him, she marries him.

ALICE S. ROSSI (b. 1922), U.S. sociologist. *Dissent,* p. 533 (November-December 1970).

Rossi and her husband were both prominent sociologists.

3 I concluded that I was skilled, however poorly, at only one thing: marriage. And so I set about the business of selling myself and two children to some unsuspecting man who might think me a desirable second-hand mate, a man of good means and disposition willing to support another man's children in some semblance of the style to which they were accustomed. My heart was not in the chase, but I was tired and there was no alternative. I could not afford freedom.

BARBARA HOWAR (b. 1934), U.S. socialite and author. *Laughing all the Way,* ch. 12 (1973).

The former North Carolina debutante and current Washington socialite was describing the dilemma she faced when she decided to divorce her rich husband and raise her children, aged three and six, alone.

4 I began quite early in life to sense the thrill a girl attains in supplying money to a man.

ANITA LOOS (1894–1981), U.S. humorist, screenwriter, and dramatist. *Cast of Thousands,* ch. 8 (1977).

Loos's husband, John Emerson, was often dependent, directly or indirectly, on her salary.

MARRIAGE: UNDESIRABILITY

1 I would rather be a beggar and single than a queen and married.

ELIZABETH I (1533–1603), Queen of England (1558–1603). As quoted in *The Sayings of Queen Elizabeth,* ch. 7, by Frederick Chamberlin (1923).

Said in 1564 to the Ambassador of the Duke of Wurtemberg. Elizabeth never married and died leaving no heir.

2 I do not choose that my grave should be dug while I am still alive.

ELIZABETH I (1533–1603), British monarch, Queen of England (1558–1603). As quoted in *The Sayings of Queen Elizabeth,* ch. 24, by Frederick Chamberlin (1923).

Said to a deputation of peers who urged her to marry.

3 . . . bringing up daughters for nothing but marriage, mingles poison in the cup of domestic life, is traitorous to the virtue of both sexes, for neither suffers alone—is adverse to the happiness, to the development of conscience and to religion, and introduces to the dwellings of wretchedness and despair. The result of this degradation is pride, intemperance, licentiousness—nay, every vice, misery, and degradation.

HARRIOT K. HUNT (1805–1875), U.S. physician and feminist. *Glances and Glimpses,* ch. 4 (1856).

4 Gentlemen, no one objects to the husband being the head of the wife as Christ was the head of the church—to crucify himself; what we object to is his crucifying his wife.

SUSAN B. ANTHONY (1820–1906), U.S. suffragist. As quoted in *The Life and Work of Susan B. Anthony,* ch. 33, by Ida Husted Harper (1898).

Responding, c. 1884, to the antisuffrage argument that the Bible exhorts wives to "submit yourselves unto your own husbands."

5 White men have always controlled their wives' wages. Colored men were not able to do so until they themselves became free. Then they owned both their wives and their wages.

SUSAN B. ANTHONY (1820–1906), U.S. suffragist. As quoted in *History of Woman Suffrage,* vol. 4, ch. 15, by Susan B. Anthony and Ida Husted Harper (1902).

Addressing the twenty-seventh annual convention of the National Woman Suffrage Association, held January 31–February 5, 1895, in Atlanta, Georgia. Anthony was referring to the fact that employed married women had no right of control over their own wages.

6 Widows are more skillful anglers for husbands than spinsters, and

many marry several times. This is a social injustice to spinsters. "One man one woman," is surely as fair a cry as "One man one vote." As there is scarcely one man for each woman, what right has one woman to two, three, or four men in succession? She may reply, "By the right of conquest." But, then, is she not reducing others to unhappy courses or to become old maids? . . . Society, for the interests of all, should discourage the remarriage of widows.

TENNESSEE CLAFLIN (1846–1923), U.S. journalist, lecturer, and social reform advocate; relocated to England. *Talks and Essays,* vol. 1, ch. 10 (1897).

When she wrote this, Claflin was married to her second husband, Francis Cook, having been divorced from her first.

7 [On Harvard President Charles William Eliot's lamentation that the average Harvard graduate had fewer than two children:] That is quite enough. Harvard graduates do not always make the best fathers. Why should we be agitated over the too small families of the rich when there are so many children of the poor that are not cared for? The rich should make it their duty to raise up these children to a higher standard. . . . Men of the world hate to give up their tobacco, liquor, sports, clubs, their luxurious habits, their freedom from responsibility. They prefer to flock together and so women are compelled to do the same. President Eliot talks as though the young women were sitting around anxiously and aimlessly waiting for the graduates to come and get them. He would find, if he should make the proper investigation, that a class of women is being developed who are demanding a higher standard of morals in men than did those of past generations, and if they cannot get husbands who reach this standard they are making very satisfactory careers for themselves outside of marriage.

SUSAN B. ANTHONY (1820–1906), U.S. suffragist. As quoted in *Life and Work of Susan B. Anthony,* vol. 3, ch. 62, by Ida Husted Harper (1908).

Said to a newspaper reporter in 1903.

8 In any service where a couple hold down jobs as a team, the male generally takes his ease while the wife labors at his job as well as her own.

ANITA LOOS (1888–1981), U.S. screenwriter, author, and humorist. *Kiss Hollywood Good-by,* ch. 2 (1974).

9 There have been several Duchesses of Westminster—but there is only *one* Chanel!

COCO CHANEL (1883–1971), French fashion designer. As quoted in *Famous Actors and Actresses on the American Stage,* vol. 2, by William C. Young (1975).

Chanel, who never married, said this to the Duke of Westminster when he proposed.

10 No husband of mine will say, "I could have been a drummer, but I had to think about the wife and kids. You know how it is." Nobody supports me at the expense of his own adventure.

MAXINE HONG KINGSTON (b. 1940), U.S. author. *The Woman Warrior,* ch. 2 (1976).

11 I don't know whether I could have managed marriage and a career.

Personally, I preferred a career. There are no distractions.

ADELE DELEEUW (1899–1988), U.S. author. As quoted in *Past and Prologue,* by Marjorie Keyishian and Annemarie Kraume Hayles (1979).

deLeeuw wrote seventy-five books, most of them intended for young adults.

12 [My mother told me:] "You must decide whether you want to get married someday, or have a career." . . . I set my sights on the career. I thought, what does any man really have to offer me?

ANNIE ELIZABETH DELANY (1891–1995), African American dentist. *Having Our Say* (1993).

One of 10 children of a former slave, she would earn her D.D.S. from Columbia University in 1923, become the second African American woman dentist licensed in New York State, and practice in Harlem for 27 years.

MARRIAGE: UNMARRIED WOMEN

1 We have not the motive to prepare ourselves for a "life-work" of teaching, of social work—we know that we would lay it down with hallelujah in the height of our success, to make a home for the right man. And all the time in the background of our consciousness rings the warning that perhaps the right man will never come. A great love is given to very few. Perhaps this make-shift time filler of a job is our life work after all.

RUTH BENEDICT (1887–1948), U.S. anthropologist. *An Anthropologist at Work,* part 2 (1959).

Written in her journal during October 1912, while teaching in a girls' boarding school. Two years later, she married a biochemist. They had no children; eventually, she became a noted anthropologist.

MARTYRDOM

1 If they want to hang me, let them. And on the scaffold I will shout "Freedom for the working class!"

MOTHER JONES (1830–1930), U.S. labor organizer. *The Autobiography of Mother Jones,* ch. 27 (1925).
From a 1916 address to a mass meeting of the wives of the striking streetcarmen in New York City.

MATERIALISM

1 We go on multiplying our conveniences only to multiply our cares. We increase our possessions only to the enlargement of our anxieties.

ANNA C. BRACKETT (1836–1911), U.S. author. *The Technique of Rest,* ch. 2 (1892).
On the changes wrought in people's material lives by industrialization.

2 To-day . . . when material prosperity and well earned ease and luxury are assured facts from a national standpoint, woman's work and woman's influence are needed as never before; needed to bring a heart power into this money getting, dollar-worshipping civilization; needed to bring a moral force into the utilitarian motives and interests of the time; needed to stand for God and Home and Native Land *versus gain and greed and grasping selfishness.*

ANNA JULIA COOPER (1859–1964), U.S. educator and feminist. *A Voice from the South,* part 1 (1892).

3 Most men have always wanted as much as they could get; and possession has always blunted the fine edge of their altruism.

KATHERINE FULLERTON GEROULD (1879–1944), U.S. author. *Modes and Morals,* ch. 1 (1920).

4 Science has done great things for us; it has also pushed us hopelessly back. For, not content with filling its own place, it has tried to supersede everything else. It has challenged the super-eminence of religion; it has turned all philosophy out of doors except that which clings to its skirts; it has thrown contempt on all learning that does not depend on it; and it has bribed the skeptics by giving us immense material comforts.

KATHERINE FULLERTON GEROULD (1879–1944), U.S. author. *Modes and Morals,* ch. 4 (1920).

5 . . . dependence upon material possessions inevitably results in the destruction of human character.

AGNES E. MEYER (1887–1970), U.S. journalist. *Out of These Roots,* ch. 1 (1953).

6 It is difficult to generalize why so many Latino/as moved toward conservative . . . views. . . . for many, I believe it is basically a matter of desiring material acquisitions. It is difficult to maintain a collective ideology in a society where possessions and power-status equal self-worth.

ANA CASTILLO (b. 1953), Mexican–American poet, essayist, and feminist. *Massacre of the Dreamers,* ch. 1 (1994).

MATHEMATICS

1 . . . geometry became a symbol for human relations, except that it was better, because in geometry things never go bad. If certain things occur, if certain lines meet, an angle is born. You cannot fail. It's not going to fail; it is eternal. I found in rules of mathematics a peace and a trust that I could not place in human beings. This sublimation was total and remained total. Thus, I'm able to avoid or manipulate or process pain.

LOUISE BOURGEOIS (b. 1911), U.S. sculptor. As quoted in *Lives and Works,* by Lynn F. Miller and Sally S. Swenson (1981).

MEDIOCRITY

1 Mediocrity would always win by force of numbers, but it would win only more mediocrity.

ELLEN GLASGOW (1873–1945), U.S. novelist. *The Woman Within,* ch. 21 (1954). Written in 1937.

MEMORY

1 When I try to classify my earliest impressions, I find that fact and fancy look alike across the years that link the past with the present. The woman paints the child's experience in her own fantasy.

HELEN KELLER (1880–1968), U.S. author. *The Story of My Life,* ch. 1 (1905). Born in the small Alabama town of Tuscumbia, and rendered deaf and blind at the age of nineteen months, Keller was untaught and largely isolated within her handicaps for the next five years.

2 It is painful to be consciously of two worlds. The Wandering Jew in me seeks forgetfulness. I am not afraid to live on and on, if only I do not have to remember too much. A long past vividly remembered is like a heavy garment that clings to your limbs when you would run.

MARY ANTIN (1881–1949), U.S. Jewish socialite and author; born in Russia. *The Promised Land,* Introduction (1912). Antin, a Russian Jew, had emigrated to America at age fifteen.

3 The memory . . . experiencing and re-experiencing, has such power over one's mere personal life, that one has merely lived.

REBECCA WEST (1892–1983), British author. *The Strange Necessity,* ch. 5 (1928).

4 If you do not remember while you are writing, it may seem confused to others but actually it is clear and eventually that clarity will be clear, that is what a master-piece is, but if you remember while you are writing it will seem clear at the time to any one but the clarity will go out of it that is what a master-piece is not.

GERTRUDE STEIN (1874–1946), U.S. author and patron of the arts; relocated to France. *What Are Masterpieces and Why Are There So Few of Them* (1936).

5 When I read a story, I relive the moment from which it sprang. A scene burned itself into me, a building magnetized me, a mood or season of Nature's penetrated me, history suddenly appeared to me in some tiny act, or a face had begun to haunt me before I glanced at it.

ELIZABETH BOWEN (1899–1973), British novelist, story writer, essayist, and memoirist; born in Ireland. *Seven Winters,* part 2, sect. 2, ch. 5 (1962).

From the preface to her 1959 *Selected Stories.*

6 I made a list of things I have
to remember and a list
of things I want to forget,
but I see they are the same list.

LINDA PASTAN (b. 1932), U.S. poet. "Lists," lines 1–4 (1982).

7 When the memory of one's prede-
cessors is buried, the assumption
persists that there were none and
each generation of women believes
itself to be faced with the burden of
doing everything for the first time.
And if no one ever did it before . . .
why do we think we can succeed
now?

JOANNA RUSS (b. 1937), U.S. science fiction writer and feminist. *How to Suppress Women's Writing,* ch. 9 (1983).

Explaining the importance of female students having the opportunity for objectively-guided study of the work of important women writers.

8 Writing fiction has developed in me
an abiding respect for the unknown
in a human lifetime and a sense of
where to look for the threads, how
to follow, how to connect, find in
the thick of the tangle what clear
line persists. The strands are all
there: to the memory nothing is
ever really lost.

EUDORA WELTY (b. 1909), U.S. fiction writer. *One Writer's Beginnings,* ch. 3 (1984).

9 Why is it that people refuse, or are
unwilling, to go back to a place
where once they have been happy?

If you ask them, they will say that
they do not want to spoil a beautiful memory, or that nothing can
ever be the same (a wonderful thing
can only happen once!). . . . Actually I think they may feel afraid that
they will be disillusioned, if indeed
they have had to convince themselves that a privately dull or ugly
event was indeed a glamourous one.
Or they may suspect that they are
less attractive than they wanted to
be, or that the other people are.

M. F. K. FISHER (1908–1992), U.S. culinary writer and autobiographer. *The Sophisticated Traveler,* Afterword (1985).

10 Appealing workplaces are to be
avoided. One wants a room with no
view, so imagination can meet
memory in the dark.

ANNIE DILLARD (b. 1945), U.S. author. *The Writing Life,* ch. 2 (1989).

On the kind of study a writer needs.

11 All water has a perfect memory and
is forever trying to get back to
where it was.

TONI MORRISON (b. 1931), U.S. fiction writer and essayist. As quoted in *Grace Notes,* Epigram, section 1, by Rita Dove (1989).

12 Our sense of worth, of well-being,
even our sanity depends upon our
remembering. But, alas, our sense
of worth, our well-being, our sanity
also depend upon our forgetting.

JOYCE APPLEBY (b. 1929), U.S. historian. "Recovering America's Historic Diversity," *Journal of American History,* p. 430 (September 1992).

13 I don't avoid pain by not remembering something; I try to remem-

ber. . . . Memory is empowering, and it's what gives you your sense of continuity in the world.

MELINDA WORTH POPHAM (b. 1944), U.S. author. As quoted in *Listen to Their Voices*, ch. 20, by Mickey Pearlman (1993).

14 . . . memory is the only way home.

TERRY TEMPEST WILLIAMS, U.S. author. As quoted in *Listen to Their Voices*, ch. 10, by Mickey Pearlman (1993).

MEN'S NATURE

1 Mixed dinner parties of ladies and gentlemen . . . are very rare, which is a great defect in the society; not only as depriving them of the most social and hospitable manner of meeting, but as leading to frequent dinner parties of gentlemen without ladies, which certainly does not conduce to refinement.

FRANCES TROLLOPE (1780–1863), British author. *Domestic Manners of the Americans*, ch. 30 (1832).
Trollope had been travelling through the United States; here, she was referring to New York City.

2 If men had to do their vile work without the assistance of woman and the stimulant of strong drink they would be obliged to be more divine and less brutal.

CAROLINE NICHOLS CHURCHILL (1833–?), U.S. author. *Active Footsteps*, preface (1909).

3 Any romantic notions that a woman may entertain regarding the stern sex are apt to be very badly damaged if she meets men outside of domestic and social circles, say as fellow collegians, or fellow workers in professional or commercial life. Here drawing-room etiquette does not prevail and the aboriginal man, divested of conventional veneer, stands forth in his true colors as a very fallible, commonplace human being.

JOSEPHINE REDDING (1892– ?), U.S. editor. As quoted in *Always in Vogue*, ch. 2, by Edna Woolman Chase and Ilka Chase (1954).
Redding, the first editor of *Vogue* magazine, wrote this in an early editorial.

MENTAL ILLNESS

1 Many a woman shudders . . . at the terrible eclipse of those intellectual powers which in early life seemed prophetic of usefulness and happiness, hence the army of martyrs among our married and unmarried women who, not having cultivated a taste for science, art or literature, form a corps of nervous patients who make fortunes for agreeable physicians . . .

SARAH M. GRIMKÉ (1792–1873), U.S. abolitionist and feminist. As quoted in *The Female Experience*, ch. 87, by Gerda Lerner (1977). Written in 1852.

2 The funny part of it all is that relatively few people seem to go crazy, relatively few even a little crazy or even a little weird, relatively few, and those few because they have nothing to do that is to say they have nothing to do or they do not do anything that has anything to do with the war only with food and cold and little things like that.

GERTRUDE STEIN (1874–1946), U.S. author; relocated to France. *Wars I Have Seen* (1945).
Written in 1943.

3   When one of us dies of cancer, loses her mind, or commits suicide, we must not blame her for her inability to survive an ongoing political mechanism bent on the destruction of that human being. Sanity remains defined simply by the ability to cope with insane conditions.

ANA CASTILLO (b. 1953), Mexican–American poet, essayist, and feminist. *Massacre of the Dreamers*, ch. 7 (1994).

MIDWEST, THE (U.S.)

I   The hurry of life in the Western part of the country, the rapidity, energy, and enterprise with which civilization is there being carried forward baffles all description, and, I think, can hardly be believed but by those who have seen it. Cities of magnificent streets and houses, with wharves, and quays, and warehouses, and storehouses, and shops full of Paris luxuries, and railroads from and to them in every direction, and land worth its weight in gold by the foot, and populations of fifty and hundreds of thousands, where, within the memory of men, no trace of civilization existed, but the forest grew and the savage wandered.

FANNY KEMBLE (1809–1893), British actor. *Further Records, 1848–1883*, vol. 2; entry dated April 6, 1857 (1891).
Kemble had just returned from a series of Shakespeare readings in the midwestern United States.

MIDWIFERY

I   I was supposed to retire when I was seventy-two years old, but I was seventy-seven when I retired. On my seventy-sixth birthday a lady had triplets. It was quite a birthday present.

JOSEPHINE RILEY MATTHEWS (b. 1897), African American midwife. As quoted in *I Dream a World,* by Brian Lanker (1989).
A licensed midwife in South Carolina, she safely delivered more than 1,300 babies. Matthews graduated from high school in 1971 at age seventy-four and, in 1976, was named South Carolina's Woman of the Year and Outstanding Older American.

MILITARY

I   I was only one woman alone, and had no power to move to action full-fed, sleek-coated, ease-loving, pleasure-seeking, well-paid, and well-placed countrymen in this war-trampled, dead, old land, each one afraid that he should be called upon to do something.

CLARA BARTON (1821–1912), U.S. Civil War nurse and founder of the American Red Cross. As quoted in *Angel of the Battlefield,* ch. 9, by Ishbel Ross (1956).
Written c. 1870 on the coolness of Civil War General Burnside to her proposal that a headquarters be established in Brussels, Belgium for distributing American goods to combatants during the Franco-Prussian War.

2   The consequence of . . . centuries of warfare is that military men assume a position of too great importance in the country, which is always a mistake, not because they are men of blood, but because they lead too exemplary lives of industry and devotion to duty. The business of the

statesman is to form sound general ideas, and that cannot be done by people who specialize early in an exacting profession. The same reason makes business men's pronouncements on political matters hardly ever worthy of attention.

REBECCA WEST (1892–1983), British author. *The Strange Necessity,* ch. 10 (1928).

3 On the whole our armed services have been doing pretty well in the way of keeping us defended, but I hope our State Department will remember that it is really the department of achieving peace . . .

ELEANOR ROOSEVELT (1884–1962), U.S. author, speaker, and First Lady. As quoted in *Eleanor: The Years Alone,* ch. 4, by Joseph P. Lash (1972).
From her "My Day" column, published in the *Ladies' Home Journal* on November 11, 1946.

4 When men talk about defense, they always claim to be protecting women and children, but they never ask the women and children what they think.

PATRICIA SCHROEDER (b. 1940), U.S. politician. As quoted in *The Decade of Women,* by Suzanne Levine and Harriet Lyons (1980).

5 Nothing changes my twenty-six years in the military. I continue to love it and everything it stands for and everything I was able to accomplish in it. To put up a wall against the military because of one regulation would be doing the same thing that the regulation does in terms of negating people.

MARGARETHE CAMMERMEYER (b. 1942), quoted in *Time* magazine, p. 63 (July 6, 1992).

An Army Colonel and a nurse, she admitted homosexuality during a routine background check and was dismissed after a career in which she had earned a Bronze Star for Vietnam War duty and was once the Veterans Administration Nurse of the Year.

MINING

1 Men's hearts are cold. They are indifferent. Not all the coal that is dug warms the world. It remains indifferent to the lives of those who risk their life and health down in the blackness of the earth; who crawl through dark, choking crevices with only a bit of lamp on their caps to light their silent way; whose backs are bent with toil, whose very bones ache, whose happiness is sleep, and whose peace is death.

MOTHER JONES (1830–1930), U.S. labor organizer. *Autobiography of Mother Jones,* ch. 22 (1925).
On her work with and for miners in a number of states, including Colorado, Virginia, West Virginia, and Pennsylvania.

2 The origin of storms is not in clouds,
our lightning strikes when the earth rises,
spillways free authentic power:
dead John Brown's body walking from a tunnel
to break the armored and concluded mind.

MURIEL RUKEYSER (1913–1980), U.S. poet. "The Bill," last five lines (1938).
Two years earlier, Rukeyser, who was then aligned with the Communist Party, had gathered information on a corporate cover-up of unsafe mining conditions in Gauley Bridge, West Virginia; they had caused illness and death among many miners. The situation had been disclosed by the Communist Party USA. A Congressional

subcommittee had investigated and found the mining company, a subsidiary of Union Carbide and Carbon, to be in the wrong.

MISTAKES

I It is so conceited and timid to be ashamed of one's mistakes. Of *course* they are mistakes. Go on to the next.

BRENDA UELAND (1891–1985), U.S. author and writing teacher. *If You Want to Write*, 2nd. ed., ch. 18 (1938).

MOBILITY

I ... the mass migrations now habitual in our nation are disastrous to the family and to the formation of individual character. It is impossible to create a stable society if something like a third of our people are constantly moving about. We cannot grow fine human beings, any more than we can grow fine trees, if they are constantly torn up by the roots and transplanted ...

AGNES E. MEYER (1887–1970), U.S. journalist. *Out of These Roots*, ch. 2 (1953).

Reflecting on the personal trauma that accompanied her parents' relocation from rural Pelham Heights, New York, to New York City when she was a teenager.

MODELS, FASHION

I ... your problem is your role models were models.

JANE WAGNER (b. 1935), U.S. playwright. *The Search for Signs of Intelligent Life in the Universe* (1986).

2 I'd like to be the first model who becomes a woman.

LAUREN HUTTON (b. 1944), U.S. fashion model. As quoted in the *New York Times Magazine*, p. 31 (July 18, 1993).

A major model for decades, Hutton was still modelling at age forty-nine and was writing a history of fashion. With an offbeat look, not classically beautiful, Hutton had always dressed casually and worn little makeup.

3 When you model, the focus is completely on you, and some people really appreciate the attention, especially if they didn't get it growing up. You're being drawn; you're being looked at. There's a sense of acceptance that comes from that.

ALEXANDRA RHEAULT, U.S. model. As quoted in the *New York Times*, p. 9 (September 6, 1993).

On life modelling—i.e., nude modelling for artists.

4 I can never see fashion models, lean angular cheeks, strutting hips and blooming hair, without thinking of
the skulls at the catacombs in Lima, Peru.

NAOMI SHIHAB NYE (b. 1952), U.S. poet. "Morning Paper, Society Page," lines 1–4 (1994).

MONARCHY

I Have a care over my people. You have my people—do you that which I ought to do. They are my people. ... See unto them—see unto them, for they are my charge. ... I care not for myself; my life is not dear to me. My care is for my people. I pray God, whoever succeedeth me, be as careful of them as I am.

ELIZABETH I (1533–1603), Queen of England (1558–1603). As quoted in *The Sayings of Queen Elizabeth,* ch. 2, by Frederick Chamberlin (1923).

Said to her judges in 1559, as they took office.

2   The word "must" is not to be used to princes.

ELIZABETH I (1533–1603), British monarch, Queen of England (1558–1603). As quoted in *The Sayings of Queen Elizabeth,* ch. 24, by Frederick Chamberlin (1923).

3   . . . there has been a comparatively greater proportion of good queens, than of good kings.

SARAH M. GRIMKÉ (1792–1873), U.S. abolitionist and feminist. *Letters on the Equality of the Sexes and the Condition of Woman,* letter #9: dated August 25, 1837 (1838).

MONEY

1   The man possessed of a dollar, feels himself to be not merely one hundred cents richer, but also one hundred cents *better,* than the man who is penniless; so on through all the gradations of earthly possessions— the estimate of our own moral and political importance swelling always in a ratio exactly proportionate to the growth of our purse.

FRANCES WRIGHT (1795–1852), Scottish author and speaker; relocated to America. *Course of Popular Lectures,* lecture 7 (1829).

2   Expenditure—like ugliness and errors—becomes a totally new thing when we attach our own personality to it, and measure it by that wide difference which is manifest (in our own sensations) between ourselves and others.

GEORGE ELIOT (1819–1880), British novelist. *Middlemarch,* ch. 58 (1871–1872).

3   I never thought that the possession of money would make me feel rich: it often does seem to have an opposite effect. But then, I have never had the opportunity of knowing, by experience, how it does make one feel. It is something to have been spared the responsibility of taking charge of the Lord's silver and gold.

LUCY LARCOM (1824–1893), U.S. poet and teacher. *A New England Girlhood,* ch. 11 (1889).

4   I can't earn my own living. I could never make anything turn into money. It's like making fires. A careful assortment of paper, shavings, faggots and kindling nicely tipped with pitch will never light for me. I have never been present when a cigarette butt, extinct, thrown into a damp and isolated spot, started a conflagration in the California woods.

MARGARET ANDERSON (1886–1973), U.S. literary editor and autobiographer. *My Thirty Years' War,* ch. 1 (1930).

Anderson founded and edited a charming, influential literary and arts magazine, *The Little Review,* which never made money.

5   . . . there is something quixotic in me about money, something meek and guilty. I want it and like it. But I cannot imagine insisting on it, pressing it out of people. I always vaguely feel: why should I have money when other people have it not? It is like taking the biggest piece of cake. And I can never feel that I have earned it.

BRENDA UELAND (1891–1985), U.S. magazine writer. *Me*, ch. 6 (1939).

On why she found it difficult to ask for salary increases, even when she knew she was more capable than men earning the same as she.

6 Wild honey smells of freedom
The dust—of sunlight
The mouth of a young girl, like a
    violet
But gold—smells of nothing.

ANNA AKHMATOVA (1889–1966), Russian poet. "Wild Honey Smells of Freedom," lines 1–4, as translated by Lenore Mayhew and William McNaughton (1943).

7 Money is only congealed snow.

DOROTHY PARKER (1893–1967), U.S. author and humorist. As quoted in *The Late Mrs. Dorothy Parker*, ch. 25, by Leslie Frewin (1986).

A popular writer who had earned considerable sums of money, Parker spent carelessly and always seemed to be in need.

8 Why? It paid the rent.

MARILYN MONROE (1926–1962), U.S. actor. As quoted in *Ms.* magazine, p. 38 (August 1972).

The "sex symbol" answering why she had posed nude for a calendar photograph early in her career.

9 People say, "Do you know how much a million dollars is?" I don't have a clue. How many Big Macs will it buy me?

BILLIE JEAN KING (b. 1943), U.S. tennis player. As quoted in *WomenSports* magazine, p. 31 (May 1977).

King, who by this time had earned an impressive income as a tennis champion, was the daughter of a firefighter and had been raised in very modest circumstances.

10 . . . today, you just walk on the court, throw up the ball, roll over your arm, and make $100,000. I killed myself for $100,000.

BILLIE JEAN KING (b. 1943), U.S. tennis player. As quoted in *WomenSports* magazine, p. 52 (January 1978).

On what was then the recent great increase in prize money for women tennis players. King's activism, and her great popularity with tennis audiences, had been major reasons for the increase.

11 . . . I'm not money hungry. . . . People who are rich want to be richer, but what's the difference? You can't take it with you. The toys get different, that's all. The rich guys buy a football team, the poor guys buy a football. It's all relative.

MARTINA NAVRATILOVA (b. 1956), U.S. tennis player; born in Czechoslovakia. *Martina*, ch. 44 (1985).

She would become the leading money-winning woman tennis player in history.

12 To be perfectly honest, what I'm really thinking about are dollar signs.

TONYA HARDING (b. 1970), U.S. ice skater. As quoted in the *New York Times*, p. A1 (January 15, 1994).

After winning the American national figure skating championship following withdrawal of the favorite, Nancy Kerrigan (b. 1969), because of an attack that injured her right leg. A few days after Harding said this, her bodyguard confessed to planning the attack. Later, her ex-husband (with whom she was living) also admitted involvement and implicated Harding. Though denying prior knowledge of the attack, she pled guilty to obstructing the criminal investigation, was expelled from the United States Figure Skating Association, and had to abandon her amateur career. In this quotation, Harding, who came from a family of very modest means, was referring to the lucrative product-endorsement contracts that she expected to be offered. They never materialized.

13 Money is that dear thing which, if you're not careful, you can squander your whole life thinking of. . . .

MARY JO SALTER (b. 1954), U.S. poet. "A Benediction," part [6], lines 1–3 (1994).

MORALITY

1 Virtue and vice suppose the freedom to choose between good and evil; but what can be the morals of a woman who is not even in possession of herself, who has nothing of her own, and who all her life has been trained to extricate herself from the arbitrary by ruse, from constraint by using her charms? ... As long as she is subject to man's yoke or to prejudice, as long as she receives no professional education, as long as she is deprived of her civil rights, there can be no moral law for her!

FLORA TRISTAN (1803–1844), French author. As quoted in *Victorian Women,* ch. 90, by Erna Olafson Hellerstein, Leslie Parker Hume, and Karen M. Offen (1981).

From an 1840 book first published in French under the title, *Promenades dans Londres.*

2 Said an opponent to me after my last protest was sent in, what party would you vote for, if you could? Neither. I would have a moral sentiment party. I would know the *private* character of my candidate, would know also whether he takes care of *his own* property—whether *he* had failed in business—if so, whether he had paid back every dollar of debt as fast as he had earned them. Yes, every candidate should be examined *morally,* and if it be found that he has not been true to the monitions of conscience in one direction, he cannot or *will not* be in another ...

HARRIOT K. HUNT (1805–1875), U.S. physician and feminist. *Glances and Glimpses,* ch. 22 (1856).

3 ... goodness is of a modest nature, easily discouraged, and when much elbowed in early life by unabashed vices, is apt to retire into extreme privacy, so that it is more easily believed in by those who construct a selfish old gentleman theoretically, than by those who form the narrower judgments based on his personal acquaintance.

GEORGE ELIOT (1819–1880), British novelist. *Middlemarch,* ch. 34 (1871–1872).

4 Moral qualities rule the world, but at short distances the senses are despotic.

MRS. H. O. WARD (1824–1899), U.S. author. *Sensible Etiquette of the Best Society Customs, Manners, Morals, and Home Culture, Compiled from the Best Authorities,* ch. 5 (1878).

5 ... life *is* moral responsibility. Life is several other things, we do not deny. It is beauty, it is joy, it is tragedy, it is comedy, it is psychical and physical pleasure, it is the interplay of a thousand rude or delicate motions and emotions, it is the grimmest and the merriest motley of phantasmagoria that could appeal to the gravest or the maddest brush ever put to palette; but it is steadily and sturdily and always moral responsibility.

ELIZABETH STUART PHELPS (1844–1911), U.S. novelist and short story writer. *Chapters from a Life,* ch. 12 (1897).

6 ... men's double standard of sex morals, whereby the victims of their lust are counted as outcasts, while the men themselves escape all social censure, really applies to morals in all departments of life. Men make the moral code and they expect women to accept it. They have decided that it is entirely right and proper for men to fight for their liberties and their rights, but that it is not right and proper for women to fight for theirs.

EMMELINE PANKHURST (1858–1928), British suffragist and politician. *My Own Story,* book 3, ch. 3 (1914).

7 The society girl meets more dangers than the girl on the stage. There is more danger at a tango tea than in the theatre. The actor is less dangerous than the dancing master.

LILLIAN RUSSELL (1861–1922), U.S. actor. As quoted in *Famous Actors and Actresses on the American Stage,* vol. 2, by William C. Young (1975).

From an article entitled, "Is the Stage a Perilous Place for a Young Girl?," first published in *Theatre* magazine in January 1916. Russell, a renowned beauty and very popular musical comedy star, was reacting to the "bad name" that the stage had at the time. She herself had been married four times and observed: "If a girl is pretty she will be tempted."

8 The very notion of *tabu* is one of the rightest notions in the world. Better any old *tabu* than none, for a man cannot be said to be "on the side of the stars" at all, unless he makes refusals.

KATHERINE FULLERTON GEROULD (1879–1944), U.S. author. *Modes and Morals,* ch. 7 (1920).

9 Each man's private conscience ought to be a nice little self-registering thermometer: he ought to carry his moral code incorruptibly and explicitly within himself, and not care what the world thinks. The

mass of human beings, however, are not made that way; and many people have been saved from crime or sin by the simple dislike of doing things they would not like to confess . . .

KATHERINE FULLERTON GEROULD (1879–1944), U.S. author. *Modes and Morals,* ch. 7 (1920).

10 While it is generally agreed that the visible expressions and agencies are necessary instruments, civilization seems to depend far more fundamentally upon the moral and intellectual qualities of human beings— upon the spirit that animates mankind.

MARY BEARD (1876–1958), U.S. historian. *Woman as Force in History,* ch. 12 (1946).

11 . . . the art of acting morally is behaving *as if everything we do matters.*

GLORIA STEINEM (b. 1934), U.S. feminist, author, and editor. *New York* magazine, p. 134 (April 19, 1993).

12 Allowing our government to kill citizens compromises the deepest moral values upon which this country was conceived: the inviolable dignity of human persons.

HELEN PRÉJEAN (b. 1940), U.S. nun and activist against the death penalty. *Dead Man Walking,* ch. 9 (1993).

13 . . . the Department of Justice is committed to asking one central question of everything we do: What is the right thing to do? Now that can produce debate, and I want it to be spirited debate. I want the lawyers of America to be able to call me and tell me: Janet, have you lost your mind?

JANET WOOD RENO (b. 1938), U.S. lawyer. As quoted in the *New York Times Magazine*, p. 43 (May 15, 1994).

The first woman Attorney General of the United States was speaking before the American Law Institute.

MORTALITY

I Sometimes the hardest part of my job is the incessant reminder of the fact we're all trying so assiduously to ignore: we are here temporarily . . . life is only ours on loan.

SUE GRAFTON (b. 1940), U.S. murder mystery novelist. *K is for Killer* (1994).

Stated by Grafton's detective-heroine, Kinsey Millhone, referring to her continual investigations of murders.

2 You only live once—and that's a curse
living within our means makes worse.

MARY JO SALTER (b. 1954), U.S. poet. "A Benediction," part [6], lines 27–28 (1994).

MOTHER-DAUGHTER RELATIONSHIPS

I One day my mother called me . . . and she said, "Forty-nine million Americans saw you on television tonight. One of them is the father of my future grandchild, but he's never going to call you because you wore your glasses."

LESLEY STAHL (b. 1941), U.S. television newswoman. As quoted in *Women in Television News*, ch. 3 (1976).

Said on May 11, 1973. At the time, Stahl was the only television newswoman who regularly wore glasses on the air.

2 Janie works hard, of course, and she's a good wife and mother, but do you know she's never once made a gingerbread house with her children?

MILDRED HASTINGS (b. 1924), U.S. housewife. As quoted in the *New York Times*, p. A1 (December 21, 1993).

Hastings, who had raised seven children and always been a full-time housewife, was speaking disapprovingly of her daughter, Jane Eagen, a successful insurance broker and mother of three. The "gingerbread house" to which Hastings referred was an elaborate creation requiring hours of work for the family when Eagen was a child.

MOTHER-SON RELATIONSHIPS

I . . . to many a mother's heart has come the disappointment of a loss of power, a limitation of influence when early manhood takes the boy from the home, or when even before that time, in school, or where he touches the great world and begins to be bewildered with its controversies, trade and economics and politics make their imprint even while his lips are dewy with his mother's kiss.

J. ELLEN FOSTER (1840–1910), U.S. attorney, temperance activist, and suffragist. *What America Owes to Women*, ch. 33 (1893).

Making the point that women should be educated, politically active, and should vote, even though they might limit their employment to housekeeping and childrearing.

2 If that's the world's smartest man, God help us.

LUCILLE FEYNMAN, Mother of American

physicist Richard Feynman (1918–1988). As quoted in *Genius*, part 6, by James Gleick (1992).

Of her son, a Nobel laureate, after *Omni* magazine labelled him the world's smartest man.

Anthony said this in 1854, on being told that she should marry and have children. She was referring to the fact that married women enjoyed few legal rights; they did not have equal say in decisions regarding their children and lost custody of them in case of divorce.

MOTHERHOOD

1   I appeal to you, my friends, as mothers: are you willing to enslave your children? You start back with horror and indignation at such a questions. But why, if slavery is *not wrong* to those upon whom it is imposed?

ANGELINA GRIMKÉ (1805–1879), U.S. abolitionist and feminist. As quoted in *The Grimké Sisters from South Carolina*, ch. 9, by Gerda Lerner (1967).
Said in 1836.

2   . . . the physical and domestic education of daughters should occupy the principal attention of mothers, in childhood: and the stimulation of the intellect should be very much reduced.

CATHERINE E. BEECHER (1800–1878), U.S. educator and author. *Treatise on Domestic Economy for the Use of Young Ladies at Home and at School*, ch. 4 (1843).

3   I think it a much wiser thing to secure for the thousands of mothers in this State the legal control of the children they now have, than to bring others into the world who would not belong to me after they were born.

SUSAN B. ANTHONY (1820–1906), U.S. suffragist. As quoted in *The Life and Work of Susan B. Anthony*, ch. 7, by Ida Husted Harper (1898).

4   I have met few men in my life, worth repeating eight times.

ELIZABETH CADY STANTON (1815–1902), U.S. suffragist, author, and social reformer. *Eighty Years and More (1815–1897)*, ch. 18 (1898).
Replying to a man at an 1872 constitutional convention in Lincoln, Nebraska. He had said, "My wife has presented me with eight beautiful children; is this not a better life-work than that of exercising the right of suffrage?"

5   I am not a suffragist, nor do I believe in "careers" for women, especially a "career" in factory and mill where most working women have their "careers." A great responsibility rests upon woman—the training of children. This is her most beautiful task.

MOTHER JONES (1830–1930), U.S. labor organizer. *Autobiography of Mother Jones*, ch. 27 (1925).
Jones preferred to emphasize the need for all men to earn adequate wages so that wives would not need to work outside their homes.

MOUNTAIN CLIMBING

1   Nothing to mountaineering, just a little physical endurance, a good deal of brains, lots of practice, and plenty of warm clothing.

ANNIE SMITH PECK (1850–1935), U.S. mountain climber. As quoted in *WomenSports* magazine, pp. 13–14 (December 1977).
Said c. 1895 by the pioneering climber who mastered her last peak at age 82: the 5,363-foot Mt. Madison in New Hampshire.

MOVIES

1 If I were twenty or thirty years younger, I would start afresh in this field with the certainty of accomplishing much. But I should have to learn from the bottom up, forgetting the theatre entirely and concentrating on the special medium of this new art. My mistake, and that of many others, lay in employing "theatrical" techniques despite every effort to avoid them. Here is something quite, quite fresh, a penetrating form of visual poetry, an untried exponent of the human soul. Alas, I am too old for it!

ELEONORA DUSE (1858–1924), Italian actor. As quoted in *Actors on Acting,* rev. ed., part 11, by Toby Cole and Helen Krich (1970).

Said by the great stage actor near the end of her life, after having made a poor movie, her only one, and having had the reels destroyed.

2 I wish to apologize for this picture and for my performance. I think they are both inexcusably bad.

MARY PICKFORD (1893–1979), U.S. actor. *Sunshine and Shadow,* ch. 3 (1955).

The extremely popular Pickford claimed that she had never liked any one of her movies "in its entirety." She jumped to her feet and said this at a Pasadena preview of one of her movies when the audience "called for a speech."

3 Too many Broadway actors in motion pictures lost their grip on success—had a feeling that none of it had ever happened on that sun-drenched coast, that the coast itself did not exist, there was no California. It had dropped away like a hasty dream and nothing could ever have been like the things they thought they remembered.

MAE WEST (1892–1980), U.S. actor. *Goodness Had Nothing to Do With It,* ch. 13 (1959).

4 An actress is not a machine, but they treat you like a machine. A money machine.

MARILYN MONROE (1926–1962), U.S. actor. As quoted in *Ms.* magazine, p. 38 (August 1972).

Monroe was an extremely popular movie star who made a great deal of money for her studio.

5 I'm an expert in hookers. I'm an expert in doormats. I'm an expert in victims. They were the best parts. And when I woke up—sociologically, politically, and creatively—I could no longer take those parts and look in the mirror.

SHIRLEY MACLAINE (b. 1934), U.S. actor and social/political activist. As quoted in *Ms.* magazine, p. 55 (February 1975).

MacLaine, a major American movie actor, was referring to Hollywood's offensively limited representations of women.

6 When I got [to Hollywood], all the movie moguls claimed to be astounded by the reality of my films. *How did I do it?* And I'd say, "Well, it wasn't hard to make Harlem look like Harlem."

SHIRLEY CLARKE (b. 1925), African American filmmaker. As quoted in *Ms.* magazine, p. 108 (April 1975).

On Hollywood moviemakers' reaction to her independently-made "fictional documentary" about Harlem (New York City), *The Cool World.* It had, of course, been filmed in Harlem itself rather than on a studio set.

7 The movies were my textbooks for everything else in the world. When it wasn't, I altered it. If I saw a college, I would see only cheerleaders or blonds. If I saw New York City, I would want to go to the slums I'd seen in the movies, where the tough kids played. If I went to Chicago, I'd want to see the brawling factories and the gangsters.

JILL ROBINSON (b. 1936), U.S. novelist. As quoted in *American Dreams*, part 1, by Studs Terkel (1980).

The daughter of movie producer Dore Schary, Robinson had grown up in Hollywood, deeply immersed in movies.

8 There in the narrow,
mote-filled finger of light, is a blonde
so blonde, so blinding, she is a blizzard, a huge
spook, and lights up like the sun
the audience
in its galoshes. She bulges like a deuce coupe.
When we see her we say good-bye to Kansas.

LYNN EMANUEL (b. 1949), U.S. poet. "Blonde Bombshell" [poem], lines 10–15 (1992).

9 ... the movie woman's world is designed to remind us that a woman may live in a mansion, an apartment, or a yurt, but it's all the same thing because what she really lives in is the body of a woman, and that body is allowed to occupy space only according to the dictates of polite society.

JEANINE BASINGER (b. 1936), U.S. movie and social historian. *A Woman's View*, ch. 7 (1993).

10 I think it's awful and ugly and a complete waste of talent. Why is he wasting his talent? ... why doesn't he make a movie that would uplift

kids and teach them something? All this sex and violence, sex and violence. He's like a dog chasing his tail.

ELIZABETH STONE, U.S. ex-wife of filmmaker Oliver Stone. As quoted in the *New Yorker*, p. 53 (August 8, 1994).

Stone was commenting on her celebrated exhusband's most recent movie, *Natural Born Killers*. Interviewer Stephen Schiff noted that Oliver Stone (b. 1946), who was present, was listening to her with a "coaxing grin," looking "triumphant, as though this were the response he had hoped for."

MUSIC

1 ... the ... radio station played a Chopin polonaise. On all the following days news bulletins were prefaced by Chopin—preludes, etudes, waltzes, mazurkas. The war became for me a victory, known in advance, Chopin over Hitler.

MARGARET ANDERSON (1886–1973), U.S. editor and memoirist. *The Fiery Fountains,* part 2 (1951).

The year was 1939, and Anderson was living in France; Neville Chamberlain (1869–1940) was the Prime Minister of England, 1937–1940. A dedicated though amateur pianist, Anderson loved the music of Chopin.

2 The secret breathed within
And never spoken, woken
By music; the garlands in
Her hands no one has seen.
She wreathes the air with green
and weaves the stillness in.

MAY SARTON (1912–1995), U.S. poet, novelist, and memoirist. "The Clavichord," lines 13–18 (1948).

3 Music proposes. Sound disposes.

BABETTE DEUTSCH (1895–1982), U.S. poet. "Electronic Concert," line 1 (1969).

4 The blues women had a commanding presence and a refreshing robustness. They were nurturers, taking the yeast of experience, kneading it into dough, molding it and letting it grow in their minds to bring the listener bread for sustenance, shaped by their sensibilities.

ROSETTA REITZ, U.S. author. As quoted in *The Political Palate,* ch. 10, by Betsey Beaven et al. (1980).

5 I traveled and made money and I wouldn't let anybody get between me and my music. If I belong to anything, I belong to my music. . . . What you were born to do, you don't stop to think, should I? could I? would I? I only think, will I? And, I shall!

EVA JESSYE (b. 1895), African American choral director. As quoted in *I Dream a World,* by Brian Lanker (1989).

MYSTERY

1 The creeks . . . are an active mystery, fresh every minute. Theirs is the mystery of continuous creation and all that providence implies: the uncertainty of vision, the horror of the fixed, the dissolution of the present, the intricacy of beauty, the pressure of fecundity, the elusiveness of the free, and the flawed nature of perfection. The mountains . . . are a passive mystery, the oldest of all. Theirs is the one simple mystery of creation from nothing, of matter itself, anything at all, the given. Mountains are giant, restful, absorbent. You can heave your spirit into a mountain and the mountain will keep it, folded, and not throw it back as some creeks will. The creeks are the world with all its stimulus and beauty; I live there. But the mountains are home.

ANNIE DILLARD (b. 1945), U.S. essayist and autobiographer. *Pilgrim at Tinker Creek,* ch. 1 (1974).

2 Billie Holiday's burned voice
had as many shadows as lights,
a mournful candelabra against a
sleek piano,
the gardenia her signature under
that ruined face.
. . .
If you can't be free, be a mystery.

RITA DOVE (b. 1952), African American poet and fiction writer. "Canary," lines 1–4 and last line (1989).

Billie Holiday (1915–1959) was a great African American jazz singer with a tragic personal life.

3 Silence is the best response to mystery.

KATHLEEN NORRIS (b. 1947), U.S. poet and farmer. *Dakota,* ch. 3 (1993).

NATIONAL CHARACTER

1 . . . the condition of women affords, in all countries, the best criterion by which to judge the character of men.

FRANCES WRIGHT (1795–1852), Scottish author and speaker; relocated to America. *Views of Society and Manners in America,* March 1820 entry (1821).

2 . . . it has always proved that the grandeur of a nation was shown by the respect paid to woman.

CLARA BARTON (1821–1912), U.S. nurse; founder of the American Red Cross. As quoted in *History of Woman Suffrage,* vol. 5, ch. 2, by Ida Husted Harper (1922).

In an address delivered in February 1902 to the thirty-fourth annual convention of the National Woman Suffrage Association.

3 Countries are either mothers or fathers, and engender the emotional bristle secretly reserved for either sire.

EDNA O'BRIEN (b. c. 1932), Irish author; relocated to England. *Mother Ireland,* ch. 1 (1976).

NATIVE AMERICANS

1 The white dominant culture seemed to think that once the Indians were off the reservations, they'd eventually become like everybody else. But they aren't like everybody else. When the Indianness is drummed out of them, they are turned into hopeless drunks on skid row.

ELIZABETH MORRIS (b. c. 1933), Native American service agency administrator. As quoted in *Ms.* magazine, p. 50 (January 1973).

An Athabascan Indian from Alaska, Morris was director of the Indian Center, a multiservice agency in Seattle, Washington.

NATURE

1 I'll tell you how the Sun rose—
A Ribbon at a time—

EMILY DICKINSON (1831–1886), U.S. poet. "I'll tell you how the Sun rose": poem no. 318 in her *Collected Poems,* lines 1–2 (c. 1860).

2 Nothing natural can be wholly unworthy.

ANNA JULIA COOPER (1859–1964), U.S. educator and feminist. *A Voice from the South,* part 2 (1892).

3 Sentimentality about nature denatures everything it touches.

JANE JACOBS (b. 1916), U.S. urban analyst. *The Death and Life of Great American Cities,* ch. 22 (1961).

4 If the sight of the blue skies fills you with joy, if a blade of grass springing up in the fields has power to move you, if the simple things of nature have a message that you understand, rejoice, for your soul is alive . . .

ELEONORA DUSE (1858–1924), Italian actor. As quoted in *Actors on Acting,* rev. ed., part 11, by Toby Cole and Helen Krich (1970).

NEEDLEWORK

1 Woman has relied heretofore too entirely for her support on the *needle*—that one-eyed demon of destruction that slays thousands annually; that evil genius of our sex, which, in spite of all our devotion, will never make us healthy, wealthy, or wise.

ELIZABETH CADY STANTON (1815–1902), U.S. feminist, social reformer, and author. As quoted in *The Female Experience,* ch. 75, by Gerda Lerner (1977).

In a speech delivered on May 25, 1851, at the Woman's Rights Convention held in Akron, Ohio. Commercial sewing work was always available to women, but it was poorly paid, the hours were long, and the working conditions were destructive of health and eyesight.

2 Tailor's work—the finishing of men's outside garments—was the "trade" learned most frequently by women in [the 1820s and 1830s], and one or more of my older sisters worked at it; I think it must have been at home, for I somehow or somewhere got the idea, while I was a small child, that the chief end of woman was to make clothing for mankind.

LUCY LARCOM (1824–1893), U.S. poet and teacher. *A New England Girlhood*, ch. 6 (1889).

3 I'm good at embroidery. It's what I always wanted to do. . . . Yep, instead of whoring, I just wanted to do fancy embroidery.

LILLIAN HELLMAN (1905–1984), U.S. playwright and memoirist. *Another Part of the Forest*, Act 2 (1946).

Spoken by the character named Laurette Sincee. Engaged to marry Oscar Hubbard, a member of a distinguished Alabama family in 1880, she is telling her betrothed of her career ambitions. "Laurette is about twenty, pig-face cute, a little too fashionably dressed."

4 The textile and needlework arts of the world, primarily because they have been the work of women have been especially written out of art history. It is a male idea that to be "high" and "fine" both women and art should be beautiful, but not useful or functional.

PATRICIA MAINARDI (b. 1942), U.S. quilter. As quoted in *The Decade of Women*, by Suzanne Levine and Harriet Lyons (1980).

NEIGHBORHOODS

I . . . people are almost always better than their neighbours think they are.

GEORGE ELIOT (1819–1880), British novelist. *Middlemarch*, ch. 72 (1871–1872).

NETHERLANDS

I Holland is a land of intense paradox. It is quite impossible, but it is there.

M. E. W. SHERWOOD (1826–1903), U.S. socialite, traveller, and author. *An Epistle to Posterity*, ch. 15 (1897).

NEW DEAL (1930–40s)

I . . . [Washington] is always an entertaining spectacle. Look at it now. The present President has the name of Roosevelt, marked facial resemblance to Wilson, and no perceptible aversion, to say the least, to many of the policies of Bryan. The New Deal, which at times seems more like a pack of cards thrown helter skelter, some face up, some face down, and then snatched in a free-for-all by the players, than it does like a regular deal, is going on before our interested, if puzzled eyes.

ALICE ROOSEVELT LONGWORTH (1884–1980), U.S. socialite; daughter and cousin of U.S. Presidents. *Crowded Hours*, ch. 21 (1933).

Longworth's distant cousin, Franklin Delano Roosevelt (1882–1945), was beginning the first of his three-plus terms as President. "New Deal" was his label for his domestic reform program.

2 One thing I hate about the New Deal is that it is killing what, to me, is the American pioneering spirit. I simply do not know what to tell my own boys, leaving school and confronting this new world whose ideal is Security and whose practice is dependence upon government instead of upon one's self. . . . All the old character-values seem simply insane from a practical point of view; the self-reliant, the independent, the courageous man is penalized from every direction . . . [ellipses in source]

ROSE WILDER LANE (1886–1968), U.S. author. As quoted in *The Ghost in the Little House*, ch. 14, by William V. Holtz (1993).

In a journal entry dated April 15, 1937, commenting on the domestic policies of President Franklin Delano Roosevelt (1882–1945; President, 1933–1945).

NEW YORK, NY

1 Everything in the neighbourhood of this city exhibits the appearance of life and cheerfulness. The purity of the air, the brilliancy of the unspotted heavens, the crowd of moving vessels, shooting in various directions, up and down and across the bay and the far-stretching Hudson, and the forest of masts crowded round the quays and wharfs at the entrance of the East River. There is something in all this—in the very air you breathe, and the fair and moving scene that you rest your eye upon—which exhilarates the spirits and makes you in good humour with life and your fellow creatures. We approached these shores under a fervid sun, but the air, though of a higher temperature than I had ever before experienced, was so entirely free of vapor, that I thought it was for the first time in my life that I had drawn a clear breath.

FRANCES WRIGHT (1795–1852), U.S. social reformer and author; born and raised in Scotland. *Views of Society and Manners in America*, entry for September 18, 1818 (1821). Making her first trip to America.

2 . . . were all America like this fair city, and all, no, only a small proportion of its population like the friends we left there, I should say, that the land was the fairest in the world.

FRANCES TROLLOPE (1780–1863), British author. *Domestic Manners of the Americans*, ch. 34 (1832).
Trollope had been travelling through the United States; here, she referred to her departure from New York City as she embarked on her trip home to England.

3 New York . . . appeared to us . . . a lovely and a noble city. . . . I think New York one of the finest cities I ever saw, and as much superior to every other in the Union, (Philadelphia not excepted), as London to Liverpool, or Paris to Rouen. Its advantages of position are, perhaps, unequalled any where. Situated on an island, which I think it will one day cover, it rises, like Venice, from the sea, and like that fairest of cities in the days of her glory, receives into its lap tribute of all the riches of the earth. . . . I think it covers nearly as much ground as Paris, but is much less thickly peopled. The extreme point is fortified towards the sea by a battery, and forms an admirable point of defence; but in these piping days of peace, it is converted into a public promenade, and one more beautiful, I should suppose, no city could boast.

FRANCES TROLLOPE (1780–1863), British author. *Domestic Manners of the Americans*, ch. 30 (1832).

Trollope had spent seven weeks in New York City.

4 It is not likely, . . . let me live as I will, that I shall ever be a rich woman, if I am to live in America; the cost of one's existence here is something fabulous, and the amount of *dis*comfort one obtains for money, that purchases a liberal allowance of luxury as well as comfort in Europe, is by no means a small item of annoyance in one's daily life.

FANNY KEMBLE (1809–1893), British actor. *Further Records, 1848–1883,* vol. 2; entry dated November 29, 1857 (1891).

Kemble had married an American and was living in New York City when she wrote this. Now widowed, she was remaining in America to be near her children.

5 Rome, like Washington, is small enough, quiet enough, for strong personal intimacies; Rome, like Washington, has its democratic court and its entourage of diplomatic circle; Rome, like Washington, gives you plenty of time and plenty of sunlight. In New York we have annihilated both.

M. E. W. SHERWOOD (1826–1903), U.S. socialite, traveller, and author. *An Epistle to Posterity,* ch. 3 (1897).

6 We arrived in New York, by rail, the day before Christmas. Everything looked bright and gay in our streets. It seemed to me that the sky was clearer, the air more refreshing, and the sunlight more brilliant than in any other land!

ELIZABETH CADY STANTON (1815–1902), U.S. suffragist, author, and social re-

former. *Eighty Years and More (1815–1897),* ch. 6 (1898).

Remembering her return to America in 1840 after an extended European honeymoon.

7 New York was a new and strange world. Vast, impersonal, merciless. . . . Always before I had felt like a person, an individual, hopeful that I could mold my life according to some desire of my own. But here in New York I was ignorant, insignificant, unimportant—one in millions whose destiny concerned no one. New York did not even know of my existence. Nor did it care.

AGNES SMEDLEY (1890–1950), U.S. journalist and socialist. *Daughter of Earth,* part 5 (1943).

In this autobiographical novel, the Missouri native was describing her first reactions to the New York City of the 1920s.

8 This place is prose.

YVONNE (b. 1945), African American poet. "Harlem 1972," first and last lines; also lines 10, 11, 21, and 29 (1972).

On Harlem, a largely African American inner-city neighborhood in upper Manhattan.

9 New York is the last true city.

TONI MORRISON (b. 1931), U.S. (New York) novelist and essayist. As quoted in *New York,* p. 72 (December 21–28, 1992).

NOVELS

1 A novel which survives, which withstands and outlives time, does do something more than merely survive. It does not stand still. It accumulates round itself the understanding of all these persons who bring to it something of their own. It acquires associations, it becomes a form of experience in itself, so that two people who meet can often make friends, find an approach to each other, because of this one great common experience they have had . . .

ELIZABETH BOWEN (1899–1973), British novelist, story writer, essayist, and memoirist; born in Ireland. *Seven Winters,* part 2, sect. 4, ch. 2 (1962).

From "Truth and Fiction," a 1956 talk which Bowen gave on a British Broadcasting Company (BBC) Home Service radio program.

2 Writing a novel is a terrible experience, during which the hair often falls out and the teeth decay.

FLANNERY O'CONNOR (1925–1964), U.S. fiction writer and essayist. *Mystery and Manners,* part 3 (1969).

Written c. 1960.

NURSING

1 I don't know how long it has been since my ear has been free from the roll of a drum. It is the music I sleep by, and I love it. . . . I shall remain here while anyone remains, and do whatever comes to my hand. I may be compelled to *face* danger, but *never fear it,* and while our soldiers can stand and *fight,* I can stand and feed and nurse them.

CLARA BARTON (1821–1912), U.S. Civil War nurse and founder of the American Red Cross. As quoted in *Angel of the Battlefield,* ch. 3, by Ishbel Ross (1956).

In an 1861 letter to her father.

2 Many young girls are . . . becoming trained nurses, whose gentle ministrations in the sick-room, skilled

touch, patient watchfulness and unwearied vigils, are as great factors in the care of the sick, as are the professional physicians.

LYDIA HOYT FARMER (1842–1903), U.S. author. *What America Owes to Women,* ch. 17 (1893).

Written at a time when nursing was becoming an organized, honored profession.

3 There were times when I felt that I could bear no more. It was the Emergency Ward which almost broke me. I stood one night beside a man who had been caught in a flywheel, and whose body felt like jelly. I wanted him to die quickly, not to go on breathing. Oh, stop breathing. I can't stand it. Die and stop suffering. I can't stand it. I can't.

MARY ROBERTS RINEHART (1876–1958), U.S. novelist. *My Story,* ch. 12 (1931). On her experience as a nursing student, c. 1900.

4 When I started out as a nurse I did so with the highest ideals. . . . But I found that steady work in my profession—like every woman's work in the world—depended upon the giving of myself. . . . Two-thirds of the physicians I met made a nurse's virtue the price of their influence in getting her steady work. Is it any wonder that I determined to become a member of this privileged sex, if possible?

CORA ANDERSON, U.S. male impersonator. As quoted in *Gay American History,* part 3, by Jonathan Katz (1976).

Said in 1914; for the previous thirteen years, Anderson had successfully impersonated a man, using the name "Ralph Kerwinieo" and doing "men's work." She lived with one woman for many years, then left her and married a second woman. The abandoned lover, Marie White, revealed Anderson/Kerwinieo's deception. She was charged with "disorderly conduct" and freed on the condition that she dress in women's clothes and stop posing as a man.

5 A baby nurse is one that changes diapers and loves 'em dearly. Get up at all hours of the night to give 'em the bottle and change their pants. If the baby coughs or cries, you have to find out the need. I had my own room usually, but I slept in the same room with the baby. I would take full charge. It was twenty-four hours. I used to have one day a week off and I'd go home and see my own two little ones.

RUTH LINDSTROM (c. 1892–?), U.S. practical nurse; born in Sweden. As quoted in *Working*, book 8, by Studs Terkel (1973).

Nearing eighty when Terkel interviewed her, she had emigrated from Sweden in 1913 and worked as a domestic. In 1918, she had become a practical nurse specializing in infant care. She had continued to perform housework as well as baby and child care for families.

OBSCENITY

1 . . . though not invariably the worst choice, war is always an obscene horror.

ELLEN GLASGOW (1873–1945), U.S. novelist. *The Woman Within*, ch. 18 (1954).

Written in 1944, near the end of World War II.

2 When you can use dirty words in every situation with everyone, that's a real big liberation.

LINA WERTMULLER (b. 1928), Italian filmmaker. As quoted in *Ms.* magazine, p. 45 (May 1975).

Contrasting the American attitude toward obscenity with the more relaxed, humorous Italian attitude.

3 Obscenity is sublime.

MOANA POZZI (1961–1994), Italian pornographic movie star. As quoted in the *New Yorker*, p. 38 (October 31, 1994).

Asserted by Italy's "most famous porn star" in an interview with a journalist. It was said that Pozzi herself "never used profanity."

OCEANS

1 . . . living out of sight of any shore does rich and powerfully strange things to humans.

M. F. K. FISHER (1908–1992), U.S. author. *The Gastronomical Me*, "Sea Change" chapter (1943).

OLD PEOPLE

1 Neither lemonade nor anything else can prevent the inroads of old age. At present, I am stoical under its advances, and hope I shall remain so. I have but one prayer at heart; and that is, to have my faculties so far preserved that I can be useful, in *some* way or other, to the last.

LYDIA MARIA CHILD (1802–1880), U.S. author, abolitionist, and suffragist. *Selected Letters, 1817–1880,* ch. 9 (1982).

In an 1869 letter to her friend Harriet Sewall, a suffragist who was married to a former abolitionist, Samuel E. Sewall. Child was sixty-seven years old and suffering from rheumatism.

2 Oh, if I could but live another century and see the fruition of all the work for women! There is so much yet to be done.

SUSAN B. ANTHONY (1820–1906), U.S. suffragist. As quoted in *Life and Work of Susan B. Anthony,* vol. 3, ch. 60, by Ida Husted Harper (1908).

In a 1902 interview. At age 82, Anthony was still active but in poor health. She had worked ceaselessly for woman suffrage for 50 years;

once ridiculed and reviled, she had lived to be an internationally honored figure. However, American women would not gain the vote until 1920, fourteen years after her death.

3 I find in myself to-day the same spring of desire to learn all that I can, to read and study that has been mine from childhood; the same impulse to undertake the difficult enterprise whatever it may be, and the same readiness to throw caution overboard and attempt a task that requires labour and pains, that I have had at any previous moment.

MARGARET E. SANGSTER (1838–1912), U.S. author. *An Autobiography from My Youth Up*, ch. 26 (1909).

At age seventy-one, Sangster was still an active author.

4 Old age is the verdict of life.

AMELIA E. BARR (1831–1919), U.S. author; born in Scotland. *All the Days of My Life*, ch. 26 (1913).

5 I have formed a strong theory that there is no such thing as "turning into" a Nasty Old Man or an Old Witch. I believe that such people, and of course they are legion, were born nasty and witchlike, and that by the time they were about five years old they had hidden their rotten bitchiness and lived fairly decent lives until they no longer had to conform to rules of social behavior, and could revert to their original horrid natures.

M. F. K. FISHER (1908–1992), U.S. culinary writer and autobiographer. *Sister Age*, Afterword (1983).

6 When I am an old woman I shall wear purple

With a red hat which doesn't go, and doesn't suit me.
And I shall spend my pension on brandy and summer gloves
And satin sandals, and say we've no money for butter.

JENNY JOSEPH (b. 1932), British author. "Warning," lines 1–4 (1987).

7 People who have had power, when they become powerless, are really tragic. . . . We just allow ourselves to be conditioned by a society so we become as important as we're supposed to be.

MAGGIE KUHN (b. 1905), U.S. senior rights activist. As quoted in *The Great Divide*, book 2, section 6, by Studs Terkel (1988).

Kuhn was the grand convener of the Gray Panthers, a militant organization that advocated the rights of the elderly.

8 [On being asked "what sort of future she anticipates having":] A very short one.

JEANNE CALMENT (b. c. 1875), French: "oldest known living person." As quoted in *Newsweek* magazine, p. 23 (March 6, 1995).

OPERA

1 Almost everyone admits to hunger during the Opera. . . . Hunger is so exalting that during a last act you practically levitate.

ELIZABETH BOWEN (1899–1973), British novelist, story writer, essayist, and memoirist; born in Ireland. As quoted in *Elizabeth Bowen*, ch. 7, by Victoria Glendinning (1979). Said in 1947.

2 The others "acted" a role; I *was* the role. She who was Mary Garden died that it might live. That was my genius . . . and my sacrifice. It drained off so much of me that by comparison my private life was empty. I could not give myself completely twice.

MARY GARDEN (1874–1967), Scottish opera singer; relocated to America. *Mary Garden's Story*, ch. 21 (1951).
She never married.

OPINION

1   Opinions are not to be learned by rote, like the letters of an alphabet, or the words of a dictionary. They are conclusions *to be formed*, and formed by each individual in the sacred and free citadel of the mind, and there enshrined beyond the arm of law to reach, or force to shake; ay! and beyond the right of impertinent curiosity to violate, or presumptuous arrogance to threaten.

FRANCES WRIGHT (1795–1852), Scottish author and speaker; relocated to America. *Course of Popular Lectures*, lecture 6 (1829).

2   If Rosa Parks had taken a poll before she sat down in that bus in Montgomery, she'd still be standing.

MARY FRANCES BERRY (b. 1938), African American author. As quoted in *I Dream a World*, by Brian Lanker (1989).
Rosa Parks (b. 1913) sparked the African American civil rights movement when, in December 1955, she broke the law by refusing to yield her seat on a Montgomery, Alabama, municipal bus to a white man. This led to the successful Montgomery bus boycott and the rise to prominence of the Rev. Dr. Martin Luther King, Jr. (1929–1968).

OPPORTUNISM

1   Judge Thomas was a man who had used the system to get where he wanted to be, but then felt that everyone else should pull themselves up by their own bootstraps.

JOYCELYN ELDERS (b. 1933), U.S. pediatrician and educator; first woman (and second African American) Surgeon General of the United States. As quoted in the *New York Times Magazine*, p. 18 (January 30, 1994).
On Judge Clarence Thomas, the second African American U. S. Supreme Court Justice. Elders was the second African American U. S. Surgeon General. Thomas, a conservative, opposed many liberal programs that were supported by most African Americans including affirmative action, which once had benefitted him.

OPPORTUNITY

1   When a little girl opens her bright eyes in the sunlight, there is no variety of options.

JEAN ARNOLD, U.S. inventor. As quoted in *Feminine Ingenuity*, ch. 9, by Anne L. MacDonald (1992).
Said in 1876.

2   . . . the door that nobody else will go in at, seems always to swing open widely for me.

CLARA BARTON (1821–1912), U.S. Civil War nurse and founder of the American Red Cross. As quoted in *Angel of the Battlefield*, ch. 14, by Ishbel Ross (1956).
Written in 1892.

3   There are no little events in life, those we think of no consequence may be full of fate, and it is at our own risk if we neglect the acquaintances and opportunities that seem to be casually offered, and of small importance.

AMELIA E. BARR (1831–1919), U.S. author; born in Scotland. *All the Days of My Life,* ch. 13 (1913).

4 Either you will
go through this door
or you will not go through.
. . .
The door itself
makes no promises.
It is only a door.

ADRIENNE RICH (b. 1929), U.S. poet, essayist, and lesbian feminist. "Prospective Immigrants Please Note," lines 1–3, 19–21 (1962).

5 Women have begun to see that if I
go through that doorway, I take everybody through it.

DIANNE FEINSTEIN (b. 1933), U.S. politician. As quoted in *Dianne Feinstein,* ch. 14, by Jerry Roberts (1994).

Said by the former San Francisco Mayor in 1990, the year when she was narrowly defeated for the California Governorship. Two years later, she would be elected a United States Senator from California. Feinstein, one of whose "Rules for Getting Ahead" was "Don't wear your sex like a badge on your sleeve," had sometimes been criticized for inadequate commitment to feminist causes.

OPPOSITES

I I've always felt that complement of opposites: body and soul, solitude and companionship, and in the dance studio, contraction and release, rise and fall.

JUDITH JAMISON (b. 1943), African American dancer. *Dancing Spirit,* ch. 1 (1993).

2 We live in a polarized world of contrived dualisms, dichotomies and paradoxes: light vs. dark and good vs. evil. We as Mexic Amerindians/

mestizas are the dark. We are the evil . . . or at least, the questionable.

ANA CASTILLO (b. 1953), Mexican–American poet, essayist, and feminist. *Massacre of the Dreamers,* ch. 1 (1994).

Castillo was born in the United States to Mexican immigrants with some Indian ancestry.

OPPRESSION

I Women ought to feel a peculiar sympathy in the colored man's wrong, for, like him, she has been accused of mental inferiority, and denied the privileges of a liberal education.

ANGELINA GRIMKÉ (1805–1879), U.S. abolitionist and feminist. As quoted in *The Grimke Sisters from South Carolina,* ch. 10, by Gerda Lerner (1967).

From a paper prepared for a May 1837 antislavery convention of women. Grimke, the daughter of a South Carolina slaveowner, had severed relations with her family and moved North.

2 The Negro has no name. He is Cuffy Douglas or Cuffy Brooks, just whose Cuffy he may chance to be. The Woman has no name. She is Mrs. Richard Roe or Mrs. John Doe, just whose Mrs. she may chance to be. Cuffy has no right to his earnings; he can not buy or sell, or lay up. Mrs. Roe has no right to her earnings; she can neither buy nor sell, make contracts, nor lay up anything that she can call her own. Cuffy has no right to his children; they can be sold from him at any time. Mrs. Roe has no right to her children; they may be bound out to cancel a father's debt of honor. The unborn child, even by the last will of the father, may be placed under the guardianship of a stranger and a foreigner. Cuffy has no legal existence; he is subject to restraint and moderate chastisement. Mrs. Roe has no legal existence; she has not the best right to her own person. The husband has the power to restrain, and administer moderate chastisement. . . . The prejudice against color, of which we hear so much, is no stronger than that against sex. It is produced by the same cause, and manifested very much in the same way. The Negro's skin and the woman's sex are both *prima facie* evidence that they were intended to be in subjection to the white Saxon man. The few social privileges which the man gives the woman, he makes up to the (free) Negro in civil rights.

ELIZABETH CADY STANTON (1815–1902), U.S. suffragist, social reformer, and author. As quoted in *History of Woman Suffrage*, vol. 1, ch. 14, by herself, Susan B. Anthony, and Matilda Joslyn Gage (1881).
Speaking before the New York State legislature in 1860. Stanton was accurately describing the legal circumstances of slaves and of women at that time.

3   . . . women feel the humiliation of their petty distinctions of sex precisely as the black man feels those of color. It is no palliation of our wrongs to say that we are not socially ostracized, so long as we are politically ostracized as he is not.

ELIZABETH CADY STANTON (1815–1902), U.S. suffragist, social reformer, and author. As quoted in *History of Woman Suffrage*, vol. 4, ch. 11, by Susan B. Anthony and Ida Husted Harper (1902).
In an address entitled "The Degradation of Disfranchisement," delivered before the first triennial convention of the National Council of

Women, a prosuffrage organization that had been founded in 1888; the convention was held in February 1891. Stanton was referring to the fact that African American men had been enfranchised in 1870 by the Fifteenth Amendment to the Constitution. Susan B. Anthony read the address, as Stanton was abroad.

4   All oppression creates a state of war.

SIMONE DE BEAUVOIR (1908–1986), French novelist, philosopher, autobiographer, and social critic. *The Second Sex*, foreword (1953; first French edition: 1949).

5   *When a system of oppression has become institutionalized it is unnecessary for individuals to be oppressive.*

FLORYNCE KENNEDY, African American lawyer, author, speaker, and social activist. "Institutionalized Oppression vs. The Female," (1970).

6   What you must understand is oppression does not end with the niggers. It does not end with the poor people, it doesn't end with the women, or the pregnant women. It goes on up the line to the executive who has his bag searched in the airport.

FLORYNCE KENNEDY (b. 1916), African American lawyer, activist, speaker, and author. *Color Me Flo*, ch. 3 (1976).

7   Usually, when people talk about the "strength" of black women they are referring to the way in which they perceive black women coping with oppression. They ignore the reality that to be strong in the face of oppression is not the same as overcoming oppression, that endurance is not to be confused with transformation.

BELL HOOKS (b. c. 1955), African American author, feminist, and civil rights advocate. *Ain't I a Woman?* Introduction (1981).

CHERRÍE MORAGA (b. 1952), Hispanic American lesbian feminist author. As quoted in *Yours in Struggle,* part 2, by Barbara Smith (1984).

8 The "Otherizing" of women is the oldest oppression known to our species, and it's the model, the template, for all other oppressions.

ROBIN MORGAN (b. 1941), U.S. author, feminist, and child actor. *The Word of a Woman,* part 2 (1992). Written in 1982.

9 . . . there is no way of measuring the damage to a society when a whole texture of humanity is kept from realizing its own power, when the woman architect who might have reinvented our cities sits barely literate in a semilegal sweatshop on the Texas-Mexican border, when women who should be founding colleges must work their entire lives as domestics . . .

ADRIENNE RICH (b. 1929), U.S. poet, essayist, and feminist. *Blood, Bread and Poetry,* ch. 12 (1986).

From a lecture given at Scripps College in Claremont, California, on February 15, 1984: the 164th anniversary of Susan B. Anthony's birthday (1820–1906).

10 Being oppressed means the *absence of choices.*

BELL HOOKS (b. 1955), African American author and educator. *Feminist Theory,* ch. 1 (1984).

hooks had grown up poor in Hopkinsville, Kentucky.

11 Oppression does not make for hearts as big as all outdoors. Oppression makes us big and small. Expressive and silenced. Deep and dead.

12 My philosophy is such that I am not going to vote against the oppressed. I have been oppressed, and so I am always going to have a vote for the oppressed, regardless of whether that oppressed is black or white or yellow or the people of the Middle East, or what. I have that feeling.

SEPTIMA CLARK (1898–1987), African American teacher and civil rights activist. *Ready from Within,* part 2, ch. 3 (1986).

13 I always draw a parallel between oppression by the regime and oppression by men. To me it is just the same. I always challenge men on why they react to oppression by the regime, but then they do exactly the same things to women that they criticize the regime for.

SETHEMBILE N., South African black anti-apartheid activist. As quoted in *Lives of Courage,* ch. 19, by Diana E. H. Russell (1989).

Said in a May 7, 1987 interview. A Zulu and a black liberation activist, she opposed Inkatha, the movement headed by Zulu Chief Buthelezi. Fearful of retaliation, she became a refugee from Inkatha and used a pseudonym during her interview.

14 . . . Jews must learn to say without excuse, without equivocation: despite our history and our powerlessness in the past, despite all the injustices that we have endured— today, now, the Palestinians are the victims of oppression, and their oppressors are the Israelis.

IRENA KLEPFISZ (b. 1941), U.S. Jewish author; born in Poland. *Dreams of an Insomniac,* part 3 (1990).

Klepfisz, a Jew born in Poland in 1941, escaped the 1943 Warsaw Uprising after her father was killed in its second day. After some years in Sweden, she and her mother emigrated to New York City–the only members of either side of the family to survive the Holocaust.

15 . . . black progress and progress for women are inextricably linked in contemporary American politics, and . . . each group suffers when it fails to grasp the dimensions of the other's struggle.

MARGARET A. BURNHAM (b. 1944), African American author. *Race-ing Justice, Engendering Power,* ch. 13 (1992).

16 It was dreadful. They tried to put the little redhead in a cage.

SARAH FERGUSON (b. 1959), British royalty, Duchess of York. As quoted in *the New York Times,* p. C10 (February 16, 1994).

After receiving much unfavorable publicity because of her free-wheeling ways, the red-haired Duchess separated from her husband, Prince Andrew, who was the third of Queen Elizabeth II's four children. Here she was remembering the constraints imposed by his family.

17 The horror of class stratification, racism, and prejudice is that some people begin to believe that the security of their families and communities depends on the oppression of others, that for some to have good lives there must be others whose lives are truncated and brutal.

DOROTHY ALLISON (b. 1949), U.S. author and lesbian feminist. *Skin,* ch. 2 (1994).

Allison had grown up in a very poor and dysfunctional South Carolina family.

18 Oppression has no logic—just a self-fulfilling prophecy, justified by a self-perpetuating system.

GLORIA STEINEM (b. 1934), U.S. feminist, author, and editor. *Moving Beyond Words,* part 2 (1994).

OPTIMISM

I I ignore all the doomsaying nonsense. I'm in a business where the odds of ever earning a living are a zillion to one, so I know it can be done. I know the impossible can become possible.

MARCIA WALLACE (b. 1942), U.S. actor. As quoted in *People* magazine (March 2, 1992).

Wallace, once a regular supporting actor on *The Bob Newhart Show* (television), was commenting on the poor prognosis for her husband, who had been stricken with pancreatic cancer.

ORATORY

I . . . the worst horror of the Russian Revolution was the letting loose of one hundred million orators, for their passion for talk was immediately responsible for all the other horrors . . . Oratory prevented Russia from becoming a constitutional country. Oratory tore the Revolution from the patriots and gave it into the bloody hands of the mob. Oratory murdered the Czar, his wife, and their innocent children. Oratory almost wiped out the educated classes. Oratory held the stupid populace spellbound while the Germans invaded the country, boosted Lenine [sic] into power, and paved the way for the treaty of Brest-Litovsk. I never want to hear any more oratory as long as I live.

RHETA CHILDE DORR (1866–1948), U.S. journalist. *A Woman of Fifty,* 2nd. ed., ch. 19 (1924).

Dorr was in Russia on a journalistic assignment at the outbreak of the Russian Revolution.

ORGANIZATION

1 The tendency of organization is to kill out the spirit which gave it birth. Organizations do not protect the sacredness of the individual; their tendency is to sink the individual in the mass, to sacrifice his rights, and to immolate him on the altar of some fancied good.

ANGELINA GRIMKÉ (1805–1879), U.S. abolitionist and feminist. As quoted in *The Grimké Sisters from South Carolina,* ch. 18, by Gerda Lerner (1967).

In a letter to the 1852 Woman's Rights Convention, held in Syracuse, New York. The major topic of the convention was to be the future organizational structure of the women's rights movement, which was only a few years old.

2 I cry out for order and find it only in art.

HELEN HAYES (1900–1993), U.S. actor. *On Reflection,* ch. 14 (1968).

ORIGINALITY

1 Originality usually amounts only to plagiarizing something unfamiliar.

KATHERINE FULLERTON GEROULD (1879–1944), U.S. author. *Modes and Morals,* ch. 7 (1920).

OVERWEIGHT

1 My chance, when it came, was due, literally, to the fact that I was slen-

der. . . . You cannot make an opera audience believe that a man will endanger his soul, and commit robbery and murder for a very stout lady's sake.

MARIA JERITZA (1887–1982), Austrian opera singer. *Sunlight and Song,* ch. 21 (1924).

Explaining why she was selected to sing the role of Aphrodite, the Greek goddess of beauty and love.

2 Once *Vogue* showed two or three dresses for stout women, but we were so shaken by the experience we haven't repeated it in fifty-seven years. Today . . . we must acknowledge that a lady may grow mature, but she never grows fat.

EDNA WOOLMAN CHASE (1877–1957), U.S. editor (*Vogue* magazine). *Always in Vogue,* ch. 2 (1954).

3 . . . I will not be a sight gag for anybody. I will not do anything degrading to myself or other fat people.

DARLENE CATES (b. 1947), U.S. actor.

Cates, a 489-pound arthritic woman who had been virtually housebound, had her first acting role in the 1993 film *What's Eating Gilbert Grape?* Her character was sympathetic and dignified; her portrayal was acclaimed. Here, Cates was setting forth her condition for accepting any future film role.

PAIN AND SUFFERING

1 I said to myself, "The only thing they can do is kill my body. They are not going to get my mind, and my soul will live on in my children and in other people."

SHAHIEDA ISSEL (b. 1957), South African black anti-apartheid activist. As quoted in *Lives of Courage,* ch. 4, by Diana E. H. Russell (1989).

Said in a 1987 interview, describing her reaction to abuse by the police.

PAINTING AND PAINTERS

1   . . . the true seeing is within; and
painting stares at you with an insis-
tent imperfection.

GEORGE ELIOT (1819–1880), British
novelist. *Middlemarch*, ch. 19 (1871–
1872).

2   . . . to paint with oil paints for the
first time . . . is like trying to make
something exquisitely accurate and
microscopically clear out of mud
pies with boxing gloves on.

BRENDA UELAND (1891–1985), U.S. au-
thor and writing teacher. *If You Want to Write*,
2nd. ed., ch. 6 (1938).

PALESTINE LIBERATION
ORGANIZATION

1   I have told my husband that if he
denies women equality, I will be in
the vanguard of women on the
streets, protesting outside his office
in the new Palestinian state.

SUHA TAWIL (b. 1963), Palestinian feminist. As quoted in the *New Yorker*, p. 83 (May
16, 1994).

Tawil, a strong-willed Christian feminist, was
married to Yasir Arafat, chairman of the Pales-
tine Liberation Organization.

PARENT-CHILD
RELATIONSHIPS

1   My parents think I'm a bum.

JACKI HANSON (b. 1948), U.S. marathon
runner. As quoted in *WomenSports* magazine,
p. 10 (February 1977).

Hansen, the women's world record holder in
the marathon, was describing her parents' reaction to her having quit several jobs because
they cut into her training time. She was living in
an old hunter's cabin in the hills outside Los
Angeles and selling glucose supplements to
other runners to earn some money.

PARIS, FRANCE

1   Paris is a hard place to leave, even
when it rains incessantly and one
coughs continually from the damp-
ness.

WILLA CATHER (1876–1947), U.S. novelist. *Willa Cather in Europe*, ch. 11 (1956).
Written on September 3, 1902.

2   Paris is the city in which one loves
to live. Sometimes I think this is because it is the only city in the world
where you can step out of a railway
station—the Gare D'Orsay—and
see, simultaneously, the chief en-
chantments: the Seine with its bridges and bookstalls, the Louvre, No-
tre Dame, the Tuileries Gardens,
the Place de la Concorde, the beginning of the Champs Elysees—nearly
everything except the Luxembourg
Gardens and the Palais Royal. But
what other city offers as much as
you leave a train?

MARGARET ANDERSON (1886–1973),
U.S. editor and memoirist. *The Fiery Fountains*,
part 1 (1951).

Anderson lived in France for nearly twenty
years.

3   . . . in the movies Paris is designed
as a backdrop for only three
things—love, fashion shows, and
revolution.

JEANINE BASINGER (b. 1936), U.S. movie
and social historian. *A Woman's View*, ch. 7
(1993).

PASSIVITY

1   Things happen to us, all the time. It
was like that for a century, and it is
again. It's not like here: People always do things, because you are

born with it; you are brought up in this spirit, the active approach to life: "Stand up and go." We were not. We were always passive in our lives.

NATASHA DUDINSKA (b. c. 1967), Czechoslovakian Jew; attending college in America. As quoted in the *New York Times*, sect. 4, p. 7 (June 13, 1993).

A Czechoslovakian citizen and New York City resident, Dudinska was comparing Slovakian passivity in the face of the breakup of Czechoslovakia to what she saw as the characteristic American approach to events. Before coming to the United States to earn a Master's degree from Columbia University, she had been a student protest leader in Communist Czechoslovakia and had helped to bring about the downfall of the Communist regime. She did not approve of the subsequent division of the country into the Czech and Slovak republics.

PAST, THE

1 The past cannot be cured.

ELIZABETH I (1533–1603), British monarch, Queen of England (1558–1603). As quoted in *The Sayings of Queen Elizabeth*, ch. 11, by Frederick Chamberlin (1923).

To the Spanish Ambassador.

2 Faithfulness to the past can be a kind of death above ground. Writing of the past is a resurrection; the past then lives in your words and you are free.

JESSAMYN WEST (1902–1984), U.S. novelist. *The Life I Really Lived*, ch. 15 (1979).

3 Life . . . is not simply a series of exciting new ventures. The future is not always a whole new ball game. There tends to be unfinished business. One trails all sorts of things around with one, things that simply won't be got rid of.

ANITA BROOKNER (b. 1928), British novelist. *Lewis Percy*, ch. 14 (1989).

Percy, the novel's protagonist, works in a library where computers are being introduced. Here he explains his resistance to computerizing his accustomed manual work processes.

PATRIARCHY

1 Why is it that many contemporary male thinkers, especially men of color, repudiate the imperialist legacy of Columbus but affirm dimensions of that legacy by their refusal to repudiate patriarchy?

BELL HOOKS (b. c. 1955), African American author, feminist, and human rights advocate. *Outlaw Culture*, ch. 19 (1994).

PATRIOTISM

1 If you think it will only add one sprig to the wreath the country twines to bind the brows of my hero, I will run the risk of being sneered at by those who criticize female productions of all kinds. . . . Though a female, I was born a patriot.

ANNIE BOUDINOT STOCKTON (1736–1801), U.S. poet. As quoted in *Past and Promise*, part 1, by Wendy Pfeffer (1990).

In a letter to her brother Elias Boudinot dated May 1, 1789, in which she discussed publishing her poetry, which often featured patriotic themes. For a woman to publish her writing was generally considered somewhat inappropriate.

2 It is to be lamented that the principle of *national* has had very little nourishment in our country, and, instead, has given place to *sectional* or *state* partialities. What more promising method for remedying

this defect than by uniting American women of every state and every section in a common effort for *our whole country*.

CATHERINE E. BEECHER (1800–1878), U.S. educator and author. As quoted in *Catherine Beecher*, ch. 12, by Kathryn Kish Sklar (1973).

Written in 1846, before the Civil War. There was tension among different states and regions because of their differing attitudes and laws regarding slavery.

3 What is Americanism? Every one has a different answer. Some people say it is never to submit to the dictation of a King. Others say Americanism is the pride of liberty and the defence of an insult to the flag with their gore. When some half-developed person tramples on that flag, we should be ready to pour out the blood of the nation, they say. But do we not sit in silence when that flag waves over living conditions which should be an insult to all patriotism?

ANNA HOWARD SHAW (1847–1919), U.S. minister, suffragist, and speaker; born in England. As quoted in *History of Woman Suffrage*, vol. 5, ch. 13, by Ida Husted Harper (1922).

Speaking in September 1916 before the forty-eighth annual convention of the National Woman Suffrage Association. Many active suffragists and sympathizers with the movement were also active in efforts to eradicate poverty.

4 Patriotism . . . is a superstition artificially created and maintained through a network of lies and falsehoods; a superstition that robs man of his self-respect and dignity, and increases his arrogance and conceit.

EMMA GOLDMAN (1869–1940), U.S. anarchist and author; born in Russia. *Anarchism and Other Essays*, 3rd rev. ed., ch. 5 (1917).

5 . . . a friend told me that she had read of a woman who had knitted a wash rag for President Wilson. She was eighty years old and her friends thought it remarkable that she could knit a wash rag! I thought that if a woman of eighty could knit a wash rage for a Democratic President it behooved one of ninety-six to make something more than a wash rag for a Republican President.

MARIA D. BROWN (1827–1927), U.S. homemaker. As quoted in *Grandmother Brown's Hundred Years*, ch. 10, by Harriet Connor Brown (1929).

On hand-embroidering a dresser scarf for President and Mrs. Coolidge in 1923; she sent it to them with a letter observing: "I have five sons, all Republican."

6 Women realize that we are living in an ungoverned world. At heart we are all pacifists. We should love to talk it over with the war-makers, but they would not understand. Words are so inadequate, and we realize that the hatred must kill itself; so we give our men gladly, unselfishly, proudly, patriotically, since the world chooses to settle its disputes in the old barbarous way.

GENERAL FEDERATION OF WOMEN'S CLUBS (GFWC), As quoted in *Everyone Was Brave*, ch. 6, by William L. O'Neill (1971).

From an editorial first published in the *GFWC Magazine* (June 1917).

7 . . . patriotism cannot go back to an innocent time before the murderous excesses of twentieth-century nationalism.

JEAN BETHKE ELSHTAIN (b. 1941), U.S. political scientist and feminist. *Power Trips and Other Journeys*, ch. 12 (1990).

PAY EQUITY

1 Women should have equal pay for equal work and they should be considered equally eligible to the offices of principal and superintendent, professor and president. So you must insist that qualifications, not sex, shall govern appointments and salaries.

SUSAN B. ANTHONY (1820–1906), U.S. suffragist. As quoted in *Life and Work of Susan B. Anthony,* vol. 3, ch. 62, by Ida Husted Harper (1908).
In a letter dated July 6, 1903, to Margaret A. Haley, President of the National Federation of Teachers. Decades later, "equal pay for equal work" would be a goal of the "second wave" feminist movement that commenced in the 1960s; many would then consider it to be a new, and radical, slogan.

2 I believe that if a man does a job as well as a woman, he should be paid as much.

CELESTE HOLM (b. 1919), U.S. actress and singer. As quoted in *Past and Promise,* part 4, by Sandra Lee Jackson (1990).
Said jokingly in an interview with the author on April 3, 1986.

PEACE

1 . . . peace produced by suppression is neither natural nor desirable.

ANNA JULIA COOPER (1859–1964), U.S. educator and feminist. *A Voice from the South,* part 2 (1892).

2 In the whole round of human affairs little is so fatal to peace as misunderstanding.

MARGARET E. SANGSTER (1838–1912), U.S. author. *An Autobiography from My Youth Up,* ch. 13 (1909).
Remembering the Civil War.

3 The contention that a standing army and navy is the best security of peace is about as logical as the claim that the most peaceful citizen is he who goes about heavily armed. The experience of every-day life fully proves that the armed individual is invariably anxious to try his strength. The same is historically true of governments. Really peaceful countries do not waste life and energy in war preparations, with the result that peace is maintained.

EMMA GOLDMAN (1869–1940), U.S. anarchist and author; born in Russia. *Anarchism and Other Essays,* 3rd rev. ed., ch. 5 (1917).

4 The peace conference must not adjourn without the establishment of some ordered system of international government, backed by power enough to give authority to its decrees. . . . Unless a league something like this results at our peace conference, we shall merely drop back into armed hostility and international anarchy. The war will have been fought in vain . . .

VIRGINIA CROCHERON GILDER-SLEEVE, (1877–1965) U.S. educator. Quoting herself in *Many a Good Crusade,* part 2 (1954).
In a speech given on February 22, 1918, before the Congress of National Service of the National Security League in Chicago. The speech was entitled "The Relationship of Nations" and was published by the League to Enforce Peace. The "war" referred to was World War I. Gildersleeve supported formation of the League of Nations, which failed largely because the United States ultimately rejected it.

5 The basis of world peace is the teaching which runs through almost all the great religions of the world. "Love thy neighbor as thyself."

Christ, some of the other great Jewish teachers, Buddha, all preached it. Their followers forgot it. What is the trouble between capital and labor, what is the trouble in many of our communities, but rather a universal forgetting that this teaching is one of our first obligations.

ELEANOR ROOSEVELT (1884–1962), First Lady of the United States, author, speaker, and diplomat. As quoted in *Eleanor and Franklin,* ch. 27, by Joseph P. Lash (1971).

Written in 1925, before her husband, Franklin Delano Roosevelt, had yet been elected President.

6 . . . peace is a militant thing . . . any peace movement must have behind it a higher passion than the desire for war. No one can be a pacifist without being ready to fight for peace and die for peace.

MARY HEATON VORSE (1874–1966), U.S. journalist and labor activist. *A Footnote to Folly,* ch. 5 (1935).

7 Even the propagandists on the radio find it very difficult to really say let alone believe that the world will be a happy place, of love and peace and plenty, and that the lion will lie down with the lamb and everybody will believe anybody.

GERTRUDE STEIN (1874–1946), U.S. author; relocated to France. *Wars I Have Seen* (1945).

Written in 1943, about what people were expecting at the close of World War II, which was then in progress.

8 . . . in spite of everything, I still believe that people are really good at heart. I simply can't build up my hopes on a foundation consisting of confusion, misery, and death. I see

the world gradually being turned into a wilderness, I hear the ever approaching thunder, which will destroy us too, I can feel the sufferings of millions and yet, if I look up into the heavens, I think that it will all come right, that this cruelty too will end, and that peace and tranquillity will return again.

ANNE FRANK (1929–1945), Dutch Jewish diarist; born in Germany. *Diary of a Young Girl,* entry dated July 15, 1944 (1947).

Frank and her family were in hiding in Holland when she wrote this. On August 4, their hiding place would be raided by the police, and they would be sent to German and Dutch concentration camps. All of them except Otto Frank, the father, would perish; Anne died in Bergen-Belsen, a German camp, just two months before the liberation of Holland.

9 Almost everybody wore a curious limpidity of expression, like newborn babies or souls just after death. Dazed but curiously dignified. . . . after a *crise* . . . of hysterical revulsion and tiredness, I passed beyond . . . and became entered by a rather sublime feeling.

ELIZABETH BOWEN (1899–1973), British novelist, story writer, essayist, and memoirist; born in Ireland. As quoted in *Elizabeth Bowen,* ch. 3, by Victoria Glendinning (1979).

In a 1945 letter to the author Charles Ritchie, her lover, describing Londoners on V-E Day, which marked the end of World War II.

10 . . . I still have faith occasionally in the brotherhood of man, and in spite of all the tragedies that have intervened since [1945], believe that sometime, somehow, all the nations of the world can work together for the common good.

VIRGINIA CROCHERON GILDERSLEEVE, (1877–1965) U.S. educator. *Many a Good Crusade,* part 5 (1954).

Dean of Barnard College in New York City, Gildersleeve was also active in international political affairs and had strongly supported the League of Nations, which failed. She was a delegate to the 1945 San Francisco Conference, which drafted the charter of the United Nations. That year also saw the end of World War II.

11 What shall we do with country quiet now?
A motor drones insanely in the blue
Like a bad bird in a dream.

BABETTE DEUTSCH (1895–1982), U.S. poet. "Lines Written in Time of Peace," lines 1–3 (late 1960s).

PERFORMING ARTS

1 . . . we performers are monsters. We are a totally different, far-out race of people. I totally and completely admit, with no qualms at all, my egomania, my selfishness, coupled with a really magnificent voice.

LEONTYNE PRICE (b. 1927), African American opera singer. As quoted in *I Dream a World,* by Brian Lanker (1989).

PERSECUTION

1 It is funny that men who are supposed to be scientific cannot get themselves to realise the basic principle of physics, that action and reaction are equal and opposite, that when you persecute people you always rouse them to be strong and stronger.

GERTRUDE STEIN (1874–1946), U.S. author; relocated to France. *Wars I Have Seen* (1945).

Written in 1944, during World War II; France, which had been defeated and occupied by Germany in 1940, was finally liberated in late 1944.

PERSEVERANCE

1 [Asked if American women would ever win full suffrage:] Assuredly. I firmly believed at one time that I should live to see that day. I have never for one moment lost faith. It will come but I shall not see it . . . it is inevitable.

SUSAN B. ANTHONY (1820–1906), U.S. suffragist. As quoted in *Life and Work of Susan B. Anthony,* vol. 3, ch. 60, by Ida Husted Harper (1908).

In a 1902 interview. At age 82, Anthony was still active but in poor health; she had worked ceaselessly for woman suffrage for 50 years. Her prediction was correct, of course. American women gained the vote in 1920, a century after her birth and fourteen years after her death.

2 I never saw that great woman, Mary Wollstonecraft, but I have read her eloquent and unanswerable arguments in behalf of the liberty of womankind. I have met and known most of the progressive women who came after her—Lucretia Mott, the Grimké sisters, Elizabeth Cady Stanton, Lucy Stone—a long galaxy of great women. . . . Those older women have gone on, and most of those who worked with me in the early years have gone. I am here for a little time only and then my place will be filled as theirs was filled. The fight must not cease; you must see that it does not stop.

SUSAN B. ANTHONY (1820–1906), U.S. suffragist. As quoted in *Life and Work of Susan B. Anthony,* vol. 3, ch. 69, by Ida Husted Harper (1908).

Speaking in Baltimore, Maryland, in February 1906, at the thirty-eighth annual convention of the National Woman Suffrage Association. Anthony was nearing her eighty-sixth birthday and was in very uncertain health. She had been a leader of the woman suffrage movement for 54 years, almost since its inception. Mary Wollstonecraft (1759–1797), a British author, wrote one of the earliest feminist tracts, *A Vindication of the Rights of Woman* (1792); Anthony had never met her, of course, because she died before Anthony was born. Lucretia Mott (1793–1880) was an American suffragist and abolitionist; she also supported a number of other social reforms. Angelina (1805–1879) and Sarah (1792–1873) Grimké were passionate abolitionists and suffragists. Elizabeth Cady Stanton (1816–1902) had been Anthony's closest friend and colleague, working with her for decades on prosuffrage activism. Lucy Stone (1818–1893) was an abolitionist and suffragist who married another active suffragist, Henry Brown Blackwell, but retained her birth name. Mott and Stanton had organized the first women's rights convention ever held in the United States, from which the woman suffrage movement dates: it opened in Seneca Falls, New York, on July 19, 1848.

3 To be a good actor . . . it is necessary to have a firmly tempered soul, to be surprised at nothing, to resume each minute the laborious task that has barely just been finished.

SARAH BERNHARDT (1845–1923), French actor. *The Art of the Theatre*, ch. 3 (1924). Written in 1923.

4 This life is a war we are not yet winning for our daughters' children.
Don't do your enemies' work for them.
Finish your own.

MARGE PIERCY (b. 1936), U.S. poet, novelist, and political activist. "Memo To: . . . Subject:," lines 53–56 (1980). Directed to "female poets" and naming twenty strongly feminist women poets, this poem argued the importance of persevering in the face of problems and frustrations.

5 I never let prejudice stop me from what I wanted to do in this life.

SARAH LOUISE DELANY (b. 1889), African American educator. *Having Our Say*, ch. 11 (1992).
One of ten children born to a former slave and his wife, she had earned Bachelor's and Master's degrees from Columbia University and taught in the New York City schools.

PHILADELPHIA, PA

1 I never walked through the streets of any city with as much satisfaction as those of Philadelphia. The neatness and cleanliness of all animate and inanimate things, houses, pavements, and citizens, is not to be surpassed.

FRANCES WRIGHT (1795–1852), U.S. social reformer and author; born and raised in Scotland. *Views of Society and Manners in America,* entry for May 1819 (1821).
Making her first trip to America.

2 I've never known a Philadelphian who wasn't a downright "character;" possibly a defense mechanism resulting from the dullness of their native habitat.

ANITA LOOS (1888–1981), U.S. screenwriter, author, and humorist. *Kiss Hollywood Good-by,* ch. 10 (1974).

PHILANTHROPY

1 If the sewing societies, the avails of whose industry are now expended in supporting and educating young men for the ministry, were to withdraw their contributions to these objects, and give them where they are *more needed,* to their advancement of their *own sex* in useful learning, the next generation might furnish sufficient proof, that in intelligence and ability to master the whole circle of sciences, woman is not inferior to man . . .

SARAH M. GRIMKÉ (1792–1873), U.S. abolitionist and feminist. *Letters on the Equality of the Sexes and the Condition of Woman,* letter #15: dated October 20, 1837 (1838).

2 How can the physique be braced if no fresh breath from the outer world is suffered to permeate the languid, enervating air of the drawing-room? How can the grasp of the mind be vigorous, without action? Daughters of inherited wealth, or accumulated labor! the wide door of philanthropy is open peculiarly to *you!* Your life-work lies beyond your threshold: your wealth has placed you above the sorrowful struggle for daily bread which takes up the whole time of so many of your brothers and sisters. You are the almoners of God. A double accountability is yours.

HARRIOT K. HUNT (1805–1875), U.S. physician and feminist. *Glances and Glimpses,* ch. 4 (1856).

3 . . . we all know the wag's definition of a philanthropist: a man whose charity increases directly as the square of the distance.

GEORGE ELIOT (1819–1880), British novelist. *Middlemarch,* ch. 38 (1871–1872).

4 . . . every woman who has any margin of time or money to spare should adopt some one public interest, some philanthropic undertaking, or some social agitation of reform, and give to that cause what-

ever time and work she may be able to afford . . .

FRANCES POWER COBBÉ (1822–1904), U.S. author and feminist. *The Duties of Women,* lecture 6 (1882).

5 . . . our scholarships should be bestowed on those whose ability and earnestness in the primary department have been proved, and whose capacity for a higher education is fully shown. This is the best work women of wealth can do, and I hope in the future they will endow scholarships for their own sex instead of giving millions of dollars to institutions for boys, as they have done in the past.

ELIZABETH CADY STANTON (1815–1902), U.S. suffragist, author, and social reformer. *Eighty Years and More (1815–1897),* ch. 27 (1898).
Said in a June 1892 address at the dedication of the Gurley Memorial Building at Emma Willard Seminary in Troy, New York, from which she had graduated sixty years earlier.

PHILOSOPHY

I Chinese were born . . . with an accumulated wisdom, a natural sophistication, an intelligent naivete, and unless they were transplanted too young, these qualities ripened in them. . . . If ever I am homesick for China, now that I am home in my own country, it is when I discover here no philosophy. Our people have opinions and creeds and prejudices and ideas but as yet no philosophy.

PEARL S. BUCK (1892–1973), U.S. author. *My Several Worlds* (1954).
The daughter of American missionaries to China, Buck had spent her childhood and

much of her adulthood in that country. She left unwillingly after the revolution.

SUSAN SONTAG (b. 1933), U.S. author. *On Photography*, ch. 3 (1977).

PHOTOGRAPHY

1 Modern photographers can reduce bones to formlessness, and change a face of the most strange, exquisite and unfathomable beauty into the face of a clubwoman.

MARGARET ANDERSON (1886–1973), U.S. editor and memoirist. *The Strange Necessity*, part 1 (1969).

Anderson was reacting to a type of portrait photography that was currently fashionable, and exposed, rather than idealized, the subject's face; Diane Arbus and Richard Avedon were prominent among the photographers who popularized it. Their subjects often appeared grotesque and probably looked much worse than they did in person.

2 I always thought of photography as a naughty thing to do—that was one of my favorite things about it, and when I first did it, I felt very perverse.

DIANE ARBUS (1923–1971), U.S. photographer. As quoted in *On Photography*, ch. 1, by Susan Sontag (1977).

Arbus was known for rather emotionless, objectifying photographs of people who were physically abnormal or somehow grotesque; her style was sometimes described as voyeuristic.

3 ... the most grandiose result of the photographic enterprise is to give us the sense that we can hold the whole world in our heads—as an anthology of images.

SUSAN SONTAG (b. 1933), U.S. author. *On Photography*, ch. 1 (1977).

4 ... [photographs] trade simultaneously on the prestige of art and the magic of the real.

PHYSICIANS

1 I felt more than ever the necessity of my mission. But I went home out of spirits, I hardly know why. I must work by myself all life long.

ELIZABETH BLACKWELL (1821–1910), U.S. physician. *Pioneer Work for Women*, ch. 3 (1895).

From a journal entry dated December 4, 1847, when she was a medical student. She had just examined an impoverished sick woman. A major rationale for women learning medicine was the necessity of women examining sick women out of respect for sexual modesty. Blackwell would become the first female American physician.

2 The prevailing idea ... is, that the *doctor* is to cure the disease. It is not so. The doctor and the patient *together*, are to cure or mitigate the disease. They must be coworkers. In order to be so, there must be the ... the most cordial sympathy and frankness between them. It is rarely that this can be so between a male physician and a female patient. Therefore, the female physician, is *the* physician for the female patient. ... In a few years the medical profession will be equally shared between men and women; public opinion is fast tending to bring this about.

HARRIOT K. HUNT (1805–1875), U.S. physician and feminist. *Glances and Glimpses*, ch. 11 (1856).

3 Trust a *woman*—as a DOCTOR!— NEVER!

FANNY KEMBLE (1809–1893), British actress. As quoted in *Pioneer Work for Women,* ch. 5, by Elizabeth Blackwell (1895).

The reaction of the prominent Shakespearean actress when approached in 1857 by Drs. Blackwell and Maria E. Zackrzewska for a donation to their "New York Infirmary for Women and Children," which had opened in May of that year.

4   . . . it is seldom a medical man has true religious views—there is too much pride of intellect.

GEORGE ELIOT (1819–1880), British novelist. *Middlemarch,* ch. 31 (1871–1872).

The novel's character named Mrs. Bulstrode is warning her beautiful niece, Rosamond Vincy, about the likely impiety of the latter's prospective fiance, Dr. Lydgate.

5   These doctors, they've got no mercy on you, 'specially if you're black. Ah! I've seen 'em, many a time, but, they never come after me, I never gave 'em a chance—not the first time.

SILVIA DUBOIS (1788?–1889), African American slave and hog breeder. As quoted in *Silvia Dubois, a Biografy of the Slav Who Whipt Her Mistres and Gand Her Fredom,* interview dated January 27, 1883, by C. W. Larison (1883).

Larison, Dubois's interviewer, was a physician.

6   When a doctor refuses money, even the most ethical ones, you usually start driving a good bargain with the undertaker.

SUE SANDERS, U.S. oil producer. *Our Common Herd,* ch. 30 (1940).

An insight gained from a siege of bad health which was erroneously expected to cause her death.

7   Nobody, but nobody, is going to stop breathing on me.

VIRGINIA APGAR (1909–1974), U.S. physician. As quoted in *Past and Promise,* by Rebecca Berry Creswell (1990).

A pediatrician and anesthesiologist who specialized in prenatal care, Apgar was speaking about her use of an "airway tube" at the site of auto accidents to revive victims.

8   A cynic might conclude that the real purpose of the $500 million-a-year implant business is the implantation of fat in the bellies and rumps of underemployed plastic surgeons.

BARBARA EHRENREICH (b. 1941), U.S. author and feminist. *Time* magazine, p. 88 (February 17, 1992).

In an article which satirically criticized breast implants in particular.

PLACE

I   . . . anybody is as their land and air is. Anybody is as the sky is low or high, the air heavy or clear and anybody is as there is wind or no wind there. It is that which makes them and the arts they make and the work they do and the way they eat and the way they drink and the way they learn and everything.

GERTRUDE STEIN (1874–1946), U.S. author and patron of the arts; relocated to France. *An American and France* (1936).

Born, raised, and educated in America, Stein settled in Paris, where she built her reputation as an innovative writer and patron of young artists and avant-garde art.

2   After all anybody is as their land and air is. Anybody is as the sky is low or high. Anybody is as there is wind or no wind there. That is what makes a people, makes their kind of looks, their kind of thinking, their subtlety and their stupidity, and their eating and their drinking and their language.

GERTRUDE STEIN (1874–1946), U.S. author; relocated to France. *Wars I Have Seen* (1945).
Written in France in 1944.

3 The writer operates at a peculiar crossroads where time and place and eternity somehow meet. His problem is to find that location.

FLANNERY O'CONNOR (1925–1964), U.S. fiction writer and essayist. *Mystery and Manners*, part 2 (1969).
Written in 1957. O'Connor, who wrote in and of Georgia, was speaking of so-called "regional" writing.

4 Nothing can happen nowhere. The locale of the happening always colours the happening, and often, to a degree, shapes it.

ELIZABETH BOWEN (1899–1973), British novelist, essayist, and memoirist; born in Ireland. *Pictures and Conversations*, ch. 1 (1975).

5 The sense of place is unavoidable in western Dakota, and maybe that's our gift to the world. . . . In these places you wait, and the places mold you.

KATHLEEN NORRIS (b. 1947), U.S. poet and farmer. *Dakota*, ch. 31 (1993).

PLAGIARISM

1 It is an old error of man to forget to put quotation marks where he borrows from a woman's brain!

ANNA GARLIN SPENCER (1851–1931), U.S. educator, author, feminist, and Unitarian minister. *Woman's Share in Social Culture*, Introduction (1913).

POETRY

1 I regard a love for poetry as one of the most needful and helpful elements in the life-outfit of a human being. It was the greatest of blessings to me, in the long days of toil to which I was shut in much earlier than most young girls are, that the poetry I held in my memory breathed its enchanted atmosphere through me and around me, and touched even dull drudgery with its sunshine.

LUCY LARCOM (1824–1893), U.S. poet and teacher. *A New England Girlhood*, ch. 6 (1889).
At age 11, Larcom had become a mill worker. Eventually, she was able to return to school and became a poet.

2 Since I know nothing of the merits of poetry, I am not able to pass any opinion upon this, but I can see that "reap" and "deep," "prayers" and "bears," "ark" and "dark," "true" and "grew" do rhyme, and so I suppose it is a splendid effort, but if you had written it in plain prose, I could have understood it a great deal better and read it a great deal more easily.

SUSAN B. ANTHONY (1820–1906), U.S. suffragist. As quoted in *The Life and Work of Susan B. Anthony*, ch. 49, by Ida Husted Harper (1898).
Responding in 1897 to an admirer who had written a poem in her honor.

3 Breathe-in experience, breathe-out poetry.

MURIEL RUKEYSER (1913–1980), U.S. poet. "Poem Out of Childhood," line 1 (1935).

4 Poetry is important. No less than science, it seeks a hold upon reality, and the closeness of its approach is the test of its success.

BABETTE DEUTSCH (1895–1982), U.S. poet. *This Modern Poetry,* Foreword (1935).

5 When . . . I comprehended that poetry had no provision in it for ultimate practical attainment of the rightness of work that *is* truth, but led on ever only to a temporizing less-than-truth . . . I stopped.

LAURA (RIDING) JACKSON (1901– 1991), U.S. author. As quoted in *Contemporary Poets,* 3rd ed., by James Vinson (1980). On why she stopped writing poetry in 1939.

6 I cannot say what poetry is; I know that our sufferings and our concentrated joy, our states of plunging far and dark and turning to come back to the world—so that the moment of intense turning seems still and universal—all are here, in a music like the music of our time, like the hero and like the anonymous forgotten; and there is an exchange here in which our lives are met, and created.

MURIEL RUKEYSER (1913–1980), U.S. poet. *The Life of Poetry,* ch. 10 (1949).

7 Poetry, whose material is language, is perhaps the most human and least worldly of the arts, the one in which the end product remains closest to the thought that inspired it. . . . Of all things of thought, poetry is the closest to thought, and a poem is less a thing than any other work of art . . .

HANNAH ARENDT (1906–1975), U.S. philosopher. *The Human Condition,* ch. 23 (1958).

8 I have no connections here; only gusty collisions,
rootless seedlings forced into bloom, that collapse.

. . .

I am the Visiting Poet: a real unicorn,
a wind-up plush dodo, a wax museum of the Movement.
People want to push the buttons and see me glow.

MARGE PIERCY (b. 1936), U.S. poet, novelist, and political activist. "Three Weeks in a State of Loneliness," lines 22–23, 28–30 (1976). On a "Visiting Poet" stint at the University of Kansas. Piercy had been a prominent activist in the movement opposing the United States' involvement in the Vietnam War and had written many political poems.

9 For women . . . poetry is not a luxury. It is a vital necessity of our existence. It forms the quality of light within which we can predicate our hopes and dreams toward survival and change, first made into language, then into idea, then into more tangible action. Poetry is the way we help give name to the nameless so it can be thought. The farthest horizons of our hopes and fears are cobbled by our poems, carved from the rock experiences of our daily lives.

AUDRE LORDE (1934–1992), African American poet, autobiographer, and lesbian feminist. *Sister Outsider,* ch. 3 (1984). From "Poetry is Not a Luxury," an essay first published in *Chrysalis,* number 3 (1977).

10 Poetry is above all a concentration of the *power* of language, which is the power of our ultimate relationship to everything in the universe.

ADRIENNE RICH (b. 1929), U.S. poet, essayist, and feminist. *The Work of a Common Woman*, by Judy Grahn, introductory essay (1978).

11 The necessity of poetry has to be stated over and over, but only to those who have reason to fear its power, or those who still believe that language is "only words" and that an old language is good enough for our descriptions of the world we are trying to transform.

ADRIENNE RICH (b. 1929), U.S. poet, essayist, and feminist. *The Work of a Common Woman*, by Judy Grahn, preface: "Power and Danger," (1978).

12 I try to make a rough music, a dance of the mind, a calculus of the emotions, a driving beat of praise out of the pain and mystery that surround me and become me. My poems are meant to make your mind get up and shout.

JUDITH JOHNSON SHERWIN (b. 1936), U.S. poet. As quoted in *Contemporary Poets*, 3rd ed., by James Vinson (1980).

13 My verse forms are relatively traditional (traditions alter). In general they have moved away from strict classical patterns in the direction of greater freedom—as is usual with most artists learning a trade. It takes courage, however, to leave all props behind, to cast oneself, like Matisse, upon pure space. I still await that confidence.

FLEUR ADCOCK (b. 1934), New Zealand poet. As quoted in *Contemporary Poets*, 3rd ed., by James Vinson (1980).

Henri Matisse (1869–1954) was an important French painter, sculptor, and lithographer.

14 When I was a young girl salmon fishing with my father in the Straits of Juan de Fuca in Washington State I used to lean out over the water and try to look past my own face, past the reflection of the boat, past the sun and darkness, down to where the fish were surely swimming. I made up charm songs and word-hopes to tempt the fish, to cause them to mean biting my hook. I believed they would do it if I asked them well and patiently and with the right hope. I am writing my poems like this. I have used the fabric and the people of my life as the bait.

TESS GALLAGHER (b. 1944), U.S. poet. As quoted in *Contemporary Poets*, 3rd ed., by James Vinson (1980).

15 For me, poetry is always a search for order.

ELIZABETH JENNINGS (b. 1926), British poet. As quoted in *Contemporary Poets*, 3rd ed., by James Vinson (1980).

16 If I fail, it is difficult to believe that it matters. Poetry runs in our veins, and over the centuries will flower now here, now there. If it does not come from my pen it will come from another's.

RUTH DALLAS (b. 1919), U.S. poet. As quoted in *Contemporary Poets*, 3rd ed., by James Vinson (1980).

17 That I am a poet in an age where the "unintellectual" (i.e., almost everybody) think of poetry as some-

thing they didn't like when they were at school, and the intellectual think it something the masses should be excluded from, is sad for me. This age has far too much reverence for poetry and too little respect—for by the same token it is very difficult indeed to earn a living from poetry.

JENI COUZYN (b. 1942), South African poet; relocated to England. As quoted in *Contemporary Poets*, 3rd ed., by James Vinson (1980).

18 Poetry isn't a profession, it's a way of life. It's an empty basket; you put your life into it and make something out of that.

MARY OLIVER (b. 1935), U.S. poet. *Georgia Review*, p. 733 (Winter 1981).

19 . . . the attempt to control poetry, to subordinate it to extrapoetic ends, constitutes misuse. . . . it may be poetry's stubborn quality of rockbottom, intrinsic *uselessness* which . . . constitutes the guarantee of its integrity, and hence of its ultimate value to us.

JAN CLAUSEN (b. 1943), U.S. poet, fiction writer, and lesbian feminist. *A Movement of Poets* (1982).

Referring to some feminists' "political" use of poetry.

20 When one's not writing poems— and I'm not at the moment—you wonder how you ever did it. It's like another country you can't reach.

MAY SARTON (1912–1995), U.S. author. As quoted in *Women Writers Talking*, ch. 1, by Janet Todd (1983).

21 Poetry asks people to have values, form opinions, care about some other part of experience besides making money and being successful on the job.

TOI DERRICOTTE (b. 1941), African American poet. As quoted in *A Gift That Cannot Be Refused*, ch. 8, by Mary Biggs (1990). Written in 1983.

22 We tend to be so bombarded with information, and we move so quickly, that there's a tendency to treat everything on the surface level and process things quickly. This is antithetical to the kind of openness and perception you have to have to be receptive to poetry. . . . poetry seems to exist in a parallel universe outside daily life in America.

RITA DOVE (b. 1952), U.S. poet. As quoted in the *New York Times*, sect. 4, p. 7 (June 20, 1993).

23 Poetry is a matter of life, not just a matter of language.

LUCILLE CLIFTON (b. 1936), U.S. poet. As quoted in *Listen to Their Voices*, ch. 9, by Mickey Pearlman (1993).

24 Poetry uses the hub of a torque converter for a jello mold.

DIANE GLANCY (b. 1941), U.S. poet. As quoted in *What Is Found There*, ch. 12, by Adrienne Rich (1993).

25 Poetry transforms and redeems the common, the hurtful, the humiliating.

SUSAN MONTEZ (b. c. 1956), U.S. poet. As quoted in the *Chronicle of Higher Education*, p. A43 (July 13, 1994).

26 Poetry
makes nothing happen.
It survives
in the valley of its saying.

MAXINE KUMIN (b. 1925), U.S. poet.
"Lines Written in the Library of Congress After
the Cleanth Brooks Lecture," lines 224–227.
"Poetry/makes nothing happen" are, as Kumin
acknowledged, lines borrowed from W. H.
Auden's (1907–1973) poem, "In Memory of
W. B. Yeats."

POETRY AND WRITING

I I write poetry in order to live more
fully.

JUDITH RODRIGUEZ (b. 1936), Australian poet. As quoted in *Contemporary Poets*,
3rd ed., by James Vinson (1980).

POETS

I To be a poet is to have a soul so
quick to discern, that no shade of
quality escapes it, and so quick to
feel, that discernment is but a hand
playing with finely ordered variety
on the chords of emotion—a soul
in which knowledge passes instanta-
neously into feeling, and feeling
flashes back as a new organ of
knowledge. One may have that condition by fits only.

GEORGE ELIOT (1819–1880), British novelist. *Middlemarch*, ch. 22 (1871–1872).

2 Herman has taken to writing poetry. You need not tell anyone, for
you know how such things get
around.

ELIZABETH SHAW MELVILLE (1822–
1906), U.S. letter writer, wife of U.S. author
Herman Melville. As quoted in *The Life of Poetry*, ch. 1, by Muriel Rukeyser (1949).

Written in a letter to her mother. Melville
(1819–1891) wrote in several forms but was
known chiefly for his novels; of those, *Moby-
Dick* (1851) was his masterpiece, though it was
not immediately appreciated by the public. In
the last three decades of his life, he published a
number of poetic works.

3 Logic, reason, disease, and the menace of death, these things meant
nothing at all to us. We were committed to other values by which the
poet has always lived in defiance
of all that society demanded
of him.

KAY BOYLE (1903–1993), U.S. author. *Being Geniuses Together*, "Kay Boyle: 1926–
1928" chapter (1968).
Of her life in France in 1926 with Ernest Walsh,
expatriate editor of the important literary magazine *This Quarter*. They were living together in
poverty; Walsh was dying of the tuberculosis to
which he succumbed that October, at age
thirty-one; and Boyle, still married to another
man, was expecting Walsh's baby, who was
born after his death.

4 It is not possible, for a poet, writing
in any language, to protect himself
from the tragic elements in human
life. . . . [ellipsis in source] Illness,
old age, and death—subjects as ancient as humanity—these are the
subjects that the poet must speak of
very nearly from the first moment
that he begins to speak.

LOUISE BOGAN (1897–1970), U.S. poet.
As quoted in *Our Ground Time Here Will be
Brief*, Epigram, by Maxine Kumin (1982).

5 . . . the reason why there are so few
first-class poets is that many people
have intense feelings or first-class
minds but to get the two together
so that you will be willing to put a
poem through sixty drafts, to be
that self-critical, to keep breaking it

down, that is what is rare. Right now most poetry is just self-indulgence.

MAY SARTON (1912–1995), U.S. author. As quoted in *Women Writers Talking*, ch. 1, by Janet Todd (1983).

6 Perceiving myself through others' ideas of what it means to be a woman has made it difficult for me to achieve the necessary commitment [to be a poet].

NAOMI CLARK (b. 1932), U.S. poet. As quoted in *A Gift That Cannot Be Refused*, ch. 2, by Mary Biggs (1990). Written in 1983 in a questionnaire response.

7 Can you remember? when we thought
the poets taught how to live?

ADRIENNE RICH (b. 1929), U.S. poet and essayist. "Poetry: I," lines 15–16 (1985).

8 A poet can read. A poet can write. A poet is African in Africa, or Irish in Ireland, or French on the left bank of Paris, or white in Wisconsin. A poet writes in her own language. A poet writes of her own people, her own history, her own vision, her own room, her own house where she sits at her own table quietly placing one word after another word until she builds a line and a movement and an image and a meaning that somersaults all of these into the singing, the absolutely individual voice of the poet: at liberty. A poet is somebody free. A poet is someone at home. How should there be Black poets in America?

JUNE JORDAN (b. 1936), African American poet and social critic. *On Call*, ch. 11 (1985).

9 . . . to a poet, the human community is like the community of birds to a bird, singing to each other. Love is one of the reasons we are singing to one another, love of language itself, love of sound, love of singing itself, and love of the other birds.

SHARON OLDS (b. 1942), U.S. poet. As quoted in *Listen to Their Voices*, ch. 18 (1993). On why writing poetry, though "always difficult," is easier than not writing it.

POLITICAL CORRECTNESS

1 Trying to be a perfect feminist . . . is not really a big improvement on trying to be a perfect wife, mother, and lady.

JANE O'REILLY, U.S. feminist and humorist. *The Girl I Left Behind*, ch. 7 (1980). O'Reilly, a free-lance writer, won her first major notice with her humorous essays in *Ms.* magazine.

2 When my dreams showed signs
of becoming
politically correct
no unruly images
escaping beyond borders
. . .
then I began to wonder

ADRIENNE RICH (b. 1929), U.S. poet and feminist. "North American Time," sect. 1, lines 1–5 and 10 (1983).

3 What I think the political correctness debate is really about is the power to be able to define. The definers want the power to name. And the defined are now taking that power away from them.

TONI MORRISON (b. 1931), African American novelist and essayist. As quoted in the *New York Times Magazine*, p. 74 (September 11, 1994).

POLITICAL PARTIES

1 I care nothing for all the political parties in the world except as they stand for justice.

ANNA HOWARD SHAW (1847–1919), U.S. suffragist. As quoted in *The Life and Work of Susan B. Anthony*, ch. 43, by Ida Husted Harper (1898–1908).
Said in 1894.

2 If you believe that a nation is really better off which achieves for a comparative few, those who are capable of attaining it, high culture, ease, opportunity, and that these few from their enlightenment should give what they consider best to those less favored, then you naturally belong to the Republican Party. But if you believe that people must struggle slowly to the light for themselves, then it seems to me that you are a Democrat.

ELEANOR ROOSEVELT (1884–1962), First Lady of the United States, author, speaker, and diplomat. As quoted in *Eleanor and Franklin*, ch. 27, by Joseph P. Lash (1971).
Roosevelt wrote this before her husband, Franklin Delano Roosevelt, had yet been elected President.

POLITICIANS: MEN

1 It's all sorts of middle-aged white men in suits—forests of middle-aged men in dark suits. All slightly

red-faced from eating and drinking too much.

DIANE ABBOTT (b. 1953), Black British politician. As quoted in *Newsweek* magazine, p. 15 (June 13, 1988).
The only black woman Member of Parliament, she was describing her colleagues.

POLITICIANS: WOMEN

1 I'm not into smoke-filled rooms. I don't have the time for byzantine political intrigues.

BENAZIR BHUTTO (b. 1953), Pakistani politician. As quoted in *Newsweek* magazine, p. 34 (July 7, 1986).
The daughter of Zulfikar Ali Bhutto (1928–1979), a Pakistani President who was overthrown and hanged, she was intent on unseating the responsible parties. She would become the first woman President of Pakistan.

2 [When asked, as a prospective Presidential candidate, whether she had ever committed adultery:] No. But then most congresswomen don't have 25-year-old lifeguards throwing themselves at their feet around this place.

PATRICIA SCHROEDER (b. 1940), U.S. politician. As quoted in *Newsweek* magazine, p. 11 (August 10, 1987).
Schroeder was, of course, implying that Congressmen had more sexual opportunities, and temptations, than Congresswomen.

3 All I really want to be is boring. When people talk about me, I'd like them to say, "Carol's basically a short Bill Bradley." Or, "Carol's kind of like Al Gore in a skirt."

CAROL MOSELEY-BRAUN (b. 1947), African American politician. As quoted in *Newsweek* magazine, p. 21 (February 8, 1993).
Moseley-Braun, a new United States Senator from Illinois, was reacting to the exaggerated attention she was receiving as the first African American woman United States Senator. Bill

Bradley (b. 1943), a Senator from New Jersey, and Vice-President Al Gore (b. 1948), formerly a Senator from Tennessee, were, like Moseley-Braun, liberal and comparatively young Democrats; both were also white, rather staid, pedestrian public speakers, and unsullied by personal scandal.

4 When I first got here, every time you'd say "breast feeding" on the House floor there would be a snicker. . . . this has been happening since creation. Can we finally get a grip on it?

SUSAN MOLINARI (b. 1958), U.S. politician. As quoted in the *New York Times*, p. B7 (March 18, 1993).

On discussions of women's health issues in the United States House of Representatives, where she began serving as a Representative from Staten Island, New York, in March 1990. Molinari was one of only twelve women among the 176 Republican Representatives.

POLITICS

1 What people do who go into politics I can't think; it drives me almost mad to see mismanagement over only a few hundred acres.

GEORGE ELIOT (1819–1880), British novelist. *Middlemarch*, ch. 40 (1871–1872).

Said by the novel's character named Caleb Garth, a property manager.

2 A political place with no power, only influence, is not to my taste.

ELLEN HENRIETTA SWALLOW RICHARDS, (1842–1911) U.S. chemist and educator. As quoted in *The Life of Ellen H. Richards*, ch. 10, by Caroline L. Hunt (1912).

Said c. 1885. Richards was explaining why she did not wish to become Supervisor of Schools in Boston.

3 *Party action should follow, not precede* the creation of a dominant popular sentiment.

J. ELLEN FOSTER (1840–1910), U.S. attorney, temperance activist, and suffragist. *What America Owes to Women*, ch. 33 (1893).

4 I would not have a woman go to Congress merely because she is a woman.

CRYSTAL EASTMAN (1881–1928), U.S. social/political activist and author. *On Women and Revolution*, (1978). Quoted in an article by Elisabeth Smith, which was reprinted in the Appendix: "Feminist for Equality, Not 'Women as Women'," *New York Telegram and Evening Mail* (October 21, 1924).

Eastman was secretary of the Women for Congress Campaign Committee of the National Woman's Party (NWP) and was explaining that she supported the NWP's candidates only because they were capable people and because the NWP strongly backed the Equal Rights Amendment to the Constitution (which was never passed). Only four years earlier, the Nineteenth Amendment to the Constitution had taken effect, enfranchising American women after a 72–year struggle for suffrage.

5 You can't make a souffle rise twice.

ALICE ROOSEVELT LONGWORTH (1884–1980), U.S. socialite; daughter of President Theodore Roosevelt. As quoted in *A Dictionary of Contemporary American History*, by Stanley Hochman and Eleanor Hochman (1993).

Said in 1948 on the defeat of Republican Thomas H. Dewey in that year's Presidential election, by incumbent President Harry S. Truman. In 1944, Dewey had been defeated by Longworth's kinsman, Franklin Delano Roosevelt.

6 Whether you want it or not, your genes have a political past, your skin a political tone. your eyes a political color.

. . .

you walk with political steps on political ground.

WISLAWA SZYMBORSKA (b. 1923), Polish poet. "Children of the Epoch," lines 6–9, 14–15, translated by Grazyna Drabik and Austin Flint.

On Poland during the Communist era. I know that Symborska's first book of poetry was published in 1948, but I don't know whether this poem was in it. In any event, that book was attacked by her government and had to be withdrawn. Neither do I know the date of the translation.

On Republican Ed Meese's investigating the "Iran-contra scandal," which, critics alleged, involved illegal, secret agreements by the administration of President Ronald Reagan, probably with the full knowledge of Vice-President George Bush, who was considered likely to be the next Republican Presidential nominee. (He won the Presidency in 1988.)

7   It has been years since I have seen anyone who could even look as if he were in love. No one's face lights up any more except for political conversation.

MARGARET ANDERSON (1886–1973), U.S. editor and memoirist. *The Fiery Fountains,* part 1 (1951).

8   Make Policy Not Coffee

FEMINIST POLITICAL BUTTON, C. 1970, ?.

9   I have never felt a placard and a poem are in any way similar.

KRISTIN HUNTER (b. 1931), African American author. *Black Women Writers at Work,* ch. 6, by Claudia Tate (1983).

On why her writing was not directly "political."

10   People would say, "We need a man on the ticket."

PATRICIA SCHROEDER (b. 1940), U.S. politician. As quoted in *Newsweek* magazine, p. 19 (April 27, 1987).

Schroeder, a Democratic Congresswoman from Colorado, was giving a tongue-in-cheek explanation of why she thought Republican Presidential nominee George Bush would not choose a woman running mate.

11   If he had been sent to check out Bluebeard's castle, he would have come back with a glowing report about the admirable condition of the cutlery.

MARY MCGRORY (b. 1918), U.S. newspaper columnist. As quoted in *Newsweek* magazine, p. 11 (August 10, 1987).

POLITICS AND POWER

1   There never seems to be any difficulty in stretching the laws and the constitution to fit any kind of a political deal, but when it is proposed to make some concession to women they loom up like an unscalable wall.

SUSAN B. ANTHONY (1820–1906), U.S. suffragist. As quoted in *Life and Work of Susan B. Anthony,* vol. 3, ch. 54, by Ida Husted Harper (1908).

Said in November 1899, of men's resistance to putting women on the school board in Rochester, New York.

2   ... the word "education" has an evil sound in politics; there is a pretense of education,
when the real purpose is coercion without the use of force.

HANNAH ARENDT (1906–1975), U.S. philosopher and political theorist; born in Germany. *Between Past and Future,* ch. 5 (1961).

3   My function in life is not to be a politician in Parliament: it is to get something done.

BERNADETTE DEVLIN (b. 1947), Irish politician and activist. *The Price of My Soul,* ch. 13 (1969).

The fiery young activist had just been elected to Parliament.

4   ... the art of politics is to be ahead of your time—about six months will do it. Any more than that, and people forget you were there.

GLORIA STEINEM (b. 1934), U.S. feminist, author, and editor. As quoted in *Ms.* magazine, p. 41 (October 1972).

Steinem was thinking of Senator (and Democratic Presidential candidate) George McGovern's often-unacknowledged, early opposition to American involvement in the Vietnam War.

5 When feminism does not explicitly oppose racism, and when antiracism does not incorporate opposition to patriarchy, race and gender politics often end up being antagonistic to each other and both interests lose.

KIMBERLÉ CRENSHAW (b. 1959), African American author. *Race-ing Justice, En-gendering Power,* ch. 14 (1992).

6 The man who promised to reinforce American families is now eager to pull the plug on Big Bird and Barney.

LESLIE HARRIS, U.S. political activist. As quoted in *Newsweek* magazine, p. 23 (December 19, 1994).

Harris, a spokesperson for the liberal organization People for the American Way, was referring to conservative Congressman Newt Gingrich's (b. 1943) wish to cut funding for the Public Broadcasting System. Among the popular programs on federally-subsidized PBS were two trailblazing children's shows: *Sesame Street,* which featured a character named Big Bird; and *Barney and Friends,* starring a purple dinosaur named Barney. Gingrich's opposition to public television was especially significant because he was about to become Speaker of the House of Representatives and because he and his like-minded colleagues were vocal exponents of "family values."

POLITICS AND WOMEN

1 . . . the black woman can never forget—however lukewarm the party may to-day appear—that it was a Republican president who struck the manacles from her own wrists and gave the possibilities of manhood to her helpless little ones; and to her mind the Democratic Negro is a traitor and a time-server.

ANNA JULIA COOPER (1859–1964), African American educator and feminist. *A Voice from the South,* part 1 (1892).

Cooper was born to a slave and her white master.

2 It's not that we want the political jobs themselves . . . but they seem to be the only language the men understand. We don't really want these $200 a year jobs. But the average man doesn't understand working for a cause.

JENNIE CAROLYN VAN NESS, (b. c. 1890– ?) U.S. educator, suffragist, and politician. As quoted in *Past and Promise,* part 3, by Susan Booker Welsh and Gloria S. Dittman (1990).

After suffrage was granted to women in 1919, Van Ness became involved in Republican politics in Essex County, New Jersey; in 1920, she and Margaret B. Laird became the first women elected to the New Jersey State legislature.

3 It is not so much that women have a different point of view in politics as that they give a different emphasis. And this is vastly important, for politics is so largely a matter of emphasis.

CRYSTAL EASTMAN (1881–1928), U.S. social/political activist and author. *On Women and Revolution,* part 1 (1978). From an article first published in *Time and Tide* on June 5, 1925.

American women had gained the right to vote only five years earlier.

4 I would like to be the first ambassador to the United States *from* the United States.

BARBARA MIKULSKI (b. 1936), U.S. politician. As quoted in *Ms.* magazine, p. 108 (November 1973).

At the time, the former liberal United States Congresswoman was serving on the Baltimore City Council and as head of the Commission on Delegate Selection and Party Structure of the Democratic National Committee.

5 . . . by and large, wife-changing and high office are not compatible. This inequity accounts for the many dull women in Washington and is the cause of much smug complacency on the distaff side of political marriages.

BARBARA HOWAR (b. 1934), U.S. socialite and author. *Laughing all the Way,* ch. 6 (1973).

Howar was a Washington socialite who had had an adulterous affair with a United States Senator.

6 I never felt I left the stage.

HELEN GAHAGAN DOUGLAS (1900–1980), U.S. actor, opera singer, and politician. As quoted in *Center Stage,* ch. 13, by Ingrid Winther Scobie (1992).

Said in 1976.

7 The presidency has become a series of visuals I don't know how a woman fits into.

PATRICIA SCHROEDER (b. 1940), U.S. politician. As quoted in *Newsweek* magazine, p. 13 (September 25, 1989).

A U. S. Representative from Colorado, Schroeder had briefly been a candidate for the Democratic Presidential nomination. She was criticized for weeping openly, an event caught on camera and widely publicized.

8 I am available to make love with Saddam Hussein to achieve peace in the Middle East.

ILONA STALLER (b. 1951), Italian politician and pornographic movie star. As quoted in *Newsweek* magazine, p. 15 (September 3, 1990).

Staller was serving as Deputy of the Italian Radical Party; Hussein was the President of Iraq.

9 I think it's about time we voted for senators with breasts. After all, we've been voting for boobs long enough.

CLAIRE SARGENT, U.S. politician. As quoted in *Newsweek* magazine, p. 27 (October 5, 1992).

At the time, Sargent was a senatorial candidate in Arizona.

10 I am not a jogger. I'm not a photo opportunity kind of person. I am at an age where I have better sense than to make a fool of myself.

LYNN SCHENK, U.S. politician. As quoted in the *New York Times,* p. A12 (July 26, 1993).

The United States Representative (Democrat—California) was explaining why she had declined an invitation to go jogging with President Bill Clinton. Politicians had been attempting to win jogging invitations ever since Clinton's inauguration and had often been embarrassed by their inability to keep up with him; a "straggler van" had to accompany the jogs to pick up those joggers who had dropped out.

11 . . . people will sometimes say, "Why don't you write more politics?" And I have to explain to them that writing the lives of women *is* politics.

GRACE PALEY (b. 1922), U.S. story writer, poet, and peace activist. As quoted in *Listen to Their Voices,* ch. 1, by Mickey Pearlman (1993).

12 . . . there has been a very special man in my life for the past year. All I'll say about him is that he's kind, warm, mature, someone I can trust—and he's not a politician.

DONNA RICE (b. c. 1962), U.S. model and actress. As quoted in *People* magazine, p. 266 (March 7–14, 1994).

In 1987, Rice had been pursued by the news media and abandoned by her lover, Gary Hart. a married U.S. Senator and candidate for the Democratic Presidential nomination, after public disclosure of their affair.

POLITICS: FAMILY

1   When your parents are in political life, you aren't normal. Everybody talks about the benefits, but I don't know what the benefits are. . . . But I'd rather have that kind of mother than an overweight housewife.

KATHERINE BERMAN MARIANO (b. 1957), U.S. housewife. As quoted in *Dianne Feinstein*, ch. 6, by Jerry Roberts (1994).

The only child of Dianne Feinstein (b. 1933), former San Francisco Mayor and current United States Senator from California, Mariano was reflecting on the resulting unwelcome attention she had received as a child and adolescent, as well as on her upbringing by a time-pressed mother and a succession of babysitters. Feinstein was known for being slim, stylish, and attractive.

PORNOGRAPHY

1   Pornography is a theatre of types, never of individuals.

SUSAN SONTAG (b. 1933), U.S. author. "The Pornographic Imagination," (1967).

2   *Pornography is the theory, and rape the practice.*

ROBIN MORGAN (b. 1941), U.S. author, feminist, and child actor. *The Word of a Woman*, part 1 (1992). Written in 1974.

3   . . . porn [is] . . . anything that people are ashamed of getting a kick out of.

NORA EPHRON (b. 1941), U.S. author and humorist. *Scribble Scrabble*, ch. 12 (1978). Written in 1976.

4   I think if a woman has a right to an abortion and to control her body, then she has the right to exploit her body and make money from it. We have it hard enough. Why give up one of our major assets?

KATHY KEETON (b. 1939), U.S. magazine publisher. As quoted in *Newsweek* magazine, p. 15 (December 16, 1991).

Keeton, president of the highly risque and controversial *Penthouse* magazine, was defending nude photographs of women.

5   What could I do? I couldn't paint, I couldn't write poetry. What could I do to make him sit up?

DOMINIQUE AURY [PAULINE RÉAGE], (b. 1908) French journalist. As quoted in the *New Yorker*, p. 43 (August 1, 1994).

On why, more than forty years earlier, she had written *The Story of O*, a sadomasochistic, pornographic romance, for her lover Jean Paulhan. A renowned intellectual more than twenty years her senior, he had arranged for its publication under the pseudonym Pauline Réage.

POVERTY

1   Talk of politeness when humanity is perishing—of the sacred sphere of woman when thousands of my sisters are prostitutes—how many from necessity, God only knows. I have not the least patience with the exquisite dandy and the fashionable flirt attempting to define proprieties—they have money, let them define *dollars*. Neither have I patience with a set of croakers who *regret* the present state of things; but how can it be helped? say they with a yawn.

Look at your widowed sister struggling to preserve a home—the hectic on that cheek, produced by overtasking her physical strength, tells you death will soon set his seal upon her. Look at that married woman—sleepless nights and toilsome days cloud her brow and irritate her temper. Shall woman's voice be hushed when woman's shrieks are heard? Shall woman quench her light, when clouds of invisible sorrows gather thick round woman's head?

HARRIOT K. HUNT (1805–1875), U.S. physician and feminist. *Glances and Glimpses,* ch. 18 (1856).

2 We all bear traces of the starvation struggle which for so long made up the life of the race. Our very organism holds memories and glimpses of that long life of our ancestors which still goes on among so many of our contemporaries. Nothing so deadens the sympathies and shrivels the power of enjoyment as the persistent keeping away from the great opportunities for helpfulness and a continual ignoring of the starvation struggle which makes up the life of at least half the race. To shut one's self away from that half of the race life is to shut one's self away from the most vital part of it; it is to live out but half the humanity to which we have been born heir.

JANE ADDAMS (1860–1935), U.S. social worker and social reformer. *Twenty Years at Hull-House,* ch. 6 (1910).

From a lecture, "The Subjective Necessity for Social Settlements," delivered in 1892 at a summer school run by the Ethical Culture Society. Addams was the founding director of Hull-House, a pioneer "settlement house" in a poor, largely immigrant, Chicago neighborhood.

3 The poor are always ragged and dirty, in very picturesque clothes, and on their poor shoes lies the earth of the Lacustrine period. And yet what a privilege it is to be even a beggar in Rome!

M. E. W. SHERWOOD (1826–1903), U.S. socialite, traveller, and author. *An Epistle to Posterity,* ch. 14 (1897).

Sherwood, a born-rich member of New York City "society," seldom expressed such a romantic view of the poor, though she was always condescendingly benign toward them.

4 . . . money trials are not the hardest, and somehow or other, they are always overcome.

AMELIA E. BARR (1831–1919), U.S. author; born in Scotland. *All the Days of My Life,* ch. 15 (1913).

Recalling a period of severe economic stress when she had six young children; serious illnesses were afflicting the family; her husband's employment was uncertain; and Texas, where they were living, was being rent by the Civil War.

5 . . . nothing seems completely to differentiate the poor but poverty. We find no adjectives to fit them, as a whole, only those of which Want is the mother. "Miserable" covers many; "shabby" most, and I am sadly aware that, in a large majority of minds, "disagreeable" includes them all.

ALBION FELLOWS BACON (1865–1933), U.S. social worker and housing reform advocate. *Beauty for Ashes,* ch. 6 (1914).

Reacting against the common belief that the poor typically were "lazy, shiftless, improvident, spendthrift, intemperate, lacking in honour, in honesty."

6 The daily lesson of slum life, visualised, reiterated, of low standards, vile living, obscenity, profanity, impurity, is bound to be dwarfing and debasing to the children who are in the midst of it.

ALBION FELLOWS BACON (1865–1933), U.S. social worker and housing reform advocate. *Beauty for Ashes,* ch. 6 (1914).

7 . . . we see the poor as a mass of shadow, painted in one flat grey wash, at the remote edges of our sunshine.

ALBION FELLOWS BACON (1865–1933), U.S. social worker and housing reform advocate. *Beauty for Ashes,* ch. 6 (1914).

8 With the present wage conditions there are thousands of young women who are living in a state of semi-starvation and they are always surrounded by the most terrible temptation. Oh, I know that some of [the] greatest reformers insist that a girl's virtue is not affected by under-nourishment, disease and nervous collapse; but if these well housed, well fed, well dressed people were put in a dirty, ugly room, if their clothes did not protect them from the cold, if their stomachs were never filled, would not even the staunchest lose some of her self-respect when looking forward to an old age? It is only a matter of wonder to me that so many girls keep clean and decent through it all.

CORA ANDERSON, U.S. male impersonator. As quoted in *Gay American History,* part 3, by Jonathan Katz (1976).

Said in 1914; for the previous thirteen years, Anderson had successfully impersonated a man, permitting her to earn a better living than she could as a woman.

9 Poor America, of what avail is all her wealth, if the individuals comprising the nation are wretchedly poor? If they live in squalor, in filth, in crime, with hope and joy gone, a homeless, soilless army of human prey.

EMMA GOLDMAN (1869–1940), U.S. anarchist and author; born in Russia. *Anarchism and Other Essays,* 3rd rev. ed., ch. 1 (1917).

10 Making the best of things is . . . a damn poor way of dealing with them. . . . My whole life has been a series of escapes from that quicksand [ellipses in source].

ROSE WILDER LANE (1886–1968), U.S. author. As quoted in *The Ghost in the Little House,* ch. 3, by William V. Holtz (1993).

In letters to Guy Moyston dated August 25, 1924, and July 11, 1925. The daughter of Laura Ingalls Wilder, author of the famous "Little House" books for children, Lane had grown up very poor.

11 What matters poverty? What matters anything to him who is "enamoured" of our art? Does he not carry in himself every joy and every beauty?

SARAH BERNHARDT (1845–1923), French actor. *The Art of the Theatre,* ch. 3 (1924).

The "art" she spoke of was dramatic theater.

12 . . . hunger and cold, ill-health and pain are nothing. They pass. The thing that remains is ignorant criticism, well-meaning but futile advice, the contempt of a subordinate, the feelings of the underdog.

ALICE FOOTE MACDOUGALL, (1867–1945) U.S. businesswoman. *The Autobiography of a Business Woman,* ch. 7 (1928).

On her reactions to the period of poverty that followed her affluent childhood and preceded her eventual business success.

13 Very early in my childhood I associated poverty, toil, unemployment, drunkenness, cruelty, quarreling, fighting, debts, jail with large families.

MARGARET SANGER (1879–1966), U.S. birth control advocate. *My Fight for Birth Control,* ch. 1 (1931).

Sanger, one of eleven children in a financially stressed family, became the first prominent advocate of birth control and of the dissemination (then illegal) of birth control information.

14 If you've ever been without money, or food, something very strange happens when you get a bit of money, a kind of madness. You don't care. You can't remember that you had no money before, that the money will be gone. You can remember nothing but that there is the money for which you have been suffering. Now here it is. A lust takes hold of you. You see food in the windows. In imagination you eat hugely; you taste a thousand meals. You look in windows. Colors are brighter; you buy something to dress up in. An excitement takes hold of you. You know it is suicide but you can't help it. You must have food, dainty, splendid food and a bright hat so once again you feel blithe, rid of that ratty gnawing shame.

MERIDEL LE SUEUR (b. 1900), U.S. author. *Women on the Breadlines* (1932).

Written in America during the Great Depression.

15 . . . it is only after years and years that you can speak of penury in the midst of opulence, of hunger in the midst of almost sinful plenty. You must never speak of the immediate experience unless and until you have learned its consequent value. Otherwise you grow old in bitterness which is barren and futile. . . .

E. M. ALMEDINGEN (1898–1971), Russian author. *Tomorrow Will Come,* ch. 2 (1936–1937).

Remembering the Russian Revolution, during which she and her affluent family were living in St. Petersburg, Russia, and lost all of their wealth.

16 We are things of dry hours and the involuntary plan,
Grayed in, and gray. "Dream"
makes a giddy sound, not strong
Like "rent," "feeding a wife," "satisfying a man."

GWENDOLYN BROOKS (b. 1917), African American poet and fiction writer. "Kitchenette building," lines 1–3 (1945).

A Chicago native, Brooks wrote about African American inner-city neighborhoods.

17 We have been weakened in our resistance to the professional anti-Communists because we know in our hearts that our so-called democracy has excluded millions of citizens from a normal life and the normal American privileges of health, housing and education.

AGNES E. MEYER (1887–1970), U.S. journalist. *Out of These Roots,* ch. 14 (1953).

18 I am very much afraid that to the fiction writer the fact that we shall always have the poor with us is a source of satisfaction, for it means, essentially, that he will always be able to find someone like himself.

FLANNERY O'CONNOR (1925–1964), U.S. fiction writer and essayist. *Mystery and Manners,* part 4 (1969). Written in 1963.

19 My family's lives were not on television, not in books, not even comic books. There was a myth of the poor in this country, but it did not include us, no matter how hard I tried to squeeze us in. There was an idea of the good poor—hard-working, ragged but clean, and intrinsically honorable. I understood that we were the bad poor . . .

DOROTHY ALLISON (b. 1949), U.S. author and lesbian feminist. *Skin,* ch. 2 (1994).

Allison described her poor, violence-ridden Southern childhood in her well-received autobiographical novel, *Bastard Out of Carolina* (1992).

POWER

1 I do not wish [women] to have power over men, but over themselves.

MARY WOLLSTONECRAFT (1759–1797), British author and feminist. *Vindication of the Rights of Woman,* ch. 4 (1792).

2 A sense of power is the most intoxicating stimulant a mortal can enjoy . . .

ELLEN HENRIETTA SWALLOW RICHARDS, (1842–1911) U.S. chemist and educator. As quoted in *The Life of Ellen H. Richards,* ch. 11, by Caroline L. Hunt (1912).

Written in the 1870s. Richards had in mind the "sense of power" derived from a strong education.

3 There is a Restlessness springing from the consciousness of power not fully utilized, which must be present wherever there is unused power of whatever kind. This is the restlessness of the germ within the seed, struggling upward and downward towards its proper life. . . . it is a striving full of pain, the cutting of tender flesh by the fetters of the captive as he struggles against their pitilessness.

ANNA C. BRACKETT (1836–1911), U.S. author. *The Technique of Rest,* ch. 4 (1892).

4 . . . people with heavy physical vibrations rule the world.

MARGARET ANDERSON (1886–1973), U.S. literary editor and autobiographer. *My Thirty Years' War,* ch. 6 (1930).

5 . . . the power-loving temperament is more dangerous when it either prefers or is forced to operate in what is materially a void. We have everything to dread from the dispossessed.

ELIZABETH BOWEN (1899–1973), British author; born in Ireland. *Bowen's Court,* afterword (1942).

6 Power corrupts . . . when the weak band together in order to ruin the strong, but not before. The will to power . . . far from being a characteristic of the strong, is, like envy and greed, among the vices of the weak, and possibly even their most dangerous one.

HANNAH ARENDT (1906–1975), U.S. philosopher. *The Human Condition,* ch. 28 (1958).

7 Dead power is everywhere among us—in the forest, chopping down the songs; at night in the industrial landscape, wasting and stiffening the new life; in the streets of the city, throwing away the day. We wanted something different for our people: not to find ourselves an old, reactionary republic, full of ghost-fears, the fears of death and the fears of birth. We want something else.

MURIEL RUKEYSER (1913–1980), U.S. poet. As quoted in *What is Found There*, page preceding preface, by Adrienne Rich (1993).

8 Popular culture entered my life as Shirley Temple, who was exactly my age and wrote a letter in the newspapers telling how her mother fixed spinach for her, with lots of butter. . . . I was impressed by Shirley Temple as a little girl my age who had power: she could write a piece for the newspapers and have it printed in her own handwriting.

ADRIENNE RICH (b. 1929), U.S. poet, essayist, and lesbian feminist. *What Is Found There*, ch. 21 (1993).

Shirley Temple (b. 1928), who in fact was slightly older than Rich, was an extremely popular child movie performer.

9 . . . anything a powerful group has is perceived as good, no matter what it is, and anything a less powerful group has is not so good, no matter how intrinsically great it might be.

GLORIA STEINEM (b. 1934), U.S. feminist, author, and editor. *Moving Beyond Words*, part 1 (1994).

10 . . . members of a powerful group are raised to believe (however illogically) that whatever affects it will also affect them. On the other hand, members of less powerful groups are raised to believe (however illogically) that each individual can escape the group's fate. Thus, cohesion is encouraged on the one hand, and disunity is fostered on the other.

GLORIA STEINEM (b. 1934), U.S. feminist, author, and editor. *Moving Beyond Words*, part 6 (1994).

11 It is an absolute impossibility in this society to reversely sexually objectify heterosexual men, just as it is impossible for a poor person of color to be a racist. Such extreme prejudice must be accompanied by the power of society's approval and legislation. While women and poor people of color may become intolerant, personally abusive, even hateful, they do not have enough power to be racist or sexist.

ANA CASTILLO (b. 1953), Mexican–American poet, essayist, and feminist. *Massacre of the Dreamers*, ch. 6 (1994).

POWER: NEGATIVE ASPECTS

1 I am more and more convinced that man is a dangerous creature; and that power, whether vested in many or a few, is ever grasping, and, like the grave, cries, "Give, give!" The great fish swallow up the small; and he who is most strenuous for the rights of the people, when vested with power, is as eager

after the prerogatives of government. You tell me of degrees of perfection to which human nature is
capable of arriving, and I believe it,
but at the same time lament that
our admiration should arise from
the scarcity of the instances.

ABIGAIL ADAMS (1744–1818), U.S. matriarch; wife and mother of United States President. *Familiar Letters of John Adams and His
Wife Abigail Adams, During the Revolution,* letter dated November 27, 1775 (1875).

In a letter to her husband John Adams, who was
away fighting in the American colonies' revolution against Britain.

2   Every white man in this country has
been raised with a false sense of
power.

ROXANNE DUNBAR (b. 1938), U.S. feminist. *Female Liberation as the Basis for Social
Revolution,* [unpaginated pamphlet] (1969).

PRAYER

1   Does any one suppose that private
prayer is necessarily candid—necessarily goes to the roots of action!
Private prayer is inaudible speech,
and speech is representative: who
can represent himself just as he is,
even in his own reflections?

GEORGE ELIOT (1819–1880), British novelist. *Middlemarch,* ch. 70 (1871–1872).

2   I have always found that when men
have exhausted their own resources,
they fall back on "the intentions of
the Creator." But their platitudes
have ceased to have any influence
with those women who believe they
have the same facilities for communication with the Divine mind as
men have.

ELIZABETH CADY STANTON (1815–
1902), U.S. suffragist, social reformer, and author. As quoted in *History of Woman Suffrage,*
vol. 4, ch. 7, by Susan B. Anthony and Ida
Husted Harper (1902).

In a letter read before the nineteenth annual
convention of the National Woman Suffrage Association, held in Washington, D.C., January
1887. Stanton was referring to the antisuffrage
argument that God did not intend women to
have equal rights.

3   Your organization is not a praying
institution. It's a fighting institution. It's an educational institution
right along industrial lines. Pray for
the dead and fight like hell for the
living!

MOTHER JONES (1830–1930), U.S. labor
organizer. *The Autobiography of Mother Jones,*
ch. 6 (1925).

Commanding members of a miners' union in
the Fairmont district of West Virginia to leave
the church where they were meeting and gather
instead in the fields.

PREJUDICE

1   How prone we are to come to the
consideration of every question
with heads and hearts pre-occupied!
How prone to shrink from any
opinion, however reasonable, if it
be opposed to any, however unreasonable, of our own! How disposed
are we to judge, in anger, those who
call upon us to think, and encourage us to enquire! To question our
prejudices seems nothing less than
sacrilege; to break the chains of our
ignorance, nothing short of impiety!

FRANCES WRIGHT (1795–1852),
Scottish author and speaker; relocated to
America. *Course of Popular Lectures,* lecture 1
(1829).

2 If the underdog were always right, one might quite easily try to defend him. The trouble is that very often he is but obscurely right, sometimes only partially right, and often quite wrong; but perhaps he is never so altogether wrong and pig-headed and utterly reprehensible as he is represented to be by those who add the possession of prejudices to the other almost insuperable difficulties of understanding him.

JANE ADDAMS (1860–1935), U.S. social worker and social reformer. *Twenty Years at Hull-House,* ch. 17 (1910).

3 This philosophy of hate, of religious and racial intolerance, with its passionate urge toward war, is loose in the world. It is the enemy of democracy; it is the enemy of all the fruitful and spiritual sides of life. It is our responsibility, as individuals and organizations, to resist this.

MARY HEATON VORSE (1874–1966), U.S. journalist and labor activist. *A Footnote to Folly,* ch. 25 (1935).

4 If people are informed they will do the right thing. It's when they are not informed that they become hostages to prejudice.

CHARLAYNE HUNTER-GAULT (b. 1942), African American journalist. As quoted in *I Dream a World,* by Brian Lanker (1989). In 1961, Hunter-Gault (then Hunter) had been one of two African American students to integrate the University of Georgia. She went on to become a journalist and television news correspondent, covering, among other issues, apartheid in South Africa.

5 . . . prejudice marks a mental land mine.

GLORIA STEINEM (b. 1934), U.S. feminist, author, and editor. *Moving Beyond Words,* part 2 (1994).

PRIDE

1 . . . pride is not a bad thing when it only urges us to hide our own hurts—not to hurt others.

GEORGE ELIOT (1819–1880), British novelist. *Middlemarch,* ch. 6 (1871–1872).

2 You can be slum-born and slum-bred and still achieve something worth while; but it is a stupid inverted snobbishness to be proud of it. If one had a right to be proud of anything, it would be of a continued decent tradition back of one.

KATHERINE FULLERTON GEROULD (1879–1944), U.S. author. *Modes and Morals,* ch. 4 (1920).

3 The people who resent me do so because I'm a woman, I'm young, and I'm a Bhutto. Well, the simple answer is, it doesn't matter that I'm a woman, it doesn't matter that I'm young, and it's a matter of pride that I'm a Bhutto.

BENAZIR BHUTTO (b. 1953), Pakistani politician. As quoted in *Newsweek* magazine, p. 33 (July 7, 1986). The daughter of Zulfikar Ali Bhutto (1928–1979), a Pakistani President who was overthrown and hanged, she would become the first woman President of Pakistan.

4 When I show my grandchildren, I have a wonderful feeling of pride. I say, "See that crane way, way up there? Grandma used to run a crane like that during the war."

JENNETTE HYMAN NUTTALL, U.S. (former) crane operator. As quoted in *A Mouthful of Rivets*, Introduction, by Nancy Baker Wise and Christy Wise (1994).

Nuttall was one of the many women who were welcomed into traditionally male trades during World War II, filling in for men who were needed in military service. Most of these women were ejected from their jobs—some willingly, others unwillingly—at the war's end.

PRISON

1 Fear, coercion, punishment, are the masculine remedies for moral weakness, but statistics show their failure for centuries. Why not change the system and try the education of the moral and intellectual faculties, cheerful surroundings, inspiring influences? Everything in our present system tends to lower the physical vitality, the self-respect, the moral tone, and to harden instead of reforming the criminal.

ELIZABETH CADY STANTON (1815–1902), U.S. suffragist, author, and social reformer. *Eighty Years and More (1815–1897)*, ch. 18 (1898).

On prison conditions.

2 . . . the way to reform has always led through prison.

EMMELINE PANKHURST (1858–1928), British suffragist and politician. *My Own Story*, book 2, ch. 8 (1914).

Pankhurst and her daughters Christabel and Sylvia, all leaders in the British woman suffrage movement, were imprisoned repeatedly for their protest activities.

3 . . . imprisonment itself, entailing loss of liberty, loss of citizenship, separation from family and loved ones, is punishment enough for most individuals, no matter how fa-

vorable the circumstances under which the time is passed.

MARY B. HARRIS (1874–1957), U.S. prison administrator. *I Knew Them in Prison*, author's foreword (1936).

When she wrote this, Harris was Superintendent of the Federal Industrial Institution for Women.

4 What was really horrifying about jail is that it really isn't horrifying. You adjust very easily.

ROBERTA VICTOR, U.S. prostitute. As quoted in *Working*, book 2, by Studs Terkel (1973).

On being jailed for prostitution.

5 That was the most horrible day of my detention. The whole day I could see my baby's face and wanted to call her name, "Dudu," "Dudu," but my mind was blank. I couldn't recollect it. "Can a mother forget her baby's name?" I wondered.

EMMA MASHININI (b. 1929), South African black labor activist. As quoted in *Lives of Courage*, ch. 13, by Diana E. H. Russell (1989).

Said in 1987. Mashinini founded the Commercial Catering and Allied Workers' Union in 1975 and guided its growth into the second largest labor union in South Africa. She was describing her experience in police detention.

6 I didn't think I'd come out alive; in fact, I was seeing death. But I was prepared to die as long as I died for the truth, and I knew that people would know that this was the case.

CONNIE MOFOKENG (b. 1959), South African black political activist. As quoted in *Lives of Courage*, ch. 2, by Diana E. H. Russell (1989).

Said in 1987. Mofokeng was recalling her experiences as a political prisoner; she was poisoned and subjected to electric shocks and solitary confinement, but she refused to inform.

7 I almost wished that I was still in prison. I felt I wasn't ready to be out making decisions. . . . Even now over three years after my release, I can carry around fifty rand for two weeks and not spend it. I go into shops, but I find it hard to choose things.

FEZIWE BOOKHOLANE (b. 1942), South African black anti–apartheid activist. As quoted in *Lives of Courage,* ch. 3, by Diana E. H. Russell (1989).

Commenting, in a 1987 interview, on the psychological impact of six years of political imprisonment.

8 The years of imprisonment hardened me. . . . Perhaps if you have been given a moment to hold back and wait for the next blow, your emotions wouldn't be blunted as they have been in my case. When it happens every day of your life, when that pain becomes a way of life, I no longer have the emotion of fear. . . . there is no longer anything I can fear. There is nothing the government has not done to me. There isn't any pain I haven't known.

WINNIE MANDELA (b. 1936), South African black anti–apartheid activist. As quoted in *Lives of Courage,* ch. 6, by Diana E. H. Russell (1989).

Said in a 1987 interview. Approximately one year later, Mandela was charged with complicity in the beating of four young anti-apartheid activists, including a fourteen-year-old boy, Stompie Moeketsi, who died as a result.

PRIVACY

1 All violations of essential privacy are brutalizing.

KATHERINE FULLERTON GEROULD (1879–1944), U.S. author. *Modes and Morals,* ch. 7 (1920).

2 Poverty is relative, and the lack of food and of the necessities of life is not necessarily a hardship. Spiritual and social ostracism, the invasion of your privacy, are what constitute the pain of poverty.

ALICE FOOTE MACDOUGALL, (1867–1945) U.S. businesswoman. *The Autobiography of a Business Woman,* ch. 7 (1928).

Before making a great success in the restaurant and wholesale beverage businesses, MacDougall and her three children had been thrust into deep poverty by her husband's financial failure. Raised in wealth and high social standing, she had been forced to ask relatives for help and was humiliated by their presumptuous inquiries about her life style and expenditures.

3 . . . privacy is . . . connected to a politics of *domination.*

BELL HOOKS (b. 1955), African American author, feminist, and human rights advocate. *Outlaw Culture,* ch. 19 (1994).

PRIVATE LIFE

1 [A writer] should try not to be too far, personally, below the level of his work.

ELIZABETH BOWEN (1899–1973), British novelist, story writer, essayist, and memoirist; born in Ireland. As quoted in *Elizabeth Bowen,* ch. 5, by Victoria Glendinning (1979).

2 I shouldn't say I'm looking forward to leading a normal life, because I don't know what normal is. This has been normal for me.

MARTINA NAVRATILOVA (b. 1956), U.S. tennis player; born and raised in Czechoslovakia. As quoted in the *New York Times,* p. B19 (September 30, 1993).

Announcing her decision to retire from professional tennis at the end of the 1994 season, which would be her twenty-second year of competitive singles play.

PROBLEMS

1 As life developed, I faced each problem as it came along. As my activities and work broadened and reached out, I never tried to shirk. I tried never to evade an issue. When I found I had something to do—I just did it.

ELEANOR ROOSEVELT (1884–1962), U.S. First Lady, author, and speaker. As quoted in *Eleanor and Franklin,* ch. 35, by Joseph P. Lash (1971).

In a *Washington Herald* interview in 1933, her first year as First Lady. She had been asked how she overcame her youthful shyness to become an influential political personage.

2 . . . I have wanted to believe people could make their dreams come true . . . that problems could be solved. However, this is a national illness. As Americans, we believe all problems can be solved, that all questions have answers.

KRISTIN HUNTER (b. 1931), African American author. *Black Women Writers at Work,* ch. 6, by Claudia Tate (1983).

PROCRASTINATION

1 If we still advise we shall never do.

ELIZABETH I (1533–1603), Queen of England (1558–1603). As quoted in *The Sayings of Queen Elizabeth,* ch. 11, by Frederick Chamberlin (1923).

To Sir Henry Sidney, governor of Ireland.

2 I somehow always have this idea that as soon as I can get through this work that's piled up ahead of me, I'll really write a beautiful thing. But I never do. I always have the idea that someday, somehow,

I'll be living a beautiful life. And that, too . . . [ellipsis in source]

ROSE WILDER LANE (1886–1968), U.S. author. As quoted in *The Ghost in the Little House,* ch. 8, by William V. Holtz (1993). Written sometime in the 1920s.

PROGRESS

1 . . . till women are more rationally educated, the progress of human virtue and improvement in knowledge must receive continual checks.

MARY WOLLSTONECRAFT (1759–1797), British feminist. *A Vindication of the Rights of Woman,* ch. 3 (1792).

2 . . . these great improvements of modern times are blessings or curses on us, just in the same ratio as the mental, moral, and religious rule over the animal; or the animal propensities of our nature predominate over the intellectual and moral. The spider elaborates *poison* from the same flower, in which the *bee* finds materials out of which she manufactures *honey.*

HARRIOT K. HUNT (1805–1875), U.S. physician. *Glances and Glimpses,* ch. 18 (1856).

3 The idealists dream and the dream is told, and the practical men listen and ponder and bring back the truth and apply it to human life, and progress and growth and higher human ideals come into being and so the world moves ever on.

ANNA HOWARD SHAW (1847–1919), U.S. minister, suffragist, and speaker; born in

England. As quoted in *History of Woman Suffrage,* vol. 5, ch. 5, by Ida Husted Harper (1922).
Speaking in the summer of 1905 at the thirty-seventh annual convention of the National Woman Suffrage Association.

PROGRESSIVISM

1 If we fail to meet our problems here, no one else in the world will do so. If we fail, the heart goes out of progressives throughout the world.

ELEANOR ROOSEVELT (1884–1962), U.S. author, speaker, and First Lady. As quoted in *Eleanor: The Years Alone,* ch. 4, by Joseph P. Lash (1972).
In a January 4, 1947, keynote address delivered at the founding meeting of the liberal organization, Americans for Democratic Action.

PROSTITUTION

1 *Prostitution is the most hideous of the afflictions produced by the unequal distribution of the world's goods;* this infamy stigmatizes the human species and bears witness against the social organization far more than does crime.

FLORA TRISTAN (1803–1844), French author. As quoted in *Victorian Women,* ch. 90, by Erna Olafson Hellerstein, Leslie Parker Hume, and Karen M. Offen (1981).
From an 1840 book first published in French under the title, *Promenades dans Londres.*

2 . . . the danger of illicit sex influences is, and always has been, in inverse proportion to the degree to which women approximated to equality with men, in social dignity and in opportunity for public responsibility.

MARY PUTNAM JACOBI (1842–1906), U.S. suffragist. *"Common Sense" Applied to Woman Suffrage,* ch. 3 (1894).
By "illicit sex influences," Jacobi meant prostitution.

3 If in this wide world, teeming with abundant supplies for human want, to thousands of wretched creatures no choice is open, save between starvation and sin, may we not justly say that there is something utterly wrong in the system that permits such things to be?

TENNESSEE CLAFLIN (1846–1923), U.S. journalist, lecturer, and social reform advocate; relocated to England. *Talks and Essays,* vol. 3, ch. 4 (1897).
Arguing for compassion for prostitutes and for social reform.

4 Nowhere is woman treated according to the merit of her work, but rather as a sex. It is therefore almost inevitable that she should pay for her right to exist, to keep a position in whatever line, with sex favors. Thus it is merely a question of degree whether she sells herself to one man, in or out of marriage, or to many men! . . . the economic and social inferiority of woman is responsible for prostitution.

EMMA GOLDMAN (1869–1940), U.S. anarchist, labor organizer, and author. *Feminism,* ch. 5 (1910).

5 Prostitution, although hounded, imprisoned, and chained, is nevertheless the greatest triumph of Puritanism.

EMMA GOLDMAN (1869–1940), U.S. anarchist and author; born in Russia. *Anarchism and Other Essays,* 3rd rev. ed., ch. 7 (1917).

6 The elements of success in this business do not differ from the elements of success in any other. Competition is keen and bitter. Advertising is as large an element as in any other business, and since the usual avenues of successful exploitation are closed to the profession, the adage that the best advertisement is a pleased customer is doubly true for this business.

MADELEINE [BLAIR], U.S. prostitute and "madam." *Madeleine,* ch. 5 (1919).

7 The prostitute is the scapegoat for everyone's sins, and few people care whether she is justly treated or not. Good people have spent thousands of pounds in efforts to reform her, poets have written about her, essayists and orators have made her the subject of some of their most striking rhetoric; perhaps no class of people has been so much abused, and alternatively sentimentalized over as prostitutes have been *but one thing they have never yet had, and that is simple legal justice.*

ALISON NEILANS, As quoted in *On Women and Revolution,* part 1, by Crystal Eastman (1978). From an article first published in *Equal Rights* on September 19, 1925.

8 Monogamy and prostitution go together.

"J", U.S. prostitute. As quoted in *Woman in Sexist Society,* ch. 3, by Kate Millett (1971).

9 When I was a call girl, men were not paying for sex. They were paying for something else. They were either paying to act out a fantasy or they were paying for companionship or they were paying to be seen with a well-dressed young woman. Or they were paying for someone to listen to them. . . . What I did was no different from what ninety-nine percent of American women are taught to do. I took the money from under the lamp instead of in Arpege.

ROBERTA VICTOR, U.S. prostitute. As quoted in *Working,* book 2, by Studs Terkel (1973).

10 Prostitutes are accused even by feminists of selling their bodies; but prostitutes don't sell their bodies, they rent their bodies. Housewives sell their bodies when they get married.

FLORYNCE KENNEDY (b. 1916), U.S. lawyer, activist, speaker, and author. *Color Me Flo,* ch. 1 (1976).

11 I swear people don't want sex so much as they want somebody who'll listen to 'em . . . the first thing you learn after fellatio is how to listen.

JANE WAGNER (b. 1935), U.S. playwright. *The Search for Signs of Intelligent Life in the Universe* (1986).

12 There is no difference between the client and the prostitute. If a man goes to a prostitute, he is also a prostitute.

SISTER MICHELE, Indian nun. As quoted in the *New York Times Magazine,* p. 35 (January 16, 1994).

She counselled child prostitutes in Thailand.

PROTECTION OF WOMEN

1 Women are told from their infancy, and taught by the example of their mothers, that a little knowledge of human weakness, justly termed cunning, softness of temper, *outward* obedience, and a scrupulous attention to a puerile kind of propriety, will obtain for them the protection of man; and should they be beautiful, every thing else is needless, for, at least, twenty years of their lives.

MARY WOLLSTONECRAFT (1759–1797), British feminist. *A Vindication of the Rights of Woman*, ch. 2 (1792).

2   Until about the age of thirty, a young lady can never go out without being accompanied.

ELISABETH-FÉLICITÉ BAYLE-MOUILLARD, (1796–1865) French author. As quoted in *Victorian Women*, ch. 19, by Erna Olafson Hellerstein, Leslie Parker Hume, and Karen M. Offen (1981).

From an 1834 advice manual, first published in French under the title, *Manuel de la bonne compagnie, ou guide de la politesse et de la bienséance.*

3   Dat man ober dar say dat womin needs to be helped into carriages, and lifted ober ditches, and to hab de best place everywhar. Nobody eber helps me into carriages, or ober mud-puddles, or gibs me any best place! And a'n't I a woman? Look at me! Look at my arm! I have ploughed, and planted, and gathered into barns, and no man could head me! And a'n't I a woman? I could work as much and eat as much as a man—when I could get it—and bear de lash as well! And a'n't I a woman? I have borne thirteen chilern, and seen 'em mos' all sold off to slavery, and when I cried out with my mother's grief, none

but Jesus heard me! And a'n't I a woman?

SOJOURNER TRUTH (1797–1883), African American human rights activist and preacher. As represented by Frances D. Gage and printed in *The History of Woman Suffrage,* vol. 1, ch. 6 (1881).

Remarks made on the second day of the Woman's Rights Convention held in Akron, Ohio, May 28–29, 1851; Truth was responding to male supremacist comments made by some men in attendance. Gage, the President of the Convention, wrote up Truth's remarks from memory. Born a slave in Ulster County, New York, and named Isabella Baumfree, Truth had been freed by New York State law in 1827. In 1843, she had a religious vision which led her to change her name and become an itinerant preacher. She also became a prominent and beloved figure in the woman suffrage and anti-slavery movements.

4   My profession brought me in contact with various minds. Earnest, serious discussion on the condition of woman enlivened my business room; failures of banks, no dividends from railroads, defalcations of all kinds, public and private, widows and orphans and unmarried women beggared by the dishonesty, or the mismanagement of men, were fruitful sources of conversation; confidence in man as a protector was evidently losing ground, and women were beginning to see that they must protect themselves.

HARRIOT K. HUNT (1805–1875), U.S. physician and feminist. *Glances and Glimpses,* ch. 18 (1856).

Hunt's patients were women and children.

5   It is better to have the power of self-protection than to depend on any man, whether he be the Governor in his chair of State, or the hunted outlaw wandering through the night, hungry and cold and with murder in his heart.

LILLIE DEVEREUX BLAKE (1835–1913), U.S. suffragist. As quoted in *History of Woman Suffrage*, vol. 4, ch. 2, by Susan B. Anthony and Ida Husted Harper (1902).

In a speech entitled "The Unknown Quantity in Politics," delivered at an 1884 convention of the National Woman Suffrage Association; Blake was a delegate from New York.

6 We hear much of chivalry of men towards women; but . . . it vanishes like dew before the summer sun when one of us comes into competition with the manly sex. Let a woman sit, weep, wring her hands, and exult in her own helplessness, and the modern knight buckles on his imaginary breastplate and draws his sword in her behalf; but when the woman girds up her loins for the battle of life, ready to fight like a lioness, if need be, to put food in the mouths of her children, let her select for her field the living-room or the cooking range.

MARTHA J. COSTON (1828–1886), U.S. author. *Signal Success*, ch. 42 (1886).

7 . . . while our men seem thoroughly abreast of the times on almost every other subject, when they strike the woman question they drop back into sixteenth century logic. They leave nothing to be desired generally in regard to gallantry and chivalry, but they actually do not seem sometimes to have outgrown that old contemporary of chivalry—the idea that women may stand on pedestals or live in doll houses, . . . but they must not furrow their brows with thought or attempt to help

men tug at the great questions of the world.

ANNA JULIA COOPER (1859–1964), U.S. educator and feminist. *A Voice from the South*, part 1 (1892).

8 The talk of sheltering woman from the fierce storms of life is the sheerest mockery, for they beat on her from every point of the compass, just as they do on man, and with more fatal results, for he has been trained to protect himself, to resist, to conquer.

ELIZABETH CADY STANTON (1815–1902), U.S. suffragist, social reformer, and author. As quoted in *History of Woman Suffrage*, vol. 4, ch. 12, by Susan B. Anthony and Ida Husted Harper (1902).

From the 1892 address which was perhaps the great suffragist's most famous: "The Solitude of the Self." She was referring to the antisuffrage argument that women should be protected from the rough-and-tumble of the larger world, including politics.

9 . . . the sentimentalist . . . exclaims: "Would you have a woman step down from her pedestal in order to enter practical life?" Yes! A thousand times, yes! If we can really find, after a careful search, any women mounted upon pedestals, we should willingly ask them to step down in order that they may meet and help to uplift their sisters. Freedom and justice for all are infinitely more to be desired than pedestals for a few.

BERTHA HONORÉ POTTER PALMER, (1849–1918) U.S. socialite. As quoted in *The Fair Women*, ch. 11, by Jeanne Madeline Weimann (1981).

Palmer, President of the Board of Lady Managers for the World's Columbian Exposition in Chicago, was speaking on May 1, 1893, the Exposition's Opening Day.

10 . . . we shall never be the people we should and might be until we have learned that it is the first and most important business of a nation to protect its women, not by any puling sentimentality of queenship, chivalry or angelhood, but by making it possible for them to earn an honest living.

KATHARINE PEARSON WOODS (1853–1923), U.S. author, teacher, and social service worker. *What America Owes to Women*, ch. 43 (1893).

In an essay deploring the low pay and poor working conditions of the less fortunate employed women.

11 There are, undoubtedly, women who are weak and silly, and simple, and who are taken advantage of by designing men. Until we have such systems of education as will tend to prevent women from being weak, simple, and silly, it is undoubtedly right to have laws punishing seduction with the utmost severity; but we have also . . . ninnies among men, and ought we not, therefore, to have laws for their protection? An Act of the Legislature entitled "An Act for the Protection of Ninnies against Designing Women" would be refreshing.

TENNESSEE CLAFLIN (1846–1923), U.S. journalist, lecturer, and social reform advocate; relocated to England. *Talks and Essays*, vol. 2, ch. 4 (1897).

12 [Men say:] "Don't you know that we are your natural protectors?" But what is a woman afraid of on a lonely road after dark? The bears and wolves are all gone; there is nothing to be afraid of now but our natural protectors.

FRANCES A. GRIFFIN, U.S. suffragist. As quoted in *History of Woman Suffrage*, vol. 4, ch. 19, by Susan B. Anthony and Ida Husted Harper (1902).

Speaking before the thirty-first annual convention of the National Woman Suffrage Association, held April 27–May 3, 1899, in Grand Rapids, Michigan. Griffin's address was entitled "The Effects of our Teaching"; here, she was referring to the antisuffrage argument that male voters would attend to women's needs and protect them from harm. Griffin was from Alabama.

13 The anti-suffragist talk of sheltering women from the fierce storms of life is a lot of cant. I have no patience with it. These storms beat on woman just as fiercely as they do on man, and she is not trained to defend herself against them.

SUSAN B. ANTHONY (1820–1906), U.S. suffragist. As quoted in *Life and Work of Susan B. Anthony*, vol. 3, ch. 67, by Ida Husted Harper (1908).

In a 1905 interview with Edwin Tracey of the New York *Press*.

14 We agree fully that the mother and unborn child demand special consideration. But so does the soldier and the man maimed in industry. Industrial conditions that are suitable for a stalwart, young, unmarried woman are certainly not equally suitable to the pregnant woman or the mother of young children. Yet "welfare" laws apply to all women alike. Such blanket legislation is as absurd as fixing industrial conditions for men on a basis of their all being wounded soldiers would be.

NATIONAL WOMAN'S PARTY, Quoted in *Everyone Was Brave. As*, ch. 8, by William L. O'Neill (1969).

From an article first published in *Equal Rights*, the Woman's Party's journal, on October 6,

1923. It refers to protective legislation which often had the effect of unnecessarily limiting women's work opportunities.

15 . . . it must be obvious that in the agitation preceding the enactment of [protective] laws the zeal of the reformers would be second to the zeal of the highly paid night-workers who are anxious to hold their trade against an invasion of skilled women. To this sort of interference with her working life the modern woman can have but one attitude: *I am not a child.*

CRYSTAL EASTMAN (1881–1928), U.S. social/political activist and author. *On Women and Revolution,* part 1 (1978). From an article first published in *Equal Rights* on March 15, 1924.
Eastman was referring to "protective" labor laws that limited women's ability to work; they prohibited, for instance, women's working at certain hours or performing certain types of work.

16 I could make out a good case for specially protecting men. It is time some attention was paid to vital statistics. More boys are born than girls, yet more girls survive. There are always more widows than widowers, there are two million more women than men. In other words, woman's survival rate is greater than man's, and women are getting stronger all the time. If either sex needs protection, it would seem to be the men.

JANE WALKER, British physician. As quoted in *On Women and Revolution,* part 1, by Crystal Eastman (1978). From an article first published in *Equal Rights* on June 19, 1927.
Walker, said to be "a leading woman physician of London," was referring to protective labor laws that limited the amount and types of work women might do—allegedly because of their

physical weakness. These laws put women at a disadvantage in the competition for jobs.

17 One fellow I was dating in medical school . . . was a veterinarian and he wanted to get married. I said, but you're going to be moving to Minneapolis, and he said, oh, you can quit and I'll take care of you. I said, "Go."

SYLVIA BECKMAN (b. c. 1931), U.S. ophthalmologist. As quoted in *The Fifties,* ch. 8, by Brett Harvey (1993).
Beckman, an interviewee in Harvey's oral history of the 1950s, was recalling her years as a student at the Women's Medical College of Pennsylvania in the late fifties.

PSYCHOLOGY

1 Psychologists have set about describing the true nature of women with a certainty and a sense of their own infallibility rarely found in the secular world.

NAOMI WEISSTEIN, U.S. psychologist, feminist, and author. *Psychology Constructs the Female* (1969).

2 Psychology has nothing to say about what women are really like, what they need and what they want, essentially, because psychology does not know.

NAOMI WEISSTEIN (b. 1939), U.S. author and feminist. *Kinder, Kuche, Kirche as Scientific Law* (1970).

3 A major difference between witches and psychotherapists is that witches see the mental health of women as having important political consequences.

NAOMI R. GOLDENBERG (b. 1947), U.S. author. As quoted in *The Political Palate,* ch. 1, by Betsey Beaven, et al. (1980).

PUBLIC LIFE

1 Only as we live, think, feel, and work outside the home, do we become humanly developed, civilized, socialized.

CHARLOTTE PERKINS GILMAN (1860–1935), U.S. author, editor, feminist, and social reformer. *Women and Economics,* ch. 10 (1898).

2 I was perfectly certain that I had nothing to offer of an individual nature and that my only chance of doing my duty as the wife of a public official was to do exactly as the majority of women were doing . . .

ELEANOR ROOSEVELT (1884–1962), First Lady of the United States, author, speaker, and diplomat. *This Is My Story,* ch. 10 (1937).

On her conventionality in 1913, when her husband, Franklin Delano Roosevelt, became Assistant Secretary of the Navy. She would go on to become the most individualistic, publicly active, and personally distinguished First Lady in history.

3 . . . it is a rather curious thing to have to divide one's life into personal and official compartments and temporarily put the personal side into its hidden compartment to be taken out again when one's official duties are at an end.

ELEANOR ROOSEVELT (1884–1962), U.S. First Lady, author, and speaker. As quoted in *Eleanor and Franklin,* ch. 50, by Joseph P. Lash (1971).

Written on October 17, 1940, as her husband, Franklin Delano Roosevelt, approached his third Presidential election, which he won.

4 One of the great penalties those of us who live our lives in full view of the public must pay is the loss of that most cherished birthright of man's privacy.

MARY PICKFORD (1893–1979), U.S. actor. *Sunshine and Shadow,* ch. 22 (1955).

On the publicity that surrounded her break from her second husband, actor Douglas Fairbanks (1883–1939). He had become quite publicly involved with another woman.

5 I gambled on having the strength to live two lives, one for myself and one for the world.

RUTH BENEDICT (1887–1948), U.S. anthropologist. As quoted in *An Anthropologist at Work,* part 1, by Margaret Mead (1959).

From a prefatory essay to this collection of Benedict's writings: "Search: 1920–1930." Benedict was in her late thirties when she said this. She was both a noted anthropologist and a wife; she did not, however, have children.

6 All my life
I have been restless—
I have felt there is something
more wonderful than gloss—
than wholeness—
than staying at home.

MARY OLIVER (b. 1935), U.S. poet. "Whelks," lines 12–17 (c. 1991).

PUBLIC SPEAKING

1 . . . the only way in which Mr. Brooke could be coerced into thinking of the right arguments at the right time was to be well plied with them till they took up all the room in his brain. But here there was the difficulty of finding room, so many things having been taken in beforehand. Mr. Brooke himself observed that his ideas stood rather in his way when he was speaking.

GEORGE ELIOT (1819–1880), British novelist. *Middlemarch,* ch. 47 (1871–1872).

Of a well-meaning but intellectually limited character in the novel who was active in local politics.

2 One of the things that I discovered in lecturing was that gradually one ceased to hear what one said one heard what the audience hears one say.

GERTRUDE STEIN (1874–1946), U.S. author and patron of the arts; relocated to France. *What Are Masterpieces and Why Are There So Few of Them* (1936).

make up the bulk of American women, slaves to society and fashion.

ELLEN HENRIETTA SWALLOW RICHARDS, (1842–1911) U.S. chemist and educator. As quoted in *The Life of Ellen H. Richards,* ch. 3, by Caroline L. Hunt (1912).

Written when she was a student at Vassar College, in a May 16, 1869, letter responding to her parents' question about what they should tell people who asked about the purpose of her college preparation.

PURITANISM

1 Mr. Doctor, that loose gown becomes you so well I wonder your notions should be so narrow.

ELIZABETH I (1533–1603), Queen of England (1558–1603). As quoted in *The Sayings of Queen Elizabeth,* ch. 6, by Frederick Chamberlin (1923).

Said during a visit to Oxford in 1566, to Dr. Humphreys, leader of the Puritans, who was clad in an academic gown.

2 ... our great-grandmothers were prudes. The reason why they talked so much about their souls, I fancy, is that there was hardly a limb or a feature of the human body that they thought it proper to mention.

KATHERINE FULLERTON GEROULD (1879–1944), U.S. author. *Modes and Morals,* ch. 7 (1920).

PURPOSE

1 ... my aim is now, as it has been for the past ten years, to make myself a true woman, one worthy of the name, and one who will unshrinkingly follow the path which God marks out, one whose aim is to do all of the good she can in the world and not be one of the delicate little dolls or the silly fools who

2 ... my one aim and concentrated purpose *shall be* and *is* to show that women *can learn, can reason, can compete* with men in the grand fields of literature and science ... that a woman can be a woman and a *true* one without having all her time engrossed by dress and society.

M. CAREY THOMAS (1857–1935), U.S. educator. As quoted in *Carey Thomas of Bryn Mawr,* ch. 1, by Edith Finch (1947).

Written when the future doctoral recipient and Bryn Mawr College president was fourteen years old.

3 We never can tell how our lives may work to the account of the general good, and we are not wise enough to know if we have fulfilled our mission or not.

ELLEN HENRIETTA SWALLOW RICHARDS, (1842–1911) U.S. chemist and educator. As quoted in *The Life of Ellen H. Richards,* ch. 9, by Caroline L. Hunt (1912).

Written in the 1870s to a student whom she was urging to persevere in the face of difficulties.

4 What do we live for, if it is not to make life less difficult to each other?

GEORGE ELIOT (1819–1880), British novelist. *Middlemarch,* ch. 72 (1871–1872).

5 I began reviewing my life in relation to its objectives. I saw no objects, I saw only states.

MARGARET ANDERSON (1886–1973), U.S. literary editor and autobiographer. *My Thirty Years' War,* ch. 6 (1930).

6 I have never been able to accept the two great laws of humanity—that you're always being suppressed if you're inspired and always being pushed into the corner if you're exceptional. I won't be cornered and I won't stay suppressed.

MARGARET ANDERSON (1886–1973), U.S. literary editor and autobiographer. *My Thirty Years' War,* ch. 1 (1930).

Anderson founded and edited a charming, influential literary and arts magazine, *The Little Review.*

7 Some lives drift here and there like reeds in a stream, depending on changing currents for their activity. Others are like swimmers knowing the depth of the water. Each stroke helps them onward to a definite objective.

MARGARET SANGER (1879–1966), U.S. birth control advocate. *My Fight for Birth Control,* ch. 1 (1931).

8 Life seems to be an experience in ascending and descending. You think you're beginning to live for a single aim—for self-development, or the discovery of cosmic truths—when all you're really doing is to move from place to place as if devoted primarily to real estate.

MARGARET ANDERSON (1886–1973), U.S. editor and memoirist. *The Fiery Fountains,* part 1 (1951).

For much of her life, Anderson moved around from city to city and home to home. Among the places where she lived were Chicago, New York, and Paris.

9 When I was in high school I thought a vocation was a particular calling. Here's a voice: "Come, follow me." My idea of a calling now is not: "Come." It's like what I'm doing right now, not what I'm going to be. Life is a calling.

REBECCA SWEENEY (b. 1938), U.S. ex–nun. As quoted in *Working,* book 9, by Studs Terkel (1973).

Thirty-five years old and unmarried, Sweeney had held a variety of jobs, including six years as a nun.

10 It beats sitting around with my butt in a sling.

ANTOINETTE CANCELLO, U.S. circus aerialist. As quoted in *WomenSports* magazine, p. 35 (January 1976).

On why she became a circus aerialist (or "flyer"); she was nicknamed "the Queen of the Air." Later, she became Aerial Director for Ringling Brothers.

11 When I was going through my transition of being famous, I tried to ask God why was I here? what was my purpose? Surely, it wasn't just to win three gold medals. There has to be more to this life than that.

WILMA RUDOLPH (1940–1994), U.S. runner. As quoted in *I Dream a World,* by Brian Lanker (1989).

In Rome in 1960, Rudolph had become the first American woman to win three gold medals in track and field at a single Olympics.

12 I take enormous pleasure every time I see something that I've done that cannot be wiped out. In some way . . . I guess it's a protest against mortality. But it's been so much fun! It's the curiosity that drives me. It's making a difference in the world that prevents me from ever giving up.

DEBORAH MEIER (b. 1931), U.S. educator. As quoted in *New York* magazine, p. 78 (December 21–28, 1992).
An urban educator, she co-founded the innovative Central Park East High School in the Harlem neighborhood of New York City.

QUILTS

1   this quilt might be
the only perfect artifact a woman
would ever see, yet she did not doubt
what we had forgotten, that out of her
potatoes and colic, sawdust and blood
she could create . . .

MARGE PIERCY (b. 1936), U.S. poet, novelist, and political activist. "Looking at Quilts," lines 44–49 (1976).

2   I question the negative connotations of fabric, of ribbon, of lace. I turn these symbols of our imprisonment around.

MIRIAM SCHAPIRO (b. 1923), U.S. quilter. As quoted in *The Decade of Women*, by Suzanne Levine and Harriet Lyons (1980). Said in 1977.

3   In the quilts I had found good objects—hospitable, warm, with soft edges yet resistant, with boundaries yet suggesting a continuous safe expanse, a field that could be bundled, a bundle that could be unfurled, portable equipment, light, washable, long-lasting, colorful, versatile, functional and ornamental,

private and universal, mine and thine.

RADKA DONNELL-VOGT, U.S. quiltmaker. As quoted in *Lives and Works*, by Lynn F. Miller and Sally S. Swenson (1981).

QUOTATIONS

1   The taste for quotations . . . is a Surrealist taste.

SUSAN SONTAG (b. 1933), U.S. author. *On Photography*, ch. 3 (1977).

2   For anyone addicted to reading commonplace books . . . finding a good new one is much like enduring a familiar recurrence of malaria, with fever, fits of shaking, strange dreams. Unlike a truly paludismic ordeal, however, the symptoms felt while savoring a collection of one man's pet quotations are voluptuously enjoyable . . .

M. F. K. FISHER (1908–1992), U.S. culinary writer and autobiographer. Preface (1985). The book's compiler is Robert Grabhorn.

RACE

1   . . . I cannot help being astonished at the furious and ungoverned execration which all reference to the possibility of a fusion of the races draws down upon those who suggest it, because nobody pretends to deny that, throughout the South, a large proportion of the population is the offspring of white men and colored women.

FANNY KEMBLE (1809–1893), British actor and abolitionist. *Journal of a Residence on a Georgian Plantation in 1838–1839,* ch. 1 (1863).

From a letter written in Philadelphia during December 1838, to her friend Elizabeth Dwight Sedgwick. A few years earlier, Kemble had unwittingly married into a slave-owning family; the marriage failed, and she and Pierce Butler were divorced in 1849. Here, Kemble was referring to the children born as a result of illicit sex between slave owners and their slaves. The same men who fathered these children, and the men's legal families, hypocritically reacted with horror to the notions of interracial sex and marriage, and cited the possibility of racial mixing as a reason to oppose emancipation and African American rights.

2   A race cannot be purified from without.

ANNA JULIA COOPER (1859–1964), African American educator and feminist. *A Voice from the South,* part 1 (1892).

Cooper was born in Raleigh, North Carolina, to a slave and her white master, a lawyer. Later, she would say that her mother was "the finest woman I have ever known."

3   The arrogance of race prejudice is an arrogance which defies what is scientifically known of human races.

RUTH BENEDICT (1887–1948), U.S. anthropologist. *An Anthropologist at Work,* part 5 (1959).

4   The writer in me can look as far as an African-American woman and stop. Often that writer looks through the African-American woman. Race is a layer of being, but not a culmination.

THYLIAS MOSS, African American poet. As quoted in the *Wall Street Journal* (May 12, 1994).

5   The notion that black folks have nothing to learn from scholarship that may reflect racial or racist biases is dangerous. It promotes closed-mindedness and a narrow

understanding of knowledge to hold that "race" is such an overwhelming concept that it negates the validity of *any* insights contained in a work that may have some racist or sexist aspects.

BELL HOOKS (b. 1955), African American author, educator, feminist, and human rights advocate. *Chronicle of Higher Education,* p. A44 (July 13, 1994).

6   We have yet to deal successfully with American transraciality in real terms, as we have failed to redefine race in light of the modern, twenty-first century progress of human kind.

VIRGINIA HAMILTON (b. 1936), African American writer of children's books. *Illusion and Reality.*

Hamilton's children were interracial.

RACE CAR DRIVING

1   Drag racing is a sport of egos, and it's all male egos.

SHIRLEY "CHA CHA" MULDOWNEY, (b. 1940) U.S. drag racer. As quoted in *WomenSports* magazine, p. 39 (December 1976).

Muldowney was the first licensed woman top fuel driver in drag racing.

2   I'd like to say I'm ready to kick ass and show the guys how it's done. But I'm not here to prove anything about being a woman. I'm here to drive a race car and try to win a race.

LYN ST. JAMES (b. 1947), U.S. race–car driver. As quoted in *People* magazine, p. 84 (May 31, 1993).

St. James was the second woman in history to qualify to race a car in the Indianapolis 500, the first having been Janet Guthrie in 1977–79; she was speaking shortly before the 1993 race.

RACE DIFFERENCES

1 . . . I really hope no white person ever has cause to write about me because they never understand Black love is Black wealth and they'll probably talk about my hard childhood and never understand that all the while I was quite happy.

NIKKI GIOVANNI (b. 1943), African American poet. "Nikki Rose," lines 24–27 (April 1968).

2 Take away an accident of pigmentation of a thin layer of our outer skin and there is no difference between me and anyone else. All we want is for that trivial difference to make no difference.

SHIRLEY CHISHOLM (b. 1924), African American politician. *Unbought and Unbossed,* ch. 13 (1970).

Chisholm was a Congresswoman from a poor African American district in Brooklyn.

3 I can't really hear the audience applause when I'm on stage. I'm totally immersed in the piece. But sometimes I get a lot of it and wonder, "Now, why did they applaud here?" If it's a white crowd, they usually applaud because they think it's a pretty movement. If it's a black crowd, it's usually because they identify with the message.

JUDITH JAMISON (b. 1944), African American dancer. As quoted in *WomenSports* magazine, p. 14 (September 1975).

4 . . . black women write differently from white women. This is the most marked difference of all those combinations of black and white,

male and female. It's not so much that women write differently from men, but that black women write differently from white women. Black men don't write very differently from white men.

TONI MORRISON (b. 1931), African American novelist and essayist. *Black Women Writers at Work,* ch. 9, by Claudia Tate (1983).

RACE DISCRIMINATION

1 . . . I am . . . one of the wretched and miserable daughters of the descendants of fallen Africa. Do you ask, why are you wretched and miserable? I reply, look at many of the most worthy and interesting of us doomed to spen our lives in gentlemen's kitchens. Look at our young men, smark, active and energetic, with souls filled with ambitious fire; if they can look forward, alas! what are their prospects? they can be nothing but the humblest laborers, on account of their dark complexions; hence many of them lose their ambition, and become worthless. Look at our middle-aged men, clad in their rusty plaids and coats; in winter, every cent they earn goes to buy their wood and pay their rents; their poor wives also toil beyond their strength, to help support their families. Look at our aged sires, whose heads are whitened with the frosts of seventy winters, with their old wood-saws on their backs. Alas, what keeps us so? Prejudice, ignorance, and poverty.

MARIA STEWART (1803–1879), African American abolitionist and schoolteacher. As quoted in *Black Women in Nineteenth-Century American Life*, part 3, by Bert James Loewenberg and Ruth Bogin (1976).

Stewart, a free black, said this in a September 21, 1832 speech delivered at Franklin Hall in Boston. She was speaking of the miserable, albeit "free," condition of Northern blacks.

2   I cannot help wondering sometimes what I might have become and might have done if I had lived in a country which had not circumscribed and handicapped me on account of my race, but had allowed me to reach any height I was able to attain.

MARY CHURCH TERRELL (1863–1954), African American author, speaker, and social reformer. *A Colored Woman in a White World,* ch. 42 (1940).

Graduating from Oberlin College in the late 1800s, Terrell was among the first African American college graduates. She then built a distinguished career in public life.

3   If Americans could understand what a painful, searing experience it is when Negro children first begin to realize that the mere color of their skin is to be the source of a lifelong discrimination, it might do more to end our cruelty toward the Negro than all the preaching on justice and equality.

AGNES E. MEYER (1887–1970), White American journalist. *Out of These Roots,* ch. 1 (1953).

4   . . . you don't have to be as good as white people, you have to be *better or the best.* When Negroes are average, *they fail,* unless they are very, very lucky. Now, if you're average and *white,* honey, you can go far. Just look at Dan Quayle. If that boy

was colored he'd be washing dishes somewhere.

ANNIE ELIZABETH DELANY (1891–1995), African American dentist. *Having Our Say,* ch. 17 (1992).

One of ten children born to an ex-slave and his wife, Delany had graduated from Columbia University's dental school in 1923 and become only the second African American woman dentist licensed to practice in New York State. Dan Quayle was Vice-President of the United States under President George Bush and considered by many to possess only mediocre intelligence.

RACE RELATIONS

1   *One who is a slaveholder at heart never recognizes a human being in a slave.*

ANGELINA GRIMKÉ (1805–1879), U.S. abolitionist. As quoted in *American Slavery As It Is,* by Theodore D. Weld (1839).

Said on April 6, 1839. The daughters of a South Carolina slaveholding family, Angelina and her sister Sarah had moved north to escape the presence of the slave system and become active abolitionists.

2   [Upon being asked if, in the primitive Hunterdon County, New Jersey, mountain town where she lived, there was "any distinction of color" among the residents]: No, not a bit, The niggers and whites all live together. The whites are just as good as the niggers, and both are as bad as the devil can make 'em.

SILVIA DUBOIS (1788?–1889), African American slave and hog breeder. As quoted in *Silvia Dubois, a Biografy of the Slav Who Whipt Her Mistres and Gand Her Fredom,* interview dated January 27, 1883, by C. W. Larison (1883).

3   [When asked: "Will not woman suffrage make the black woman the political equal of the white woman and does not political equality mean social equality?":] If it does then men by keeping both white and black women disfranchised have already established social equality!

ANNA HOWARD SHAW (1847–1919), U.S. minister, suffragist, and speaker; born in England. As quoted in *History of Woman Suffrage*, vol. 5, ch. 3, by Ida Husted Harper (1922).

Speaking in March 1903 at the thirty-fifth annual convention of the National Woman Suffrage Association.

4 They had supposed their formula was fixed.
They had obeyed instructions to devise
A type of cold, a type of hooded gaze.
But when the Negroes came they were perplexed.
These Negroes looked like men. . . .

GWENDOLYN BROOKS (b. 1917), African American poet, fiction writer, and autobiographer. "Gay Chaps at the Bar: the white troops had their orders but the Negroes looked like men," lines 1–5 (1945).

At this time, American military units were racially segregated.

5 I have known no experience more distressing than the discovery that Negroes didn't love me. Unutterable loneliness claimed me. I felt without roots, like a man without a country . . .

SARAH PATTON BOYLE, U.S. civil rights activist and author. *The Desegregated Heart*, part 1, ch. 10 (1962).

An affluent white Virginian who was cared for in her childhood by African American servants, Boyle was reflecting her eventual realization that many African Americans actually resented her.

6 I do not think white America is committed to granting equality to the American Negro. So committed are only a minority of white Americans, mostly educated and affluent, few of whom have had any prolonged social contact with Negroes.

SUSAN SONTAG (b. 1933), U.S. author. *What's Happening in America* (1966).

Written in response to a summer 1966 questionnaire sent to her and other prominent American intellectuals by *Partisan Review*. All of their answers were published in the magazine's Winter 1967 issue, but Sontag also published hers separately as an essay.

7 . . . white people, like black ones, are victims of a racist society. They are products of their time and place.

SHIRLEY CHISHOLM (b. 1924), African American politician and feminist. *Unbought and Unbossed,* ch. 15 (1970).

8 The air has finally gotten to the place that we can breathe it together.

SEPTIMA CLARK (1898–1987), African American teacher and civil rights activist. *Ready from Within*, part 2, ch. 3 (1986).

Quoting a statement she made in 1970 at the banquet held for her by the Southern Christian Leadership Conference (SCLC) when she won its Martin Luther King, Jr., Award "for Great Service to Humanity." King had founded SCLC.

9 I can't think of a single supposedly Black issue that hasn't wasted the original Black target group and then spread like the measles to outlying white experience.

JUNE JORDAN (b. 1936), African American poet, essayist, and social critic. *On Call,* ch. 4 (1985).

Written in 1982, with reference to such problems as drug abuse and unwed teenage pregnancy.

10 A major problem for Black women, and all people of color, when we are challenged to oppose anti-Semitism, is our profound skepticism that white people can actually be oppressed.

BARBARA SMITH (b. 1946), African American author. *Yours in Struggle,* part 2 (1984).

11 Strictly speaking, one cannot legislate love, but what one can do is legislate fairness and justice. If legislation does not prohibit our living side by side, sooner or later your child will fall on the pavement and I'll be the one to pick her up. Or one of my children will not be able to get into the house and you'll have to say, "Stop here until your mom comes here." Legislation affords us the chance to see if we might love each other.

MAYA ANGELOU (b. 1928), African American author and performer. As quoted in *I Dream a World,* by Brian Lanker (1989).

12 Once in a while, God sends a good white person my way, even to this day. I think it's God's way of keeping me from becoming too mean. And when he sends a nice one to me, then I have to eat crow. And honey, crow is a tough old bird to eat, let me tell you.

ANNIE ELIZABETH DELANY (1891–1995), African American dentist. *Having Our Say,* ch. 12 (1992).

Delany was the daughter of a former slave and his wife.

13 He looked at Senator Hatch and said, "I'm going to make her cry. I'm going to sing 'Dixie' until she

cries." And I looked at him and said, "Senator Helms, your singing would make me cry if you sang 'Rock of Ages'."

CAROL MOSELEY-BRAUN (b. 1947), African American politician. As quoted in *Newsweek* magazine, p. 17 (August 16, 1993).

Moseley-Braun, a United States Senator from Illinois, was recalling a conversation with Senator Jesse Helms, in the presence of Senator Orrin Hatch, in the Senate elevator. Helms, a long-time Senator from South Carolina, had a negative record on civil rights. Moseley-Braun, a staunch advocate of civil rights and other liberal causes, was new to the Senate. Helms's spokesman later characterized the encounter as "a good-natured exchange."

14 I never feel so conscious of my race as I do when I stand before a class of twenty-five young men and women eager to learn about what it is to be black in America.

CLAIRE OBERON GARCÍA, African American college professor. As quoted in the *Chronicle of Higher Education,* p. B3 (July 27, 1994).

One of only two African American women on the faculty of Colorado College, García was teaching American and African American literature.

RACIAL INTEGRATION

1 I do not like forced integration. . . . I do not like forced anything. . . . as a youngster I lived in a white neighborhood with a white neighbor next door. We would go to them, they would go to us. If they had anything, we had it. We lived just like one. We didn't think about no integration.

RUBY MIDDLETON FORSYTHE (b. 1905), African American schoolteacher. As quoted in *I Dream a World,* by Brian Lanker (1989).

Raised in Charleston, S. C., Forsythe had taught in that state for more than sixty years.

RACIAL SOLIDARITY

1 The confirmation of Clarence Thomas, one of the most conservative voices to be added to the [Supreme] Court in recent memory, carries a sobering message for the African-American community. . . . As he begins to make his mark upon the lives of African Americans, we must acknowledge that his successful nomination is due in no small measure to the support he received from black Americans.

KIMBERLÉ CRENSHAW (b. 1959), African American author. *Race-ing Justice, En-gendering Power*, ch. 14 (1992).

Thomas, an African American Supreme Court Justice appointed by President George Bush, had taken many stands traditionally opposed by liberals; for example, he opposed affirmative action and abortion rights and supported the death penalty.

2 . . . the outcome of the Clarence Thomas hearings and his subsequent appointment to the Supreme Court shows how misguided, narrow notions of racial solidarity that suppress dissent and critique can lead black folks to support individuals who will not protect their rights.

BELL HOOKS (b. c. 1955), African American author, feminist, and human rights advocate. *Outlaw Culture*, ch. 5 (1994).

In 1991, hearings were held on Republican President George Bush's nomination of Clarence Thomas (b. 1948), an African American conservative judge, for appointment to the Supreme Court. hooks was speaking of those hitherto liberal African Americans who supported Thomas even though he took positions that were antithetical to theirs: e.g., he opposed affirmative action.

RACISM

1 On fields all drenched with blood he made his record in war, abstained from lawless violence when left on the plantation, and received his freedom in peace with moderation. But he holds in this Republic the position of an alien race among a people impatient of a rival. And in the eyes of some it seems that no valor redeems him, no social advancement nor individual development wipes off the ban which clings to him.

FRANCES ELLEN WATKINS HARPER, (1825–1911) African American author, speaker, and rights advocate. As quoted in *The Female Experience*, ch. 66, by Gerda Lerner (1977).

Speaking in 1891 to the National Council of Women of the United States; she was referring to black veterans.

2 As sure as time is—*these mists will clear away*. And the world—our world, will surely and unerringly see us as we are. Our only care need be the intrinsic worth of our contributions. If we represent the ignorance and poverty, the vice and destructiveness, the vagabondism and parasitism in the world's economy, no amount of philanthropy and benevolent sentiment can win for us esteem: and if we contribute a positive value in those things the world prizes, no amount of negrophobia can ultimately prevent its recognition. And our great "problem" after all is to be solved not by brooding over it, and orating about it, but by *living into it*.

ANNA JULIA COOPER (1859–1964), African American educator and feminist. *A Voice from the South*, part 2 (1892).

Cooper, the daughter of a former slave, was referring to the "mists" of race bigotry.

McCabe was President of the National Coalition of 100 Black Women.

3 Seeing their children touched and seared and wounded by race prejudice is one of the heaviest crosses which colored women have to bear.

MARY CHURCH TERRELL (1863–1954), African American author, speaker, and social reformer. *A Colored Woman in a White World,* ch. 2 (1940).

4 Racism keeps people who are being managed from finding out the truth through contact with each other.

SHIRLEY CHISHOLM (b. 1924), African American politician. *Unbought and Unbossed,* ch. 13 (1970).

5 . . . all Americans are the prisoners of racial prejudice.

SHIRLEY CHISHOLM (b. 1924), African American politician. *Unbought and Unbossed,* ch. 13 (1970).

Chisholm was a Congresswoman from a poor African American district in Brooklyn.

6 People in Stamps used to say that the whites in our town were so prejudiced that a Negro couldn't buy vanilla ice cream. Except on July Fourth. Other days he had to be satisfied with chocolate.

MAYA ANGELOU (b. 1928), African American poet, autobiographer, and performer. *I Know Why the Caged Bird Sings,* ch. 8 (1970).

Remembering her childhood in strictly segregated, harshly racist Stamps, Arkansas, during the 1930s.

7 You factor in racism as a reality and you keep moving.

JEWELL JACKSON MCCABE, (b. 1945) African American professional. As quoted in *I Dream a World,* by Brian Lanker (1989).

8 Everybody's scared for their ass. There aren't too many people ready to die for racism. They'll kill for racism but they won't die for racism.

FLORYNCE KENNEDY (b. 1916), African American lawyer, civil rights activist, and feminist. As quoted in *This Little Light of Mine,* ch. 10, by Hay Mills (1993).

In a February 22, 1990 interview, recalling her civil rights work in Ruleville, Mississippi, in 1964.

9 Assumptions that racism is more oppressive to black men than black women, then and now . . . based on acceptance of patriarchal notions of masculinity.

BELL HOOKS (b. c. 1955), African American feminist author and educator. *Yearning,* ch. 8 (1990).

10 There are those who would keep us slipping back into the darkness of division, into the snake pit of racial hatred, of racial antagonism and of support for symbols of the struggle to keep African-Americans in bondage.

CAROL MOSELEY-BRAUN (b. 1947), African American politician. As quoted in *Newsweek* magazine, p. 15 (December 16, 1991).

Moseley-Braun, a United States Senator from Illinois, said this in a speech that led the Senate to reverse a vote to extend the patent on a society insignia that incorporated an image of the Confederate flag.

11 I am the kind of Negro that most white people don't know about. They either don't know, or maybe they don't *want* to know, I'm not sure which I mean, just listen to that fella, David Duke, down in

Louisiana—the fella that was with the Klan and then he was going to run for president. David Duke doesn't think there are Negroes like me and Sadie, colored folks who have never done nothin' except *contribute* to America. Well, I'm just as good an American as he is—*better!* . . . I think I'm going to write a letter, and I'm going to say, "Dear Mr. Duke: This is just to set the record straight. I am a Negro woman. I was brought up in a good family. My Papa was a devoted father. I went to college; I paid my own way. I am not stupid. I'm not on welfare. And I'm not scrubbing floors. Especially not yours."

Annie Elizabeth Delany (1891–1995), African American dentist. *Having Our Say*, ch. 25 (1992).

Delany and her sister Sarah Louise ("Sadie") were two of ten children born to an ex-slave and his wife. She had earned a D.D.S. degree from Columbia University and was the second licensed African American woman dentist in New York State.

RADIO

1 Now they can do the radio in so many languages that nobody any longer dreams of a single language, and there should not any longer be dreams of conquest because the globe is all one, anybody can hear everything and everybody can hear the same thing, so what is the use of conquering.

Gertrude Stein (1874–1946), U.S. author; relocated to France. *Wars I Have Seen* (1945).

Written in 1943.

READING

1 I don't read such small stuff as letters, I read men and nations. I can see through a millstone, though I can't see through a spelling-book. What a narrow idea a reading qualification is for a voter!

Sojourner Truth (1797–1883), African American suffragist and abolitionist. As quoted in *History of Woman Suffrage*, appendix—ch. 19, by Elizabeth Cady Stanton (1882).

The former slave, itinerant preacher, and beloved activist in the woman suffrage movement said this during an 1867 visit with Elizabeth Cady Stanton and her family. This is from a letter that Stanton wrote to the *World*, which, she said, "seemed to please Sojourner more than any other journal." Truth was illiterate but enjoyed having newspapers read aloud to her.

2 The common reader . . . differs from the critic and the scholar. He is worse educated, and nature has not gifted him so generously. He reads for his own pleasure rather than to impart knowledge or correct the opinions of others. Above all, he is guided by an instinct to create for himself, out of whatever odds and ends he can come by, some kind of whole—a portrait of a man, a sketch of an age, a theory of the art of writing. He never ceases, as he reads, to run up some rickety and ramshackle fabric which shall give him the temporary satisfaction of looking sufficiently like the real object to allow of affection, laughter, and argument. Hasty, inaccurate, and superficial, snatching now this poem, now that scrap of old furniture without caring where he finds it or of what nature it may be

so long as it serves his purpose and rounds his structure; his deficiencies as a critic are too obvious to be pointed out.

VIRGINIA WOOLF (1882–1941), British novelist, essayist, and diarist. *The Common Reader*, ch. 1 (1925).

3   Our poems will have failed if our readers are not brought by them beyond the poems.

MURIEL RUKEYSER (1913–1980), U.S. poet. *The Life of Poetry*, ch. 5 (1949).

4   The poem has a social effect of some kind whether or not the poet wills it to have. It has kinetic force, it sets in motion . . . [ellipsis in source] elements in the reader that would otherwise be stagnant.

DENISE LEVERTOV (b. 1923), U.S. poet. As quoted in *Against Forgetting*, sect. 5, by Carolyn Forche (1993).

Written in 1965, during the Vietnam War; Levertov was active in the movement opposing American involvement in that war.

5   During those years in Stamps, I met and fell in love with William Shakespeare. He was my first white love. . . . it was Shakespeare who said, "When in disgrace with fortune and men's eyes." It was a state of mind with which I found myself most familiar. I pacified myself about his whiteness by saying that after all he had been dead so long it couldn't matter to anyone any more.

MAYA ANGELOU (b. 1928), African American poet, autobiographer, and performer. *I Know Why the Caged Bird Sings*, ch. 2 (1970).

Remembering her childhood in strictly segregated, harshly racist Stamps, Arkansas, during the 1930s. Shakespeare had, of course, "been dead" for more than three centuries: since 1616. "When, in disgrace with fortune and men's eyes" is the first line of sonnet no. 29.

6   The writer studies literature, not the world. . . . He is careful of what he reads, for that is what he will write.

ANNIE DILLARD (b. 1945), U.S. author. *The Writing Life*, ch. 5 (1989).

REALISM

1   . . . there is no point in being realistic about here and now, no use at all not any, and so it is not the nineteenth but the twentieth century, there is no realism now, life is not real it is not earnest, it is strange which is an entirely different matter.

GERTRUDE STEIN (1874–1946), U.S. author; relocated to France. *Wars I Have Seen* (1945).

Written in 1943.

2   Realism to be effective must be a matter of selection. . . . genius chooses its materials with a view to their beauty and effectiveness; mere talent copies what it thinks is nature, only to find it has been deceived by the external grossness of things.

JULIA MARLOWE (1866–1950), U.S. actor; born in England. As quoted in *Famous Actors and Actresses on the American Stage*, vol. 2, by William C. Young (1975).

3   the tide lays down its wet throat and alters the land to island—even as I watch

I say there is no shore
apart from stories of it,
no smoke, no hut, no beacon . . .
LYNN EMANUEL (b. 1949), U.S. poet.
"Shipwrecked," lines 15–19 (1979).

REALITY

1 . . . the ordinary is simply the universal observed from the surface,
that the direct approach to reality is
not without, but within. Touch life
anywhere . . . and you will touch
universality wherever you touch the
earth.
ELLEN GLASGOW (1873–1945), U.S. novelist. The Woman Within, ch. 10 (1954).
Written in 1944. Glasgow said that she gained
this insight from reading the great Russian novelist, Leo Tolstoy (1828–1910).

2 What staggers me is not the persistence of illusion, but the persistence
of the world in the face of illusion.
A. G. MOJTABAI (b. 1937), U.S. novelist.
Mundome (1974).

3 . . . parables are unnecessary for
recognizing the blatant absurdity
of everyday life. Reality is lesson
enough.
JANE O'REILLY, U.S. feminist and humorist. The Girl I Left Behind, ch. 2 (1980).
This is drawn from O'Reilly's famous essay first
published in Ms. magazine: "Click! The Housewife's Moment of Truth."

REALITY AND REALISM

1 We had to take the world as it was
given:
The nursemaid sitting passive in the
park

Was rarely by a changeling prince
accosted,
The mornings happened similar
and stark
In rooms of selfhood where we
woke and lay
Watching today unfold like
yesterday.
ADRIENNE RICH (b. 1929), U.S. poet
and feminist. "Ideal Landscape," lines 1–6
(1955).

REASON

1 . . . the conduct of an accountable
being must be regulated by the op-
erations of its own reason . . .
MARY WOLLSTONECRAFT (1759–1797),
British feminist. A Vindication of the Rights of
Woman, ch. 2 (1792).

2 . . . a large portion of those who demand woman suffrage are persons
who have not been trained to reason, and are chiefly guided by their
generous sensibilities.
CATHERINE E. BEECHER (1800–1878),
U.S. educator and author. Woman's Profession
as Mother and Educator, with Views in Opposition to Woman Suffrage, "An Address to the
Christian Women of America," (1872).
Beecher was both an anti-suffragist and a passionate advocate of education for girls and
women.

3 Human beings lose their logic in
their vindictiveness.
ELIZABETH CADY STANTON (1815–
1902), U.S. author, suffragist, and social reformer. Elizabeth Cady Stanton as Revealed in
her Letters, Diary and Reminiscences, vol. 2,
letter dated November 28, 1890 (1922).

4 Reason is a passion; an instinct, a
drive.

BETTE HOWLAND (b. 1937), U.S. author. *Blue in Chicago*, ch. 3 (1978).

REBELLION

1   . . . it is one thing to like defiance, and another thing to like its consequences.

GEORGE ELIOT (1819–1880), British novelist. *Middlemarch*, ch. 46 (1871–1872).

2   I refuse to be. In the madhouse of the inhuman I refuse to live.
With the wolves of the market place I refuse to howl . . .

MARINA TSVETAYEVA (1892–1941), Russian poet; relocated to Czechoslovakia. "Poems for Czechoslovakia," part 8, lines 9–13, as translated by Elaine Feinstein (1938).

From a poem cycle written to protest the Nazi occupation of Czechoslovakia, where she was living in exile from her native Russia.

3   The best thing in life is doing things people say you can't do.

JENNIFER MOORE (b. 1972), U.S. college student and ROTC midshipman captain. As quoted in the *Chronicle of Higher Education*, p. A5 (April 21, 1993).

Said by the Boston University senior who was the nation's highest-ranking woman member of the Navy ROTC (Reserve Officer Training Corps).

4   When you come to a place where you have to go left or right, go straight ahead.

SISTER RUTH, U.S. nun. As quoted in *Dakota*, ch. 30, by Kathleen Norris (1993).

RELIGION

1   Those who appear the most sanctified are the worst.

ELIZABETH I (1533–1603), Queen of England (1558–1603). As quoted in *The Sayings of Queen Elizabeth*, ch. 11, by Frederick Chamberlin (1923).

Said to the Spanish Ambassador when he protested her arrest of Catholics. (Elizabeth, a Protestant, was embattled against Roman Catholics throughout her reign.)

2   Religion . . . may be defined thus: *a belief in, and homage rendered to, existences unseen and causes unknown.*

FRANCES WRIGHT (1795–1852), Scottish author and speaker; relocated to America. *Course of Popular Lectures*, lecture 5 (1829).

3   . . . so far from entrenching human conduct within the gentle barriers of peace and love, religion has ever been, and now is, the deepest source of contentions, wars, persecutions for conscience sake, angry words, angry feelings, backbitings, slanders, suspicions, false judgments, evil interpretations, unwise, unjust, injurious, inconsistent actions.

FRANCES WRIGHT (1795–1852), Scottish author and speaker; relocated to America. *Course of Popular Lectures*, lecture 5 (1829).

4   No person can be considered as possessing a good education without religion. A good education is that which prepares us for our future sphere of action and makes us contented with that situation in life in which God, in his infinite mercy, has seen fit to place us, to be perfectly resigned to our lot in life, whatever it may be.

ANN PLATO (1820– ?), U.S. teacher and author. As quoted in *Black Women in Nineteenth-Century American Life*, part 2, by Bert James Loewenberg and Ruth Bogin (1976).

Plato, a free African American who was a schoolmistress in Hartford, Connecticut, said this in 1841.

quoted in *The Narrative of Sojourner Truth,* Memorial Chapter, by Frances W. Titus (added 1883; book originally copyrighted in 1875). Said near the end of her life.

5 In her present ignorance, woman's religion, instead of making her noble and free, by the wrong application of great principles of right and justice, has made her bondage but more certain and lasting, her degradation more hopeless and complete.

ELIZABETH CADY STANTON (1815–1902), U.S. suffragist, social reformer, and author. As quoted in *The Life and Work of Susan B. Anthony,* vol. 1, ch. 5, by Ida Husted Harper (1898).

From a September 8, 1852, letter sent to the Woman's Rights Convention in Syracuse, NY, and read aloud by Susan B. Anthony, who was attending such a convention for the first time; she served as one of the convention secretaries. She and Stanton had met in 1850. Before long, Anthony (1820–1906) would establish herself as a major leader in the movement.

6 When I was young . . . there never was any question about right and wrong. We knew our catechism, and that was enough; we learned our creed and our duty. Every respectable Church person had the same opinions. But, now if you speak out of the Prayer-book itself, you are liable to be contradicted.

GEORGE ELIOT (1819–1880), British novelist. *Middlemarch,* ch. 17 (1871–1872).

Said by the novel's character named Mrs. Farebrother, mother of the village Vicar. This part of the novel is set in 1829, and Mrs. Farebrother is said to be "still under seventy," so she would have been "young" c. 1760–1780.

7 Religion without humanity is a poor human stuff.

SOJOURNER TRUTH (1797–1883), African American slave; later an itinerant preacher and advocate of various social reforms including abolition, woman suffrage, and temperance. As

8 You may go over the world and you will find that every form of religion which has breathed upon this earth has degraded women. There is not one which has not made her subject to man.

ELIZABETH CADY STANTON (1815–1902), U.S. suffragist, social reformer, and author. As quoted in *History of Woman Suffrage,* vol. 4, ch. 4, by Susan B. Anthony and Ida Husted Harper (1902).

Speaking before the seventeenth annual convention of the National Woman Suffrage Association, held January 20–22, 1885, in Washington, D.C.

9 . . . religion (ought to be if it isn't) a great deal more than mere gratification of the instinct for worship linked with the straight-teaching of irreproachable credos. Religion must be *life made true;* and life is action, growth, development—begun now and ending never.

ANNA JULIA COOPER (1859–1964), U.S. educator and feminist. *A Voice from the South,* part 2 (1892).

10 I care not for the theoretical symmetry and impregnable logic of your moral code, I care not for the hoary respectability and traditional mysticisms of your theological institutions, I care not for the beauty and solemnity of your rituals and religious ceremonies, I care not even for the reasonableness and unimpeachable fairness of your social ethics,—if it does not turn out better, nobler, truer, men and women,—if it does not add to the world's stock of valuable souls,—if it does not give us a sounder, healthier, more reliable product from this great factory of *men*—I will have none of it.

ANNA JULIA COOPER (1859–1964), African American educator and feminist. *A Voice from the South,* part 2 (1892).

11 While we honour religion and believe it to be a powerful factor in elevating our race, we discriminate, as we hope our readers will also do, between it and dogmatism. Dogmatism has been the bane of civilization and a curse to mankind. It has degraded our sex, stifled intelligent inquiry, and persecuted every independent reformer and every noble cause.

TENNESSEE CLAFLIN (1846–1923), U.S. journalist, lecturer, and social reform advocate; relocated to England. *Talks and Essays,* vol. 1, ch. 7 (1897).

12 . . . all the cares and anxieties, the trials and disappointments of my whole life, are light, when balanced with my sufferings in childhood and youth from the theological dogmas which I sincerely believed, and the gloom connected with everything associated with the name of religion, the church, the parsonage, the graveyard, and the solemn, tolling bell.

ELIZABETH CADY STANTON (1815–1902), U.S. suffragist, author, and social reformer. *Eighty Years and More (1815–1897),* ch. 2 (1898).

13 Religion! How it dominates man's mind, how it humiliates and de-

grades his soul. God is everything, man is nothing, says religion. But out of that nothing God has created a kingdom so despotic, so tyrannical, so cruel, so terribly exacting that naught but gloom and tears and blood have ruled the world since gods began.

EMMA GOLDMAN (1869–1940), U.S. anarchist and author; born in Russia. *Anarchism and Other Essays,* 3rd rev. ed., ch. 1 (1917).

14 I shall never send for a priest or recite an Act of Contrition in my last moments. I do not mind if I lose my soul for all eternity. If the kind of God exists Who would damn me for not working out a deal with Him, then that is unfortunate. I should not care to spend eternity in the company of such a person.

MARY MCCARTHY (1912–1989), U.S. author. *Memories of a Catholic Girlhood,* ch. 1 (1957).

Raised in a strictly religious, unsympathetic Irish-Catholic home, McCarthy had become an unbeliever.

15 It's Hard to be Proud of Being Jewish When Your Only Religious Experience Was Seeing *Exodus*

LYNNE SAVITT, U.S. Jewish poet. "It's Hard to Be Proud of Being Jewish When Your Only Religious Experience Was Seeing *Exodus,*" title (of poem) (1979).

Exodus was a popular movie (1960) based on Leon Uris's novel of the same name (1958) about the founding of the modern state of Israel.

16 . . . I can't see (or feel) the conflict between love and religion. To me they're the same thing.

ELIZABETH BOWEN (1899–1973), British novelist, story writer, essayist, and memoirist;

born in Ireland. As quoted in *Elizabeth Bowen,* ch. 13, by Victoria Glendinning (1979). To her lover, the author Charles Ritchie, in the late 1960s.

17 ... the meanest life, the poorest existence, is attributed to God's will, but as human beings become more affluent, as their living standard and style begin to ascend the material scale, God descends the scale of responsibility at a commensurate speed.

MAYA ANGELOU (b. 1928), African American poet, autobiographer, and performer. *I Know Why the Caged Bird Sings,* ch. 18 (1970).

RELIGIOUS FEELING

1 The best piety is to enjoy ...

GEORGE ELIOT (1819–1880), British novelist. *Middlemarch,* ch. 22 (1871–1872).

2 I pray every single second of my life; not on my knees, but with my work. My prayer is to lift woman to equality with man. Work and worship are one with me. I can not imagine a God of the universe made happy by my getting down on my knees and calling him "great."

SUSAN B. ANTHONY (1820–1906), U.S. suffragist, speaker, and editor. As quoted in *The Life and Work of Susan B. Anthony,* ch. 46, by Ida Husted Harper (1898–1908). Said in 1896.

3 Life is a thin narrowness of taken-for-granted, a plank over a canyon in a fog. There is something under our feet, the taken-for-granted. A table is a table, food is food, we are we—because we don't question

these things. And science is the enemy because it is the questioner. Faith saves our souls alive by giving us a universe of the taken-for-granted.

ROSE WILDER LANE (1886–1968), U.S. author. As quoted in *The Ghost in the Little House,* ch. 7, by William V. Holtz (1993). From a 1923 journal entry.

4 Religion engaged her feelings in the hard grapple she knew as love.

ELIZABETH BOWEN (1899–1973), British author; born in Ireland. *Bowen's Court,* ch. 8 (1942). Of Eliza Galwey Bowen, wife of her nineteenth-century forbear, Robert Bowen.

5 The problem of the novelist who wishes to write about a man's encounter with God is how he shall make the experience—which is both natural and supernatural—understandable, and credible, to his reader. In any age this would be a problem, but in our own, it is a well-nigh insurmountable one. Today's audience is one in which religious feeling has become, if not atrophied, at least vaporous and sentimental.

FLANNERY O'CONNOR (1925–1964), U.S. fiction writer and essayist. *Mystery and Manners,* part 5 (1969). From "Novelist and Believer," a paper given in March 1963 at a symposium at Sweet Briar College, Virginia. O'Connor was a devout Roman Catholic.

6 Irish Catholics are more interested in the rosary beads than in the rosary ...

BERNADETTE DEVLIN (b. 1947), Irish Catholic politician. *The Price of My Soul,* ch. 5 (1969).

REPETITION

I   . . . there was the first Balkan war and the second Balkan war and then there was the first world war. It is extraordinary how having done a thing once you have to do it again, there is the pleasure of coincidence and there is the pleasure of repetition, and so there is the second world war, and in between there was the Abyssinian war and the Spanish civil war.

GERTRUDE STEIN (1874–1946), U.S. author; relocated to France. *Wars I Have Seen* (1945).

Written in 1943.

REPRODUCTIVE RIGHTS

I   Shall we who have heard the cries and seen the agony of dying women respect the law which has caused their deaths? Shall we watch in patience the murdering of 25,000 women each year in the Untied States from criminal abortions? Shall we fold our hands and wait until a body of sleek and well-fed politicians get ready to abolish the cause of such slaughter?

MARGARET SANGER (1879–1966), U.S. birth control rights activist. *My Fight for Birth Control,* ch. 6 (1931).

From an editorial published in her pro-birth control magazine, *The Woman Rebel.* She was at the time facing trial for publishing and distributing the magazine, which was defined as "obscene."

REPUTATION

I   I would rather go to any extreme than suffer anything that is unworthy of my reputation, or of that of my crown.

ELIZABETH I (1533–1603), Queen of England (1558–1603). As quoted in *The Sayings of Queen Elizabeth,* ch. 13, by Frederick Chamberlin (1923).

To Fenelon, the French Ambassador.

2   Reputation is not of enough value to sacrifice character for it.

"MISS CLARK", U.S. charity worker. As quoted in *Petticoat Surgeon,* ch. 9, by Bertha Van Hoosen (1947).

Clark was chair of the Committee for Delinquent Girls [i.e., unmarried young mothers] in Detroit in the 1880s.

RESEARCH

I   I think, for the rest of my life, I shall refrain from looking up things. It is the most ravenous time-snatcher I know. You pull one book from the shelf, which carries a hint or a reference that sends you posthaste to another book, and that to successive others. It is incredible, the number of books you hopefully open and disappointedly close, only to take down another with the same result.

CAROLYN WELLS (1862–1942), U.S. author. *The Rest of My Life,* ch. 8 (1937).

2   . . . research is never completed . . . Around the corner lurks another possibility of interview, another book to read, a courthouse to explore, a document to verify.

CATHERINE DRINKER BOWEN (1897–1973), U.S. biographer. *Adventures of a Biographer,* ch. 4 (1959).

Bowen wrote widely read biographies of several famous men, including two lawyers: Oliver Wendell Holmes and John Adams.

3 I did my research and decided I just had to live it.

KARINA O'MALLEY, U.S. sociologist and educator. As quoted in the *Chronicle of Higher Education*, p. A5 (September 16, 1992).

A sociology professor at St. Norbert College who studied the homeless, O'Malley was explaining why she had moved into a homeless shelter.

4 Almost all scholarly research carries practical and political implications. Better that we should spell these out ourselves than leave that task to people with a vested interest in stressing only some of the implications and falsifying others. The idea that academics should remain "above the fray" only gives ideologues license to misuse our work.

STEPHANIE COONTZ (b. 1944), U.S. social historian. *Chronicle of Higher Education*, p. B2 (October 21, 1992).

A scholar specializing in the subject of the American family, Coontz was reacting to inaccuracies and distortions in the conservative political emphasis on "family values."

RESPONSIBILITY

1 To be a king and wear a crown is more glorious to them that see it than it is pleasure to them that bear it.

ELIZABETH I (1533–1603), Queen of England (1558–1603). As quoted in *The Sayings of Queen Elizabeth*, ch. 6, by Frederick Chamberlin (1923).

Said to the House of Commons when she disbanded Parliament in 1601 for the last time in her life.

2 . . . I believe it is *now the duty of the slaves of the South to rebuke their masters* for their robbery, oppression and crime. . . . No station or character can destroy individual responsibility, in the matter of reproving sin.

ANGELINA GRIMKÉ (1805–1879), U.S. abolitionist and feminist. *Letters to Catherine Beecher,* letter #9 (1837).

In a letter dated August 17, 1837.

3 Nothing strengthens the judgment and quickens the conscience like individual responsibility. Nothing adds such dignity to character as the recognition of one's self-sovereignty; the right to an equal place, everywhere conceded—a place earned by personal merit, not an artificial attainment by inheritance, wealth, family and position.

ELIZABETH CADY STANTON (1815–1902), U.S. suffragist, social reformer, and author. *The Solitude of Self* (February 20, 1894).

From a famous speech delivered before a Senate committee which was considering arguments in favor of woman suffrage. Printed in the *Congressional Record* and reprinted in the *Women's Tribune,* the speech was remarkable for its refusal to engage the usual practical and democratic pro-suffrage arguments.

4 I dreamed night after night that everyone in the world was dead excepting myself, and that upon me rested the responsibility of making a wagon wheel.

JANE ADDAMS (1860–1935), U.S. settlement house founder and social reformer. *Twenty Years at Hull-House,* ch. 2 (1910).

Describing an experience that she had at age six, in her hometown of Cedarville, Illinois.

RETIREMENT

1 Being sixty-five . . . became a crossroads. We said, We have nothing to lose, so we can raise hell.

MAGGIE KUHN (b. 1905), U.S. senior rights activist. As quoted in *The Great Divide,* book 2, section 6, by Studs Terkel (1988).

On the effect of forced retirement (now illegal in the United States for most employee categories).

2 Look at the trees now, aren't they bare? But you let a certain day come for spring and they'll come out. They won't be the same leaves that was there last year, but when they come out they're so pretty. I look out at those trees and just think, Oh, you're so beautiful. God sure dressed you up. I say that to a tree. The work I have done, if I have to do it over, I'm willin'. But I don't want to go back. Let me be the leaf just laying at the foot of the tree giving it substance to grow.

WILLIE MAE FORD SMITH, (1904–1994) African American gospel singer. As quoted in *I Dream a World,* by Brian Lanker (1989).

Smith was a major talent in American gospel singing.

3 People who refuse to rest honorably on their laurels when they reach "retirement" age seem very admirable to me.

HELEN HAYES (1900–1993), U.S. actor. *My Life in Three Acts,* ch. 19 (1990).

Hayes was an actor from age five until into her seventies, and thereafter a speaker and an activist on behalf of the elderly. She also wrote, with assistance, four volumes of memoirs; this was her last.

4 I want a place where I can sit back in the rocker and say, "Do you remember when we picketed the White House in 1965?"

BARBARA GITTINGS (b. 1932), U.S. gay and lesbian rights activist. As quoted in *Making History,* part 3, by Eric Marcus (1992).

Commenting on her future goal, suggested half-jokingly by her partner, Kay Tobin, of founding a "gay retirement home."

5 I think it beats the heck out of life after death, that's for sure.

MARTINA NAVRATILOVA (b. 1956), U.S. tennis player; born and raised in Czechoslovakia. As quoted in *People* magazine, p. 116 (September 13, 1993).

On how she envisioned life after tennis. A competitive player for twenty-one years, she was planning to retire.

6 I retired from work and I didn't want to just sit there and do nothing; I don't knit and I don't like TV and I'm no gardener.

MARGARET DEMERS (b. c. 1917), U.S. college student. As quoted in *On Campus with Women,* p. 2 (Spring 1993).

A 76-year-old retired office worker, she was explaining why she had enrolled as an undergraduate student at Worcester State College in Massachusetts.

REVOLUTION

I There is nothing in the world I hold in greater horror than to see a body moving against its head: and I shall be very careful not to ally myself with such a monster.

ELIZABETH I (1533–1603), Queen of England (1558–1603). As quoted in *The Sayings of Queen Elizabeth,* ch. 16, by Frederick Chamberlin (1923).

To the French Ambassador.

2 I . . . really think I should consider my own throat and those of my children well cut if some night the people were to take it into their head to clear off scores in that fashion.

FANNY KEMBLE (1809–1893), British actor and abolitionist. *Journal of a Residence on a Georgian Plantation in 1838–1839,* ch. 19 (1863).
From a letter written from St. Simons Island, Georgia, on February 28, 1839, to her friend Elizabeth Dwight Sedgwick. A few years earlier, Kemble had unwittingly married into a slave-owning family; the marriage failed, and she and Pierce Butler were divorced in 1849. At this time, however, they were staying together on the Butler family plantation. She wrote this after hearing a young slave woman tell of savage ill treatment.

3 Last night you wrote on the wall:
Revolution is poetry.
Today you needn't write; the wall
has tumbled down.

ADRIENNE RICH (b. 1929), U.S. poet and feminist. "Ghazals: Homage to Ghalib," lines 1–2 (July 26, 1968).

4 . . . a legitimate revolution must be led by, *made* by those who have been most oppressed: black, brown, yellow, red, and white *women—* with men relating to that the best they can.

ROBIN MORGAN (b. 1941), U.S. author, feminist, and child actor. *Goodbye to All That* (January 1970).

5 We live in a highly industrialized society and every member of the Black nation must be as academically and technologically developed as possible. To wage a revolution, we need competent teachers, doctors, nurses, electronics experts, chemists, biologists, physicists, political scientists, and so on and so forth. Black women sitting at home reading bedtime stories to their children are just not going to make it.

FRANCES BEALE, African American feminist and civil rights activist. *The Black Woman,* ch. 14 (1970).

6 . . . in order to be a true revolutionary, you must understand love. Love, sacrifice, and death.

SONIA SANCHEZ (b. 1934), U.S. poet. *Black Women Writers at Work,* ch. 10, by Claudia Tate (1985).

7 Like art, revolutions come from combining what exists into what has never existed before.

GLORIA STEINEM (b. 1934), U.S. feminist, author, and editor. *Moving Beyond Words,* part 4 (1994).

REVOLUTION AND REVOLUTIONARY ACTIVITY

1 Split by a tendril of revolt stone cedes to blossom everywhere.

MURIEL RUKEYSER (1913–1980), U.S. poet. "City of Monuments," lines 36–37 (1934). The "city" is Washington, DC.

2 The poet who speaks out of the deepest instincts of man will be heard. The poet who creates a myth beyond the power of man to realize is gagged at the peril of the group that binds him. He is the true revolutionary: he builds a new world.

BABETTE DEUTSCH (1895–1982), U.S. poet. *This Modern Poetry,* ch. 9 (1935).

3 Did all of us feel interested in bombing buildings only when the men we slept with were urging us on?

JANE ALPERT (b. 1947), U.S. revolutionary and convicted bomber. *Growing Up Underground,* ch. 13 (1981).

Reflecting on the instigation of her lover, Sam Melville, who led a tiny revolutionary commune in New York City during the late 1960s; Melville was imprisoned in Attica, in western New York State, and died in a revolt there.

REVOLUTIONARY ACTIVITY

1   I shall earnestly and persistently continue to urge all women to the practical recognition of the old Revolutionary maxim. "Resistance to tyranny is obedience to God."

SUSAN B. ANTHONY (1820–1906), U.S. suffragist. As quoted in *Feminism: The Essential Historical Writings*, part 3, by Miriam Schnier (1972).

Said by the famous woman suffrage leader in federal court on June 18, 1873, upon its being judged that she "did knowingly, wrongfully and unlawfully vote for a Representative in the Congress of the United States"; the case was *United States vs. Susan B. Anthony*. This was the last statement she made in court that day. American women would not gain the right to vote for another forty-seven years.

2   Some day the workers will take possession of your city hall, and when we do, no child will be sacrificed on the altar of profit!

MOTHER JONES (1830–1930), U.S. labor organizer. *The Autobiography of Mother Jones*, ch. 10 (1903).

Shouted outside City Hall in Independence Park, Philadelphia, while leading a 1903 demonstration of child textile workers from Kensington, Pennsylvania; 75,000 Kensington textile workers were on strike, of whom 10,000 were children.

3   There is something that governments care for more than human life, and that is the security of property, and so it is through property that we shall strike the enemy. . . . Those of you who can break windows—break them. Those of you who can still further attack the secret idol of property, so as to make the Government realize that property is as greatly endangered by women's suffrage as it was by the Chartists of old—do so. And my last word is to the Government: I incite this meeting to rebellion!

EMMELINE PANKHURST (1858–1928), British suffragist. As quoted in *Feminism: The Essential Historical Writings*, part 5, by Miriam Schnier (1972).

In a speech delivered at London's Royal Albert Hall on October 17, 1912 following her release from imprisonment for attacking shop windows, and the windows of Prime Minister's residence at 10 Downing Street, with a hammer. Approximately 150 other suffragists had been arrested with her. Chartists (1838–1848) were English working-class political reformists who called for universal male suffrage; they held public demonstrations which led to some riots and confrontations with the military.

4   Revolution begins with the self, in the self. . . . We'd better take the time to fashion revolutionary selves, revolutionary lives, revolutionary relationships. Mouth don't win the war.

TONI CADE (b. 1939), African American author and political activist. *The Black Woman*, ch. 15 (1970).

Excerpted from "The Scattered Sopranoes," an autobiographical essay delivered as a lecture to the Livingston College Black Woman's Seminar in December 1969. Cade was speaking of the African American militant movement. She would become well known as a fiction writer, under the name Toni Cade Bambara.

5   This tendency to consider only bombings or picking up the gun as revolutionary, with the glorification of the heavier the better, we've called the military error.

BERNARDINE DOHRN (b. 1942), U.S. political activist and lawyer. As quoted in *The War Within*, ch. 8, by Tom Wells (1994).

Said in 1970, when Dohrn was a leader of Weather Underground (originally Weathermen), a radical, violent anti-Vietnam war and anti-establishment organization that grew out of the Students for a Democratic Society. At this time, she was a fugitive from justice and was on the FBI's Ten Most Wanted list.

6   To be revolutionary is to be original, to know where we came from, to validate what is ours and help it to flourish, the best of what is ours, of our beginnings, our principles, and to leave behind what no longer serves us.

INES HERNANDEZ, U.S. Chicana political activist. As quoted in *What Is Found There,* ch. 28, by Adrienne Rich (1993).

7   A revolutionary poem will not tell you who or when to kill, what and when to burn, or even how to theorize. It reminds you . . . where and when and how you are living and might live—it is a wick of desire.

ADRIENNE RICH (b. 1929), U.S. poet, essayist, and lesbian feminist. *What Is Found There,* ch. 28 (1993).

REVOLUTIONARY WAR: AMERICAN

1   . . . I feel anxious for the fate of our monarchy, or democracy, or whatever is to take place. I soon get lost in a labyrinth of perplexities; but, whatever occurs, may justice and righteousness be the stability of our times, and order arise out of confusion. Great difficulties may be surmounted by patience and perseverance.

ABIGAIL ADAMS (1744–1818), U.S. matriarch; wife and mother of United States President. *Familiar Letters of John Adams and His Wife Abigail Adams, During the Revolution,* letter dated November 27, 1775 (1875).

In a letter to her husband John Adams, who was away fighting in the American colonies' revolution against Britain.

RHETORIC

1   . . . rhetoric never won a revolution yet.

SHIRLEY CHISHOLM (b. 1924), African American politician and human rights advocate. *Unbought and Unbossed,* ch. 13 (1970).

RISK

1   I am willing, for a money consideration, to test this physical strength, this nervous force, and muscular power with which I've been gifted, to show that they will bear a certain strain. If I break down, if my brain gives way under want of sleep, my heart ceases to respond to the calls made on my circulatory system, or the surcharged veins of my extremities burst—if, in short, I fall helpless, or it may be, dead on the track, then I lose my money.

ADA ANDERSON (1860– ?), U.S. marathon walker. As quoted in *WomenSports* magazine, p. 17 (June 1976).

Said c. 1878, the year in which Anderson amazed the world by "walking a quarter mile every fifteen minutes for a month." During that month, she never slept for more than ten minutes at a time. For her efforts, she won $10,000.

2   A lot of people refuse to do things because they don't want to go naked, don't want to go without guarantee. But that's what's got to happen. You go naked until you die.

NIKKI GIOVANNI (b. 1943), U.S. poet.

Black Women Writers at Work, ch. 5, by Claudia Tate (1983).

3 One of the few things I know about writing is this: spend it all, shoot it, play it, lose it, all, right away, every time. Do not hoard what seems good for a later place in the book, or for another book; give it, give it all, give it now.

ANNIE DILLARD (b. 1945), U.S. author. *The Writing Life,* ch. 5 (1989).

ROLE MODELS

1 I had a consuming ambition to possess a miller's thumb. I believe I have never since wanted anything more desperately than I wanted my right thumb to be flattened as my father's had become, during his earlier years of a miller's life.

JANE ADDAMS (1860–1935), U.S. settlement house founder and social reformer. *Twenty Years at Hull-House,* ch. 1 (1910).
Of her early-childhood yearning to be like her father, her mother having died when she was a baby.

2 . . . if women once learn to be something themselves, that the only way to teach is to be fine and shining examples, we will have in one generation the most remarkable and glorious children.

BRENDA UELAND (1891–1985), U.S. author and writing teacher. *If You Want to Write,* 2nd. ed., ch. 10 (1938).

3 . . . no young colored person in the United States today can truthfully offer as an excuse for lack of ambition or aspiration that members of

his race have accomplished so little, he is discouraged from attempting anything himself. For there is scarcely a field of human endeavor which colored people have been allowed to enter in which there is not at least one worthy representative.

MARY CHURCH TERRELL (1863–1954), African American author, speaker, and social reformer. *A Colored Woman in a White World,* ch. 8 (1940).

4 . . . you can't love yourself unless you know that somebody that looks like you has done something good.

OPHELIA DEVORE-MITCHELL (b. 1923), African American fashion model and businesswoman. As quoted in *I Dream a World,* by Brian Lanker (1989).
Referring to the importance of documenting the accomplishments of African American people. DeVore-Mitchell was a founder of the African American press archives at Howard University, Washington, DC.

5 . . . I didn't come to this with any particular cachet. I was just a person who grew up in the United States. And when I looked around at the people who were sportscasters, I thought they were just people who grew up in the United States, too. So I thought, Why can't a woman do it? I just assumed everyone else would think it was a swell idea.

GAYLE GARDNER, U.S. sports reporter. As quoted in *Sports Illustrated,* p. 85 (June 17, 1991).
Gardner, who was the first female sports anchor to appear weekly on a major television network, did encounter sex discrimination in her career but succeeded nonetheless.

6 She's me. She represents everything I feel, everything I want to be. I'm so locked into her that what she says is unimportant.

DIANE VALLETA, American suburbanite. As quoted in the *New York Times,* p. A13 (July 29, 1992).

Valleta, a white woman from a Chicago suburb, was explaining her support for Carol Moseley-Braun (b. 1947), an African American U. S. Senatorial candidate from the largely African American South Side of Chicago.

7 You can't be what you don't see. I didn't think about being a doctor. I didn't even think about being a clerk in a store—I'd never seen a black clerk in a clothing store.

JOYCELYN ELDERS (b. 1933), U.S. pediatrician and educator; first woman (and second African American) Surgeon General of the United States. As quoted in the *New York Times Magazine,* p. 18 (January 30, 1994).

Elders, who was the U. S. Surgeon General at the time, was noting the importance of professional role models for African American children. Explaining why, growing up African American in Arkansas, she wanted to be a lab technician, she said: "That was the only thing I'd ever heard about." Eventually, she met Dr. Edith Irby Jones, the first African American woman to study at the University of Arizona Medical School, and was inspired to become a physician.

8 My generation had Doris Day as a role model, then Gloria Steinem— then Princess Diana. We are the most confused generation.

ERICA JONG (b. 1942), U.S. poet and novelist. As quoted in *People* magazine, p. 36 (March 7–14, 1994).

Day (b. 1924) was a blond, wholesome, ever-virginal star of Hollywood movies in the 1950s and sixties; she performed dramatic roles but achieved her greatest popularity in romantic comedies. Steinem (b. 1934) was a prominent feminist. Lady Diana Spencer (b. 1961) became a Princess when she married Charles, Prince of Wales and heir to the British throne; like Day, she represented traditional values and ideals of femininity. All three women were extremely attractive physically.

ROMAN CATHOLIC CHURCH

1 . . . the average Catholic perceives no connection between religion and morality, unless it is a question of someone else's morality.

MARY MCCARTHY (1912–1989), U.S. author. *Memories of a Catholic Girlhood,* ch. 1 (1957).

Raised in a strictly Catholic, unsympathetic, Irish-American home, McCarthy would later become an unbeliever.

ROMANCE

1 Adventure is making the distant approach nearer but romance is having what is where it is which is not where you are stay where it is.

GERTRUDE STEIN (1874–1946), U.S. author and patron of the arts; relocated to France. *An American and France* (1936).

2 . . . to be "literary" appeared to my deluded innocence as an unending romance.

ELLEN GLASGOW (1873–1945), U.S. novelist. *The Woman Within,* ch. 9 (1954).

Written in 1944. She was recalling her early infatuation with the idea of having a literary career.

3 The importance of a lost romantic vision should not be underestimated. In such a vision is power as well as joy. In it is meaning. Life is flat, barren, zestless, if one can find one's lost vision nowhere.

SARAH PATTON BOYLE, U.S. civil rights activist and author. *The Desegregated Heart,* part 1, ch. 19 (1962).

Boyle was a white Virginian who publicly advocated integration from the earliest days of the civil rights movement. The "vision" whose loss she lamented was that of sentimental, fully reciprocal love between white Southerners and the African American Southerners who served them. She had come to learn that this had always been merely a white illusion.

4 As a novelist, I cannot occupy myself with "characters," or at any rate central ones, who lack panache, in one or another sense, who would be incapable of a major action or a major passion, or who have not a touch of the ambiguity, the ultimate unaccountability, the enlarging mistiness of persons "in history." History, as more austerely I now know it, is not romantic. But I am.

ELIZABETH BOWEN (1899–1973), British novelist, essayist, and memoirist; born in Ireland. *Pictures and Conversations,* ch. 1 (1975).

ROME, ITALY

1 Rome . . . seems to me the place in the world where one can best dispense with happiness. . . .

FANNY KEMBLE (1809–1893), British actor. *Further Records, 1848–1883,* vol. 2; entry dated December 22, 1853 (1891).

Kemble was travelling through Europe and staying briefly in Rome.

ROYALTY

1 It is better to pay court to a queen . . . than to worship, as we too often do, some unworthy person whose wealth is his sole passport into society. I believe that a habit of respect is good for the human race.

M. E. W. SHERWOOD (1826–1903), U.S. socialite, traveller, and author. *An Epistle to Posterity,* ch. 8 (1897).

2 The prince in disguise makes the most charming beggar in the world, no doubt; but that is because—as all fairy-tales from the beginning of time have taught us—the prince wears his rags as if they were purple. And, to do that, he not only must once have worn purple, but must never forget the purple that he has worn. And to the argument that all cannot wear purple, I can . . . only reply that that seems to me to be no reason why all should wear rags.

KATHERINE FULLERTON GEROULD (1879–1944), U.S. author. *Modes and Morals,* ch. 3 (1920).

3 I see no cameras! *Where* are the cameras?

MARY, QUEEN OF GREAT BRITAIN, (1867–1953) As quoted in *Kiss Hollywood Good-by,* ch. 8, by Anita Loos (1974).

The wife of King George V, who reigned 1910–1936, she allegedly said this "whenever [she] graced a public gathering" and no photographers were in evidence.

RUNNING

1 Something in me wanted to find out how far I could run without stopping.

JACKI HANSON (b. 1948), U.S. marathon runner. As quoted in *WomenSports* magazine, p. 10 (February 1977).

The women's world record holder in the marathon was explaining why she became involved in the sport.

2 All I want to do is speed, speed.

MIKI GORMAN (b. 1935), U.S. marathon runner; born in China. As quoted in *WomenSports* magazine, p. 26 (November 1977).

At 5'1" and 89 pounds, Gorman was the first woman to win the Boston Marathon (1974 and 1977). She also won the New York City Marathon (1976) and other important races.

3 It's not like I was out there running and not knowing what's going on in the country. I knew what was going on, but I felt this is not something that is going to bog me down and not let me participate. The only way I was going to make a difference for myself or any other black person is to say the hurdles were there and do what I had to do.

WYOMIA TYUS (b. 1945), African American runner. As quoted in *I Dream a World*, by Brian Lanker (1989).

Referring to white racism. Born in humble circumstances in Georgia, Tyus became a champion runner, winning gold medals in the 1964 and 1968 Olympics.

4 I think I've been good, but I want to be better. I think women reach their peak in their mid-thirties.

MARY DECKER SLANEY (b. 1958), U.S. runner. As quoted in *Sports Illustrated*, p. 55 (July 29, 1991).

At thirty-three, Slaney had been running competitively for eighteen years; at age fifteen, she had already been ranked fourth in the world. She had suffered setbacks recently and was professionally threatened by emerging African track stars.

5 The real reason I run is to bring honor to Jesus.

CHARITY FILLMORE (b. 1982), U.S. runner. As quoted in the *New York Times*, p. B16 (June 15, 1994).

The sixty-pound twelve-year-old already held a national 5-K record for the under-twelve age group. She was running forty miles per week and cherished goals of setting world and Olympic records. Her father was a Baptist minister and principal of the Baptist school she was attending.

RURAL LIFE

1 There is a city myth that country life was isolated and lonely; the truth is that farmers and their families then had a richer social life than they have now. They enjoyed a society organic, satisfying and whole, not mixed and thinned with the life of town, city and nation as it now is.

ROSE WILDER LANE (1886–1965), U.S. author. *Old Hometown*, ch. 1 (1935).

Of life in rural Nebraska when she was growing up there in the late 1800s.

2 It may be romantic to search for the salves of society's ills in slow-moving rustic surroundings, or among innocent, unspoiled provincials, if such exist, but it is a waste of time.

JANE JACOBS (b. 1916), U.S. urban analyst. *The Death and Life of Great American Cities*, ch. 22 (1961).

Jacobs lived in the lively, diverse Greenwich Village section of Manhattan (New York City).

SACRIFICE

1 We now come to the *grand law* of the system in which we are placed, as it has been developed by the experience of our race, and that, in one word, is SACRIFICE!

CATHERINE E. BEECHER (1800–1878), U.S. educator and author. *Common Sense Applied to Religion, or the Bible and the People*, ch. 4 (1857).

2 *Renunciation:* that is the great fact we all, individuals and classes, have to learn. In trying to avoid it we bring misery to ourselves and others.

BEATRICE WEBB (1858–1943), British author and socialist. As quoted in *Beatrice Webb*, ch. 10, by Carole Seymour-Jones (1992).
Written in her diary on February 1, 1885, upon determining to forsake romance and the affluent high society into which she had been born for service to society.

3 ... I swore I would battle not only for myself but for freedom and opportunity for everything living that wore chains, especially sex chains. It that meant poverty for myself and my boy then poverty we should have to suffer. If it meant social ostracism, if it meant relinquishing the literary success that lay within my grasp, then let the success go.

RHETA CHILDE DORR (1866–1948), U.S. journalist. *A Woman of Fifty,* 2nd. ed., ch. 9 (1924).
On the personal transformation that followed her visits to Czarist Russia, and to England during the radical woman suffrage activism that was occurring there in the early 1900s. Dorr was a divorced mother entirely responsible for her son's support.

4 I think there is choice possible at any moment to us, as long as we live. But there is no sacrifice. There is a choice, and the rest falls away. Second choice does not exist. Beware of those who talk about sacrifice.

MURIEL RUKEYSER (1913–1980), U.S. poet. *The Life of Poetry,* ch. 11 (1949).

SALES WORK

1 No one who has not experienced the condescension of a buyer to-

ward an ordinary salesgirl can have any conception of its withering effect.

MARY BARNETT GILSON (1877– ?), U.S. factory personnel manager, economist, and educator. *What's Past is Prologue,* ch. 4 (1940).
As a young woman, Gilson had worked as a salesclerk.

SATISFACTION

1 ... one's self-satisfaction is an untaxed kind of property which it is very unpleasant to find depreciated.

GEORGE ELIOT (1819–1880), British novelist. *Middlemarch,* ch. 16 (1871–1872).

2 Climbing is unadulterated hard labor. The only real pleasure is the satisfaction of going where no man has been before and where few can follow.

ANNIE SMITH PECK (1850–1935), U.S. mountain climber. As quoted in *WomenSports* magazine, p. 15 (December 1977).
Said c. 1925 by the pioneering climber who, at seventy-five, was still scaling mountains. She conquered her last peak at age 82: the 5,363–foot Mt. Madison in New Hampshire.

3 In all our contacts it is probably the sense of being really needed and wanted which gives us the greatest satisfaction and creates the most lasting bond.

ELEANOR ROOSEVELT (1884–1962), First Lady of the United States, author, speaker, and diplomat. *This Is My Story,* ch. 18 (1937).

SCANDAL

1 Falling in love with a United States Senator is a splendid ordeal. One is nestled snugly into the bosom of power but also placed squarely in the hazardous path of exposure.

BARBARA HOWAR (b. 1934), U.S. socialite and author. *Laughing all the Way,* ch. 6 (1973).

Of an adulterous affair which the Washington, DC, socialite began in 1964.

SCHEDULES

1 . . . I'm a slave to this leaf in a diary that lists what I must do, what I must say, every half hour.

GOLDA MEIR (1898–1978), Israeli Prime Minister; born in Russia. As quoted in *Ms.* magazine, p. 103 (April 1973).

2 How we spend our days is, of course, how we spend our lives. What we do with this hour, and that one, is what we are doing. A schedule defends from chaos and whim. It is a net for catching days. It is a scaffolding on which a worker can stand and labor with both hands at sections of time. A schedule is a mock-up of reason and order—willed, faked, and so brought into being; it is a peace and a haven set into the wreck of time; it is a lifeboat on which you find yourself, decades later, still living.

ANNIE DILLARD (b. 1945), U.S. author. *The Writing Life,* ch. 2 (1989).

SCHOLARSHIP

1 . . . it is an uneasy lot at best, to be what we call highly taught and yet not to enjoy: to be present at this great spectacle of life and never to be liberated from a small hungry shivering self—never to be fully possessed by the glory we behold, never to have our consciousness rapturously transformed into the vividness of a thought, the ardour of a passion, the energy of an action, but always to be scholarly and uninspired, ambitious and timid, scrupulous and dim-sighted.

GEORGE ELIOT (1819–1880), British novelist. *Middlemarch,* ch. 29 (1871–1872).

2 The belief that established science and scholarship—which have so relentlessly excluded women from their making—are "objective" and "value-free" and that feminist studies are "unscholarly," "biased," and "ideological" dies hard. Yet the fact is that all science, and all scholarship, and all art are ideological; there is no neutrality in culture!

ADRIENNE RICH (b. 1929), U.S. poet, essayist, and feminist. *Blood, Bread and Poetry,* ch. 1 (1986).

From a 1979 commencement address delivered at Smith College, Northampton, Massachusetts.

SCIENCE

1 The best road to correct reasoning is by physical science; the way to trace effects to causes is through physical science; the only corrective, therefore, of superstition is physical science.

FRANCES WRIGHT (1795–1852), Scottish author and speaker; relocated to America. *Course of Popular Lectures,* lecture 3 (1829).

2 Science is properly more scrupulous than dogma. Dogma gives a charter to mistake, but the very breath of science is a contest with mistake, and must keep the conscience alive.

GEORGE ELIOT (1819–1880), British novelist. *Middlemarch,* ch. 73 (1871–1872).

3 The insidiousness of science lies in its claim to be not a subject, but a method. You could ignore a subject; no subject is all-inclusive. But a method can plausibly be applied to anything within the field of consciousness.

KATHERINE FULLERTON GEROULD (1879–1944), U.S. author. *Modes and Morals,* ch. 4 (1920).

4 ... the nineteenth century believed in science but the twentieth century does not. Not.

GERTRUDE STEIN (1874–1946), U.S. author; relocated to France. *Wars I Have Seen* (1945).
Written in 1943.

5 We're designing a new spacecraft to be launched and there are no women. Where are they? I wonder. I worry.

ANDREA DUPREE (b. 1939), U.S. astronomer. As quoted in the *New York Times,* p. A16 (August 2, 1993).
A senior scientist at the Harvard-Smithsonian Center for Astrophysics, Dupree was reflecting on how little women's level of participation had changed since her youth.

SECRECY

I Do not tell secrets to those whose faith and silence you have not already tested.

ELIZABETH I (1533–1603), Queen of England (1558–1603). As quoted in *The Sayings of Queen Elizabeth,* ch. 11, by Frederick Chamberlin (1923).
Said in 1561 to the King of Sweden.

SECURITY

I Safe upon the solid rock the ugly houses stand:
Come and see my shining palace built upon the sand!

EDNA ST. VINCENT MILLAY, (1892–1950) U.S. poet. "Second Fig," entire poem (1920).

2 All my life I have said, "Whatever happens there will always be tables and chairs"—and what a mistake.

ELIZABETH BOWEN (1899–1973), British novelist, story writer, essayist, and memoirist; born in Ireland. As quoted in *Elizabeth Bowen,* ch. 8, by Victoria Glendinning (1979).
In a 1940 letter to the novelist Virginia Woolf, upon learning that the Woolfs' London home had been destroyed in the World War II "blitz."

3 It's unlikely I'll ever submit to a psychiatrist's couch. I don't want some stranger prowling around through my psyche, monkeying with my id. I don't need an analyst to tell me that I have never had any sense of security. Who has?

TALLULAH BANKHEAD (1903–1968), U.S. actor. *Tallulah,* ch. 1 (1952).

4 It was occasions like this that made me more resolved than ever that my family would someday know real se-

curity. I never for a moment doubted that I myself would ultimately provide it for them.

MARY PICKFORD (1893–1979), U.S. actor. *Sunshine and Shadow,* ch. 6 (1955).
Speaking of spring 1909, when she was sixteen. Her widowed mother and younger sister and brother, as well as she, acted on the New York stage and also toured with shows. There was very little money; they dreaded the touring, which economic necessity forced upon them, because it meant separation. By spring 1909, after a period together in New York City, they once again had to seek work on tour. Pickford's assumption of responsibility for the whole family extended back to her father's death when she was five. Ultimately, she would become a hugely popular movie star who was notorious for driving a hard business bargain.

SEGREGATION

1 ... many of the things which we deplore, the prevalence of tuberculosis, the mounting record of crime in certain sections of the country, are not due just to lack of education and to physical differences, but are due in great part to the basic fact of segregation which we have set up in this country and which warps and twists the lives not only of our Negro population, but sometimes of foreign born or even of religious groups.

ELEANOR ROOSEVELT (1884–1962), U.S. First Lady, author, and speaker. As quoted in *Eleanor and Franklin,* ch. 44, by Joseph P. Lash (1971).
Written on November 15, 1941.

2 It seemed a long way from 143rd Street. Shaking hands with the Queen of England was a long way from being forced to sit in the colored section of the bus going into downtown Wilmington, North Car-

olina. Dancing with the Duke of Devonshire was a long way from not being allowed to bowl in Jefferson City, Missouri, because the white customers complained about it.

ALTHEA GIBSON (b. 1927), African American tennis player. As quoted in *Women-Sports* magazine, p. 23 (March 1976).
Gibson said this c. 1957, on being the first African American to win a major tennis title at the prestigious Wimbledon tournament in England; she won the women's singles title in 1957 and 1958. New York City's largely African American and Hispanic Harlem community includes 143rd Street.

3 In Stamps the segregation was so complete that most Black children didn't really, absolutely know what whites looked like.

MAYA ANGELOU (b. 1928), African American poet, autobiographer, and performer. *I Know Why the Caged Bird Sings,* ch. 4 (1970).
Remembering her childhood in strictly segregated, harshly racist Stamps, Arkansas, during the 1930s.

4 You are not a doctor of dentistry! You are a doctor of segregation!

ANNIE ELIZABETH DELANY (1891–1995), African American dentist. Quoting herself in *Having Our Say,* ch. 19 (1992).
Delany, African American and a retired dentist in New York City, was recalling what she had told a white male dentist, her former classmate at Columbia University's dental school, who sent her his African American maid as a patient because he did not want to work on a African American person's teeth.

SELF-CONFIDENCE

1 The small perplexities of small minds eddy and boil about you. Confident from the experience that has led you out of these same dangers, you attack each problem as it appears, unafraid.

ALICE FOOTE MACDOUGALL, (1867–1945) U.S. businesswoman. *The Autobiography of a Business Woman,* ch. 7 (1928).
On what is learned from struggling, and succeeding, in business.

2   First, I'm trying to prove to myself that I'm a person. Then maybe I'll convince myself that I'm an actress.

MARILYN MONROE (1926–1962), U.S. actor. As quoted in *Ms.* magazine, p. 42 (August 1972).
A beautiful and famous movie star, Monroe was emotionally vulnerable and had a troubled personal life. Long after she had become famous, she privately studied acting to improve her skills. It is believed that she committed suicide.

SELF-CONSCIOUSNESS

1   Actors cannot choose the manner in which they are born. Consequently, it is the one gesture in their lives completely devoid of self-consciousness.

HELEN HAYES (1900–1993), U.S. actor. *On Reflection,* ch. 1 (1968).

SELF-DECEPTION

1   They are most deceived that trusteth most in themselves.

ELIZABETH I (1533–1603), British monarch, Queen of England (1558–1603). As quoted in *The Sayings of Queen Elizabeth,* ch. 1, by Frederick Chamberlin (1923).
Written in 1549, when she was still Princess Elizabeth, to Edward Seymour, Duke of Somerset. Somerset had custody of her half-brother and his nephew, the "boy king" Edward VI (1537–1553; became King in 1547), and was serving as protector of the realm. Somerset's scheming brother, Admiral Thomas Seymour (1508?-1549), had marital designs on the 15-year-old Elizabeth, and his attentions to her had led to scandal, including the unfounded rumor

that she was pregnant with his child. Later that year, Seymour was executed.

2   . . . people were so ridiculous with their illusions, carrying their fools' caps unawares, thinking their own lies opaque while everybody else's were transparent, making themselves exceptions to everything, as if when all the world looked yellow under a lamp they alone were rosy.

GEORGE ELIOT (1819–1880), British novelist. *Middlemarch,* ch. 33 (1871–1872).

SELF-DESTRUCTIVENESS

1   I try to live [the Golden Rule] and I certainly expect it of some particular others. But I'll be damned if I want most folk out there to do unto me what they do unto themselves.

TONI CADE BAMBARA (b. 1939), U.S. fiction writer. *Black Women Writers at Work,* ch. 2, by Claudia Tate (1983).

SELF-DETERMINATION

1   Every individual, like a statue, develops in his life the laws of harmony, integrity, and freedom; or those of deformity, immorality, and bondage. Whether we wish to or not, we are all drawing our own pictures in the lives we are living . . .

HARRIOT K. HUNT (1805–1875), U.S. physician and feminist. *Glances and Glimpses,* ch. 25 (1856).

2   . . . self-determination and self-defense go hand in hand.

ANONYMOUS, U.S. woman. As quoted in *Fugitive Information,* ch. 8, by Kay Leigh Hagan (1993).

SELF-DEVELOPMENT

I   The highest form of development is to govern one's self.

ZERELDA G. WALLACE (1817–1901), U.S. suffragist. As quoted in *History of Woman Suffrage*, vol. 4, ch. 7, by Susan B. Anthony and Ida Husted Harper (1902).

In an address entitled "Women's Ballot a Necessity for the Permanence of Free Institutions," delivered before the nineteenth annual convention of the National Woman Suffrage Association, held in Washington, D.C., January 1887. Wallace, a representative from Indiana, was quoted in a Washington, D.C. newspaper. This was said to be "an imperfect abstract" which, nonetheless, conveyed "the trend of her argument."

2   Emancipation should make it possible for woman to be human in the truest sense. Everything within her that craves assertion and activity should reach its fullest expression; all artificial barriers should be broken, and the road towards greater freedom cleared of every trace of centuries of submission and slavery.

EMMA GOLDMAN (1869–1940), U.S. anarchist and author; born in Russia. *Anarchism and Other Essays*, 3rd rev. ed., ch. 10 (1917).

3   . . . I . . . know the bitter fact that most lives are incredibly wasted, that opportunities for developing identity, for receiving pleasure, for achieving a sense of self-worth are limited and, not only underdeveloped, but in most cases not developed at all—because no one thinks that a housewife, or a mother, or a typist has anything to develop.

IRENA KLEPFISZ (b. 1941), U.S. Jewish lesbian author; born in Poland. *Dreams of an Insomniac*, part 1 (1990).

SELF-EXPRESSION

I   . . . everybody who is human has something to express. Try *not* expressing yourself for twenty-four hours and see what happens. You will nearly burst. You will want to write a long letter or draw a picture or sing, or make a dress or a garden.

BRENDA UELAND (1891–1985), U.S. author and writing teacher. *If You Want to Write*, 2nd. ed., ch. 1 (1938).

SELF-FULFILLMENT

I   Thus far woman has struggled through life with bandaged eyes, accepting the dogma of her weakness and inability to take care of herself not only physically but intellectually. She has held out a trembling hand and received gratefully the proffered aid. She has foregone her right to study, to know the laws and purposes of government to which she is subject. But there is now awakened in her a consciousness that she is defrauded of her legitimate Rights and that she never can fulfill her mission until she is placed in that position to which she feels herself called by the divinity within. Hitherto she has surrendered her person and her individuality to man, but she can no longer do this and not feel that she is outraging her nature and her God.

SARAH M. GRIMKÉ (1792–1873), U.S. abolitionist and feminist. As quoted in *The Female Experience*, ch. 87, by Gerda Lerner (1977).

Written in 1857.

2 The work of the world is common
as mud.
Botched, it smears the hands, crumbles to dust.
But the thing worth doing well
done
has a shape that satisfies, clean and
evident.

. . .

The pitcher cries for water to carry
and a person for work that is real.

MARGE PIERCY (b. 1936), U.S. poet, novelist, and political activist. "To Be of Use," lines 19–22, 26–27 (1973).

SELF-KNOWLEDGE

I . . . the majority of us scarcely see
more distinctly the faultiness of our
own conduct than the faultiness of
our own arguments, or the dulness
[sic] of our own jokes.

GEORGE ELIOT (1819–1880), British novelist. *Middlemarch*, ch. 18 (1871–1872).

2 When we talk about the writer's
country we are liable to forget that
no matter what particular country it
is, it is inside as well as outside him.
. . . The writer's value is lost, both
to himself and to his country, as
soon as he ceases to see that country as a part of himself, and to
know oneself is, above all, to know
what one lacks. It is to measure oneself against Truth, and not the other
way around. The first product of
self-knowledge is humility, and this
is not a virtue conspicuous in any
national character.

FLANNERY O'CONNOR (1925–1964),
U.S. fiction writer and essayist. *Mystery and Manners*, part 2 (1969).
Written in 1957.

SELF-REALIZATION

I Weak as we are, compared to the
health strength we are conscious
would be desirable; ignorant as we
are, compared to the height, and
breadth, and depth of knowledge
which extends around us as far as
the universal range of matter itself;
miserable as we are, compared to
the happiness of which we feel ourselves capable; yet in this living
principle we see nothing beyond or
above us, nothing to which we or
our descendants may not attain, of
great, of beautiful, of excellent. But
to *feel* the power of this mighty
principle, to urge it forward in its
course and accelerate the change in
our condition which it promises, we
must awaken to its observation.

FRANCES WRIGHT (1795–1852), U.S. social reformer and author; born and raised in Scotland. *Course of Popular Lectures*, lecture 1 (1829).

2 I shall have the veil withdrawn and
be allowed to gaze unblinded on the
narrow limits of my own possibilities.

BEATRICE WEBB (1858–1943), British author and socialist. As quoted in *Beatrice Webb*, ch. 6, by Carole Seymour-Jones (1992).
Written in her diary on April 24, 1883. A wealthy, protected young woman who longed for a good education, Webb was expressing hope for her future.

3 No life if it is properly realized is
without its cosmic importance.

HORTENSE ODLUM (1892– ?), U.S. businesswoman. *A Woman's Place,* ch. 17 (1939).

4 Somewhere along the line of development we discover who we really are, and then we make our real decision for which we are responsible. Make that decision primarily for yourself because you can never really live anyone else's life not even your child's. The influence you exert is through your own life and what you become yourself.

ELEANOR ROOSEVELT (1884–1962), U.S. First Lady, author, and speaker. As quoted in *Eleanor and Franklin,* ch. 23, by Joseph P. Lash (1971).

In a June 1941 letter to her friend Trude Lash.

5 . . . this world gives no room to be what we dreamt of being

ADRIENNE RICH (b. 1929), U.S. poet and feminist. "Pieces," section 3, lines 12–13 (1969).

6 I never wanted to live an unembellished life, and I have never done it. . . . Living under such a compulsion has been like painting pictures of life, and I don't take kindly to suggestions that I might have been less egotistically employed had I become a trained nurse.

MARGARET ANDERSON (1886–1973), U.S. editor and memoirist. *The Strange Necessity,* part 1 (1969).

A devotee, editor, publisher, and promoter of the arts—especially the avant-garde—Anderson often survived on very little income and never held a "regular" job. She was beautiful, stylish, and flamboyant. Openly lesbian, she lived at various times in Chicago, New York, and Paris, becoming familiar with the visual and literary artists of each locale.

7 Only when we break the mirror and climb into our vision,
only when we are the wind together streaming and singing,
only in the dream we become with our bones for spears,
we are real at last
and wake.

MARGE PIERCY (b. 1936), U.S. poet, novelist, and political activist. "The Provocation of the Dream," lines 81–85 (1976).

Piercy was a prominent activist in the movement opposing the United States' involvement in the Vietnam War. These are the last lines in the last poem of her first post-Vietnam War collection, *Living in the Open.*

SELF-RELIANCE

1 A young man is stirred and stimulated by the consciousness of how much depends upon his own exertions: a young girl is . . . oppressed by it.

ELIZABETH MISSING SEWELL (1815–1906), British author. *Principles of Education, Drawn from Nature and Revelation, and Applied to Female Education in the Upper Classes,* ch. 29 (1866).

2 The isolation of every human soul and the necessity of self-dependence must give each individual the right to choose his own surroundings. The strongest reason for giving woman all the opportunities for higher education, for the full development of her faculties, her forces of mind and body; for giving her the most enlarged freedom of thought and action; a complete emancipation from all forms of bondage, of custom, dependence, superstition; from all the crippling influences of fear—is the solitude and personal responsibility of her own individual life.

ELIZABETH CADY STANTON (1815–1902), U.S. suffragist, social reformer, and author. *The Solitude of Self* (February 20, 1894).

From a famous speech delivered before a Senate committee which was considering arguments in favor of woman suffrage. Printed in the *Congressional Record* and reprinted in the *Women's Tribune*, the speech was remarkable for its refusal to engage the usual practical and democratic pro-suffrage arguments.

SELF-RESPECT

1 . . . even if the right to vote brought to women no better work, no better pay, no better conditions in any way, she should have it for her own self-respect and to compel man's respect for her.

SUSAN B. ANTHONY (1820–1906), U.S. suffragist. As quoted in *Life and Work of Susan B. Anthony*, vol. 3, ch. 62, by Ida Husted Harper (1908).

In a letter dated June 27, 1903, to Margaret A. Haley, President of the National Federation of Teachers. Anthony believed, and counselled Haley to argue, that women could force improvement in their salaries and working conditions if they had to the power of the ballot; she emphasized, nonetheless, that the vote was *inherently* essential.

SELF-SUPPORT

1 The girl must early be impressed with the idea that she is to be "a hand, not a mouth"; a worker, and not a drone, in the great hive of human activity. Like the boy, she must be taught to look forward to a life of self-dependence, and early prepare herself for some trade or profession.

ELIZABETH CADY STANTON (1815–1902), U.S. feminist, social reformer, and author. As quoted in *The Female Experience*, ch. 75, by Gerda Lerner (1977).

In a speech delivered on May 25, 1851, at the Woman's Rights Convention held in Akron, Ohio.

2 Of all existing forms of injustice there is none so cruel and inconsistent as is the position in which women are placed with regard to self-maintenance—the calm ignoring of their rights and responsibilities which has gone on for centuries. If the economic conditions are hard for men to meet, subjected as they are to the constant weeding out of the less expert and steady hands, it is evident that women, thrown upon their own resources, have a frightful struggle to endure, especially as they have always to contend against a public sentiment which discountenances their seeking industrial employment as a means of livelihood.

BERTHA HONORE POTTER PALMER, (1849–1918) U.S. socialite. As quoted in *The Fair Women*, ch. 11, by Jeanne Madeline Weimann (1981).

Palmer, President of the Board of Lady Managers for the World's Columbian Exposition in Chicago, was speaking on May 1, 1893, the Exposition's Opening Day.

3 Women of all classes are awakening to the necessity of self-support, but few are willing to do the ordinary useful work for which they are fitted.

ELIZABETH CADY STANTON (1815–1902), U.S. suffragist, author, and social reformer. *Eighty Years and More (1815–1897)*, ch. 24 (1898).

Reflecting on the large number of untalented girls hoping to gain distinction as artists.

4 I think the girl who is able to earn her own living and pay her own way should be as happy as anybody on earth. The sense of independence and security is very sweet.

SUSAN B. ANTHONY (1820–1906), U.S. suffragist. As quoted in *Life and Work of Susan B. Anthony,* vol. 3, ch. 67, by Ida Husted Harper (1908).

In a 1905 interview with Edwin Tracey of the New York *Press.*

5 . . . I'm thirteen years old, and I think I'm at the crossroads of my life. I've got to make good between now and the time I'm twenty, and I have only seven years to do it in. Besides, I'm the father of my family and I've got to earn all the money I can.

MARY PICKFORD (1893–1979), U.S. actor. *Sunshine and Shadow,* ch. 6 (1955).

Self-quoting a statement she made to the theatrical producer David Belasco in 1906 when he asked her why she had said that her "life depended on" seeing him. Her father had died when she was five, and she had two younger siblings. The entire family, including her mother, had been acting on the stage without much pecuniary return.

6 I was always pretending that I was a poor-working-girl, always forgetting that I was really poor—also a working girl.

MARGARET ANDERSON (1886–1973), U.S. literary editor and autobiographer. *My Thirty Years' War,* ch. 1 (1930).

On her first full year in Chicago, as a working woman independent of her parents. Raised in affluence, she was now on her own, living hand-to-mouth as a book reviewer and literary editor.

7 I complacently accepted the social order in which I was brought up. I probably would have continued in my complacency if the happy necessity of self-support had not fallen to my lot; if self-support had not deepened and widened my contacts and my experience.

MARY BARNETT GILSON (1877– ?), U.S. factory personnel manager, economist, and educator. *What's Past is Prologue,* ch. 27 (1940).

Gilson never married.

8 I'm tired of earning my own living, paying my own bills, raising my own child. I'm tired of the sound of my own voice crying out in the wilderness, raving on about equality and justice and a new social order. . . . Self-sufficiency is exhausting. Autonomy is lonely. It's so hard to be a feminist if you are a woman.

JANE O'REILLY, U.S. feminist and humorist. *The Girl I Left Behind,* ch. 7 (1980).

O'Reilly was a divorced mother struggling to support herself and her young child by freelance writing.

9 . . . there was always the assumption, even when I was getting a graduate degree in education, that any work I did was temporary, something to do until I assumed my principal role in life which was to be the perfect wife and mother, supported by my husband. As it turned out, I never had children, and I've supported myself for thirty years. If I'd known I was going to have to do that I would have made some very different decisions. I would have approached work with more seriousness and purpose.

SALLY ANN CARTER (b. 1934), U.S. realtor. As quoted in *The Fifties,* ch. 3, by Brett Harvey (1993).

Carter was an interviewee in Harvey's oral history of the 1950s.

SELFISHNESS

1   Will not a tiny speck very close to our vision blot out the glory of the world, and leave only a margin by which we see the blot? I know no speck so troublesome as self.

GEORGE ELIOT (1819–1880), British novelist. *Middlemarch*, ch. 42 (1871–1872).

2   This is the great truth life has to teach us . . . that gratification of our individual desires and expression of our personal preferences without consideration for their effect upon others brings in the end nothing but ruin and devastation.

HORTENSE ODLUM (1892– ?), U.S. businesswoman. *A Woman's Place*, ch. 17 (1939).

SENSES

1   Women have seldom sufficient employment to silence their feelings; a round of little cares, or vain pursuits frittering away all strength of mind and organs, they become naturally only objects of sense.

MARY WOLLSTONECRAFT (1759–1797), British feminist. *A Vindication of the Rights of Woman*, ch. 9 (1792).

SEPARATISM

1   Separatism of any kind promotes marginalization of those unwilling to grapple with the whole body of knowledge and creative works avail-able to others. This is true of black students who do not want to read works by white writers, of female students of any race who do not want to read books by men, and of white students who only want to read works by white writers.

BELL HOOKS (b. 1955), African American author, educator, feminist, and human rights advocate. *Chronicle of Higher Education*, p. A44 (July 13, 1994).

hooks was thinking of the students she encountered as a professor of English at City College of the City University of New York.

SERVANTS

1   . . . such is the horrible idea that I entertain respecting a life of servitude, that if I conceived of there being no possibility of my rising above the condition of servant, I would gladly hail death as a welcome messenger.

MARIA STEWART (1803–1879), African American abolitionist and schoolteacher. As quoted in *Black Women in Nineteenth-Century American Life*, part 3, by Bert James Loewenberg and Ruth Bogin (1976).

Stewart, a free African American, said this in a September 21, 1832 speech delivered at Franklin Hall in Boston. She was arguing for education for Northern African Americans, especially girls, so that they would have career choices beyond that of servant.

2   A good many causes tend to make good masters and mistresses quite as rare as good servants. . . . The large and rapid fortunes by which vulgar and ignorant people become possessed of splendid houses, splendidly furnished, do not, of course, give them the feelings and manners of gentle folks, or in any way really raise them above the servants they

employ, who are quite aware of this fact, and that the possession of wealth is literally the only superiority their employers have over them.

FANNY KEMBLE (1809–1893), British actor. *Further Records, 1848–1883*, vol. 1; entry dated February 12, 1874 (1891).

3 A master or mistress should refrain from speaking to their servants at dinner, let what will go wrong. Care should be taken that they wear thin-soled shoes, that their steps may be noiseless. . . . A good servant . . . avoids coughing, breathing hard, or treading on a lady's dress; never lets any article drop, and deposits plates, glasses, knives, forks and spoons noiselessly. It is now considered good form for a servant not to wear gloves in waiting at table, but to use a damask napkin, with one corner wrapped around the thumb, that he may not touch the plates and dishes with the naked hand.

MRS. H. O. WARD (1824–1899), U.S. author. *Sensible Etiquette of the Best Society Customs, Manners, Morals, and Home Culture, Compiled from the Best Authorities*, ch. 5 (1878).

SERVICE

1 Let the good service of well-deservers be never rewarded with loss. Let their thanks be such as may encourage more strivers for the like.

ELIZABETH I (1533–1603), Queen of England (1558–1603). As quoted in *The Sayings of Queen Elizabeth*, ch. 11, by Frederick Chamberlin (1923).

To Sir Henry Sidney, governor of Ireland.

2 How difficult the task to quench the fire and the pride of private ambition, and to sacrifice ourselves and all our hopes and expectations to the public weal! How few have souls capable of so noble an undertaking! How often are the laurels worn by those who have had no share in earning them! But there is a future recompense of reward, to which the upright man looks, and which he will most assuredly obtain, provided he perseveres unto the end.

ABIGAIL ADAMS (1744–1818), U.S. matriarch; wife and mother of United States President. *Familiar Letters of John Adams and His Wife Abigail Adams, During the Revolution*, letter dated July 10, 1775 (1875).

In a letter written from Braintree, Massachusetts, to her husband John Adams, who was away fighting in the American colonies' revolution against Britain.

3 . . . it is more than petty treason to the Republic, to call a free citizen a *servant*. The whole class of young women, whose bread depends upon their labour, are taught to believe that the most abject poverty is preferable to domestic service. Hundreds of half-naked girls work in the paper-mills, or in any other manufactory, for less than half the wages they would receive in service; but they think their equality is compromised by the latter, and nothing but the wish to obtain some particular article of finery will ever induce them to submit to it.

FRANCES TROLLOPE (1780–1863), British author. *Domestic Manners of the Americans*, ch. 6 (1832).

Trollope had recently travelled extensively in the United States, to which she was referring here.

4 The Service without Hope
Is tenderest, I think—. . .
There is no Diligence like that
That knows not an Until—

EMILY DICKINSON (1831–1886), U.S.
poet. "The Service with Hope": poem no. 779
in her *Collected Poems*, lines 1–2 and 7–8 (c.
1863).

5 Each is under the most sacred obligation not to squander the material
committed to him, not to sap his
strength in folly and vice, and to see
at the least that he delivers a product worthy the labor and cost which
have been expended on him.

ANNA JULIA COOPER (1859–1964),
African American educator and feminist. *A
Voice from the South*, part 2 (1892).

Cooper, the daughter of a former slave and her
white master, was speaking specifically of the
obligation of African Americans to strive and, if
possible, to help others of their race; she had
cited Booker T. Washington and his school at
Tuskegee, Alabama as an example. However,
she also meant this as a general principle,
applying to all people.

6 Any woman who does not live for
unselfish service is a useless cumb-
erer of the earth.

ANNA HOWARD SHAW (1847–1919),
U.S. suffragist, minister, and speaker; born in
England. As quoted in *History of Woman Suffrage*, vol. 5, ch. 1, by Ida Husted Harper
(1922).

The Rev. Dr. Shaw may have been the first
woman to earn both divinity and medical
degrees. She said this in an address delivered in 1901 to the thirty-third annual convention of the National Woman Suffrage Association.

7 It is not alone the fact that women
have generally had to spend most of
their strength in doing for others
that has handicapped them in individual effort; but also that they have

almost universally had to care
wholly for themselves.

ANNA GARLIN SPENCER (1851–1931),
U.S. educator, author, feminist, and Unitarian
minister. *Woman's Share in Social Culture*, ch.
3 (1913).

8 In business you get what you want
by giving other people what they
want.

ALICE FOOTE MACDOUGALL, (1867–
1945) U.S. businesswoman. *The Autobiography of a Business Woman*, ch. 7 (1928).

MacDougall was a successful coffee house proprietor and coffee, tea, and cocoa merchant.

9 It is not serving, but servility, that is
menial.

HORTENSE ODLUM (1892– ?), U.S. businesswoman. *A Woman's Place*, ch. 6 (1939).

10 Service . . . is love in action, love
"made flesh"; service is the body,
the incarnation of love. Love is the
impetus, service the act, and creativity the result with many by-prod-
ucts.

SARAH PATTON BOYLE, U.S. civil rights
activist and author. *The Desegregated Heart*,
part 3, ch. 3 (1962).

11 I can't be servile. I give service.
There is a difference.

DOLORES DANTE, U.S. waitress. As quoted
in *Working*, book 5, by Studs Terkel (1973).

12 Service is the rent that you pay for
room on this earth.

SHIRLEY CHISHOLM (b. 1924), African
American politician. As quoted in *I Dream a
World*, by Brian Lanker (1989).

Chisholm was the first African American
woman to be elected to the United States Congress, serving 1969–1982. In 1972, she attempted to win the Democratic Party's Presidential nomination.

SERVITUDE

1 Whether our feet are compressed in iron shoes, our faces hidden with veils and masks; whether yoked with cows to draw the plow through its furrows, or classed with idiots, lunatics and criminals in the laws and constitutions of the State, the principle is the same; for the humiliations of the spirit are as real as the visible badges of servitude.

ELIZABETH CADY STANTON (1815–1902), U.S. suffragist, social reformer, and author. As quoted in *History of Woman Suffrage*, vol. 4, ch. 8, by Susan B. Anthony and Ida Husted Harper (1902).

In an opening-day speech before a meeting of the International Council of Women, which was held in Washington, D.C., March 25–April 1, 1888. Stanton was referring to the fact that only women, "idiots, lunatics and criminals" were denied the vote in America.

SEX

1 Nowhere is woman treated according to the merit of her work, but rather as a sex. It is therefore almost inevitable that she should pay for her right to exist, or keep a position in whatever line, with sex favors. Thus it is merely a question of degree whether she sells herself to one man, in or out of marriage, or to many men.

EMMA GOLDMAN (1869–1940), U.S. anarchist and author; born in Russia. *Anarchism and Other Essays*, 3rd rev. ed., ch. 8 (1917).

2 . . . I do see, still, a beautiful result of the old order that the new order does not tend to produce. The conventional avoidance as a general subject of conversation of sex in all its phases was a safeguard to sensibilities.

KATHERINE FULLERTON GEROULD (1879–1944), U.S. author. *Modes and Morals*, ch. 7 (1920).

3 While American men are fighting to rid the old world of autocracy let American women set to and rid the new world of this intolerable old burden of sex ignorance.

CRYSTAL EASTMAN (1881–1928), U.S. author and political activist. *On Women and Revolution*, part 1 (1978).

From an article originally published in *Birth Control Review* (January 1918) during World War I. To dispense information about birth control was then illegal.

4 From early Colonial days, sex life in America had been based on the custom of men supporting women. That situation reached its heyday in the Twenties when it was easy for any dabbler in stocks to flaunt his manhood by lavishing an unearned income on girls. But with the stock-market crash, men were hard put even to keep their wives, let alone spend money on sex outside the home. The adjustment was much easier on women than on men, who jumped out of windows in droves, whereas I can't recall a single headline that read: KEPT GIRL LEAPS FROM LOVE NEST.

ANITA LOOS (1888–1981), U.S. screenwriter, author, and humorist. *Kiss Hollywood Good-by*, ch. 2 (1974).

5 I think the reason we're so crazy sexually in America is that all our responses are acting. We don't

know how to feel. We know how it looked in the movies.

JILL ROBINSON (b. 1936), U.S. novelist. As quoted in *American Dreams,* part 1, by Studs Terkel (1980).

The daughter of movie producer Dore Schary, Robinson had grown up rich in Hollywood; her notions of the world were shaped by the movies in which she was immersed.

6 Human sexuality has been regulated and shaped by men to serve men's needs.

ANA CASTILLO (b. 1953), Mexican–American poet, essayist, and feminist. *Massacre of the Dreamers,* ch. 6 (1994).

SEX DIFFERENCES: IN PERSPECTIVE

1 I claim . . . that there is a feminine as well as a masculine side to truth . . . That as the man is more noble in reason, so the woman is more quick in sympathy. That as he is indefatigable in pursuit of abstract truth, so is she in caring for the interests by the way—striving tenderly and lovingly that not one of the least of these "little ones" should perish. That while we not unfrequently see women who reason, we say, with the coolness and precision of a man, and men as considerate of helplessness as a woman, still there is a general consensus of mankind that the one trait is essentially masculine and the other as peculiarly feminine. That both are needed to be worked into the training of children, in order that our boys may supplement their virility by tenderness and sensibility, and our girls may round out their gentleness by strength and self-reliance. That, as both are alike necessary in giving symmetry to the individual, so a nation or a race will degenerate into mere emotionalism on the one hand, or ballism on the other, if dominated by either exclusively; lastly, and most emphatically, that the feminine factor can have its proper effect only through woman's development and education so that she may fitly and intelligently stamp her force on the forces of her day, and add her modicum to the riches of the world's thought.

ANNA JULIA COOPER (1859–1964), U.S. educator and feminist. *A Voice from the South,* part 1 (1892).

The daughter of a former slave, Cooper was widowed soon after her marriage and never bore children. At age 57, she adopted five orphaned siblings, ranging in age from six months to twelve years. At age 67, she became the fourth African American woman to earn a Ph.D. (from the University of Paris).

2 I have often been asked why I am so fond of playing male parts. . . . As a matter of fact, it is not male parts, but male brains that I prefer.

SARAH BERNHARDT (1845–1923), French actor. *The Art of the Theatre,* ch. 3 (1924).

Bernhardt played, among other male characters, Hamlet and the title role in *L'Aiglon,* by Edmond Rostand.

3 It would be a thousand pities if women wrote like men, or lived like men, or looked like men, for if two sexes are quite inadequate, considering the vastness and variety of the world, how should we manage with one only? Ought not education to bring out and fortify the differences rather than the similarities?

VIRGINIA WOOLF (1882–1941), British author. *A Room of One's Own*, ch. 6 (1929).

HARRIOT K. HUNT (1805–1875), U.S. physician and feminist. *Glances and Glimpses*, ch. 18 (1856).

Commenting on the Harvard students' publication of "resolutions" opposing the Medical Faculty's decision to allow her to attend lectures.

SEX DIFFERENCES: IN UPBRINGING

1 A boy's mind is not so easily sullied as a girl's. . . . Undesirable knowledge is not an equal shock to the moral nature.

ELIZABETH MISSING SEWELL (1815–1906), British author. *Principles of Education, Drawn from Nature and Revelation, and Applied to Female Education in the Upper Classes*, ch. 28 (1866).

SEX DIFFERENCES: PHYSICAL

1 I don't know what immutable differences exist between men and women apart from differences in their genitals; perhaps there are some other unchangeable differences; probably there are a number of irrelevant differences. But it is clear that until social expectations for men and women are equal, until we provide equal respect for both men and women, our answers to this question will simply reflect our prejudices.

NAOMI WEISSTEIN (b. 1939), U.S. psychologist and feminist. *Kinder, Kuche, Kirche as Scientific Law* (1970).

2 You are, or you are not the President of The National University Law School. If you are its President I wish to say to you that I have been passed through the curriculum of study of that school, and am entitled to, and demand my Diploma. If you are not its President then I ask you to take your name from its papers, and not hold out to the world to be what you are not.

BELVA LOCKWOOD (1830–1917), U.S. lawyer and political activist. As quoted in *The Female Experience*, ch. 76, by Gerda Lerner (1977).

Written in an 1873 letter to Ulysses S. Grant, who was then President of the United States and therefore also President of the National University Law School. Lockwood had been among the first women admitted to the school, but after completing the course of study along with one other woman, she was denied her diploma because of her sex. Following her petition to Grant, she received her diploma and was later admitted to the bar in the District of Columbia. In 1879, after a three-year fight for admission, she became the first woman to practice before the U. S. Supreme Court. In 1884 and 1888, she ran for President of the United States as the candidate of the National Equal Rights Party. She also claimed to be the first woman in the District of Columbia to ride a bicycle.

SEX DISCRIMINATION: IN EDUCATION

1 The class at Harvard in 1851, have purchased for themselves a notoriety they will not covet in years to come.

3 There are no golden geese. There are only fat geese eating the food that could nourish more athletic opportunities for women.

DONNA A. LOPIANO (b. 1946), U.S. sports executive. As quoted in the *Chronicle of Higher Education*, p. B1 (December 2, 1992).

Lopiano, who was the executive director of the Women's Sports Foundation, was pointing out the disproportionately small amounts of money being spent on women's athletics by colleges and universities, and the large deficits being run by many Division I men's basketball and football programs—programs that were often said, erroneously, to be "golden geese" whose profits fuelled the rest of the institution's athletic programs.

SEX DISCRIMINATION: IN SOCIETY

1   . . . I do earnestly wish to see the distinction of sex confounded in society, unless where love animates the behaviour.

MARY WOLLSTONECRAFT (1759–1797), British feminist. *A Vindication of the Rights of Woman,* ch. 4 (1792).

2   They aroused me to a determination to understand more fully the position of women, and the character of those men who talk so much of the need of our being "*protected*"—removing from us, meanwhile, what are often the very weapons of our defence [sic], occupations, and proper and encouraging remuneration.

HARRIOT K. HUNT (1805–1875), U.S. physician and feminist. *Glances and Glimpses,* ch. 10 (1856).
Reflecting on the seduction and illicit pregnancy of a young woman betrayed by her lover, a store clerk.

3   No matter how well-born, how intelligent, how highly educated, how virtuous, how rich, how refined, the women of to-day constitute a political class below that of every man,

no matter how base-born, how stupid, how ignorant, how vicious, how poverty-stricken, how brutal. The pauper in the almshouse may vote; the lady who devotes her philanthropic thought to making that almshouse habitable, may not. The tramp who begs cold victuals in the kitchen may vote; the heiress who feeds him and endows universities may not.

MARY PUTNAM JACOBI (1842–1906), U.S. suffragist. *"Common Sense" Applied to Woman Suffrage,* ch. 4 (1894).
African American men had been granted suffrage by the Fifteenth Amendment to the Constitution, which took effect in 1870. Thus women were the only free and sane class of United States citizens still denied the vote. Jacobi was not, of course, protesting enfranchisement of "paupers" or "tramps"; she was simply pointing out the ironies inherent in sex discrimination.

4   To the young man confronting life the world lies wide. Such powers as he had he may use, must use. . . . What he wants to be, he may strive to be. What he wants to get, he may strive to get. Wealth, power, social distinction, fame,—what he wants he can try for. To the young woman confronting life there is the same world beyond, there are the same human energies and human desires and ambitions within. But all that she may wish to have, all that she may wish to do, must come through a single channel and a single choice. Wealth, power, social distinction, fame,—not only these, but home and happiness, reputation, ease and pleasure, her bread

and butter,—all, must come to her through a small gold ring.

CHARLOTTE PERKINS GILMAN (1860–1935), U.S. author and feminist. *Women and Economics*, ch. 4 (1898).

5 The failure of women to produce genius of the first rank in most of the supreme forms of human effort has been used to block the way of all women of talent and ambition for intellectual achievement.

ANNA GARLIN SPENCER (1851–1931), U.S. educator, author, feminist, and Unitarian minister. *Woman's Share in Social Culture,* ch. 3 (1913).

On the rationalization that women should be denied access to intellectual opportunities because they had not yet demonstrated excellence equivalent to men's in intellectually demanding pursuits.

6 Until the sky is the limit [for women], as it is for men, men as well as women will suffer, because all society is affected when half of it is denied equal opportunity for full development.

MARY BARNETT GILSON (1877– ?), U.S. factory personnel manager, economist, and educator. *What's Past is Prologue,* ch. 26 (1940).

7 The only difference between a man and woman climbing the ladder of success is that a woman is expected to put it in the closet when she's finished with it.

BARBARA DALE (b. 1940), U.S. cartoonist. *The Working Woman Book,* ch. 10 (1985).

SEX DISCRIMINATION: IN THE WORKPLACE

1 I have done a great deal of work, as much as a man, but did not get so much pay. I used to work in the field and bind grain, keeping up with the cradler; but men doing no more, got twice as much pay. . . . We do as much, we eat as much, we want as much.

SOJOURNER TRUTH (1797–1883), African American human rights activist and preacher. As quoted in *Feminism: The Essential Historical Writings,* part 3, by Miriam Schnier (1972).

Speaking at an 1867 meeting of the American Equal Rights Association held in New York City. Born a slave in Ulster County, New York, and named Isabella Baumfree, Truth had been freed by New York State law in 1827. In 1843, she had a religious vision which led her to change her name and become an itinerant preacher. She also became a prominent and beloved figure in the woman suffrage and anti-slavery movements.

2 . . . many of the so-called grievances of women are false. No man ever unfairly discriminated against me. If one tried to, I . . . was equal to the emergency, and such experience really added a great deal to the zest of life. . . . women, as a habit, over-estimated their ability, and . . . they were too untrained even to appreciate the magnitude of their undertaking.

ALICE FOOTE MACDOUGALL, (1867–1945) U.S. businesswoman. *The Autobiography of a Business Woman,* ch. 3 (1928). A flourishing merchant and the proprietor of five successful New York City coffee houses, MacDougall had opposed woman suffrage.

3 An editor once said to me, "If I didn't know that you, a woman, had written these poems, I would

like your work." And once an editor wrote me, "Your poems are dynamic, colorful, exciting, but too strong for a woman."

DAISY ALDAN (b. 1923), U.S. poet and publisher. As quoted in *The Little Magazine in America*, ch. [17], by Elliott Anderson and Mary Kinzie (1978).

On the literary climate for women in the 1950s; Aldan was herself a publisher of poetry, bringing out the notable arts journal, *Folder.*

4 In the end, I think you really only get as far as you're allowed to get.

GAYLE GARDNER, U.S. sports reporter. As quoted in *Sports Illustrated*, p. 87 (June 17, 1991).

Gardner, who was the first female sports anchor to appear weekly on a major television network, was describing the sex-based limitations she perceived.

SEX ROLES

1 ... intellect is not sexed; ... strength of mind is not sexed; and ... our views about the duties of men and the duties of women, the sphere of man and the sphere of woman, are mere arbitrary opinions, differing in different ages and countries, and dependent solely on the will and judgment of erring mortals.

SARAH M. GRIMKÉ (1792–1873), U.S. abolitionist and feminist. *Letters on the Equality of the Sexes and the Condition of Woman,* letter #9: dated August 25, 1837 (1838).

2 The aim of education is to fit children for the position in life which they are hereafter to occupy. Boys are to be sent out into the world to buffet with its temptations, to mingle with bad and good, to govern and direct. ... girls are to dwell in quiet homes, amongst a few friends; to exercise a noiseless influence, to be submissive and retiring. There is no connection between the bustling mill-wheel life of a large school and that for which they are supposed to be preparing. ... to educate girls in crowds is to educate them wrongly.

ELIZABETH MISSING SEWELL (1815–1906), British author. *Principles of Education, Drawn from Nature and Revelation, and Applied to Female Education in the Upper Classes,* ch. 28 (1866).

3 I was born a mechanic, and made a barrel before I was ten years old. The cooper told my father, "Fanny made that barrel, and has done it quicker and better than any boy I have had after six months' training." My father looked at it and said, "What a pity that you were not born a boy so that you could be good for something. Run into the house, child, and go to knitting."

FRANCES D. GAGE (1808–1884), U.S. suffragist. As quoted in *History of Woman Suffrage*, vol. 2, ch. 18, by Susan B. Anthony, Matilda Joslyn Gage, and herself (1882).

Gage said this on May 10, 1867, at a national convention of the American Equal Rights Association.

4 In the older times it was seldom said to little girls, as it always has been said to boys, that they ought to have some definite plan, while they were children, what to be and do when they were grown up. There was usually but one path open before them, to become good wives and housekeepers. And the ambition of most girls was to follow their mothers' footsteps in this di-

rection; a natural and laudable ambition. But girls, as well as boys, must often have been conscious of their own peculiar capabilities,— must have desired to cultivate and make use of their individual powers.

Lucy Larcom (1824–1893), U.S. poet and teacher. *A New England Girlhood*, ch. 7 (1889).

5 The universal social pressure upon women to be all alike, and do all the same things, and to be content with identical restrictions, has resulted not only in terrible suffering in the lives of exceptional women, but also in the loss of unmeasured feminine values in special gifts. The Drama of the Woman of Genius has too often been a tragedy of misshapen and perverted power.

Anna Garlin Spencer (1851–1931), U.S. educator, author, feminist, and Unitarian minister. *Woman's Share in Social Culture*, ch. 3 (1913).

6 . . . social roles vary in the extent to which it is culturally permissible to express ambivalence or negative feelings toward them. Ambivalence can be admitted most readily toward those roles that are optional, least where they are considered primary. Thus men repress negative feelings toward work and feel freer to express negative feelings toward leisure, sex and marriage, while women are free to express negative feelings toward work but tend to repress them toward family roles.

Alice S. Rossi (b. 1922), U.S. sociologist. *Dissent*, p. 535 (November-December 1970).

7 . . . if you're a woman, all they can think about your relationship with a politician is that you're either sleeping with him or advising him about clothes.

Gloria Steinem (b. 1934), U.S. feminist and author. As quoted in *Crazy Salad*, ch. 6, by Nora Ephron (1972).

Steinem said this in January 1972 about an inaccurate news story that she had given then-Presidential candidate George McGovern advice about what to wear.

8 I seemed intent on making it as difficult for myself as possible to pursue my "male" career goal. I not only procrastinated endlessly, submitting my medical school application at the very last minute, but continued to crave a conventional female role even as I moved ahead with my "male" pursuits.

Margaret S. Mahler (1897–1985), U.S. psychoanalyst and author; born in Austria. *The Memoirs of Margaret S. Mahler*, compiled and edited by Paul E. Stepansky, ch. 1 (1988).

Said sometime in the 1970s. Mahler became an important figure in her field, specializing in childhood psychosis.

9 Freedom of choice for women, at the expense of the caring, warmth, and sensitivity to others so often associated with them, may be empty. In the thrust to redefine male and female roles, women must not become men; nor can men be permitted the continual dehumanization of their roles.

KATHLEEN WEIBEL (b. 1945), U.S. librarian and feminist. *Library Journal,* p. 267 (January 1976).

SEX ROLES: FEMALE

1 . . . what is especially insufferable in a woman is a restless, bold, domineering manner, for this manner goes against nature. . . . [ellipsis in source] No matter what her worth, no matter that she never forgets that she could be a man by virtue of her superiority of mind and the force of her will, on the outside she must be a woman! She must present herself as that creature made to please, to love to seek support, that being who is inferior to man and who approaches the angels.

ELISABETH-FÉLICITÉ BAYLE-MOUILLARD (1796–1865), French author. As quoted in *Victorian Women,* ch. 19, by Erna Olafson Hellerstein, Leslie Parker Hume, and Karen M. Offen (1981).

From an 1834 advice manual, first published in French under the title, *Manuel de la bonne compagnie, ou guide de la politesse et de la bienséance.*

2 One of the reasons, surely, why women have been credited with less perfect veracity than men is that the burden of conventional falsehood falls chiefly on them.

KATHERINE FULLERTON GEROULD (1879–1944), U.S. author. *Modes and Morals,* ch. 8 (1920).

3 . . . the opportunity offered by life to women is far in excess of any offered to men. To be the inspiration is more than to be the tool. To cre-ate the world, a greater thing than to reform it.

ALICE FOOTE MACDOUGALL (1867–1945), U.S. businesswoman. *The Autobiography of a Business Woman,* ch. 3 (1928).

Driven by her husband's financial failure to the necessity of supporting her three young children by establishing her own business, MacDougall lamented her children's first material, then emotional, deprivation. Despite her remarkable worldly success, she did not romanticize the benefits of "emancipation" and opposed woman suffrage.

4 A life I didn't choose
chose me: even
my tools are the wrong ones
for what I have to do.

ADRIENNE RICH (b. 1929), U.S. poet, essayist, and lesbian feminist. *The Roofwalker,* lines 22–25 (1961).

Later in the 1960s and the 1970s, Rich developed into a prominent feminist; in the mid-1970s, she also "came out" as a lesbian. When she wrote this poem, she was married and raising three young sons.

5 I'm the only woman reporter they have, so I get all the meat boycott stories and all the meatless food stories. . . . Actually, I've only cooked three meals in my life. The most uncomfortable place for me in the whole world is in a kitchen.

THERESA BROWN (b. 1957), U.S. television newswoman. As quoted in *Women in Television News,* ch. 4, by Judith S. Gelfman (1976).

Said on April 3, 1973.

6 I don't think the ladies in town accepted the fact that I worked. That was the point at which I said to myself, well, you're always going to be out of step and you might as well face it.

ELLEN RODGERS (b. c. 1930), U.S. civil engineer. As quoted in *The Fifties*, ch. 8, by Brett Harvey (1993).

Rodgers, an interviewee in Harvey's oral history of the 1950s, was recalling moving to a Kansas town with her husband in 1957 and taking an engineering job.

SEX SYMBOLS

1   I'm a failure as a woman. My men expect so much of me, because of the image they've made of me—and that I've made of myself—as a sex symbol. They expect bells to ring and whistles to whistle, but my anatomy is the same as any other woman's and I can't live up to it.

MARILYN MONROE (1926–1962), U.S. actor. As quoted in *Marilyn*, ch. 27, by Peter Harry Brown and Patte B. Barham (1992).

Said c. 1962 by the beautiful Hollywood star who was heavily promoted as a "sex symbol"; she had three husbands and was said to have had many lovers as well.

2   A sex symbol becomes a thing. . . . I just hate to be a thing.

MARILYN MONROE (1926–1962), U.S. actor. As quoted in *Ms.* magazine, p. 40 (August 1972).

The beautiful movie star was considered her era's prime example of a "sex symbol."

SEXISM

1   Mr. Douglass talks about the wrongs of the negro; but with all the outrages that he to-day suffers, he would not exchange his sex and take the place of Elizabeth Cady Stanton.

SUSAN B. ANTHONY (1820–1906), U.S. suffragist. As quoted in *History of Woman Suffrage*, vol. 2, ch. 22, by Elizabeth Cady Stanton, Matilda Joslyn Gage, and herself (1882).

Speaking at a May 12, 1869, anniversary celebration of the Equal Rights Association, held in New York. Anthony was disagreeing with Frederick Douglass (c. 1817–1895), the distinguished African American advocate of African American rights and universal suffrage. Douglass had argued that African American men's need for suffrage was more urgent than women's. Stanton (1815–1902) was a prominent suffragist and was Anthony's closest colleague and friend.

SEXISM: IN SOCIETY

1   The prejudice against color, of which we hear so much, is no stronger than that against sex. It is produced by the same cause, and manifested very much in the same way. The Negro's skin and the woman's sex are both *prima facie* evidence that they were intended to be in subjection to the white Saxon man. The few social privileges which the man gives the woman, he makes up to the Negro in civil rights. The woman may sit at the same table and eat with the white man; the free Negro may hold property and vote. The woman may sit in the same pew with the white man in church; the free Negro may enter the pulpit and preach. Now, with the black man's right to suffrage, the right unquestioned, even by Paul, to minister at the altar, it is evident that the prejudice against sex is more deeply rooted and unreasonably maintained than that against color . . .

ELIZABETH CADY STANTON (1815–1902), U.S. suffragist, author, and social reformer. As quoted in *Feminism: The Essential Historical Writings*, part 3, by Miriam Schnier (1972).

From an 1860 address to the New York State legislature. One month later, the New York State Married Women's Property Act became law.

2 . . . social evils are dangerously contagious. The fixed policy of persecution and injustice against a class of women who are weak and defenseless will be necessarily hurtful to the cause of all women.

FANNIE BARRIER WILLIAMS (1855–1944), African American advocate of civil rights and women's rights. As quoted in *Black Women in Nineteenth-Century American Life,* ch. 3, by Bert James Loewenberg and Ruth Bogin (1976).

Williams was speaking, in 1893, of discrimination against African American women.

3 Profound as race prejudice is against the Negro American, it is not practically as far-reaching as the prejudice against women. For stripping away the sentimentality which makes Mother's Day and Best American Mother Contests, the truth is that women suffer all the effects of a minority.

PEARL S. BUCK (1892–1973), U.S. author; born in China. *Of Men and Women,* ch. 8 (1941).

4 . . . the struggle against sexism demands the destruction of the American state, and . . . the immediate personal nature of sexism requires struggle against men who enforce that oppression as well as its institutions.

WOMEN OF THE WEATHER UNDERGROUND, *Ms. Magazine,* p. 105 (February 1974).

This was a small group of women who were living as fugitives after indictment for crimes related to left-radical politics and opposition to American involvement in the Vietnam War;

they included such well-known activists as Kathy Boudin and Bernardine Dohrn, both of whom later surfaced and served prison time.

5 I came along at a time when there was a demand to give men greater visibility and opportunity. In white society they were saying, "Women can't do it." In black society, they were saying, "Women do too much." It's a diabolical situation.

YVONNE BRAITHWAITE BURKE (b. 1932), African American attorney and politician. As quoted in *I Dream a World,* by Brian Lanker (1989).

The first African American woman ever elected to the U. S. House of Representatives from California, she served three terms, then practiced law with a specialty in public finance.

6 . . . not all black women have silently acquiesced in sexism and misogyny within the African-American community. Indeed, many writers, activists, and other women have voiced their opposition and paid the price: they have been ostracized and branded as either man-haters or pawns of white feminists, two of the more predictable modes of disciplining and discrediting black feminists.

KIMBERLÉ CRENSHAW (b. 1959), African American author. *Race-ing Justice, En-gendering Power,* ch. 14 (1992).

SEXISM: IN THE WORKPLACE

1 Every single day, sexism plays a part in my life. . . . Not from my company, from people outside the company: people who want to send a tape, lawyers or managers. . . . Because I'm a girl, they don't think

I'm powerful enough to be in a position of authority.

Anna Statman, U.S. recording company executive. As quoted in the *New York Times,* sect. 2, p. 33 (June 6, 1993).

Statman was an executive of the small independent recording company, Interscope.

SEXISM: OF MEN

1 Assumptions of male superiority are as widespread and deep rooted and every bit as crippling to the woman as the assumptions of white supremacy are to the Negro. . . . this is no more a man's world than it is a white world.

Student Non-violent Coordinating Committee, African American civil rights organization. *SNCC Position Paper (Women in the Movement)* (November 1974).

SNCC was founded in Atlanta, Georgia, in 1959; this paper was written by a subgroup of women.

2 Sexism has always been a political stance mediating social domination, enabling white men and black men to share a common sensibility about sex roles and the importance of male domination.

bell hooks (b. c. 1955), African American author and educator. *Yearning,* ch. 7 (1990).

SEXISM: OF WOMEN

1 I would not trust a mouse to a woman if a man's judgment could be had.

Elizabeth Gaskell (1810–1865), British novelist. As quoted in *Woman in Sexist Society,* ch. 20, by Elaine Showalter (1971).

2 Please do not take counsel of women who are so prejudiced that, as I once heard said, they would not allow a male grasshopper to chirp on their lawn; but out of your own great heart, refuse to set an example to such folly.

Frances E. Willard (1839–1898), U.S. temperance leader and suffragist. As quoted in *The Life and Work of Susan B. Anthony,* ch. 40, by Ida Husted Harper (1898–1908).

In an 1892 letter to suffrage leader Susan B. Anthony (1820–1906), asking her to reverse her decision not to sit for a bust by male sculptor Lorado Taft for exhibition at the following year's World Columbian Exposition. Anthony had at first agreed to sit for Taft but later yielded to those feminists who said that the bust should be sculpted by a woman. Finally, Anthony sat for Taft, and he completed a bust.

SEXUAL HARASSMENT

1 I worked as a waitress till I was fired because I dumped a cup of hot coffee in the lap of a half-drunk guy who was pinching my butt.

Juli Loesch (b. c. 1953), U.S. ex-waitress. As quoted in *The Great Divide,* book 2, section 1, by Studs Terkel (1988).

2 . . . they think that Miss America *belongs* to them! That they can touch her and give her a kiss on the cheek—or even on the lips!

Ellie Ross, Travelling companion for Miss Americas. As quoted in *Miss America,* ch. 17, by Ann-Marie Bivans (1991).

Ross "laughed" as she described the public's reaction to her charges.

3 One of the oddest episodes I remember was an occasion in which [Clarence] Thomas was drinking a Coke in his office, he got up from the table, at which we were work-

ing, went over to his desk to get the Coke, looked at the can and asked, "Who has put pubic hair on my coke?"

ANITA HILL (b. 1956), U.S. lawyer and law professor. As quoted in *The Real Anita Hill,* introduction, by David Brock (1991).

Describing to a Senate panel on October 12, 1991, her experience of sexual harassment by Clarence Thomas (b. 1948), her former boss and, at this time, President George Bush's Supreme Court nominee. Thomas's appointment to the Court was approved.

4 [There is a] no-win decision that innumerable people make, or try to make, or try to put off making daily: Whether to give up the job, the place, the people, the future one holds dear, denying one's own mental capacities, independence, and desires (what are left of them, what one remembers of them) just to get away. They will find themselves disgusting if they let their tormentor get his way, not . . . by touching their body . . . but by forcing them to flee, to change anything they would not have changed if they were free to keep it: their white collar career or their cash register at the supermarket, it doesn't matter in the slightest.

CLAUDIA BRODSKY LACOUR, U.S. author. *Race-ing Justice, En-gendering Power,* ch. 5 (1992).

On why women who are sexually harassed at work may not leave their jobs.

SHOPPING

I When a lady of wealth, is seen roaming about in search of cheaper articles, or trying to beat down a shopkeeper, or making a close bar-

gain with those she employs, the impropriety is glaring to all minds. A person of wealth has no occasion to spend time in looking for extra cheap articles; her time could be more profitably employed in distributing to the wants of others. And the practice of beating down tradespeople, is vulgar and degrading, in any one.

CATHERINE E. BEECHER (1800–1878), U.S. educator and author. *Treatise on Domestic Economy for the Use of Young Ladies at Home and at School,* ch. 17 (1843).

2 Shopping seemed to take an entirely too important place in women's lives. You never saw men milling around in men's departments. They made quick work of it. I used to wonder if shopping was a form of escape for women who had no worthwhile interests.

MARY BARNETT GILSON (1877– ?), U.S. factory personnel manager, economist, and educator. *What's Past is Prologue,* ch. 4 (1940).

Remembering her youthful days as a salesclerk.

3 . . . I've found out it's fun to go shopping. It's such a feminine thing to do.

MARILYN MONROE (1926–1962), U.S. actor. As quoted in *Ms.* magazine, p. 41 (August 1972).

Raised in very modest circumstances, Monroe had recently gained fame and wealth as a movie star.

SILENCE

I I have always noticed that in portraits of really great writers the mouth is always firmly closed.

GERTRUDE STEIN (1874–1946), U.S. author and patron of the arts; relocated to France. As quoted in *What Are Masterpieces,* afterword, by Robert Haas (1970). Said in a January 1946 interview with Haas.

2   Silence remains, inescapably, a form of speech.

SUSAN SONTAG (b. 1933), U.S. author. "The Aesthetics of Silence," (1967).

SIMPLICITY

I   Simplicity is a great element of good breeding.

FANNY KEMBLE (1809–1893), British actor. *Further Records, 1848–1883,* vol. 1; entry dated January 20, 1875 (1891).

2   Economy, prudence, and a *simple life* are the sure masters of need, and will often accomplish that which, their opposites, with a fortune at hand, will fail to do.

CLARA BARTON (1821–1912), U.S. Civil War nurse and founder of the American Red Cross. As quoted in *Angel of the Battlefield,* ch. 19, by Ishbel Ross (1956).
In a letter written c. 1912 to Mrs. John A. Logan, who had succeeded Barton in the Presidency of the American Red Cross after her retirement in 1904.

3   . . . it is always the simple that produces the marvelous.

AMELIA E. BARR (1831–1919), U.S. novelist. *All the Days of My Life,* ch. 1 (1913).

4   The real drawback to "the simple life" is that it is not simple. If you are living it, you positively can do nothing else. There is not time.

KATHERINE FULLERTON GEROULD (1879–1944), U.S. author. *Modes and Morals,* ch. 3 (1920).

5   I like a thing simple but it must be simple through complication. Everything must come into your scheme, otherwise you cannot achieve real simplicity.

GERTRUDE STEIN (1874–1946), U.S. author and patron of the arts; relocated to France. As quoted in *What Are Masterpieces,* Afterword, by Robert Haas (1970). Said in a January 1946 interview with Haas.

6   To shut the door at the end of the workday, which does not spill over into evening. To throw away books after reading them so they don't have to be dusted. To go through boxes on New Year's Eve and throw out half of what is inside. Sometimes for extravagance to pick a bunch of flowers for the one table. Other women besides me must have this daydream about a carefree life.

MAXINE HONG KINGSTON (b. 1940), U.S. author. *The Woman Warrior,* ch. 3 (1976).

SINCERITY

I   Sincerity and the correct use of the voice are the greatest things in the art of acting.

ALLA NAZIMOVA (1879–1945), U.S. actor; born in Russia. As quoted in *Actors on Acting,* rev. ed., part 13, by Toby Cole and Helen Krich (1970). Said in 1937.

SKEPTICISM

I   . . . scepticism . . . can never be thoroughly applied, else life would come to a standstill . . .

GEORGE ELIOT (1819–1880), British novelist. *Middlemarch,* ch. 23 (1871–1872).

2 The great, the fundamental need of any nation, any race, is for heroism, devotion, sacrifice; and there cannot be heroism, devotion, or sacrifice in a primarily skeptical spirit.

ANNA JULIA COOPER (1859–1964), African American educator and feminist. *A Voice from the South,* part 2 (1892).

3 I read ... an article by a highly educated man wherein he told with what conscientious pains he had brought up all his children to be skeptical of everything, never to believe anything in life or religion or their own feelings without submitting it to many rational doubts, to have a persistent, thoroughly skeptical, doubting attitude toward everything. ... I think he might as well have taken them out in the backyard and killed them with an ax.

BRENDA UELAND (1891–1985), U.S. author and writing teacher. *If You Want to Write,* 2nd. ed., ch. 17 (1938).

SLANDER

1 I would gladly chastise those who represent things as different from what they are. Those who steal property or make counterfeit money are punished, and those ought to be still more severely dealt with who steal away or falsify the good name of a prince.

ELIZABETH I (1533–1603), Queen of England (1558–1603). As quoted in *The Sayings of Queen Elizabeth,* ch. 13, by Frederick Chamberlin (1923).

To Fenelon, the French Ambassador.

2 It will be the mistake of your life if you go into print in your own defence [sic]. Your denial will reach a new set of people and start them to talking, while the ones who read the original charges will never see the refutation of them.

SUSAN B. ANTHONY (1820–1906), U.S. suffragist, speaker, and editor. As quoted in *The Life and Work of Susan B. Anthony,* ch. 48, by Ida Husted Harper (1898–1908).

Said in 1896 to a colleague who was considering publishing a response to lies that had been printed about her.

SLAVERY

1 I wish most sincerely there was not a slave in this province. It always appeared a most iniquitous scheme to me—to fight ourselves for what we are daily robbing and plundering from those who have as good a right to freedom as we have.

ABIGAIL ADAMS (1744–1818), U.S. matriarch; wife and mother of United States President. *Familiar Letters of John Adams and His Wife Abigail Adams, During the Revolution,* letter dated September 24, 1774 (1875).

In a letter written from Boston, Massachusetts, to her husband John Adams.

2 To give liberty to a slave before he understands its value is, perhaps, rather to impose a penalty than to bestow a blessing ...

FRANCES WRIGHT (1795–1852), Scottish author and speaker; relocated to America. *Views of Society and Manners in America,* April 1820 entry (1821).

Wright, a visiting Scotswoman who later settled in Cincinnati, Ohio, would eventually advocate a program of gradual emancipation from slavery.

3　To emancipate [the slaves] entirely throughout the Union cannot, I conceive, be thought of, consistently with the safety of the country.

FRANCES TROLLOPE (1780–1863), British author. *Domestic Manners of the Americans,* ch. 22 (1832).

Trollope had been travelling in the United States.

4　... this nation is *rotten at the heart,* and ... nothing but the most tremendous blows with the sledgehammer of abolition truth, could ever have broken the false rest which we had taken up for ourselves on the very brink of ruin.

ANGELINA GRIMKÉ (1805–1879), U.S. abolitionist and feminist. *Letters to Catherine Beecher,* letter #8 (1837).

In a letter dated June 1837, on the morally degrading effect of the slave system.

5　Though the Negroes are fed, clothed, and housed, and though the Irish peasant is starved, naked, and roofless, the bare name of freemen—the lordship over his own person, the power to choose and will—are blessings beyond food, raiment, or shelter; possessing which, the want of every comfort of life is yet more tolerable than their fullest enjoyment without them.

FANNY KEMBLE (1809–1893), British actor and abolitionist. *Journal of a Residence on a Georgian Plantation in 1838–1839,* ch. 1 (1863).

From a letter written in Philadelphia during December 1838, to her friend Elizabeth Dwight Sedgwick. Kemble was responding to a comment made by a man of their acquaintance that European peasants were poorer than American slaves. A few years earlier, Kemble had unwittingly married into a slave-owning family; the marriage failed, and she and Pierce Butler were divorced in 1849.

6　... no one who has not been an integral part of a slaveholding community, can have any idea of its abominations. ... even were slavery no curse to its victims, the exercise of arbitrary power works such fearful ruin upon the hearts of *slaveholders,* that I should feel impelled to labor and pray for its overthrow with my last energies and latest breath.

ANGELINA GRIMKÉ (1805–1879), U.S. abolitionist. As quoted in *American Slavery As It Is,* by Theodore D. Weld (1839).

Said on April 6, 1839. The daughters of a South Carolina slaveholding family, Angelina and her sister Sarah had moved north to escape the presence of the slave system and become active abolitionists.

7　... even I am growing accustomed to slavery; so much so that I cease to think of its accursed influence and calmly eat from the hands of the bondman without being mindful that he is such. O, Slavery, hateful thing that thou art thus to blunt the keen edge of conscience!

SUSAN B. ANTHONY (1820–1907), U.S. suffragist. As quoted in *The Life of Susan B. Anthony,* vol. 1, ch. 7, by Ida Husted Harper (1897).

From an 1854 description in her diary of visits to Alexandria, Virginia and Baltimore, Maryland.

8　Slavery is malignantly aristocratic.

ANTOINETTE BROWN BLACKWELL (1825–1921), U.S. minister, suffragist, abolitionist, and temperance advocate. As quoted in *History of Woman Suffrage,* vol. 2, ch. 16, by Elizabeth Cady Stanton, Susan B. Anthony, and Matilda Joslyn Gage (1882).

Speaking on May 14, 1863, at a national convention of the Woman's National Loyal League.

9 I care not by what measure you end the war. If you allow one single germ, one single seed of slavery to remain in the soil of America, whatever may be your object, depend upon it, as true as effect follows cause, that germ will spring up, that noxious weed will thrive, and again stifle the growth, wither the leaves, blast the flowers, and poison the fair fruits of freedom. Slavery and freedom cannot exist together.

ERNESTINE L. ROSE (1810–1892), U.S. suffragist and abolitionist. As quoted in *History of Woman Suffrage*, vol. 2, ch. 16, by Elizabeth Cady Stanton, Susan B. Anthony, and Matilda Joslyn Gage (1882).

Speaking on May 14, 1863, at a national convention of the Woman's National Loyal League.

10 This is beautiful indeed; the colored people have given this to the head of the government, and that government once sanctioned laws that would not permit its people to learn enough to enable them to read this book.

SOJOURNER TRUTH (1779–1883), African American slave; later an itinerant preacher and advocate of various social reforms including abolition, woman suffrage, and temperance. As quoted in *The Narrative of Sojourner Truth*, part 2: "Book of Life," by Frances W. Titus (1875).

Said in 1864 to President Abraham Lincoln, whom Truth staunchly supported, when he showed her a Bible presented to him "by the colored people of Baltimore." Truth was illiterate; this story is taken from a letter, written by a friend at Truth's dictation, to Rowland Johnson. It was dated November 17, 1864, from Freedman's Village, Virginia. Truth was referring to laws that prohibited teaching slaves to read and write.

11 . . . where there is one slave there are always two—he who wears the chain and he who rivets it.

JEANNE DE HERICOURT (1809–1875), French feminist and author. As quoted in *History of Woman Suffrage*, vol. 2, ch. 22, by Elizabeth Cady Stanton, Susan B. Anthony, and Matilda Joslyn Gage (1882).

Speaking at a May 12, 1869, anniversary celebration of the Equal Rights Association, held in New York City. She was probably speaking of slavery generally, but within the specific context of the subordination of women by the state (i.e., by men).

12 . . . there was one of two things I had a *right* to, liberty, or death; if I could not have one, I would take de oder; for no man should take me alive; I should fight for my liberty as long as my strength lasted, and when de time came for me to go, de Lord would let dem take me.

HARRIET TUBMAN (c. 1820–1913), African American escaped slave and abolitionist. As quoted in *Harriet, the Moses of Her People*, by Sarah Bradford (1869).

Bradford was the friend and first biographer of the great abolitionist and ex-slave who, after escaping to freedom, returned nineteen times to the South and ushered other runaway slaves, including her parents and brothers, to freedom in the North. Here, Tubman was remembering her determination to flee the South after the death of her master.

13 Them old masters, when they got mad, had no mercy on a nigger— they'd cut a nigger all up in a hurry—cut 'em all up into strings, just leave the life, that's all. I've seen 'em do it, many a time.

SILVIA DUBOIS (1788?–1889), African American slave and hog breeder. As quoted in *Silvia Dubois, a Biografy of the Slav Who Whipt Her Mistres and Gand Her Fredom*, interview dated January 27, 1883, by C. W. Larison (1883).

Remembering her days as a slave in New Jersey.

14 It is said that the Negro is ignorant. But why is he ignorant? It comes with ill grace from a man who has put out my eyes to make a parade of my blindness,—to reproach me for my poverty when he has wronged me of my money. . . . If he is poor, what has become of the money he has been earning for the last two hundred and fifty years? Years ago it was said cotton fights and cotton conquers for American slavery. The Negro helped build up that great cotton power in the South, and in the North his sigh was in the whir of its machinery, and his blood and tears upon the warp and woof of its manufactures.

FRANCES ELLEN WATKINS HARPER, (1825–1911) African American author, speaker, and rights advocate. As quoted in *The Female Experience,* ch. 66, by Gerda Lerner (1977).

Speaking in 1891 to the National Council of Women of the United States, in anticipation of "the objection that the Negro is poor and ignorant."

15 In nothing was slavery so savage and relentless as in its attempted destruction of the family instincts of the Negro race in America. Individuals, not families; shelters, not homes; herding, not marriages, were the cardinal sins in that system of horrors.

FANNIE BARRIER WILLIAMS (1855– 1944), African American advocate of civil rights and women's rights. As quoted in *Black Women in Nineteenth-Century American Life,* ch. 3, by Bert James Loewenberg and Ruth Bogin (1976).

Born in Brockport, New York, to a distinguished free African American family, Williams had lived in the South before marrying a Chicago attorney. This is from "Religious Duty to the Negro," an 1893 speech she made in Chicago before the World's Parliament of Religions.

16 The cloud was so dark that it needed all the bright lights that could be turned upon it. But for four years there was a contagion of nobility in the land, and the best blood North and South poured itself out a libation to propitiate the deities of Truth and Justice. The great sin of slavery was washed out, but at what a cost!

M. E. W. SHERWOOD (1826–1903), U.S. socialite, traveller, and author. *An Epistle to Posterity,* ch. 5 (1897).

17 It would be idle to say that we were not, from time to time, aware that a volcano slumbered fitfully beneath us. There were dark sides to the Slavery Question, for master, as for slave.

MARION HARLAND (1830–1922), U.S. author. *Marion Harland's Autobiography,* ch. 18 (1910).

Harland, a Virginian, was referring to slaveowners' ever-present fear of a slave uprising in the years before the Civil War.

18 When white men were willing to put their own offspring in the kitchen and corn field and allowed them to be sold into bondage as slaves and degraded them as another man's slave, the retribution of wrath was hanging over this country and the South paid penance in four years of bloody war.

REBECCA LATIMER FELTON (1835– 1930), U.S. author. *Country Life in Georgia in the Days of My Youth,* ch. 1 (1919).

Referring to the "offspring" born of slaveowners' illicit sex with slave women. Felton herself was a slaveowner who came to oppose slavery.

19 I'll kill you, gal, if you don't stand up for yourself. Fight, and if you can't fight, kick; if you can't kick, then bite.

"CORNELIA" (1844– ?), U.S. slave. As quoted in *Black Women in Nineteenth-Century American Life,* part 1, by "Fannie" (1976).
In 1929 or 1930, Fannie recalled her mother Cornelia's admonition when they were both slaves on a small farm in Tennessee—c. the early 1860s.

20 He was high and mighty. But the kindest creature to his slaves—and the unfortunate results of his bad ways were not sold, had not to jump over ice blocks. They were kept in full view and provided for handsomely in his will. His wife and daughters in the might of their purity and innocence are supposed never to dream of what is as plain before their eyes as the sunlight, and they play their parts of unsus-pecting angels to the letter.

ANONYMOUS ANTEBELLUM CONFED-ERATE WOMAN, As quoted in *Divided Houses,* ch. 1, by Leeann Whites (1992).
On a Southern slave owner. The "unfortunate results of his bad ways" refers to the children born of his illicit sex with slave women.

21 . . . some of my people could have been left [in Africa] and are living there. And I can't understand them and they don't know me and I don't know them because all we had was taken away from us. And I became kind of angry; I felt the anger of why this had to happen to us. We were so stripped and robbed of our background, we wind up with nothing.

FANNIE LOU HAMER (1917–1977), Afri-can American civil rights activist. As quoted in *This Little Light of Mine,* ch. 7, by Hay Mills (1993).

The Mississippi civil rights leader, granddaugh-ter of a slave, was reflecting in the 1960s on Af-rican Americans' situation after visiting an Afri-can country (Guinea) for the first time.

SMALL TOWNS

1 People who live in quiet, remote places are apt to give good dinners. They are the oft-recurring excite-ment of an otherwise unemotional, dull existence. They linger, each of these dinners, in our palimpsest memories, each recorded clearly, so that it does not blot out the others.

M. E. W. SHERWOOD (1826–1903), U.S. socialite, traveller, and author. *An Epistle to Pos-terity,* ch. 4 (1897).
Recalling an elaborately formal dinner, featur-ing French cuisine, which was served to her when she was travelling in the West Indies.

2 . . . what a thing it is to lie there all day in the fine breeze, with the pine needles dropping on one, only to re-turn to the hotel at night so hungry that the dinner, however homely, is a fete, and the menu finer reading than the best poetry in the world! Yet we are to leave all this for the glare and blaze of Nice and Monte Carlo; which is proof enough that one cannot become really accli-mated to happiness.

WILLA CATHER (1876–1947), U.S. novel-ist. *Willa Cather in Europe,* ch. 13 (1956).
Written on September 10, 1902 on her first trip to France, while stopping in the village of Cava-laire, which consisted "of a station house and a little tavern by the roadside."

3 Our rural village life was a purify-ing, uplifting influence that fortified us against the later impacts of urbanization; Church and State, because they were separated and friendly, had spiritual and ethical standards that were mutually enriching; freedom and discipline, individualism and collectivity, nature and nurture in their interaction promised an ever stronger democracy. I have no illusions that those simpler, happier days can be resurrected.

AGNES E. MEYER (1887–1970), U.S. journalist. *Out of These Roots,* ch. 1 (1953). Recalling her childhood in quiet Pelham Heights, New York.

4 A small town is automatically a world of pretense. Since everyone knows everyone else's business, it becomes the job of the populace to act as if they don't know what is going on instead of its being their job to try to find out.

JEANINE BASINGER (b. 1936), U.S. film and social historian. *A Woman's View,* ch. 7 (1993).

SMOKING

1 Without infringing on the liberty we so much boast, might we not ask our professional Mayor to call upon the smokers, have them register their names in each ward, and then appoint certain thoroughfares in the city for their use, that those who feel no need of this envelopment of curling vapor, to insure protection may be relieved from a nuisance as disgusting to the olfactories as it is prejudicial to the lungs.

HARRIOT K. HUNT (1805–1875), U.S. physician. *Glances and Glimpses,* ch. 12 (1856). Hunt was taking an early stand against what is now termed "second-hand smoke."

2 Smoking . . . is downright dangerous. Most people who smoke will eventually contract a fatal disease and die. But they don't brag about it, do they? Most people who ski, play professional football or drive race cars, will not die—at least not in the act—and yet they are the ones with the glamorous images, the expensive equipment and the mythic proportions. Why this should be I cannot say, unless it is simply that the average American does not know a daredevil when he sees one.

FRAN LEBOWITZ (b. 1950), U.S. humorist. *Social Studies,* ch. 18 (1981). Lebowitz, a dedicated cigarette smoker, often wrote satirically about smoking, laws restricting smoking, and "smokers' rights."

3 The same people who tell us that smoking doesn't cause cancer are now telling us that advertising cigarettes doesn't cause smoking.

ELLEN GOODMAN (b. 1941), U.S. political columnist. As quoted in *Newsweek* magazine, p. 17 (July 28, 1986).

SOCIAL CHANGE

1 We are now going through a period of demolition. In morals, in social life, in politics, in medicine, and in religion there is a universal upturning of foundations. But the day of reconstruction seems to be looming, and now the grand question is:

Are there any sure and universal principles that will evolve a harmonious system in which we shall all agree?

CATHERINE BEECHER (1800–1878), U.S. educator and author. *Common Sense Applied to Religion, or the Bible and the People,* ch. 1 (1857).

2   Mr. Roosevelt, this is my principal request—it is almost the last request I shall ever make of anybody. Before you leave the presidential chair, recommend Congress to submit to the Legislatures a Constitutional Amendment which will enfranchise women, and thus take your place in history with Lincoln, the great emancipator. I beg of you not to close your term of office without doing this.

SUSAN B. ANTHONY (1820–1906), U.S. suffragist. As quoted in *Life and Work of Susan B. Anthony,* vol. 3, ch. 68, by Ida Husted Harper (1908).

In a meeting with President Theodore Roosevelt (1858–1919) on November 15, 1904, shortly after his election to a second term of office (first full term: he had succeeded to the Presidency when President McKinley was assassinated). She did not secure the desired assurance; Roosevelt never actively supported woman suffrage. At age 84, Anthony had been in uncertain health for four years and had greatly curtailed her public work. Also present at her meeting with Roosevelt were Ida Husted Harper, who transcribed the quotation, and Harriet Taylor Upton.

3   This is rather different from the receptions I used to get fifty years ago. They threw things at me then—but they were not roses.

SUSAN B. ANTHONY (1820–1906), U.S. suffragist. As quoted in *Life and Work of Susan B. Anthony,* vol. 3, ch. 68, by Ida Husted Harper (1908).

Upon being deluged with tossed bouquets of flowers at a reception in her honor which was held on June 30—"Woman's Day"—at the Lewis and Clark Exposition of 1905, Portland, Oregon. In her fifty-three years as a suffrage leader, Anthony had seen the typical public response to her appearance evolve from hostility and ridicule into affectionate respect.

4   The correct rate of speed in innovating changes in long-standing social customs has not yet been determined by even the most expert of the experts. Personally I am beginning to think there is more danger in lagging than in speeding up cultural change to keep pace with mechanical change.

MARY BARNETT GILSON (1877– ?), U.S. factory personnel manager, economist, and educator. *What's Past is Prologue,* ch. 17 (1940).

5   It's like pushing marbles through a sieve. It means the sieve will never be the same again.

ANONYMOUS, Delegate to the meeting of the National Women's Political Caucus held before the 1972 Democratic Convention. As quoted in *Crazy Salad,* ch. 6, by Nora Ephron (1972).

On the gains women had recently made as active participants in politics.

6   What would it mean to live in a city whose people were changing each other's despair into hope?— You yourself must change it.

ADRIENNE RICH (b. 1929), U.S. poet and essayist. "Dreams Before Waking," lines 66–69 (1983).

SOCIAL CLASS

I   It hurts me to hear the tone in which the poor are condemned as "shiftless," or "having a pauper spirit," just as it would if a crowd mocked at a child for its weakness, or laughed at a lame man because he could not run, or a blind man because he stumbled.

ALBION FELLOWS BACON (1865–1933), U.S. social worker and housing reform advocate. *Beauty for Ashes,* ch. 6 (1914).

2 The principle of avoiding the unnecessary expenditure of energy has enabled the species to survive in a world full of stimuli; but it prevents the survival of the aristocracy.

REBECCA WEST (1892–1983), British author. *The Strange Necessity,* ch. 10 (1928).

SOCIAL CUSTOMS

1 . . . it was not very unusual at Washington for a lady to take the arm of a gentleman, who was neither her husband, her father, nor her brother. This remarkable relaxation of American decorum has been probably introduced by the foreign legations.

FRANCES TROLLOPE (1780–1863), British author. *Domestic Manners of the Americans,* ch. 20 (1832).
Trollope had been travelling in the United States.

2 . . . in no part of the world is genteel visiting founded on esteem, in the absence of suitable furniture and complete dinner-service.

GEORGE ELIOT (1819–1880), British novelist. *Middlemarch,* ch. 23 (1871–1872).

3 . . . to most mortals there is a stupidity which is unendurable and a stupidity which is altogether accept-

able—else, indeed, what would become of social bonds?

GEORGE ELIOT (1819–1880), British novelist. *Middlemarch,* ch. 58 (1871–1872).

4 Society in general do not like originality, especially in woman, as it looks like defying man's authority for a woman to prefer her own methods to accepting those laid down for the majority.

CAROLINE NICHOLS CHURCHILL (1833–?), U.S. author. *Active Footsteps,* ch. 24 (1909).

5 . . . I cannot conceive a more odious society than one where nothing is considered indecent or impious.

KATHERINE FULLERTON GEROULD (1879–1944), U.S. author. *Modes and Morals,* ch. 7 (1920).

6 Conventions, at the present moment, are really menaced. The most striking sign of this is that people are now making unconventionality a social virtue, instead of an unsocial vice. The switches have been opened, and the laden trains must take their chance of a destination.

KATHERINE FULLERTON GEROULD (1879–1944), U.S. author. *Modes and Morals,* ch. 7 (1920).

7 No convention gets to be a convention at all except by grace of a lot of clever and powerful people first inventing it, and then imposing it on others. You can be pretty sure, if you are strictly conventional, that you are following genius—a long way off. And unless you are a genius yourself, that is a good thing to do.

KATHERINE FULLERTON GEROULD (1879–1944), U.S. author. *Modes and Morals,* ch. 7 (1920).

SOCIAL GATHERINGS

1   That man is to be pitied who cannot enjoy social intercourse without eating and drinking. The lowest orders, it is true, cannot imagine a cheerful assembly without the attractions of the table, and this reflection alone should induce all who aim at intellectual culture to endeavor to avoid placing the choicest phases of social life on such a basis.

MRS. H. O. WARD (1824–1899), U.S. author. *Sensible Etiquette of the Best Society Customs, Manners, Morals, and Home Culture, Compiled from the Best Authorities,* ch. 5 (1878).

2   . . . if a person is to be unconventional, he must be amusing or he is intolerable: for, in the nature of the case, he guarantees you nothing but amusement. He does not guarantee you any of the little amenities by which society has assured itself that, if it must go to sleep, it will at least sleep in a comfortable chair.

KATHERINE FULLERTON GEROULD (1879–1944), U.S. author. *Modes and Morals,* ch. 7 (1920).

3   I went to a literary gathering once. . . . The place was filled with people who looked as if they had been scraped up out of drains. The ladies ran to draped plush dresses—for Art; to wreaths of silken flowerets in the hair—for Femininity; and, somewhere between the two adornments, to chain-drive *pince-nez*—

for Astigmatism. The gentlemen were small and somewhat in need of dusting.

DOROTHY PARKER (1893–1967), U.S. author and humorist. *Constant Reader,* ch. 13 (1970). From a column dated February 11, 1928.

4   It has lately been drawn to your correspondent's attention that, at social gatherings, she is not the human magnet she would be. Indeed, it turns out that as a source of entertainment, conviviality, and good fun, she ranks somewhere between a sprig of parsley and a single ice-skate. It would appear, from the actions of the assembled guests, that she is about as hot company as a night nurse.

DOROTHY PARKER (1893–1967), U.S. author and humorist. *Constant Reader,* column dated November 17, 1928 (1970).

5   All through the nineties I met people. Crowds of people. Met and met and met, until it seemed that people were born and hastily grew up, just to be met.

CAROLYN WELLS (1862–1942), U.S. author. *The Rest of My Life,* ch. 14 (1937).

6   . . . I prefer not to have among my guests two people or more, of any sex, who are in the first wild tremours of love. It is better to invite them after their new passion has settled, has solidified into a quieter reciprocity of emotions. (It is also a waste of good food, to serve it to new lovers.)

M. F. K. FISHER (1908–1992), U.S. author and food expert. *Serve it Forth,* ch. 9 (1937).

7 A party, like a meeting for worship, is not operating on the level of reason. . . . It transcends logic. It slides willingly and consciously (if it is a good party) toward a celebration of the fact of being alive. The celebrants at a party share bread and wine and reach toward a communal touching, for a moment, of an existence that is not limited by the individual ego. The sound of a party is a sound of amity, of human beings who have become for a moment, and for nonaggressive reasons, something outside themselves.

JESSAMYN WEST (1902–1984), U.S. novelist. *To See the Dream,* part 1 (1956).

8 Few enjoy noisy overcrowded functions. But they are a gesture of goodwill on the part of host or hostess, and also on the part of guests who submit to them.

FANNIE HURST (1889–1968), U.S. novelist. *Anatomy of Me,* book 4 (1958).

SOCIAL JUSTICE

I . . . when the right of the individual is made sacred, when the image of God in human form, whether in marble or in clay, whether in alabaster or in ebony, is consecrated and inviolable, when men have been taught to look beneath the rags and grime, the pomp and pageantry of mere circumstance and have regard unto the celestial kernel uncontaminated at the core,—when race, color, sex, condition, are realized to be the accidents, not the substance of life, and consequently as not obscuring or modifying the inalienable title to life, liberty, and the pursuit of happiness,—then is mastered the science of politeness, the art of courteous contact, which is naught but the practical application of the principal [sic] of benevolence, the back bone and marrow of all religion; then woman's lesson is taught and woman's cause is won—not the white woman nor the black woman nor the red woman, but the cause of every man or woman who has writhed silently under a mighty wrong.

ANNA JULIA COOPER (1859–1964), African American educator and feminist. *A Voice from the South,* part 1 (1892).

Cooper had been born to a slave.

2 For twelve successive Congresses we have appeared before committees of the two Houses making this plea, that the underlying principle of our Government, the right of consent, shall have practical application to the other half of people. Such a little simple thing we have been asking for a quarter of a century. For over forty years, longer than the children of Israel wandered through the wilderness, we have been begging and praying and pleading for this act of justice. We shall some day be heeded.

SUSAN B. ANTHONY (1820–1906), U.S. suffragist. As quoted in *History of Woman Suffrage,* vol. 4, ch. 14, by Susan B. Anthony and Ida Husted Harper (1902).

From the opening address of the twenty-sixth annual convention of the National Woman Suffrage Association, held February 15–20, 1894, in Washington, D.C.

3   ... my soul stood erect, exultant,
     envisioning a new world where the
     light of justice for every individual
     will be unclouded.

HELEN KELLER (1880–1968), U.S. author.
As quoted in *Eleanor: The Years Alone,* ch. 3,
by Joseph P. Lash (1972).
Keller, who was deaf and blind but intellectually accomplished, wrote this in a 1948 letter to
former First Lady Eleanor Roosevelt, after reading the Declaration of Human Rights drafted by
the Commission on Human Rights of the new
United Nations. Roosevelt had represented
the United States and had chaired the Commission.

4   Apart from letters, it is the vulgar
     custom of the moment to deride
     the thinkers of the Victorian and
     Edwardian eras; yet there has not
     been, in all history, another age ...
     when so much sheer mental energy
     was directed toward creating a
     fairer social order.

ELLEN GLASGOW (1873–1945), U.S. novelist. *The Woman Within,* ch. 12 (1954).

SOCIAL PROBLEMS

1   We have had nineteen centuries of
     ecclesiastical teaching and preach-
     ing, and what do we see in our
     midst? Tens of thousands of honest
     and industrious poor begging—not
     for bread, but for labour; thousands
     of malicious loafers looking evilly
     aslant at wealth; myriads of fallen
     women pacing the streets and alleys
     of our towns that they may degrade
     for temporary hire, to men more
     debased than themselves, those frail
     bodies which should be "temples of
     the living God." We see millions
     toiling early and late for the mere

necessaries of life. We see an inordi-
nate desire for wealth and luxury,
to the exclusion of duty and of pity
and consideration for others. We
see the wealthy and gifted too often
abandoned to sensuality and frivolity.

TENNESSEE CLAFLIN (1846–1923), U.S.
journalist, lecturer, and social reform advocate;
relocated to England. *Talks and Essays,* vol. 1,
ch. 7 (1897).
Reflecting on nineteenth-century London.

2   One cannot be too extreme in
     dealing with social ills; the ex-
     treme thing is generally the true
     thing.

EMMA GOLDMAN (1869–1940), U.S.
anarchist and author; born in Russia. *Anarchism and Other Essays,* 3rd rev. ed., ch. 1
(1917).

3   As our disorderly, competitive tech-
     nological society is piling up its vic-
     tims and constantly developing new
     problems of maladjustment, we
     must use our scientific knowledge
     to determine the cause and preven-
     tion of suffering rather than putting
     all our emphasis on its allevia-
     tion ...

AGNES E. MEYER (1887–1970), U.S.
journalist. *Out of These Roots,* ch. 8
(1953).

4   Overall, white men run America.
     From nuclear armaments to the
     filth and jeopardy of New York City
     subways to the cruel mismanage-
     ment of health care, is there any-
     thing to boast about?

JUNE JORDAN (b. 1936), African American
poet, essayist, and social critic. *On Call,* ch. 5
(1985).
Written in 1982.

SOCIAL REFORM

1 . . . the great mistake of the reformers is to believe that life begins and ends with health, and that happiness begins and ends with a full stomach and the power to enjoy physical pleasures, even of the finer kind.

KATHERINE FULLERTON GEROULD (1879–1944), U.S. author. *Modes and Morals,* ch. 1 (1920).

2 . . . every woman's organization recognizes that reformers are far more common than feminists, that the passion to look after your fellow man, and especially woman, to do good to her in your way is far more common than the desire to put into every one's hand the power to look after themselves.

CRYSTAL EASTMAN (1881–1928), U.S. social/political activist and author. *On Women and Revolution,* part 1 (1978). From an article first published in *The World* on June 27, 1926.

3 Reformation, like education, is a journey, not a destination.

MARY B. HARRIS (1874–1957), U.S. prison administrator. *I Knew Them in Prison,* ch. 34 (1936).

4 People who know what is good for other people all the time are as big a menace in our society as the capitalists.

MAY HOBBS (b. 1938), British author. *Born to Struggle,* Postlude (1973).
Of the destruction of her old neighborhood—Hoxton Street in the London borough of Hackney, on the city's East End—as the result of a government slum clearance project.

5 There's a difference between Vaselining the rapee and catching the rapist.

FLORYNCE KENNEDY (b. 1916), U.S. lawyer, activist, speaker, and author. *Color Me Flo,* ch. 1 (1976).

SOCIAL RESPONSIBILITY

1 The denial of our duty to act in this case is a denial of our right to act; and if we have no right to act, then may *we* well be termed "the white slaves of the North," for like our brethren in bonds, we must seal our lips in silence and despair.

ANGELINA GRIMKE (1805–1879), U.S. abolitionist and feminist. As quoted in *The Grimke Sisters from South Carolina,* ch. 10, by Gerda Lerner (1967).
Referring, in May 1837, to the common criticism that women should not speak out on a "political" subject such as slavery.

2 . . . we should be miserable but for the consciousness that we have done all in our power to help forward every measure for the freedom and equality of the races and the sexes.

SUSAN B. ANTHONY (1820–1906), U.S. suffragist. As quoted in *The Life and Work of Susan B. Anthony,* ch. 41, by Ida Husted Harper (1898).
Written in an 1893 letter to Robert Purvis, an African American advocate of racial equality and woman suffrage.

3 . . . God allows the wheat and the tares to grow up together, and . . . the tares frequently get the start of the wheat and kill it out. The only difference between the wheat and human beings is that the latter have intellect and ought to combine and pull out the tares, root and branch.

SUSAN B. ANTHONY (1820–1906), U.S. suffragist. As quoted in *The Life and Work of Susan B. Anthony*, ch. 6, by Ida Husted Harper (1898).

Said in 1897, on the need for good people to join forces in order to achieve such goals as woman suffrage and temperance.

4 Everyone in the full enjoyment of all the blessings of his life, in his normal condition, feels some individual responsibility for the poverty of others. When the sympathies are not blunted by any false philosophy, one feels reproached by one's own abundance.

ELIZABETH CADY STANTON (1815–1902), U.S. suffragist, author, and social reformer. *Eighty Years and More (1815–1897)*, ch. 6 (1898).

5 . . . the selfishness that is bred of great success is our shame. We have subdued the wilderness and made it ours. We have conquered the earth and the richness thereof. We have indelibly stamped upon its face the seal of our dominating will. Now, unlike Alexander sighing for more worlds to conquer, we should address ourselves to adding beauty to that glory and grandeur.

ALICE FOOTE MACDOUGALL, (1867–1945) U.S. businesswoman. *The Autobiography of a Business Woman*, ch. 6 (1928).

MacDougall was a highly successful, self-made merchant and restaurateur in New York City.

6 . . . education fails in so far as it does not stir in students a sharp awareness of their obligations to society and furnish at least a few guideposts pointing toward the implementation of these obligations.

MARY BARNETT GILSON (1877– ?), U.S. factory personnel manager, economist, and educator. *What's Past is Prologue*, ch. 25 (1940).

7 For me being a poet is a job rather than an activity. I feel I have a function in society, neither more nor less meaningful than any other simple job. I feel it is part of my work to make poetry more accessible to people who have had their rights withdrawn from them.

JENI COUZYN (b. 1942), South African poet; relocated to England. As quoted in *Contemporary Poets*, 3rd ed., by James Vinson (1980).

8 Our responsibility as privileged human beings is to pay back for the opportunities we've received.

KATHRYN ANASTOS (b. 1950), U.S. physician. As quoted in *New York* magazine, p. 90 (December 21–28, 1992).

On why she left teaching at Montefiore Medical Center in New York City for medical practice.

SOCIAL WORK

1 . . . life cannot be administered by definite rules and regulations; that wisdom to deal with a man's difficulties comes only through some knowledge of his life and habits as a whole . . .

JANE ADDAMS (1860–1935), U.S. social worker and social reformer. *Twenty Years at Hull-House*, ch. 8 (1910).

Addams was the founding director of Hull-House, a pioneer "settlement house" in a poor, largely immigrant, Chicago neighborhood.

2 . . . I remembered the rose bush that had reached a thorny branch out through the ragged fence, and caught my dress, detaining me when I would have passed on. And again the symbolism of it all came over me. These memories and visions of the poor—they were the clutch of the thorns. Social workers have all felt it. It holds them to their work, because the thorns curve backward, and one cannot pull away.

Albion Fellows Bacon (1865–1933), U.S. social worker and housing reform advocate. *Beauty for Ashes*, ch. 3 (1914).

SOCIAL/POLITICAL ACTIVISM: 19TH CENTURY

1 . . . to be successful a person must attempt but one reform. By urging two, both are injured, as the average mind can grasp and assimilate but one idea at a time.

Susan B. Anthony (1820–1906), U.S. suffragist. As quoted in *The Life and Work of Susan B. Anthony*, ch. 7, by Ida Husted Harper (1898).

Anthony said this in 1854, on the inadvisability of advocating woman suffrage while wearing a controversial "bloomer" outfit in an attempt to advance dress reform.

2 . . . women of the North, I ask you to rise up with earnest, honest purpose, and go forward in the way of right, fearlessly, as independent human beings, responsible to God alone for the discharge of every duty, for the faithful use of every gift, the good Father has given you. Forget conventionalisms; forget what the world will say, whether you are in your place or out of your place; think your best thoughts, speak your best words, do your best

works, looking to your own conscience for approval.

Susan B. Anthony (1820–1906), U.S. suffragist. As quoted in *History of Woman Suffrage*, vol. 2, ch. 16, by Elizabeth Cady Stanton, Matilda Joslyn Gage, and herself (1882). Speaking on May 14, 1863, at a national convention of the Woman's National Loyal League.

3 My business is stanching blood and feeding fainting men; my post the open field between the bullet and the hospital. I sometimes discuss the application of a compress or a wisp of hay under a broken limb, but not the bearing and merits of a political movement. I make gruel—not speeches; I write *letters home* for wounded soldiers, not political addresses.

Clara Barton (1821–1912), U.S. Civil War nurse and founder of the American Red Cross. As quoted in *Angel of the Battlefield*, ch. 5, by Ishbel Ross (1956). Written on June 24, 1863, during the Civil War, to editor T. W. Meighan, who had urged her to use her influence to help bring about peace.

4 Dead niggers tell no tales; you go on or die!

Harriet Tubman (*c.* 1820–1913), African American escaped slave and abolitionist. As quoted in *Harriet, the Moses of Her People*, by Sarah Bradford (1869). Bradford was the friend and first biographer of the great abolitionist and ex-slave who, after escaping to freedom, returned nineteen times to the South and ushered more than 300 other runaway slaves, including her parents and brothers, to freedom in the North. While carrying out these extremely dangerous missions, Tubman carried a revolver. Should one of her charges tire and refuse to go on, she would point it at the runaway's head and say this, knowing that to leave anyone behind would jeopardize her rescue program and could cost many lives.

5 . . . it is the right and duty of every woman to employ the power of or-

ganization and agitation in order to gain those advantages which are given to the one sex and unjustly withheld from the other.

CATHERINE E. BEECHER (1800–1878), U.S. educator and author. *Woman's Profession as Mother and Educator with Views in Opposition to Woman Suffrage* (1872).

From an address delivered on December 10, 1870, at the Music Hall of Boston. Beecher, an important advocate of the systematization of housework and of education and economic independence for women, nonetheless was never captivated by the era's woman suffrage movement. She favored suffrage only for women whose names appeared on the tax rolls; hers probably did, as she was single and self-supporting.

6 If I wrote at all, I must throw myself headlong into the great political maelstrom, and would of course be swallowed up like a fishing-boat in the great Norway horror which decorated our school geographies; for no woman had ever done such a thing, and I could never again hold up my head under the burden of shame and disgrace which would be heaped upon me. But what matter? I had no children to dishonor; all save one who had ever loved me were dead, and she no longer needed me, and if the Lord wanted some one to throw into that gulf, no one could be better spared than I.

JANE GREY SWISSHELM (1815–1884), U.S. newspaperwoman, abolitionist, and human rights activist. *Half a Century,* ch. 18 (1880).

Recalling her decision to write against the Mexican War (1846–1848) and against slavery.

7 Ours is the old, old story of every uprising race or class or order. The

work of elevation must be wrought by ourselves or not at all.

FRANCES POWER COBBÉ (1822–1904), U.S. author and feminist. *The Duties of Women,* Preface (1882).

8 Long ago I added to the true old adage of "What is everybody's business is nobody's business," another clause which, I think, more than any other principle has served to influence my actions in life. That is, What is nobody's business is my business.

CLARA BARTON (1821–1912), U.S. Civil War nurse and founder of the American Red Cross. As quoted in *Angel of the Battlefield,* ch. 13, by Ishbel Ross (1956).

In a letter dated March 7, 1888, written to orator Robert G. Ingersoll (1833–1899), urging him to speak on behalf of the residents of Mount Vernon, Illinois, whose town had been ravaged by a tornado the month before.

9 They tell us sometimes that if we had only kept quiet, all these desirable things would have come about of themselves. I am reminded of the Greek clown who, having seen an archer bring down a flying bird, remarked, sagely: "You might have saved your arrow, for the bird would anyway have been killed by the fall."

ELIZABETH CADY STANTON (1815–1902), U.S. suffragist, social reformer, and author. As quoted in *"Common Sense" Applied to Woman Suffrage,* ch. 1, by Mary Putnam Jacobi (1894).

Said on May 7, 1894, at a mass meeting during the 1894 Woman's Rights Convention in New York City. Stanton was referring to successes of the women's rights movement, which included the securing of independent property rights for women and of personal rights in contracts and business.

10 ... it seems to have been my luck to stumble into various forms of progress, to which I have been of the smallest possible use; yet for whose sake I have suffered the discomfort attending all action in moral improvements, without the happiness of knowing that this was clearly quite worth while.

ELIZABETH STUART PHELPS (1844–1911), U.S. novelist and short story writer. *Chapters from a Life*, ch. 12 (1897).

Phelps had worked for temperance and for women's education and enfranchisement. When she wrote this, prohibition and woman suffrage were still many years from enactment, and women were still barred from most colleges, though their opportunities for higher education were increasing.

11 We are told it will be of no use for us to ask this measure of justice—that the ballot be given to the women of our new possessions upon the same terms as to the men—because we shall not get it. It is not our business whether we are going to get it; our business is to make the demand. . . . Ask for the whole loaf and take what you can get.

SUSAN B. ANTHONY (1820–1906), U.S. suffragist. As quoted in *History of Woman Suffrage*, vol. 4, ch. 19, by Susan B. Anthony and Ida Husted Harper (1902).

Speaking before the thirty-first annual convention of the National Woman Suffrage Association, held April 27–May 3, 1899, in Grand Rapids, Michigan. She was explaining why equal suffrage should be demanded in Hawaii and other new United States possessions, even though it was unlikely to be granted.

SOCIAL/POLITICAL ACTIVISM: EARLY 20TH CENTURY

1 I know no East or West, North or South, when it comes to my class fighting the battle for justice. If it is my fortune to live to see the industrial chain broken from every workingman's child in America, and if then there is one black child in Africa in bondage, there shall I go.

MOTHER JONES (1830–1930), U.S. labor organizer. *The Autobiography of Mother Jones*, ch. 13 (1925).

From an address before a 1903 convention of the Federation of Labor.

2 These have been wonderful years. How many happy, happy times we have traveled about together! Day and night, in stage coaches, on freight trains, over the mountains and across the prairies, hungry and tired, we have wandered. The work was sometimes hard and discouraging but those were happy and useful years.

SUSAN B. ANTHONY (1820–1906), U.S. suffragist. As quoted in *Life and Work of Susan B. Anthony*, vol. 3, ch. 71, by Anna Howard Shaw, to Ida Husted Harper (1908).

In March 1906, on her death bed, reminiscing with her sister suffragist, Rev. Anna Howard Shaw (1847–1919).

3 You have to make more noise than anybody else, you have to make yourself more obtrusive than anybody else, you have to fill all the papers more than anybody else, in fact you have to be there all the time and see that they do not snow you under, if you are really going to get your reform realized.

EMMELINE PANKHURST (1858–1928), British suffragist. As quoted in *Feminism: The Essential Historical Writings*, part 5, by Miriam Schnier (1972).

In a speech that the fiery militant suffragist gave in Hartford, Connecticut, on November 13, 1913, during an American lecture tour.

4 [When asked by the judge, after her first arrest, at age 15: "Do you expect to convert people to socialism by talking on Broadway?":] Indeed I do.

ELIZABETH GURLEY FLYNN (1890–1964), U.S. labor organizer and Communist Party activist. As quoted in *The Nation*, p. 175, by Mary Heaton Vorse (February 17, 1926).

This arrest, in 1906, was the first of many for Flynn.

5 The militancy of men, through all the centuries, has drenched the world with blood, and for these deeds of horror and destruction men have been rewarded with monuments, with great songs and epics. The militancy of women has harmed no human life save the lives of those who fought the battle of righteousness. Time alone will reveal what reward will be allotted to women.

EMMELINE PANKHURST (1858–1928), British feminist. *My Own Story*, January 1920 entry (1921).

" . . . written in the late summer of 1914," while Europe prepared for the war now referred to as World War I.

6 . . . the moving spirit of militancy is deep and abiding reverence for human life.

EMMELINE PANKHURST (1858–1928), British suffragist and politician. *My Own Story*, book 3, ch. 4 (1914).

Pankhurst used militant techniques in her agitation for woman suffrage, including hunger strikes and deliberate provocation of arrest and imprisonment.

7 Indifference is harder to fight than hostility, and there is nothing that kills an agitation like having everybody admit that it is fundamentally right.

CRYSTAL EASTMAN (1881–1928), U.S. social/political activist and author. *On Women and Revolution*, part 1 (1978). From an article first published in *Time and Tide* on July 20, 1923.

8 I don't really know how most of my ventures in this work were ever financed. I am of no economical turn of mind. I do things first, and somehow or another they get paid for. If I had waited to finance my various battles for birth control, I do not suppose they ever would have become realities. I suppose here is the real difference between the idealist—or the "fanatic, as we are called—and the ordinary "normal" human being.

MARGARET SANGER (1879–1966), U.S. birth control advocate. *My Fight for Birth Control*, ch. 4 (1931).

Of her passionate work to legitimize birth control and disseminate information about it.

SOCIAL/POLITICAL ACTIVISM: LATE 20TH CENTURY

1 . . . most reform movements in our country have been cursed by a lunatic fringe and have mingled sound ideas for social progress with utopian nonsense.

AGNES E. MEYER (1887–1970), U.S. journalist. *Out of These Roots*, ch. 4 (1953).

2 Women have had the vote for over forty years and their organizations lobby in Washington for all sorts of causes; why, why, why don't they take up their own causes and obvious needs?

DOROTHY THOMPSON (1894–1961), U.S. journalist. *Ladies' Home Journal*, p. 19 (May 1960).

Written three years before publication of Betty Friedan's milestone book, *The Feminine Mystique*, and six years before the National Organization for Women was founded.

3 I cannot say to a person who suffers injustice, "Wait." Perhaps you can. I can't. And having decided that I cannot urge caution I must stand with him.

SANDRA "CASEY" CASON (b. c. 1940), U.S. political activist. As quoted in *Personal Politics*, ch. 3, by Sara Evans (1979).

From a 1960 speech given at the congress of the National Student Association. She was referring to injustice toward Southern African Americans. Cason was later known as Casey Hayden, an activist in the Students for a Democratic Society (SDS) and among the earliest post-1950s feminist theorists in the United States.

4 . . . Negroes must concern themselves with every single means of struggle: legal, illegal, passive, active, violent and non-violent. . . . They must harass, debate, petition, boycott, sing hymns, pray on steps—and shoot from their windows when the racists come cruising through their communities. . . . The acceptance of our condition is the only form of extremism which discredits us before our children [ellipses in source].

LORRAINE HANSBERRY (1930–1965), African American playwright and essayist. As

quoted in *Blood, Bread and Poetry*, ch. 2, by Adrienne Rich (1986).

Written in 1962.

5 This is the 184th Demonstration.

. . .

What we do is not beautiful
hurts no one makes no one
    desperate
we do not break the panes of safety
    glass
stretching between people on the
    street
and the deaths they hire.

MARGE PIERCY (b. 1936), U.S. poet, novelist, and political activist. "The 184th Demonstration," lines 1, 27–31 (1968).

On the countless demonstrations mounted to protest the United States' involvement in the Vietnam War; Piercy was a prominent activist in the antiwar movement.

6 The will to change begins in the
    body not in the mind
My politics is in my body, accruing
    and expanding with every act of
    resistance and each of my failures.

ADRIENNE RICH (b. 1929), U.S. poet and feminist. "Tear Gas," lines 38–39 (1969).

7 Basically, I have no place in organized politics. By coming to the British Parliament, I've allowed the people to sacrifice me at the top and let go the more effective job I should be doing at the bottom.

BERNADETTE DEVLIN (b. 1947), Irish politician. *The Price of My Soul*, ch. 6 (1969).

The fiery Northern Irish political activist had been elected to Parliament in the preceding year.

8 Divide and conquer—that's what they try to do to any group trying to make social change. I call it D&

C. Black people are supposed to turn against Puerto Ricans. Women are supposed to turn against their mothers and mothers-in-law. We're all supposed to compete with each other for the favors of the ruling class.

FLORYNCE KENNEDY (b. 1916), African American lawyer, author, activist, and humorist. As quoted in *The Decade of Women,* by Suzanne Levine and Harriet Lyons (1980). Said in 1973.

9 Determination and skill come out of a depth of political and cultural experiences. Women resist and are brave in the most ordinary-seeming situations: on a welfare line, after being told that medical benefits are going to cut; on a street late at night helping a sister who is being harassed; as a mother demanding that the hospital stop experimenting with sterilization on her daughters; one sister to another trying to convince her to stop shooting up because it's giving the man a victory, swallowing up her life.

WOMEN OF THE WEATHER UNDERGROUND, *Ms. Magazine,* p. 106 (February 1974). This was a small group of women who were living as fugitives after indictment for crimes related to left-radical politics and opposition to American involvement in the Vietnam War; they included such well-known activists as Kathy Boudin and Bernardine Dohrn, both of whom later surfaced and served prison time.

10 The difference between poetry and rhetoric
is being
ready to kill
yourself
instead of your children.

AUDRE LORDE (1934–1992), African American author and lesbian feminist. "Power," lines 1–5 (1978). Lorde was the mother of two.

11 it was not enough to be for abolition
while the spirit of the masters
flickered in the abolitionist's heart
. . .
With whom do you believe your lot is cast?

ADRIENNE RICH (b. 1929), U.S. poet and feminist. "The Spirit of Place," section 1, lines 21–23 and 27 (1980).

12 We must remember the past, define the future, and challenge the present—wherever and however we can. It will take the rest of our lives even to begin. But then, what else have we to do?

JANE O'REILLY, U.S. feminist and humorist. *The Girl I Left Behind,* Introduction (1980).

13 As a practicing member of several oppressed minority groups, I feel that I have on the whole conducted myself with the utmost decorum. I have . . . refrained from marching, chanting . . . or in any other way making anything that could even vaguely be construed as a fuss.

FRAN LEBOWITZ (b. 1950), U.S. humorist. *Social Studies,* ch. 18 (1981). Lebowitz did not specify the minority groups to which she belonged, but probably meant that she was female, Jewish, and a smoker.

14 The sixties were characterized by a heady belief in instantaneous solutions.

AUDRE LORDE (1934–1992), African American poet, autobiographer, and lesbian feminist. *Sister Outsider,* ch. 14 (1984).

From a speech delivered during Malcolm X Weekend at Howard University, in February 1982. It was entitled "Learning from the Sixties."

15 . . . all my letters are read. I like that. I usually put something in there that I would like the staff to see. If some of the staff are lazy and choose not to read the mail, I usually write on the envelope "Legal Mail." This way it will surely be read. It's important that we educate everybody as we go along.

JEAN GUMP, U.S. pacifist. As quoted in *The Great Divide,* book 2, section 10, by Studs Terkel (1988).

A militant activist, Gump was serving time in the Correctional Institution for Women at Alderson, West Virginia, for destroying government property. Her husband, Joe Gump, also participated in the attack and was sentenced to prison as well. She said this during an August 15, 1987, interview.

16 The demonstrations are always early in the morning, at six o'clock. It's wonderful, because I'm not doing anything at six anyway, so why not demonstrate? . . . When you've written to your president, to your congressman, to your senator and nothing, nothing has come of it, you take to the streets.

ERICA BOUZA, U.S. jewelry designer and social activist. As quoted in *The Great Divide,* book 2, section 7, by Studs Terkel (1988).

The wife of a Minneapolis police chief, Bouza was an activist with a history of five arrests.

17 I have to change how people view themselves in the world. I have to get people to believe they can in fact make a difference. . . . We view ourselves . . . as people trained to develop people. Issues are only

tools. Think about the guy who works in a factory. He's on the assembly line. He's a nobody. He doesn't do the kind of work that's ever gonna get him recognition. Take that same person and he's a key leader in the parish or in a union. Suddenly that same man, who from Monday to Friday stands on the assembly line at General Motors and is a nobody, is somebody over here. People look to him. He makes a difference and he knows it. He counts.

MARY GONZALES, Mexican American neighborhood organizer. As quoted in *The Great Divide,* book 1, section 2, by Studs Terkel (1988).

The cofounder and associate director of a Chicago neighborhood organization, she was explaining what motivated her.

18 I am not going to have 2,000 condoms hanging in my window. I don't care what it represents.

SHARON ZUCKERBROD, U.S. business executive. As quoted in *Newsweek* magazine, p. 23 (November 20, 1989).

The Vice-President of the Houston, Texas, Tiffany's—an extremely elite jewelry store—she was explaining why she would not allow a window display, containing many condoms, to promote AIDS research.

19 I have not been animated in my life to fight against race and sex discrimination simply because of my own identity. That would mean that one must be South African to fight apartheid, or a poor white in Appalachia to fight poverty, or Jewish to fight anti-Semitism. And I just reject that conception of how struggles should be waged.

ELEANOR HOLMES NORTON (b. 1937), African American lawyer and educator. As quoted in *I Dream a World,* by Brian Lanker (1989).

A graduate of Yale Law School, Norton was the first woman to the Equal Employment Opportunity Commission (1977–1981). She also worked for the American Civil Liberties Union and, in 1970, headed the New York City Commission on Human Rights.

20 I've never been afraid to step out and to reach out and to move out in order to make things happen.

VICTORIA GRAY, African American civil rights activist. As quoted in *This Little Light of Mine,* ch. 3, by Hay Mills (1993).

From an interview conducted by Mills on April 4, 1990. Gray, a Mississippi native, joined activists Fannie Lou Hamer and Annie Devine in their 1964 challenge to the United States House of Representatives over the seating of five white Mississippi men. Representing the Mississippi Freedom Democratic Party, the women argued that because African American Mississippians "were effectively denied the vote," the election in which the men had won their seats was illegal.

21 I will cut the head off my baby and swallow it if it will make Bush lose.

ZAINAB ISMAEL, Iraqi housewife. As quoted in *Newsweek* magazine, p. 31 (November 16, 1992).

On the day of the United States' 1992 Presidential election; the incumbent President George Bush lost to Democratic challenger Bill Clinton.

22 The important thing is that when you come to understand something you act on it, no matter how small that act is. Eventually it will take you where you need to go.

HELEN PRÉJEAN (b. 1940), U.S. nun and activist against the death penalty. As quoted in the *New York Times Magazine,* p. 31 (May 9, 1993).

On her evolution into an activist, carrying out a ministry to both death row inmates and the families of their victims.

23 . . . dealing with being a lesbian— and part of that is by being politi-

cally activist—has caused me to have a less carefree adolescence. But I don't think that's a bad thing. It has its rewards.

KARINA LUBOFF (b. 1974), U.S. college student and gay/lesbian rights activist. As quoted in the *New York Times,* sect. 9, p. 7 (June 13, 1993).

Luboff had been active in lesbian and gay rights causes since she was sixteen.

24 I wish I could take back some of the things I said and some of the things I did. But in the bigger picture, I don't feel that it was violent and terrible. I feel like it was *primarily*— obviously not completely—moral, based on a vision that the government should be better, and that people could be better, and that democracy should be real.

BERNARDINE DOHRN (b. 1942), U.S. lawyer and political activist. As quoted in the *Chronicle of Higher Education,* p. A5 (July 14, 1993).

Reflecting on her political activism in the 1960s. A founder of Weatherman, a small radical group that splintered off from the Students for a Democratic Society (SDS), Dohrn went "underground" in 1969 to escape prosecution for her part in instigating the "Days of Rage," a series of riots in Chicago that caused extensive property damage. She had established a reputation for fiery revolutionary rhetoric and for advocating violence.

25 A movement is only composed of people moving. To feel its warmth and motion around us is the end as well as the means.

GLORIA STEINEM (b. 1934), U.S. feminist, author, and editor. *Moving Beyond Words,* part 6 (1994).

On the satisfactions of social activism. Steinem was an early, prominent feminist beginning in the late 1960s and a cofounder of the first widely-distributed, "slick" feminist magazine, *Ms.* (1973–)

SOCIALISM

1   . . . this dream that men shall cease to waste strength in competition and shall come to pool their powers of production is coming to pass all over the earth.

JANE ADDAMS (1860–1935), U.S. social worker and social reformer. *Twenty Years at Hull-House,* ch. 7 (1910).

Addams was the founding director of Hull-House, a pioneer "settlement house" in a poor, largely immigrant, Chicago neighborhood.

2   I nearly always find, when I ask a vegetarian if he is a socialist, or a socialist if he is a vegetarian, that the answer is in the affirmative.

KATHERINE FULLERTON GEROULD (1879–1944), U.S. author. *Modes and Morals,* ch. 3 (1920).

3   Successful socialism depends on the perfectibility of man. Unless all, or nearly all, men are high-minded and clear-sighted, it is bound to be a rotten failure in any but a physical sense. Even through it is altruism, socialism means materialism. You can guarantee the things of the body to every one, but you cannot guarantee the things of the spirit to every one; you can guarantee only that the opportunity to seek them shall not be denied to any one who chooses to seek them.

KATHERINE FULLERTON GEROULD (1879–1944), U.S. author. *Modes and Morals,* ch. 1 (1920).

SOCIETY, FASHIONABLE

1   Fashionable women regard themselves, and are regarded by men, as pretty toys or as mere instruments of pleasure; and the vacuity of mind, the heartlessness, the frivolity which is the necessary result of this false and debasing estimate of women, can only be fully understood by those who have mingled in the folly and wickedness of fashionable life . . .

SARAH M. GRIMKÉ (1792–1873), U.S. abolitionist and feminist. *Letters on the Equality of the Sexes and the Condition of Woman,* letter #8: dated 1837 (1838).

Grimké, born into a wealthy Southern family, wrote: "During the early part of my life, my lot was cast among the butterflies of the fashionable world." She moved north and, with her sister Angelina, became active on behalf of African Americans and women.

2   The radical changes in society from the small, well-considered hundreds to the countless thousands have of course destroyed the neighborly character of the strange conglomerate. It is more ornamental and much more luxurious now than then.

M. E. W. SHERWOOD (1826–1903), U.S. socialite, traveller, and author. *An Epistle to Posterity,* ch. 11 (1897).

Comparing New York "society" of the 1870s and the 1890s.

3   And then came the most devastating thought of all: I was one of them. I who used to swing upside down on a living horse, who always danced when mere walking would have done, so glad was I of life, so full of health. It was the most gruesome thought I had ever had in my life.

JOSEPHINE DEMOTT ROBINSON (1865–1948), U.S. circus performer. *The Circus Lady,* ch. 10 (1926).

On retiring from a long career in the circus to become a Congressman's wife, spending hours in the confines of staid social circles.

4 I pity people who do not care for Society. They are poorer for the oblation they do not make.

ELIZABETH BOWEN (1899–1973), British novelist, story writer, essayist, and memoirist; born in Ireland. *Seven Winters,* part 1, ch. 10 (1962).

5 Socialite women meet socialite men and mate and breed socialite children so that we can fund small opera companies and ballet troupes because there is no government subsidy.

SUGAR RAUTBORD, U.S. socialite fundraiser and self-described "trash" novelist. As quoted in *The Great Divide,* book 2, section 7, by Studs Terkel (1988).

SOLIDARITY

1 [The Settlement House] must be grounded in a philosophy whose foundation is on the solidarity of the human race, a philosophy which will not waver when the race happens to be represented by a drunken woman or an idiot boy.

JANE ADDAMS (1860–1935), U.S. social worker and social reformer. *Twenty Years at Hull-House,* ch. 6 (1910).
From a lecture, "The Subjective Necessity for Social Settlements," delivered in 1892 at a summer school run by the Ethical Culture Society. Addams was the founding director of Hull-House, a pioneer "settlement house" in a poor, largely immigrant, Chicago neighborhood.

2 I know we're termites. But if all the termites got together, the house would fall down.

FLORYNCE KENNEDY (b. 1916), African American lawyer, activist, speaker, and author. *Color Me Flo,* ch. 3 (1976).
Of the various social movements of the time, none of which had generous funding or direct access to power.

3 I have more in common with a Mexican man than with a white woman. . . . This opinion . . . chagrins women who sincerely believe our female physiology unequivocally binds all women throughout the world, despite the compounded social prejudices that daily affect us all in different ways. Although women everywhere experience life differently from men everywhere, white women are members of a race that has proclaimed itself globally superior for hundreds of years.

ANA CASTILLO (b. 1953), Mexican–American poet, essayist, and feminist. *Massacre of the Dreamers,* ch. 1 (1994).
Castillo was born in the United States to Mexican immigrants.

SOLITUDE

1 . . . solitude is such a potential thing. We hear voices in solitude, we never hear in the hurry and turmoil of life; we receive counsels and comforts, we get under no other condition . . .

AMELIA E. BARR (1831–1919), U.S. author; born in Scotland. *All the Days of My Life,* ch. 17 (1913).

2 Solitary and *farouche* people don't have relationships; they are quite unrelatable. If you and I were capable of being altogether house-trained and made jolly, we should be nicer people, but not writers.

Elizabeth Bowen (1899–1973), British novelist, story writer, essayist, and memoirist; born in Ireland. As quoted in *Elizabeth Bowen,* ch. 3, by Victoria Glendinning (1979).

In a 1948 letter to the writer V. S. Pritchett. "Farouche" is a French word meaning (roughly) fierce, shy, and untamed.

3   The things men come to eat when they are alone are, I suppose, not much stranger than the men themselves. . . . A writer years ago told me of living for five months on hen mash.

M. F. K. Fisher (1908–1992), U.S. author and food expert. *An Alphabet for Gourmets,* "M is for Monastic" chapter (1949).

4   Anyone with a real taste for solitude who indulges that taste encounters the dangers of any other drug-taker. The habit grows. You become an addict. . . . Absorbed in the visions of solitude, human beings are only interruptions. What voice can equal the voices of solitude? What sights equal the movement of a single day's tide of light across the floor boards of one room? What drama be as continuously absorbing as the interior one?

Jessamyn West (1902–1984), U.S. novelist. *To See the Dream,* part 1 (1956).

5   I restore myself when I'm alone. A career is born in public—talent in privacy.

Marilyn Monroe (1926–1962), U.S. actor. As quoted in *Ms.* magazine, p. 40 (August 1972).

Monroe was a very popular and pressured movie star. Hoping to develop her skills and reputation as a serious actor, she quietly studied

acting in New York City after she had become famous in Hollywood.

SOPHISTICATION

1   Out in Hollywood, where the streets are paved with Goldwyn, the word "sophisticate" means, very simply, "obscene." A sophisticated story is a dirty story. Some of that meaning was wafted eastward and got itself mixed up into the present definition. So that a "sophisticate" means: one who dwells in a tower made of a DuPont substitute for ivory and holds a glass of flat champagne in one hand and an album of dirty post cards in the other.

Dorothy Parker (1893–1967), U.S. author and humorist. As quoted in *You Might as Well Live,* part 3, ch. 6, by John Keats (1970).

From a speech given in 1939 to the left-wing Congress of American Voters: "Sophisticated Verse and the Hell With It." Samuel Goldwyn (1882–1974) was a movie producer.

SORROW

1   Interpretation is the evidence of growth and knowledge, the latter through sorrow—that great teacher.

Eleonora Duse (1858–1924), Italian actor. As quoted in *Actors on Acting,* rev. ed., part 11, by Toby Cole and Helen Krich (1970).

The great stage actor had an omnipresent aura of sadness and was reticent and retiring.

SOUTH, THE (U.S.)

1   One of the most singular facts about the unwritten history of this country is the consummate ability

with which Southern influence, Southern ideas and Southern ideals, have from the very beginning even up to the present day, dictated to and domineered over the brain and sinew of this nation.

ANNA JULIA COOPER (1859–1964), African American educator and feminist. *A Voice from the South,* part 1 (1892).

Cooper was born to a slave.

2   . . . I had grown up in a world that was dominated by immature age. Not by vigorous immaturity, but by immaturity that was old and tired and prudent, that loved ritual and rubric, and was utterly wanting in curiosity about the new and the strange. Its era has passed away, and the world it made has crumbled around us. Its finest creation, a code of manners, has been ridiculed and discarded.

ELLEN GLASGOW (1873–1945), U.S. novelist. *The Woman Within,* ch. 12 (1954).

Written in 1944, on growing up in Richmond, Virginia.

3   The Southerner is usually tolerant of those weaknesses that proceed from innocence.

FLANNERY O'CONNOR (1925–1964), U.S. fiction writer and essayist. As quoted in review of *The Devil's Dream,* a book by Lee Smith, by Robert Houston (1992).

O'Connor was a lifelong resident of Georgia.

4   It was the world of Southern, rural, black growing up, of folks sitting on porches day and night, of folks calling your mama, 'cause you walked by and didn't speak, and of the switch waiting when you got home so that you could be taught some manners. It was a world of single black older women schoolteachers, dedicated, tough; they had taught your mama, her sisters, and her friends. They knew your people in ways that you never would and shared their insight, keeping us in touch with generations. It was a world where we had a history.

BELL HOOKS (b. c. 1955), African American feminist author and educator. *Yearning,* ch. 4 (1990).

On growing up in a small African American Southern community.

5   [President Ellen Wood Hall is] short, with short gray hair that is not in the least bit attractive, and wears godawful clothes.

PEGGY HITE SELF (b. c. 1921), U.S. college alumna. As quoted in the *Chronicle of Higher Education,* p. A17 (December 16, 1992).

A 1943 alumna of all-women Converse College (Spartanburg, S.C.), Self was criticizing the college's first woman president. She and another alumna, Harriet B. Wilder, complained to the college's governing board and declared that they would discontinue their $100 annual donations. Among the other criticisms made by President Hall's opponents were her hiring of an African American dean of students and the informal meeting of a college counselor with a group of lesbian students. Sally H. Coughman, president of the Alumnae Association, said: "She [Hall] is not the white-glove Southern lady that I think many, many of the older alums see themselves as and see Converse girls as being— which is absolutely not who those students are anymore." Katherine F. Reeves, chair of the Board of Trustees, lamented: "To have this happen at a women's college is really depressing." And President Hall observed: "Couched in all this is the idea that one isn't as feminine as one should be, and I think that's a way of trying to keep women from being as independent as they need to be to function in leadership positions." Soon after saying this, she resigned.

SOVIET UNION

I   Have convictions. Be friendly. Stick to your beliefs as they stick to theirs. Work as hard as they do.

Eleanor Roosevelt (1884–1962), U.S. author, speaker, and First Lady. As quoted in *Eleanor: The Years Alone*, ch. 3, by Joseph P. Lash (1972).

From a statement made on February 16, 1946, to the *New York Times*, on how to deal with the Soviet Union.

SPECIALIZATION

I   . . . to a specialist his specialty is the whole of everything and if his specialty is in good order and it generally is then everything must be succeeding.

Gertrude Stein (1874–1946), U.S. author; relocated to France. *Wars I Have Seen* (1945).

Written in 1943.

SPIRIT

I   The coarser forms of slavery all can see and deplore, but the subjections of the spirit, few either comprehend or appreciate. In our day women carrying heavy burdens on their shoulders while men walk by their side smoking their pipes, or women harnessed to plows and carts with cows and dogs while men drive, are sights which need no eloquent appeals to move American men to pity and indignation. But the subtle humiliations of women possessed of wealth, education, and genius, men on the same plane can not see or feel, and yet can any misery be more real than invidious distinctions on the ground of sex in the laws and constitution, in the political, religious, and moral position of those who in nature stand the peers of each other?

Elizabeth Cady Stanton (1815–1902), U.S. suffragist, social reformer, and author. *History of Woman Suffrage*, vol. 2, ch. 19 (1882).

2   . . . the spiritual world is *here* and *now* and indisputably and preeminently real. It is the material world that is the realm of shadows.

Amelia E. Barr, U.S. novelist. *All the Days of My Life*, ch. 1 (1913).

3   The sources of poetry are in the spirit seeking completeness.

Muriel Rukeyser (1913–1980), U.S. poet. *The Life of Poetry*, ch. 13 (1949).

4   . . . in a history of spiritual rupture, a social compact built on fantasy and collective secrets, poetry becomes more necessary than ever: it keeps the underground aquifers flowing; it is the liquid voice that can wear through stone.

Adrienne Rich (b. 1929), U.S. poet, essayist, and lesbian feminist. *What Is Found There*, ch. 16 (1993).

SPIRITUALITY

I   I distrust those people who know so well what God wants them to do, because I notice it always coincides with their own desires.

Susan B. Anthony (1820–1906), U.S. suffragist. As quoted in *History of Woman Suffrage*, vol. 4, ch. 16, by Susan B. Anthony and Ida Husted Harper (1902).

Said at the twenty-eighth annual convention of the National Woman Suffrage Association, held January 23–28, 1896, in Washington, D.C.

SPORTS

1 ... though it is by no means requisite that the American women should emulate the men in the pursuit of the whale, the felling of the forest, or the shooting of wild turkeys, they might, with advantage, be taught in early youth to excel in the race, to hit a mark, to swim, and in short to use every exercise which could impart vigor to their frames and independence to their minds.

FRANCES WRIGHT (1795–1852), Scottish author and speaker; relocated to America. *Views of Society and Manners in America,* March 1820 entry (1821).

2 Loosen your girdle and let 'er fly!

BABE DIDRIKSON ZAHARIAS (1911–1956), U.S. athlete. As quoted in *WomenSports* magazine, p. 28 (November 1975).

In the 1930s, the multitalented, blunt-spoken Zaharias said this was her formula for female athletic success.

3 People tend to box little girls in. They teach them to sit properly and stand quietly and not attract attention. Sports is one place where girls can be free and enjoy the exhilaration of movement.

TENLEY ALBRIGHT (b. 1935), U.S. ice skater. As quoted in *WomenSports* magazine, p. 16 (January 1975).

4 I looked so much like a guy you couldn't tell if I was a boy or a girl. I had no hair, I wore guys' clothes, I walked like a guy ... [ellipsis in

source] I didn't do anything right except sports. I was a social dropout, but sports was a way I could be acceptable to other kids and to my family.

KAREN LOGAN (b. 1949), U.S. athlete. As quoted in *WomenSports* magazine, p. 37 (January 1976).

On why she became a basketball and volleyball player.

5 The one nice thing about sports is that they prove men do have emotions and are not afraid to show them.

JANE O'REILLY, U.S. feminist and humorist. *The Girl I Left Behind,* ch. 5 (1980).

6 The whole idea of image is so confused. On the one hand, Madison Avenue is worried about the image of the players in a tennis tour. On the other hand, sports events are often sponsored by the makers of junk food, beer, and cigarettes. What's the message when an athlete who works at keeping her body fit is sponsored by a sugar-filled snack that does more harm than good?

MARTINA NAVRATILOVA (b. 1956), U.S. tennis player; born in Czechoslovakia. *Martina,* ch. 33 (1985).

The tennis champion was reacting to sponsors' dropping another tennis star, Billie Jean King (b. 1943), when she was sued for "palimony" by a former woman lover; and to criticism of the Virginia Slims tennis tournament because of its sponsorship by a cigarette company known for specifically targeting women consumers. Navratilova, like King, had women lovers.

7 Picture a room. It can be a bar, a fraternity, a living room and there are thirty men in it, sitting around a television, watching football. The door opens, and they turn, and you walk in. And you're staying. Here's what they think. A) Do we really want her here? B) Can we still do what we usually do? C) Why would she want to be here anyway?

GAYLE GARDNER, U.S. sports reporter. As quoted in *Sports Illustrated,* p. 82 (June 17, 1991).

On being a woman sports reporter. She was the first female sports anchor to appear weekly on a major television network.

8 The lesson learned here is a costly one: If you stand up for your principles, follow the law, and win massively, you lose totally.

LINDA J. CARPENTER, U.S. educator. As quoted in the *Chronicle of Higher Education,* p. A38 (July 15, 1992).

On the total elimination of intercollegiate sports at Brooklyn College, following the federal government's finding that the college had discriminated against its women athletes.

9 It is odd that the NCAA would place a school on probation for driving an athlete to class, or providing a loan, but would have no penalty for a school that violates Title IX, a federal law.

CARDISS L. COLLINS (b. 1931), U.S. politician. As quoted in the *Chronicle of Higher Education,* p. A32 (May 26, 1993).

On the National College Athletic Association's failure to support the law requiring gender equity in college sports. Most special favors for college athletes are prohibited by the Association. Collins was a member of the U.S. House of Representatives.

10 I knew I had to do it. It was an order from the coach.

CHARLOTTE SMITH (b.c. 1974), U.S. college basketball player. As quoted in the *New York Times,* p. C7 (April 3, 1994).

On shooting a three-point basket at the game-ending buzzer to carry her team, the University of North Carolina, to the National College Ath-

letic Association's women's basketball championship. Smith had made only eight of thirty-one three-point attempts all season; her coach was Sylvia Hatchell. Trailing 59–57 with less than one second left to play, North Carolina beat the favored team from Louisiana Tech 60–59.

SPRINGTIME

1 The American spring is by no means so agreeable as the American autumn; both move with faltering step, and slow; but this lingering pace, which is delicious in autumn, is most tormenting in the spring.

FRANCES TROLLOPE (1780–1863), British author. *Domestic Manners of the Americans,* ch. 14 (1832).

Trollope was residing temporarily in America when she wrote this.

2 Spring is the Period
Express from God.

EMILY DICKINSON (1831–1886), U.S. poet. "Spring is the Period": poem no. 844 in her *Collected Poems,* lines 1–2 (c. 1864).

3 Life in itself
Is nothing,
An empty cup, a flight of
uncarpeted stairs.
It is not enough that yearly, down
this hill,
April
Comes like an idiot, babbling and
strewing flowers.

EDNA ST. VINCENT MILLAY, (1892–1950) U.S. poet. "Spring," lines 13–18 (1921).

STATUS

1 . . . it would be impossible for women to stand in higher estimation than they do here. The defer-

383 • STATUS QUO

ence that is paid to them at all times and in all places has often occasioned me as much surprise as pleasure.

FRANCES WRIGHT (1795–1852), Scottish author and speaker; relocated to America. *Views of Society and Manners in America,* March 1820 entry (1821).

The Scotswoman had been travelling in the United States since September 1818.

2 It's really amazing what a money reputation will do for your social standing . . .

SUE SANDERS, U.S. oil producer. *Our Common Herd,* ch. 21 (1940).

Having earned, lost, and then again earned, large amounts of money, Sanders was reflecting on people's changed treatment of her when her fortunes improved.

3 There are of course people who are more important than others in that they have more importance in the world but this is not essential and it ceases to be. I have no sense of difference in this respect because every human being comprises the combination form.

GERTRUDE STEIN (1874–1946), U.S. author and patron of the arts; relocated to France. As quoted in *What Are Masterpieces,* afterword, by Robert Haas (1970).

Said in a January 1946 interview with Haas.

4 To photograph is to confer importance.

SUSAN SONTAG (b. 1933), U.S. author. *On Photography,* ch. 2 (1977).

5 When you're crowned Miss America, they put you up on a pedestal. People really look up to you and they think you're perfect. They

think that you have everything that you've ever wanted or dreamed about in life.

KAYE LANI RAE RAFKO (b. c. 1968), U.S. beauty contest winner, Miss America, 1988. As quoted in *Miss America,* ch. 17, by Ann-Marie Bivans (1991).

6 . . . a lot of my people are models. I like that for them. I admire models, so I think that's right for my people. . . . I love it when I have an important [client]. And the pictures and awards. One of my clients has these television awards—a beautiful statue of a woman. I think it's an Emmy. People would be lucky to get one. She has two. I think that's great.

ELAINE STRONG (b. 1934), U.S. maid. As quoted in the *New York Times,* sect. 14, p. 12 (May 8, 1994).

Strong worked for a New York City agency which sent her to clean apartments; she was explaining how she imagined lives for her clients based on the clues in their homes.

STATUS QUO

1 . . . it is a great mistake to confuse conventionality with simplicity . . . it takes a good deal of intelligence and a great many inhibitions to follow a social code.

KATHERINE FULLERTON GEROULD (1879–1944), U.S. author. *Modes and Morals,* ch. 7 (1920).

2 Activities that seem to represent choices are often inert reproductions of accepted practice.

SHOSHANA ZUBOFF (b. 1951), U.S. social scientist. *In the Age of the Smart Machine,* Conclusion (1988).

STEREOTYPES

1   ... the constructive power of an image is not measured in terms of its truth, but of the love it inspires.

SARAH PATTON BOYLE, U.S. civil rights activist and author. *The Desegregated Heart,* part 1, ch. 15 (1962).

On African American resentment of such stereotypical figures as Uncle Remus and Ol' Black Joe, which whites still regarded with affection. Boyle, a Southern white who advocated integration in the 1950s, understood African Americans' resentment but thought it perhaps ill-advised.

2   Women have the right to say: this is surface, this falsifies reality, this degrades.

TILLIE OLSEN (b. 1912), U.S. essayist and story writer. *Silences,* part 1 (1978).

Written in 1971, on being critical of writing that depicts women stereotypically or inaccurately.

3   Hispanic gives us all one ultimate paternal cultural progenitor: Spain. The diverse cultures already on the American shores when the Europeans arrived, as well as those introduced because of the African slave trade, are completely obliterated by the term. Hispanic is nothing more than a concession made by the U. S. legislature when they saw they couldn't get rid of us. If we won't go away, why not at least Europeanize us, make us presentable guests at the dinner table, take away our feathers and rattles and civilize us once and for all.

ANA CASTILLO (b. 1953), Mexican-American poet, essayist, and feminist. *Massacre of the Dreamers,* ch. 1 (1994).

Castillo was born in the United States to Mexican immigrants.

STOCK MARKET

1   The more kites that are up, the more string they need, and when it runs out, the bigger the loss. ... no one ever got a balloon up quite as high or hit bottom as hard as I did. I figure the lessons I learned were worth the money. Wounds made by these gambles soon heal, and before long the boys are back, looking at the board again. ... it's just life, and we all join in the game one way of another.

SUE SANDERS, U.S. oil producer. *Our Common Herd,* ch. 29 (1940).

On what she had learned about playing the stock market.

2   When you're right in the market, it's the best high you can imagine. It's a high without any alcohol. When you're wrong, it's the lowest low you can imagine.

MICHELLE MILLER (b. c. 1950), U.S. commodities broker. As quoted in *The Great Divide,* book 1, section 5, by Studs Terkel (1988).

STORIES

1   The universe is made of stories, not of atoms.

MURIEL RUKEYSER (1913–1980), U.S. poet. "The Speed of Darkness," part 9, lines 3–4 (1958).

STORY

1   All sorrows can be borne if you put them into a story or tell a story about them.

ISAK DINESEN (1885–1962), Danish author. As quoted in *The Human Condition,* Epigram, ch. 5, by Hannah Arendt (1958).

2 There is a certain embarrassment about being a storyteller in these times when stories are considered not quite as satisfying as statements and statements not quite as satisfying as statistics; but in the long run, a people is known, not by its statements or its statistics, but by the stories it tells.

FLANNERY O'CONNOR (1925–1964), U.S. fiction writer and essayist. *Mystery and Manners,* part 5 (1969). Written in 1963.

3 Long before I wrote stories, I listened for stories. Listening *for* them is something more acute than listening *to* them. I suppose it's an early form of participation in what goes on. Listening children know stories are *there.* When their elders sit and begin, children are just waiting and hoping for one to come out, like a mouse from its hole.

EUDORA WELTY (b. 1909), U.S. fiction writer. *One Writer's Beginnings,* ch. 1 (1984).

4 If it had not been for storytelling, the black family would not have survived. It was the responsibility of the Uncle Remus types to transfer philosophies, attitudes, values, and advice, by way of storytelling using creatures in the woods as symbols.

JACKIE TORRENCE (b. 1944), African American storyteller. As quoted in *I Dream a World,* by Brian Lanker (1989). Torrence was a professional storyteller specializing in "ghost stories, African American tales, and Appalachian mountain lore."

5 . . . there is . . . a big aspect of play in writing novels, and making the story more and more elaborate is just more and more fun.

GISH JEN (b. 1956), U.S. novelist. As quoted in *Listen to Their Voices,* ch. 2, by Mickey Pearlman (1993).

6 A good story is one that isn't demanding, that proceeds from A to B, and above all doesn't remind us of the bad times, the cardboard patches we used to wear in our shoes, the failed farms, the way people you love just up and die. It tells us instead that hard work and perseverance can overcome all obstacles; it tells lie after lie, and the happy ending is the happiest lie of all.

KATHLEEN NORRIS (b. 1947), U.S. poet and farmer. *Dakota,* ch. 14 (1993). Describing the reading preferences of the townspeople of rural Lemmon, South Dakota, where Norris lived and farmed.

STRENGTH (PHYSICAL)

1 Only when women rebel against patriarchal standards does female muscle become more accepted.

GLORIA STEINEM (b. 1934), U.S. feminist, author, and editor. *Moving Beyond Words,* part 2 (1994).

STRUGGLE

1 [Asked, upon the death of her fast friend and sister suffragist Elizabeth Cady Stanton (1816–1902), which period of their association she had enjoyed the most:] The days when the struggle was the hardest and the fight the thickest; when the whole world was against us and we had to stand the closer to each other; when I would go to her home and help with the children and the housekeeping through the day and then we would sit up far into the night preparing our ammunition and getting ready to move on the enemy. The years since the rewards began to come have brought no enjoyment like that.

Susan B. Anthony (1820–1906), U.S. suffragist. As quoted in *Life and Work of Susan B. Anthony,* vol. 3, ch. 61, by Ida Husted Harper (1908).

In an interview on October 16, 1902, the day of Stanton's death. The two women had worked together for fifty years. Anthony had remained single; Stanton had married and raised a large family.

2   I wasn't born to be a fighter. I was born with a gentle nature, a flexible character and an organism as equilibrated as it is judged hysterical. I shouldn't have been forced to fight constantly and ferociously. The causes I have fought for have invariably been causes that should have been gained by a delicate suggestion. Since they never were, I made myself into a fighter.

Margaret Anderson (1886–1973), U.S. literary editor and autobiographer. *My Thirty Years' War,* ch. 4 (1930).

Devoted to literature and the arts, Anderson founded, and for fifteen years sustained, a literary and arts magazine entitled *The Little Review;* it acquired a remarkable reputation and place in literary history but never made money. She was also the defiant daughter of a tense, affluent family with conventional expectations, and an open lesbian.

3   A liberation struggle is like a struggle against dirt. No matter what type of bath you take . . . in three weeks you'll smell like you've never seen a bathtub. What we don't understand about a liberation struggle is you never win it, any more than you "win" clean dishes. As soon as you eat on them, the dishes are dirty again.

Florynce Kennedy (b. 1916), African American lawyer, activist, speaker, and author. *Color Me Flo,* ch. 3 (1976).

SUBORDINATION OF WOMEN

1   All over this land women have no political existence. Laws pass over our heads that we can not unmake. Our property is taken from us without our consent. The babes we bear in anguish and carry in our arms are not ours.

Lucy Stone (1818–1893), U.S. suffragist. As quoted in *History of Woman Suffrage,* vol. 2, ch. 16, by Elizabeth Cady Stanton, Susan B. Anthony, and Matilda Joslyn Gage (1882).

Speaking on May 14, 1863, at a national convention of the Woman's National Loyal League; Stone was president of the convention.

2   So long as State constitutions say that all may vote when twenty-one, save idiots, lunatics, convicts and women, you are brought down politically to the level of those others disfranchised.

Susan B. Anthony (1820–1906), U.S. suffragist. As quoted in *The Life and Work of Susan B. Anthony,* ch. 44, by Ida Husted Harper (1898).

In a November 16, 1895, speech in Cleveland to the national convention of the Women's Christian Temperance Union, which strongly supported woman suffrage.

SUBORDINATION OF WOMEN: BY GOVERNMENT

1   . . . it is high time that the women of Republican America should

know how much the laws that govern *them* are like the *slave laws* of the South . . .

HARRIOT K. HUNT (1805–1875), U.S. physician and feminist. *Glances and Glimpses,* ch. 18 (1856).

SUBORDINATION OF WOMEN: BY MEN

1 That your sex are naturally tyrannical is a truth so thoroughly established as to admit of no dispute; but such of you as wish to be happy willingly give up the harsh title of master for the more tender and endearing one of friend. . . . Men of sense in all ages abhor those customs which treat us only as the vassals of your sex; regard us then as being placed by Providence under your protection, and in imitation of the Supreme Being make use of that power only for our happiness.

ABIGAIL ADAMS (1744–1818), U.S. matriarch; wife and mother of United States President. *Familiar Letters of John Adams and His Wife Abigail Adams, During the Revolution,* letter dated March 3, 1776 (1875).

In a letter from Braintree, Massachusetts, to her husband John Adams, who was away at war.

2 . . . I ask no favors for my sex. I surrender not our claim to equality. All I ask of our brethren is, that they will take their feet from off our necks, and permit us to stand upright on that ground which God designed us to occupy.

SARAH M. GRIMKE (1792–1873), U.S. abolitionist and feminist. *Letters on the Equality of the Sexes and the Condition of Woman,* letter #2: dated July 17, 1837 (1838).

3 Let every woman ask herself: "Why am I the slave of man? Why is my brain said not to be the equal of his brain? Why is my work not paid equally with his? Why must my body be controlled by my husband? Why may he take my labor in the household, giving me in exchange what he deems fit? Why may he take my children from me? Will them away while yet unborn?" Let every woman ask.

VOLTAIRINE DECLEYRE (1866–1912), U.S. anarchist, feminist, author, and teacher. As quoted in *Fugitive Information,* ch. 2, by Kay Leigh Hagan (1993). Written in 1890.

4 The history of woman is the history of the continued and universal oppression of one sex by the other. The emancipation of woman is her restoration to equal rights and privileges with man. . . . Need we wonder, then, at the sad spectacle which humanity offers us? Its hideous wars, its social abominations, its foul creeds, its treacheries, vices, wants, diseases, lusts, tyrannies, and crimes are the natural outcome of the subjugation of one half of the human race by the other.

TENNESSEE CLAFLIN (1846–1923), U.S. journalist, lecturer, and social reform advocate; relocated to England. *Talks and Essays,* vol. 1, ch. 4 (1897).

5 If woman alone had suffered under these mistaken traditions [of women's subordination], if she could have borne the evil by herself, it would have been less pitiful, but her brother man, in the laws he created and ignorantly worshipped, has suffered with her. He has lost her high-

est help; he has crippled the intelligence he needed; he has belittled the very source of his own being and dwarfed the image of his Maker.

CLARA BARTON (1821–1912), U.S. nurse; founder of the American Red Cross. As quoted in *History of Woman Suffrage*, vol. 5, ch. 2, by Ida Husted Harper (1922).
In an address delivered in February 1902 to the thirty-fourth annual convention of the National Woman Suffrage Association.

6   She has been man's slave. He has been educated at her expense. If he bought the ice cream, she was expected to pay for all his luxuries in reduced wages. She has done the drudgery and borne the insults of those who wronged her, assuming to be her protector.

CAROLINE NICHOLS CHURCHILL (1833–?), U.S. author. *Active Footsteps*, ch. 8 (1909).

7   In civilized societies today . . . clitoris envy, or womb envy, takes subtle forms. Man's constant need to disparage woman, to humble her, to deny her equal rights, and to belittle her achievements—all are expressions of his innate envy and fear.

ELIZABETH GOULD DAVIS (b. 1910), U.S. feminist and author. *The First Sex*, ch. 9 (1971).

SUBORDINATION OF WOMEN: BY SOCIETY

1   Women are not so well united as to form an Insurrection. They are for the most part wise enough to love their Chains, and to discern how becomingly they fit.

MARY ASTELL (1666–1731), British author. *Some Reflections Upon Marriage*, 4th ed., Appendix (1730).

2   . . . whilst you are proclaiming peace and good will to men, Emancipating all Nations, you insist upon retaining absolute power over wives. But you must remember that Arbitrary power is like most other things which are very hard, very liable to be broken—and notwithstanding all your wise Laws and Maxims we have it in our power not only to free ourselves but to subdue our Masters, and without violence throw both your natural and legal authority at our feet . . .

ABIGAIL ADAMS (1744–1818), U.S. matriarch, wife and mother of United States Presidents. In a letter reprinted in *The Feminist Papers*, part 1, by Alice S. Rossi (1973).
In a letter dated May 7, 1776 and written from Braintree, MA to her husband, John Adams, during the Revolutionary War, less than two months before the Declaration of Independence was signed.

3   There is a vulgar persuasion, that the ignorance of women, by favoring their subordination, ensures their utility. 'Tis the same argument employed by the ruling few against the subject many in aristocracies; by the rich against the poor in democracies; by the learned professions against the people in all countries.

FRANCES WRIGHT (1795–1852), Scottish author and speaker; relocated to America. *Course of Popular Lectures*, lecture 2 (1829).

4   That a majority of women do not wish for any important change in their social and civil condition,

merely proves that they are the un-reflecting slaves of custom.

LYDIA MARIA CHILD (1802–1880), U.S. author, abolitionist, and suffragist. *Selected Letters, 1817–1880,* ch. 9 (1982).

In an 1870 letter to the Advocates of Woman's Suffrage, an Iowa organization.

5 The principle of subordination is the great bond of union and harmony through the universe.

CATHERINE E. BEECHER (1800–1878), U.S. educator and author. *Woman's Profession as Mother and Educator, with Views in Opposition to Woman Suffrage,* "An Address to the Christian Women of America," (1872).

Beecher argued that, just as all people were properly subordinate to God, so employees should be subordinate to their employers and women subordinate to men. She herself was a hard-working, independent educator and proponent of education for women; she never married.

6 I think it is worse to be poor in mind than in purse, to be stunted and belittled in soul, made a coward, made a liar, made mean and slavish, accustomed to fawn and prevaricate, and "manage" by base arts a husband or a father,—I think this is worse than to be kicked with hobnailed shoes.

FRANCES POWER COBBÉ (1822–1904), U.S. author and feminist. *The Duties of Women,* lecture 1 (1882).

7 They who say that women do not desire the right of suffrage, that they prefer masculine domination to self-government, falsify every page of history, every fact in human experience. It has taken the whole power of the civil and canon law to hold woman in the subordinate po-sition which it is said she willingly accepts.

ELIZABETH CADY STANTON (1815–1902), U.S. suffragist, author, and social reformer. As quoted in *History of Woman Suffrage,* vol. 4, ch. 3, by Susan B. Anthony and Ida Husted Harper (1902).

From her paper entitled "Self-Government the Best Means of Self-Development," which was read to the United States Senate Committee on Woman Suffrage at a hearing on March 7, 1884.

8 ... today we round out the first century of a professed republic,—with woman figuratively representing freedom—and yet all free, save woman.

PHOEBE W. COUZINS (1845–1913), U.S. suffragist. As quoted in *The History of Woman Suffrage,* vol. 3, ch. 27, by Elizabeth Cady Stanton, Susan B. Anthony, and Matilda Joslyn Gage (1886).

At a convention of the National Woman Suffrage Association held on the centennial of American independence in the First Unitarian Church, Philadelphia.

9 Thus far women have been the mere echoes of men. Our laws and constitutions, our creeds and codes, and the customs of social life are all of masculine origin. The true woman is as yet a dream of the future. A just government, a humane religion, a pure social life await her coming.

ELIZABETH CADY STANTON (1815–1902), U.S. suffragist, social reformer, and author. As quoted in *History of Woman Suffrage,* vol. 4, ch. 8, by Susan B. Anthony and Ida Husted Harper (1902).

In a speech before a meeting of the International Council of Women, which was held in Washington, D.C., March 25–April 1, 1888.

10 The abominable doctrine taught in the pulpit, the press, in books and elsewhere, is that the whole duty of women is self-abasement and self-sacrifice. I do not believe subjection is woman's duty any more than it is the duty of a man to be under subjection to another man or many men. Women have the right of independence, of conscience, of will and of responsibility.

ANNA HOWARD SHAW (1847–1919), U.S. minister and suffragist. As quoted in *History of Woman Suffrage*, vol. 4, ch. 14, by Susan B. Anthony and Ida Husted Harper (1902). From a Sunday sermon preached in February 1894 to attendees of the twenty-sixth annual convention of the National Woman Suffrage Association. Shaw's text was "Let no man take thy crown."

11 With all her masculine vigour and glory, Greece fell, gradually atrophied, because one half of her had been, of set purpose, intellectually and politically paralyzed.

TENNESSEE CLAFLIN (1846–1923), U.S. journalist, lecturer, and social reform advocate; relocated to England. *Talks and Essays*, vol. 4, ch. 7 (1897). Hypothesizing that the Greek Empire fell because of the subordination of its women.

12 . . . no community where more than one-half of the adults are disfranchised and otherwise incapacitated by law and custom, can be free from great vices. Purity is inconsistent with slavery.

TENNESSEE CLAFLIN (1846–1923), U.S. journalist, lecturer, and social reform advocate; relocated to England. *Talks and Essays*, vol. 1, ch. 11 (1897). Referring primarily to women's exclusion from voting.

13 No more astounding relic of the subjection of women survives in western civilization than the status of the prostitute. . . . In connection with what other illegal vice is the seller alone penalized, and not the buyer?

CRYSTAL EASTMAN (1881–1928), U.S. social/political activist and author. *On Women and Revolution*, part 1 (1978). From an article first published in *Equal Rights* on September 19, 1925. In England, prostitution was not technically illegal, but prostitutes were routinely arrested and convicted of "solicitation, loitering, etc." Lady Astor had introduced in the House of Commons a bill for "Repeal of the Solicitation Laws."

14 The subtlest and most vicious aspect of women's oppression is that we have been conditioned to believe we are not oppressed, blinded so as not to see our own condition.

ROBIN MORGAN (b. 1941), U.S. author, feminist, and child actor. *The Word of a Woman*, part 1 (1992). Written in 1969.

15 Woman is the nigger of the world.

YOKO ONO (b. 1933), U.S. artist; born in Japan. "Some Time in New York City" [song lyric written with John Lennon] (1972).

16 of artists dying in childbirth, wise-women charred at the stake, centuries of books unwritten piled behind these shelves; and we still have to stare into the absence of men who would not, women who could not, speak to our life—this still unexcavated hole called civilization, this act of translation, this half-world.

ADRIENNE RICH (b. 1929), U.S. poet and feminist. *Twenty-One Love Poems*, poem #5, lines 15–20 (1974–76). Reflecting on her large personal library and on what, due to women's subordination over the centuries, was probably "missing" from it.

SUCCESS

1 Success is counted sweetest
By those who ne'er succeed.

EMILY DICKINSON (1830–1886), U.S.
poet. "Success is counted sweetest": Poem #67
in her *Complete Poems,* lines 1–2 (c. 1859).

2 I am succeeding quite well in my
work and the future looks well.
What special mission is God preparing me for? Cutting off all earthly
ties and isolating me as it were.

ELLEN HENRIETTA SWALLOW RICHARDS, (1842–1911) U.S. chemist and educator. As quoted in *The Life of Ellen H. Richards,*
ch. 5, by Caroline L. Hunt (1912).
Written to her friend Flora Hughes on April 30,
1871, a few months after she entered the Massachusetts Institute of Technology, as its first
woman student, to study chemistry. Her beloved father had recently died, which added to
her loneliness. Richards would eventually become a chemist and professor.

3 The only way to get along is to seek
the difficult job, always do it well,
and see that you get paid for it
properly. Oh, yes, and don't forget
to exploit men all you can. Because
if you don't they will exploit you.

EL DORADO JONES (1861–1932), U.S. inventor. As quoted in *Feminine Ingenuity,* ch. 12,
by Anne L. MacDonald (1992).
Said in the early 1900s.

4 Permanent success cannot be
achieved except by incessant intellectual labour, always inspired by
the ideal.

SARAH BERNHARDT (1845–1923), French
actor. *The Art of the Theatre,* ch. 3 (1924).

5 Success is an absurd, erratic thing.
She arrives when one least expects
her and after she has come may depart again almost because of a
whim.

ALICE FOOTE MacDOUGALL (1867–1945), U.S. businesswoman. *The Autobiography of a Business Woman,* ch. 3
(1928).
MacDougall was a self-made, and very successful, wholesale merchant and restaurateur.

6 Nothing succeeds like reports of
success.

SUE SANDERS, U.S. oil producer. *Our Common Herd,* ch. 24 (1940).

7 A tragic irony of life is that we so often achieve success or financial independence after the chief reason
for which we sought it has passed
away.

ELLEN GLASGOW (1873–1945), U.S. novelist. *The Woman Within,* ch. 16 (1954).
Written in 1944. Glasgow, who became a
widely recognized novelist only after decades
of writing, was reflecting on the fact that her
mother, whom she would have liked to aid financially, died before her first book was published.

8 . . . the most extreme conditions require the most extreme response,
and for some individuals, the call to
that response is vitality itself. . . .
The integrity and self-esteem gained
from winning the battle against extremity are the richest treasures in
my life.

DIANA NYAD (b. 1949), U.S. long-distance swimmer. *Other Shores,* ch. 8 (1978).
The champion marathon swimmer had
swum extremely difficult and even dangerous
courses, some taking dozens of hours to complete.

9 In my time and neighborhood (and
in my soul) there was only one

standard by which a woman measured success: did some man want her?

JESSAMYN WEST (1907–1984), U.S. novelist and autobiographer. *The Life I Really Lived,* part 7 (1979).

10 Every day, in this mostly male world, you have to figure out, "Do I get this by charming somebody? By being strong? Or by totally allowing my aggression out?" You've got to risk failure. The minute you want to keep power—you've become subservient, somebody who does work you don't believe in.

PAULA WEINSTEIN (b. 1945), U.S. movie company executive. As quoted in *The Decade of Women,* by Suzanne Levine and Harriet Lyons (1980).

11 Sometimes you're overwhelmed when a thing comes, and you do not realize the magnitude of the affair at that moment. When you get away from it, you wonder, did it really happen to you.

MARIAN ANDERSON (1902–1993), African American singer. As quoted in *I Dream a World,* by Brian Lanker (1989).

Anderson was a great contralto singer who wanted, and if not for racism probably would have had, an important operatic career. In 1955, she finally became the first African American soloist to sing at the Metropolitan Opera House in New York City. Here, she was remembering that experience.

12 Nothing is as seductive as the assurance of success.

GERTRUDE HIMMELFARB (b. 1922), U.S. author. *On Looking into the Abyss,* ch. 3 (1994).

From a paper delivered in 1990 at the American Enterprise Institute: "From Marx to Hegel."

SUFFRAGE

1 Universal suffrage is the only guarantee against despotism.

MAY WRIGHT SEWALL (1844–1920), U.S. suffragist. As quoted in *History of Woman Suffrage,* vol. 4, ch. 5, by Susan B. Anthony and Ida Husted Harper (1902).

Speaking before the eighteenth annual convention of the National Woman Suffrage Association, held February 17–19, 1886, in Washington, D.C.

2 In all history no class has been enfranchised without some selfish motive underlying. If to-day we could prove to Republicans or Democrats that every woman would vote for their party, we should be enfranchised.

CARRIE CHAPMAN CATT (1859–1947), U.S. suffragist. As quoted in *History of Woman Suffrage,* vol. 4, ch. 17, by Susan B. Anthony and Ida Husted Harper (1902).

Speaking before the twenty-ninth annual convention of the National Woman Suffrage Association, held January 26–29, 1897, in Des Moines, Iowa.

3 . . . in every State there are more women who can read and write than the whole number of illiterate male voters; more white women who can read and write than all Negro voters; more American women who can read and write than all foreign voters.

NATIONAL WOMAN SUFFRAGE ASSOCIATION, As quoted in *History of Woman Suffrage,* vol. 4, ch. 13, by Susan B. Anthony and Ida Husted Harper (1902).

From a resolution passed unanimously by the association in 1893 at its twenty-fifth annual convention. The women were stung by the fact that male illiterates, male ex-slaves, and male immigrants were all permitted to vote, while women—even those who were well educated, free-born, and native-born—were not. It should be noted, however, that most suffragists had also opposed slavery and championed the civil rights of African Americans. Their point was not that these men should be denied the vote, only that women should be accorded it.

4 I have seen in my time two enormous extensions of the suffrage to men—one in America and one in England. But neither the negroes in the South nor the agricultural laborers in Great Britain had shown before they got the ballot any capacity of government; for they had never had the opportunity to take the first steps of political action. Very different has been the history of the march of women toward a recognized position in the State. We have had to prove our ability at each stage of progress, and have gained nothing without having satisfied a test of capacity.

HARRIOT STANTON BLATCH (1856–1940), British suffragist; born in the United States. As quoted in *History of Woman Suffrage*, vol. 4, ch. 18, by Susan B. Anthony and Ida Husted Harper (1902).
Speaking before the thirtieth annual convention of the National Woman Suffrage Association, held February 13–19, 1898, in Washington, D.C. In her address, which was entitled "Woman as an Economic Factor," Blatch contrasted women with "the negroes in the [American] South" and "the agricultural laborers in Great Britain," who had won the right to vote before having had the opportunity to demonstrate political aptitude.

5 There are whole precincts of voters in this country whose united intelligence does not equal that of one representative American woman.

CARRIE CHAPMAN CATT (1859–1947), U.S. suffragist. As quoted in *History of Woman Suffrage*, vol. 4, ch. 20, by Susan B. Anthony and Ida Husted Harper (1902).
In the closing address at the thirty-second annual convention of the National Woman Suffrage Association, held February 8–14, 1900, in Washington, D.C. The address was entitled

"Why We Ask for the Submission of an [Constitutional] Amendment." Catt was referring to the fact that although no woman, no matter how accomplished, was allowed to vote (except for limited voting rights in some states), virtually all men were, regardless of education, background, or ability.

6 . . . woman does not see what people of intellect perceived fifty years ago: that suffrage is an evil, that it has only helped to enslave people, that it has but closed their eyes that they may not see how craftily they were made to submit.

EMMA GOLDMAN (1869–1940), U.S. anarchist and author; born in Russia. *Anarchism and Other Essays*, 3rd rev. ed., ch. 9 (1917).
A socialist and anarchist, she was also anti-democratic and an anti-suffragist.

SUNDAY

1 Jesus would recommend you to pass the first day of the week rather otherwise than you pass it now, and to seek some other mode of bettering the morals of the community than by constraining each other to look grave on a Sunday, and to consider yourselves more virtuous in proportion to the idleness in which you pass one day in seven.

FRANCES WRIGHT (1795–1852), Scottish author and speaker; relocated to America. *Course of Popular Lectures*, lecture 6 (1829).

2 . . . this is "society's" Sunday. The majority of Londoners of the middle class still keep to their chapels, churches, gardens, and homes; it is a beautifully quiet and respectable day in the London suburbs. It is true that people seek the fresh air, couples go out on their bicycles, immense numbers of pedestrians are turning out towards the parks, and there is a great deal of movement, but it is decorous and becoming. It is one of the distinctions of New York that it is also a Sunday-keeping city. We of the small contingent of the Anglo-Saxon race are the only people who observe the Lord's day in this fashion.

M. E. W. SHERWOOD (1826–1903), U.S. socialite, traveller, and author. *An Epistle to Posterity*, ch. 15 (1897).

3   Even the street, the sunshine, the very air had a special Sunday quality. We walked differently on Sundays, with greater propriety and stateliness. Greetings were more formal, more subdued, voices more meticulously polite. Everything was so smooth, bland, polished. And genuinely so, because this was Sunday. In church the rustling and the stillness were alike pervaded with the knowledge that all was for the best. Propriety ruled the universe. God was in His Heaven, and we were in our Sunday clothes.

ROSE WILDER LANE (1886–1965), U.S. author. *Old Hometown*, ch. 1 (1935).

Remembering Sundays in the small Nebraska town where she grew up.

SUPERSTITION

1   . . . woman's narrow and purist attitude toward life makes her a greater danger to liberty wherever she has political power. Man has long overcome the superstitions that still engulf women.

EMMA GOLDMAN (1869–1940), U.S. anarchist and author; born in Russia. *Anarchism and Other Essays*, 3rd rev. ed., ch. 9 (1917).

SURFING

1   I plan to be reincarnated as a dolphin.

MARGO GODFREY OBERG (b. c. 1955), U.S. surfer. As quoted in *WomenSports* magazine, p. 12 (June 1977).

Oberg was a five-time winner of the women's world championship in surfing.

SURREALISM

1   Surrealism is a bourgeois disaffection; that its militants thought it universal is only one of the signs that it is typically bourgeois.

SUSAN SONTAG (b. 1933), U.S. author. *On Photography*, ch. 3 (1977).

SURVIVAL

1   Mortua—sed non sepulta! Mortua—sed non sepulta! [Dead—but not buried! Dead—but not buried!]

ELIZABETH I (1533–1603), Queen of England (1558–1603). As quoted in *The Sayings of Queen Elizabeth*, ch. 3, by Frederick Chamberlin (1923).

Said in 1599, upon learning of rumors that she had died. She would repeat this often until her actual death.

2   Self-preservation is the first responsibility.

MARGARET ANDERSON (1886–1973), U.S. literary editor and autobiographer. *My Thirty Years' War*, ch. 5 (1930).

3   You survived because you were the first.

You survived because you were the last.

Because alone. Because the others.

Because on the left. Because on the right.

Because it was raining. Because it was sunny.

Because a shadow fell.

WISLAWA SZYMBORSKA (b. 1923), Polish poet. "Any Case," lines 6–11 (1948); tr. By Grazyna Drabik and Sharon Olds (1993).

Symborska, who has always lived in Poland, wrote a great deal of protest poetry during the Communist era.

4 . . . having bowed to the inevitability of the dictum that we must eat to live, we should ignore it and live to eat . . .

M. F. K. FISHER (1908–1992), U.S. author and food expert. *An Alphabet for Gourmets,* "A is for Dining Alone" chapter (1949).

5 World, do not ask those snatched from death
where they are going,
they are always going to their graves.
The pavements of the foreign city were not laid for the music of fugitive footsteps -

NELLY SACHS (1891–1970), German Jewish poet and translator; relocated to Sweden. "World, do not ask those snatched from death," lines 1–5, translated by Michael Hamburger, et al. (1967; first edition in German: 1949).

Sachs was cowinner of the 1966 Nobel Prize for Literature. A German Jew who escaped to Sweden in 1940, she was always keenly conscious of being a survivor of the Holocaust and an exile from her native land.

6 . . . passion for survival is the great theme of women's poetry.

ADRIENNE RICH (b. 1929), U.S. poet, essayist, and feminist. *The Work of a Common Woman,* by Judy Grahn, introductory essay (1978).

7 I think the main thing, don't you, is to keep the show on the road.

ELIZABETH BOWEN (1899–1973), British novelist, story writer, essayist, and memoirist; born in Ireland. As quoted in *Elizabeth Bowen,* ch. 13, by Victoria Glendinning (1979).

On being asked by television interviewer James Mossman, near the end of her life, "what her feelings were about aging—and, by implication, about death." (Soon afterward, Mossman committed suicide.)

8 . . . she learned survival
depends on complete distrust. Even today she is still
fierce in her refusal to rely on others. Some would call
it alienation. Others pride. I think it's only
the necessary stance of any survivor.

IRENA KLEPFISZ (b. 1941), U.S. Jewish poet and essayist; born in Poland. "A Visit," lines 29–33 (1981).

Of her mother, a Polish Jew and widow of a fighter for Jewish rights, who fled Warsaw after the death of her husband and eventually settled with her small daughter in New York City.

9 Think of the life of the working woman as the decathlon. If you even finish it's a miracle.

BARBARA DALE (b. 1940), U.S. cartoonist. *The Working Woman Book,* ch. 7 (1985).

10 I think the American Dream for most people is just survival.

SANDY SCHOLL, U.S. owner of a small cleaning service. As quoted in *The Great Divide,* book 1, section 2, by Studs Terkel (1988).

11 The Holocaust was not an event that ended in 1945—at least not for the survivors. Not for me. It contin-

ued on and on because my mother and I were alone. Because my father's family no longer existed and I was its sole survivor. It continued on in the struggle of extreme poverty that we experience in the early years in this country. It continued on and on, coloring every thought I had, every decision I made. It continued on in the Bronx, on ordinary streets, at the kitchen table. It continued on invisible.

IRENA KLEPFISZ (b. 1941), U.S. Jewish author; born in Poland. *Dreams of an Insomniac*, part 2 (1990).

Klepfisz, a Jew born in Poland in 1941, escaped the 1943 Warsaw Uprising; her father had been killed on the second day of the Uprising. After some years in Sweden, she and her mother emigrated to New York City.

12 . . . when I have formed the sounds, said the words out loud, those who had assumed Yiddish was a language of the past only, suddenly felt it had been revived. As my tongue, mouth, lips, throat, lungs physically pushed Yiddish into the world—as I, a Jew, spoke a Jewish language to other Jews—Yiddish was very much alive. Not unlike a *lebn geblibene*, a survivor, of an overwhelming catastrophe, it seemed to be saying *'khbin nisht vos ikh bin amol geven.* I am not what I once was. *Ober 'khbin nisht geshtorbn. Ikh leb.* But I did not die. I live.

IRENA KLEPFISZ (b. 1941), U.S. Jewish author; born in Poland. *Dreams of an Insomniac*, part 4 (1990).

Klepfisz, a Jew born in Poland in 1941, escaped the 1943 Warsaw Uprising after her father was killed in its second day. After some years in Sweden, she and her mother emigrated to New York City—the only members of either side of the family to survive the Holocaust. She became an expert in, and teacher of, Yiddish.

13 . . . survival is the least of my desires.

DOROTHY ALLISON (b. 1949), U.S. author and lesbian feminist. *Skin*, ch. 22 (1994).

Allison had suffered a poverty-stricken, violence-ridden, Southern childhood.

SWIMMING

1 When we're in the water, we're not in this world.

GERTRUDE EDERLE (b. 1906), U.S. swimmer. As quoted in *WomenSports* magazine, p. 16 (May 1977).

Ederle was the fifth person, and the first woman, to swim across the English Channel.

2 . . . marathon swimming is the most difficult physical, intellectual and emotional battleground I have encountered, and each time I win, each time I touch the other shore, I feel worthy of any other challenge life has to offer.

DIANA NYAD (b. 1949), U.S. long-distance swimmer. *Other Shores*, ch. 8 (1978).

The champion marathon swimmer had swum extremely difficult and even dangerous courses, some taking dozens of hours to complete.

SWITZERLAND

1 In a war everybody always knows all about Switzerland, in peace times it is just Switzerland but in war time it is the only country that everybody has confidence in, everybody.

GERTRUDE STEIN (1874–1946), U.S. author; relocated to France. *Wars I Have Seen* (1945).

Written in 1943.

SYMPATHY

1 It is in the comprehension of the physically disabled, or disordered . . . that we are behind our age. . . . sympathy as a fine art is backward in the growth of progress . . .

ELIZABETH STUART PHELPS (1844–1911), U.S. novelist and short story writer. *Chapters from a Life,* ch. 11 (1897).

2 . . . while many people pride themselves, and with no exaggeration, on their ability to hear with sympathy of the downfall, sickness, and death of others, very few people seem to know what to do with a report of joy, happiness, good luck.

JESSAMYN WEST (1902–1984), U.S. novelist. *To See the Dream,* part 2 (1956).

TALENT

1 Everybody is talented, original and has something important to say.

BRENDA UELAND (1891–1985), U.S. author and writing teacher. *If You Want to Write,* 2nd. ed., ch. 1 (1938).

2 My talents fall within definite limitations. I am not as versatile an actress as some think.

GRETA GARBO (1905–1990), Swedish actor; relocated to the United States. As quoted in *The Divine Garbo,* ch. 5, by Frederick Sands and Sven Broman (1979).

Said at some time in the second half of her life, after she had retired. Many critics considered her the greatest actress in the history of the movies.

3 I have no patience with this dreadful idea that whatever you have in you has to come out, that you

can't suppress true talent. People can be destroyed; they can be bent, distorted, and completely crippled.

KATHERINE ANNE PORTER (1890–1980), U.S. novelist and story writer. As quoted in "Contexts" [poem], Epigram, by Irena Klepfisz (1982).

4 . . . talent is like electricity. We don't understand electricity. We use it.

MAYA ANGELOU (b. 1928), U.S. author and performer. *Black Women Writers at Work,* ch. 1, by Claudia Tate (1983).

5 I traded my childhood for my good left hand.

YEOU-CHENG MA (b. c. 1950), U.S. musician and pediatrician. As quoted in the *New York Times,* p. 39 (October 3, 1993).

Referring to her childhood as a violin prodigy. Ma's father gave her a violin when she was seven months old, and she won her first competition at three-and-a-half, playing against teenagers. Practicing eight hours per day, she did not attend school and took corespondence courses instead. But by the time she was eleven, her more talented younger brother, cellist Yo-Yo Ma (b. 1955), was attracting attention, and she studied the piano so that she could accompany him. Four years later, when her violin teacher told her to stick with the piano, she was crushed. She eventually became a developmental pediatrician but continued to be involved in music as executive director of the Children's Orchestra Society in New York City.

TASTE

1 I am continually fascinated at the difficulty intelligent people have in distinguishing what is controversial from what is merely offensive.

NORA EPHRON (b. 1941), U.S. author and humorist. *Scribble Scrabble,* ch. 10 (1978). Written in 1976, with reference to a book publisher.

TAXES

1 ... dissatisfied with city expenditures, the inequality of public school education, (*sexualizing education*), your remonstrant pays her taxes *compulsorily* instead of *cheerfully*, feeling within her that element of patriotism which inspired *her* as well as *your* forefathers, in the utterance of that deep, full, and clear sentiment, "Taxation *without representation* is tyranny."

HARRIOT K. HUNT (1805–1875), U.S. physician and feminist. *Glances and Glimpses,* ch. 21 (1856).

These are the closing lines of her letter "To the Authorities of the city of Boston, Massachusetts, and the Citizens generally," in which she protested having to pay a city tax when, as a woman, she lacked the right to vote.

2 Only the little people pay taxes.

LEONA HELMSLEY (b. 1921), U.S. hotelier and real estate magnate. As quoted in *Newsweek* magazine, p. 11 (July 24, 1989).

Helmsley, along with her husband and business partner Harry Helmsley, was convicted of tax evasion.

TEACHING

1 So long as the mental and moral instruction of man is left solely in the hands of hired servants of the public—let them be teachers of religion, professors of colleges, authors of books, or editors of journals or periodical publications, dependent upon their literary incomes for their daily bread, so long shall we hear but half the truth; and well if we hear so much. Our teachers, political, scientific, moral, or religious; our writers, grave or gay, are com-

pelled to administer to our prejudices and to perpetuate our ignorance.

FRANCES WRIGHT (1795–1852), Scottish author and speaker; relocated to America. *Course of Popular Lectures,* lecture 1 (1829).

2 I trust the time is coming, when the occupation of an instructer [sic] to children will be deemed the most honorable of human employment. If it is a drudgery to teach these little ones, then it is the duty of men to bear a part of that burthen; if it is a privilege and an honor, then we generously invite them to share that honor and privilege with us.

ANGELINA GRIMKÉ (1805–1879), U.S. abolitionist and feminist. *Letters to Catherine Beecher,* letter #13 (1837).

In a letter dated October 23, 1837, opposing the view of Beecher (1800–1878), a prominent educator, that women were peculiarly suited to the teaching of children. It was probably significant to Grimké, a determined abolitionist, that Beecher had cited the need for teachers as a reason for women not to give their time to antislavery activism.

3 Soon, in all parts of our country, in each neglected village, or new settlement, the Christian female teacher will quietly take her station, collecting the ignorant children around her, teaching them habits of neatness, order and thrift; opening the book of knowledge, inspiring the principles of morality, and awakening the hope of immortality. Soon her influence in the village will create a demand for new laborers, and then she will summon from among her friends at home, the nurse for the young and sick, the seamstress and the mantuamaker; and these

will prove her auxiliaries in good moral influence, and in sabbath school training. And often as the result of these labors, the Church will arise, and the minister of Christ be summoned to fill up the complement of domestic, moral and religious blessing.

CATHERINE E. BEECHER (1800–1878), U.S. educator and author. As quoted in *Catherine Beecher*, ch. 12, by Kathryn Kish Sklar (1973).
Written in 1846.

4 Do you not see that so long as society says woman has not brains enough to be a doctor, lawyer or minister, but has plenty to be a teacher, every man of you who condescends to teach, tacitly admits before all Israel and the sun that he has no more brains than a woman?

SUSAN B. ANTHONY (1820–1906), U.S. suffragist. As quoted in *The Life and Work of Susan B. Anthony*, ch. 6, by Ida Husted Harper (1898).
Anthony said this on August 3, 1853, at a State Teachers' Convention in Rochester, New York, during a discussion of "why the profession of teacher is not as much respected as that of lawyer, doctor, or minister?" Anthony was the first woman ever to speak publicly at a teachers' convention and caused a great stir.

5 What an infernal set of fools those schoolmarms must be! Well, if in order to please men they wish to live on air, let them. The sooner the present generation of women dies out, the better. We have idiots enough in the world now without such women propagating any more.

ELIZABETH CADY STANTON (1815–1902), U.S. suffragist, social reformer, and author. As quoted in *The Life and Work of Susan B. Anthony*, vol. 1, ch. 10, by Ida Husted Harper (1898).

In an 1857 letter to Susan B. Anthony, her close friend and sister activist, on women schoolteachers' acceptance of salaries much smaller than those received by their male counterparts.

6 The great want of our race is *perfect educators* to train new-born minds, who are *infallible teachers of what is right and true.*

CATHERINE E. BEECHER (1800–1878), U.S. educator and author. As quoted in *Catherine Beecher*, ch. 17, by Kathryn Kish Sklar (1973).
Written in 1857.

7 Education is considered the peculiar business of women; perhaps for that very reason it is one of the worst-paid businesses in the world . . .

KATHARINE PEARSON WOODS (1853–1923), U.S. author, teacher, and social service worker. *What America Owes to Women*, ch. 43 (1893).

8 No one should teach who is not in love with teaching.

MARGARET E. SANGSTER (1838–1912), U.S. author. *An Autobiography from My Youth Up*, ch. 23 (1909).

9 In a world that holds books and babies and canyon trails, why should one condemn oneself to live day-in, day-out with people one does not like, and sell oneself to chaperone and correct them?

RUTH BENEDICT (1887–1948), U.S. anthropologist. *An Anthropologist at Work*, part 2 (1959).
Written in her journal on May 20, 1913, during her brief career as a boarding-school teacher.

10 . . . teaching to me was anathema, chiefly because it would condemn me to a world of petticoats.

AGNES E. MEYER (1887–1970), U.S. journalist. *Out of These Roots*, ch. 4 (1953).

On why, upon graduation from Barnard College, she chose to pursue a career in journalism rather than in teaching, which would have been a more conventional choice.

11 The first rule of education for me was discipline. Discipline is the keynote to learning. Discipline has been the great factor in my life. I discipline myself to do everything—getting up in the morning, walking, dancing, exercise. If you won't have discipline, you won't have a nation. We can't have permissiveness. When someone comes in and says, "Oh, your room is so quiet," I know I've been successful.

ROSE HOFFMAN, U.S. public school third-grade teacher. As quoted in *Working*, book 8, by Studs Terkel (1973).

She had been teaching for thirty-three years.

12 ... anybody with the brains and energy to become a teacher ought to want to become something better.

FLORYNCE KENNEDY (b. 1916), U.S. lawyer, activist, speaker, and author. *Color Me Flo*, ch. 2 (1976).

13 Mrs. Zajac knows you didn't try. You don't just hand in junk to Mrs. Zajac. She's been teaching an awful lot of years. She didn't fall off the turnip cart yesterday. She told you she was an old-lady teacher.

CHRISTINE ZAJAC, U.S. fifth-grade teacher. As quoted in *Among Schoolchildren*, "September" section, part 1, by Tracy Kidder (1989).

A teacher with high standards, this was part of Zajac's ongoing spiel to her students.

14 A long time ago people often said, "Why did you become a teacher?"

Well, that was about the only decent thing when I was growing up for a girl to be. If you became a secretary ... you got a hard name.

KNOWLES WITCHER TEEL (b. c. 1906), U.S. schoolteacher. As quoted in *Hill Country Teacher*, ch. 2, by Diane Manning (1990).

Teel taught in Texas from 1924 until her retirement in 1972; she was rare among teachers of her generation in that she continued working despite marriage and motherhood.

TECHNOLOGY

1 In the end we will listen to the voice of the machines. We will have to. There is no choice. We will not go back to tallow dips while the great shining wheels are there to bring us light.

MARY HEATON VORSE (1874–1966), U.S. journalist and labor activist. *A Footnote to Folly*, ch. 25 (1935).

2 It is high time we realized that the havoc wrought in human life and ideals by a technological revolution and too long ignored has caught up with us.

AGNES E. MEYER (1887–1970), U.S. journalist. *Out of These Roots*, ch. 13 (1953).

3 The discussion of the whole problem of technology ... has been strangely led astray through an all-too-exclusive concentration upon the service or disservice the machines render to men. The assumption here is that every tool and implement is primarily designed to make human life easier and human labor less painful. ... But ... *homo faber*, the toolmaker, invented tools

and equipment in order to erect a world, not . . . to help the human life process. The question therefore is not so much whether we are the masters or the slaves of our machines, but whether machines still serve the world and its things, or if, on the contrary, they and the automatic motion of their processes have begun to rule and even destroy world and things.

HANNAH ARENDT (1906–1975), U.S. philosopher. *The Human Condition,* ch. 20 (1958).

4 A mechanism of some kind stands between us and almost every act of our lives.

SARAH PATTON BOYLE, U.S. civil rights activist and author. *The Desegregated Heart,* part 3, ch. 2 (1962).

5 Technological innovation has done great damage . . . to eating habits. Food is now available in such unpleasant forms that one frequently finds smoking between courses to be an aid to digestion.

FRAN LEBOWITZ (b. 1950), U.S. humorist. *Metropolitan Life,* part 2 (1978).

6 Technology makes the world a new place.

SHOSHANA ZUBOFF (b. 1951), U.S. social scientist. *In the Age of the Smart Machine,* Conclusion (1988).

TELECOMMUNICATION

1 The telephone, which interrupts the most serious conversations and cuts short the most weighty observations, has a romance of its own.

VIRGINIA WOOLF (1882–1941), British novelist, essayist, and diarist. *The Common Reader,* ch. 21 (1925).

2 It's a hard feeling when everyone's in a hurry to talk to somebody else, but not to talk to you. Sometimes *you* get a feeling of need to talk to somebody. Somebody who wants to listen to you other than "Why didn't you get me the right number?"

HEATHER LAMB, U.S. telephone operator. As quoted in *Working,* book 2, by Studs Terkel (1973).

3 In Hell all the messages you ever left on answering machines will be played back to you.

JUDY HORACEK (b. 1961), Australian cartoonist. *Life on the Edge* (1992).

TELEVISION

1 Television could perform a great service in mass education, but there's no indication its sponsors have anything like this on their minds.

TALLULAH BANKHEAD (1903–1968), U.S. actress. *Tallulah,* ch. 1 (1952).

At this point, Bankhead had never appeared on television. Later, she would.

2 . . . there is no reason to confuse television news with journalism.

NORA EPHRON (b. 1941), U.S. author and humorist. *Scribble Scrabble,* ch. 5 (1978).

Written in 1975 at the end of an essay harshly criticizing CBS-TV for paying H. R. Haldeman, a key figure in the "Watergate" political scandal, to appear on its *60 Minutes* news program.

3 There was a girl who was running the traffic desk, and there was a woman who was on the overnight for radio as a producer, and my desk assistant was a woman. So when the world came to an end, we took over.

MARYA MCLAUGHLIN, U.S. television newswoman. As quoted in *Women in Television News*, ch. 3, by Judith S. Gelfman (1976). On working the midnight to 8:00 a.m. shift for CBS network news.

4 Putting people in a room and strapping wires to their wrist to find out if I make them tingle when I'm telling them about Beirut is a long way from Edward R. Murrow.

LINDA ELLERBEE (b. 1932), U.S. television newswoman. As quoted in *Newsweek* magazine, p. 8 (June 16, 1986). On the increased use of "image consultants" in television news. Edward R. Murrow (1908–1965) had been a highly respected television journalist.

5 One good thing came out of the summit. We got to see that Dan Rather is definitely a he-man and no wimp.

LIZ SMITH (b. 1923), U.S. gossip columnist. As quoted in *Newsweek* magazine, p. 15 (June 13, 1988). Statement made during a visit to Russia by President Ronald Reagan. Dan Rather, a famous news anchorman who covered the event wore an open-necked shirt and no tie, revealing a hairy chest.

6 We're a Madison Avenue country. I'm not sure that we make a distinction between newspeople and celebrities. And I think there is a distinction. The distinction lies in what you do every day—and what you do to get stories and how far you

will go and how much you will dig for them. All the rest of the attention that comes to you because you're on the air seems to me an irrelevance.

DIANE SAWYER (b. 1945), U.S. television newswoman. As quoted in *Time* magazine, p. 51 (August 7, 1989).

7 I'm not ugly. I'm cute as hell.

CHRISTINE CRAFT (b. c. 1944), U.S. newswoman. As quoted in *People* magazine, p. 177 (March 7–14, 1994). In 1981, Craft, an attractive news anchorwoman at KMBC-TV in Kansas City, Missouri, had been demoted for being, in her bosses' opinion, "too old, too ugly, not deferential to men." She had sued for sex discrimination but ultimately lost her case, which was highly publicized.

TENNIS

1 In the complete overall history of tennis, I figure I'll be worth a sentence or two. . . . That's why my place in the all-time rankings means so very little to me, because I know I won't be anybody's number one, and it's that same old thing: if you're not number one, then what does it really matter?

BILLIE JEAN KING (b. 1943), U.S. tennis player. *Billie Jean*, ch. 16 (1982). Winner of many Grand Slam tennis events, including a record twenty Wimbledon titles, King was correct when she said that she would not be considered the all-time top woman tennis player; she would, however, be highly ranked.

2 It's about learning your craft. That's a wonderful thing—especially with today's consumerism and instant gratification. You can't buy that. It's about making decisions, corrections, choices. I don't think it's so much about becoming a tennis player. It's about becoming a person.

BILLIE JEAN KING (b. 1943), U.S. tennis player. As quoted in *Sports Illustrated,* p. 72 (April 29, 1991).

On learning to play tennis.

3   If you give me a short shot I will attack you. I'm not a baseliner who rallies. I try to get the point over with.

VENUS WILLIAMS (b. 1980), African American tennis player. As quoted in *Sports Illustrated,* p. 48 (June 10, 1991).

A tennis prodigy from a poor African American and Hispanic neighborhood in Compton, California, Williams was describing her playing style.

4   When I was in grade school and we had to write papers about what we wanted to be when we grew up, I wanted to be a social worker or a missionary or a teacher. Then I got involved with tennis, and everything was just me, me, me. I was totally selfish and thought about myself and nobody else, because if you let up for one minute, someone was going to come along and beat you. I really wouldn't let anyone or any slice of happiness enter. . . . I didn't like the characteristics that it took to become a champion.

CHRIS EVERT (b. 1954), U.S. tennis player. As quoted in *Sports Illustrated,* p. 64 (May 25, 1992).

Evert said this after marrying for the second time, retiring from professional tennis, and having her first child.

5   I know some of my self-worth comes from tennis, and it's hard to think of doing something else where you know you'll never be the best. Tennis players are rare creatures: where else in the world can you know that you're the best? The definitiveness of it is the beauty of it, but it's not all there is to life and I'm ready to explore the alternatives.

MARTINA NAVRATILOVA (b. 1956), U.S. tennis player; born and raised in Czechoslovakia. As quoted in the *New York Times,* p. B19 (September 30, 1993).

Announcing her decision to retire from professional tennis at the end of the 1994 season, which would be her twenty-second year of competitive singles play. For several years, she had been the top-ranked woman singles player in the world (and, some said, the best in history); by this time, she had slipped to third ranking.

6   I decided that I want to live the rest of my life happy with what I'm doing. So when I play tennis again, I have to play it for the right reason. I don't want to play to get my No. 1 ranking back. I don't want to play for the attention, or to earn more. I don't even want to play because the world wants to see me do it, even though it's nice to know that the world is interested. I only want to play because I love the game, which is the reason I began to play at age seven in the first place.

MONICA SELES (b. 1973), Yugoslavian tennis player; relocated to America. As quoted in *Tennis* magazine, p. 42 (March 1994).

The former top-ranked woman singles tennis player in the world, she was reflecting on decisions she had made in her year off from competing. She was recovering, physically and psychologically, from being stabbed a year earlier by Gunther Parche, a deranged fan of rival player Steffi Graf. At the time of the attack, Graf had been second-ranked; with Seles out of competition, she rose to number one, which had been Parche's goal.

7 This is reality, not a dream.

MARTINA NAVRATILOVA (b. 1957), U.S. tennis player; born in Czechoslovakia. As quoted in *USA Today*, p. 3C (June 29, 1994).

On advancing to the women's singles semifinal round at Wimbledon, the world's oldest and most prestigious major international tennis tournament. Navratilova had won the Wimbledon singles title a record nine times, but at this point, she had slipped from top ranking, and she was clearly in the twilight of her career. She had already announced that she would retire at the end of the year. She went on to win the semifinal round and lose in the final, performing far better than most people had expected.

8 Manuela, why are you crying? Hit the ball down the line, please. Stop crying, thank you. Use some topspin on your backhand now. Please stop crying. *Thank you.*

YOULIA MALEEVA (b. 1945), Bulgarian tennis coach and manager; former tennis champion. As quoted in the *New Yorker*, p. 38 (July 25, 1994).

A former Bulgarian tennis champion, and a coach and manager of her three tennis-star daughters, Maleeva was recounting her outside imprecations to the oldest daughter when she played in the United States for the first time, c. 1986, wearing "a homemade dress" and equipped "with only three racquets." Her opponent was Chris Evert's sister Jeanne.

TERRORISM

I . . . I never drink wine . . . I keep my hands soft and supple . . . I sleep in a soft bed and never overtire my body. It is because when my hour strikes I must be a perfect instrument. My eyes must be steady, my brain clear, my nerves calm, my aim true. I must be prepared to do my work, successfully if God wills. But if I perish, I perish.

"LISA", Russian terrorist (anonymous) during reign of Czar Nicholas II. As quoted in *A Woman of Fifty*, 2nd. ed., ch. 8, by Rheta Childe Dorr (1924).

Said c. 1917.

THEATER

I I have come to believe . . . that the stage may do more than teach, that much of our current moral instruction will not endure the test of being cast into a lifelike mold, and when presented in dramatic form will reveal itself as platitudinous and effete. That which may have sounded like righteous teaching when it was remote and wordy will be challenged afresh when it is obliged to simulate life itself.

JANE ADDAMS (1860–1935), U.S. social reformer and author. *Twenty Years at Hull-House*, ch. 16 (1910).

2 . . . the modern drama, operating through the double channel of dramatist and interpreter, affecting as it does both mind and heart, is the strongest force in developing social discontent, swelling the powerful tide of unrest that sweeps onward and over the dam of ignorance, prejudice, and superstition.

EMMA GOLDMAN (1869–1940), U.S. anarchist and author; born in Russia. *Anarchism and Other Essays*, 3rd rev. ed., ch. 12 (1917).

The concluding statement of an essay that dealt with modern plays informed by "radical" thought.

3 People whose understanding and taste in literature, painting, and music are beyond question are, for the most part, ignorant of what is good or bad art in the theater.

MINNIE MADDERN FISKE (1865–1932), U.S. actor. As quoted in *Mrs. Fiske: Her Views on Actors, Acting and the Problems of Production*, ch. 1, by Alexander Woollcott (1917).

4 . . . actresses require protection in their art from blind abuse, from savage criticism. Their work is their religion, if they are seeking the best in their art, and to abuse that faith is to rob them, to dishonor them.

NANCE O'NEIL (1874–1965), U.S. actor. As quoted in *Famous Actors and Actresses on the American Stage*, vol. 2, by William C. Young (1975).

From an article first published in *Theatre* magazine in 1920.

5 The theatre is the involuntary reflex of the ideas of the crowd.

SARAH BERNHARDT (1845–1923), French actor. *The Art of the Theatre*, ch. 3 (1924).

6 To save the theatre, the theatre must be destroyed, the actors and actresses must all die of the plague. They poison the air, they make art impossible. It is not drama that they play, but pieces for the theatre. We should return to the Greeks, play in the open air: the drama dies of stalls and boxes and evening dress, and people who come to digest their dinner.

ELEONORA DUSE (1858–1924), Italian actor. As quoted in *Actors on Acting*, rev. ed., part 11, by Toby Cole and Helen Krich (1970).

7 . . . there is something shameful about the death of a play. It does not die with pity, but contempt.

MARY ROBERTS RINEHART (1876–1958), U.S. novelist. *My Story*, ch. 23 (1931).

The immensely popular novelist was recalling the failure of her play, *Cheer Up*.

8 This play holds the season's record [for early closing], thus far, with a run of four evening performances and one matinee. By an odd coincidence it ran just five performances too many.

DOROTHY PARKER (1893–1967), U.S. author and humorist. As quoted in *The Late Mrs. Dorothy Parker*, ch. 10, by Leslie Frewin (1986).

In a review, written for *Vanity Fair* magazine, of a bad play.

9 The theater is a baffling business, and a shockingly wasteful one when you consider that people who have proven their worth, who have appeared in or been responsible for successful plays, who have given outstanding performances, can still, in the full tide of their energy, be forced, through lack of opportunity, to sit idle season after season, their enthusiasm, their morale, their very talent dwindling to slow gray death. Of finances we will not even speak; it is too sad a tale.

ILKA CHASE (1905–1978), U.S. actor. As quoted in *Famous Actors and Actresses on the American Stage*, vol. 2, by William C. Young (1975).

From her autobiography, *Past Imperfect* (1942).

10 It's one of the tragic ironies of the theater that only one man in it can count on steady work—the night watchman.

TALLULAH BANKHEAD (1903–1968), U.S. actress. *Tallulah*, ch. 1 (1952).

11 We have played this show everywhere except underwater.

TALLULAH BANKHEAD (1903–1968), U.S. actress. As quoted in *Tallulah*, introduction, by Brendan Gill (1972).

Of Noel Coward's *Private Lives,* with which she toured over a period of many years and played many times in many cities and towns.

12   . . . the theatre demanded of its members stamina, good digestion, the ability to adjust, and a strong sense of humor. There was no discomfort an actor didn't learn to endure. To survive, we had to be horses and we were.

HELEN HAYES (1900–1993), U.S. actor. *On Reflection,* ch. 3 (1968).

Hayes, who began acting at age five and made her New York stage debut in 1909, was recalling the gruelling road travel and hard physical work required of actors in the early years of her career–trials that, she said, diminished "with the death of 'the road' and the birth of microphones."

13   The stage was our school, our home, our life.

LILLIAN GISH (1893–1993), U.S. actress. *The Movies, Mr. Griffith and Me,* ch. 7 (1969).

Describing her and her sister Dorothy's (1898–1968) childhood experiences as theatrical performers. Later, they would become movie stars.

14   Show business is the best possible therapy for remorse. I've known deserted brides to take fresh interest in life by sweeping up the stage in some godforsaken regional theater.

ANITA LOOS (1888–1981), U.S. screenwriter, author, and humorist. *Kiss Hollywood Good-by,* ch. 13 (1974).

15   If you're an actor, a real actor, you've got to be on the stage. But you mustn't go on the stage unless it's absolutely the only thing you can do.

DAME EDITH EVANS (1888–1976), British actor. As quoted in *Dame Edith Evans,* ch. 12, by Bryan Forbes (1977).

THINKING AND THOUGHT

1   . . . we all of us, grave or light, get our thoughts entangled in metaphors, and act fatally on the strength of them . . .

GEORGE ELIOT (1819–1880), British novelist. *Middlemarch,* ch. 10 (1871–1872).

2   . . . there is no human being who having both passions and thoughts does not think in consequence of his passions.

GEORGE ELIOT (1819–1880), British novelist. *Middlemarch,* ch. 47 (1871–1872).

3   . . . so long as woman sat with bandaged eyes and manacled hands, fast bound in the clamps of ignorance and inaction, the world of thought moved in its orbit like the revolutions of the moon; with one face (the man's face) always out, so that the spectator could not distinguish whether it was disc or sphere.

ANNA JULIA COOPER (1859–1964), African American educator and feminist. *A Voice from the South,* part 1 (1892).

Born to a slave and her white master, Cooper held ardently feminist views. At age 67, she became the fourth African American woman to earn a Ph.D. (from the University of Paris).

4   The most unpardonable sin in society is independence of thought.

EMMA GOLDMAN (1869–1940), U.S. anarchist and author; born in Russia. *Anarchism and Other Essays,* 3rd rev. ed., ch. 2 (1917).

5   The tragedy of bold, forthright, industrious people is that they act so

continuously without much thinking, that it becomes dry and empty.

BRENDA UELAND (1891–1985), U.S. author and writing teacher. *If You Want to Write,* 2nd. ed., ch. 6 (1938).

6   . . . writing is the action of thinking, just as drawing is the action of seeing and composing music is the action of hearing. And all that is inward must be expressed in action, for that is the true life of the spirit and the only way we can be continually discarding our dead and mistaken (sinful) selves and progressing and knowing more.

BRENDA UELAND (1891–1985), U.S. magazine writer. *Me,* ch. 8 (1939).

7   Temperamentally, the writer exists on happenings, on contacts, conflicts, action and reaction, speed, pressure, tension. Were he a contemplative purely, he would not write.

ELIZABETH BOWEN (1899–1973), British novelist, story writer, essayist, and memoirist; born in Ireland. *Seven Winters,* part 2, sect. 1, ch. 1 (1962).

8   As information technology restructures the work situation, it abstracts thought from action.

SHOSHANA ZUBOFF (b. 1951), U.S. social scientist. *In the Age of the Smart Machine,* ch. 2 (1988).

9   When the whole world is writing letters, it's easy to lap into the quiet within, tell the story of an hour, keep alive the narrating inner life. To be alone in the presence of one's thought is not a value, only a common practice.

VIVIAN GORNICK (b. 1935), U.S. author. *New York Times Book Review,* p. 24 (July 31, 1994).

TIME

1   . . . [ellipsis in source] it is true that the world was made in six days, but it was by God, to whose power the infirmity of men is not to be compared.

ELIZABETH I (1533–1603), British monarch, Queen of England (1558–1603). As quoted in *The Sayings of Queen Elizabeth,* ch. 23, by Frederick Chamberlin (1923).

Said in 1565 to de Foix, the French Ambassador, who complained that he had waited six days without getting an answer to his proposition that she marry a French prince.

2   Time should be imaged with a paint-brush instead of a scythe; he knows how to wield the former even better than the latter.

M. E. W. SHERWOOD (1826–1903), U.S. socialite, traveller, and author. *An Epistle to Posterity,* ch. 8 (1897).

3   . . . when there is a war the years are longer that is to say the days are longer the months are longer the years are much longer but the weeks are shorter that is what makes a war.

GERTRUDE STEIN (1874–1946), U.S. author; relocated to France. *Wars I Have Seen* (1945).

Written in 1943.

4   I like old people when they have aged well. And old houses with an accumulation of sweet honest living in them are good. And the timelessness that only the passing

of Time itself can give to objects both inside and outside the spirit is a continuing reassurance.

M. F. K. Fisher (1908–1992), U.S. culinary writer and autobiographer. *Sister Age*, Afterword (1983).

5 Who wants always to look at a cafe or an altar or an oak tree with the first innocence and the limited understanding of a naive lovesick girl, or a born-again Byron? Five minutes or five centuries from now, we will see changeless realities with new eyes, and the sounds of sheep bleating and a new child's wail will be the same but heard through new ears. How can we pretend to be changeless, then? . . . Is it wrong to see the phony, painted mushroom-bollard on the quay and accept it, as part of the whole strong song that keeps on singing there, in spite of wars and movies and the turtling-on of time?

M. F. K. Fisher (1908–1992), U.S. culinary writer and autobiographer. Afterword (1985).

6 Time rushes by and yet time is frozen. Funny how we get so exact about time at the end of life and at its beginning. She died at 6:08 or 3:46, we say, or the baby was born at 4:02. But in between we slosh through huge swatches of time—weeks, months, years, decades even.

Helen Prejéan (b. 1940), U.S. nun and activist against the death penalty. *Dead Man Walking*, ch. 4 (1993).

Acting as spiritual advisor to a prison inmate scheduled for execution, Prejean ruminates as the time draws near.

TOKENISM

1 The token woman carries a bouquet of hothouse celery and a stenographer's pad; she will take the minutes, perk the coffee, smile like a plastic daisy and put out the black cat of her sensuous anger to howl on the fence all night.

Marge Piercy (b. 1936), U.S. poet, novelist, and political activist. "The Token Woman," lines 4–9 (1976).

2 To become a token woman— whether you win the Nobel Prize or merely get tenure at the cost of denying your sisters—is to become something less than a man . . . since men are loyal at least to their own world-view, their laws of brotherhood and self-interest.

Adrienne Rich (b. 1929), U.S. feminist poet and essayist. As quoted in *Ms.* magazine, p. 44 (September 1979).

In a May 7, 1979, Smith College commencement address.

3 It was so hard to pry this door open, and if I mess up I know the people behind me are going to have it that much harder. Because then there's living proof. They can sit around and say, "See? It doesn't work." I don't want to be their living proof.

Gayle Gardner, U.S. sports reporter. As quoted in *Sports Illustrated*, p. 87 (June 17, 1991).

Describing the tendency of people to judge women sportscasters like her more harshly than their male counterparts. She called this "the black quarterback syndrome" because for a long time, it had been assumed that African Americans lacked the leadership qualities or the mental agility to be successful quarterbacks. As the color bar to quarterbacking broke down and a number of skilled African American quarterbacks emerged, this was proven false. Gardner was the first female sports anchor to appear weekly on a major television network.

4 I've tried to open the door. My knock isn't that big a sound. But it is like the knock in "The Wizard of Oz." It set up this echo through the halls until it was heard by everyone.

SHANNON FAULKNER (b. c. 1975), U.S. college student. As quoted in the *New York Times Magazine*, p. 59 (September 11, 1994).

Faulkner was the first woman admitted to The Citadel, a publicly funded, all-male military academy; the admission had been granted accidentally, Citadel staff having been misled by her gender-ambiguous name. At this time, she was fighting for the right to become a full cadet with all attendant responsibilities and opportunities. She won her fight, but decided to leave the academy in August 1995 after falling ill during basic training. Her illness was attributed variously to the extreme heat, great psychological stress, and her apparent deficient physical conditioning.

TOLERANCE

1 . . . the structure of our public morality crashed to earth. Above its grave a tombstone read, "Be tolerant—even of evil." Logically the next step would be to say to our commonwealth's criminals, "I disagree that it's all right to rob and murder, but naturally I respect your opinion." Tolerance is only complacence when it makes no distinction between right and wrong.

SARAH PATTON BOYLE, U.S. civil rights activist and author. *The Desegregated Heart*, part 2, ch. 2 (1962).

Boyle, a white Virginian pro-integration activist from the beginning of the 1950s, was recalling the mild, accommodating reaction of her state's political leaders to those segregationists who, following the 1954 Supreme Court decision outlawing segregation in public schools but setting no deadline for desegregation, still resisted.

2 Never to despise in myself what I have been taught
to despise. Nor to despise the other.
Not to despise the *it.* To make this relation
with the it: to know that I am it.

MURIEL RUKEYSER (1913–1980), U.S. poet. "Despisals," lines 21–24 (1973).

Raised in wealth, Rukeyser affiliated with the Communist Party in the 1930s and was a strong advocate of social reform, social justice, and nonviolence. She was also a feminist and was bisexual or lesbian. Homosexuality is mentioned earlier in this poem.

3 Advocating the mere tolerance of difference between women is the grossest reformism. It is a total denial of the creative function of difference in our lives. Difference must be not merely tolerated, but seen as a fund of necessary polarities between which our creativity can spark like a dialectic.

AUDRE LORDE (1934–1992), African American poet, autobiographer, and lesbian feminist. *Sister Outsider,* ch. 11 (1984).

From comments made on September 29, 1979, at the Second Sex Conference in New York City.

4 Being offended is the natural consequence of leaving one's home. I do not like after-shave lotion, adults who roller-skate, children who speak French, or anyone who is unduly tan. I do not, however, go around enacting legislation and putting up signs.

FRAN LEBOWITZ (b. 1950), U.S. humorist. *Social Studies,* ch. 18 (1981).

Lebowitz, a dedicated smoker, was reacting against strictures on public smoking.

5 Human beings tolerate what they understand they have to tolerate.

Jane Rule (b. 1931), Canadian fiction writer and essayist; born in the U. S.. *Outlander*, part 2, essay 6 (1981).

Rule, a lesbian, was living with her lover of twenty-three years in a small Canadian community on a "cranky little island" where people were forced to depend on the help of one another.

6 A leaky faucet, a barking dog— those are things you tolerate.

Candace Gingrich (b. c. 1967), U.S. computer technician and gay/lesbian rights activist. As quoted in *Newsweek* magazine, p. 24 (March 13, 1995).

The half-sister of conservative Speaker of the House Newt Gingrich (b. 1943), she was responding to remarks he had made that she considered offensive to homosexuals and to his recommendation that homosexuality be "tolerated."

TRADITION

1 Your favor containing the question, as to whether I consider myself a "new woman" is before me. As a rule I do not consider myself at all. I am, and always have been a progressive woman, and while never directly attacking the conventionalities of society, have always done, or attempted to do those things which I have considered conducive to my health, convenience or emolument . . .

Belva Lockwood (1830–1917), U.S. lawyer and political activist. As quoted in *The Female Experience*, ch. 76, by Gerda Lerner (1977).

Written on November 21, 1897.

2 Few countries have produced such arrogance and snobbishness as America. Particularly is this true of the American woman of the middle class. She not only considers herself the equal of man, but his superior, especially in her purity, goodness, and morality. Small wonder that the American suffragist claims for her vote the most miraculous powers. In her exalted conceit she does not see how truly enslaved she is, not so much by man, as by her own silly notions and traditions. Suffrage can not ameliorate that sad fact; it can only accentuate it, as indeed it does.

Emma Goldman (1869–1940), U.S. anarchist and author; born in Russia. *Anarchism and Other Essays*, 3rd rev. ed., ch. 9 (1917).

3 Tradition has made women cowardly.

Nance O'Neil (1874–1965), U.S. actor. As quoted in *Famous Actors and Actresses on the American Stage*, vol. 2, by William C. Young (1975).

From an article first published in *Theatre* magazine in 1920.

4 One must eliminate the traditional and cling to the essential.

Alice Foote MacDougall, (1867–1945) U.S. businesswoman. *The Autobiography of a Business Woman*, ch. 7 (1928).

On overcoming poverty and succeeding in business as a woman entrepreneur.

TRAINING

1 I said, "That was a very brave thing to do." He said, "Och, it was just the training." I have a feeling that, in the end, probably that is the answer to a great many things.

Queen Elizabeth II (b. 1926), British monarch. As quoted in *Time* magazine, p. 58 (November 30, 1992).

On giving an award to a soldier.

TRAINS

1 . . . there isn't a train I wouldn't take,
No matter where it's going.
EDNA ST. VINCENT MILLAY, (1892–1950) U.S. poet. "Travel," lines 11–12 (1921).

2 . . . more and more I like to take a train I understand why the French prefer it to automobiling, it is so much more sociable and of course these days so much more of an adventure, and the irregularity of its regularity is fascinating.
GERTRUDE STEIN (1874–1946), U.S. author; relocated to France. *Wars I Have Seen* (1945).
Written in 1943, during World War II.

3 Women on trains
have a life
that is exactly livable
the precision of days flashing past
AUDRE LORDE (1934–1992), U.S. author. "Women on Trains," lines 24–27 (c. 1992).

TRANSLATION

1 I do wish that as long as they are translating the thing, they would go right on ahead, while they're at it, and translate Fedor Vasilyevich Protosov and Georgei Dmitrievich Abreskov and Ivan Petrovich Alexandrov into Joe and Harry and Fred.
DOROTHY PARKER (1893–1967), U.S. author and humorist. As quoted in *The Late Mrs. Dorothy Parker*, ch. 9, by Leslie Frewin (1986).
On the long names characteristic of Russia and common in Russian literature.

2 With a broad shoehorn
I am unstuffing a big bird in this dream
—somebody else's holiday feast—
and repacking the crop of my own,
knowing it will burst with such onion, oyster, savory bread crust.
MAXINE KUMIN (b. 1925), U.S. poet. "In the Uneasy Sleep of the Translator," lines 1–6 (1975).

TRAVEL

1 Put me on a moving train if I'm sick, and I'll get well. It's good for mind and body to get out and see the world.
MARIA D. BROWN (1827–1927), U.S. homemaker. As quoted in *Grandmother Brown's Hundred Years*, ch. 9, by Harriet Connor Brown (1929).
Said sometime between 1907 and 1913. Following the death of her husband in 1906, when she was 79, Brown began to travel alone by train and continued to do so for the next seven years.

2 There was a road ran past our house
Too lovely to explore.
I asked my mother once—she said
That if you followed where it led
It brought you to the milk-man's door.
(That's why I have not travelled more.)
EDNA ST. VINCENT MILLAY (1892–1950), U.S. poet. "The Unexplorer," entire poem (1920).

3 There is a mystery that floats between
The tourist and the town.
Imagination

Estranges it from her. She need not
suffer
Or die here. It is none of her affair,
Its calm heroic vistas make no
claim.

ADRIENNE RICH (b. 1929), U.S. poet and
feminist. "The Tourist and the Town," lines 17–
21 (1955).

4 A way of certifying experience, taking photographs is also a way of refusing it—by limiting experience to a search for the photogenic, by converting experience into an image, a souvenir. Travel becomes a strategy for accumulating photographs.

SUSAN SONTAG (b. 1933), U.S. author. On
Photography, ch. 1 (1977).

5 . . . I never thought of anything but a long full life with my love, but a heavy foreboding hit me about two years into this planned bliss, when he said firmly that we must never go back to the fishing village where we had spent our first Christmas. And a cruel mixture of disbelief and sadness filled me as I came to understand how thoroughly and firmly he stood by his conviction, that if people know real happiness anywhere, they must never expect to find it there again. . . . So that year we went to Nuremberg, and the next year Strasbourg and and and, but we never returned to any place we had been before, because once, according to his private calendar, we had been there. And in a few more years we parted. You might say that we ran out of places.

M. F. K. FISHER (1908–1992), U.S. culinary writer and autobiographer. Afterword
(1985).

Recalling her first marriage, which began when
she was twenty-one.

TREASON AND TREACHERY

1 The stone often recoils on the head
of the thrower.

ELIZABETH I (1533–1603), Queen of England (1558–1603). As quoted in The Sayings of
Queen Elizabeth, ch. 18, by Frederick Chamberlin (1923).

To Mary, Queen of Scots (1542–1587), who
had been helping enemies of Elizabeth's. Elizabeth was a daughter of King Henry VIII; after
Henry's offspring, Mary had the strongest claim
to the throne and schemed to win it. Eventually,
and with great sorrow, Elizabeth had Mary executed.

2 My loving people,—We have been
persuaded by some that are careful
of our safety, to take heed how we
commit ourselves to armed multitudes for fear of treachery; but, I do
assure you, I do not desire to live to
distrust my faithful and loving people. Let tyrants fear.

ELIZABETH I (1533–1603), Queen of England (1558–1603). As quoted in The Sayings of
Queen Elizabeth, ch. 2, by Frederick Chamberlin (1923).

In a stirring speech to England's troops in 1588
on the hill at Tilbury; it was they who would
have to defend her reign against the Armada,
the fleet which had been sent by Philip II of
Spain, a Roman Catholic, to overthrow Elizabeth, who was a Protestant, and take her
throne. The English defeated the Armada.

TREES

1 I want to celebrate these elms which
have been spared by the plague,
these survivors of a once flourishing
tribe commemorated by all the Elm

Streets in America. But to celebrate them is to be silent about the people who sit and sleep underneath them, the homeless poor who are hauled away by the city like trash, except it has no place to dump them. To speak of one thing is to suppress another.

LISEL MUELLER (b. 1924), U.S. poet; born in Germany. *Triage,* sentences 3–5 (1989).

2 Everybody who's anybody longs to be a tree—

RITA DOVE (b. 1952), U.S. poet and fiction writer. "Horse and Tree," line 1 (1989).

TRUST

I I shall lend credit to nothing against my people which parents would not believe against their own children.

ELIZABETH I (1533–1603), British Monarch, Queen of England (1558–1603). As quoted in *The Sayings of Queen Elizabeth,* ch. 2, by Frederick Chamberlin (1923).
Said in the late 1500s.

2 The natural order will emerge only if we let go of the fear of the disorder, we trust each other.

JUDITH MALINA (b. 1926), U.S. actor and stage producer. As quoted in *Actors on Acting,* rev. ed., part 13, by Toby Cole and Helen Krich (1970).

3 It might be that some day I shall be drowned by the sea, or die of pneumonia from sleeping out at night, or be robbed and strangled by strangers. These things happen. Even so, I shall be ahead because of trusting the beach, the night and strangers.

JANET WOOD RENO (b. 1913), U.S. mother of U.S. Attorney General Janet Reno. As quoted in the *New York Times Magazine,* p. 44 (May 15, 1994).
Reno had "once walked 104 miles up the Florida coast alone."

TRUTH

I . . . what a weak barrier is truth when it stands in the way of an hypothesis!

MARY WOLLSTONECRAFT (1759–1797), British feminist. *A Vindication of the Rights of Woman,* ch. 3 (1792).

2 If we bring not the good courage of minds covetous of truth, and truth only, prepared to hear all things, and decide upon all things, according to evidence, we should do more wisely to sit down contented in ignorance, than to bestir ourselves only to reap disappointment.

FRANCES WRIGHT (1795–1852), Scottish author and speaker; relocated to America. *Course of Popular Lectures,* lecture 1 (1829).

3 . . . the truth is the hardest missile one can be pelted with.

GEORGE ELIOT (1819–1880), British novelist. *Middlemarch,* ch. 38 (1871–1872).

4 My name was Isabella; but when I left the house of bondage, I left everything behind. I wa'n't goin' to keep nothin' of Egypt on me, an' so I went to the Lord an' asked him to give me a new name. And the Lord gave me Sojourner, because I was to travel up an' down the land, showin' the people their sins, an' bein' a sign unto them. Afterward I told the Lord I wanted another

name, 'cause everybody else had two names; and the Lord gave me Truth, because I was to declare Truth to the people.

SOJOURNER TRUTH (1797–1883), African American slave; later an itinerant preacher and advocate of various social reforms including abolition, woman suffrage, and temperance. As quoted in *The Narrative of Sojourner Truth,* part 2: "Book of Life," by Frances W. Titus (1875). Explaining her change of name. She was originally named Isabella, with the surname Van Wagener, after her last master, actually a humane person who offered her refuge and employment after she escaped from slavery. She had a flair for speaking and hymn-singing and, in 1851, left her home in Northampton, Massachusetts, on a lecture tour sponsored by abolitionists. She did not know her birthdate but did know that she was born in Ulster County, New York, and claimed to have been freed by that state's act of 1817 which liberated all slaves who were forty or older. Truth was illiterate, but several of her listeners recorded her words. In this case, Harriet Beecher Stowe (1811–1896), the famous abolitionist author of *Uncle Tom's Cabin* (1852), was recalling Truth's conversation during a visit to the Stowe home. Stowe described the visit in "Sojourner Truth, the Libyan Sibyl," an article first published in the *Atlantic Monthly* (April 1863) and reprinted by Titus in this book.

5 Truth, like climate, is common property . . .

ELIZABETH STUART PHELPS (1844–1911), U.S. novelist and short story writer. *Chapters from a Life,* ch. 12 (1897).

6 . . . in writing you cannot possibly be interesting if what you say is not true, if it is what I call "a true lie," i.e., a truth which gives the wrong impression. For no matter how subtly you lie in writing, people know it and don't believe you, and the whole secret of being interesting is to be believed.

BRENDA UELAND (1891–1985), U.S. magazine writer. *Me,* ch. 6 (1939).

7 . . . instinct is the direct connection with truth.

LAURETTE TAYLOR (1887–1946), U.S. actor. As quoted in *Actors on Acting,* rev. ed., part 13, by Toby Cole and Helen Krich (1970). Referring to acting.

8 The times are so peculiar now, so mediaeval so unreasonable that for the first time in a hundred years truth is really stranger than fiction. Any truth.

GERTRUDE STEIN (1874–1946), U.S. author; relocated to France. *Wars I Have Seen* (1945). Written in 1943.

9 To be against war is not enough, it is hardly a beginning. And all things strive; we who try to speak know the ideas trying to be more human, we know things near their birth that try to become real. The truth here goes farther, there is another way of being against war and for poetry. We are against war and the sources of war. We are for poetry and the sources of poetry.

MURIEL RUKEYSER (1913–1980), U.S. poet. *The Life of Poetry,* ch. 13 (1949).

10 Once the pursuit of truth begins to haunt the mind, it becomes an ideal never wholly attained.

AGNES E. MEYER (1887–1970), U.S. journalist. *Out of These Roots,* ch. 3 (1953).

11 I learned early to understand that there is no such condition in human affairs as absolute truth. There is only truth as people see it, and truth, even in fact, may be kaleidoscopic in its variety. The damage such perception did to me I have felt ever since . . . I could never belong entirely to one side of any question.

PEARL S. BUCK (1892–1973), U.S. author. *My Several Worlds* (1954).

12 The basis of art is truth, both in matter and in mode.

FLANNERY O'CONNOR (1925–1964), U.S. fiction writer and essayist. *Mystery and Manners*, part 3 (1969). Written c. 1960.

13 The novelist is required to open his eyes on the world around him and look. If what he sees is not highly edifying, he is still required to look. Then he is required to reproduce, with words, what he sees.

FLANNERY O'CONNOR (1925–1964), U.S. fiction writer and essayist. *Mystery and Manners*, part 5 (1969). Written in 1964.

14 What would happen if one woman told the truth about her life? The world would split open

MURIEL RUKEYSER (1913–1980), U.S. poet. "Kathe Kollwitz," part 3, lines 25–26 (1968).
Kollwitz (1867–1945) was a German graphic artist and sculptor whose work had great emotional impact and haunting qualities.

15 Curse of the orchard,
Blemish on the land's fair
    countenance,
I have grown strong for strength
denied, for struggle
In hostile woods. I keep alive by
    being the troublesome,
Indestructible
Stinkweed of truth.

NAOMI LONG MADGETT (b. 1923), African American poet. "Tree of Heaven," lines 13–18 (1970).
On being an African American.

16 As a child I was taught that to tell the truth was often painful. As an adult I have learned that not to tell the truth is more painful, and that the fear of telling the truth—whatever the truth may be—that fear is the most painful sensation of a moral life.

JUNE JORDAN (b. 1936), U.S. poet, essayist, and social critic. *On Call,* ch. 10 (1985). Written in 1984.

17 . . . I have a duty to speak the truth as I see it and to share not just my triumphs, not just the things that felt good, but the pain, the intense, often unmitigating pain. It is important to share how I know survival is survival and not just a walk through the rain.

AUDRE LORDE (1934–1992), African American lesbian author and feminist. *Black Women Writers at Work,* ch. 8, by Claudia Tate (1985).
Lorde had recently survived a bout with breast cancer, the disease that would kill her seven years later.

18 Fiction is a piece of truth that turns lies to meaning.

DOROTHY ALLISON (b. 1949), U.S. author and lesbian feminist. *Skin,* ch. 18 (1994).
Allison—a lesbian feminist essayist, fiction writer, and poet—described her poor, violence-ridden Southern childhood in her well-received autobiographical novel, *Bastard Out of Carolina* (1992).

19 . . . the generation of the 20's was truly secular in that it still knew its theology and its varieties of religious experience. We are post-secular, inventing new faiths, without any sense of organizing truths. The truths we accept are so multiple that honesty becomes little more than a strategy by which you manage your tendencies toward duplicity.

Ann Douglas (b. 1942), U.S. cultural scholar. As quoted in the *New York Times Book Review*, p. 37, by Tobin Harshaw (February 12, 1995).

TYRANNY

1 A strength to harm is perilous in the hand of an ambitious head.

Elizabeth I (1533–1603), Queen of England (1558–1603). As quoted in *The Sayings of Queen Elizabeth*, ch. 13, by Frederick Chamberlin (1923).

To Sir Henry Sidney, governor of Ireland.

2 . . . tyrants deserve to be the victims of tyrants.

Jeanne De Hericourt (1809–1875), French feminist and author. As quoted in *History of Woman Suffrage*, vol. 2, ch. 22, by Elizabeth Cady Stanton, Susan B. Anthony, and Matilda Joslyn Gage (1882).

Speaking at a May 12, 1869, anniversary celebration of the Equal Rights Association, held in New York City. She was speaking of tyranny generally, but within the specific context of tyranny over women.

3 . . . resistance to tyranny is man's highest ideal.

Emma Goldman (1869–1940), U.S. anarchist and author; born in Russia. *Anarchism and Other Essays*, 3rd rev. ed., ch. 3 (1917).

4 A good deal of tyranny goes by the name of protection.

Crystal Eastman (1881–1928), U.S. social/political activist and author. *On Women*

and Revolution, part 1 (1978). From an article published in *Equal Rights* on March 15, 1924.

5 Better to die, or not to have been born,
than hear that plaining, piteous convict wail
about these beautiful dark eyebrowed women.
It's soldiers who sing these days. O Lord God.

Marina Tsvetayeva (1892–1941), Russian poet; relocated to Czechoslovakia. "A low white sun . . . ," lines 13–16, as translated by Elaine Feinstein (1938).

Written to protest the Nazi occupation of Czechoslovakia, where she was living in exile from her native Russia.

6 . . . the idea of a classless society is . . . a disastrous mirage which cannot be maintained without tyranny of the few over the many. It is even more pernicious culturally than politically, not because the monolithic state forces the party line upon its intellectuals and artists, but because it has no social patterns to reflect.

Agnes E. Meyer (1887–1970), U.S. journalist. *Out of These Roots*, ch. 17 (1953).

7 Until recently the word fascist was considered shameful. Fortunately, that period has passed. In fact, there is now a reassessment of how much grandpa Benito did for Italy.

Alessandra Mussolini, Italian actor, politician, and medical student. As quoted in *Newsweek* magazine, p. 19 (February 17, 1992).

The granddaughter of the Italian fascist dictator Benito Mussolini (1883–1945) was announcing that she intended to run for Parliament as a neo-fascist candidate.

UNDERSTANDING

1   ... the deep experience of the lonely climb on the mountain of success brings a wealth beyond power to compute. To you all suffering is understandable and your heart opens wide in sympathy.

ALICE FOOTE MACDOUGALL (1867–1945), U.S. businesswoman. *The Autobiography of a Businesswoman,* ch. 7 (1928).

2   I do not think I will ever become deadened, because I live in other people's lives, I must admit there are times when it weighs me down because I can't do some of the things I want.

ELEANOR ROOSEVELT (1884–1962), U.S. First Lady, author, and speaker. As quoted in *Eleanor and Franklin,* ch. 51, by Joseph P. Lash (1971).

Written to Esther Lape on December 19, 1940, as her husband, President Franklin Delano Roosevelt, prepared to begin his third term as President. She had been an active and compassionate First Lady.

UNEMPLOYMENT

1   ... of all the aspects of social misery nothing is so heartbreaking as unemployment ...

JANE ADDAMS (1860–1935), U.S. social worker and social reformer. *Twenty Years at Hull-House,* ch. 10 (1910).

2   When I quit working, I lost all sense of identity in about fifteen minutes.

PAIGE RENSE (b. 1929), U.S. author and editor. As quoted in the *New York Times,* p. 37 (February 21, 1994).

The writer and *Architectural Digest* editor was recalling her brief period of being a housewife.

UNITY

1   ... a nation to be strong, must be united; to be united, must be equal in condition; to be equal in condition, must be similar in habits and feeling; to be similar in habits and feeling, *must be raised in national institutions as the children of a common family, and citizens of a common country.*

FRANCES WRIGHT (1795–1852), Scottish author and speaker; relocated to America. *Course of Popular Lectures,* lecture 7 (1829).

From a lecture given on June 2, 1829. Wright had recently become an American citizen.

2   I think unity is a mistake. ... If I were the Establishment and had the big loaded guns of the various oppressive institutions. ... I would much prefer to see one lion come through the door than 500 mice.

FLORYNCE KENNEDY (b. 1916), African American lawyer, activist, speaker, and author. *Color Me Flo,* ch. 3 (1976).

Kennedy had been a visible supporter of numerous social causes, including African American rights, women's rights, prostitutes' rights, and anti-Vietnam War movements.

UPWARD MOBILITY

1   ... social advance depends quite as much upon an increase in moral sensibility as it does upon a sense of duty ...

JANE ADDAMS (1860–1935), U.S. social worker and social reformer. *Twenty Years at Hull-House,* ch. 15 (1910).

Addams was the founding director of Hull-House, a pioneer "settlement house" in a poor, largely immigrant, Chicago neighborhood.

2 Outside America I should hardly be believed if I told how simply, in my experience, Dover Street merged into the Back Bay.

MARY ANTIN (1881–1949), U.S. socialite and author; born in Russia. *The Promised Land,* ch. 20 (1912).

A Russian Jew who emigrated to the United States at age 15 and settled on Dover Street in the Boston slums, Antin attended prestigious Barnard College and made her way up into the social world represented by Boston's elite Back Bay neighborhood.

that our civilization itself means the uses of everything it has—the inventions, the histories, every scrap of fact. But there is one kind of knowledge—infinitely precious, time-resistant more than monuments, here to be passed between the generations in any way it may be: never to be used. And that is poetry.

MURIEL RUKEYSER (1913–1980), U.S. poet. *The Life of Poetry,* ch. 1 (1949).

USEFULNESS

1 One of the duties which devolve upon women in the present interesting crisis, is to prepare themselves for more extensive usefulness, by making use of those religious and literary privileges and advantages that are within their reach, if they will only stretch out their hands and possess them.

SARAH M. GRIMKÉ (1792–1873), U.S. abolitionist and feminist. *Letters on the Equality of the Sexes and the Condition of Woman,* letter #15: dated October 20, 1837 (1838).

The "interesting crisis" was slavery, which Grimke—the offspring of a wealthy slaveholding South Carolina family—passionately opposed.

2 As with all children, the feeling that I was useful was perhaps the greatest joy I experienced.

ELEANOR ROOSEVELT (1884–1962), First Lady of the United States, author, speaker, and diplomat. *This Is My Story,* ch. 1 (1937).

3 Everywhere we are told that our human resources are all *to be used,*

VALUES OF MEN

1 I feel more charity for a Mormon who has been taught from his birth that it is not only his right but his duty to God to enter into plural marriages, and that the man who has the greatest number of wives stands highest in God's favor, than I do for the man who has been taught from his cradle that the unpardonable sin is the desecration of womanhood; whose religious training and the moral code of civilization in which he is reared make it a crime to violate the Seventh Commandment and the established law of monogamy. Yet, judging from the testimony we see all about us— our . . . lying-in and foundling hospitals and our fallen womanhood— the married or single man who lives a pure life is rare.

SUSAN B. ANTHONY (1820–1906), U.S. suffragist. As quoted in *Life and Work of Susan B. Anthony,* vol. 3, ch. 54, by Ida Husted Harper (1908).

Said in 1899.

2 White males are the most responsible for the destruction of human life and environment on the planet today.

ROBIN MORGAN (b. 1941), U.S. author, feminist, and child actor. *Goodbye to All That* (January 1970).

3 There is still the feeling that women's writing is a lesser class of writing, that . . . what goes on in the nursery or the bedroom is not as important as what goes on in the battlefield, . . . that what women know about is a less category of knowledge.

ERICA JONG (b. 1942), U.S. author. As quoted in *The Craft of Poetry,* by William Packard (1974).

Many of Jong's poems and fiction works dealt with love, sex, and family.

4 For things to have value in man's world, they are given the role of commodities. Among man's oldest and most constant commodity is woman.

ANA CASTILLO (b. 1953), Mexican American poet, essayist, and feminist. *Massacre of the Dreamers,* ch. 3 (1994).

VALUES OF WOMEN

1 . . . trifling employments have rendered woman a trifler.

MARY WOLLSTONECRAFT (1759–1797), British author and feminist. *Vindication of the Rights of Woman,* ch. 4 (1792).

2 Women . . . are degraded by the . . . propensity to enjoy the present moment, and, at last, despise the free-dom which they have not sufficient virtue to struggle to attain.

MARY WOLLSTONECRAFT (1759–1797), British feminist. *A Vindication of the Rights of Woman,* ch. 3 (1792).

3 Sentiment is the mightiest force in civilization; *not sentimentality,* but sentiment. Women will bring this into politics. Home, sweet home, is as powerful on the hustings as at the fireside.

J. ELLEN FOSTER (1840–1910), U.S. attorney, temperance activist, and suffragist. *What America Owes to Women,* ch. 33 (1893).

4 May we not assure ourselves that whatever woman's thought and study shall embrace will thereby receive a new inspiration, that she will save science from materialism, and art from a gross realism; that the "eternal womanly shall lead upward and onward"?

LOUISA PARSONS HOPKINS, U.S. scientist and author. As quoted in *The Fair Women,* ch. 16, by Jeanne Madeline Weimann (1981).

From a paper published in *Art and Handicraft in the Woman's Building,* a book sponsored by the Board of Lady Managers of the Commission that planned the 1893 World's Columbian Exposition in Chicago. The Woman's Building at that Exposition, which was planned and managed by women, was considered a landmark achievement.

5 So much of the trouble is because I am a woman. To me it seems a very terrible thing to be a woman. There is one crown which perhaps is worth it all—a great love, a quiet home, and children. We all know that is all that is worthwhile, and yet we must peg away, showing off our wares on the market if we have money, or manufacturing careers for ourselves if we haven't.

Ruth Benedict (1887–1948), U.S. anthropologist. *An Anthropologist at Work*, part 2 (1959).

Written in her journal during October 1912, while teaching in a girls' boarding school. Two years later, she married Stanley Benedict, a biochemist. Greatly disappointed by their childlessness, Benedict eventually resigned herself to professional life and became an important anthropologist.

6 Just imagine for a moment what life in this country might have been if women had been properly represented in Congress. Would a Congress where women in all their diversity were represented tolerate the countless laws now on the books that discriminate against women in all phases of their lives? Would a Congress with adequate representation of women have allowed this country to reach the 1970s without a national health care system? Would it have permitted this country to rank fourteenth in infant mortality among the developed nations of the world? Would it have allowed the situation we now have in which thousands of kids grow up without decent care because their working mothers have no place to leave them? Would such a Congress condone the continued butchering of young girls and mothers in amateur abortion mills? Would it allow fraudulent packaging and cheating of consumers in supermarkets, department stores and other retail outlets? Would it consent to the perverted sense of priorities that has dominated our government for decades, where billions have been ap-

propriated for war while our human needs as a people have been neglected?

Bella Abzug (b. 1920), U.S. politician. *Bella!* "February 7" section (1972).

At this time, Abzug was a member of the United States House of Representatives. The United States was still deeply involved in the Vietnam War, an involvement that Abzug opposed. Abortion was still illegal; Abzug favored its legalization.

VALUES OF WOMEN: COURTESY

1 . . . woman's cause is the cause of the weak; and when all the weak shall have received their due consideration, then woman will have her "rights," and the Indian will have his rights, and the Negro will have his rights, and all the strong will have learned at last to deal justly, to love mercy, and to walk humbly; and our fair land will have been taught the secret of universal courtesy which is after all nothing but the art, the science, and the religion of regarding one's neighbor as one's self, and to do for him as we would, were conditions swapped, that he do for us.

Anna Julia Cooper (1859–1964), African American educator and feminist. *A Voice from the South*, part 1 (1892).

Cooper had been born to a slave.

VALUES OF WOMEN: SHARING

1 . . . probably all of the women in this book are working to make part of the same quilt to keep us from freezing to death in a world that

grows harsher and bleaker—where male is the norm and the ideal human being is hard, violent and cold: a macho rock. Every woman who makes her living something strong and good is sharing bread with us.

MARGE PIERCY (b. 1936), U.S. poet, novelist, and political activist. As quoted in *Mountain Moving Day*, by Elaine Gill (1973).

"This book" was a feminist collection of poetry by women.

VANITY

1   My lord, the crown which I have borne so long has given enough of vanity in my time. I beseech you not to augment it in this hour when I am so near my death.

ELIZABETH I (1533–1603), British monarch, Queen of England (1558–1603). As quoted in *The Sayings of Queen Elizabeth*, ch. 24, by Frederick Chamberlin (1923).

Said on the last night of her life, to the Archbishop of Canterbury, who was praying by her side and had been extolling the accomplishments of her reign. These are her last recorded words.

2   . . . overconfidence in one's own ability is the root of much evil. Vanity, egoism, is the deadliest of all characteristics. This vanity, combined with extreme ignorance of conditions the knowledge of which is the very A B C of business and of life, produces more shipwrecks and heartaches than any other part of our mental make-up.

ALICE FOOTE MACDOUGALL, (1867–1945) U.S. businesswoman. *The Autobiography of a Business Woman*, ch. 7 (1928).

VETERANS

1   [Veterans] feel disappointed, not about the 1914–1918 war but about this war. They liked that war, it was a nice war, a real war a regular war, a commenced war and an ended war. It was a war, and veterans like a war to be a war. They do.

GERTRUDE STEIN (1874–1946), U.S. author; relocated to France. *Wars I Have Seen* (1945).

Written in 1943, contrasting World War I with World War II, which was then in progress.

VICTIMS

1   Humanity from the first has had its vultures and sharks, and representatives of the fraternity who prey upon mankind may be expected no less in America than elsewhere. That this virulence breaks out most readily and commonly against colored persons in this country, is due of course to the fact that they are, generally speaking, weak and can be imposed upon with impunity. Bullies are always cowards at heart . . .

ANNA JULIA COOPER (1859–1964), African American educator and feminist. *A Voice from the South*, part 1 (1892).

Cooper was the daughter of a former slave.

2   I will not feed your hunger with my blood
Nor crown your nakedness
With jewels of my elegant pain.

NAOMI LONG MADGETT (b. 1923), African American poet. "The Race Question," lines 13–15 (1965).

The dedication of this poem reads: "For one whose fame depends upon keeping The Problem a problem."

3 I suspect victims; they win in the long run.

ELIZABETH BOWEN (1899–1973), British novelist, story writer, essayist, and memoirist; born in Ireland. As quoted in *Elizabeth Bowen*, ch. 13, by Victoria Glendinning (1979).

4 Women . . . are the permanent victims.

JANE O'REILLY, U.S. feminist and humorist. *The Girl I Left Behind*, ch. 6 (1980).

5 . . . the victim accommodates to power. The victim doesn't want anymore [sic] trouble.

JUNE JORDAN (b. 1936), African American poet, essayist, and social critic. *On Call*, ch. 4 (1985).
Written in 1982.

6 I don't see black people as victims even though we are exploited. Victims are flat, one-dimensional characters, someone rolled over by a steamroller so you have a cardboard person. We are far more resilient and more *rounded* than that. I will go on showing there's more to us than our being victimized. Victims are dead.

KRISTIN HUNTER (b. 1931), African American author. *Black Women Writers at Work*, ch. 6, by Claudia Tate (1983).

7 The victim mentality may be the last uncomplicated thing about life in America.

ANNA QUINDLEN (b. 1953), U.S. author. *New York Times*, section 4, p. 17 (November 14, 1993).

8 I'm not interested in who suffered the most.

I'm interested in people getting over it.

NAOMI SHIHAB NYE (b. 1952), U.S. poet. "Jerusalem," lines 1–4 (1994).

VICTORY

1 Victory comes late—
And is held low to freezing lips—
Too rapt with frost
To take it—

EMILY DICKINSON (1830–1886), U.S. poet. "Victory comes late": Poem #690 in her *Complete Poems*, lines 1–4 (c. 1863).

2 Peoples need a victory so bad. We've been working here since '62 and we haven't got nothing, except a helluva lot of heartaches.

FANNIE LOU HAMER (1917–1977), African American civil rights activist. As quoted in *This Little Light of Mine*, ch. 9, by Hay Mills (1993).
Said in 1967, on commencing a voter registration drive among African Americans in Sunflower County, Mississippi, which was 70% African American. Before the drive, 13% of eligible African Americans were registered to vote, compared with 85% of eligible whites.

VIETNAM WAR

1 This nation is founded on blood like a city on swamps yet its dream has been beautiful and sometimes just that now grows brutal and heavy as a burned out star.

MARGE PIERCY (b. 1936), U.S. poet, novelist, and political activist. "The Peaceable Kingdom," lines 53–55 (1968).
Written during the Vietnam War; Piercy was a prominent opponent of the United States' involvement in that war.

2 It was a heavy burden on the conscience to know that while you sat in Music 101, some contemporary—as "worthy" of a college education as you were, but one who had been denied the opportunity because he was poor, or black, or both—was getting his head blown off in Vietnam. Many students believed that such inequity was wrong, but couldn't bring themselves to redress it personally by refusing the student deferment. It's a dreadful combination: to act for self-protection yet at the same time to loathe oneself for acting that way.

MURIEL BEADLE (b. 1915), U.S. author and community organizer. *Where Has All the Ivy Gone?* Ch. 26 (1972).

Beadle was the wife of George Beadle, who served as President of the University of Chicago, 1960–1968, during part of the time that the university was besieged by a series of student anti-Vietnam War protests.

3 Many of us, whether in the jungles of Asia or on the streets of Chicago, had discovered that noble causes can lead to ignoble actions and that we were capable of sacrificing honor to a sense of efficacy.

LINDA GRANT (b. 1949), U.S. mystery writer. *Blind Trust,* ch. 27 (1990).

On the generation that came of age during the Vietnam War and the movement against American involvement in it. Major anti-war demonstrations occurred, most notably in Chicago during the 1968 Democratic Convention.

4 I realized how for all of us who came of age in the late sixties and early seventies the war was a defining experience. You went or you didn't, but the fact of it and the de-

cisions it forced us to make marked us for the rest of our lives, just as the depression and World War II had marked my parents.

LINDA GRANT (b. 1949), U.S. mystery novelist. *Blind Trust,* ch. 20 (1990).

Catherine Sayler, the private-investigator heroine of this detective series, was reflecting on the Vietnam War after hearing it discussed by a mentally disturbed veteran and her lover, who had been able to avoid the draft.

5 . . . the Wall became a magnet for citizens of every generation, class, race, and relationship to the war perhaps because it is the only great public monument that allows the anesthetized holes in the heart to fill with a truly national grief.

ADRIENNE RICH (b. 1929), U.S. poet, essayist, and feminist. *What Is Found There,* ch. 14 (1993).

Written in 1991 about the Vietnam War Memorial in Washington, D.C.: a black granite wall designed by Maya Lin and inscribed with the names of Americans who died in that war.

6 There is only one place for the women who served and that is on the same site with our brother soldiers. These women have touched thousands of those names on the wall. We have to be at that spot, physically, spiritually and emotionally.

DIANE CARLSON EVANS (b. c. 1943), U.S. nurse and military servicewoman. As quoted in *People* magazine, p. 90 (May 31, 1993).

Evans, who served as a combat nurse in Pleiku, Vietnam, 1968–1969, led the successful effort to have the Vietnam Women's Memorial Project, a sculpture by Glenna Goodacre, created and placed near the black granite Vietnam War Memorial in Washington, DC. None of the 112 monuments previously erected in Washington honored military women.

7 In Vietnam, some of us lost control of our lives. I want my life back. I almost feel like I've been missing in action for twenty-two years.

WANDA SPARKS, U.S. nurse. As quoted in the *New York Times Magazine*, p. 72 (November 7, 1993).

On the traumatic effect of the Vietnam War. Sparks had been an Air Force flight nurse in the war and had lost her fiance to it; he was listed as Missing in Action.

VIOLENCE

I The miners lost because they had only the constitution. The other side had bayonets. In the end, bayonets always win.

MOTHER JONES (1830–1930), U.S. labor organizer. *The Autobiography of Mother Jones*, ch. 22 (1925).

Commenting on the failed Colorado miners' strike while addressing a 1915 mass meeting in Cooper Union, New York City.

2 There's in people simply an urge to destroy, an urge to kill, to murder and rage, and until all mankind, without exception, undergoes a great change, wars will be waged, everything that has been built up, cultivated, and grown will be destroyed and disfigured, after which mankind will have to begin all over again.

ANNE FRANK (1929–1945), Dutch Jewish diarist; born in Germany. *Diary of a Young Girl*, entry dated May 3, 1944 (1947).

Frank and her family were in hiding in Holland when she wrote this. On August 4, their hiding place would be raided by the police, and they would be sent to German and Dutch concentration camps. All of them except Otto Frank, the father, would perish; Anne died in Bergen-Belsen, a German camp, just two months before the liberation of Holland.

3 . . . the man in the violent situation reveals those qualities least dispensable in his personality, those qualities which are all he will have to take into eternity with him.

FLANNERY O'CONNOR (1925–1964), U.S. fiction writer and essayist. *Mystery and Manners*, part 3 (1969).

Written in 1957. O'Connor's stories and novels often contained violence. She was a devout Roman Catholic.

4 Loving feels lonely in a violent world,
irrelevant to people burning like last year's weed
with bellies distended, with fish throats agape
and flesh melting down to glue.
We can no longer shut out the screaming
That leaks through the ventilation system . . .

MARGE PIERCY (b. 1936), U.S. poet, novelist, and political activist. "Community," lines 1–6 (1969).

Referring to television and photographic images of the Vietnam War, which was at its height when this was written. Piercy was a prominent activist in the antiwar movement.

5 I will try to be non-violent one more day
this morning, waking the world away
in the violent day.

MURIEL RUKEYSER (1913–1980), U.S. poet. "Waking This Morning," lines 22–25 (1973).

VIRTUE

I The sciences have ever been the surest guides to virtue.

FRANCES WRIGHT (1795–1852), Scottish author and speaker; relocated to America. *Course of Popular Lectures*, lecture 5 (1829).

2 . . . blameless people are always the most exasperating!

GEORGE ELIOT (1819–1880), British novelist. *Middlemarch*, ch. 12 (1871–1872).

3 [Women's] duty is nothing else than the fulfilment [sic] of the whole moral law, the attainment of every human virtue.

FRANCES POWER COBBÉ (1822–1904), U.S. author and feminist. *The Duties of Women*, lecture 1 (1882).

4 The happiest excitement in life is to be convinced that one is fighting for all one is worth on behalf of some clearly seen and deeply felt good, and against some greatly scorned evil.

RUTH BENEDICT (1887–1948), U.S. anthropologist. *An Anthropologist at Work*, part 2 (1959).
Written c. the early 1920s.

5 . . . the only way to become a better writer is to become a better person.

BRENDA UELAND (1891–1985), U.S. author and writing teacher. *If You Want to Write*, 2nd. ed., ch. 13 (1939).

VISION

1 Our visions begin with our desires.

AUDRE LORDE (1934–1992), U.S. author. *Black Women Writers at Work*, ch. 8, by Claudia Tate (1985).

2 . . . This is the paradox of vision:

Sharp perception softens our existence in the world.

SUSAN GRIFFIN (b. 1943), U.S. author and feminist. "Happiness," lines 110–113 (1987).

VOLUNTARISM

1 Unpaid work never commands respect . . .

HARRIOT STANTON BLATCH (1856–1940), British suffragist; born in the United States. As quoted in *History of Woman Suffrage*, vol. 4, ch. 18, by Susan B. Anthony and Ida Husted Harper (1902).
Speaking before the thirtieth annual convention of the National Woman Suffrage Association, held February 13–19, 1898, in Washington, D.C. Her address was entitled "Woman as an Economic Factor"; here, she was reflecting on women's inability to gain genuine respect for the work they did in their homes.

WAGES

1 The flour merchant, the housebuilder, and the postman charge us no less on account of our sex; but when we endeavor to earn money to pay all these, then, indeed, we find the interest.

LUCY STONE (1818–1893), U.S. suffragist. As quoted in *Feminism: The Essential Historical Writings*, part 3, by Miriam Schnier (1972).
Extemporaneous remarks at the 1855 National Woman's Rights Convention in Cincinnati, Ohio.

2 I do not want to be covetous, but I think I speak the minds of many a wife and mother when I say I would willingly work as hard as possible all day and all night, if I might be sure of a small profit, but have worked hard for twenty-five years and have never known what it was

to receive a financial compensation and to have what was really my own.

EMMA WATROUS, U.S. inventor. As quoted in *Feminine Ingenuity,* ch. 8, by Anne L. Mac-Donald (1992).

Written in 1891 in a letter to *Woman Inventor.* The holder of two patents, Watrous was frustrated by her inability to exploit their commercial potential.

3 It is impossible to forget the sense of dignity which marks the hour when one becomes a wage-earner. . . . I felt that I had suddenly acquired value—to myself, to my family, and to the world.

ELIZABETH STUART PHELPS (1844–1911), U.S. novelist and short story writer. *Chapters from a Life,* ch. 1 (1897).

On receiving her first payment for writing, She was very young and was paid $2.50 for a "pious little contribution" to "some extremely orthodox young people's periodical."

4 Not one of our national officers ever has had a dollar of salary. I retire on full pay!

SUSAN B. ANTHONY (1820–1906), U.S. suffragist. As quoted in *History of Woman Suffrage,* vol. 4, ch. 21, by Susan B. Anthony and Ida Husted Harper (1902).

On resigning the presidency of the National Woman Suffrage Association in February 1900. Then in her eightieth year of life, Anthony had held office in woman suffrage organizations continuously for forty-eight years.

5 The two most beautiful words in the English language are "check enclosed."

DOROTHY PARKER (1893–1967), U.S. author and humorist. As quoted in *The Late Mrs. Dorothy Parker,* ch. 17, by Leslie Frewin (1986).

Said in the 1920s; Parker, trying to earn her living as a writer, was referring to the financial insecurity of the profession.

6 . . . a worker was seldom so much annoyed by what he got as by what he got in relation to his fellow workers.

MARY BARNETT GILSON (1877– ?), U.S. factory personnel manager, economist, and educator. *What's Past is Prologue,* ch. 7 (1940).

7 It was obvious that the size of your chest was in direct proportion to the size of your salary.

CYNTHIA HESS, U.S. exotic dancer. As quoted in *Newsweek* magazine, p. 19 (April 25, 1994).

"Explaining why she sought—successfully—to have her size 56FF breast implants declared a tax-deductible business expense."

WAR

I I know I have the body of a weak, feeble woman; but I have the heart and stomach of a king—and of a King of England too, and think foul scorn that Parma or Spain, or any prince of Europe, should dare to invade the borders of my realm; to which, rather than any dishonour should grow by me, I myself will take up arms—I myself will be your general, judge, and rewarder of every one of your virtues in the field.

ELIZABETH I (1533–1603), Queen of England (1558–1603). As quoted in *The Sayings of Queen Elizabeth,* ch. 2, by Frederick Chamberlin (1923).

In a stirring speech to England's troops in 1588 on the hill at Tilbury; it was they who would have to defend her reign against the Armada, the fleet which had been sent by Philip II of Spain, a Roman Catholic, to overthrow Elizabeth, who was a Protestant, and take her throne. The English defeated the Armada.

2 The bugle-call to arms again sounded in my war-trained ear, the bayonets gleamed, the sabres clashed, and the Prussian helmets and the eagles of France stood face to face on the borders of the Rhine. . . . I remembered our own armies, my own war-stricken country and its dead, its widows and orphans, and it nerved me to action for which the physical strength had long ceased to exist, and on the borrowed force of love and memory, I strove with might and main.

CLARA BARTON (1821–1912), U.S. Civil War nurse and founder of the American Red Cross. As quoted in *Angel of the Battlefield,* ch. 9, by Ishbel Ross (1956).

The former war nurse was describing her reaction to the announcement of the beginning of the Franco-Prussian War (1870–1871).

3 We saw the lightning and that was the guns; and then we heard the thunder and that was the big guns; and then we heard the rain falling and that was the blood falling; and when we came to get in the crops, it was dead men that we reaped.

HARRIET TUBMAN (1820–1913), African American slave, liberator of slaves, and spy. As quoted in *Divided Houses,* ch. 7, by Lyde Cullen Sizer (1992).

Of the Civil War, during which she acted as a spy for the Union.

4 For some reason a nation feels as shy about admitting that it ever went forth to war for the sake of more wealth as a man would about admitting that he had accepted an invitation just for the sake of the food. This is one of humanity's most profound imbecilities, as perhaps the only justification for asking one's fellowmen to endure the horrors of war would be the knowledge that if they did not fight they would starve.

REBECCA WEST (1892–1983), British author. *The Strange Necessity,* ch. 10 (1928).

5 The spectacle of misery grew in its crushing volume. There seemed to be no end to the houses full of hunted starved children. Children with dysentery, children with scurvy, children at every stage of starvation. . . . We learned to know that the barometer of starvation was the number of children deserted in any community.

MARY HEATON VORSE (1874–1966), U.S. journalist and labor activist. *A Footnote to Folly,* ch. 24 (1935).

On Russia in 1921, following the Revolution. Vorse was there as a Hearst newspaper correspondent.

6 All our civilization had meant nothing. The same culture that had nurtured the kindly enlightened people among whom I had been brought up, carried around with it war. Why should I not have known this? I did know it, but I did not believe it. I believed it as we believe we are going to die. Something that is to happen in some remote time.

MARY HEATON VORSE (1874–1966), U.S. journalist and labor activist. *A Footnote to Folly,* ch. 8 (1935).

On being in France during World War I.

7 I believe that one of the most dignified ways we are capable of, to assert and then reassert our dignity in the face of poverty and war's fears and pains, is to nourish ourselves

with all possible skill, delicacy, and ever-increasing enjoyment.

M. F. K. FISHER (1908–1992), U.S. author and food expert. *How to Cook a Wolf*, Conclusion (1942).

8   . . . we often ask ourselves here despairingly: "What, oh, what is the use of the war? Why can't people live peacefully together? Why all this destruction?" The question is very understandable, but no one has found a satisfactory answer to it so far. Yes, why do they make still more gigantic planes, still heavier bombs and, at the same time, prefabricated houses for reconstruction? Why should millions be spent daily on the war and yet there's not a penny available for medical services, artists, or for poor people? . . . Oh, why are people so crazy?

ANNE FRANK (1929–1945), Dutch Jewish diarist; born in Germany. *Diary of a Young Girl*, entry dated May 3, 1944 (1947).

Frank and her family were in hiding in Holland when she wrote this. On August 4, their hiding place would be raided by the police, and they would be sent to German and Dutch concentration camps. All of them except Otto Frank, the father, would perish; Anne died in Bergen-Belsen, a German camp, just two months before the liberation of Holland.

9   All the strong agonized men
Wear the hard clothes of war,
Try to remember what they are
    fighting for.
But in dark weeping helpless
    moments of peace
Women and poets believe and resist
    forever.

MURIEL RUKEYSER (1913–1980), U.S. poet. "Letter to the Front," part 1, lines 7–11 (1944).

Written during World War II.

10   I can not believe that war is the best solution. No one won the last war, and no one will win the next war.

ELEANOR ROOSEVELT (1884–1962), U.S. author, speaker, and First Lady. As quoted in *Eleanor: The Years Alone*, ch. 5, by Joseph P. Lash (1972).

In a June 28, 1947, letter to President Harry S. Truman.

11   . . . in any war a victory means another war, and yet another, until some day inevitably the tides turn, and the victor is the vanquished, and the circle reverses itself, but remains nevertheless a circle.

PEARL S. BUCK (1892–1973), U.S. author. *My Several Worlds* (1954).

12   I really don't think this war will end soon. We are completely aware of the difficulties, no food or fuel, the danger, but we want to be stronger than all that. With each child, we are fighting back with our love of life.

TINA BAJRAKTAREBIC (b. 1965), Bosnian mother-to-be. As quoted in *Newsweek* magazine, p. 60 (January 3, 1994).

Living in the city of Sarajevo in the thick of civil war, she was nine months pregnant with her first child.

WAR: NEGATIVE ASPECTS

1   Monarchs ought to put to death the authors and instigators of war, as their sworn enemies and as dangers to their states.

ELIZABETH I (1533–1603), Queen of England (1558–1603). As quoted in *The Sayings of Queen Elizabeth*, ch. 13, by Frederick Chamberlin (1923).

To Fenelon, the French Ambassador.

2 War is a most uneconomical, foolish, poor arrangement, a bloody enrichment of that soil which bears the sweet flower of peace . . .

M. E. W. SHERWOOD (1826–1903), U.S. socialite, traveller, and author. *An Epistle to Posterity,* ch. 5 (1897).

3 The utter helplessness of a conquered people is perhaps the most tragic feature of a civil war or any other sort of war.

REBECCA LATIMER FELTON (1835–1930), U.S. author. *Country Life in Georgia in the Days of My Youth,* ch. 2 (1919).
Remembering the aftermath of the Civil War. This remark comes from Felton's synopsis of an address she gave in 1900, in Augusta, Georgia, to the Daughters of the Confederacy.

4 I . . . hate with a murderous hatred those men who, having lived their youth, would send into war other youth, not lived, unfulfilled, to fight and die for them; the pride and cowardice of those old men, making their wars that boys must die.

MARY ROBERTS RINEHART (1876–1958), U.S. novelist. *My Story,* ch. 36 (1931).

5 Raids are slightly constipating.

ELIZABETH BOWEN (1899–1973), British novelist, story writer, essayist, and memoirist; born in Ireland. As quoted in *Elizabeth Bowen,* ch. 8, by Victoria Glendinning (1979).
In a letter to her friend, Noreen Colley Butler, dated September 24, 1940, referring to the air raids on London during the World War II "blitz," which had begun the previous month. Butler was in Ireland.

6 Anyone who thinks must think of the next war as they would of suicide.

ELEANOR ROOSEVELT (1884–1962), U.S. First Lady, author, and speaker. As quoted in *El-*

eanor and Franklin, ch. 51, by Joseph P. Lash (1971).
In a January 21, 1941, speech at the National Conference on the Cause and Cure of War.

7 War is never fatal but always lost. Always lost.

GERTRUDE STEIN (1874–1946), U.S. author; relocated to France. *Wars I Have Seen* (1945).
Written in 1943.

8 The worst thing about war is that so many people enjoy it.

ELLEN GLASGOW (1873–1945), U.S. novelist. *The Woman Within,* ch. 19 (1954).
Written in 1944, near the end of World War II.

9 How can anyone be *interested* in war?—that glorious pursuit of annihilation with its ceremonious bellowings and trumpetings over the mangling of human bones and muscles and organs and eyes, its inconceivable agonies which could have been prevented by a few well-chosen, reasonable words. How, why, did this unnecessary business begin? Why does anyone want to read about it—this redundant human madness which men accept as inevitable?

MARGARET ANDERSON (1886–1973), U.S. editor and memoirist. *The Strange Necessity,* part 1 (1969).

10 War is bestowed like electroshock on the depressive nation; thousands of volts jolting the system, an artificial galvanizing, one effect of which is loss of memory. War comes at the end of the twentieth century as absolute failure of imagination, scientific and political. That a war can be represented as helping a people to "feel good" about themselves, their country, is a measure of that failure.

Adrienne Rich (b. 1929), U.S. poet and essayist. *What is Found There*, ch. 3 (1993). Written in January 1991.

11 I . . . toyed with the idea of going to find another war where I could at least feel alive. I was so numb that it took terror to make me feel anything.

Bess Jones, U.S. nurse. As quoted in the *New York Times Magazine*, p. 72 (November 7, 1993).
A U. S. Army nurse during the Vietnam War, she was describing the impact of war's trauma after she returned home.

12 You didn't feel there was anything you ever could enjoy again because you really were immersed in death. Other people seemed shallow. You felt a strong allegiance to the dead.

Joan Furey (b. 1946), U.S. military nurse. As quoted in the *New York Times Magazine*, p. 40 (November 7, 1993).
On returning home from duty as a military nurse in the Vietnam War.

WAR: POSITIVE ASPECTS

1 I have never believed that war settled anything satisfactorily, but I am not entirely sure that some times there are certain situations in the world such as we have in actuality when a country is worse off when it does not go to war for its principles than if it went to war.

Eleanor Roosevelt (1884–1962), U.S. First Lady, author, and speaker. As quoted in *Eleanor and Franklin*, ch. 46, by Joseph P. Lash (1971).

Written on January 2, 1938. Roosevelt was abandoning her earlier pacifism in the face of the fascist threat.

2 War is a beastly business, it is true, but one proof we are human is our ability to learn, even from it, how better to exist.

M. F. K. Fisher (1908–1992), U.S. culinary writer and autobiographer. *How to Cook a Wolf*, rev. ed., Introduction to the Revised Edition (1951).
The first edition of this book had been published in 1942, when World War II was still in progress.

3 . . . it is a commonplace that men like war. For peace, in our society, with the feeling we have then that it is feeble-minded to strive except for one's own private profit, is a lonely thing and a hazardous business. Over and over men have proved that they prefer the hazards of war with all its suffering. It has its compensations.

Ruth Benedict (1887–1948), U.S. anthropologist. *An Anthropologist at Work*, part 4 (1959).
From "Primitive Freedom," a paper written in 1942.

4 Through the particular, in wartime, I felt the high-voltage current of the general pass.

Elizabeth Bowen (1899–1973), British novelist, story writer, essayist, and memoirist; born in Ireland. As quoted in *Elizabeth Bowen*, ch. 8, by Victoria Glendinning (1979).
Written during the 1940s, about having lived in London during World War II.

5 I thought if war did not include killing, I'd like to see one every year.

Maya Angelou (b. 1928), African American author and performer. *Gather Together in My Name*, ch. 1 (1974).

On the sense of "festival" in the San Francisco African American community that followed the announcement of victory in World War II.

WASHINGTON, DC

1 . . . Washington was not only an important capital. It was a city of fear. Below that glittering and delightful surface there is another story, that of underpaid Government clerks, men and women holding desperately to work that some political pull may at any moment take from them. A city of men in office and clutching that office, and a city of struggle which the country never suspects.

MARY ROBERTS RINEHART (1876–1958), U.S. novelist. *My Story*, ch. 48 (1931).

2 Washington will ever be a city for extracurricular romance and undercover trysts, partly because of the high moral standards demanded of the politician by his constituency, and also because it is a town where women are more easily tolerated if they dabble with politicians rather than politics.

BARBARA HOWAR (b. 1934), U.S. socialite and author. *Laughing all the Way*, ch. 6 (1973).

Howar, a noted Washington socialite during the Kennedy and Johnson administrations, had an adulterous affair with a United States Senator.

3 Sometimes I think we're the only two lawyers in Washington who trust each other.

ELIZABETH DOLE (b. 1936), U.S. lawyer and government official. As quoted in *Newsweek* magazine, p. 13 (August 3, 1987).

Speaking of her husband, Senator Robert Dole, who was also a lawyer.

4 I came there as prime steak and now I feel like low-grade hamburger.

JOYCELYN ELDERS (b. 1933), U.S. pediatrician and medical educator; first woman (and second African American), Surgeon General. As quoted in *Newsweek* magazine, p. 17 (September 20, 1993).

On what she thought of Washington, DC, where she had come from her native Arkansas to be Surgeon General. She was sharply criticized throughout her tenure and in 1994 was dismissed by President Bill Clinton.

5 What you don't understand about this town is that they can fight about issues all they want, but they don't really care about them. What they really care about is who they sit next to at dinner.

ANONYMOUS "PROMINENT WOMAN," Washington, DC, socialite. As quoted in *The Agenda*, ch. 20, by Hillary Rodham Clinton, to Bob Woodward (1994).

This was said to Mrs. Clinton soon after she became First Lady of the United States; according to Woodward, she "claimed that she had been shocked."

WEALTH

1 . . . wealth and female softness equally tend to debase mankind!

MARY WOLLSTONECRAFT (1759–1797), British feminist. *A Vindication of the Rights of Woman*, ch. 3 (1792).

2 . . . so large a portion of those who hold much capital, instead of using their various advantages for the greatest good of those around them, employ the chief of them for mere selfish indulgences; thus inflicting as

much mischief on themselves, as results to others from their culpable neglect. A great portion of the rich seem to be acting on the principle, that the more God bestows on them, the less are they under obligation to practise any self-denial, in fulfilling his benevolent plan of raising our race to intelligence and holiness.

CATHERINE E. BEECHER (1800–1878), U.S. educator and author. *Treatise on Domestic Economy for the Use of Young Ladies at Home and at School*, ch. 17 (1843).

3 No one need go into alleys to hunt up wretchedness; they can find it in perfection among the rich and fashionable of every land and nation. Oh! if tesselated hearths and satin tapestries could speak, what tales of agony they might tell! If the marble statues that adorn the riches of lordly mansions could open their mouths, how would they outrival all poetry and romance in the incidents they could proclaim! and could the nuptial couch, with its silken hangings, unfold its memories, could we bear to listen to its disclosures?

ELIZA POTTER, U.S. "society" hairdresser. *A Hairdresser's Experience in High Life*, "Author's Appeal" [Introduction] (1859).

4 To exist as an advertisement of her husband's income, or her father's generosity, has become a second nature to many a woman who must have undergone, one would say, some long and subtle process of degradation before she sunk [sic] so low, or grovelled so serenely.

ELIZABETH STUART PHELPS (1844–1911), U.S. author. *What to Wear?* Ch. 1 (1873).

Referring to exorbitantly costly dress.

5 She was the first of our rich women to wear many diamonds, and she always looked as if they wearied her.

M. E. W. SHERWOOD (1826–1903), U.S. socialite, traveller, and author. *An Epistle to Posterity*, ch. 11 (1897).

Sherwood was speaking of Mrs. J. J. Astor, mother of William Waldorf Astor, in New York City in the 1870s.

6 . . . the aristocracy most widely developed in America is that of wealth.

KATHERINE FULLERTON GEROULD (1879–1944), U.S. author. *Modes and Morals*, ch. 2 (1920).

7 I had a feeling that out there, there were very poor people who didn't have enough to eat. But they wore wonderfully colored rags and did musical numbers up and down the streets together.

JILL ROBINSON (b. 1936), U.S. novelist. As quoted in *American Dreams*, part 1, by Studs Terkel (1980).

The daughter of movie producer Dore Schary, Robinson had grown up rich in Hollywood; her notions of the world were shaped by the movies in which she was immersed.

8 Throughout the 1980's, we did hear too much about individual gain and the ethos of selfishness and greed. We did not hear enough about how to be a good member of a community, to define the common good and to repair the social contract. And we also found that while prosperity does not trickle down from the most powerful to the rest of us,

all too often indifference and even intolerance do.

HILLARY RODHAM CLINTON (b. 1947), U.S. attorney; First Lady of the United States. *New York Times*, p. A17 (May 18, 1993).

From the First Lady's commencement speech a day earlier at the University of Pennsylvania, which had recently experienced racial conflicts.

9   Having money is just the best thing in the world.

MADONNA (b. 1958), U.S. singer and actress. As quoted in *People* magazine, p. 74 (August 30, 1993).

At the time she said this, the popular performer's worth was estimated at $100 million, and she claimed to have taken "only three brief vacations in 10 years."

10   I think there's a point at which money, influence, and power become so blinding that people believe they control the world.

IRIS SAWYER (b. 1933), U.S. ex–socialite. As quoted in *New York* magazine, p. 52 (May 16, 1994).

The one-time millionairess was destitute, having been treated unfairly in a real estate deal by her former lover of eight years, a Wall Street financier, and having received an inadequate divorce settlement from her husband of twenty-four years, a wealthy consultant.

WEAVING

1   I used to be angry all the time and I'd sit there weaving my anger. Now I'm not angry. I sit there hearing the sounds outside, the sounds in the room, the sounds of the treadles and heddles—a music of my own making.

BHAKTI ZIEK (b. c. 1946), U.S. weaver and textile designer. As quoted in the *Chronicle of Higher Education*, p. A51 (December 1, 1993).

Ziek was teaching woven design at the Philadelphia College of Textiles and Science.

WELDING

1   I became a journeyman welder—I did very well. I loved it. It was like crocheting . . .

MILDRED ADMIRE BEDELL, U.S. (former) welder. As quoted in *A Mouthful of Rivets*, ch. 1, by Nancy Baker Wise and Christy Wise (1994).

Bedell was one of the many women who were welcomed into traditionally male trades during World War II, filling in for men who were needed in military service. Most of these women were ejected from their jobs—some willingly, others unwillingly—at the war's end.

WELFARE SYSTEM

1   Borrow a child and get on welfare. Borrow a child and stay in the house all day with the child, or go to the public park with the child, and take the child to the welfare office and cry and say your man left you and be humble and wear your dress and your smile, and don't talk back . . .

SUSAN GRIFFIN (b. 1943), U.S. author and feminist. "An Answer to a Man's Question, 'What Can I Do About Women's Liberation?'," Lines 28–33 (c. 1970).

2   I will never accept that I got a free ride. It wasn't free at all. My ancestors were brought here against their will. They were made to work and help build the country. I worked in the cotton fields from the age of seven. I worked in the laundry for twenty-three years. I worked for the

national organization for nine years. I just retired from city government after twelve-and-a-half years.

JOHNNIE TILLMON (b. 1926), African American community organizer. As quoted in *I Dream a World*, by Brian Lanker (1989).

Tillmon, who lived in the African American Watts neighborhood of Los Angeles, was director of the National Welfare Rights Organization.

3 . . . if you're poor and ignorant, with a child, you're a slave. Meaning that you're never going to get out of it. These women are in bondage to a kind of slavery that the 13th Amendment just didn't deal with. The old master provided food, clothing and health care to the slaves because he wanted them to get up and go to work in the morning. And so on welfare: you get food, clothing and shelter—you get survival, but you can't really do anything else. You can't control your life.

JOYCELYN ELDERS (b. 1933), U.S. pediatrician and educator; first woman (and second African American) Surgeon General of the United States. As quoted in the *New York Times Magazine*, p. 18 (January 30, 1994).

Elders, who was U. S. Surgeon General at the time, was explaining why her first priority was: "To do something about unplanned and unwanted pregnancies." The Thirteenth Amendment (1865) to the U. S. Constitution abolished slavery.

ened because they were strangers to it!

HORTENSE ODLUM (1892– ?), U.S. businesswoman. *A Woman's Place*, ch. 7 (1939).

2 he would press himself between them—
hero and betrayer
legend and deserter—
so when they sat down to eat
they could taste his ashes

IRENA KLEPFISZ (b. 1941), U.S. Jewish poet and essayist; born in Poland. "The Widow and Daughter," lines 117–121 (1971).

Klepfisz's father, a Polish fighter for Jewish rights, died during the Warsaw Uprising. He was thirty, Irena an infant. She and her mother fled Poland, eventually resettling in New York City, where they lived in poverty.

WILDERNESS

I The point of the dragonfly's terrible lip, the giant water bug, birdsong, or the beautiful dazzle and flash of sunlighted minnows, is not that it all fits together like clockwork—for it doesn't . . . but that it all flows so freely wild, like the creek, that it all surges in such a free, finged tangle. Freedom is the world's water and weather, the world's nourishment freely given, its soil and sap: and the creator loves pizzazz.

ANNIE DILLARD (b. 1945), U.S. essayist and autobiographer. *Pilgrim at Tinker Creek*, ch. 8 (1974).

WIDOWHOOD

I How many wives have been forced by the death of well-intentioned but too protective husbands to face reality late in life, bewildered and fright-

WINNING

I In business everyone is out to grab, to fight, to win. Either you are the under or the over dog. It is up to you to be on top.

ALICE FOOTE MACDOUGALL (1867–1945), U.S. businesswoman. *The Autobiography of a Business Woman,* ch. 3 (1928).

MacDougall was a flourishing beverage merchant and the proprietor of five successful New York City coffee houses.

2 The I'm-going-to-win-no-matter-how-I-have-to-do-it attitude just doesn't seem to fit. For me, a contest isn't a success unless it was fun, whether or not I win.

MARGO GODFREY OBERG (b. c. 1955), U.S. surfer. As quoted in *WomenSports* magazine, p. 12 (June 1977).

When she said this, Oberg was already a five-time winner of the women's world championship in surfing.

3 I have a lot to say, and if I'm not No. 1, I can't say it.

BILLIE JEAN KING (b. 1943), U.S. tennis player. As quoted in *WomenSports* magazine, p. 52 (January 1978).

Though beset with knee problems, the tennis champion was struggling to regain her number one ranking.

4 No matter how tough, no matter what kind of outside pressure, no matter how many bad breaks along the way, I must keep my sights on the final goal, to win, win, win— and with more love and passion than the world has ever witnessed in any performance.

BILLIE JEAN KING (b. 1943), U.S. tennis player. *Billie Jean,* ch. 16 (1982).

5 Winning brought me a wonderful sense of completeness.

TENLEY ALBRIGHT (b. 1935), U.S. ice skater. As quoted in *People* magazine, p. 81 (February 24, 1992).

On winning the Olympic gold medal for women's figure skating in 1956.

6 In tennis, at the end of the day you're a winner or a loser. You know exactly where you stand. . . . I don't need that anymore. I don't need my happiness, my well-being, to be based on winning and losing.

CHRIS EVERT (b. 1954), U.S. tennis player. As quoted in *Sports Illustrated,* p. 64 (May 25, 1992).

On retiring from professional tennis, in which she had been a very frequent winner.

7 Winning is everything.

YOULIA MALEEVA (b. 1945), Bulgarian tennis coach and manager. As quoted in the *New Yorker,* p. 38 (July 25, 1994).

A former Bulgarian singles champion in tennis, and now a coach and manager of her three tennis-champion daughters, she was stating her "philosophy."

WITCHCRAFT

1 I am no more a witch than you are a wizard. If you take my life away, God will give you blood to drink.

SARAH GOOD (?–1692), Colonial American woman convicted of witchcraft. As quoted in *Great American Trials,* "1600s" section, by Edward W. Knappman (1994).

Good, a "near derelict," was among those women accused by young girls in Salem, Massachusetts, of being witches and convicted in court. On July 19, 1692, as she was about to be hanged, the Reverend Nicholas Noyes urged her to confess. She refused, saying this.

WOMAN SUFFRAGE

1 Had I represented twenty thousand voters in Michigan, that political editor would not have known nor cared whether I was the oldest or the youngest daughter of Methuselah, or whether my bonnet came from the Ark or from Worth's.

SUSAN B. ANTHONY (1820–1906), U.S. suffragist. As quoted in *Eighty Years and More*, ch. 18, by Elizabeth Cady Stanton (1898).

Anthony said this c. 1873, reacting to an editorial in a Kalamazoo, Michigan, journal which focused on her appearance, ridiculing her age (53) and her style of dress. Methuselah was the oldest man mentioned in the Bible; he died at age 969. Worth's was a store that sold fine clothing.

2   As a Tax-Paying Citizen of the United States I am entitled to a voice in Governmental affairs. . . . Having paid this *unlawful Tax under written Protest* for forty years, I am entitled to receive from the Treasury of "Uncle Sam" the full amount of both Principal and Interest.

SUSAN PECKER FOWLER (1823–1911), U.S. suffragist, tax protestor, and dress reformer. As quoted in *Past and Promise*, part 3, by Charlotte Perry-Dickerson and Joyce Bator-Rabinoff (1990).

Fowler's point was that women, as they were denied the vote, should not be expected to pay taxes. This adaptation of the principle that "taxation without representation" is unjust was common among suffragists.

3   . . . [woman suffrage] has made little difference beyond doubling the number of voters. There is no woman's vote as such. They divide up just about as men do.

ALICE ROOSEVELT LONGWORTH (1884–1980), U.S. socialite; daughter and cousin of U.S. Presidents. *Crowded Hours*, ch. 21 (1933).

4   The American struggle for the vote was much more difficult than the English for the simple reason that it was much more easy.

REBECCA WEST (1892–1983), British author. As quoted in *On Women and Revolution*, part 1: "Personalities and Powers," by Crystal Eastman (1978).

Making the point that English suffragists were more bitterly and violently opposed than their American counterparts. (However, the Americans won woman suffrage eight years earlier [1920] than the English [1928].)

WOMAN SUFFRAGE MOVEMENT

1   The True Republic—Men, their rights and nothing more; women, their rights, and nothing less.

ELIZABETH CADY STANTON (1815–1902), U.S. suffragist. As quoted in *The Life and Work of Susan B. Anthony*, vol. 1, ch. 21, by Ida Husted Harper (1898).

This was the "motto" of their newspaper, *The Revolution* (1868–1970), which advocated suffrage and other rights for women.

2   You may talk about Free Love, if you please, but we are to have the right to vote. To-day we are fined, imprisoned, and hanged, without a jury trial by our peers. You shall not cheat us by getting us off to talk about something else. When we get the suffrage, then you may taunt us with anything you please, and we will then talk about it as long as you please.

LUCY STONE (1818–1893), U.S. suffragist. As quoted in *History of Woman Suffrage*, vol. 2, ch. 22, by Elizabeth Cady Stanton, Susan B. Anthony, and Matilda Joslyn Gage (1882).

Speaking at a May 12, 1869, anniversary celebration of the Equal Rights Association, held in New York. Stone was responding to Rev. Mrs. Hanaford, who had asked that the assembly disavow "Free Loveism," as anti-suffragists sometimes taunted suffragists by accusing them of supporting it. This, she observed, was upsetting and alienating to "the Christian men and women of New England everywhere." Stone declared, "I am ashamed that the question should be asked here," and seemed to criticize Hanaford for tumbling to an anti-suffrage diversionary move.

3 You may consider me presumptuous, gentlemen, but I claim to be a citizen of the United States, with all the qualifications of a voter. I can read the Constitution, I am possessed of two hundred and fifty dollars, and the last time I looked in the old family Bible I found I was over twenty-one years of age.

ELIZABETH CADY STANTON (1816–1902), U.S. suffragist, social reformer, and author. As quoted in *History of Woman Suffrage,* vol. 2, ch. 23, by Susan B. Anthony, Matilda Joslyn Gage, and herself (1882).

Speaking before the Judiciary Committee of the U.S. Senate on January 10, 1872; Stanton was in her fifty-sixth year and had been a leading suffragist for 24 years, having been a convener of the first suffrage convention, held in Seneca Falls, New York, in 1848.

4 ... in your ordered verdict of guilty you have trampled under foot every vital principle of our government. My natural rights, my civil rights, my political rights, my judicial rights are all alike ignored. Robbed of the fundamental privilege of citizenship, I am degraded from the status of a citizen to that of a subject; and not only myself individually but all of my sex are, by your honor's verdict, doomed to political subjection under this so-called republican form of government.

SUSAN B. ANTHONY (1820–1906), U.S. suffragist. As quoted in *The Life and Work of Susan B. Anthony,* ch. 25, by Ida Husted Harper (1898).

Anthony was found guilty of having voted, in violation of the law which prohibited women from voting, on November 5, 1872, in Rochester, New York. Convicted on June 17, 1873, she said this in response to Judge Ward Hunt's question, "Has the prisoner anything to say why sentence shall not be pronounced?"

5 It is twenty-eight years ago to-day since the first woman's rights convention ever held assembled in the Wesleyan chapel at Seneca Falls, N.Y. Could we have foreseen, when we called that convention, the ridicule, persecution, and misrepresentation that the demand for woman's political, religious and social equality would involve; the long, weary years of waiting and hoping without success; I fear we should not have had the courage and conscience to begin such a protracted struggle, nor the faith and hope to continue the work.

ELIZABETH CADY STANTON (1815–1902), U.S. suffragist, author, and social reformer. As quoted in *The History of Woman Suffrage,* vol. 3, ch. 27, by Susan B. Anthony, Matilda Joslyn Gage, and herself (1886).

In a letter to suffragist Lucretia Mott (1793–1880), dated July 19, 1876. It was read aloud by Stanton's longtime friend and sister suffragist Susan B. Anthony (1820–1906) in Philadelphia, at a celebration of the twenty-eighth anniversary of the Seneca Falls convention. Mott and Stanton had called the convention and had continued as women's rights activists ever since. Neither Mott nor Stanton nor Anthony would live to see their central goal—woman suffrage—achieved. It was established through the Nineteenth Amendment to the U. S. Constitution, which took effect in 1920.

6 Courage, then, for the end draws near! A few more years of persistent, faithful work and the women of the United States will be recognized as the legal equals of men.

MARY A. LIVERMORE (1821–1905), U.S. suffragist. As quoted in *History of Woman Suffrage,* vol. 4, ch. 22, by Susan B. Anthony and Ida Husted Harper (1902).

In a letter to the sixteenth annual convention of the American Woman Suffrage Association, which was held November 19–20, 1884, in Chicago. In fact, thirty-six more years would pass before women would be granted suffrage.

7 Better lose me than lose a state.

SUSAN B. ANTHONY (1820–1906), U.S. suffragist, speaker, and editor. As quoted in *The Life and Work of Susan B. Anthony,* ch. 38, by Ida Husted Harper (1898–1908).

Said in 1890, to those who urged her not to undertake, at age 70, what promised to be a physically arduous suffrage campaign through South Dakota.

8 It is not quite the same when we are seventy-two as when we are twenty-seven; still I am glad of what is left, and wish we might both hold out till the victory we have sought is won, but all the same the victory is coming. In the aftertime the world will be the better for it.

LUCY STONE (1818–1893), U.S. suffragist. As quoted in *The Life and Work of Susan B. Anthony,* ch. 39, by Ida Husted Harper (1898–1908).

In an 1891 letter to Susan B. Anthony (1820–1906), her longtime colleague in the fight for woman suffrage. Anthony, exhausted after a difficult suffrage campaign in South Dakota, had recently fallen ill. As it turned out, neither woman lived to see "victory," represented by the passage, in 1919, of the 19th Amendment to the United States Constitution, giving women the right to vote.

9 *Organize, agitate, educate,* must be our war cry.

SUSAN B. ANTHONY (1820–1906), U.S. suffragist. As quoted in *The Life and Work of Susan B. Anthony,* ch. 41, by Ida Husted Harper (1898). Said in 1893.

10 . . . we have every reason to rejoice when there are so many gains and when favorable conditions abound on every hand. The end is not yet in sight, but it can not be far away. The road before us is shorter than the road behind.

LUCY STONE (1818–1893), U.S. suffragist. As quoted in *History of Woman Suffrage,* vol. 4, ch. 13, by Susan B. Anthony and Ida Husted Harper (1902).

From a letter read by her husband, suffragist Henry Blackwell, in 1893 to the twenty-fifth annual convention of the National Woman Suffrage Association. Stone had worked for woman suffrage since the beginning of the movement almost fifty years earlier; she died a few months after this convention. As "only" twenty-six years lay ahead before women would be granted suffrage, she was, technically, correct.

11 Think of submitting our measure to the advice of politicians! I would as soon submit the subject of the equality of a goose to a fox.

ANNA HOWARD SHAW (1847–1919), U.S. suffragist. As quoted in *The Life and Work of Susan B. Anthony,* ch. 42, by Ida Husted Harper (1898–1908).

In an 1894 letter to Laura M. Johns, President of the Kansas State Suffrage Association, on Republican pressure not to pursue getting a suffrage amendment to the state Constitution.

12 We are the only class in history that has been left to fight its battles alone, unaided by the ruling powers. White labor and the freed black men had their champions, but where are ours?

ELIZABETH CADY STANTON (1815–1902), U.S. suffragist, social reformer, speaker, author, and editor. As quoted in *The Life and Work of Susan B. Anthony,* ch. 47, by Ida Husted Harper (1898–1908).

In an 1896 letter to her closest friend and colleague, Susan B. Anthony.

13 We hope the day will soon come when every girl will be a member of a great Union of Unmarried Women, pledged to refuse an offer of marriage from any man who is not an advocate of their emancipation.

TENNESSEE CLAFLIN (1846–1923), U.S. journalist, lecturer, and social reform advocate; relocated to England. *Talks and Essays*, vol. 1, ch. 11 (1897).

14 Every man who is not for us in this prolonged struggle for liberty is responsible for the present degradation of the mothers of the race. It is pitiful to see how few men ever have made our cause their own, but while leaving us to fight our battle alone, they have been unsparing in their criticism of every failure. Of all the battles for liberty in the long past, woman only has been left to fight her own, without help and with all the powers of earth and heaven, human and divine, arrayed against her.

ELIZABETH CADY STANTON (1815–1902), U.S. suffragist, social reformer, and author. As quoted in *History of Woman Suffrage*, vol. 4, ch. 19, by Susan B. Anthony and Ida Husted Harper (1902).

In a letter read by Susan B. Anthony (1820–1906) before the thirty-first annual convention of the National Woman Suffrage Association, which was held April 27–May 3, 1899, in Grand Rapids, Michigan.

15 I expect to do more work for woman suffrage in the next decade than ever before.

SUSAN B. ANTHONY (1820–1906), U.S. suffragist. As quoted in *History of Woman Suffrage*, vol. 4, ch. 21, by Susan B. Anthony and Ida Husted Harper (1902).

On resigning the presidency of the National Woman Suffrage Association in February 1900. Then in her eightieth year of life, Anthony had held office in woman suffrage organizations continuously for forty-eight years. Carrie Chapman Catt (1859–1947) was elected to replace her. Accepting the honor, Catt said, "The papers have spoken of the new president as Miss Anthony's successor. Miss Anthony never will have a successor."

16 In 1872 I received a request like this and I did register and vote, for which I was arrested, convicted and fined $100. Excuse me if I decline to repeat the experience.

SUSAN B. ANTHONY (1820–1906), U.S. suffragist. As quoted in *Life and Work of Susan B. Anthony*, vol. 3, ch. 62, by Ida Husted Harper (1908).

Written to a political committee in 1902 upon receipt of a post card reminding her to register to vote; it had been sent to S. B. Anthony under the erroneous assumption that, as head of household, "S. B." must be a man. Her message was widely reprinted by newspapers, one headlining its front-page story: "Susan B. Anthony Scores One." (Anthony had refused to pay the $100 fine imposed upon her thirty years earlier, because she did not recognize her action as properly illegal.)

17 Now, Mr. President, we don't intend to trouble you during the campaign but after you are elected, then look out for us!

SUSAN B. ANTHONY (1820–1906), U.S. suffragist. As quoted in *History of Woman Suffrage*, vol. 5, ch. 4, by Ida Husted Harper (1922).

Attending the thirty-sixth annual convention (February 1904) of the National Woman Suffrage Association, Anthony was introduced to President Theodore Roosevelt (1858–1919), who was not a woman suffrage advocate. Having succeeded to the Presidency after the assassination of President William McKinley, Roosevelt was now running for election to his second term (first full term). Anthony quoted herself as having said this to him.

18 [On being told that "every woman should stand with bared head before Susan B. Anthony":] Yes, and every man as well.

CLARA BARTON (1821–1912), U.S. nurse; founder of the American Red Cross. As quoted in *History of Woman Suffrage*, vol. 5, ch. 6, by Ida Husted Harper (1922).

Speaking in February 1906 before the thirty-eighth annual convention of the National Woman Suffrage Association. This was the last convention that Anthony (1820–1906) would attend; she had been a suffrage leader for 54 years and was a greatly respected and beloved figure.

Equal voting rights for British women were finally granted in 1928, the year of Pankhurst's death.

19 I stand here tonight to say that we have never known defeat; we have never been vanquished. We have not always reached the goal toward which we have striven, but in the hour of our greatest disappointment we could always point to our battlefield and say: "There we fought our good fight, there we defended the principles for which our ancestors and yours laid down their lives; there is our battlefield for justice, equality and freedom. Where is yours?"

ANNA HOWARD SHAW (1847–1919), U.S. minister, suffragist, and speaker; born in England. As quoted in *History of Woman Suffrage*, vol. 5, ch. 6, by Ida Husted Harper (1922).

Speaking in February 1906 before the thirty-eighth annual convention of the National Woman Suffrage Association. The woman suffrage movement was by this time 58 years old.

20 ... I want to say to you who think women cannot succeed, we have brought the government of England to this position, that it has to face this alternative: either women are to be killed or women are to have the vote.

EMMELINE PANKHURST (1858–1928), British suffragist. As quoted in *Feminism: The Essential Historical Writings*, part 5, by Miriam Schnier (1972).

In a speech that the fiery militant suffragist gave in Hartford, Connecticut, on November 13, 1913, during an American lecture tour. She was referring to the tactic of hunger striking. During that year, she had participated in twelve hunger strikes; 182 other British suffragists had also gone on hunger strikes to win the right to vote.

21 The American suffrage movement has been, until very recently, altogether a parlor affair, absolutely detached from the economic needs of the people.

EMMA GOLDMAN (1869–1940), U.S. anarchist and author; born in Russia. *Anarchism and Other Essays*, 3rd rev. ed., ch. 9 (1917).

Goldman was concerned about the middle-class biases, and indifference or antagonism to labor issues, of the leading women suffragists. Interestingly, this same criticism was later made of post-World War II feminists—especially in the 1960s and 1970s.

22 The right of citizens of the United States to vote shall not be denied or abridged by the United States or by any State on account of sex. Congress shall have power to enforce this article by appropriate legislation.

Suffragists, hear this last call to a suffrage convention! The officers of the National American Woman Suffrage Association hereby call their State auxiliaries, through their elected delegates, to meet in annual convention at Chicago, Congress Hotel, February 12th to 18th, inclusive. In other days our members and friends have been summoned to annual conventions to disseminate the propaganda for their common cause, to cheer and encourage each other, to strengthen their organized influence, to counsel as to ways and means of insuring further progress. At this time they are called to rejoice that the struggle is over, the aim achieved and the women of the nation about to enter into the enjoyment of their hard-earned political liberty. Of all the conventions held within the past fifty-one years, this will prove the most momentous. Few people live to see the actual and final realization of hopes to which they have devoted their lives. That privilege is ours.

CARRIE CHAPMAN CATT (1859–1947), U.S. suffragist. As quoted in *History of Woman Suffrage*, vol. 5, ch. 19, by Ida Husted Harper (1922).

Passed by the United States Congress, this proposed Constitutional amendment was submitted to the State Legislatures on June 4, 1919; ratification by thirty-six of the then forty-eight states was needed. On August 23, 1920, Tennessee became the thirty-sixth state to ratify; on the following day, Governor Roberts mailed the certificate of ratification to Secretary of State Bainbridge Colby. It was delivered to him at 4:00 a.m., and five hours later, he issued a proclamation that it had "become valid to all intents and purposes as a part of the Constitution of the United States." Thus the woman suffrage movement that had begun 72 years earlier with a meeting in Seneca Falls, New York, drew to its close. All of the pioneer leaders were dead: Lucretia Mott (1793–1880) and Elizabeth Cady Stanton (1815–1906), who had organized the Seneca Falls meeting; Lucy Stone (1818–1893), and Susan B. Anthony (1820–1906). One of their most distinguished younger colleagues, and one of the movement's most dynamic speakers, the Rev. Dr. Anna Howard Shaw, had died the previous year (1847–1919). Authorship of this "Call" to the National Woman Suffrage Association's last convention, held in 1920, is not specifically credited to Catt, but she was its president at the time. The Nineteenth Amendment to the Constitution was not actually declared in effect until August 26th of that year, three days after Tennessee became the thirty-sixth, and last necessary, state to ratify it. By this time, however, victory was certain, and the convention's official title was Victory Convention of the national American Woman Suffrage Association and First Congress of the League of Women Voters. In fact, most of the prominent early suffrage leaders did not "live to see the actual and final realization of hopes to which they [had] devoted their lives."

WOMAN SUFFRAGE: ANTI

1   I wish the women's rights folks would be more sensible. I think women have a great deal to learn, before they are fit to vote.

ELLEN HENRIETTA SWALLOW RICHARDS (1842–1911), U.S. chemist and educator. As quoted in *The Life of Ellen H. Richards*, ch. 4, by Caroline L. Hunt (1912).
Written on March 13, 1870, to her parents while she was a student at Vassar College.

2   What do women want with votes, when they hold the sceptre of influence with which they can control even votes, if they wield it aright?

MRS. H. O. WARD (1824–1899), U.S. author. *Sensible Etiquette of the Best Society Customs, Manners, Morals, and Home Culture, Compiled from the Best Authorities*, ch. 4 (1878).
Referring to women's influence over the men in their families. Ward emphasized that to "wield" their influence "aright," women must be educated.

3   . . . it is probable that in a fit of generosity the men of the United States would have enfranchised its women *en masse*; and the government now staggering under the ballots of ignorant, irresponsible men, must have gone down under the additional burden of the votes which would have been thrown upon it, by millions of ignorant, irresponsible women.

JANE GREY SWISSHELM (1815–1884), U.S. newspaperwoman, abolitionist, and human rights activist. *Half a Century*, ch. 29 (1880).
Swisshelm was very critical of what she regarded as the amateurish processes and shrill, il-

logical demands of women's rights conventions.
Here, she was being sardonic.

WOMAN SUFFRAGE: PRO

I   Our fathers waged a bloody conflict
with England, because *they* were
taxed without being represented.
This is just what unmarried women
of property are now.

ANGELINA GRIMKÉ (1805–1879), U.S.
abolitionist and feminist. *Letters to Catherine
Beecher,* letter #11 (1837).

In a letter dated August 28, 1837, pointing out
that because women were not permitted to
vote, the single woman property-owner, with
not even an indirect say (through possible influence on a husband's vote) in property tax policy, had no say at all.

2   . . . I believe it is woman's right to
have a voice in all the laws and regulations by which she is to be *governed;* whether in Church or State;
and that the present arrangements
of society, on these points, are *a violation of human rights, a rank usur-
pation of power,* a violent seizure
and confiscation of what is sacredly
and inalienably hers—and thus inflicting upon woman outrageous
wrongs, working mischief incalculable in the social circle, and in its influence on the world producing
only evil, and that continually.

ANGELINA GRIMKÉ (1805–1879), U.S.
abolitionist, suffragist, feminist, and author. *Letters to Catherine E. Beecher,* Letter no. 12
(1838).

From a letter dated October 2, 1837. Beecher, a
prominent educator of women, was an anti-suffragist.

3   When in the enfranchisement of the
black men [women] saw another ig-

norant class of voters placed about
their heads, and beheld the danger
of a distinctively "male" government, forever involving the nations
of the earth in war and violence;
and demanded for the protection of
themselves and children, that woman's voice should be heard and her
opinions in public affairs be expressed by the ballot, they were
coolly told that the black man had
earned the right to vote, that he had
fought and bled and died for his
country.

It was not because the three-penny
tax on tea was so exorbitant that
our Revolutionary fathers fought
and died, but to establish the principle that such taxation was unjust. It
is the same with this woman's revolution; though every law were as
just to woman as to man, the principle that one class may usurp the
power to legislate for another is unjust, and all who are now in the
struggle from love of principle
would still work on until the establishment of the grand and immutable truth, "All governments derive
their just powers from the consent
of the governed."

SUSAN B. ANTHONY (1820–1906), U.S.
suffragist. As quoted in *The Life and Work of Susan B. Anthony,* vol. 1 ch. 11, by Ida Husted
Harper (1898).

Written in 1865. She was pointing up the
irony—which embittered many female abolition and suffrage advocates—of male ex-slaves,
for whose freedom they had long fought, being
potentially elevated above them politically.
Slaves were freed by the Thirteenth Amendment
to the U.S. Constitution (1865); male ex-slaves
would be enfranchised by the Fifteenth Amendment (1870). Women would not be enfranchised until fifty years after that. Stanton's remarks should not be interpreted as racist or ma-
lignant. Always an active supporter of abolition

and African American suffrage, she meant only that slaves were, quite literally, uneducated; it had been against the law to teach them to read and write. White women, as a group, were inevitably much better educated. In an 1859 letter to her brother Daniel, who had questioned the need for woman suffrage.

4 I am sometimes told that "Women aint fit to vote. Why, don't you know that a woman had seven devils in her: and do you suppose a woman is fit to rule the nation?" Seven devils aint no account; a man had a legion in him.

Sojourner Truth (1797–1883), African American suffragist and abolitionist. As quoted in *History of Woman Suffrage,* vol. 2, ch. 18, by Susan B. Anthony, Matilda Joslyn Gage, and herself (1882).

The former slave, itinerant preacher, and beloved activist in the woman suffrage movement said this on May 10, 1867, at a national convention of the American Equal Rights Association.

5 I must sojourn once to the ballot-box before I die. I hear the ballot-box is a beautiful glass globe, so you can see all the votes as they go in. Now, the first time I vote I'll see if the woman's vote looks any different from the rest—if it makes any stir or commotion. If it don't inside, it need not outside.

Sojourner Truth (1797–1883), African American suffragist and abolitionist. As quoted in *History of Woman Suffrage,* appendix—ch. 19, by Elizabeth Cady Stanton (1882).

The former slave, itinerant preacher, and beloved activist in the woman suffrage movement said this during an 1867 visit with Elizabeth Cady Stanton and her family. This is from a letter that Stanton wrote to the *World,* which, she said, "seemed to please Sojourner more than any other journal." Truth was illiterate but enjoyed having newspapers read aloud to her. Her name was an assumed one, which she took after experiencing a vision. She would not live to fulfill her ambition to vote; women were granted suffrage nationwide only in 1920, thirty-seven years after Truth died.

6 . . . any men who would give up the law-making power to women in order to remedy existing evils, would surely be those most ready to enact the needful laws themselves.

Catherine E. Beecher (1800–1878), U.S. educator and author. *Woman's Profession as Mother and Educator, with Views in Opposition to Woman Suffrage,* "An Address to the Christian Women of America," (1872).

Beecher was challenging the pro-suffrage argument that women needed the vote in order to influence the passage of progressive legislation. Her rather intricate argument held that if men were progressive enough to grant suffrage to women, then women didn't need suffrage, because those progressive men could be counted on to support the positions that women favored.

7 When any man expresses doubt to me as to the use that I or any other woman might make of the ballot if we had it, my answer is, What is that to you? If you have for years defrauded me of my rightful inheritance, and then, as a stroke of policy, of from late conviction, concluded to restore to me my own domain, must I ask you whether I may make of it a garden of flowers, or a field of wheat, or a pasture for kine?

Matilda Joslyn Gage (1826–1898), U.S. suffragist. As quoted in *The History of Woman Suffrage,* vol. 3, ch. 27, by Elizabeth Cady Stanton, Susan B. Anthony, and herself (1886).

Speaking before the U. S. House of Representatives on March 31, 1876, as President of the National Woman Suffrage Association. Gage was alluding to the common anti-suffrage argument that women might not vote wisely.

8 *Universal manhood suffrage,* by establishing an aristocracy of sex, imposes upon the women of this nation a more absolute and cruel despotism than monarchy; in that, woman finds a political master in her father, husband, brother, son. The aristocracies of the old world are based upon birth, wealth, refinement, education, nobility, brave deeds of chivalry; in this nation, on sex alone; exalting brute force above moral power, vice above virtue, ignorance above education, and the son above the mother who bore him.

NATIONAL WOMAN SUFFRAGE ASSOCIATION, As quoted in *The History of Woman Suffrage,* vol. 3, ch. 27, by Elizabeth Cady Stanton, Susan B. Anthony, and Matilda Joslyn Gage (1886).

From the Association's "Declaration of the Rights of Woman," written for the centennial of American independence. Susan B. Anthony (1820–1906) read it on July 4, 1876, from the steps of Independence Hall in Philadelphia.

9 Words cannot describe the indignation . . . a proud woman feels for her sex in disfranchisement.

ELIZABETH CADY STANTON (1815–1902), U.S. suffragist, social reformer, and author. *History of Woman Suffrage,* vol. 2, ch. 19 (1882).

10 It is cruel for you to leave your daughter, so full of hope and resolve, to suffer the humiliations of disfranchisement she already feels so keenly, and which she will find more and more galling as she grows into the stronger and grander woman she is sure to be. If it were your son who for any cause was denied his right to have his opinion counted, you would compass sea and land to lift the ban from him.

SUSAN B. ANTHONY (1820–1906), U.S. suffragist. As quoted in *The Life and Work of Susan B. Anthony,* vol. 2, ch. 33, by Ida Husted Harper (1898).

From a January 6, 1884, letter to U. S. Representative William De. Kelley (Republican, PA), who had voted for woman suffrage but did not accord it high priority and push it in Congress.

11 When Abraham Lincoln penned the immortal emancipation proclamation he did not stop to inquire whether every man and every woman in Southern slavery did or did not want to be free. Whether women do or do not wish to vote does not affect the question of their right to do so.

MARY E. HAGGART, U.S. suffragist. As quoted in *History of Woman Suffrage,* vol. 4, ch. 3, by Susan B. Anthony and Ida Husted Harper (1902).

In a hearing on woman suffrage held by the Judiciary Committee of the United States House of Representatives on March 8, 1884. Haggart, who was from Indiana, was responding to the antisuffrage argument that some women did not wish to vote.

12 I do not think the mere extension of the ballot a panacea for all the ills of our national life. What we need to-day is not simply more voters, but better voters.

FRANCES ELLEN WATKINS HARPER (1825–1911), U.S. suffragist and rights advocate. As quoted in *Black Women in Nineteenth-Century American Life,* part 3, by Bert James Loewenberg and Ruth Bogin (1976).

From her 1893 speech at the Columbian Exposition in Chicago: "Woman's Political Future."

13 I feel as tall as you.

ELLIS MEREDITH, U.S. suffragist. As quoted in *History of Woman Suffrage,* vol. 4, ch. 14, by Susan B. Anthony and Ida Husted Harper (1902).

At the twenty-sixth annual convention of the National Woman Suffrage Association, held February 15–20, 1894, in Washington, D.C. Meredith was a delegate from Colorado, which had recently enfranchised women. A "very small" person, she "looked up brightly at a tall

Maryland lady, who was congratulating her" and said this. The incident was reported by Alice Stone Blackwell, secretary of the convention, in a report in the *Woman's Journal,* which she edited.

14 We fully believed, so soon as we saw that woman's suffrage was right, every one would soon see the same thing, and that in a year or two, at farthest, it would be granted.

ANTOINETTE BROWN BLACKWELL (1825–1921), U.S. suffragist. As quoted in *"Common Sense" Applied to Woman Suffrage,* ch. 1, by Mary Putnam Jacobi (1894).

Blackwell made this comment at the 1894 Woman's Rights Convention, recalling the first such convention, which had been held forty-six years earlier at Seneca Falls, New York. Not until 1920—or seventy-two years after Seneca Falls—would the Nineteenth Amendment to the Constitution grant American women the vote.

15 Women, we might as well be dogs baying the moon as petitioners without the right to vote!

SUSAN B. ANTHONY (1820–1906), U.S. suffragist. As quoted in *The Life and Work of Susan B. Anthony,* ch. 44, by Ida Husted Harper (1898).

In a November 16, 1895, speech in Cleveland to the national convention of the Women's Christian Temperance Union, which strongly supported woman suffrage. Anthony considered it very difficult—perhaps futile—for that or any women's organization to effect changes in the law.

16 The millennium will not come as soon as women vote, but it will not come until they do vote.

ANNA HOWARD SHAW (1847–1919), U.S. minister and suffragist. As quoted in *History of Woman Suffrage,* vol. 4, ch. 17, by Susan B. Anthony and Ida Husted Harper (1902).

Speaking before the twenty-ninth annual convention of the National Woman Suffrage Association, held January 26–29, 1897, in Des Moines, Iowa.

17 In asking for a voice in the government under which we live, have we been pursuing a shadow for fifty years? In seeking political power, are we abdicating that social throne where they tell us our influence is unbounded? No, no! The right of suffrage is no shadow, but a substantial entity that the citizen can seize and hold for his own protection and his country's welfare. A direct power over one's own person and property, an individual opinion to be counted, on all questions of public interest, are better than indirect influence, be that ever so far-reaching.

ELIZABETH CADY STANTON (1815–1902), U.S. suffragist, author, and social reformer. *Eighty Years and More (1815–1897),* ch. 22 (1898).

It was exactly fifty years since the first Woman's Rights Convention in Seneca Falls, NY, which Stanton had helped to organize and where the first formal demand for woman suffrage in America was set forth.

18 If I were asked what are the greatest obstacles to the speedy enfranchisement of women I should answer: There are three; the first is militarism. . . . The second obstacle is the unconscious, unmeasured influence upon the estimate in which women as a whole are held that emanates from that most debasing of our evil institutions, prostitution. . . . [ellipsis in source] The third great cause is the inertia in the growth of democracy which has come as a reaction following the aggressive movements that with possibly ill-advised haste enfranchised the foreigner, the Negro and the Indian. Perilous conditions, seeming to follow from the introduction into the body politic of vast numbers of irresponsible citizens, have made the nation timid.

CARRIE CHAPMAN CATT (1859–1947), U.S. suffragist. As quoted in *History of Woman Suffrage*, vol. 5, ch. 1, by Ida Husted Harper (1922).

Responding implicitly to a paper submitted to the thirty-third annual convention of the National Woman Suffrage Association by Elizabeth Cady Stanton (1815–1902) and read aloud by Susan B. Anthony (1820–1906) on the opening day: May 30, 1901. Stanton had focused on alleged contributions of theology and organized religion to the suppression of women's rights, a view not shared by many of the conventioneers. At the time Catt said this, typical attitudes toward immigrants and African American men, many of whom were former slaves or the children of former slaves, were considerably different than they are today. This statement would not have sounded as illiberal in 1901 as it does now. Most suffragists had been staunch foes of slavery and had supported the Union during the Civil War; many were still bitter that, despite this record, they remained disfranchised even after African American men were granted suffrage by the 15th Amendment to the Constitution (1870).

women to strive against tradition, prejudice, conservatism, self-interest, political power and in addition all the forces of corruption combined, to secure the privilege which was conferred upon vast numbers of men who never even demanded it and many of whom knew nothing of its significance after it was granted. I claim, and fear no contradiction, that the women of this land are better qualified to exercise the suffrage with intelligence, honesty and patriotism than were any other class of citizens in the world at the time when it was conferred upon them.

ANNA HOWARD SHAW (1847–1919), U.S. minister, suffragist, and speaker; born in England. As quoted in *History of Woman Suffrage*, vol. 5, ch. 6, by Ida Husted Harper (1922).

Speaking in February 1906 before the thirty-eighth annual convention of the National Woman Suffrage Association.

19 When will the men do something besides extend congratulations? I would rather have President Roosevelt say one word to Congress in favor of amending the Constitution to give women the suffrage than to praise me endlessly!

SUSAN B. ANTHONY (1820–1906), U.S. suffragist. As quoted in *Life and Work of Susan B. Anthony*, vol. 3, ch. 70, by Ida Husted Harper (1908).

After listening to a long stream of politicians' congratulatory letters read aloud at a celebration of her eighty-sixth birthday held in Washington, D.C., on February 15, 1906. Despite her entreaties, President Theodore Roosevelt had not actively supported extension of the vote to women.

20 Such is the boasted chivalry of the Land of Freedom, which has left its

21 I have never had a vote, and I have raised hell all over this country. You don't need a vote to raise hell! You need convictions and a voice!

MOTHER JONES (1830–1930), U.S. labor organizer. *The Autobiography of Mother Jones*, ch. 22 (1925).

From a 1915 address to a dinner assemblage of 500 women, most of them suffragists. Five years later, the Nineteenth Amendment to the United States Constitution would take effect, granting women the vote.

WOMAN'S SPHERE

1 Are we bereft of citizenship because we are mothers, wives and daughters of a mighty people? Have women no country—no interests

staked in public weal—no liabilities in common peril—no partnership in a nation's guilt and shame?

ANGELINA GRIMKÉ (1805–1879), U.S. abolitionist and feminist. As quoted in *The Grimke Sisters from South Carolina,* ch. 1, by Gerda Lerner (1967).

Said on February 21, 1838, presenting antislavery petitions to the Massachusetts state legislature. This was the first time a woman addressed that body.

2 We must be generously willing to leave for a time the narrow boundaries in which our individual lives are passed . . . In this fresh, breezy atmosphere . . . we will be surprised to find that many of our familiar old conventional truths look very queer indeed in some of the sudden side lights thrown upon them.

BERTHA HONORE POTTER PALMER (1849–1918), U.S. socialite. As quoted in *The Fair Women,* ch. 4, by Jeanne Madeline Weimann (1981).

Said in 1890, upon being selected as President of the Board of Lady Managers of the World's Columbian Commission; the Commission was to plan the World's Columbian Exposition, which was scheduled for Chicago in 1893. The Board of Lady Managers planned the famous Woman's Building. Palmer was married to Chicago luminary Potter Palmer.

3 The old, subjective, stagnant, indolent and wretched life for woman has gone. She has as many resources as men, as many activities beckon her on. As large possibilities swell and inspire her heart.

ANNA JULIA COOPER (1859–1964), U.S. educator and feminist. *A Voice from the South,* part 1 (1892).

On the expansion of educational opportunities for women. Cooper, a former slave's daughter, had already earned two degrees from Oberlin College and would become the fourth African American woman to earn a Ph.D. (from the University of Paris).

4 It has always been thought perfectly womanly to be a scrub-woman in the Legislature and to take care of the spittoons; that is entirely within the charmed circle of woman's sphere; but for women to occupy any of those official seats would be degrading.

SUSAN B. ANTHONY (1820–1906), U.S. suffragist. As quoted in *History of Woman Suffrage,* vol. 4, ch. 15, by Susan B. Anthony and Ida Husted Harper (1902).

Addressing the twenty-seventh annual convention of the National Woman Suffrage Association, held January 31–February 5, 1895, in Atlanta, Georgia. Anthony was referring to the antisuffrage argument that any involvement in politics would "degrade" women.

5 The well-cared-for woman is a parasite, and the woman who must work is a slave.

CORA ANDERSON, U.S. male impersonator. As quoted in *Gay American History,* part 3, by Jonathan Katz (1976).

Said in 1914; for the previous thirteen years, Anderson had successfully impersonated a man, permitting her to earn a better living than she could as a woman.

6 You are wonderful. I love and honor you. . . . [ellipsis in source] Lead your own life, attend to your charities, cultivate yourself, travel when you wish, bring up the children, run your house. I'll give you all the freedom you wish and all the money I can but—leave me my business and politics.

ELEANOR ROOSEVELT (1884–1962), U.S. First Lady, author, and speaker. As quoted in *Eleanor and Franklin,* ch. 28, by Joseph P. Lash (1971).

Commenting, in a 1924 newspaper interview, on men's attitude toward women in politics.

7 For boys, the family was the place from which one sprang and to which one returned for comfort and support, but the field of action was the larger world of wilderness, adventure, industry, labor, and politics. For girls, the family was to be the world, their field of action the domestic circle. *He* was to express himself in his work and, through it and social action, was to help transform his environment; *her* individual growth and choices were restricted to lead her to express herself through love, wifehood, and motherhood— through the support and nurture of others, who would act for her.

GERDA LERNER (b. 1920), U.S. historian and feminist. *The Female Experience,* introduction (1977).

8 . . . no woman is really an insider in the institutions fathered by masculine consciousness.

ADRIENNE RICH (b. 1929), U.S. feminist poet and essayist. As quoted in *Ms.* magazine, p. 43 (September 1979).
In a May 7, 1979, Smith College commencement address.

WOMEN STUDIES

I . . . feminism never harmed anybody unless it was some feminists. The danger is that the study and contemplation of "ourselves" may become so absorbing that it builds by slow degrees a high wall that shuts out the great world of thought.

RHETA CHILDE DORR (1866–1948), U.S. journalist. *A Woman of Fifty,* 2nd. ed., ch. 16 (1924).

WOMEN'S LIBERATION MOVEMENT

I Women, because of their colonial relationship to men, have to fight for their own independence. This fight for our own independence will lead to the growth and development of the revolutionary movement in this country. Only the independent woman can be truly effective in the larger revolutionary struggle.

WOMEN'S LIBERATION WORKSHOP, STUDENTS FOR A DEMOCRATIC SOCIETY, Radical political/social activist organization. "Liberation of Women," in *New Left Notes* (July 10, 1967).

2 Let it all hang out. Let it seem bitchy, catty, dykey, frustrated, crazy, nutty, frigid, ridiculous, bitter, embarrassing, man-hating, libelous, pure, unfair, envious, intuitive, low-down, stupid, petty, liberating. *We are the women that men have warned us about.*

ROBIN MORGAN (b. 1941), U.S. author, feminist, and child actor. *Goodbye to All That* (January 1970).

3 Every so often, I turn on the television and see one of the movement leaders being asked some idiot question like, "Isn't the women's movement in favor of all women abandoning their children and going off to work?" . . . the leader usually replies that the movement isn't in favor of all women doing anything right; what the movement is about, she says, is options. She is right, of course. At its best, that is exactly what the movement is about. But it just doesn't work out that way. Because the hardest thing for us to accept is the right to those options. I hear myself saying these words: *what this movement is about is options.* I say it to my friends who are frustrated, or housebound, or guilty, or child-laden, and what I am really thinking is, if you really got it together, the option you would choose is mine.

NORA EPHRON (b. 1941), U.S. author and humorist. *Crazy Salad,* ch. 5 (1972).

4   You mean those nuts that burn their bras and walk around all disheveled and hate men? They're crazy. Crazy.

GOLDA MEIR (1898–1978), Israeli Prime Minister; born in Russia. As quoted in *Ms.* magazine, p. 100 (April 1973).

5   How can you be beautiful and be for Women's Lib?

ANONYMOUS (b. c. 1953), U.S. anti-feminist. As quoted in *Ms.* magazine, p. 46, by Wanda Urbanski (June 1974).

Urbanski, blond, beautiful, and a self-proclaimed radical feminist, was quoting a question put to her by her best friend.

6   If it's a movement, I sometimes think it needs a laxative.

FLORYNCE KENNEDY (b. 1916), U.S. lawyer, activist, speaker, and author. *Color Me Flo,* ch. 3 (1976).

On the Women's Liberation Movement; Kennedy was very active and visible in this, as well as other social movements.

7   I know black women in Tennessee who have worked all their lives,

from the time they were twelve years old to the day they died. These women don't listen to the women's liberation rhetoric because they know that it's nothing but a bunch of white women who had certain life-styles and who want to change those life-styles. They say things like they don't want men opening doors for them anymore, and they don't want men lighting their cigarettes for them anymore. Big deal. Black women have been opening doors for themselves and lighting their own cigarettes for a couple centuries in this country. Black women don't quibble about things that are not important.

WILMA RUDOLPH (1940–1994), African American runner. *Wilma,* ch. 14 (1977).

Rudolph, a track champion, was raised in a modest Tennessee home as the twentieth of twenty-two children.

8   [When asked if she believed in "women's lib":] Not really. Not when I see what most of them look like.

GRETA GARBO (1905–1990), Swedish actor; relocated to the United States. As quoted in *The Divine Garbo,* ch. 8, by Frederick Sands and Sven Broman (1979).

Said in 1977. Garbo, who never married and was reputed to enjoy intimate relationships with women as well as with men, had been an extraordinarily successful actor and legendary beauty. Her last movie was released in 1941, when she was 36; thereafter, she lived quietly and independently.

9   I'll never feel ineffectual again. I'll never feel I don't count again.

BARBARA FELDON (b. 1941), U.S. actor. As quoted in *Ms.* magazine, p. 56 (June 1978).

Reflecting on the impact of the women's liberation movement on her life. At the time, she was working actively for passage of the proposed Equal Rights Amendment to the U. S. Constitution; ultimately, it would be defeated.

10 It was heady stuff, recognizing ourselves as an oppressed class, but the level of discussion was poor. We explained systemic discrimination, and men looked prettily confused and said: "But, I *like* women."

Jane O'Reilly, U.S. feminist and humorist. *The Girl I Left Behind,* ch. 2 (1980). Recalling the early days of the contemporary feminist movement. This is drawn from O'Reilly's famous essay first published in *Ms.* magazine: "Click! The Housewife's Moment of Truth."

11 . . . contemporary black women felt they were asked to choose between a black movement that primarily served the interests of black male patriarchs and a women's movement which primarily served the interests of racist white women.

Bell Hooks (b. c. 1955), African American author, feminist, and civil rights advocate. *Ain't I a Woman?* Introduction (1981).

12 Had middle class black women begun a movement in which they had labeled themselves "oppressed," no one would have taken them seriously.

Bell Hooks (b. 1955), African American author and educator. *Feminist Theory,* ch. 1 (1984). Referring to the fact that the contemporary Women's Liberation Movement was founded largely by well-educated, middle-class white women. hooks, who was college educated but grew up in a poor African American Kentucky family, was a feminist.

13 The message of women's liberation is that women can love each other

and ourselves against our degrading education.

Jane Rule (b. 1931), Canadian lesbian, feminist, fiction writer, and essayist; born in the U.S. *A Hot-Eyed Moderate,* part 2 (1985).

WOMEN'S NATURE

1 The destiny of the whole race is comprised in four things: Religion, education, morals, politics. Woman is a religious being; she is becoming educated; she has a high code of morals; she will yet purify politics.

Zerelda G. Wallace (1817–1901), U.S. suffragist. As quoted in *History of Woman Suffrage,* vol. 4, ch. 7, by Susan B. Anthony and Ida Husted Harper (1902).

In an address entitled "Women's Ballot a Necessity for the Permanence of Free Institutions," delivered before the nineteenth convention of the National Woman Suffrage Association, held in Washington, D.C., January 1887. Wallace, a representative from Indiana, was quoted in a Washington, D.C. newspaper. This was said to be "an imperfect abstract" which, nonetheless, conveyed "the trend of her argument."

2 Slowly . . . the truth is dawning upon women, and still more slowly upon men, that woman is no stepchild of nature, no Cinderella of fate to be dowered only by fairies and the Prince; but that for her and in her, as truly as for and in man, life has wrought its great experiences, its master attainments, its supreme human revelations of the stuff of which worlds are made.

Anna Garlin Spencer (1851–1931), U.S. educator, author, feminist, and Unitarian minister. *Woman's Share in Social Culture,* Introduction (1913).

3 The dramatic art would appear to be rather a feminine art; it contains

in itself all the artifices which belong to the province of woman: the
desire to please, facility to express
emotions and hide defects, and the
faculty of assimilation which is the
real essence of woman.

SARAH BERNHARDT (1845–1923), French
actor. *The Art of the Theatre,* ch. 3 (1924).

4   Explain the antagonism women
showed me, as you will, members of
the suffrage and feminist movements. I cannot. All I know is that
while men sprang ever ready, ever
chivalrous, to put business in my
way, sometimes even when competitors, women almost invariably
turned me down. . . . The difficulty
. . . lay in the quality of the feminine mind. The subtle flattery of an
adroit salesman pleased them and
their order in consequence went to
him. Fear, also, in a dim, unrealized
way of those "higher up" crushed
their initiative, and I pitied them.

ALICE FOOTE MACDOUGALL (1867–
1945), U.S. businesswoman. *The Autobiography of a Business Woman,* ch. 3 (1928).
MacDougall, a successful coffee, tea, and cocoa merchant, was reflecting on her failure to
obtain orders from women's institutions.

5   Psychology has nothing to say
about what women are really like,
what they need and what they want,
essentially because psychology does
not know. . . . this failure is not limited to women; rather, the kind of
psychology that has addressed itself
to how people act and who they are
has failed to understand in the first
place why people act the way they
do, and certainly failed to under-

stand what might make them act
differently.

NAOMI WEISSTEIN, U.S. psychologist,
feminist, and author. *Psychology Constructs the
Female* (1969).

6   The question has been asked,
"What is a woman?" A woman is a
person who makes choices. A
woman is a dreamer. A woman is a
planner. A woman is a maker, and a
molder. A woman is a person who
makes choices. A woman builds
bridges. A woman makes children
and makes cars. A woman writes
poetry and songs. A woman is a person who makes choices. You cannot
even simply become a mother anymore. You must *choose* motherhood. Will you choose change? Can
you become its vanguard?

ELEANOR HOLMES NORTON (b. 1937),
U.S. lawyer and social activist. As quoted in
Crazy Salad, ch. 5, by Nora Ephron (1972).
Norton said this in a Wellesley College com-
mencement speech when she was New York
City Commissioner of Human Rights.

7   Being a woman is of special interest
only to aspiring transsexuals. To actual women, it is simply a good reason not to play football.

FRAN LEBOWITZ (b. 1950), U.S. humorist.
Metropolitan Life, part 4 (1978).
In a critical discussion of "women's" maga-
zines.

8   Natural law is only whatever happens in your lifetime within fifty
miles of you.

"MARCY." As quoted in *The Girl I Left Behind,* Introduction, by Jane O'Reilly (1980).
Marcy was a woman who called in to a late-
night radio talk show on which O'Reilly appeared during a promotional tour for *Ms.* maga-

zine. O'Reilly had spoken about the sexual politics of housework; a previous, male, caller had
accused her of "contravening natural law." This
was the next caller's response to him.

9   . . . why shouldn't women make
good coaches? We were brought up
to listen, to nurture, to observe.

BILLIE JEAN KING (b. 1943), U.S. tennis
player. As quoted in *Sports Illustrated,* p. 74
(April 29, 1991).

WOMEN'S RIGHTS

1   I long to hear that you have declared an independancy [sic]—and
by the way in the new Code of Laws
which I suppose it will be necessary
for you to make I desire you would
Remember the Ladies, and be more
generous and favorable to them
than your ancestors. Do not put
such unlimited power into the
hands of the Husbands. Remember
all men would be tyrants if they
could. If particular care and attention is not paid to the Laidies [sic]
we are determined to foment a Re-
belion [sic], and will not hold ourselves bound by any Laws in which
we have no voice, or Representation.

ABIGAIL ADAMS (1744–1818), U.S. matriarch, wife and mother of American Presidents.
In a letter reprinted in *The Feminist Papers,* part
1, by Alice S. Rossi (1973).
In a letter dated March 31, 1776 and written
from Braintree, MA to her husband, John Adams, during the Revolutionary War, shortly after
the British occupation of Boston was lifted.

2   Let woman share the rights and she
will emulate the virtues of man; for
she must grow more perfect when
emancipated . . .

MARY WOLLSTONECRAFT (1759–1797),
British feminist. *A Vindication of the Rights of
Woman,* ch. 13 (1792).

3   The whole land seems aroused to
discussion on the province of
woman, and I am glad of it. We are
willing to bear the brunt of the
storm, if we can only be the means
of making a break in that wall of
public opinion which lies right in
the way of woman's rights, true dignity, honor and usefulness.

ANGELINA GRIMKÉ (1805–1879), U.S.
abolitionist and feminist. As quoted in *The
Grimke Sisters from South Carolina,* ch. 12, by
Gerda Lerner (1967).
Said on July 25, 1837.

4   . . . I am persuaded that the rights
of woman, like the rights of slaves,
need only be examined to be understood and asserted.

SARAH M. GRIMKÉ (1792–1873), U.S. abolitionist and feminist. *Letters on the Equality of
the Sexes and the Condition of Woman,* letter
#3: dated July 1837 (1838).

5   Can you not see that women could
do and would do a hundred times
more for the slave, if she were not
fettered?

ANGELINA GRIMKÉ (1805–1879), U.S.
abolitionist and feminist. As quoted in *The
Grimke Sisters from South Carolina,* ch. 12, by
Gerda Lerner (1967).
Said in 1837.

6   What's dat got to do with women's
rights or niggers' rights? If my cup
won't hold but a pint and yourn
holds a quart, wouldn't ye be mean
not to let me have my little half-
measure full?

SOJOURNER TRUTH (1797–1883), African American suffragist and abolitionist; later an itinerant preacher and advocate of various social reforms including abolition, woman suffrage, an. As quoted in *The Narrative of Sojourner Truth,* part 2: "Book of Life," by Frances W. Titus (1875).

Said at the 1851 Woman's Rights Convention in Akron, Ohio, in response to a minister who had cited women's supposedly inferior intelligence as a reason to deny them suffrage and other rights.

7 In the courts women have no rights, no voice; nobody speaks for them. I wish woman to have her voice there among the pettifoggers. If it is not a fit place for women, it is unfit for men to be there.

SOJOURNER TRUTH (1797–1883), African American human rights activist and preacher. As quoted in *Feminism: The Essential Historical Writings,* part 3, by Miriam Schnier (1972).

Speaking at an 1867 meeting of the American Equal Rights Association held in New York City.

8 The women of this century are neither idle nor indifferent. They are working with might and main to mitigate the evils which stare them in the face on every side, but much of their work is without knowledge. It is aimed at the effects, not the cause; it is plucking the spoiled fruit; it is lopping off the poisonous branches of the deadly upas tree, which but makes the root more vigorous in sending out new shoots in every direction. A right understanding of physiological law teaches us that the cause must be removed; the tree must be girdled; the tap-root must be severed. The tap-root of our social upas lies deep down at the very foundations of society. It is woman's dependence. It is woman's

subjection. Hence, the first and only efficient work must be to emancipate woman from her enslavement.

SUSAN B. ANTHONY (1820–1906), U.S. suffragist. As quoted in *The Life and Work of Susan B. Anthony,* vol. 2, Appendix, by Ida Husted Harper (1898).

From "Social Purity," a speech first delivered in Chicago in the spring of 1875 as part of a "dime lecture course."

9 . . . woman was made first for her own happiness, with the absolute right to herself . . . we deny that dogma of the centuries, incorporated in the codes of all nations—that woman was made for man . . .

NATIONAL WOMAN SUFFRAGE ASSOCIATION, As quoted in *The History of Woman Suffrage,* vol. 3, ch. 27, by Elizabeth Cady Stanton, Susan B. Anthony, and Matilda Joslyn Gage (1886).

From the Association's "Declaration of the Rights of Woman," written for the centennial of American independence. Susan B. Anthony (1820–1906) read it on July 4, 1876, from the steps of Independence Hall in Philadelphia.

10 I assert that the first, and fundamental right of every woman is to be allowed the free exercise of her own belief; and that free exercise is not allowed when she is in any way restrained either morally or intellectually.

MARGARET ANNA CUSACK (1829–1899), U.S. author and founder of Sisters for Peace. As quoted in *Past and Promise,* part 3, by Rosalie McQuaide and Janet Davis Richardson (1990).

Cusack was known as Sister Mary Frances Clare after becoming a nun.

11 Her wrongs are . . . indissolubly linked with all undefended woe, all helpless suffering, and the plenitude of her "rights" will mean the final triumph of all right over might, the supremacy of the moral forces of reason and justice and love in the government of the nation. God hasten the day.

ANNA JULIA COOPER (1859–1964), African American educator and feminist. *A Voice from the South,* part 1 (1892).

Cooper had been born to a slave.

12 . . . when we shall have our amendment to the Constitution of the United States, everyone will think it was always so, just exactly as many young people believe that all the privileges, all the freedom, all the enjoyments which woman now possesses were always hers. They have no idea of how every single inch of ground that she stands upon to-day has been gained by the hard work of some little handful of women of the past.

SUSAN B. ANTHONY (1820–1906), U.S. suffragist. As quoted in *History of Woman Suffrage,* vol. 4, ch. 14, by Susan B. Anthony and Ida Husted Harper (1902).

From the opening address of the twenty-sixth annual convention of the National Woman Suffrage Association, held February 15–20, 1894, in Washington, D.C. Anthony had been a leading suffragist for fifty years, had been tried and convicted in 1872 for attempting to register to vote, and would die fourteen years before implementation of the Nineteenth Amendment to the Constitution, granting suffrage to women.

13 Let us have a fair field! This is all we ask, and we will be content with nothing less. The finger of evolution, which touches everything, is laid tenderly upon women. They have on their side all the elements of progress, and its spirit stirs within them. They are fighting, not

for themselves alone, but for the future of humanity. Let them have a fair field!

TENNESSEE CLAFLIN (1846–1923), U.S. journalist, lecturer, and social reform advocate; relocated to England. *Talks and Essays,* vol. 4, ch. 7 (1897).

At this time, British women lacked most legal rights, including the franchise.

14 When the mother of the race is free, we shall have a better world, by the easy right of birth and by the calm, slow, friendly forces of evolution.

CHARLOTTE PERKINS GILMAN (1860–1935), U.S. author and feminist. *Women and Economics,* ch. 15 (1898).

15 I beg you to speak of Woman as you do of the Negro—speak of her as a human being, as a citizen of the United States, as a half of the people in whose hands lies the destiny of this Nation.

SUSAN B. ANTHONY (1820–1906), U.S. suffragist. As quoted in *The Life and Work of Susan B. Anthony,* vol. 3, ch. 67, by Ida Husted Harper (1908).

Written to President Theodore Roosevelt in 1905, reacting to a stirring speech he had made at the Republican Club of New York City on Lincoln's birthday. The speech, "devoted principally to the race question," argued that the African American man "should be treated with regard to his merits and not his color."

16 With a generous endowment of motherhood provided by legislation, with all laws against voluntary motherhood and education in its methods repealed, with the feminist ideal of education accepted in home and school, and with all special barriers removed in every field of human activity, there is no reason why woman should not become almost a human thing. It will be time enough then to consider whether she has a soul.

CRYSTAL EASTMAN (1881–1928), U.S. social/political activist and author. *On Women and Revolution,* part 1 (1978). From an article first published in *The Liberator* in December 1920.

Earlier that year, American women had gained the constitutional right to vote, ending a 72-year struggle for suffrage. But it was still illegal to disseminate information about birth control. Eastman believed that it was "idle to talk of real economic independence for women" until they were granted "adequate economic reward from the political government" for child-rearing—hence, the demand for a "generous endowment of motherhood."

17 Having achieved political liberty for women this organization pledges itself to make an end to the subjection of women in all its remaining forms. Among our tasks we emphasize these:
1. To remove all barriers of law or custom or regulation which prevent women from holding public office—the highest as well as the lowest—from entering into and succeeding in any profession, from going into or getting on in any business, from practicing any trade of joining the union of her trade.
2. So to remake the marriage laws and so to modify public opinion that the status of the woman whose chosen work is homemaking shall no longer be that of the dependent entitled to her board and keep in return for her services, but that of a full partner.
3. To rid the country of all laws which deny women access to scientific information concerning the limitation of families.
4. To re-write the laws of divorce,

of inheritance, of the guardianship of children, and the laws for the regulation of sexual morality and disease, on a basis of equality, equal rights, equal responsibilities, equal standards.
5. To legitimatize [sic] all children.
6. To establish a liberal endowment of motherhood.

WOMAN'S PARTY. As quoted in *On Women and Revolution,* part 1, by Crystal Eastman (1978).

Paul (1885–1977), formerly a leading suffragist, was founder of the feminist Woman's Party. Women had won suffrage in 1920, when the Nineteenth Amendment to the Constitution took effect. Attempting to articulate new feminist goals, this "minority resolution" was introduced, and buried, at the 1921 Convention in Washington, DC. Interestingly, of the six recommendations, only numbers one, three, and four have been implemented.

18 . . . women were fighting for limited freedom, the vote and more education. I wanted all the freedom, all the opportunity, all the equality there was in the world. I wanted to belong to the human race, not to a ladies' aid society to the human race.

RHETA CHILDE DORR (1866–1948), U.S. journalist. *A Woman of Fifty,* 2nd ed., ch. 6 (1924).

Reflecting on the women's rights movement of the second half of the nineteenth century and how she, as a young woman, reacted to it.

19 I am not interested in women just because they're women. I am interested, however, in seeing that they are no longer classed with children and minors.

CRYSTAL EASTMAN (1881–1928), U.S. social/political activist and author. *On Women and Revolution,* appendix (1978). From an article first published in the *New York Telegram and Evening Mail* on October 31, 1924.

20 These hearings take place on the eve of Mother's Day, a ritual observance which celebrates not so much mothers and motherhood as the American genius for wedding sentimentality and profitable commercialism. . . . But Mother's Day 1970 may usher in a new era, for it comes at a time when a very strong tide is running in behalf of the proposition that American women, while they may like candy and roses, really need basic rights still denied them. Rights not roses is the watchword for an increasing number of American women . . .

OLGA M. MADAR, U.S. labor activist and feminist. As quoted in *The Female Experience*, ch. 70, by Gerda Lerner (1977).
Madar, Vice-President of the United Automobile, Aerospace and Agriculture Implement Workers of America (UAW), was speaking at the 1970 U. S. Senate hearings on the proposed Equal Rights Amendment to the Constitution; the UAW supported the amendment.

21 Women's rights is not only an abstraction, a cause; it is also a personal affair. It is not only about "us"; it is also about me and you. Just the two of us.

TONI MORRISON (b. 1931), African American fiction writer and essayist. As quoted in *Ms.* magazine, p. 42 (September 1979).
From a May 1979 commencement address at Barnard College. Morrison was commenting on women's unkindness and unhelpfulness toward one another.

WOMEN'S RIGHTS MOVEMENT: 19TH CENTURY

1 Sisters, I a'n't clear what you'd be after. Ef women want any rights more'n dey's got, why don't dey jes take 'em, an' not be talkin' about it?

SOJOURNER TRUTH (c. 1777–1883), African American slave; later an itinerant preacher and advocate of various social reforms including abolition, woman suffrage, and temperance. As quoted in *The Narrative of Sojourner Truth*, part 2: "Book of Life," by Frances W. Titus (1875).
Truth was recounting to Harriet Beecher Stowe (1811–1896) and her family what she had said when asked to address a gathering of women's rights advocates. At this time, she was a guest in the home of Stowe, the famous abolitionist author of *Uncle Tom's Cabin* (1852). Stowe described the visit in "Sojourner Truth, the Libyan Sibyl," an article first published in the *Atlantic Monthly* (April 1863) and reprinted by Titus in this book.

2 You glorify the women who made their way to the front to reach you in your misery, and nurse you back to life. You called us angels. Who opened the way for women to go and make it possible? . . . For every woman's hand that ever cooled your fevered brows, staunched your bleeding wounds, gave food to your famished bodies, or water to your parching lips, and called back life to your perishing bodies, you should bless God for Susan B. Anthony, Elizabeth Cady Stanton, Frances D. Gage and their followers.

CLARA BARTON (1821–1912), U.S. Civil War nurse and founder of the American Red Cross. As quoted in *Angel of the Battlefield*, ch. 8, by Ishbel Ross (1956).
In 1869, addressing an audience in an Iowa town when she had been extolled as a non-feminist: "Miss Barton does not belong to that class of woman." In fact, she knew and respected many active feminists—including the three she mentioned—and subscribed to some feminist ideas.

3 The *woman movement* is one which is uniting by co-operating influences, all the antagonisms that are warring on the family state. Spiritualism, free love, free divorce, the vicious indulgences consequent on unregulated civilization, the worldliness which tempts men and women to avoid *large* families, often by sinful methods, thus making the ignorant masses the chief supply of the future ruling majorities; and most powerful of all, the feeble constitution and poor health of women, causing them to dread maternity as—what it is fast becoming—an accumulation of mental and bodily tortures.

CATHERINE E. BEECHER (1800–1878), U.S. educator and author. *Woman's Profession as Mother and Educator, with Views in Opposition to Woman Suffrage,* "Dedication," (1872).

This dedication was written: "To the Ministers of Religion in the United States." Beecher herself never married.

4 It will open a door through which fools and fanatics will pour in, and make the cause ridiculous.

JANE GREY SWISSHELM (1815–1884), U.S. newspaperwoman, abolitionist, and human rights activist. *Half a Century,* ch. 29 (1880).

Explaining why she was declining the presidency of a planned women's rights convention.

WORK

I Everything overworks everybody here.

FANNY KEMBLE (1809–1893), British actor. *Further Records, 1848–1883,* vol. 1; entry dated December 31, 1874 (1891).

Kemble, who was married to an American and living in Philadelphia, was referring specifically to the strenuous work of the Christmas season, but also to the extraordinary exertions of life in the United States generally. Her point of contrast was her native England.

2 . . . possibly there is no needful occupation which is wholly unbeautiful. The beauty of work depends upon the way we meet it—whether we arm ourselves each morning to attack it as an enemy that must be vanquished before night comes, or whether we open our eyes with the sunrise to welcome it as an approaching friend who will keep us delightful company all day, and who will make us feel, at evening, that the day was well worth its fatigues.

LUCY LARCOM (1824–1893), U.S. poet and teacher. *A New England Girlhood,* ch. 9 (1889).

3 Out of my discomforts, which were small enough, grew one thing for which I have all my life been grateful—the formation of fixed habits of work.

ELIZABETH STUART PHELPS (1844–1911), U.S. novelist and short story writer. *Chapters from a Life,* ch. 11 (1897).

4 The experience of the race shows that we get our most important education not through books but through our work. We are developed by our daily task, or else demoralized by it, as by nothing else.

ANNA GARLIN SPENCER (1851–1931), U.S. feminist, educator, author, and Unitarian minister. *Woman's Share in Social Culture,* ch. 5 (1913).

Observation made in a discussion of the tendency of teen-aged girls to do menial factory work until marrying.

5 . . . aside from the financial aspect, [there] is more: the life of my work. I feel that is all I came into the world for, and have failed dismally if it is not a success.

Mary E. Wilkins Freeman (1852–1930), U.S. author. *Infant Sphinx,* letter #495, dated February 1, 1928 (1985).

6 . . . work is only part of a man's life; play, family, church, individual and group contacts, educational opportunities, the intelligent exercise of citizenship, all play a part in a well-rounded life. Workers are men and women with potentialities for mental and spiritual development as well as for physical health. We are paying the price today of having too long sidestepped all that this means to the mental, moral, and spiritual health of our nation.

Mary Barnett Gilson (1877– ?), U.S. factory personnel manager, economist, and educator. *What's Past is Prologue,* ch. 12 (1940).

7 The beaux and the babies, the servant troubles, and the social aspirations of the other girls seemed to me superficial. My work did not. I was professional. I could earn my own money, or I could be fired if I were inefficient. It was something to get your teeth into. It was living.

Edna Woolman Chase (1877–1957), U.S. editor (*Vogue* magazine). *Always in Vogue,* ch. 4 (1954).

Chase began working for *Vogue* in 1895, only three years after its founding.

8 . . . we have almost succeeded in leveling all human activities to the common denominator of securing the necessities of life and providing for their abundance. Whatever we do, we are supposed to do for the sake of "making a living;" such is the verdict of society, and the number of people, especially in the professions who might challenge it, has decreased rapidly. The only exception society is willing to grant is to the artist, who, strictly speaking, is the only "worker" left in a laboring society.

Hannah Arendt (1906–1975), U.S. philosopher. *The Human Condition,* ch. 17 (1958).

9 I am a working woman. I take care of a home. I hold down a job. I am nuts.

Barbara Dale (b. 1940), U.S. cartoonist. *The Working Woman Book,* ch. 1 (1985).

10 Work is valued by the social value of the worker.

Gloria Steinem (b. 1934), U.S. feminist, author, and editor. *Moving Beyond Words,* part 5 (1994).

WORK: NEGATIVE ASPECTS

1 God made a woman equal to a man, but He did not make a woman equal to a woman *and* a man. We usually try to do the work of a man and of a woman too; then we break down . . .

Anna Howard Shaw (1847–1919), U.S. minister and suffragist. As quoted in *History of Woman Suffrage,* vol. 4, ch. 13, by Susan B. Anthony and Ida Husted Harper (1902).

In 1893 at the twenty-fifth annual convention of the National Woman Suffrage Association. Shaw was speaking of the travails of the Rev. Anna Oliver, who had to serve as minister without the customary enormous aid of a full-time "minister's wife."

2 Work . . . becomes at once a delight and a tyrant. For even when the time comes and you can relax, you hardly know how.

ALICE FOOTE MACDOUGALL (1867–1945), U.S. businesswoman. *The Autobiography of a Business Woman,* ch. 7 (1928).
On becoming a self-made, successful, business entrepreneur.

3 Not rarely, and this is especially true of wives and mothers, the motive behind assuming a disproportionate share of work and responsibility is completely unselfish. We want to protect, to spare those of whom we are fond. We forget that, regardless of the motive, the results of such action are almost always destructive and unproductive.

HORTENSE ODLUM (1892– ?), U.S. businesswoman. *A Woman's Place,* ch. 7 (1939).

4 It seemed pathetic and terrible to me and it still does, that men and women work eight hours a day at jobs that bring them no joy, no reward save a few dollars.

HORTENSE ODLUM (1892– ?), U.S. businesswoman. *A Woman's Place,* ch. 17 (1939).
On first beginning to work at Bonwit Teller in 1932; it was a New York City women's store which was then failing. Odlum's husband, a wealthy businessman, had acquired an interest in the store. Odlum had never held a job when she acquiesced to his request that she study it and advise on how to address its problems. The workforce was understaffed, demoralized, and gloomy.

5 The blessing of life as a whole . . . can never be found in work.

HANNAH ARENDT (1906–1975), U.S. philosopher. *The Human Condition,* ch. 14 (1958).

6 Nothing is so threatening to conventional values as a man who does not want to work or does not want

to work at a challenging job, and most people are disturbed if a man in a well-paying job indicates ambivalence or dislike toward it.

ALICE S. ROSSI (b. 1922), U.S. sociologist. *Dissent,* pp. 534–535 (November-December 1970).

7 You live on hopes, I guess. You always dream that someday you might have a lot of money, your ship might come in. But if the ship doesn't come in, I'm going to work as long as I can.

MARION GRAY (b. c. 1914), U.S. salesclerk. As quoted in *Ms.* magazine, p. 99 (February 1974).
A Woolworth's clerk for more than thirty years, Gray had had to support her husband and their three children after he suffered a stroke. Now, her husband dead and her children grown, she was living with and caring for her elderly aunt and uncle.

8 It is not true that there is dignity in all work. Some jobs are definitely better than others. . . . People who have good jobs are happy, rich, and well dressed. People who have bad jobs are unhappy, poor and use meat extenders. Those who seek dignity in the type of work that compels them to help hamburgers are certain to be disappointed.

FRAN LEBOWITZ (b. 1950), U.S. humorist. *Metropolitan Life,* part 1 (1978).
Referring to a popular packaged mix called "Hamburger Helper."

9 Men decided a few centuries ago that any job they found repulsive was women's work.

FRANCES GABE, U.S. scientist. As quoted in *Feminine Ingenuity,* ch. 15, by Anne L. MacDonald (1992).
Said in 1983.

10 Across the curve of the earth, there
are women getting up before dawn,
in the blackness before the point of
light, in the twilight before sunrise;
there are women rising earlier than
men and children to break the ice,
to start the stove, to put up the pap,
the coffee, the rice, to iron the
pants, to braid the hair, to pull the
day's water up from the well, to boil
water for tea, to wash the children
for school, to pull the vegetables
and start the walk to market, to run
to catch the bus for the work that is
paid. I don't know when most
women sleep!

ADRIENNE RICH (b. 1929), U.S. poet, essayist, and feminist. *Blood, Bread and Poetry*,
ch. 15 (1986).

From a talk given at the First Summer School of
Critical Semiotics, Conference on Women, Fem-
inist Identity and Society in the 1980s, in
Utrecht, Holland, on June 1, 1984.

11 Men are allowed to have passion
and commitment for their work . . .
a woman is allowed that feeling for
a man, but not her work.

BARBRA STREISAND (b. 1942), U.S. entertainer and moviemaker. As quoted in *People*
magazine, pp. 67–68 (May 31, 1993).

12 And you're too fired up to go to
sleep, you sit at the kitchen table.
It's really late, it's really quiet,
you're tired. Don't wanna go to
bed, though. Going to bed means
this was the day. This Feb. 12, this
Aug. 3, this Nov. 20 is over and
you're tired and you made some
money but it didn't happen, nothing happened. You got through it
and a whole day of your life is over.
And all it is—is time to go to bed.

CLAUDIA SHEAR, U.S. author. *New York
Times*, p. A21 (September 29, 1993).

In an "op-ed" piece adapted from her one-
woman play, *Blown Sideways Through Life*,
Shear imagines day's end for a woman in a
dead-end, menial job.

WORK: POSITIVE ASPECTS

1 The end crowneth the work.

ELIZABETH I (1533–1603), British monarch, Queen of England (1558–1603). As
quoted in *The Sayings of Queen Elizabeth*, ch.
11, by Frederick Chamberlin (1923).

2 . . . how can a rational being be en-
nobled by any thing that is not obtained by its own exertions?

MARY WOLLSTONECRAFT (1759–1797),
British feminist. *A Vindication of the Rights of
Woman*, ch. 4 (1792).

3 Work is a sovereign remedy for all
ills, and a man who loves to work
will never be unhappy.

ELLEN HENRIETTA SWALLOW RICH-
ARDS (1842–1911), U.S. chemist and educator. As quoted in *The Life of Ellen H. Richards*,
ch. 3, by Caroline L. Hunt (1912).

Written in an April 10, 1869, letter to her parents when she was a student at Vassar College.

4 Work is and always has been my salvation and I thank the Lord for it.

LOUISA MAY ALCOTT (1832–1888), U.S.
novelist. As quoted in *Louisa May*, ch. 17, by
Martha Saxton (1977).

Written in 1873. Alcott remained single
throughout her life; among her eighteen books
was a novel entitled *Work*, published the same
year that she wrote this sentence.

5 Work elevates, idleness degrades.

MRS. H. O. WARD (1824–1899), U.S. author. *Sensible Etiquette of the Best Society Customs, Manners, Morals, and Home Culture,
Compiled from the Best Authorities*, ch. 16
(1878).

6 Perhaps I stand now on the eve of a new life, shall watch the sun rise and disappear behind a black cloud extending out into a grey sky cover. I shall not be deceived by its glory. If it is to be so, there is work and the influence that work brings, but not happiness. Am I strong enough to face that?

BEATRICE WEBB (1858–1943), British author and socialist. As quoted in *Beatrice Webb,* ch. 7, by Carole Seymour-Jones (1992).

Written in her diary on July 7, 1883. Webb, one of nine daughters of a wealthy, socially prominent English family, was working with the poor under the auspices of Octavia Hill's Charity Organisation Society. A beautiful woman who was drawn to men, maternity, and the pleasures of high society, Webb struggled to renounce these things so that she might live a life of service. Eventually, she rejected the man she loved in favor of Sidney Webb, a poor man who repelled her physically but was her intellectual match. They married and together wrote many books, founded the London School of Economics, and were major theorists of Fabian Socialism. The marriage was childless and largely celibate.

7 I don't want to die as long as I can work; the minute I can not, I want to go.

SUSAN B. ANTHONY (1820–1906), U.S. suffragist. As quoted in *The Life and Work of Susan B. Anthony,* ch. 46, by Ida Husted Harper (1898).

Anthony said this in 1896; she would live for ten more years, but would begin to suffer health problems and reduced capacity for work within four years.

8 I have everything in the world that is necessary to happiness, good faith, good friends and all the work I can possibly do. I think God's greatest blessing to the human race was when He sent man forth into the world to earn his bread by the sweat of his face. I believe in toil, in the dignity of labor, but I also believe in adequate compensation for that toil.

ANNA HOWARD SHAW (1847–1919), U.S. minister, suffragist, and speaker; born in England. As quoted in *History of Woman Suffrage,* vol. 5, ch. 8, by Ida Husted Harper (1922).

Speaking in October 1908 before the fortieth annual convention of the National Woman Suffrage Association. The last clause refers indirectly to the issue of "equal pay for equal work," by this time a frequently used slogan in the women's rights movement.

9 A perfect personality . . . is only possible in a state of society where man is free to choose the mode of work, the conditions of work, and the freedom to work. One to whom the making of a table, the building of a house, or the tilling of the soil, is what the painting is to the artist and the discovery to the scientist,— the result of inspiration, of intense longing, and deep interest in work as a creative force.

EMMA GOLDMAN (1869–1940), U.S. anarchist and author; born in Russia. *Anarchism and Other Essays,* 3rd rev. ed., ch. 1 (1917).

10 Know that it is good to work. Work with love and think of liking it when you do it.

BRENDA UELAND (1891–1985), U.S. author and writing teacher. *If You Want to Write,* 2nd. ed., ch. 18 (1938).

11 . . . no matter what happened, no one could take our heritage away from us. This heritage meant that we had strong bodies, pride, and will power. We could never get so poor that we couldn't work our way out. Through droughts, floods, and tornadoes we could stick and work.

SUE SANDERS, U.S. oil producer. *Our Common Herd,* ch. 8 (1940).

Sanders's father had died when she was five. Within two years, she, her older sister, and their mother were successfully carrying out all the work of the farm he had cultivated.

12 I must work, so as not to be a fool, to get on, to become a journalist, because that's what I want! . . . I can't imagine that I would have to lead the same sort of life as Mummy . . . and all the women who do their work and are then forgotten. I must have something besides a husband and children, something that I can devote myself to!

ANNE FRANK (1929–1945), Dutch Jewish diarist; born in Germany. *Diary of a Young Girl,* entry dated April 4, 1944 (1947).

Frank and her family were in hiding in Holland when she wrote this. Exactly four months later, their hiding place would be raided by the police, and they would be sent to German and Dutch concentration camps. All of them except Otto Frank, the father, would perish; Anne died in Bergen-Belsen, a German camp, just two months before the liberation of Holland.

13 To work and suffer is to be at home.
All else is scenery . . .

ADRIENNE RICH (b. 1929), U.S. poet, essayist, and lesbian feminist. "The Tourist and the Town," lines 31–32 (1955).

14 Never be afraid to meet to the hilt the demand of either work or friendship—two of life's major assets.

ELEANOR ROBSON BELMONT (1878–1979), U.S. stage actress and socialite. *The Fabric of Memory,* part 1, ch. 4 (1957).

From teens to early adulthood, Belmont had worked very long hours as a stage actress.

15 Work to me is a sacred thing.

MARGARET BOURKE-WHITE (1904–1971), U.S. photographer. *Portrait of Myself,* ch. 30 (1963).

An important photographer, she was known chiefly for her *Life* magazine work. She continued to work after being diagnosed with Parkinson's disease, which eventually killed her.

16 Because I have work to care about, it is possible that I may be less difficult to get along with than other women when the double chins start to form.

GLORIA STEINEM (b. 1934), U.S. feminist, author, and editor. As quoted in *Movers and Shakers,* ch. 5, by June Sochem (1973).

17 Work is an essential part of being alive. Your work is your identity. It tells you who you are. It's gotten so abstract. People don't work for the sake of working. They're working for a car, a new house, or a vacation. It's not the work itself that's important to them. There's such a joy in doing work well.

KAY STEPKIN, U.S. baker. As quoted in *Working,* book 8, by Studs Terkel (1973).

She was the director of a health-conscious bread bakery where natural ingredients were used.

18 I really feel work is gorgeous. It's the only thing you can depend upon in life. You can't depend on love.

BARBARA TERWILLIGER (b. c. 1940), U.S. unemployed woman. As quoted in *Working,* book 7, by Studs Terkel (1973).

A single woman with an independent income, she was not working. In her younger years, she had held various jobs.

19 My job is my own only land.

MAXINE HONG KINGSTON (b. 1940), Chinese–American author. *The Woman Warrior,* ch. 2 (1976).

Kingston was raised in California by Chinese immigrant parents.

20 when I work I am pure as an angel
tiger and clear is my eye and hot
my brain and silent all the whining
grunting piglets of the appetites.

MARGE PIERCY (b. 1936), U.S. poet, novelist, and political activist. "The Moon is Always Female," lines 9–12 (1980).

21 I did nothing but work. I made
work my hobby. I was lucky that
way.

MARY ROEBLING (1905–1994), U.S. banker, businesswoman, and philanthropist. As quoted in *Past and Promise,* part 4, by Denise V. Lang (1990).

Said in an interview with the author on November 17, 1985, referring to her success in building a career in banking after the sudden death of her second husband, Siegfried Roebling (Her first husband had died in 1925); the Trenton Trust, where she assumed the Presidency upon his death, was the Roebling family bank.

22 Your work is to keep cranking the
flywheel that turns the gears that
spin the belt in the engine of belief
that keeps you and your desk in
midair.

ANNIE DILLARD (b. 1945), U.S. author. *The Writing Life,* ch. 1 (1989).

On the nature of a writer's work.

23 I work hard in social work, public
relations, and raising the Grimaldi
heirs.

PRINCESS GRACE (1929–1982), Monacan princess; born in America. As quoted in *People* magazine, p. 97 (July 26, 1993).

The former Grace Kelly was explaining that, though in 1956 she had abandoned her American movie career in order to marry Prince Rainier of Monaco, she was still a worker. The couple had three children.

24 I had a wonderful job. I worked for
a big model agency in Manhattan.
. . . When I got on the subway to go
to work, it was like traveling into
another world. Oh, the shops were
beautiful, we had Bergdorf's, Bendel's, Bonwit's, DePinna. The
women wore hats and gloves. Another world. At home, it was cooking, cleaning, taking care of the
kids, going to PTA, Girl Scouts. But
when I got into the office, everything was different, I was different.

ESTELLE SHUSTER (b. c. 1923), U.S. realtor. As quoted in *The Fifties,* ch. 7, by Brett Harvey (1993).

Shuster was an interviewee in Harvey's oral history of the 1950s. Her children were eight and twelve when she began working; her husband and mother objected, but she had "to get out of the house."

25 The way I see it, God gave me the
body, so I intend to use it. It's a big
ego trip. . . . You know, you look
around a bar, you pick out a guy
and you say, that's the one: I'm going to take all of his money
tonight.

TERESA BEATY (b. c. 1975), U.S. stripper and member of the United States Air Force. As quoted in the *New York Times Magazine,* p. 60 (March 27, 1994).

An Air Force enlistee, Beaty was also an occasional stripper, earning "usually . . . $1,200 a week."

WORKING MOTHERS

1 With all the efforts made by modern society to nurture and educate the young, how stupid it is to permit the mothers of young children to spend themselves in the coarser work of the world!

Jane Addams (1860–1935), U.S. social worker and social reformer. *Twenty Years at Hull-House*, ch. 8 (1910).

Addams was the founding director of Hull-House, a pioneer "settlement house" in a poor, largely immigrant, Chicago neighborhood. Here she had in mind poor women who worked long hours in factories out of economic necessity. This is not to say, however, that she would necessarily have approved of more affluent mothers working outside the home at more congenial jobs.

2   Before devising any blueprint that includes the assumption of Having It All, we need to ask . . . Why do we need Everything?

Letty Cottin Pogrebin (b. 1939), U.S. author. As quoted in *Ms.* magazine, p. 48 (March 1978).

Commenting on the feminist notion that women could "have it all"—i.e., have a good job *and* a good marriage *and* a good home *and* a well-adjusted family of children.

WORKING WOMEN

1   Women in drudgery knew
They must be one of four:
Whores, artists, saints, and wives.
There are composite lives
that women always live

Muriel Rukeyser (1913–1980), U.S. poet. "Wreath of Women," lines 42–46 (1944).

WORKING-CLASS PEOPLE

1   For a number of years I . . . believed that political bondage was the cause of many of the ills endured by those of my own sex; until I discovered that the man without a job was about as badly off as the woman without a ballot. In fact, a little worse, for we can live without voting but we cannot live without eating. The real antagonism is not that which exists or is supposed to exist between the sexes; but between the capitalist class and the proletariat. Women are victims of class distinctions more than of sex distinctions . . .

Lena Morrow Lewis (1862–1950), U.S. political activist. As quoted in *The Female Experience*, ch. 69, by Gerda Lerner (1977).

Written in 1907, on why she shifted her emphasis from woman suffrage and temperance to socialism.

2   . . . in the working class, the process of building a family, of making a living for it, of nurturing and maintaining the individuals in it "costs worlds of pain."

Lillian Breslow Rubin (b. 1924), U.S. sociologist, family counselor, and author. *Worlds of Pain*, epilogue (1976).

These are the final words of her study. Rubin, who had herself grown up in a working-class family, drew her title from this stanza of "The Everlasting Mercy," a poem by John Masefield: "To get the whole world out of bed/And washed, and dressed, and warmed, and fed,/To work, and back to bed again,/Believe me, Saul, costs worlds of pain."

3   Before I knew that I was Jewish or a girl I knew that I was a member of the working class. At a time when I had not yet grasped the significance of the fact that in my house English was a second language, or that I wore dresses while my brother wore pants, I knew—and I knew it was important to know—that Papa worked hard all day long.

VIVIAN GORNICK (b. 1935), U.S. Jewish sociologist, feminist, and author. *The Romance of American Communism,* ch. 1 (1977).

These are the opening sentences of her study.

4   The aspirations of most people—security, pleasure, leisure, meaningful work, creative and intellectual pursuits—are to be supported. These desires and dreams are not shameful. In supporting them, we are showing solidarity with working people, for whom these are luxuries and not givens.

IRENA KLEPFISZ (b. 1941), U.S. Jewish lesbian author; born in Poland. *Dreams of an Insomniac,* part 1 (1990).

Referring to the tendency of political activists, drawn mostly from the educated middle-class, to minimize the significance of personal desires. Klepfisz had been very poor as a child and had done sub-professional office work.

5   Stupid or smart, there wasn't much choice about what was going to happen to me . . . Growing up was like falling into a hole. . . . I might not quit school, not while Mama had any say in the matter, but what difference would that make? What was I going to do in five years? Work in the textile mill? Join Mama at the diner? It all looked bleak to me. No wonder people got crazy as they grew up.

DOROTHY ALLISON (b. 1953), U.S. novelist and poet. *Bastard Out of Carolina,* ch. 12 (1992).

From the autobiographical novel based on memories of her poverty-stricken youth in South Carolina.

WORLD WAR I

1   It is the women of Europe who pay the price while war rages, and it will be the women who will pay again when war has run its bloody course and Europe sinks down into the slough of poverty like a harried beast too spent to wage the fight. It will be the sonless mothers who will bend their shoulders to the plough and wield in age-palsied hands the reaphook.

KATE RICHARDS O'HARE (1877–1948), U.S. political activist and author. As quoted in *Movers and Shakers,* ch. 2, by June Sochem (1973).

From an article published in the October 1914 issue of *Social Revolution.*

2   WHEREAS: It is our conviction that had the women of the countries of Europe, with their deep instinct of motherhood and desire for the conservation of life, possessed a voice in the councils of their governments, this deplorable war would never have been allowed to occur; therefore, be it RESOLVED: That the National American Woman Suffrage Association, in convention assembled, does hereby affirm the obligation of peace and good will toward all men and further demands the inclusion of women in the government of nations of which they are a part, whose citizens they bear and rear and whose peace their political liberty would help to secure and maintain.

NATIONAL WOMAN SUFFRAGE ASSOCIATION. Quoted in *History of Woman Suffrage,* vol. 5, ch. 14, by Ida Husted Harper (1922).

This resolution was presented at the forty-sixth annual convention of the National Woman Suffrage Association, which was held in November 1914, four months after commencement of what would become World War I.

3   We shall exchange our material thinking for something quite different, and we shall all be kin. We shall all be enfranchised, prohibition will prevail, many wrongs will be righted, vampires and grafters and slackers will be relegated to a class by themselves, stiff necks will limber up, hearts of stone will be changed to hearts of flesh, and little by little we shall begin to understand each other.

GENERAL FEDERATION OF WOMEN'S CLUBS (GFWC), As quoted in *Everyone Was Brave*, ch. 6, by William L. O'Neill (1971).

From an editorial first published in the *GFWC Magazine* (June 1917), predicting the long-range effects of World War I, which was then in progress.

4   Surely there is not a capitalist or well-informed person in this world today who believes that [World War I] is being fought to make the world safe for democracy. It is being fought to make the world safe for capital.

ROSE PORTER STOKES (1879–1933), U.S. socialist. As quoted in *Movers and Shakers*, ch. 2, by June Sochem (1973).

The once-poor wife of millionaire socialist J. G. Phelps Stokes, she was, in this speech given in Kansas City in March 1918, alluding to President Woodrow Wilson's declaration that the war would "make the world safe for democracy."

WORLD WAR II

1   . . . the next war will be a war in which people not armies will suffer, and our boasted, hard-earned civilization will do us no good. Cannot

the women rise to this great opportunity and work now, and not have the double horror, if another war comes, of losing their loved ones, and knowing that they lifted no finger when they might have worked hard?

ELEANOR ROOSEVELT (1884–1962), First Lady of the United States, author, speaker, and diplomat. As quoted in *Eleanor and Franklin*, ch. 27, by Joseph P. Lash (1971).

Written in 1925; Roosevelt's husband, Franklin Delano Roosevelt, would be elected President in 1932 and would serve through the "next war:" World War II.

2   The children won't leave without me; I won't leave without the King; and the King will never leave.

ELIZABETH (b. 1900), British royalty, Queen Consort (1936–1952) and Queen Mother (1952– present). As quoted in *Majesty*, ch. 9, by Robert Lacey (1977).

The Queen said this in 1940, responding to suggestions that the two young Princesses, Elizabeth (b. 1926) and Margaret (b. 1930), be evacuated from England for their safety during the Second World War. She was the Consort of King George VI (1895–1952).

3   This world crisis came about without women having anything to do with it. If the women of the world had not been excluded from world affairs, things today might have been different.

ALICE PAUL (1885–1977), U.S. feminist. As quoted in *Movers and Shakers*, ch. 3, by June Sochem (1973).

Said in 1941.

4   One . . . aspect of the case for World War II is that while it was still a shooting affair it taught us survivors a great deal about daily living which is valuable to us now that it is, ethically at least, a question of cold weapons and hot words.

M. F. K. FISHER (1908–1992), U.S. culinary writer and autobiographer. *How to Cook a Wolf,* rev. ed., Introduction to the Revised Edition (1951).

The first edition of this book had been published in 1942, when the war was still in progress.

5 . . . the French know that you must not succeed you must rise from the ashes and how could you rise from the ashes if there were no ashes, but the Germans never think of ashes and so when there are ashes there is no rising, not at all and every day and in every way this is clearer and clearer.

GERTRUDE STEIN (1874–1946), U.S. author; relocated to France. *Wars I Have Seen* (1945).

Written in 1943.

6 What I hated even more than the conflict was the lurid spectacle of a world of unreason.

ELLEN GLASGOW (1873–1945), U.S. novelist. *The Woman Within,* ch. 19 (1954).

Written in 1944, near the end of World War II.

7 Everything is very quiet, the streets are never crowded, and the people one dislikes are out of town.

ELIZABETH BOWEN (1899–1973), British novelist, story writer, essayist, and memoirist; born in Ireland. As quoted in *Elizabeth Bowen,* ch. 8, by Edmund Wilson, who was in turn quoted by Victoria Glendinning (1979).

On why she had enjoyed being in London during World War II.

WORLD'S COLUMBIAN EXPOSITION

1 Every woman who visited the Fair made it the center of her orbit. Here was a structure designed by a woman, decorated by women, man-

aged by women, filled with the work of women. Thousands discovered women were not only doing something, but had been working seriously for many generations . . . [ellipsis in source] Many of the exhibits were admirable, but if others failed to satisfy experts, what of it?

KATE FIELD (1838–1908), U.S. newspaper publisher. As quoted in *The Fair Women,* ch. 11, by Jeanne Madeline Weimann (1981).

Written in 1893, on the landmark Woman's Building at the World's Columbian Exposition of that same year, held in Chicago.

WRITERS

1 A person who publishes a book willfully appears before the populace with his pants down.

EDNA ST. VINCENT MILLAY (1892–1950), U.S. poet. As quoted in *The Late Mrs. Dorothy Parker,* ch. 4, by Leslie Frewin (1986).

Millay began publishing her poetry when she was still in her teens.

2 The writing career is not a romantic one. The writer's life may be colorful, but his work itself is rather drab.

MARY ROBERTS RINEHART (1876–1958), U.S. novelist. *My Story,* ch. 53 (1931).

3 I have heard it said that it took Messrs. Shipman and Hymer [the playwrights] just three-and-a-half days to write their drama. I should like to know what they were doing during the three days.

DOROTHY PARKER (1893–1967), U.S. author and humorist. As quoted in *The Late Mrs. Dorothy Parker,* ch. 10, by Leslie Frewin (1986).

On a review, written for *Vanity Fair* magazine, of a bad play.

4 The writer can choose what he writes about but he cannot choose what he is able to make live.

FLANNERY O'CONNOR (1925–1964), U.S. fiction writer and essayist. *Mystery and Manners,* part 2 (1969).

Written in 1957. O'Connor's fiction was heavily populated with extreme eccentrics.

5 . . . the writer is initially set going by literature more than by life.

FLANNERY O'CONNOR (1925–1964), U.S. fiction writer and essayist. *Mystery and Manners,* part 2 (1969).

Written in 1957.

6 . . . writers do not find subjects: subjects find them. There is not so much a search as a state of open susceptibility.

ELIZABETH BOWEN (1899–1973), British novelist, story writer, essayist, and memoirist; born in Ireland. *Seven Winters,* part 2, sect. 1, ch. 1 (1962).

7 The novelist's—any writer's—object is to whittle down his meaning to the exactest and finest possible point. What, of course, is fatal is when he does not know what he does mean: he has no point to sharpen.

ELIZABETH BOWEN (1899–1973), British novelist, essayist, and memoirist; born in Ireland. *Pictures and Conversations,* ch. 5 (1975).

8 A man who finishes a book is always alone when he finishes it . . .

NORA EPHRON (b. 1941), U.S. author and humorist. *Scribble Scribble,* ch. 6 (1978).

Written in 1975.

9 Women are not supposed to have uteruses, especially in poems.

MAXINE KUMIN (b. 1925), U.S. poet and feminist. As quoted in *Women's Studies,* p. 135 (1976).

On the restrictions on poetry's subject matter due to male editors' dismissal of peculiarly "female" topics.

10 The real writer is one
who really writes. Talent
is an invention like phlogiston
after the fact of fire.
Work is its own cure. You have to
like it better than being loved.

MARGE PIERCY (b. 1936), U.S. poet and novelist. "For the Young Who Want To," lines 31–36 (1980).

11 I sometimes have the sense that I live my life as a writer with my nose pressed against the wide, shiny plate glass window of the "mainstream" culture. The world seems full of straight, large-circulation, slick periodicals which wouldn't think of reviewing my book and bookstores which will never order it.

JAN CLAUSEN (b. 1943), U.S. author, editor, and lesbian feminist. (1982).

Clausen published her fiction and poetry through "small" or "alternative" presses and magazines.

12 Writers don't write from experience, although many are hesitant to admit that they don't. . . . If you wrote from experience, you'd get maybe one book, maybe three poems. Writers write from empathy.

NIKKI GIOVANNI (b. 1943), U.S. poet. *Black Women Writers at Work,* ch. 5, by Claudia Tate (1983).

13 . . . writing is the enemy of forgetfulness, of thoughtlessness. For the writer there is no oblivion. Only endless memory.

ANITA BROOKNER (b. 1928), British novelist. *Look at Me,* ch. 6 (1983).

14 When I think about why I would be a writer, why I should continue to be a writer, it seems to me one of the few things you can do where you're never bored.

GISH JEN (b. 1956), U.S. novelist. As quoted in *Listen to Their Voices,* ch. 2, by Mickey Pearlman (1993).

15 In a certain sense, women who write fiction and political feminists comes from two different camps. One is interested in change and revolution; the other, women who write serious fiction, believe that life doesn't change that much, that we all struggle perennially with the same old painful issues that are true for all people: how to deal with unexplained suffering, how to survive a sorrowful universe, how to heal yourself, how to restore yourself when that seems difficult and impossible (given what life deals out to people). That's not a very revolutionary approach to take—to speak of sorrow and suffering as inevitable and as part of the human condition. And yet all serious writers have always spoken that way.

SUE MILLER (b. 1943), U.S. novelist and story writer. As quoted in *Listen to Their Voices,* ch. 14 (1993).

16 I have wanted everything as a writer and a woman, but most of all a world changed utterly by my revelations.

DOROTHY ALLISON (b. 1949), U.S. author and lesbian feminist. *Skin,* ch. 18 (1994).

Allison—a lesbian feminist essayist, fiction writer, and poet—described her poor, violence-ridden Southern childhood in her well-received autobiographical novel, *Bastard Out of Carolina* (1992).

WRITING

1 . . . if we can imagine the art of fiction come alive and standing in our midst, she would undoubtedly bid us to break her and bully her, as well as honour and love her, for so her youth is renewed and her sovereignty assured.

VIRGINIA WOOLF (1882–1941), British novelist, essayist, and diarist. *The Common Reader,* ch. 13 (1925).

2 And so now you will begin to work at your writing. Remember these things. Work with all your intelligence and love. Work freely and rollickingly as though they were talking to a friend who loves you. Mentally (at least three or four times a day) thumb your nose at all know-it-alls, jeerers, critics, doubters.

BRENDA UELAND (1891–1985), U.S. author and writing teacher. *If You Want to Write,* 2nd. ed., ch. 1 (1939).

3 I can shake off everything if I write; my sorrows disappear, my courage is reborn. But, and that is the great question, will I ever be able to write anything great, will I ever become a journalist or a writer? I hope so, oh, I hope so very much, for I can recapture everything when I write, my thoughts, my ideals and my fantasies.

ANNE FRANK (1929–1945), Dutch Jewish diarist; born in Germany. *Diary of a Young Girl,* entry dated April 4, 1944 (1947).

Frank and her family were in hiding in Holland when she wrote this. Exactly four months later, their hiding place would be raided by the police, and they would be sent to German and Dutch concentration camps. All of them except Otto Frank, the father, would perish; Anne died in Bergen-Belsen, a German camp, just two months before the liberation of Holland. Although she did not live to know that she had fulfilled her ambition, she did so through the posthumous publication of her diary.

4 I would write of the universal, not the provincial, in human nature. . . . I would write of characters, not of characteristics.

ELLEN GLASGOW (1873–1945), U.S. novelist. *The Woman Within,* ch. 11 (1954). Written in 1944.

5 The writer, like a swimmer caught by an undertow, is borne in an unexpected direction. He is carried to a subject which has awaited him—a subject sometimes no part of his conscious plan. Reality, the reality of sensation, has accumulated where it was least sought. To write is to be captured—captured by some experience to which one may have given hardly a thought.

ELIZABETH BOWEN (1899–1973), British novelist, story writer, essayist, and memoirist; born in Ireland. *Seven Winters,* part 2, sect. 2, ch. 8 (1962). Written in 1952.

6 . . . in nine out of ten cases the original wish to write is the wish to make oneself felt . . . [ellipsis in source] the non-essential writer never gets past that wish.

ELIZABETH BOWEN (1899–1973), British novelist, story writer, essayist, and memoirist;

born in Ireland. As quoted in *Elizabeth Bowen,* ch. 3, by Victoria Glendinning (1979).

7 Crushed to earth and rising again is an author's gymnastic. Once he fails to struggle to his feet and grab his pen, he will contemplate a fact he should never permit himself to face: that in all probability books have been written, are being written, will be written, better than anything he has done, is doing, or will do.

FANNIE HURST (1889–1968), U.S. novelist. *Anatomy of Me,* book 4 (1958).

8 If, while watching the sun set on a used-car lot in Los Angeles, you are struck by the parallels between this image and the inevitable fate of humanity, do not, under any circumstances, write it down.

FRAN LEBOWITZ (b. 1950), U.S. humorist. *Metropolitan Life,* part 4 (1978). Advice to prospective writers.

9 Irony in writing is a technique for increasing reader self-approval.

JESSAMYN WEST (1907–1984), U.S. novelist and autobiographer. *The Life I Really Lived,* part 6 (1979).

10 I was standing in the schoolyard waiting for a child when another mother came up to me. "Have you found work yet?" she asked. "Or are you still just writing?"

ANNE TYLER (b. 1941), U.S. novelist. As quoted in *The Writer on Her Work,* ch. 2, by Janet Sternburg (1980). Tyler was among the most honored and widely read novelists in America.

11 . . . I feel more alive when I'm writing than I do at any other time—except when I'm making love. Two things when you forget time, when nothing exists except the moment—the moment of writing, the moment of love. That perfect concentration is bliss.

MAY SARTON (1912–1995), U.S. author. As quoted in *Women Writers Talking,* ch. 1, by Janet Todd (1983).

12 If I could live as a tree, as a river, as the moon, as the sun, as a star, as the earth, as a rock, I would. . . . Writing permits me to experience life as any number of strange creations.

ALICE WALKER (b. 1944), U.S. poet and fiction writer. *Black Women Writers at Work,* ch. 12, by Claudia Tate (1985).

13 It's a dismally lonely business, writing.

TONI CADE BAMBARA (b. 1939), African American fiction writer. As quoted in *Black Women Writers at Work,* ch. 2, by Claudia Tate (1985).

14 I do not so much write a book as sit up with it, as with a dying friend.

ANNIE DILLARD (b. 1945), U.S. author. *The Writing Life,* ch. 3 (1989).

15 . . . I write to keep in contact with our ancestors and to spread truth to people.

SONIA SANCHEZ (b. 1934), African American author and political activist. As quoted in *I Dream a World,* by Brian Lanker (1989).

16 It's important as a writer to do my art well and do it in a way that is powerful and beautiful and meaningful, so that my work regenerates

the people, certainly Indian people, and the earth and the sun. And in that way we all continue forever.

JOY HARJO (b. 1951), Native American (Creek) author. As quoted in *Listen to Their Voices,* ch. 7, by Mickey Pearlman (1993).

YEARNING

1 The years seemed to stretch before her like the land: spring, summer, autumn, winter, spring; always the same patient fields, the patient little trees, the patient lives; always the same yearning; the same pulling at the chain—until the instinct to live had torn itself and bled and weakened for the last time, until the chain secured a dead woman, who might cautiously be released.

WILLA CATHER (1873–1947), U.S. novelist. *O Pioneers!* Part 4 (1913).

Trapped in her situation as a young Nebraska farm wife with an unsympathetic husband, the novel's tragic heroine, Marie Shabata, longs for a larger life.

2 Is there anything better than to be longing for something, when you know it is within reach?

GRETA GARBO (1905–1990), Swedish actor; relocated to the United States. As quoted in *The Divine Garbo,* ch. 4, by Frederick Sands and Sven Broman (1979).

Written in a letter to her friend, the Swede Lars Saxon, in 1926. The previous year, Garbo had come to the United States to make movies; she was "longing" to return to Sweden and believed that after making another three films—which she thought would take "perhaps . . . another six months"—she would do so. However, she did not.

3 Yearning is the word that best describes a common psychological state shared by many of us, cutting across boundaries of race, class, gender, and sexual practice.

BELL HOOKS (b. c. 1955), African American feminist author and educator. *Yearning,* ch. 3 (1990).

YOUTH

1   If youth is the season of hope, it is often so only in the sense that our elders are hopeful about us; for no age is so apt as youth to think its emotions, partings, and resolves are the last of their kind. Each crisis seems final, simply because it is new.

GEORGE ELIOT (1819–1880), British novelist. *Middlemarch,* ch. 55 (1871–1872).

2   The most serious thing about war is the slaughter of boys. It is the boys of the country who must face the enemy. They lose education. They risk the vices of camp life, they encounter the diseases that swoop down on them, and generally bring home enough of the evils to wreck physical and moral health for all time. They are the "seed corn" of any nation and the crop fails. The political leaders force a country into bloody strife and three-fourths of the army are young men and boys who had absolutely nothing to do with bringing it on, without any real knowledge of the evils resented or principles fought for.

REBECCA LATIMER FELTON (1835–1930), U.S. author. *Country Life in Georgia in the Days of My Youth,* ch. 1 (1919).

3   The young are so old, they are born with their fingers crossed.

EDNA ST. VINCENT MILLAY (1892–1950), U.S. poet. "Fontaine, Je Ne Boirai Pas De Ton Eau!" Line 13 (1939).

4   Insolent youth rides, now, in the whirlwind. For those modern iconoclasts who are without culture possess, apparently, all the courage.

ELLEN GLASGOW (1873–1945), U.S. novelist. *The Woman Within,* ch. 12 (1954). Written in 1944, of the "New South." Glasgow had grown up in the more traditional Southern ambience of late-nineteenth-century Virginia.

5   I was too young to take it all in. I was too young to even realize I was young. I was just living my life.

TRACY AUSTIN (b. 1962), U.S. tennis player. As quoted in *Sports Illustrated,* p. 12 (August 6, 1993). On beating Chris Evert in the 1979 U. S. Open to become, at age sixteen, the youngest person ever to win that prestigious tennis tournament.

6   You're playing serious music, and you want to be taken seriously. When they get my age wrong on the program, I wish they'd make me *older*.

LEILA JOSEFOWICZ (b. c. 1973), U.S. violinist. As quoted in the *New York Times,* p. 39 (October 3, 1993). On being treated as a violin "prodigy" rather than a serious adult violinist. A student at Philadelphia's Curtis Institute of Music, she had already been a soloist with major orchestras and had appeared on television shows.

7   Boys and girls may sit together, but they know the rules. I must be able to see both heads and all hands at all times.

MELODY CLARKE, U.S. school-bus driver. As quoted in *Newsweek* magazine, p. 23 (December 19, 1994).

Clarke drove the longest school-bus route in the United States: a two-hour trip through southern Texas to Alpine High School.

GLORIA STEINEM (b. 1934), U.S. feminist, author, and editor. *Moving Beyond Words,* part 6 (1994).

8 . . . if young women have a problem, it's only that they think there's no problem.

Index of Sources